THE
PIANO BENCH
OF
CHILDREN'S
SONGS

Amsco Publications
New York/London/Paris/Sydney/Copenhagen/Madrid

COMPILED AND EDITED BY AMY APPLEBY

ORDER NO. AM 967538
US INTERNATIONAL STANDARD BOOK NUMBER: 0.8256.1823.1
UK INTERNATIONAL STANDARD BOOK NUMBER: 0.7119.8509.X

EXCLUSIVE DISTRIBUTORS:
MUSIC SALES CORPORATION
257 PARK AVENUE SOUTH, NEW YORK, NY 10010 USA
MUSIC SALES LIMITED
8/9 FRITH STREET, LONDON W1D 3JB ENGLAND
MUSIC SALES PTY. LIMITED
120 ROTHSCHILD STREET, ROSEBERY, SYDNEY, NSW 2018, AUSTRALIA

PRINTED IN THE UNITED STATES OF AMERICA BY
VICKS LITHOGRAPH AND PRINTING CORPORATION

FOREWORD

For the family that loves music, the ideal piano bench is sturdy, comfortable, and filled to the brim with delightful songs. Over the years, the music within provides hours of enjoyment for family and friends—whether learning, dancing, singing, or simply laughing together.

This illustrated volume provides kids, parents, and teachers with the ideal benchful of songs for all occasions. The easy-to-read lyrics, piano arrangements, and chord symbols allow everyone to join in the fun. Whether at home, school, or around the campfire, kids are sure to find the songs they love best in this gigantic song collection.

You hold in your hands the ultimate treasury of the world's best music literature for young singers and dancers. Here kids will find a wealth of singing pleasure and musical discovery at every developmental level. In this piano bench, parents and teachers will also find many of their own favorite friends from childhood, and perhaps a few new ones too.

The Piano Bench of Children's Songs

Fun Songs and Dances

Singing and Learning

Animal Songs

Storybook People

Holiday Songs

Golden Showstoppers

Songs of America

Songs of Many Lands

Singing with Grandma

Rounds

Three-Part Rounds

Two-Part Rounds

Four- and Five-Part Rounds

Quiet Songs and Lullabies

Fun Songs
and Dances

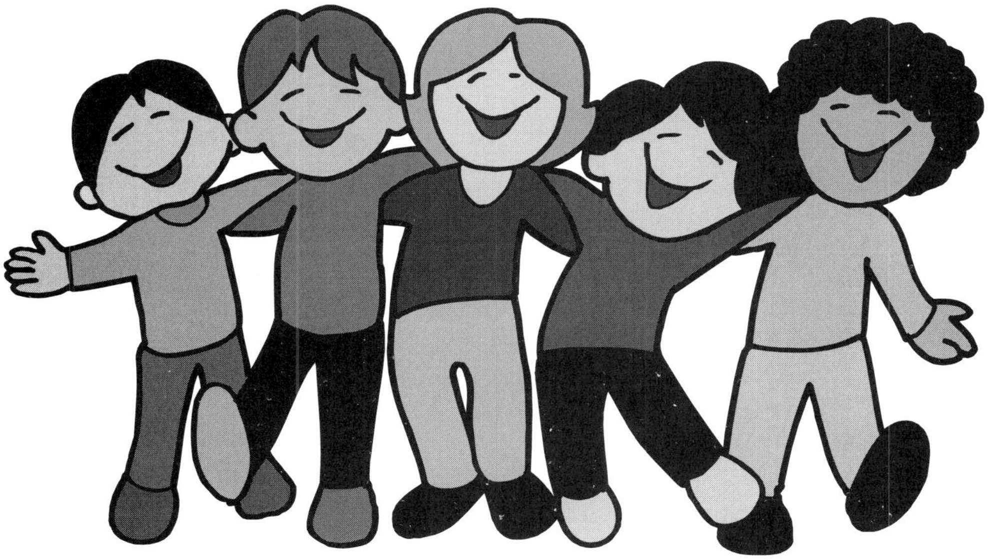

Do Your Ears Hang Low?

G
Do your ears hang low? Do they wob - ble to and
Emin
A
fro? Can you tie them in a knot? Can you tie them in a
D7
G
bow? Can you toss them o-ver your shoul-der like a con - tin - ent - al
Emin
G
D7
G
sol - dier, Do your ears hang low?

2. Yes, my ears hang low.
   They can wobble to and fro,
   I can tie them in a knot,
   I can tie them in a bow,
   I can toss them over my shoulder
   Like a continental soldier.
   Yes, my ears hang low.

Fiddle-de-dee

2. Fiddle-de-dee, fiddle-de-dee,
Says the Bee, says she, "I'll live under your wing,
And you'll never know I carry a sting."
Fiddle-de-dee, Fiddle-de-dee,
The Fly has married the Bumblebee.

3. Fiddle-de-dee, fiddle-de-dee,
And when Parson Beetle had married the pair,
They both went out to take the air.
Fiddle-de-dee, Fiddle-de-dee,
The Fly has married the Bumblebee.

Girls and Boys Come Out to Play

Girls and boys come out to play, the moon is shin-ing bright as day.

Leave your sup-per and leave your sleep and join your play-fel-lows in the street.

Here We Go Round the Mulberry Bush

F Bb F
Here we go round the mul - berry bush, the
G C7
mul - ber - ry bush, the mul - ber - ry bush.
F Bb F Dm7
Here we go round the mul - berry bush on a
G C7 F Gm7 F
cold and fros - ty morn - ing.

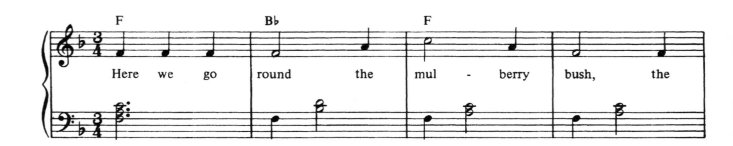

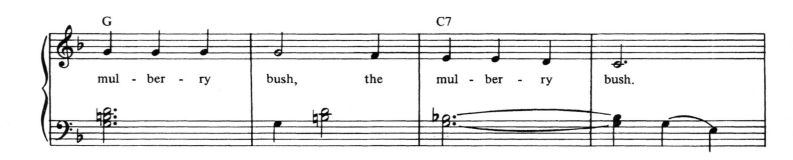

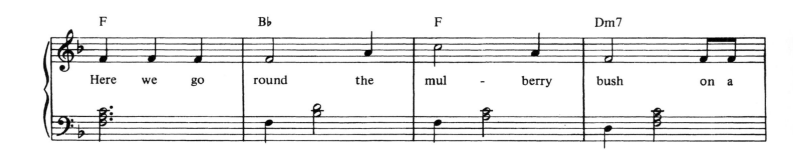

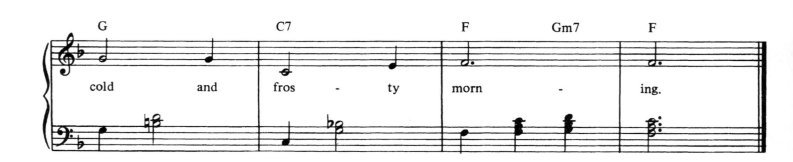

Hey Diddle Diddle

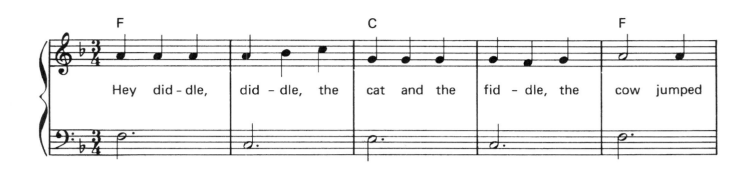

Hey did – dle, did – dle, the cat and the fid – dle, the cow jumped

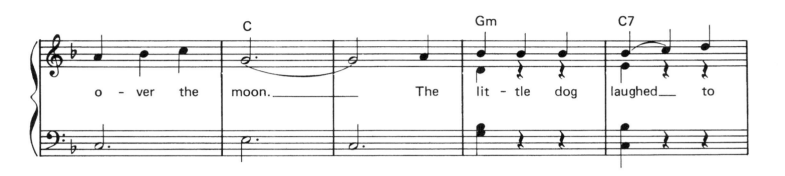

o – ver the moon. The lit – tle dog laughed to

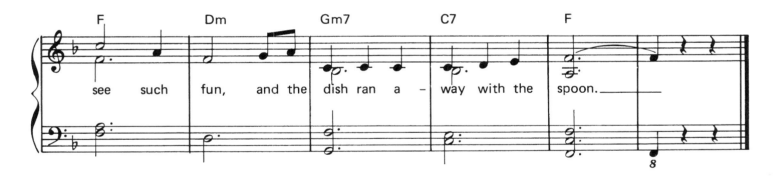

see such fun, and the dish ran a – way with the spoon.

The Hokey Pokey

F
C7
F
You put your right hand in, You put your right hand
C7
F
C7
out, You put your right hand in, And you shake it all a -
Chorus
bout. You do the ho - key po - key And you turn your-self a -
F
round. That's what it's all a - bout. Hey!

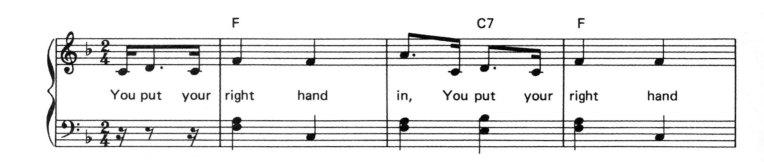

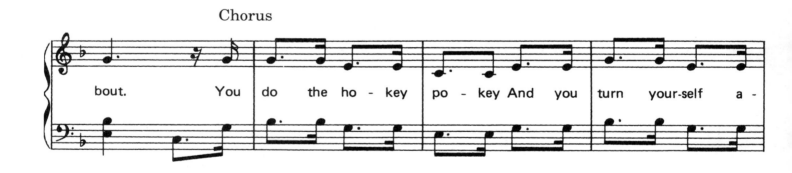

2. You put your left foot in,
   You put your left foot out,
   You put your left foot in,
   And then you shake it all about.
   Chorus

3. You put your right hand in,
   You put your right hand out,
   You put your right hand in,
   And then you shake it all about.
   Chorus

4. You put your left hand in,
   You put your left hand out,
   You put your left hand in,
   And then you shake it all about.
   Chorus

5. You put your head in,
   You put your head out,
   You put your head in,
   And then you shake it all about.
   Chorus

6. You put your back in,
   You put your back out,
   You put your back in,
   And then you shake it all about.
   Chorus

7. You put your whole self in,
   You put your whole self out,
   You put your whole self in,
   And then you shake it all about.
   Chorus

Hot Cross Buns

D7 G D7 G
Hot cross buns! Hot cross buns!
D7 B Em Cm6 D7 G
One a pen - ny, two a pen - ny, Hot cross buns!
Bm Am7 D7 G A9 D7
If you have no daugh - ters, give them to your sons.
B Em Cm6 D7 G
One a pen - ny, two a pen - ny, Hot cross buns!

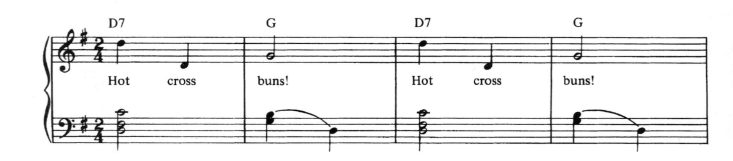

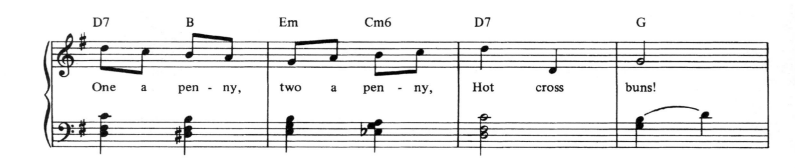

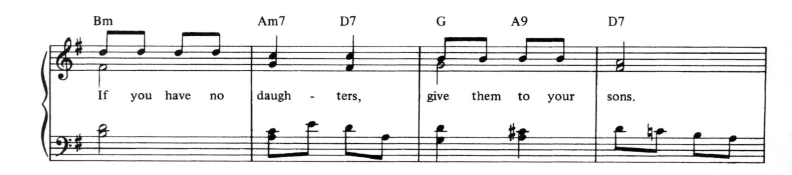

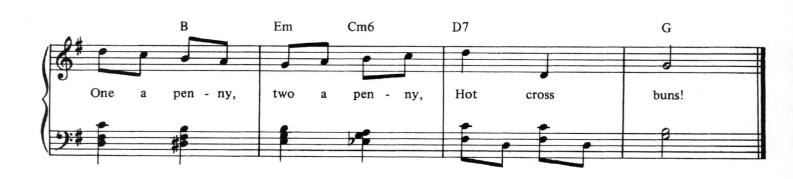

Hickory Dickory Dock

C G C G C
Hick-or-y, dick-or-y dock, the mouse ran up the clock. The
Am Em F C G G7 C
clock struck one, the mouse ran down, hick-or-y dick-or-y dock.

If All the World Were Paper

C F C F G C Amin D7 Emin A
If all the world were pa – per, And all the sea were ink And
Dmin C Dmin C F D Dmin G7 C
all the trees were bread and cheese, What should we do for drink?

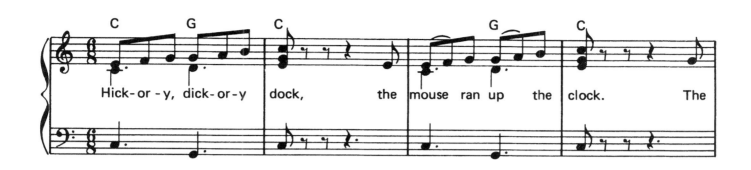

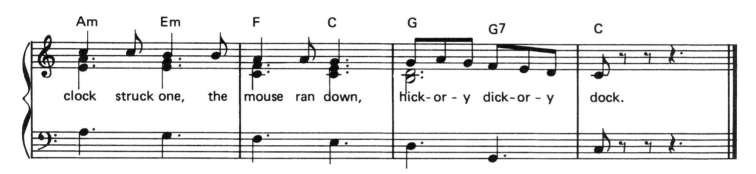

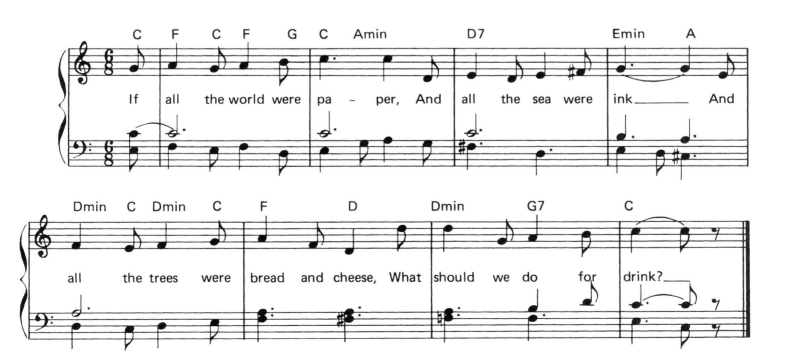

Knicky, Knicky, Knacky Noo

Put my hand on my - self, what have I here?

This is my head knock-er, my sou - ven - ir. Head knock-er, head knock-er,

knick-y, knick-y, knack-y noo; That's what they taught me when I went to school.

2. Put my hand on myself, what have I here?
   This is my nose wiper, my souvenir,
   Nose wiper, nose wiper,
   Knicky, knicky, knacky, noo;
   That's what they taught me
   when I went to school.

3. This is my tea stainer, *etc.*

4. This is my chin chopper, *etc.*

5. This is my chest bumper, *etc.*

6. This is my bread basket, *etc.*

7. This is my thigh bumper, *etc.*

8. This is my knee knocker, *etc.*

9. This is my toe tapper, *etc.*

10. This is my heel wagger, *etc.*

Lavender Blue

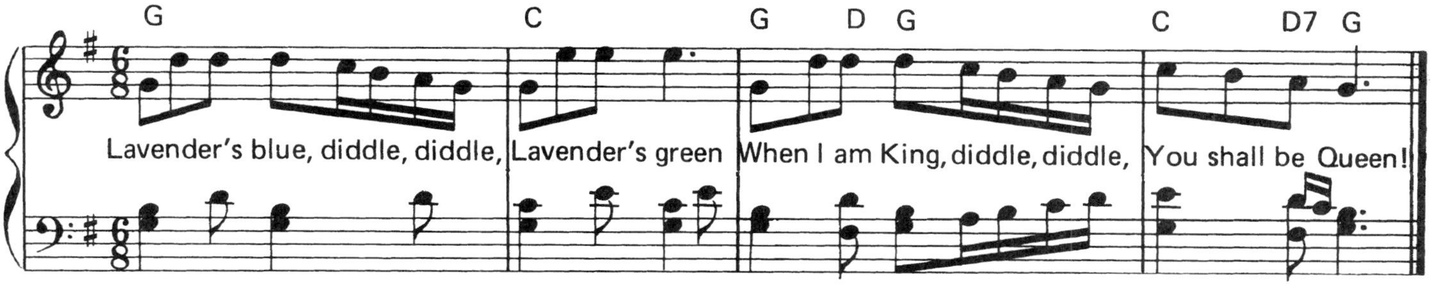

Looby Loo

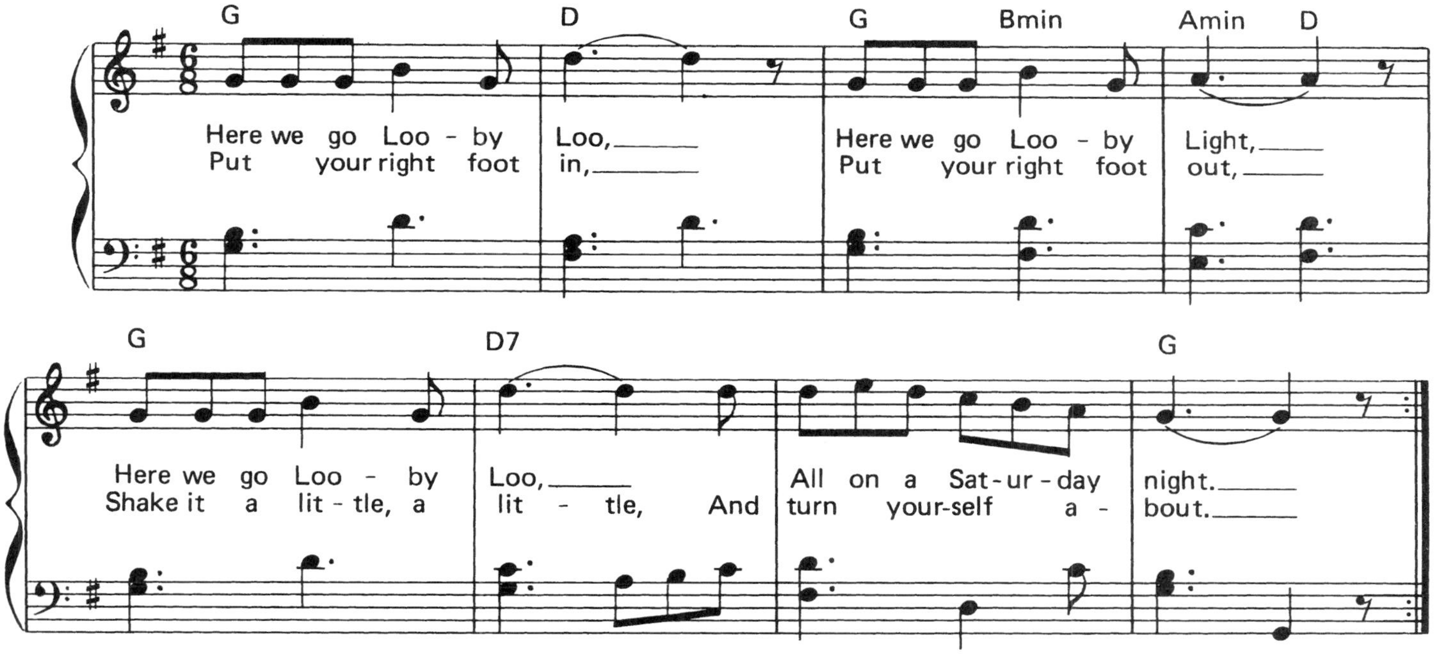

2. Here we go Looby Loo, *etc.*
   Put your left foot in, *etc.*

3. Here we go Looby Loo, *etc.*
   Put your right hand in, *etc.*

4. Here we go Looby Loo, *etc.*
   Put your left hand in, *etc.*

5. Here we go Looby Loo, *etc.*
   Put your noses in, *etc.*

London Bridge Is Falling Down

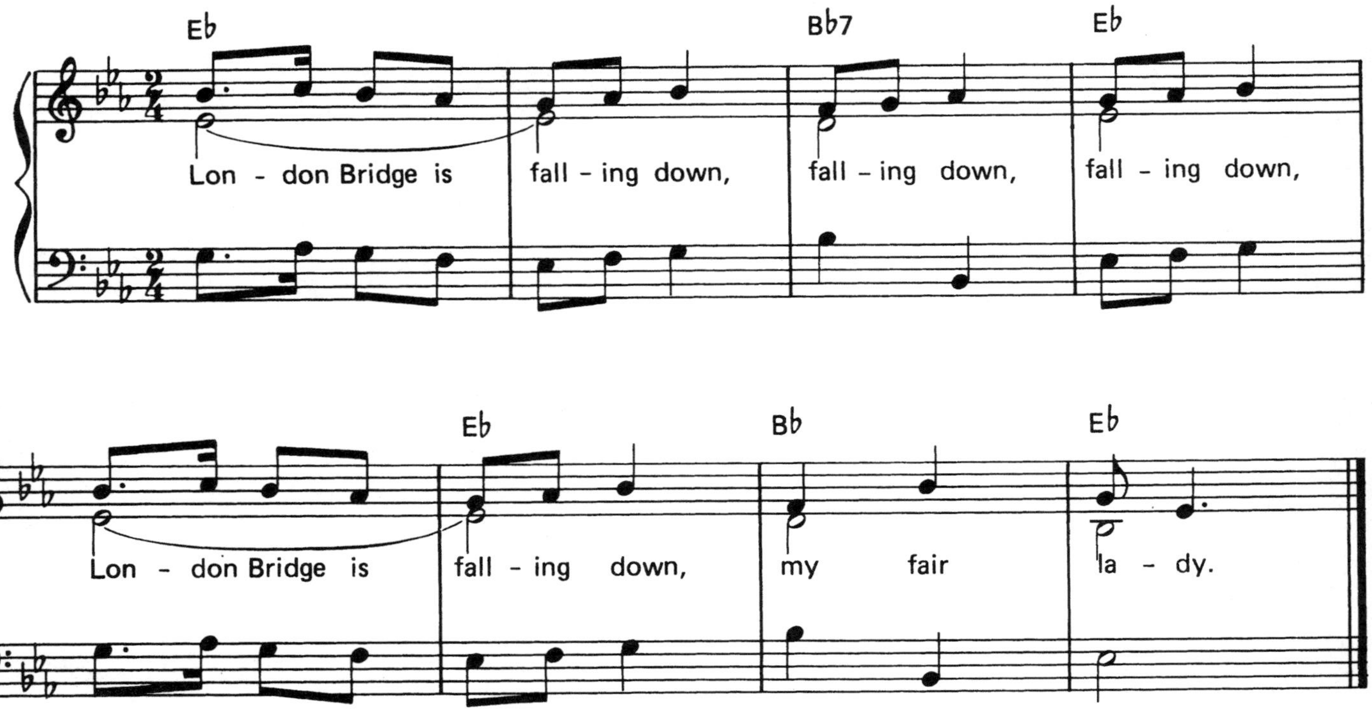

Mother May I Go Out to Swim?

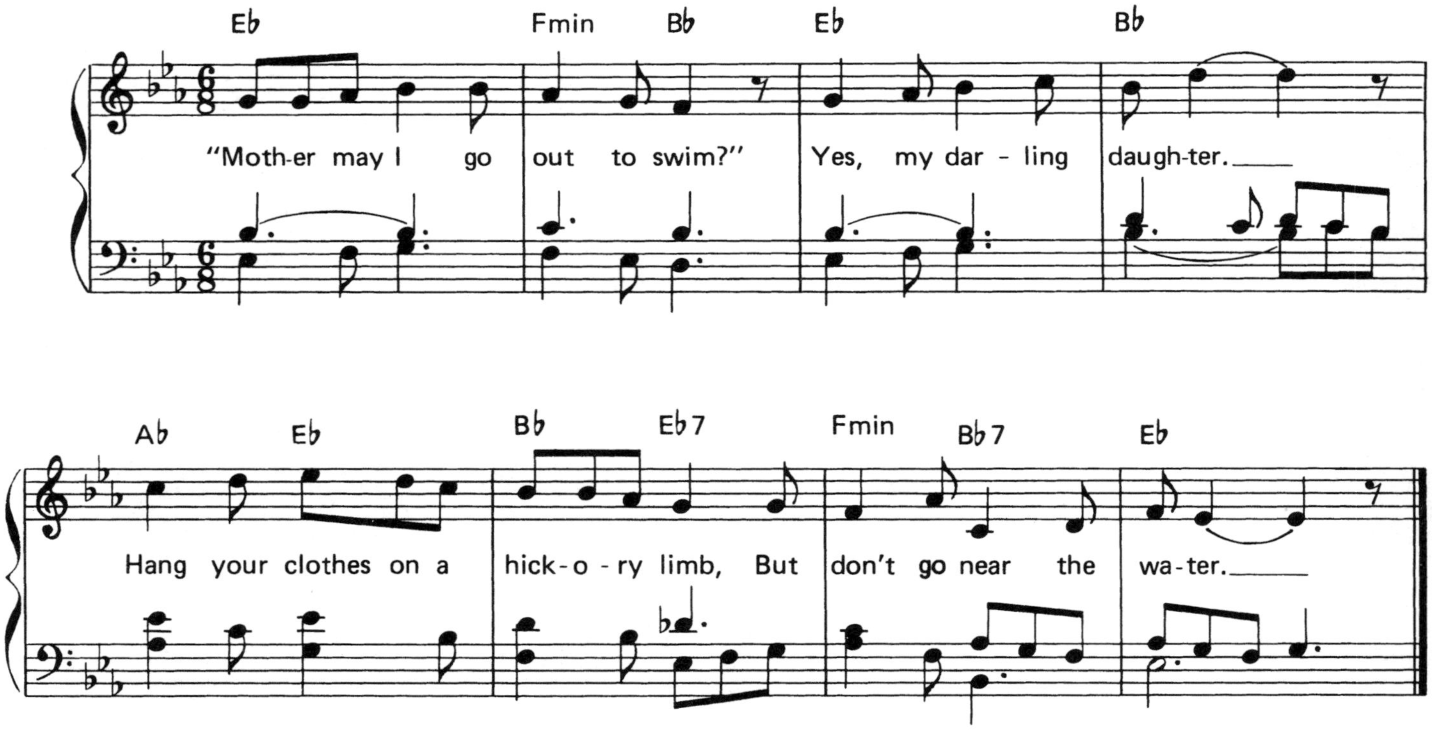

Oranges and Lemons

G Am D G Em Am D G 1 D Bm
Or-an-ges and Lem-ons, say the bells of St. Clem-ent's. You owe me five far-things, say the bells of St. Mar-tin's.
Pray, when will that be, say the bells at Step-ney. I'm sure I don't know, says the great bell at Bow.
When will you pay me? Say the
Em A7 D Bm Em A7 D D7
bells of Old Bail-ey. When I grow rich, say the bells at Shore-ditch.
2 G
Here comes a can-dle to light you to bed, and here comes a

G
chop-per to chop off your head.

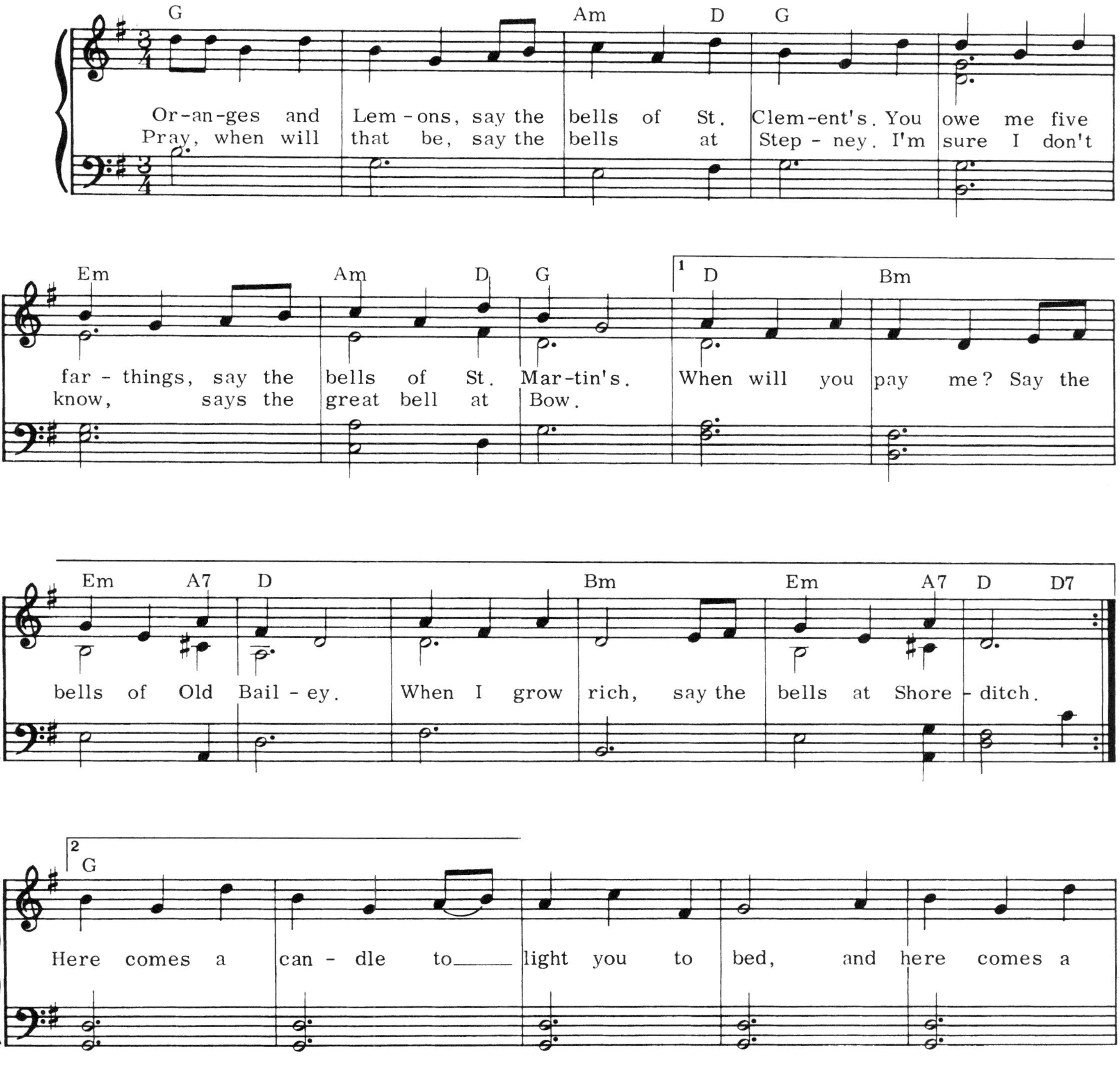

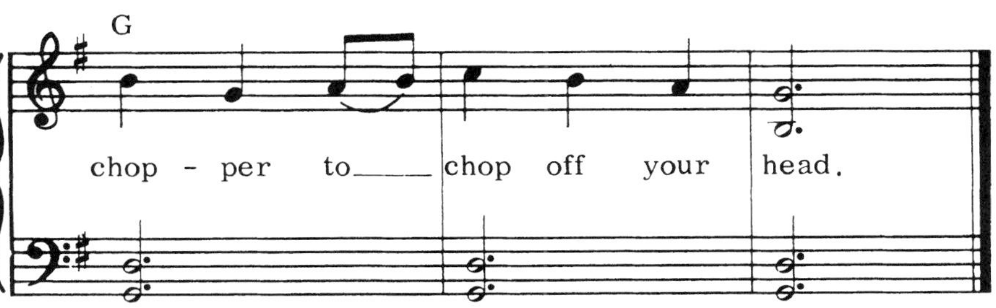

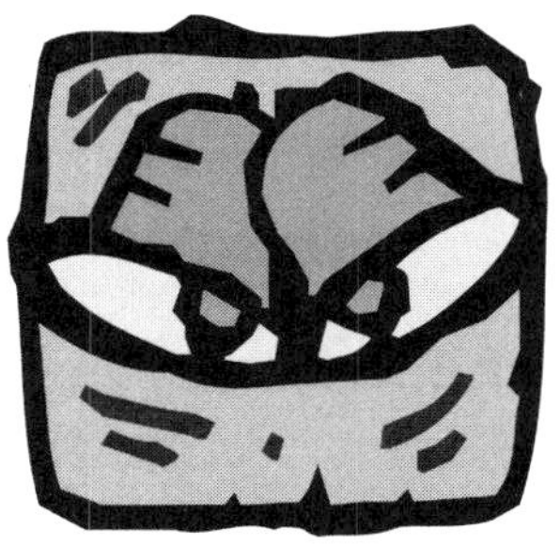

Pat-a-Cake

Eb
Bb
Pat - a - cake, pat - a - cake, ba - ker's man,
E
bake me a cake as fast as you can.
Ab
Pat it and prick it, and mark it with 'B',
Bb
Fm
Bb
Eb
Put it in the ov - en for Ba - by and me.

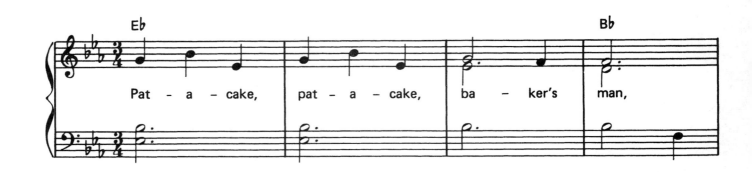

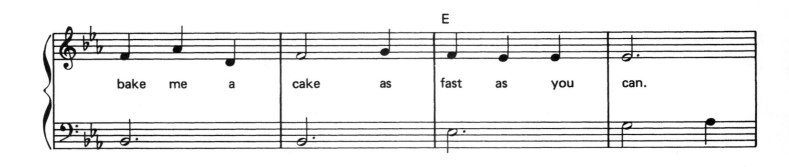

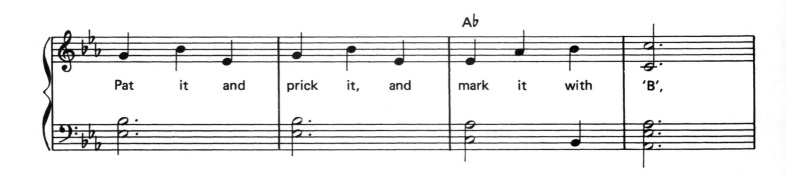

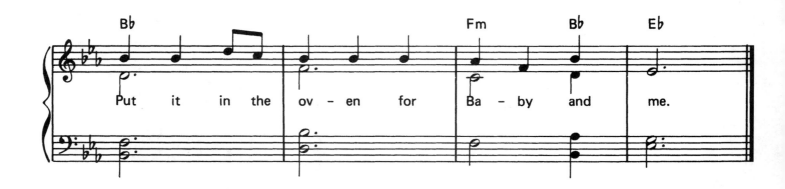

Paw-Paw Patch

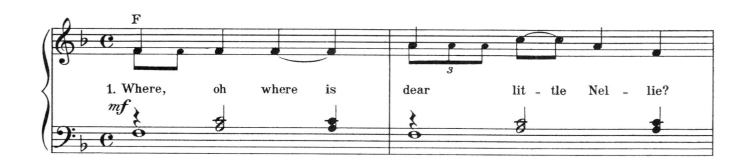

1. Where, oh where is dear lit - tle Nel - lie?

Where, oh where is dear lit - tle Nel - lie? Where, oh where is

dear lit - tle Nel - lie? 'Way down yon-der in the paw - paw patch.

2. Come on, kids, let's go find her,
Come on, kids, let's go find her,
Come on, kids, let's go find her,
'Way down yonder in the paw-paw patch.

3. Pickin' up paw-paws, puttin' 'em in your pocket,
Pickin' up paw-paws, puttin' 'em in your pocket,
Pickin' up paw-paws, puttin' 'em in your pocket,
'Way down yonder in the paw-paw patch.

Polly Put the Kettle On

F C F G C
Pol - ly put the ket - tle on, Pol - ly put the ket - tle on,
F C F B♭ C7 F
Pol - ly put the ket - tle on, we'll all have tea.
C7 F Gm C
Su - key take it off a - gain, Su - key take it off a - gain,
F C7 F B♭ C7 F
Su - key take it off a - gain, they've all gone a - way.

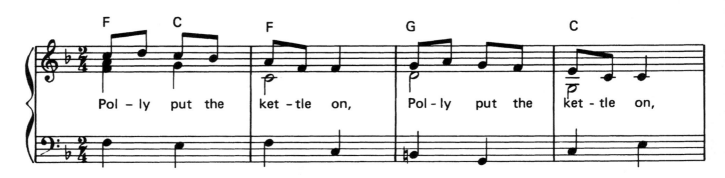

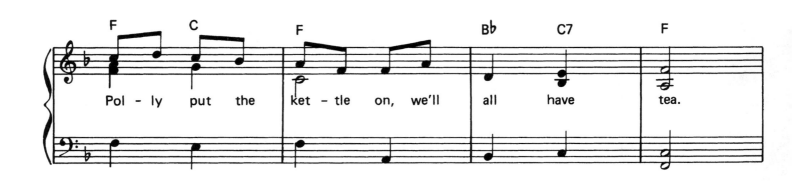

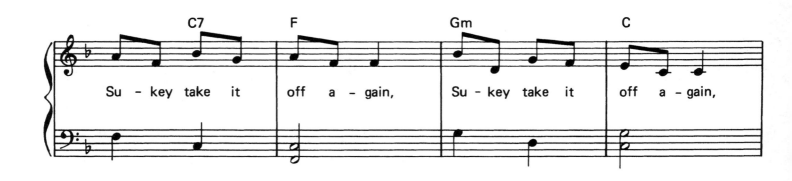

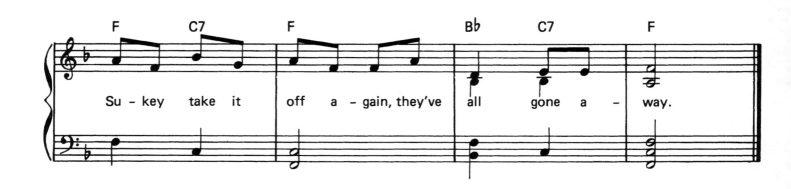

A Ring Around the Rosey

C F C F C
A ring a-round the ros - ey, a pock-et full of pos - ies. A -
C G7 C
tish - oo! A - tish - oo! We all fall down.

See-Saw Margery Daw

G D7 G D7 G A7 D
See - saw, Mar-ger-y Daw, Jack-y shall have a new mas - ter.
G D Em D G C D7 G
He shall have but a pen-ny a day, be - cause he can't work an-y fast - er.

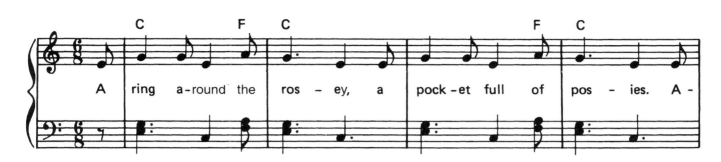

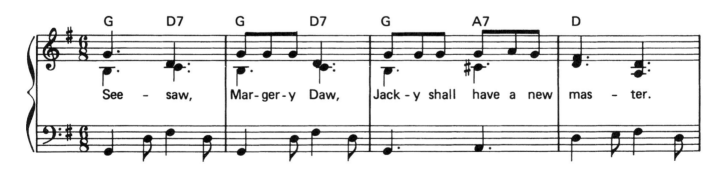

Ride a Toy Horse

C
G7
Ride a toy horse to Ban - bu - ry Cross, to
C
D7
G
see a fine la - dy get on a white horse. With
C
Am7
D7
rings on her fin - gers and bells on her toes,
C
F
G7
C
She shall have mu - sic wher - ev - er she goes.

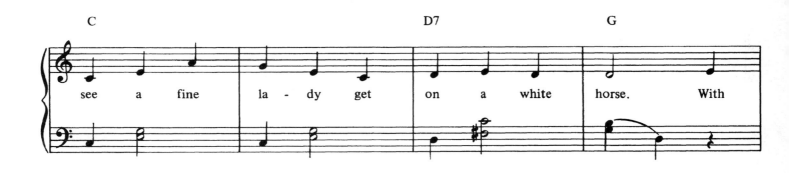

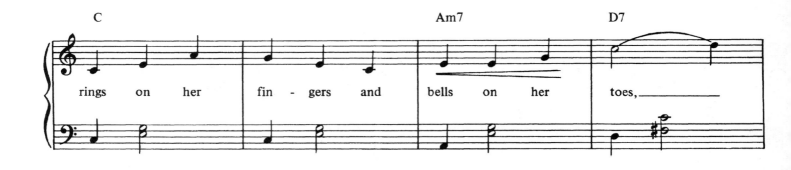

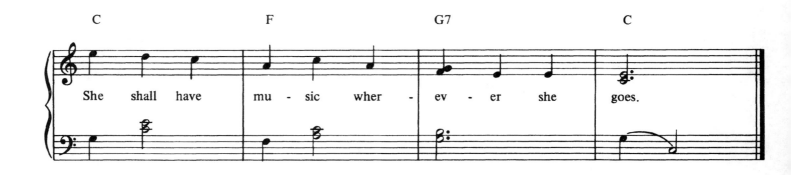

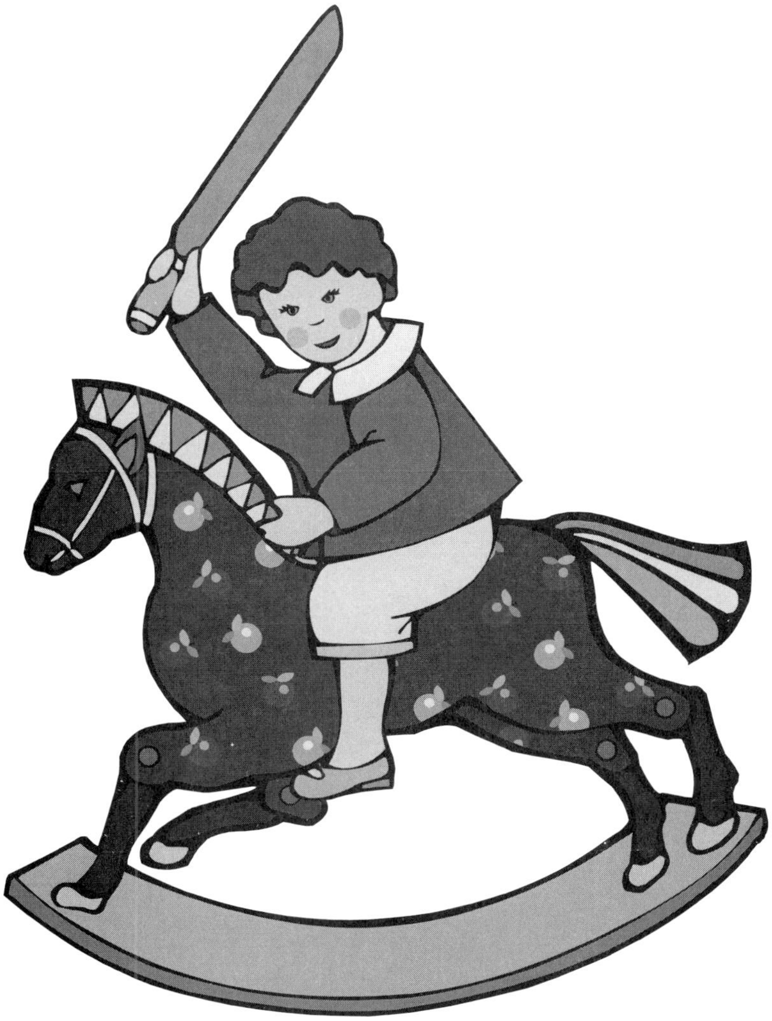

Sailing, Sailing

C F C
f
Sail - ing, Sail - ing, o - ver the bound - ing main, For
G7 C G/D D7/F♯ G G7/F
man - y a storm - y wind shall blow Ere Jack comes home a - gain.
C F C
Sail - ing, sail - ing, o - ver the bound - ing main, For
F B7/F♯ C/G Dm/F C G7 C
man- y a storm - y wind shall blow Ere Jack comes home a - gain.

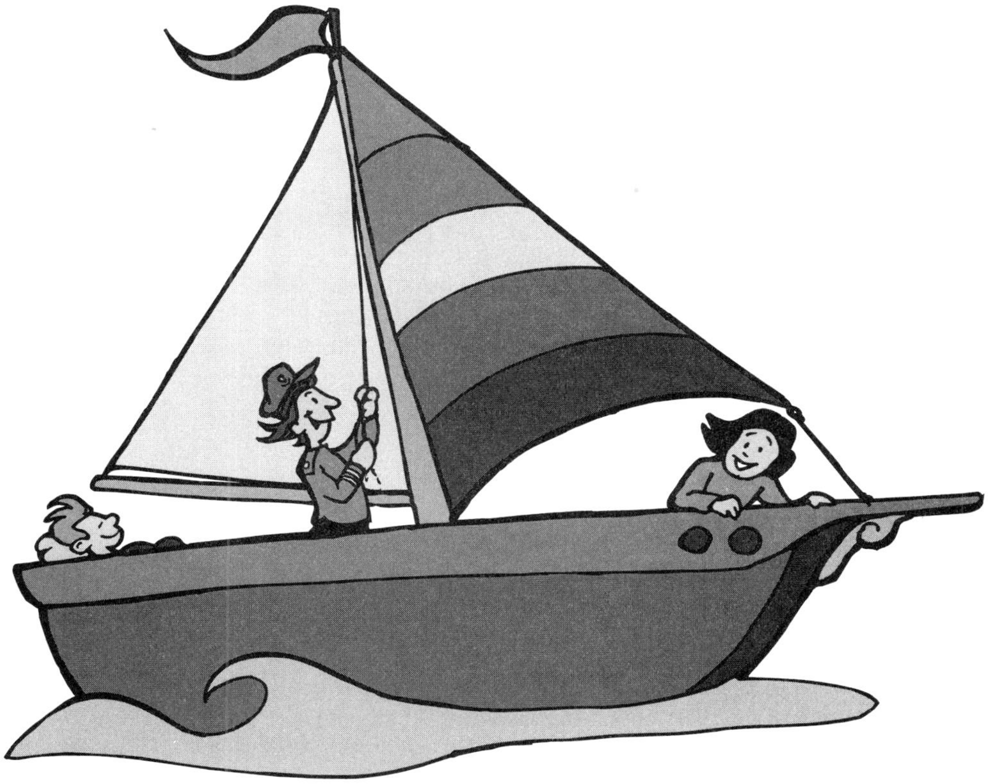

Shortnin' Bread

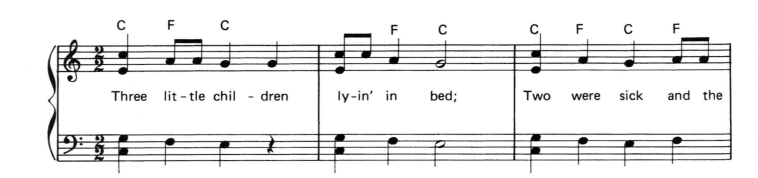

Three lit-tle chil - dren ly-in' in bed; Two were sick and the

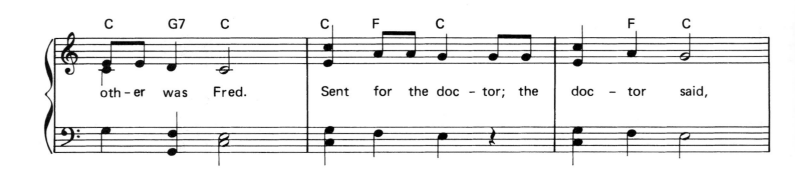

oth-er was Fred. Sent for the doc - tor; the doc - tor said,

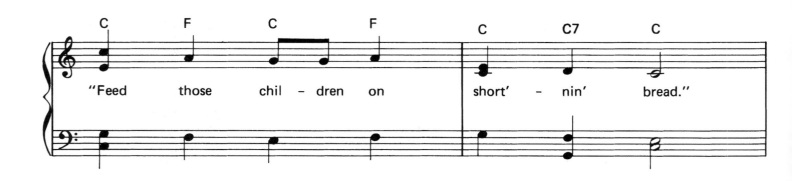

"Feed those chil - dren on short' - nin' bread."

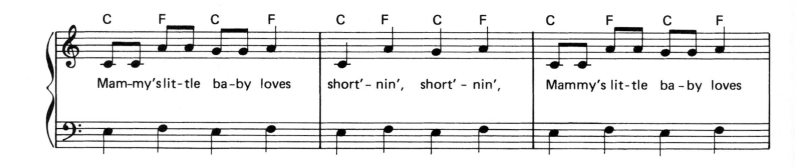

Mam-my's lit-tle ba-by loves short' - nin', short' - nin', Mammy's lit-tle ba-by loves

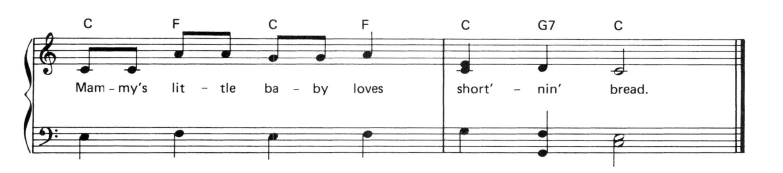

2. Put on the skillet, put on the lid,
   Mammy's goin' to bake a little short'nin' bread.
   That isn't all she's going to do,
   Mammy's goin' to make a little iced tea too.

Sing a Song of Sixpence

2. The king was in his counting house, counting out his money.
The queen was in the parlor, eating bread and honey.
The maid was in the garden, hanging out the clothes,
When down came a blackbird and pecked her on the nose.

Skip to My Lou

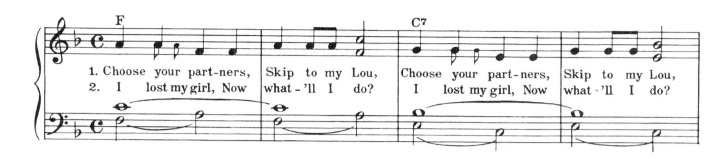

1. Choose your part-ners,
2. I lost my girl, Now

Skip to my Lou, what-'ll I do? Choose your part-ners, I lost my girl, Now Skip to my Lou, what-'ll I do?

Choose your part-ners, I lost my girl, Now Skip to my Lou, what-'ll I do? Skip to my Lou my dar-ling.

3. I'll get another one, a happy one too.

4. Can't get a red bird, a blue bird'll do.

5. I got a red bird, a pretty one too.

6. Cat's in the cream jar, what'll I do?

7. Chicken in the dough tray, what'll I do?

8. Fly's in the buttermilk, shoo fly, shoo!

9. Pickles are sour, and so are you.

10. Hurry up slowpoke, do, oh do.

11. My girl wears a number nine shoe.

12. Bear's in the rose bush, boo-hoo hoo!

13. Cow's in the stable, moo, moo, moo!

14. Come on big foot, what you goin' to do?

Take Me Out to the Ballgame

Words by Jack Norworth

Music by Albert von Tilzer

E7 A7 D
I don't care if I ev - er get back, Let me root, root
A D D7
root for the home team, If they don't win it's a
G Em7 B♭ D G
shame, For it's one, two, three strikes, you're
D D° D E7 A7 D
out, At the old ball game.

There's a Hole in the Bucket

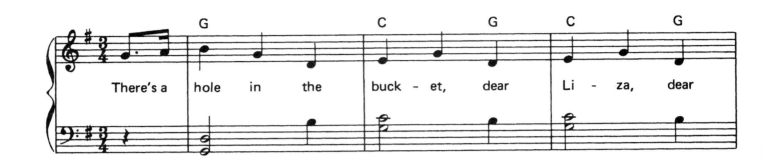

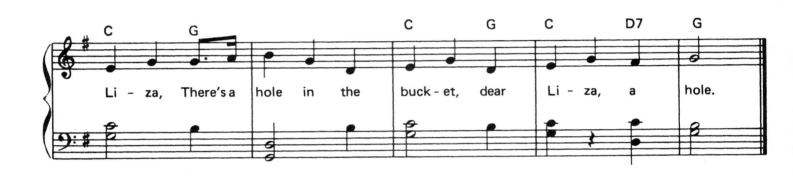

2. Then mend it, dear Henry, dear Henry, dear Henry,
Then mend it, dear Henry, dear Henry, mend it.

3. With what shall I mend it, dear Liza, dear Liza,
With what shall I mend it, dear Liza, with what?

4. With straw, dear Henry, dear Henry, dear Henry,
With straw, dear Henry, dear Henry, with straw.

5. The straw is too long, dear Liza, dear Liza,
The straw is too long, dear Liza, too long.

6. Then cut it, dear Henry, dear Henry, dear Henry,
Then cut it, dear Henry, dear Henry, cut it.

7. With what shall I cut it, dear Liza, dear Liza,
With what shall I cut it, dear Liza, with what?

8. With a knife, dear Henry, dear Henry, dear Henry,
With a knife, dear Henry, dear Henry, a knife.

9. The knife is too dull, dear Liza, dear Liza,
The knife is too dull, dear Liza, too dull.

10. Then sharpen it, dear Henry, dear Henry, dear Henry,
Then sharpen it, dear Henry, dear Henry, sharpen it.

11. With what shall I sharpen it, dear Liza, dear Liza,
With what shall I sharpen it, dear Liza, with what?

12. With a stone, dear Henry, dear Henry, dear Henry,
With a stone, dear Henry, dear Henry, with a stone.

13. The stone is too dry, dear Liza, dear Liza,
The stone is too dry, dear Liza, too dry.

14. Then wet it, dear Henry, dear Henry, dear Henry,
Then wet it, dear Henry, dear Henry, wet it.

15. With what shall I wet it, dear Liza, dear Liza,
With what shall I wet it, dear Liza, with what?

16. With water, dear Henry, dear Henry, dear Henry,
With water, dear Henry, dear Henry, with water.

17. But where shall I get it, dear Liza, dear Liza,
But where shall I get it, dear Liza, but where?

18. From the well, dear Henry, dear Henry, dear Henry,
From the well, dear Henry, dear Henry, from the well.

19. In what shall I carry it, dear Liza, dear Liza,
In what shall I carry it, dear Liza, in what?

20. In the bucket, dear Henry, dear Henry, dear Henry,
In the bucket, dear Henry, dear henry, in the bucket.

21. But there's a hole in the bucket, dear Liza, dear Liza,
There's a hole in the bucket, dear Liza, a hole!

We Whooped and We Hollered

G Em C D7
We whooped and we hol - lered and the first thing we did
G Em7 A7 E♭7
find, Was a barn on a hill ___ and that we left be -
G D G Em C
hind, ___ Look a there now. Some said it was a barn,
D7 G Em7
some said "Nay," Some said it was a church ___ with the
A7 E♭7 G D G
stee - ple cut a - way, ___ Look - a there now.

2. We whooped and we hollered and the next thing we did find.
   Was a pig in a lane and that we left behind.
   Look-a there now.
   Some said it was a pig, some said, "Nay,"
   Some said it was an elephant with his trunk put away.
   Look-a there now.

3. We whooped and we hollered and the next thing we did find.
   Was the moon in a tree and that we left behind.
   Look-a there now.
   Some said it was the moon in a tree, some said, "Nay,"
   Some said it was a cheese with a half cut away.
   Look-a there now.

4. We whooped and we hollered and the next thing we did find.
   Was a frog in a well and that we left behind.
   Look-a there now.
   Some said it was a frog in a well, some said, "Nay,"
   Some said it was a jaybird with its feathers put away.
   Look-a there now.

5. We whooped and we hollered and the last thing we did find.
   Was an owl on a log that we left behind.
   Look-a there now.
   Some said it was an owl in a tree, some said, "Nay,"
   Some said it was a ghost, so we all ran away.
   Look-a there now.

The World Turned Upside Down

C Am C+ C Am C+5
mf
If but-ter-cups buzzed af - ter the bee, If boats were on land, church-es on sea, If
Am Em Dm G G7 C Am D7 G
po-nies rode men, and if grass ate the cows, And cats should be chased in - to holes by the mouse,
Gsus4 G Em7 C G7sus4 G7 C
p
cresc.
If the ma - mas sold their ba - bies to the Gyp-sies for half a crown, If
Gsus4 G7 C C♯dim G7 C Dm7 C G7 C
rit.
f
a tempo
sum-mer were spring, and the oth - er way 'round, Then all the world would be up - side down.

Singing and Learning

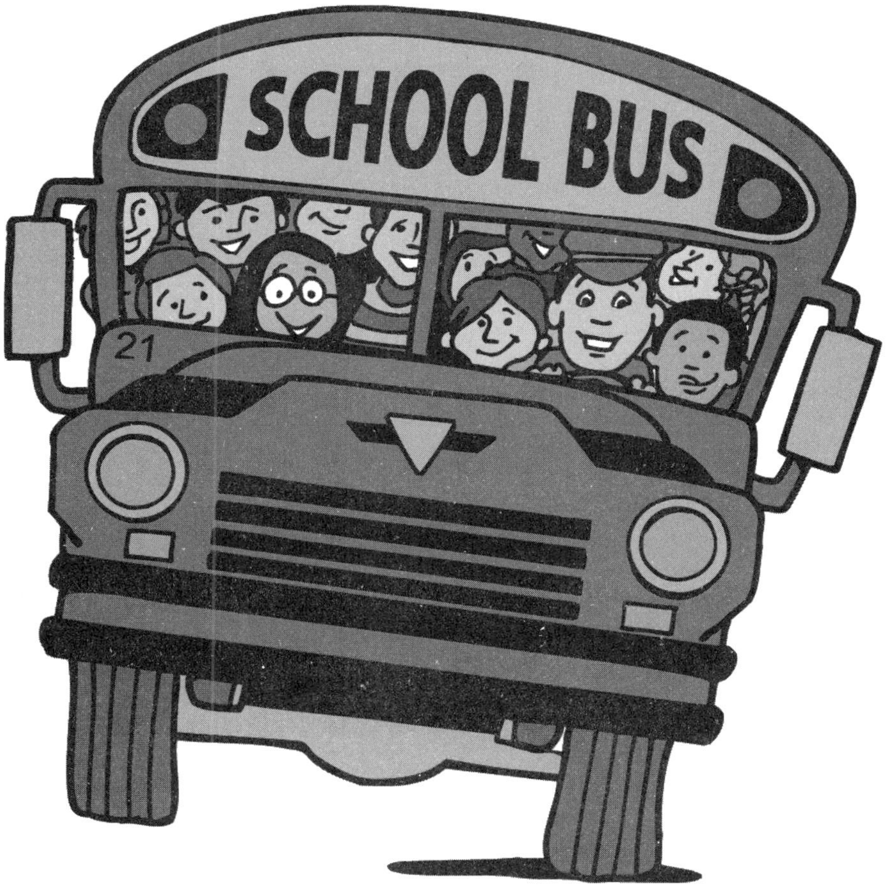

The Alphabet Song

G C G D7 G D7 G
Come, dear moth-er. hear me say What I can of A B C;
Now, my Al - pha - bet is through, Will you hear dear sis - ter too?
C G D7 G D7 G
A B C D E F G, H I J K L M N O P
A B C D E F G, She has said them all to me;
Amin G Amin G Amin G D7
Q R S and T U V, W(dou-ble - you) and X Y Z.
Q R S and T U V, W(dou-ble - you) and X Y Z.
G C G D7 G D7 G
Now you've heard my A B C, Tell me what you think of me.
Now we've said our A B C, Let us have a kiss from thee.

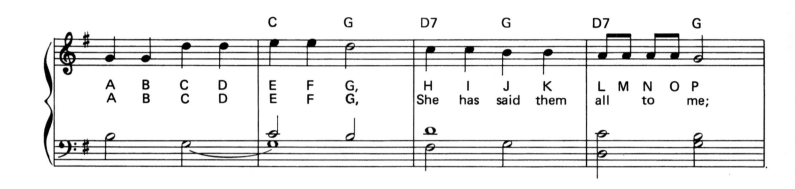

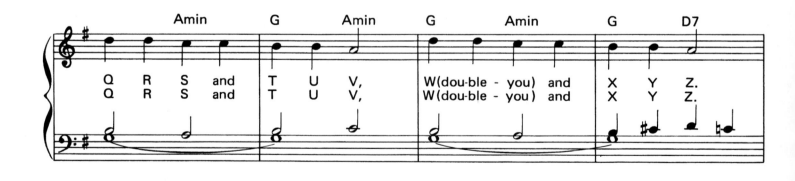

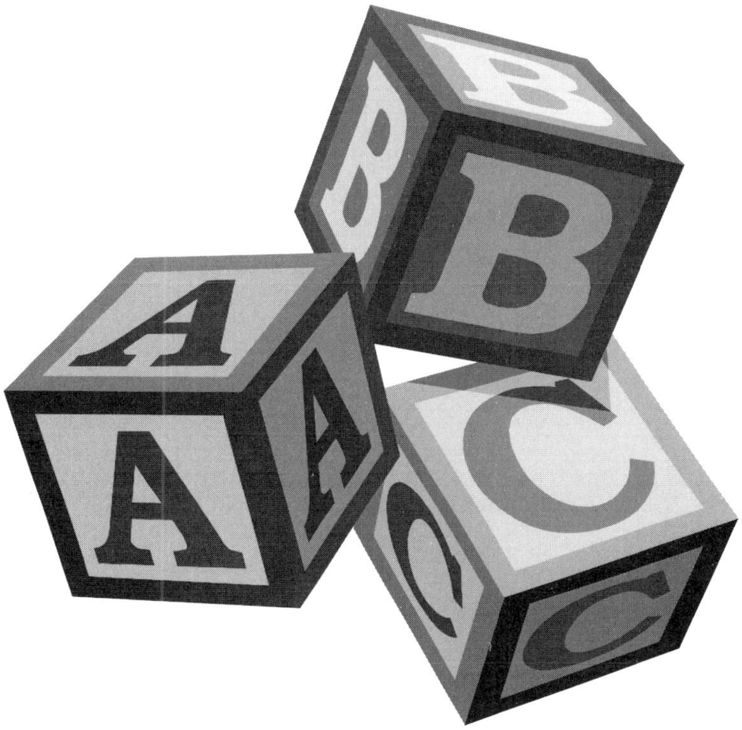

48

The Ants Came Marching

© 2001 Music Sales Corporation (ASCAP)
International Copyright Secured. All Rights Reserved.

2. The ants came marching two by two,
   Hurrah! Hurrah!
   The ants came marching two by two,
   Hurrah! Hurrah!
   The ants came marching two by two,
   The little one stopped to tie his shoe.
   And they all go marching down around the town
   (Boom, boom, boom.)

3. The ants came marching three by three, *etc.*
   The little one stopped to climb a tree, *etc.*

4. The ants came marching four by four, *etc.*
   The little one stopped to shut the door, *etc.*

5. The ants came marching five by five, *etc.*
   The little one stopped to take a dive, *etc.*

6. The ants came marching six by six, *etc.*
   The little one stopped to pick up sticks, *etc.*

7. The ants came marching seven by seven, *etc.*
   The little one stopped to go to heaven, *etc.*

8. The ants came marching eight by eight, *etc.*
   The little one stopped to shut the gate, *etc.*

9. The ants came marching nine by nine, *etc.*
   The little one stopped to scratch his spine, *etc.*

10. The ants came marching ten by ten, *etc.*
    The little one stopped to say, "The end!," *etc.*

One Finger, One Thumb, One Hand

F Gm F C7
One fin-ger, one thumb, one hand keep mov - ing, One
F Gm F Bb C Bb
fin-ger, one thumb, one hand keep mov - ing, One fin-ger, one thumb, one hand, keep
F Dm F Bb F C7 F
mov - ing, And we'll all be hap - py and gay!

One, Two, Three, Four, Five

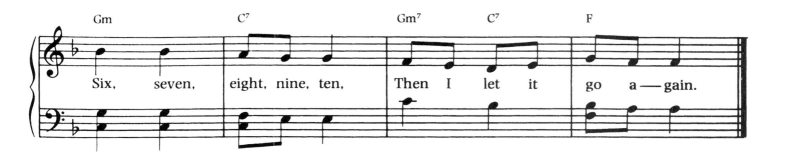

2. Why did you let it go?
   It nibbled on my finger so.
   Which finger did it bite?
   The little finger on the right.

The Orchestra

William Geisler

Moderately
I
The vi - o - lin's ring - ing like joy - - - ful
II
The clar-i - net, the clar - i - net sings dood-le, dood - le, dood - le,
III
The trum - pet is sound - ing ta ta ta ta ta ta ta, ta ta ta
IV
The horn, the horn whose song is for -
V
The drum plays on two tones and drones on the
Moderately
C
G7
PIANO
mf

sing - ing, The vi - o - lin's ring - ing like joy - ful___ song.
doodle det, The clar - i - net, the clar - i - net sings dood - le, dood - le, dood - le det.
ta ta ta ta, The trum - pet is sound - ing ta ta ta ta ta ta ta, ta ta ta ta.
lorn, The horn, the horn whose song is for - lorn.
same tones, Five one, one five, boom boom boom boom boom.
C
G7
C

Ten Little Sailors

F
C
Old Da - vey Jones had one lit-tle sail - or, Old Da-vey
C7
F
Jones had one lit - tle sail - or, Old Da - vey Jones had
Gm
C7
F
one lit - tle sail - or, One lit - tle sail - or boy. He had
C
one, he had two, he had three lit - tle sail - ors, Four, he had

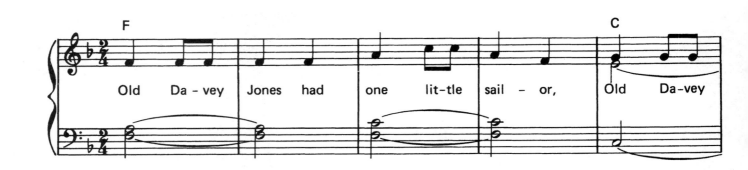

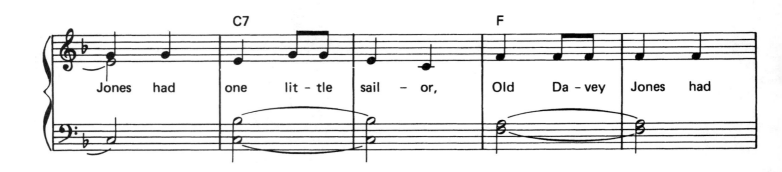

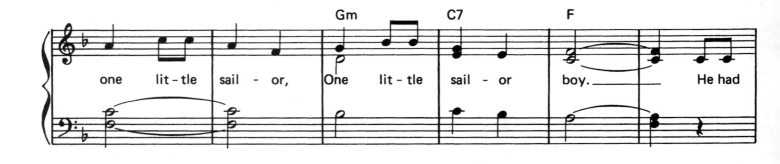

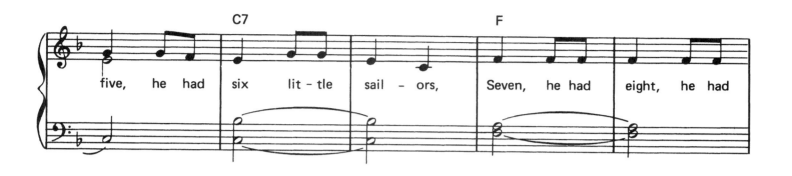

five, he had six lit – tle sail – ors, Seven, he had eight, he had

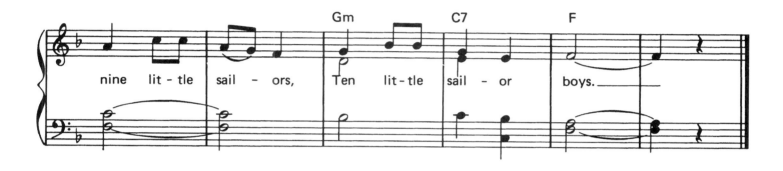

nine lit – tle sail – ors, Ten lit – tle sail – or boys.

There Were Ten in a Bed

There were ten in the bed and the lit - tle one

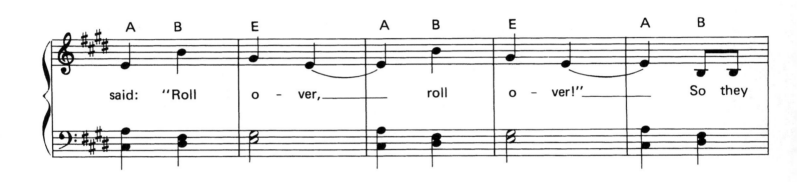

said: "Roll o - ver, roll o - ver!" So they

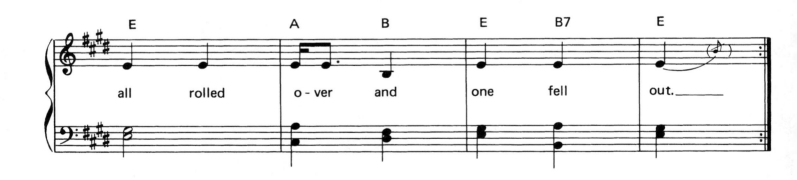

all rolled o - ver and one fell out.

2. There were nine in the bed and the little one said, *etc.*

3. There were eight in the bed and the little one said, *etc.*

4. There were seven in the bed and the little one said, *etc.*

5. There were six in the bed and the little one said, *etc.*

6. There were five in the bed and the little one said, *etc.*

7. There were four in the bed and the little one said, *etc.*

8. There were three in the bed and the little one said, *etc.*

9. There were two in the bed and the little one said, *etc.*

10. There was one in the bed and the little one said,
    "Good night!"

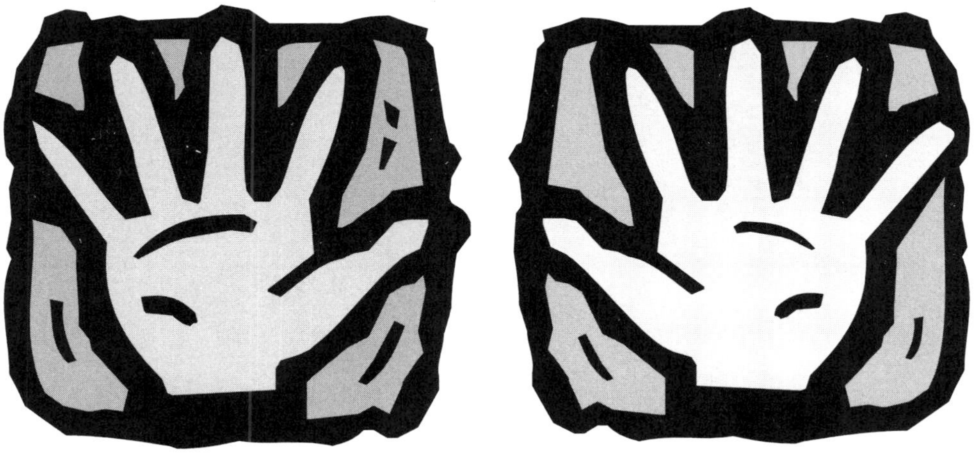

This Old Man

2. This old man, he played two,
   He played nick-nack on my shoe, *etc.*

3. This old man, he played three,
   He played nick nack on my knee, *etc.*

4. This old man, he played four,
   He played nick nack on the floor, *etc.*

5. This old man, he played five,
   He played nick-nack on a hive, *etc.*

6. This old man, he played six,
   He played nick-nack on some sticks, *etc.*

7. This old man, he played seven,
   He played nick-nack up in heaven., *etc.*

8. This old man, he played eight,
   He played nick-nack at my gate, *etc.*

9. This old man, he played nine,
   He played nick-nack on my spine, *etc.*

10. This old man, he played ten,
    He played nick-nack once again, *etc..*

Animal Songs

The Animal Fair

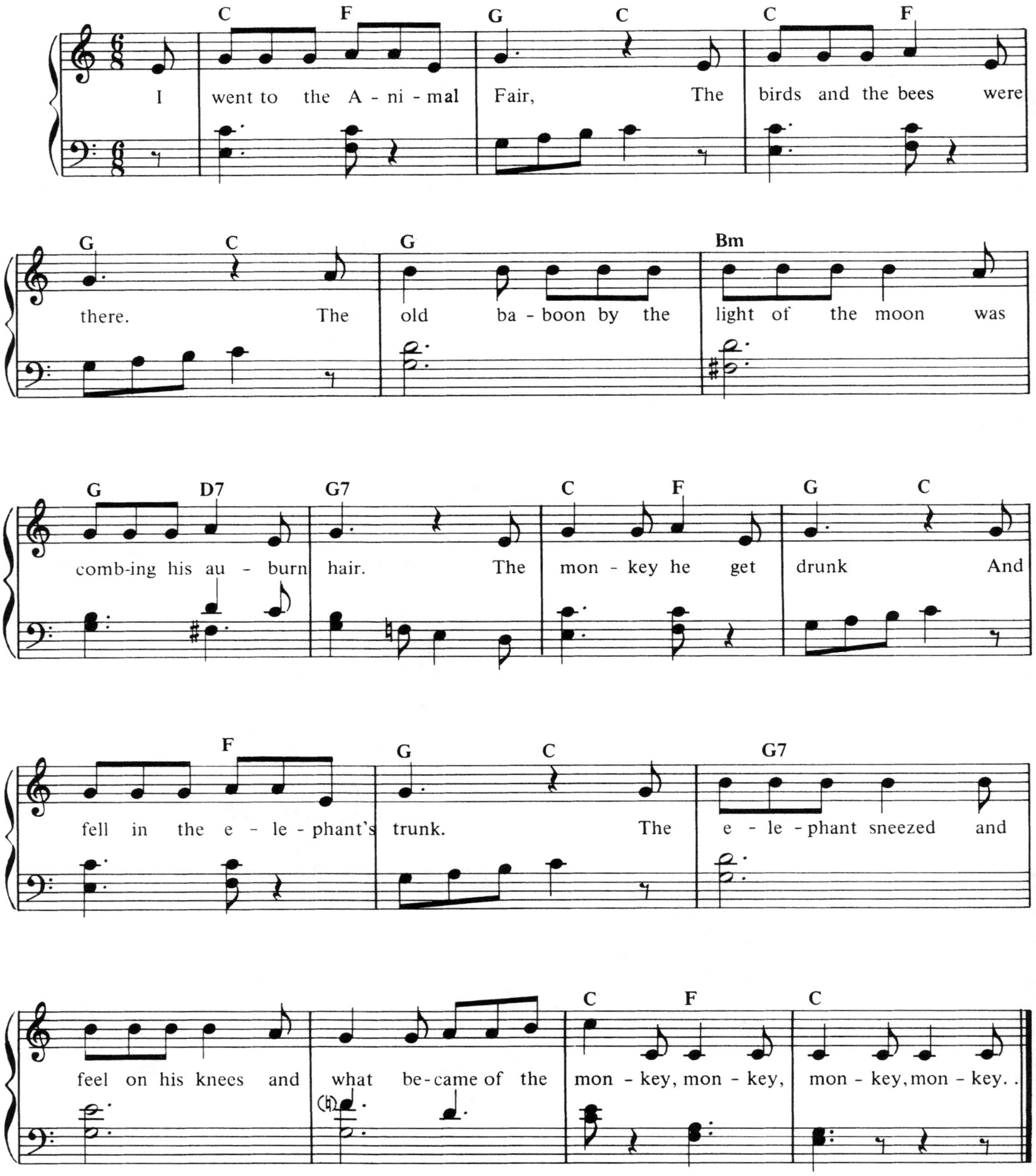
C F G C C F
I went to the A - ni - mal Fair, The birds and the bees were
G C G Bm
there. The old ba - boon by the light of the moon was
G D7 G7 C F G C
comb-ing his au - burn hair. The mon - key he get drunk And
F G C G7
fell in the e - le - phant's trunk. The e - le - phant sneezed and
C F C
feel on his knees and what be-came of the mon - key, mon - key, mon - key, mon - key. .

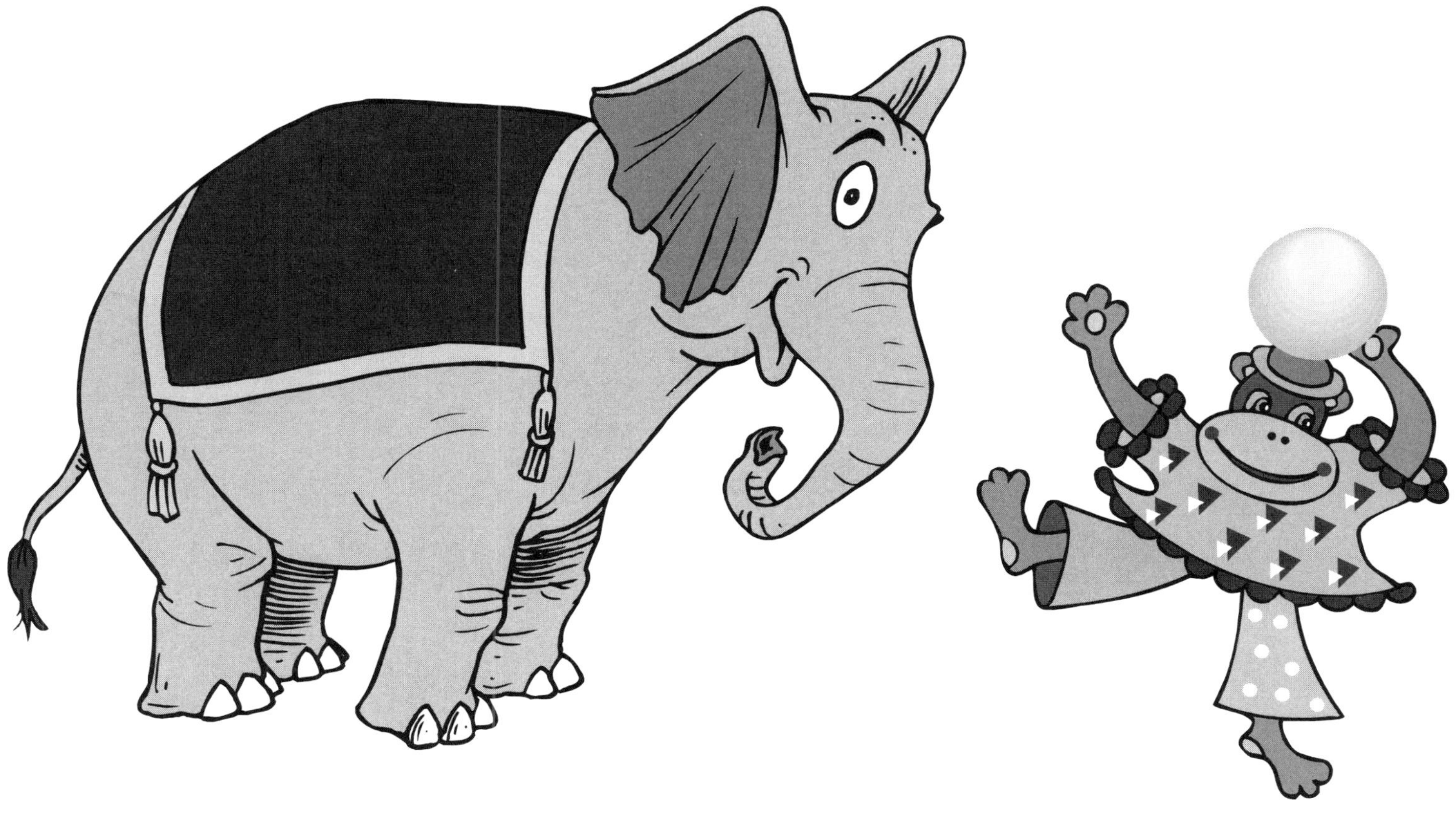

The Animal Song

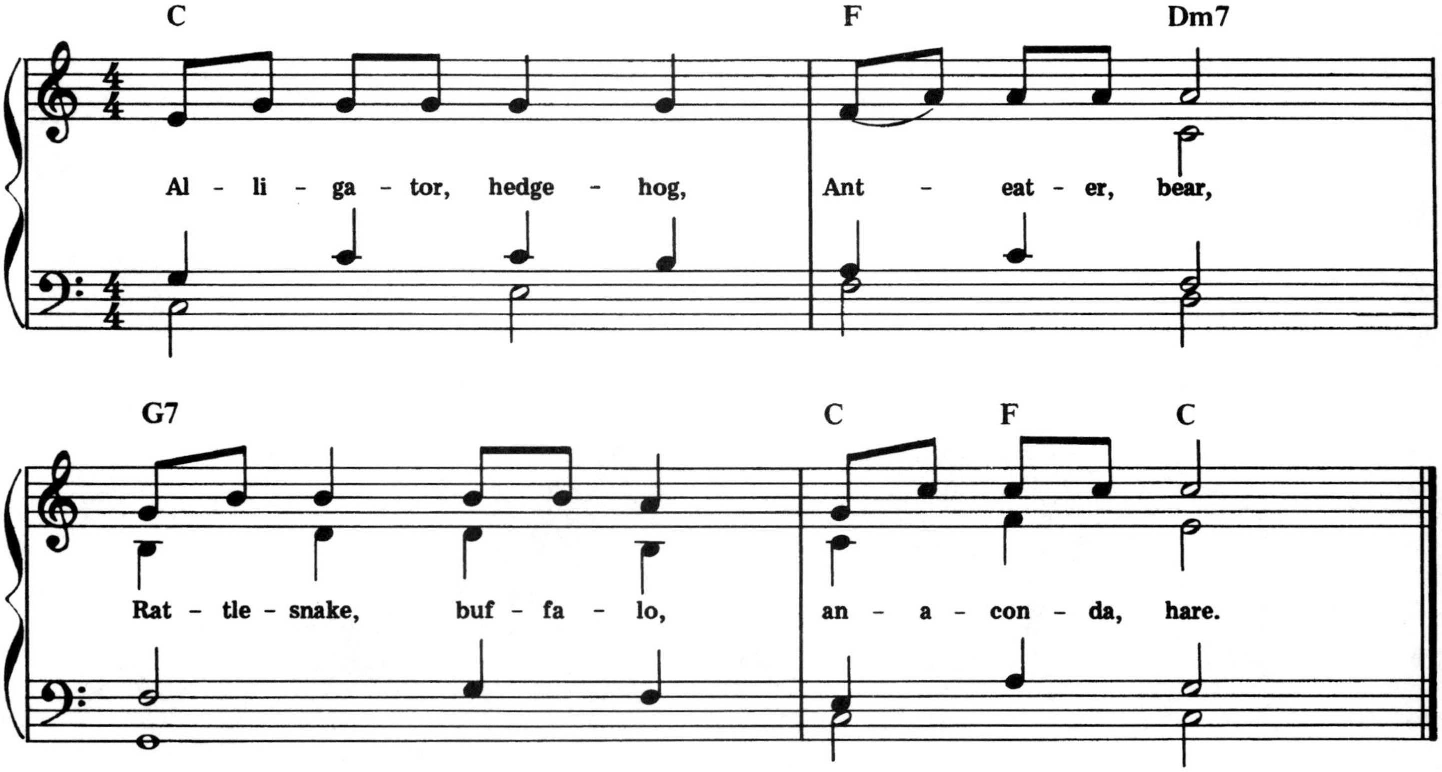

2. Bullfrog, woodchuck, wolverine, goose,
Whiipporwill, chipmunk, jackal, moose.

3. Mud turtle, whale, glowworn, bat,
Salamander, snail, Maltese cat.

4. Black squirrel, coon, opossum, wren,
Red squirrel, loon, South Guinea hen.

5. Reindeer, blacksnake, ibex, nightingale,
Martin, wild drake, crocodile, quail.

6. House rat, kitten, brown bear, doe,
Chickadee, peacock, bobolink, crow.

7. Eagle, jellyfish, sheep, duck, widgeon,
Conger, armadillo, shrew, seal, pigeon.

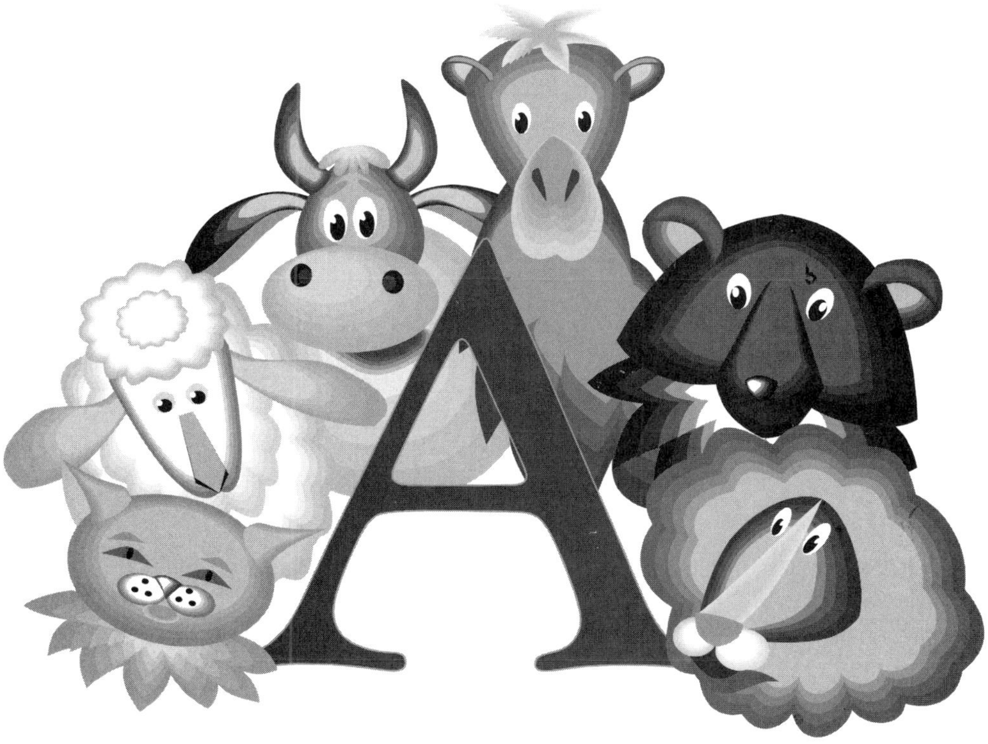

The Barnyard Song

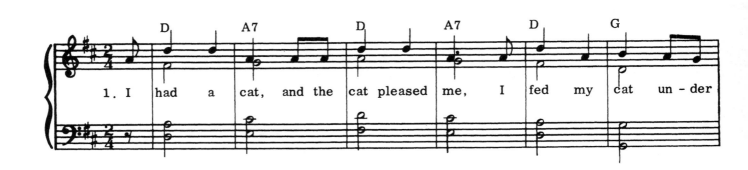

1. I had a cat, and the cat pleased me, I fed my cat un-der

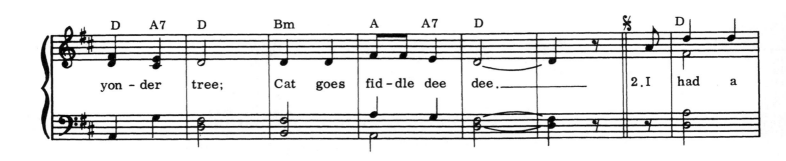

yon-der tree; Cat goes fid-dle dee dee. 2.I had a

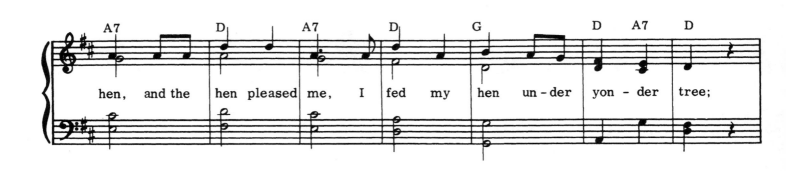

hen, and the hen pleased me, I fed my hen un-der yon-der tree;

Repeated an extra time for each verse

Hen goes chim-my chuck, chimmy chuck, Cat goes fid-dle dee dee. Back to

3. I had horse, and the horse pleased me,
   I fed my horse under yonder tree;
   Horse goes neigh, neigh,
   Hen goes chimmy chuck, chimmy chuck,
   Cat goes fiddle dee dee.

4. I had a cow, and the cow pleased me,
   I fed my cow under yonder tree;
   Cow goes moo, moo,
   Horse goes neigh, neigh,
   Hen goes chimmy chuck, chimmy chuck,
   Cat goes fiddle dee dee.

Baa! Baa! Black Sheep

D G D
Baa, baa, black sheep, have you an - y wool?
Em7 A7 D Em A D
Yes, sir, yes, sir, three bags full,
G D
One for my mas - ter, And one for my dame, And
Em7 A7 D Em A7 D
one for the lit - tle boy who lives down the lane.

Black Sheep, Where's Your Lamb?

G Emin D7 G A7 D7 G
Black sheep, black sheep, where's your lamb? Way down in the val - ley,
C Emin E♭7 G A7 D7 G
But-ter-fly, but-ter-fly, flit-ting round its eye, and the poor lit-tle thing cried, "Mam - my,"
G C G Amin Emin A D7 G
Mam-my said when she went a-way, to take good care of the ba - by, When
C Emin E♭7 G A7 D7 G
she come back she'd bring a piece of cake, and give a lit-tle bit to the ba - by.

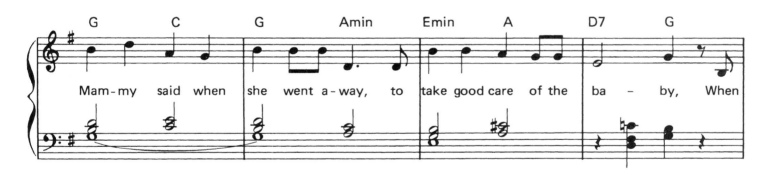

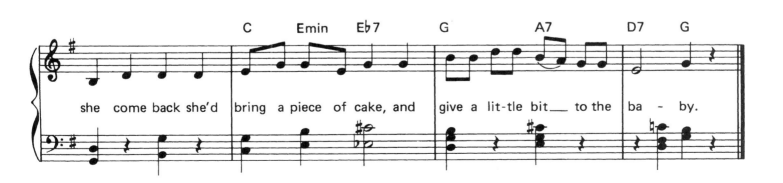

The Bear Went Over the Mountain

C F C G C
The bear went o-ver the moun - tain, The bear went o-ver the moun - tain, The
F G7 C
bear went o - ver the moun - tain To see what he could see. And
F C F C G7
all that he could see, And all that he could see was The
C F C G C
oth - er side of the moun - tain The oth - er side of the moun - tain, The

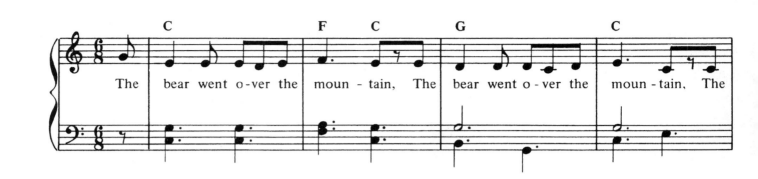

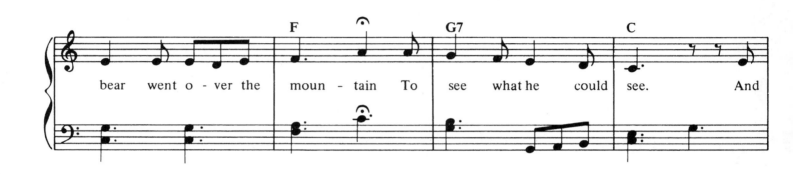

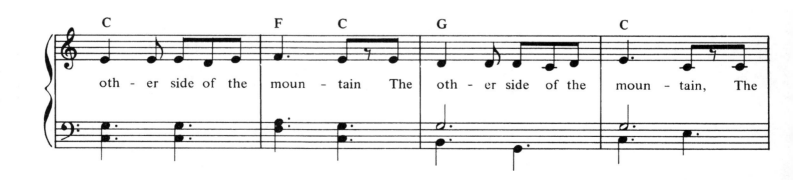

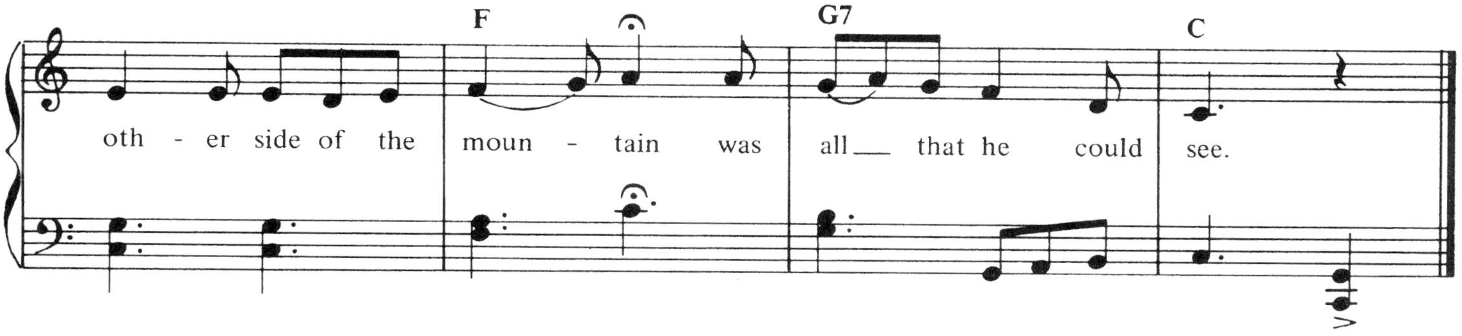

oth - er side of the moun - tain was all __ that he could see.

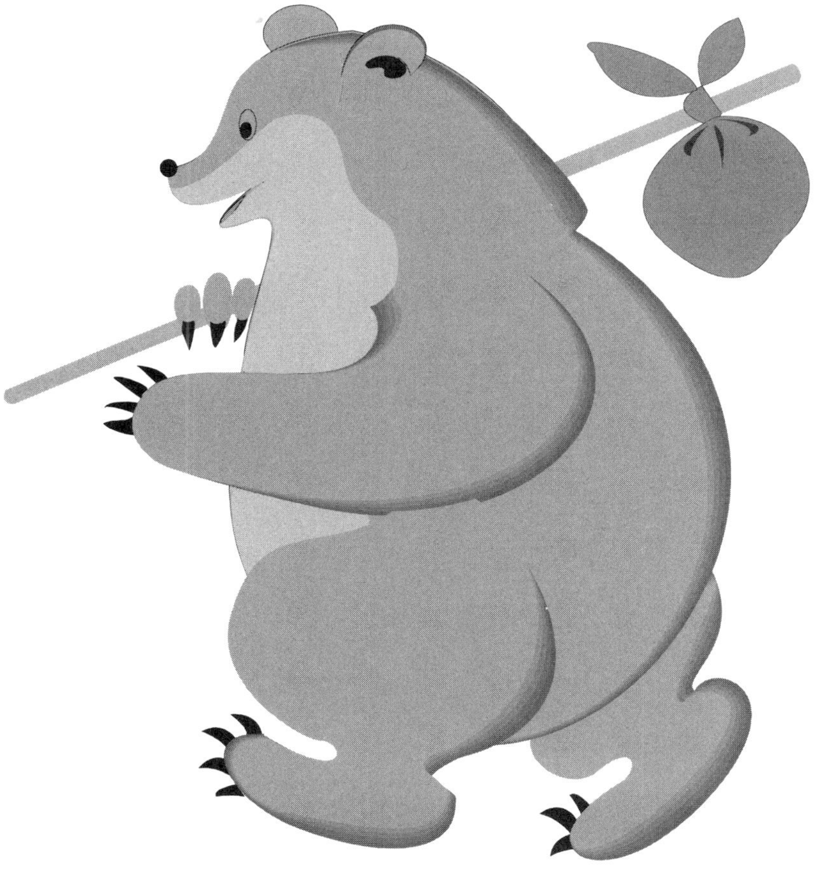

The City Rat and the Country Rat

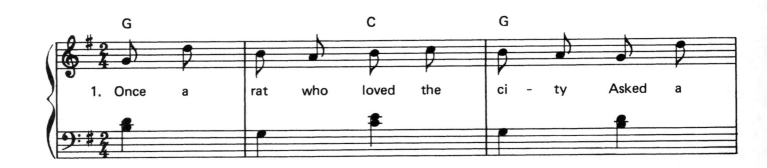

1. Once a rat who loved the ci - ty Asked a

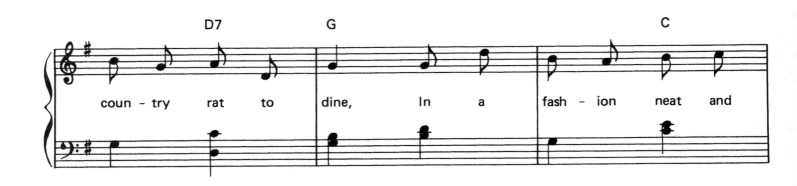

coun - try rat to dine, In a fash - ion neat and

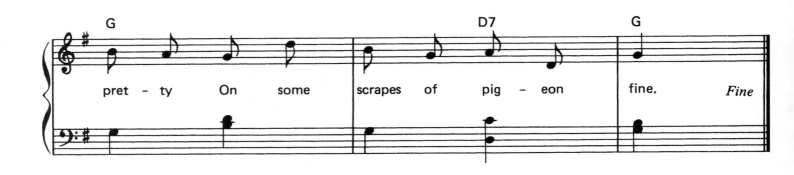

pret - ty On some scrapes of pig - eon fine. *Fine*

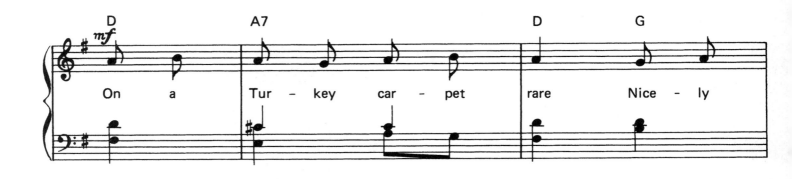

On a Tur - key car - pet rare Nice - ly

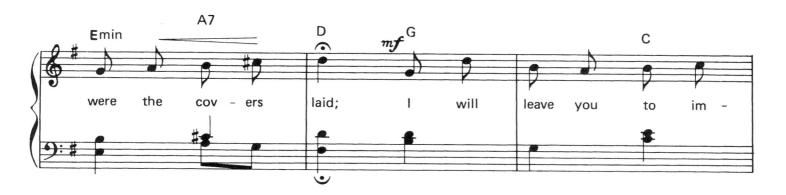

were the cov - ers laid; I will leave you to im -

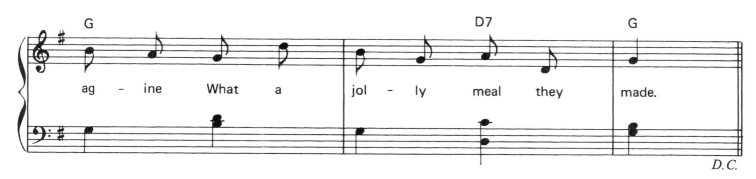

ag - ine What a jol - ly meal they made.

D.C.

2. Good the roast was found on eating,
   Naught was wanting in the least;
   But at every merry meeting
   Something will disturb the feast.
   On a Turkey carpet rare
   Nicely were the covers laid;
   I will leave you to imagine
   What a jolly meal they made.

3. Quiet all, they left their cover,
   Country rat was dumb with fright;
   City rat said to the other,
   "Come and let us finish quite!"
   Suddenly they hear a noise
   As of someone at the door;
   Soon the country rat was running,
   City rat was off before.

4. "In my barn I eat at leisure,
   Nothing will disturb us there:
   Fare you well if you have pleasure,
   You have also fear and care."

The Crawdad Song

F Gm7 F B♭ Dm7 Gm7 F B♭
1. You get a line and___ I'll get a pole,___ Ho - ney.___
2. Here comes a man with a pack on his back,___ Ho - ney.___
Am B♭ C Dmin7 C B♭ Am Gm
You get a line and___ I'll get a pole, Babe.___
Here comes a man with a pack on his back, Babe.___
F F7 B♭ F
You get a line and___ I'll get a pole, we'll, go fish-in' in the
Here comes a man with a pack on his back, To-tin the craw - dads___
G9 C7 F B♭ Am C7 F
craw-dad hole,___ Ho - ney,___ Oh Ba - by Mine.___
in his pack,___

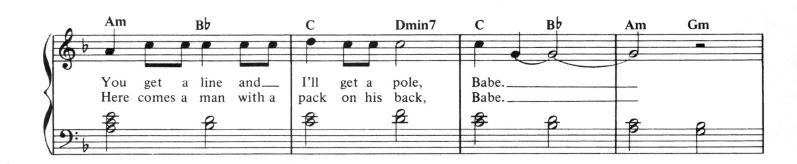

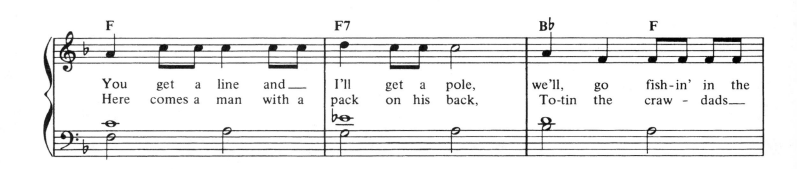

3. Whatcha gonna do when the stream runs dry, Honey?
   Whatcha gonna do when the stream runs dry, Babe?
   Whatcha gonna do when the stream runs dry?
   Sit on the bank, watch the crawdads die,
   Honey, Oh, Baby Mine.

Ding Dong Bell

F C7 F Gm7 F C7 F
Ding dong bell! Pus - sy's in the well!
C7 F Gm7 F C7 F F7
Who put her in? Lit - tle Tom - my Green. Who pulled her out?
B♭ C7 F F7 B♭ C7 F
Lit - tle Tom - my Stout. What a naught - y boy was that, to scare poor pus - sy cat, Who
G7 F G7 F C7 F B♭ F C7 F
ne'er did an - y harm, but killed all the mice in Fath - er's farm.

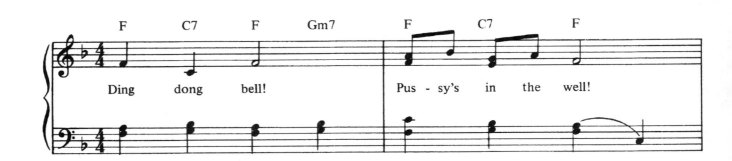

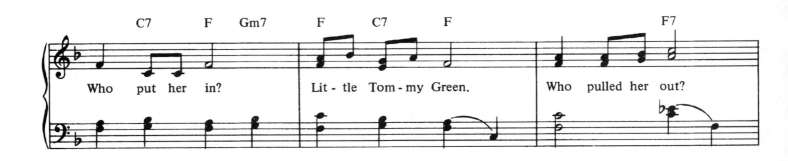

Ducks on the Millpond

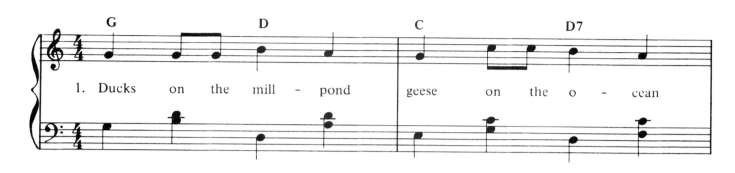

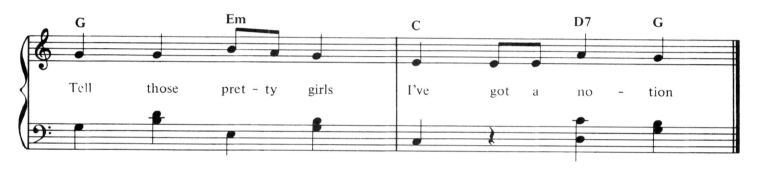

2. Ducks on the millpond, geese in clover,
   Tell those pretty girls I'm coming over.

3. All I want in this creation,
   Nice, clever wife and a green plantation.

4. All I want to make me happy,
   Two little boys to call me pappy.

5. All I want to make me gladdy,
   Two little girls to call me daddy.

Eency Weency Spider

Een - cy ween - cy spi - der went up the wa - ter spout,

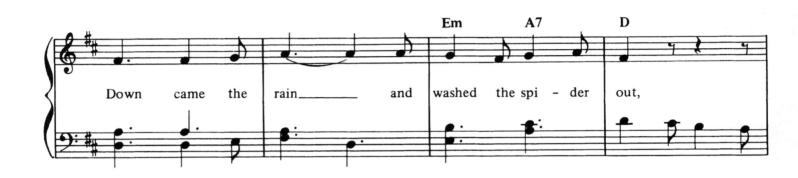

Down came the rain_____ and washed the spi - der out,

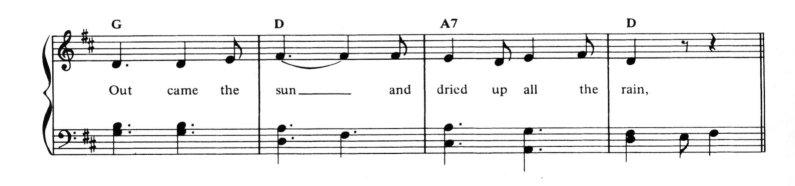

Out came the sun_____ and dried up all the rain,

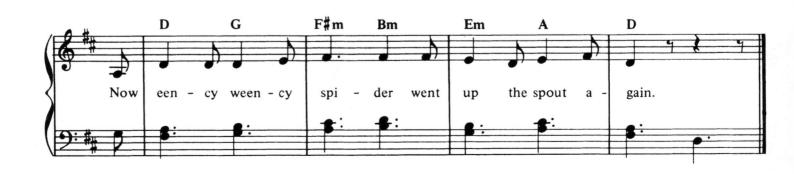

Now een - cy ween - cy spi - der went up the spout a - gain.

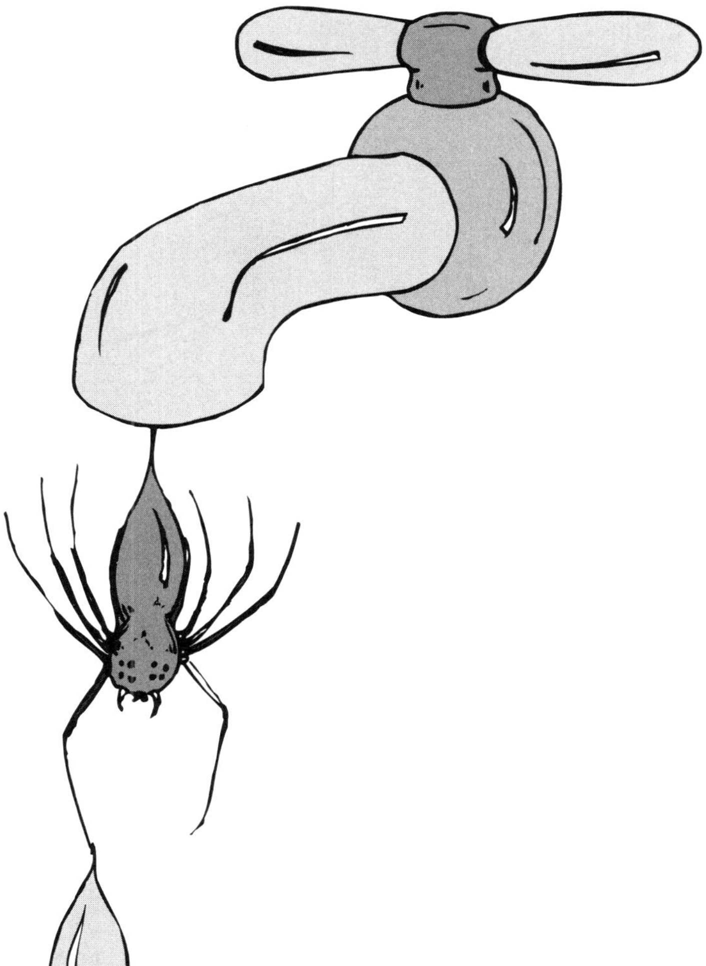

The Farmer in the Dell

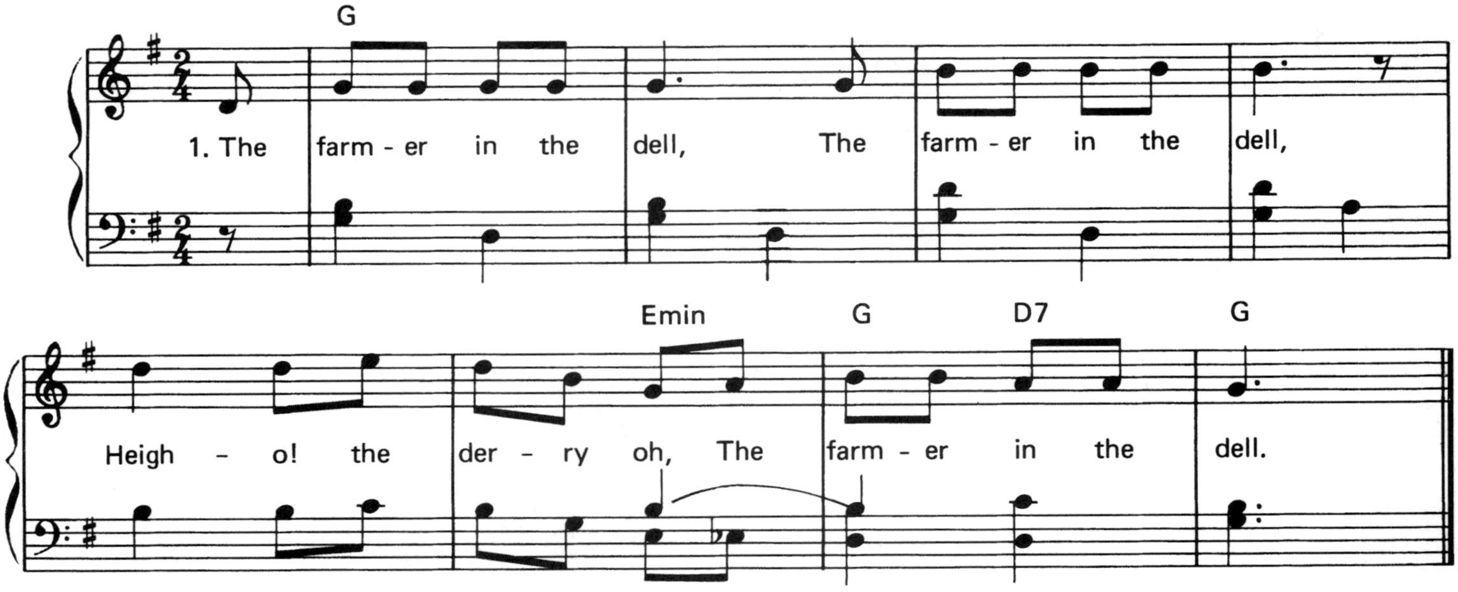

1. The farm - er in the dell, The farm - er in the dell, Heigh - o! the der - ry oh, The farm - er in the dell.

2. The farmer takes a wife, *etc.*

3. The wife takes the child, *etc.*

4. The child takes the nurse, *etc.*

5. The nurse takes the dog, *etc.*

6. The dog takes the cat, *etc.*

7. The cat takes the rat, *etc.*

8. The rat takes the cheese, *etc.*

9. The cheese stands alone, *etc.*

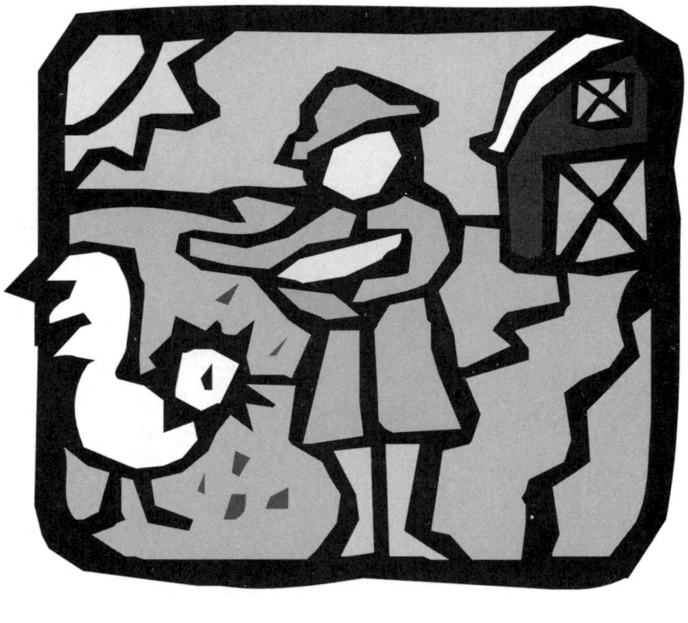

Five Fat Turkeys

Oh, five fat tur-keys are we_____ We slept all night in a tree. When the cook came a-round, We could-n't be found, And that's why we're here, You see._____

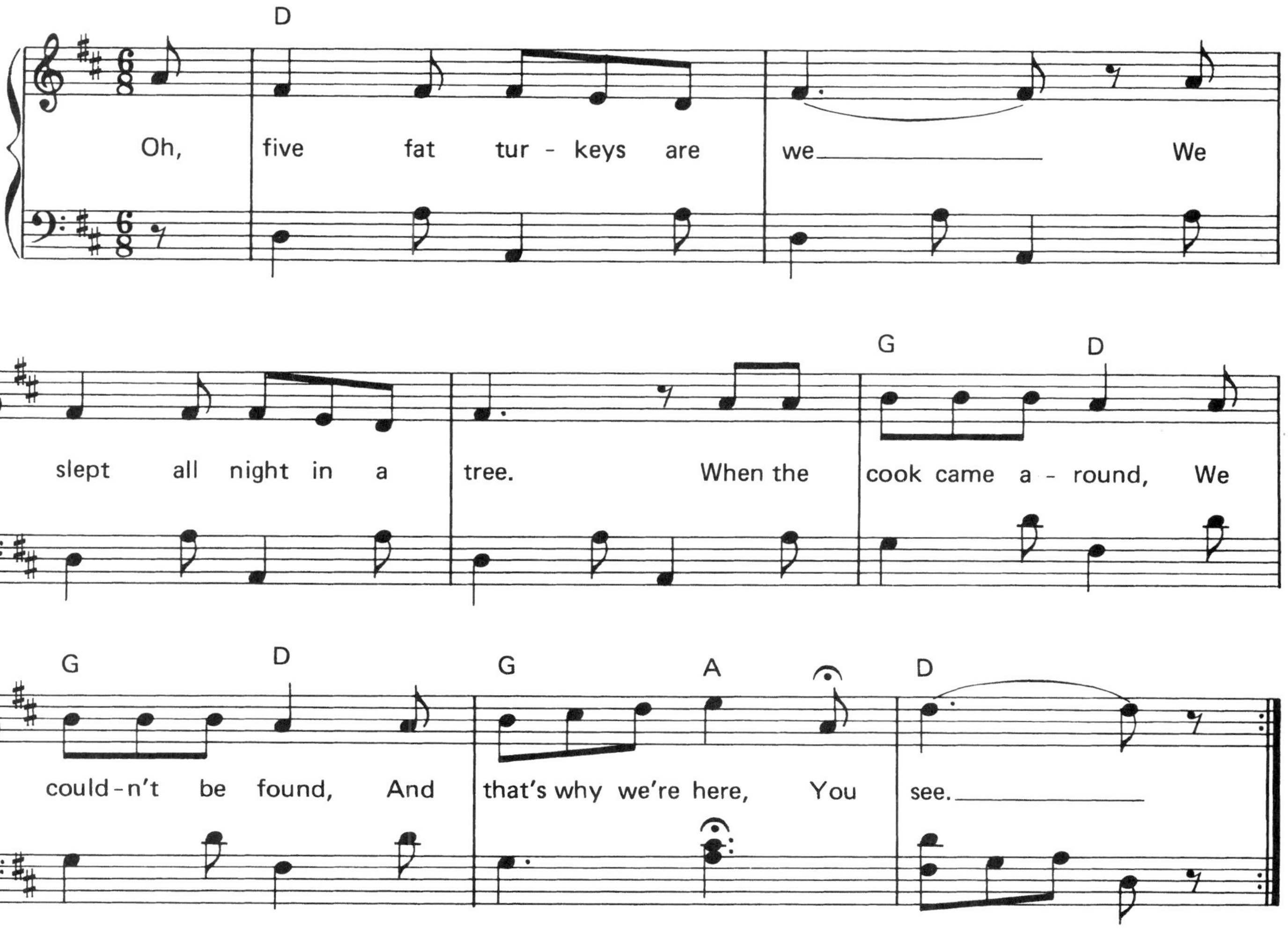

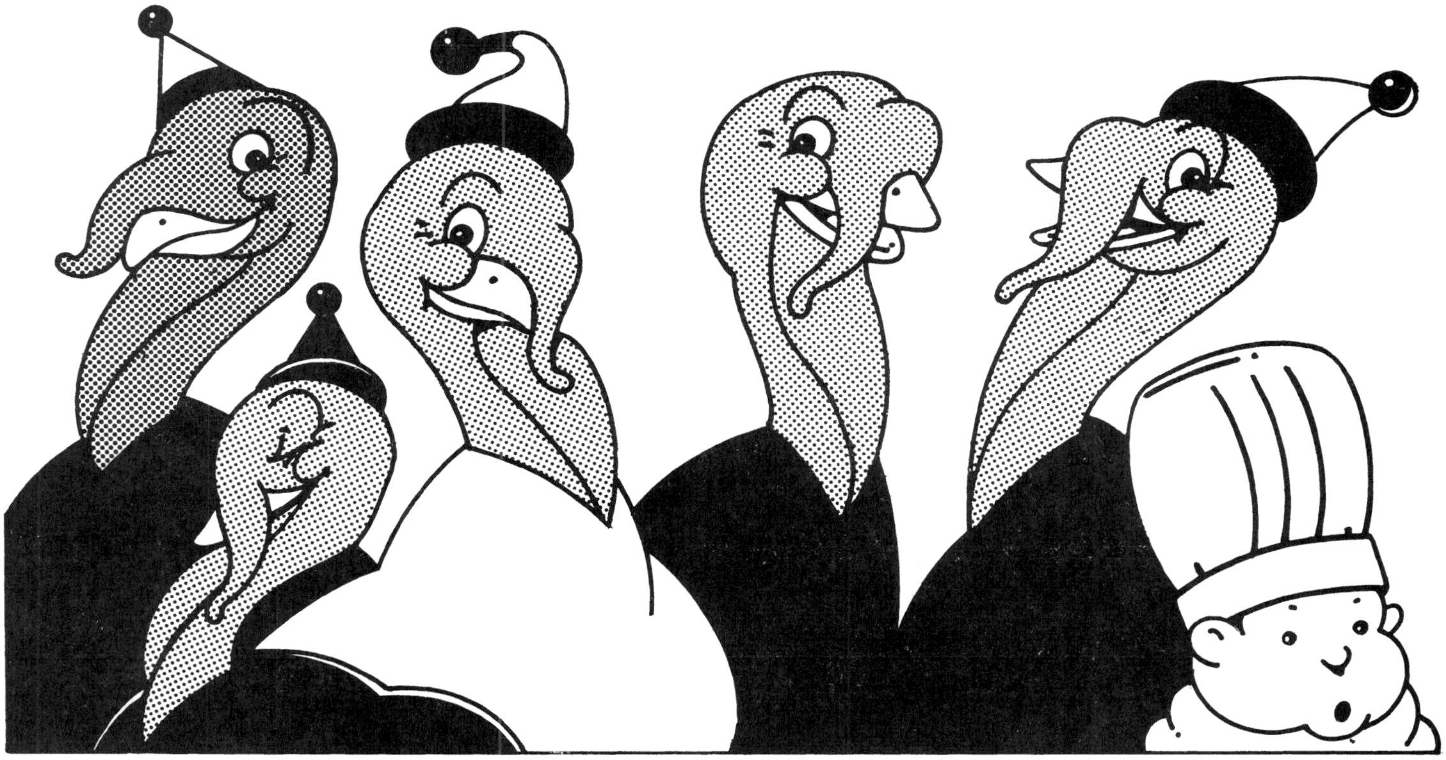

Five Little Monkeys

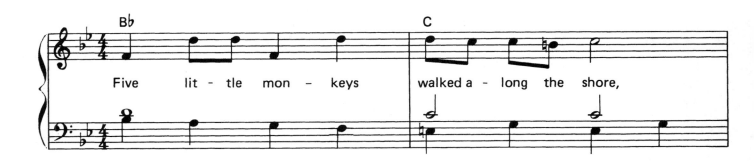

Five lit - tle mon - keys walked a - long the shore,

One went sail - ing, Then there were four. Four lit - tle mon - keys

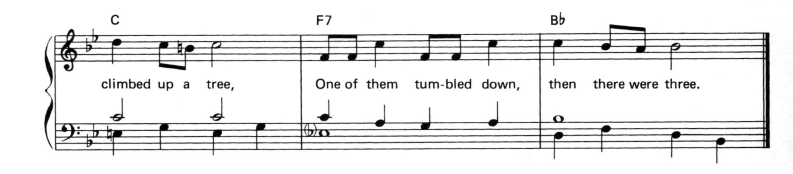

climbed up a tree, One of them tum-bled down, then there were three.

2. Three little monkeys found a pot of glue,
   One got stuck and,
   Then there were two.

3. Two little monkeys found a raisin bun,
   One ran away and
   Then there was one.

4. One little monkey, red in the face,
   They trained him as an astronaut
   And sent him out in space.

The Fox

2. He ran till he came to a great big bin,
   The ducks and the geese were kept therein,
   "A couple of you will grease my chin
   Before I leave this town-o," *etc.*

3. He grabbed the gray goose by the neck,
   Slung the little one over his back,
   He didn't mind their quack, quack, quack,
   And the legs all dangling down-o, *etc.*

4. Old Mother Pitter-Patter jumped out of bed,
   Out of the window she cocked her head,
   Crying, "John, John, the Gray goose is gone,
   And the fox is on the town-o," *etc.*

5. John he went to the top of the hill,
   Blew his horn both loud and shrill;
   The fox, he said, "Better flee with my kill
   Or they'll soon be on my trail-o," *etc.*

6. He ran till he came to his cozy den,
   There were the little ones, eight, nine, ten,
   They said, "Daddy, better go back again,
   'Cause it must be a mighty fine town-o," *etc.*

7. Then the fox and his wife without any strife
   Cut up the goose with a fork and knife,
   They never had such a supper in their life
   And the little ones chewed on the bones-o, *etc.*

Go Tell Aunt Rhody

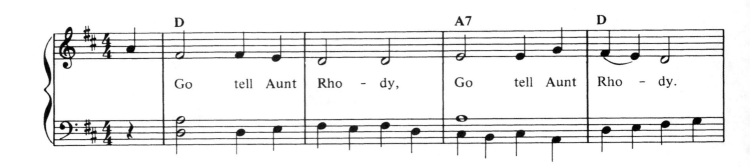

Go tell Aunt Rho - dy, Go tell Aunt Rho - dy.

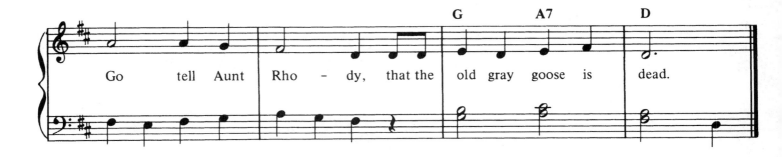

Go tell Aunt Rho - dy, that the old gray goose is dead.

2. The one she's been saving *(three times)*
   To make a feather bed.

3. She died in the millpond *(three times)*
   From standing on her head.

A Frog in a Bog

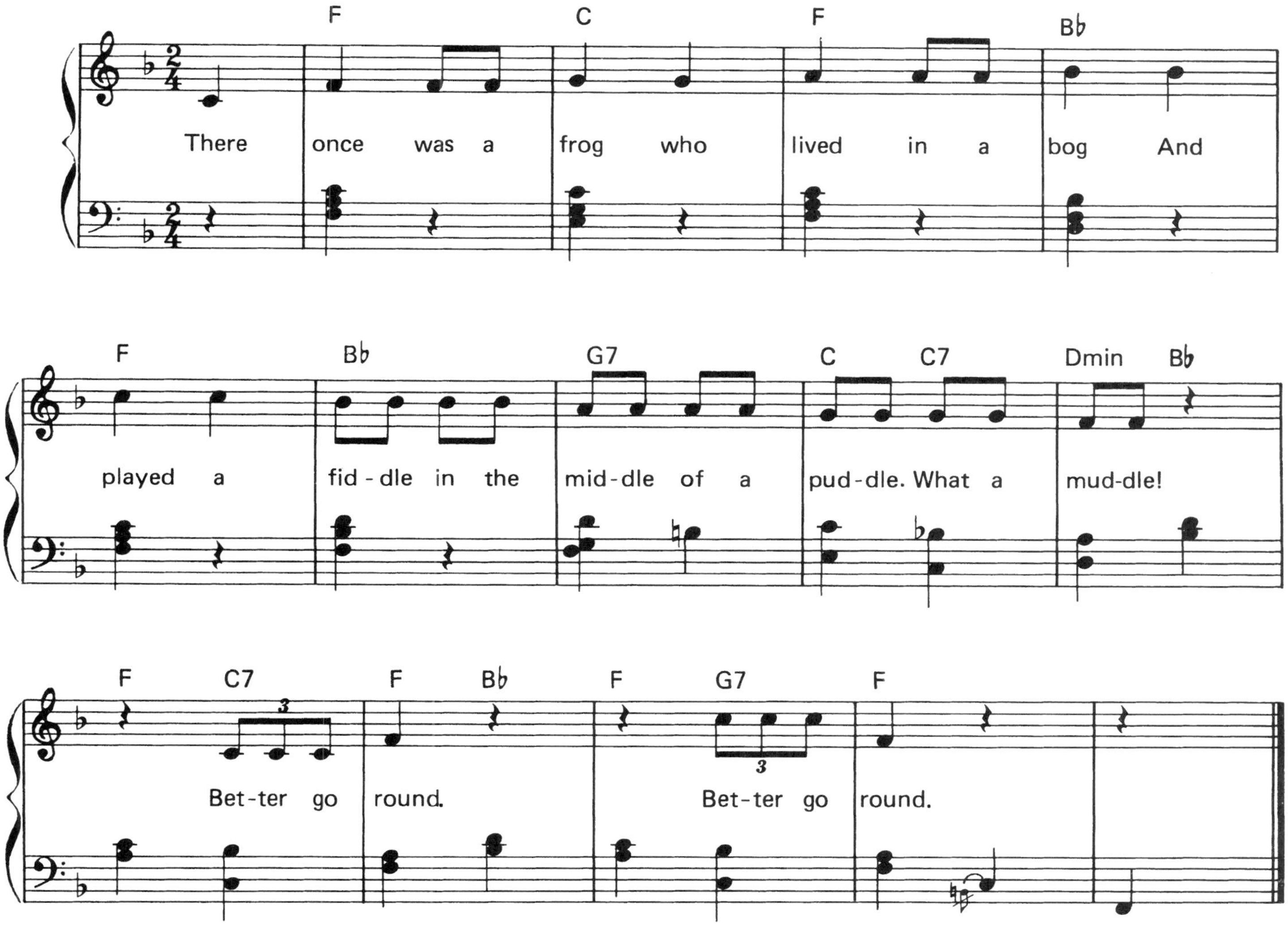

Lyrics:
There once was a frog who lived in a bog And played a fid-dle in the mid-dle of a pud-dle. What a mud-dle! Bet-ter go round. Bet-ter go round.

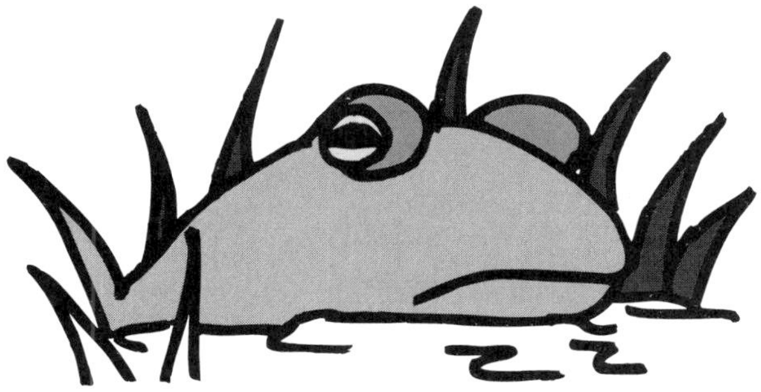

Froggie Went A-Courtin'

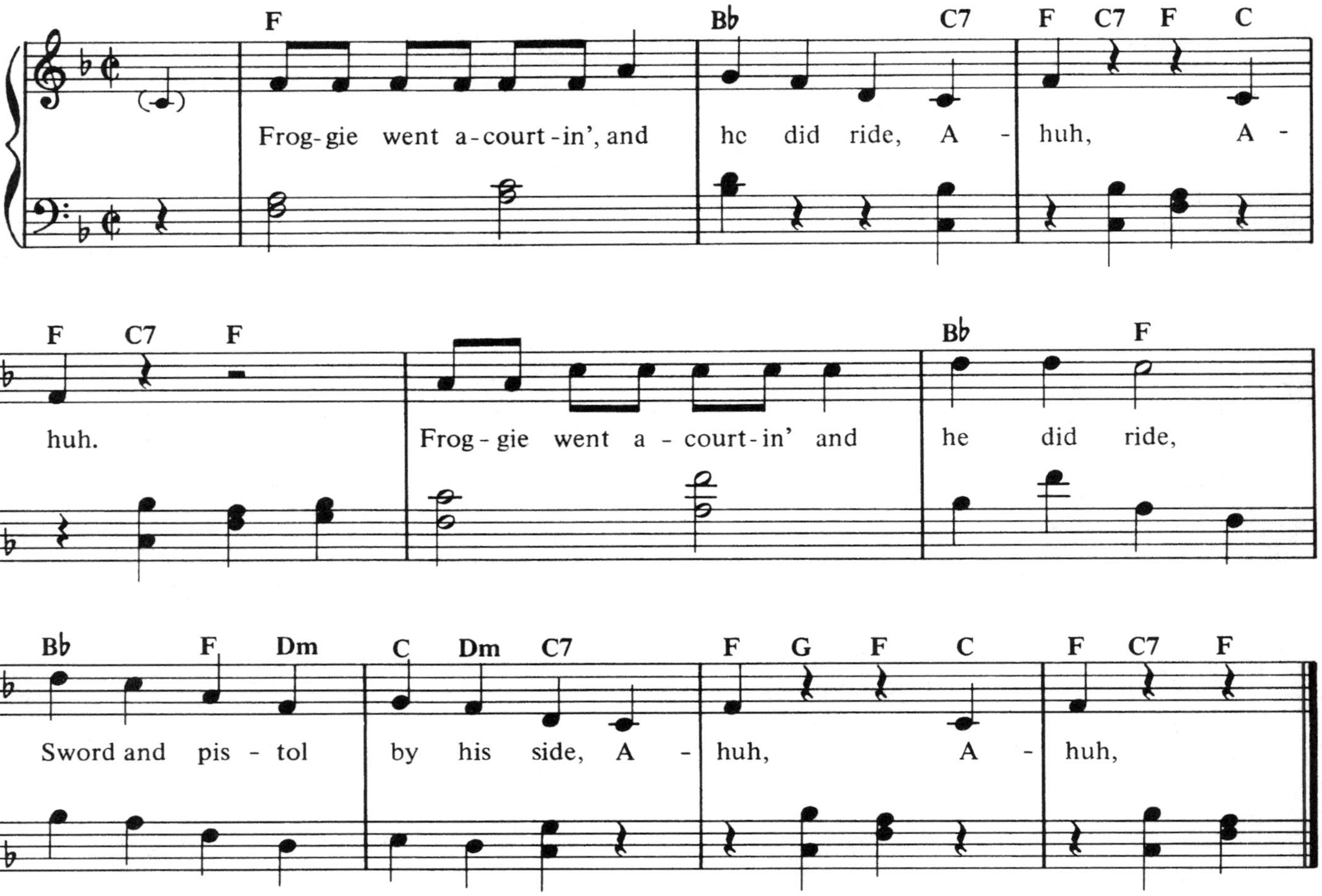

2. Well, he rode down to Miss Mouse's door,
     A-huh, A-huh,
   Well, he rode down to Miss Mouse's door,
   Where he had often been before,
     A-huh, A-huh.

3. He took Miss Mousie on his knee, *etc.*
   Said, "Miss Mousie, will you marry me?" *etc.*

4. "I'll have to ask my Uncle Rat,"
   "See what he will say to that."

5. "Without my Uncle Rat's consent,"
   "I would not marry the President."

6. Well, Uncle Rat rode off to town,
   To buy his niece a wedding gown.

7. "Where will the wedding supper be?"
   "Way down yonder in a hollow tree."

8. "What will the wedding supper be?"
   "A fried mosquito and a roasted flea."

9. First to come in were two little ants,
   Fixing around to have a dance.

10. Next to come in was a bumblebee,
    Bouncing a fiddle on his knee.

Glow-Worm

Words by Lilla Cayley Robinson

Music by Paul Lincke

Shine, lit-tle glow-worm, glim-mer, Shine, lit-tle glow-worm, glim-mer.

Lead us, lest too far we wan-der, Love's sweet voice is call-ing yon-der.

Shine, lit-tle glow-worm, glim-mer, Shine, lit-tle glow-worm, glim-mer.

Light the path, be-low, a-bove, And lead us on to love!

Have a Little Dog

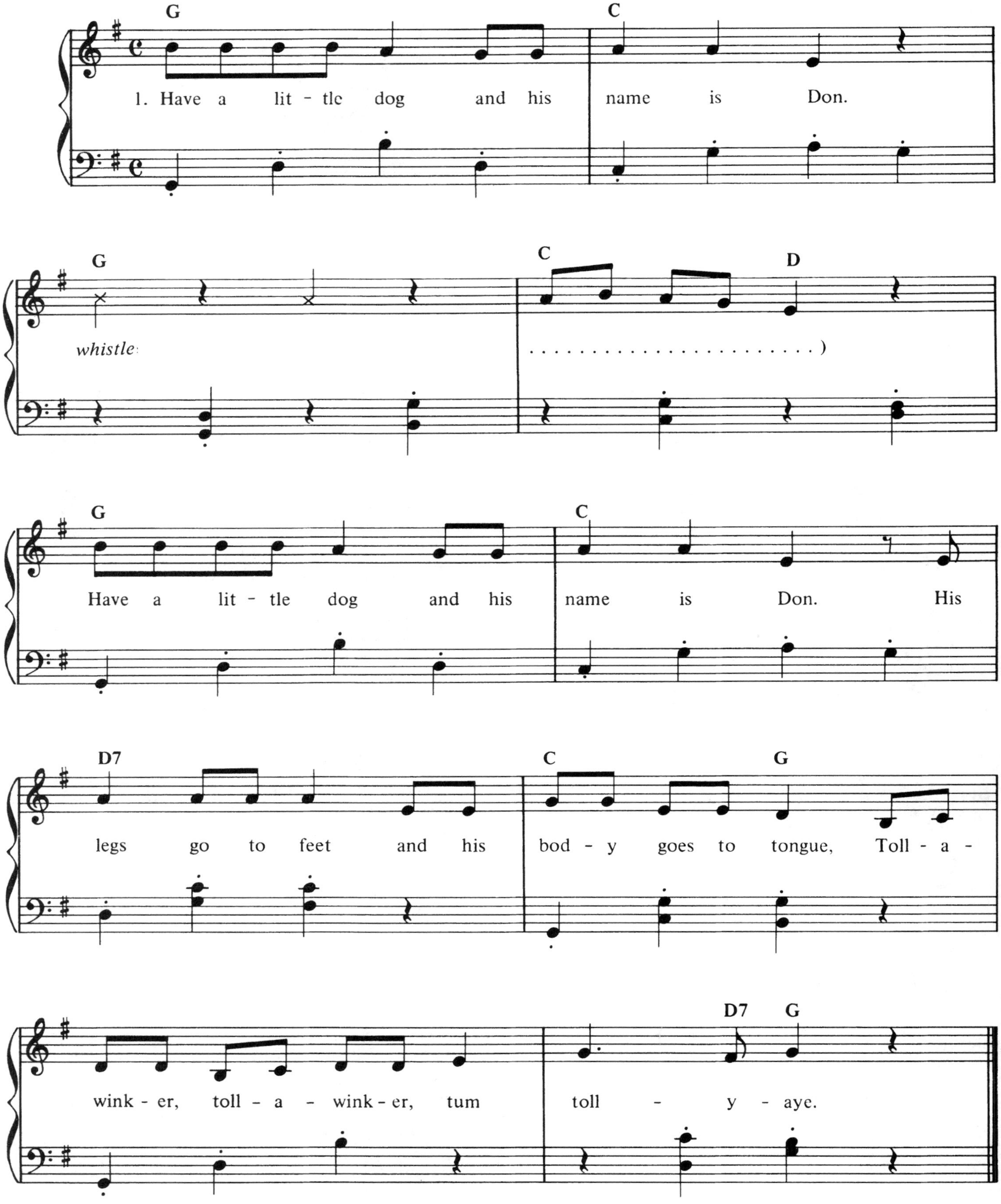
G
C
1. Have a lit - tle dog and his name is Don.
G
C
D
whistle:
. . . .)
G
C
Have a lit - tle dog and his name is Don. His
D7
C
G
legs go to feet and his bod - y goes to tongue, Toll - a -
D7
G
wink - er, toll - a - wink - er, tum toll - y - aye.

2. Have a little box about three feet square.
   Whistle
   Have a little box about three feet square.
   When I go to travel I put him in there,
   Toll-a-winker, toll-a-winker, tum tolly-aye.

3. When I travel, I travel like an ox,
   Whistle
   When I travel, I travel like an ox,
   And in my pocket, I carry that box,
   Toll-a-winker, toll-a-winker, tum tolly-aye.

4. Had a little hen and her color was fair,
   Whistle
   Had a little hen and her color was fair,
   Sat on an egg and she hatched me a hare,
   Toll-a-winker, toll-a-winker, tum tolly-aye.

5. Had a little mule that was made of hay,
   Whistle
   Had a little mule that was made of hay,
   Wind came along and it blew him all away,
   Toll-a-winker, toll-a-winker, tum tolly-aye.

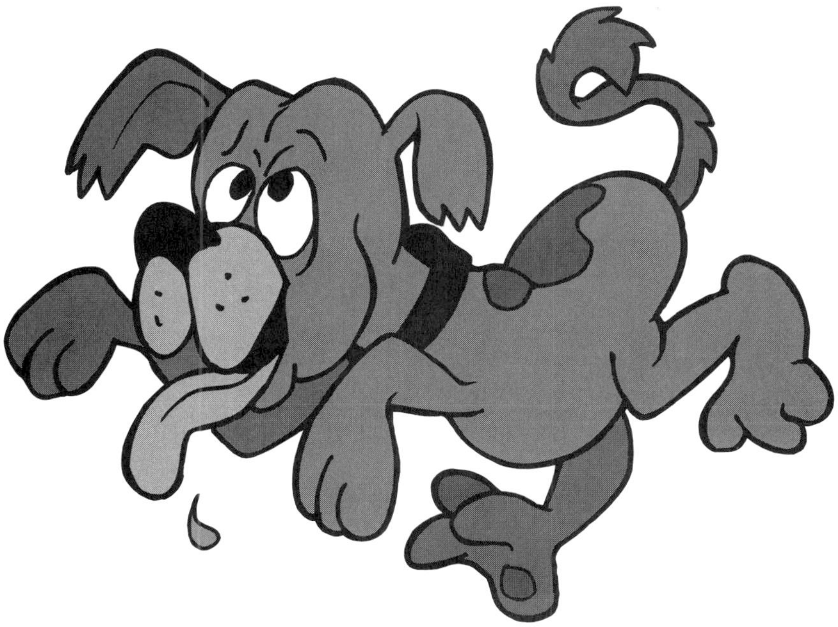

Hark! Hark! The Dogs Do Bark

C
G7
C
G7
Hark! hark! the dogs do bark,
C
G
Am7
G
C
Min - strels are com - ing to town.
F
Some in jags and some in rags and
C
G7
C
one in a vel - vet gown.

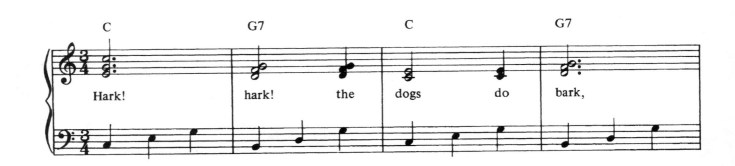

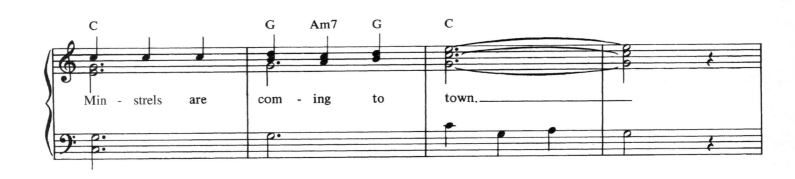

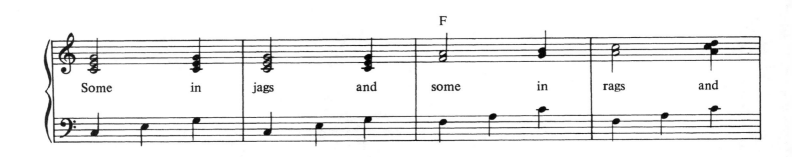

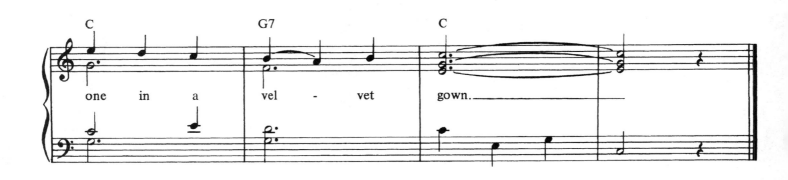

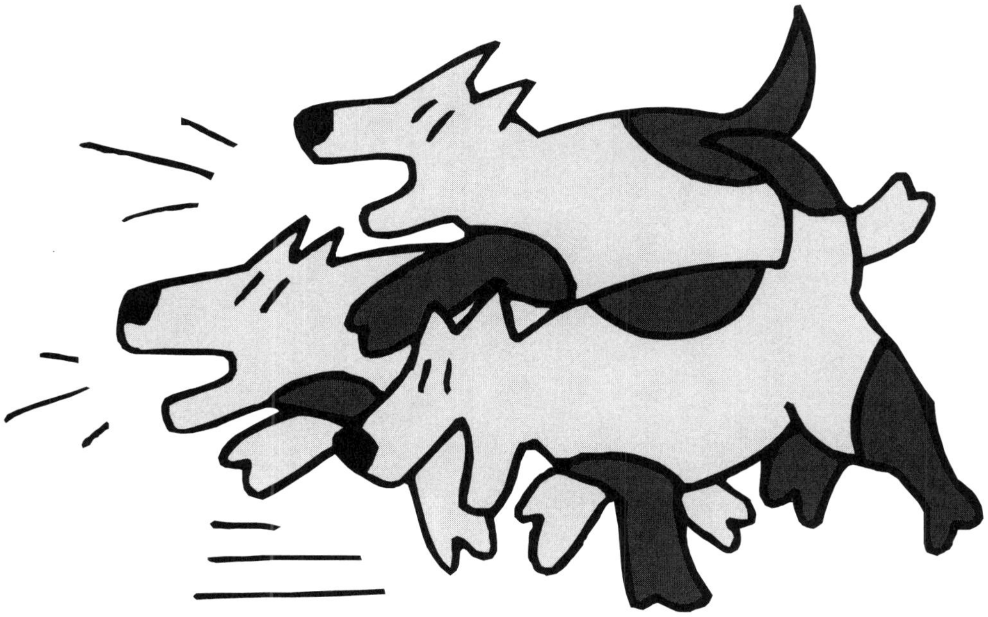

I Had a Little Rooster

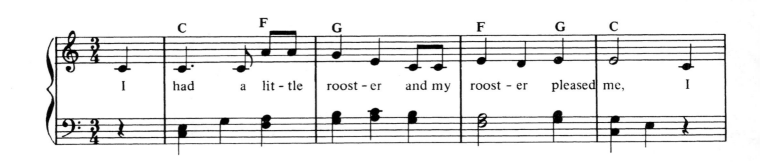

I had a lit-tle roost-er and my roost-er pleased me, I

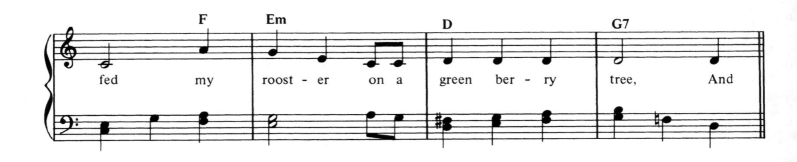

fed my roost-er on a green ber-ry tree, And

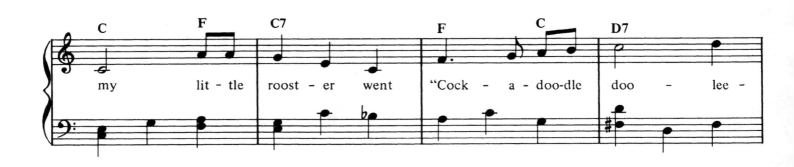

my lit-tle roost-er went "Cock-a-doo-dle doo-lee-

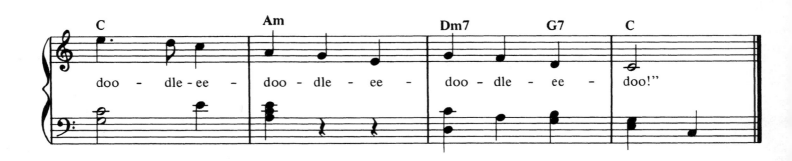

doo-dle-ee- doo-dle-ee- doo-dle-ee- doo!"

2. I had a little hen and my hen pleased me,
   I fed my hen on a green berry tree,
   And my little hen went "Cluck! Cluck! Cluck!"
   And my rooster went "Cock-a-doodle-doo-lee—
   Doodle-ee-doodle-ee-doodle-ee-doo!"

3. I had a little duck and my duck pleased me,
   I fed my duck on a green berry tree,
   And my little duck went "Quack! Quack! Quack!"
   And my little hen went "Cluck! Cluck! Cluck!"
   And my rooster went "Cock-a-doodle-doo-lee—

I Love Little Kitty

C
F
I love lit - tle kit - ty her coat is so warm, And
G7
C
if I don't hurt her she'll do me no harm. I'll
F
sit by the fire and give her some food, And
Dm
G7
C
kit - ty will love me be - cause I'm so good.

The Kicking Mule

1. My un-cle had an old mule, His name was Si-mon Slick, He
2. Went to feed that mule one morn-ing, And he met me with a smile, He

'Bove any-thing I ev-er did see was how that mule could kick.
backed one ear and he winked one eye and he kicked me half a mile.

Well, whoa there, mule, I tell you, Miss Li-za, you keep cool, I

ain't got time to kiss you now, I'm bus-y with my mule.

Little Bird, Little Bird

D
Lit - tle bird, lit - tle bird, go
G
through my
Em7
win - dow,
Lit - tle bird, lit - tle bird, go
A7
through my
D
win - dow,
Lit - tle bird, lit - tle bird, go
G
through my
D
win - dow, And
Em7
buy mo -
A7
lass - es
D
can - dy.

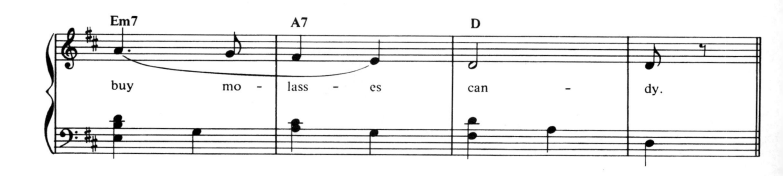

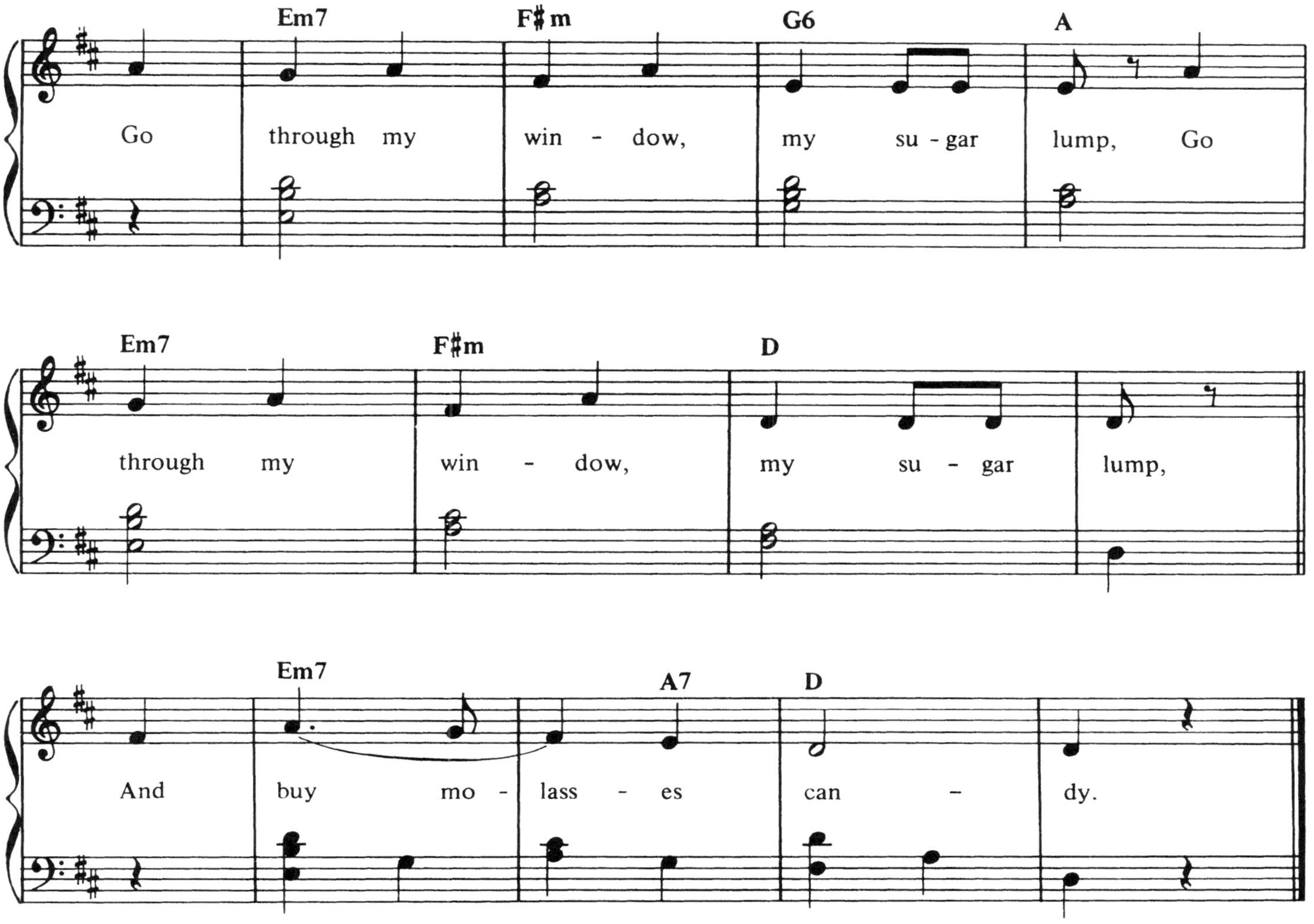
Em7 F♯m G6 A
Go through my win - dow, my su - gar lump, Go
Em7 F♯m D
through my win - dow, my su - gar lump,
Em7 A7 D
And buy mo - lass - es can - dy.

Ladybug, Ladybug

G D D7 G Bm Em Am D7 G
Lad - y - bug, lad - y - bug, fly a-way home, your house is on fire and your child-ren all gone.

Little Robin Redbreast

2. Little Robin Redbreast jumped upon a wall,
   Pussy cat jumped after him and almost had a fall.
   Little Robin chirped and sang, and what did pussy say?
   Pussy cat said naught but, "Meow," and Robin flew away.

The Little Skunk

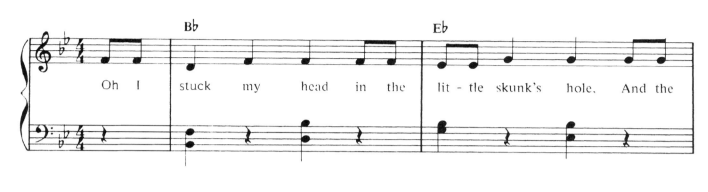

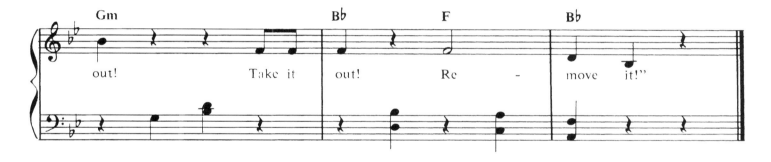

2. Oh, I didn't take it out, and the little skunk said:
"If you don't take it out, you'll wish you had.
Take it out! Take it out!" Pheeew! I removed it.

Mister Rabbit

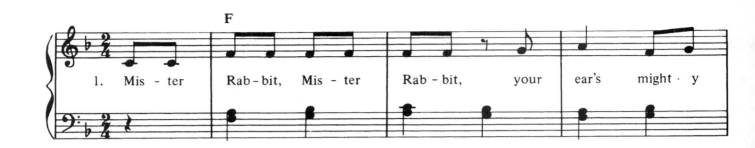

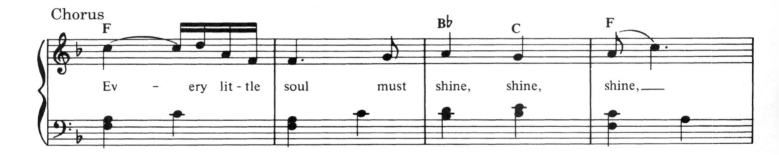

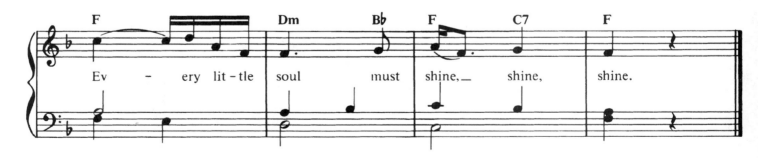

2. Mister Rabbit, Mister Rabbit,
   Your coat's mighty gray.
   Yes, oh yes, 'twas made that way.
   Chorus

3. Mister Rabbit, Mister Rabbit,
   Your tail's mighty white.
   Yes, oh yes, I'm getting out of sight.
   Chorus

4. Mister Rabbit, Mister Rabbit,
   Your feet are mighty red,
   Yes, oh yes, they feel like lead.
   Chorus

5. Mister Rabbit, Mister Rabbit,
   You look mighty thin.
   Yes, oh yes, been cutting through the wind.
   Chorus

Mole in the Ground

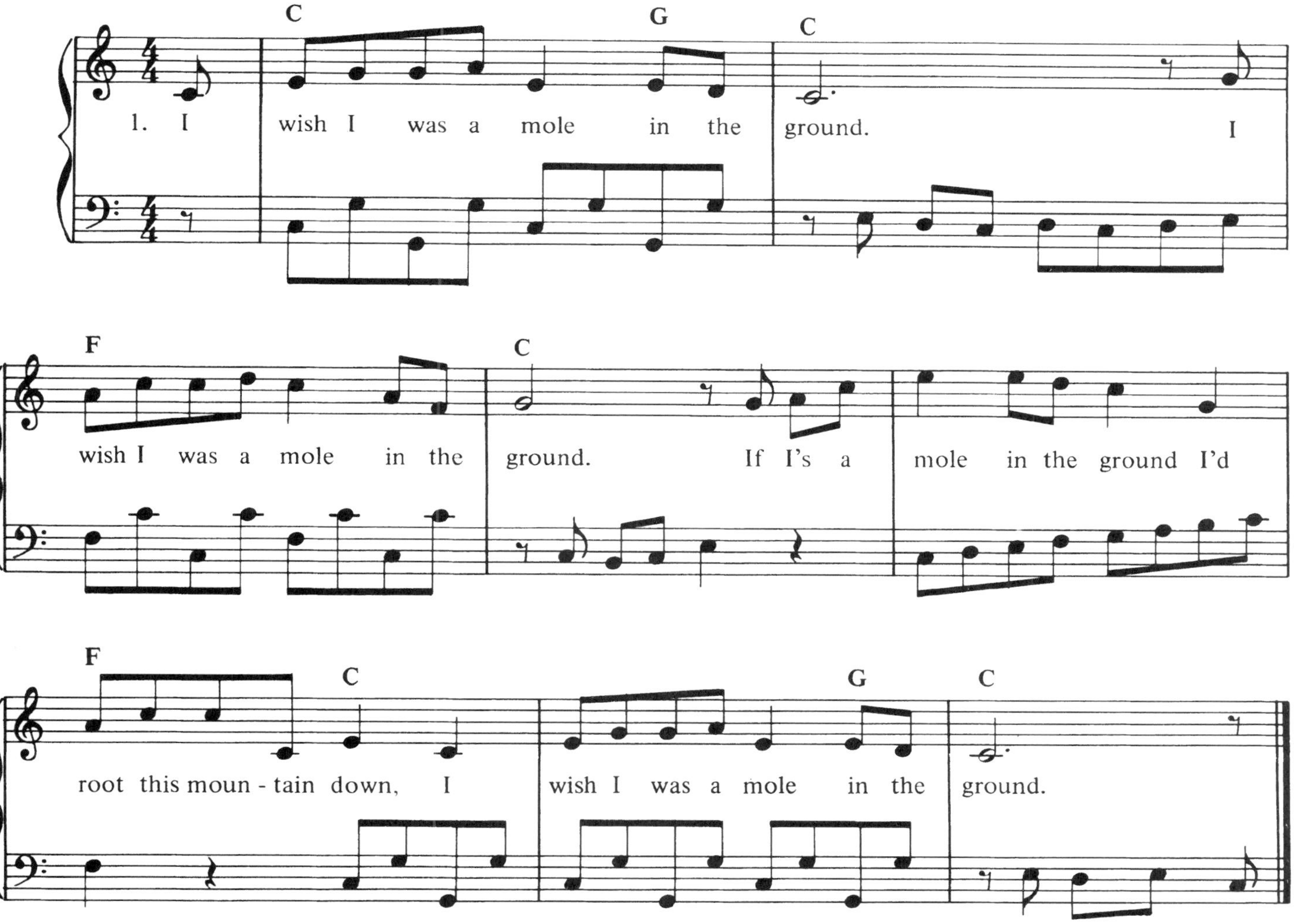

2. I wish I was a lizard in the spring.
   I wish I was a lizard in the spring.
   If I was a lizard in the spring, I could hear my darling sing,
   And I wish I was a lizard in the spring.

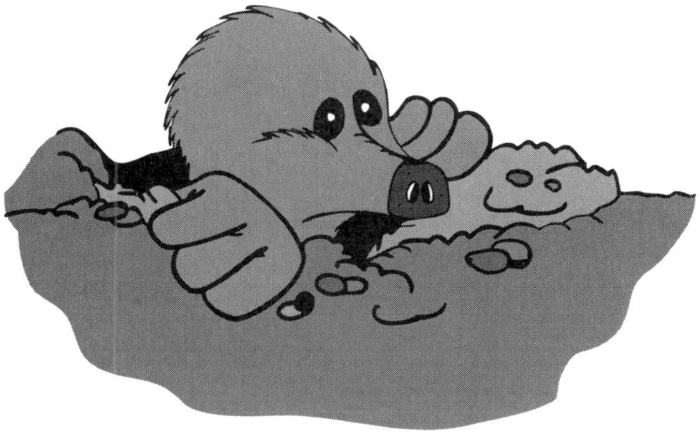

Monkey See, Monkey Do

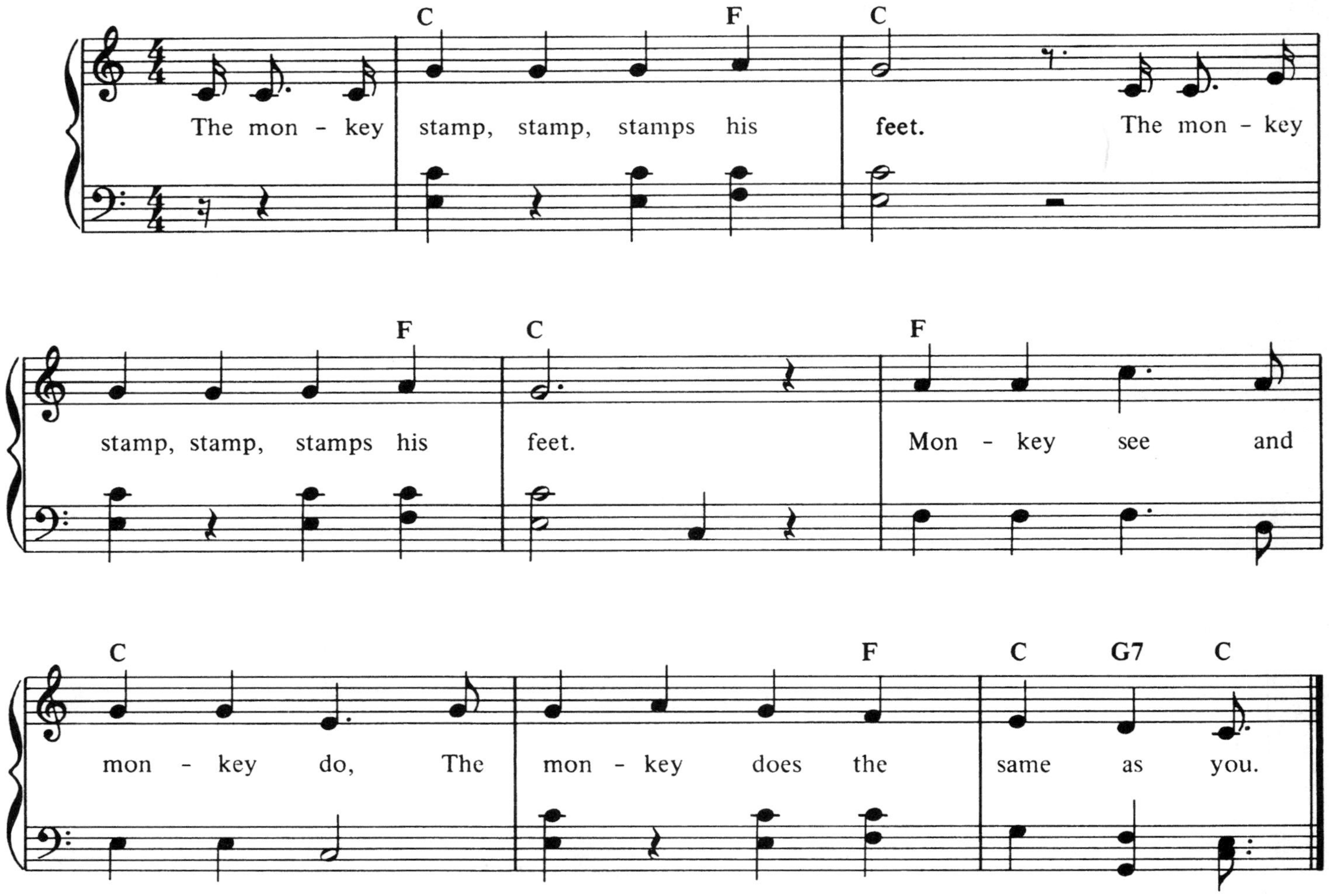

2. The monkey clap, clap, claps his hands.
   The monkey clap, clap, claps his hands.
   Monkey see and monkey do,
   The monkey does the same as you.

3. The monkey pat, pat, pats his knees.
   The monkey pat, pat, pats his knees.
   Monkey see and monkey do,
   The monkey does the same as you.

4. And when you make a funny face,
   The monkey makes a funny face.
   Monkey see and monkey do,
   The monkey does the same as you.

5. And when you turn yourself around,
   The monkey turns himself around.
   Monkey see and monkey do,
   The monkey does the same as you.

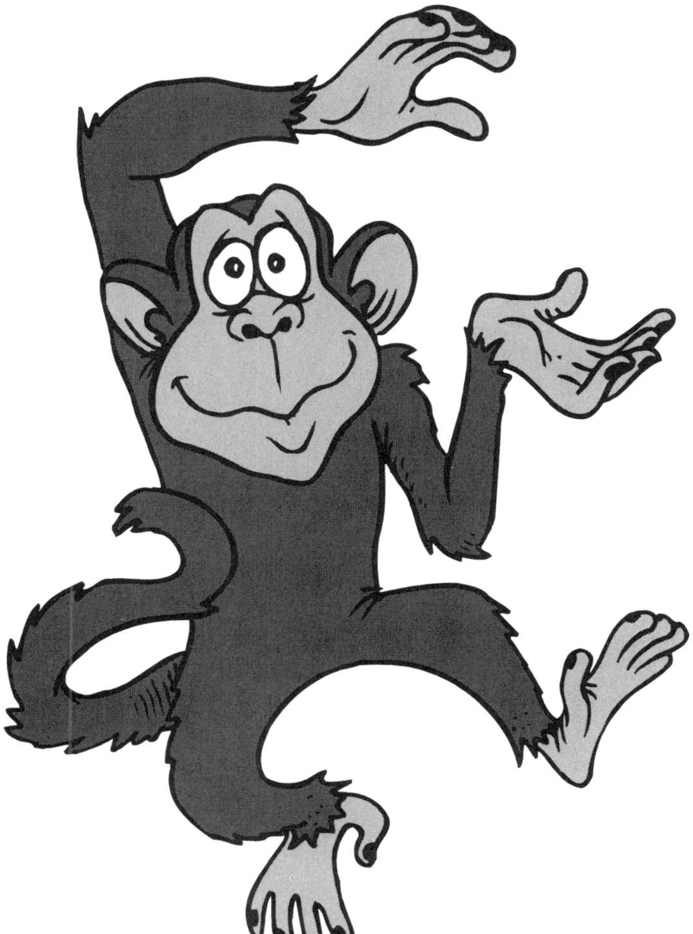

Old Blue

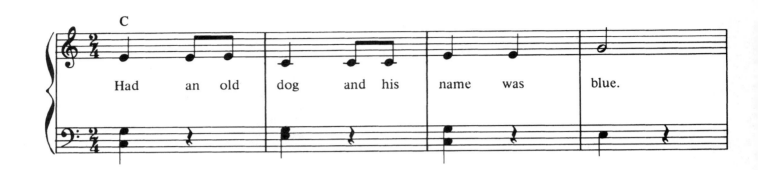

Had   an   old   dog   and his   name   was   blue.

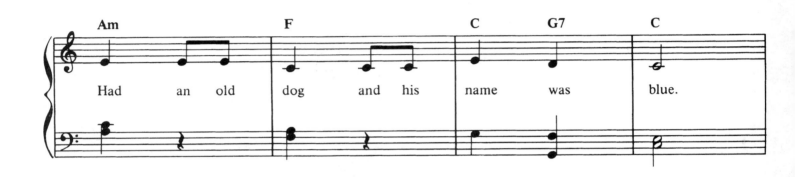

Had   an   old   dog   and his   name   was   blue.

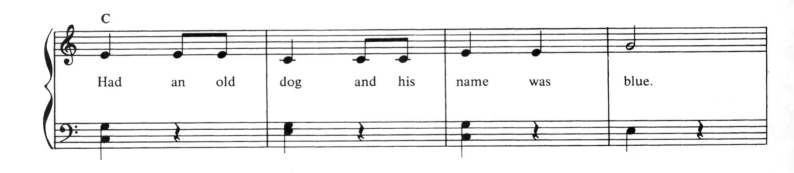

Had   an   old   dog   and his   name   was   blue.

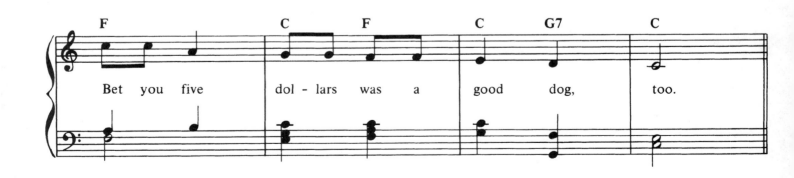

Bet   you   five   dol - lars   was   a   good   dog,   too.

Chorus

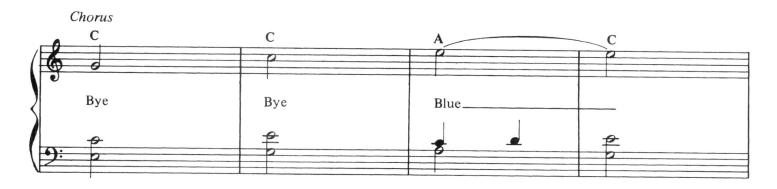

Bye   Bye   Blue____

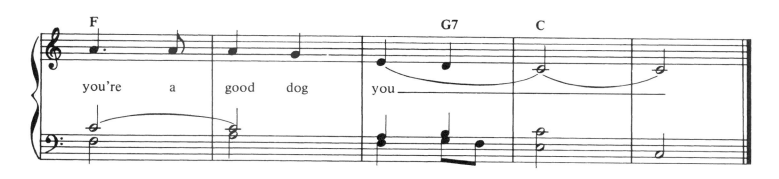

you're   a   good   dog   you____

2. Every night just about dark
      (three times)
   Blue goes out and begins to bark.
   Chorus

3. Everything just in a rush
      (three times)
   He treed a possum in a white-oak bush.
   Chorus

4. Possum walked out to the end of a limb
      (three times)
   Blue sat down and talked to him.
   Chorus

5. When I get to heaven, I'll tell you what I'll do
      (three times)
   I'll take my horn and blow for Blue.
   Chorus

Old Dog Tray

D7
G
Old dog Tray's ev - er faith - ful,
D7
G
D7
Grief can-not drive him a - way. He's gen-tle, he is kind, I'll
G
C
G
D7
G
ne-ver ne-ver find a bet-ter friend than old dog Tray.

Old Ground Hog

4. Daddy returned in an hour and a half,
   Daddy returned in an hour and a half,
   Carried a ground hog as big as a calf.
   Oh ground hog.

5. How those children whooped and cried,
   How those children whooped and cried,
   "We love ground hog stewed or fried!"
   Oh ground hog.

6. In comes Maw with a snigger and a grin,
   In comes Maw with a snigger and a grin,
   Ground hog gravy all over her chin.
   Oh ground hog.

7. Old Aunt Sal was the mother of them all,
   Old Aunt Sal was the mother of them all,
   Fed them on ground hog before they could crawl.
   Oh ground hog.

The Old Gray Mare

F
Oh the old gray mare, She ain't what she used to be,
C7
F
Ain't what she used to be, Ain't what she used to be, The
A7
Dmin
old gray mare, She ain't what she used to be
B♭
C7
F
Man - y long years a - go.

The Old Hen Cackled

1. The old hen she cack-led, she cack-led in the loft,

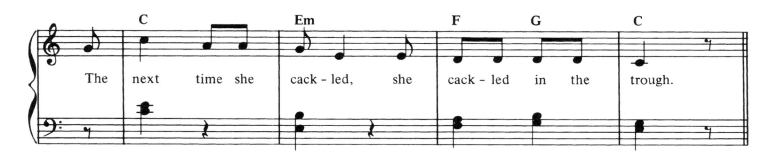

The next time she cack-led, she cack-led in the trough.

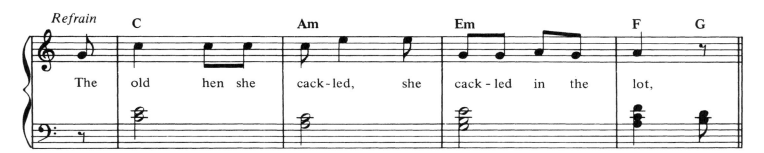

Refrain

The old hen she cack-led, she cack-led in the lot,

The next time she cack-led, she cack-led in the pot,

2. The old hen cackled, she cackled in the stable,
   She cackled on the chair, she cackled on the table.
   Chorus

3. The old hen cackled, she hopped upon one leg,
   The old hen cackled, and the rooster laid an egg.
   Chorus

108

Old MacDonald

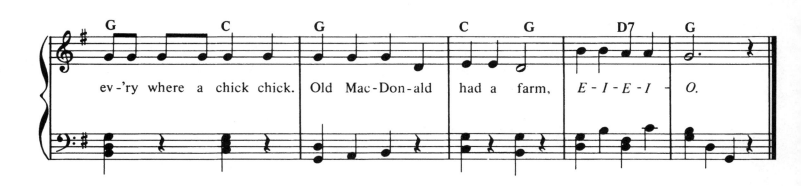

2. Old MacDonald had a farm, *E-I-E-I-O.*
   And on that farm he had some ducks, *E-I-E-I-O.*
   With a quack-quack here,
      and a quack-quack there,
   Here a quack, there a quack,
      everywhere a quack-quack.
   Old MacDonald had a farm, *E-I-E-I-O.*

3. Old MacDonald had a farm, *E-I-E-I-O.*
   And on that farm he had a cat, *E-I-E-I-O.*
   With a meow-meow here,
      and a meow-meow there,
   Here a meow, there a meow,
      everywhere a meow-meow.
   Old MacDonald had a farm, *E-I-E-I-O.*

4. Old MacDonald had a farm, *E-I-E-I-O.*
   And on that farm he had a dog, *E-I-E-I-O.*
   With a woof-woof here,
      and a woof-woof there,
   Here a woof, there a woof,
      everywhere a woof-woof.
   Old MacDonald had a farm, *E-I-E-I-O.*

5. Old MacDonald had a farm, *E-I-E-I-O.*
   And on that farm he had some sheep, *E-I-E-I-O.*
   With a baa-baa here,
      and a baa-baa there,
   Here a baa, there a baa,
      everywhere a baa-baa.
   Old MacDonald had a farm, *E-I-E-I-O.*

6. Old MacDonald had a farm, *E-I-E-I-O.*
   And on that farm he had some cows, *E-I-E-I-O.*
   With a moo-moo here,
      and a moo-moo there,
   Here a moo, there a moo,
      everywhere a moo-moo.
   Old MacDonald had a farm, *E-I-E-I-O.*

7. Old MacDonald had a farm, *E-I-E-I-O.*
   And on that farm he had a horse, *E-I-E-I-O.*
   With a neigh-neigh here,
      and a neigh-neigh there,
   Here a neigh, there a neigh,
      everywhere a neigh-neigh.
   Old MacDonald had a farm, *E-I-E-I-O.*

Oh Where Has My Little Dog Gone?

G
D7
Oh where, oh where has my lit - tle dog
gone, Oh where, oh where can he
G
be?
With his ears cut short and his
D7
tail cut
long, Oh where, oh where is
G
he?

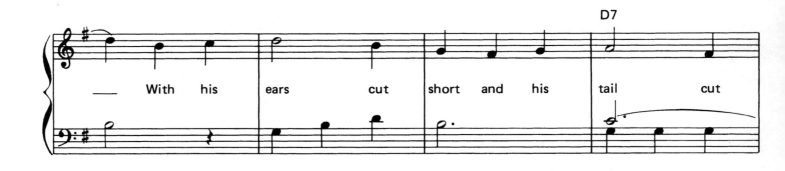

Old Molly Hare

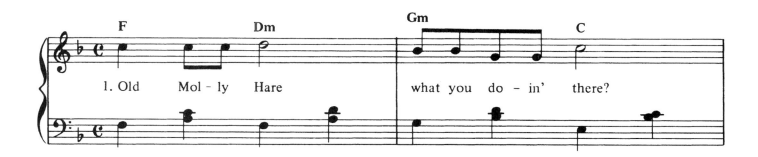

1. Old Mol - ly Hare what you do - in' there?

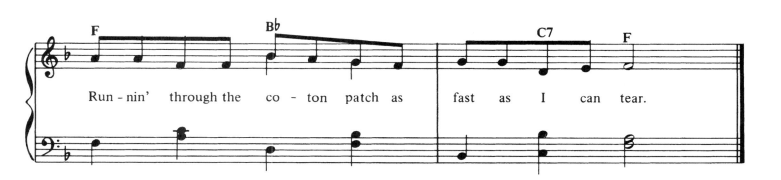

Run - nin' through the co - ton patch as fast as I can tear.

2. Old Molly Hare what you doin' there?
   Sittin' on the front porch combin' out my hair.

3. Old Molly Hare what you doin' there?
   Sittin' on a dinner plate a-lookin for my share.

5. Old Molly Hare what you doin' there?
   Runnin' with the night wind a-blowin' in my hair.

6. Ridin' of a goat, leadin' of a sheep,
   I won't be back here until the middle of next week.

One Little Elephant Balancing

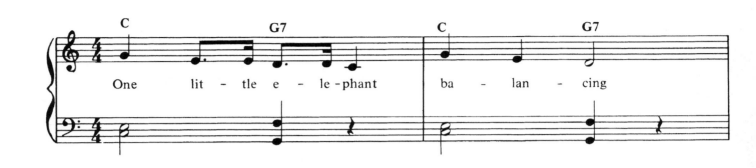

One lit - tle e - le -phant ba - lan - cing

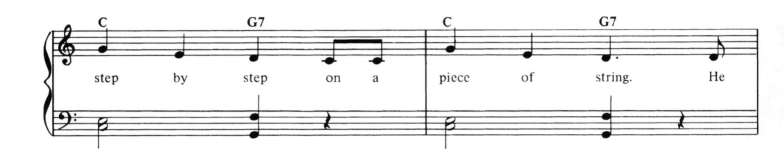

step by step on a piece of string. He

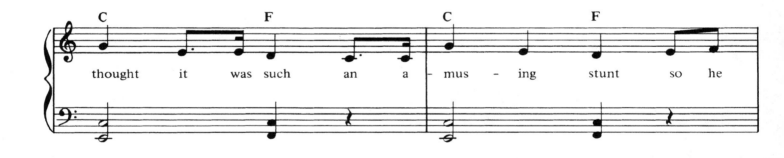

thought it was such an a - mus - ing stunt so he

called in a - no - ther lit - tle e - le - phant.

Pap's Billy Goat

1. Pap-py bought him a great big bil-ly goat Ma-ma washed most ev-'ry day.

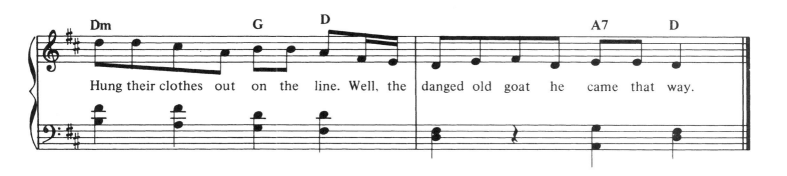

Hung their clothes out on the line. Well, the danged old goat he came that way.

2. He pulled down that old red shirt,
You ought to hear them buttons crack.
He twisted it around his neck,
And he tied himself to the railroad track.

3. Tied himself across the railroad track
The train was a-comin' at a thousand rate.
The goat belched up that old red shirt
And then flagged down that big old freight.

Pop Goes the Weasel

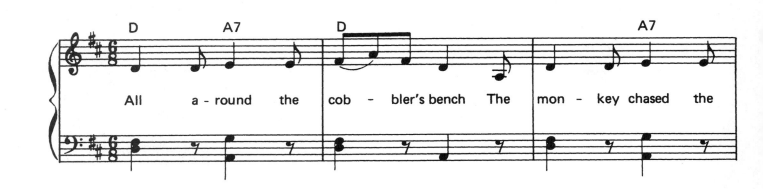

All a-round the cob-bler's bench The mon-key chased the

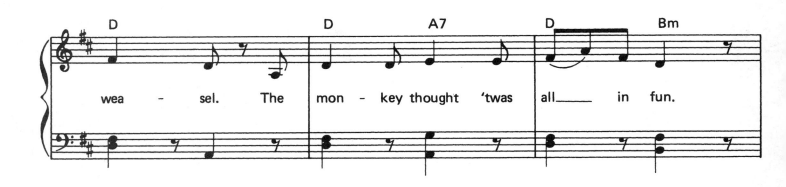

wea-sel. The mon-key thought 'twas all___ in fun.

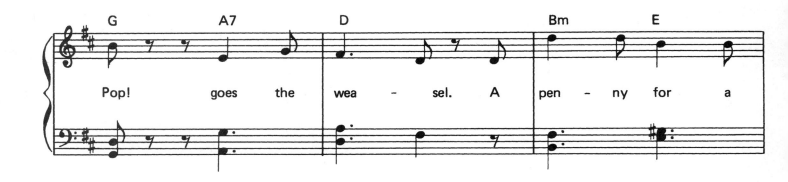

Pop! goes the wea-sel. A pen-ny for a

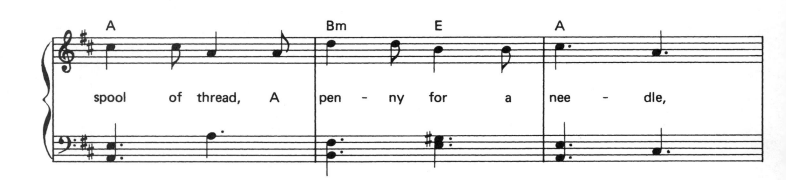

spool of thread, A pen-ny for a nee-dle,

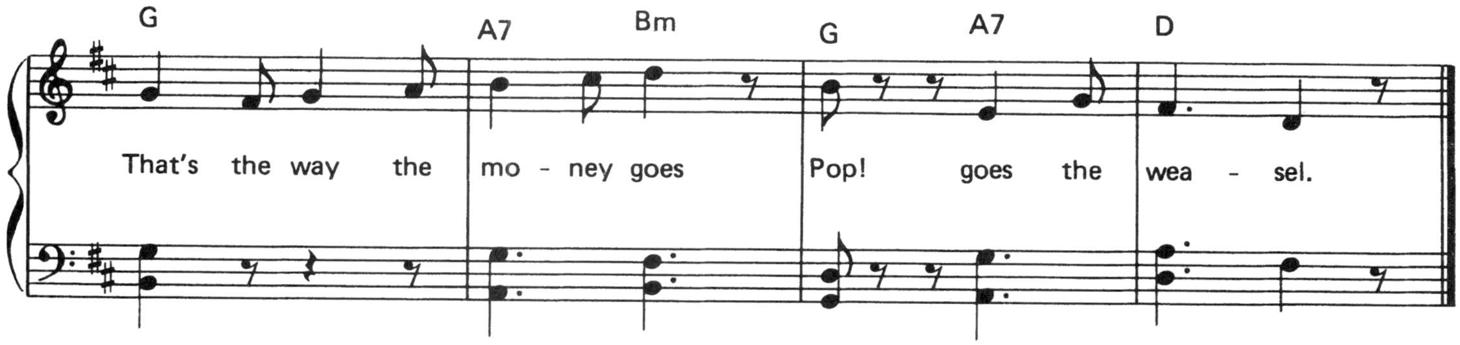

That's the way the mo - ney goes Pop! goes the wea - sel.

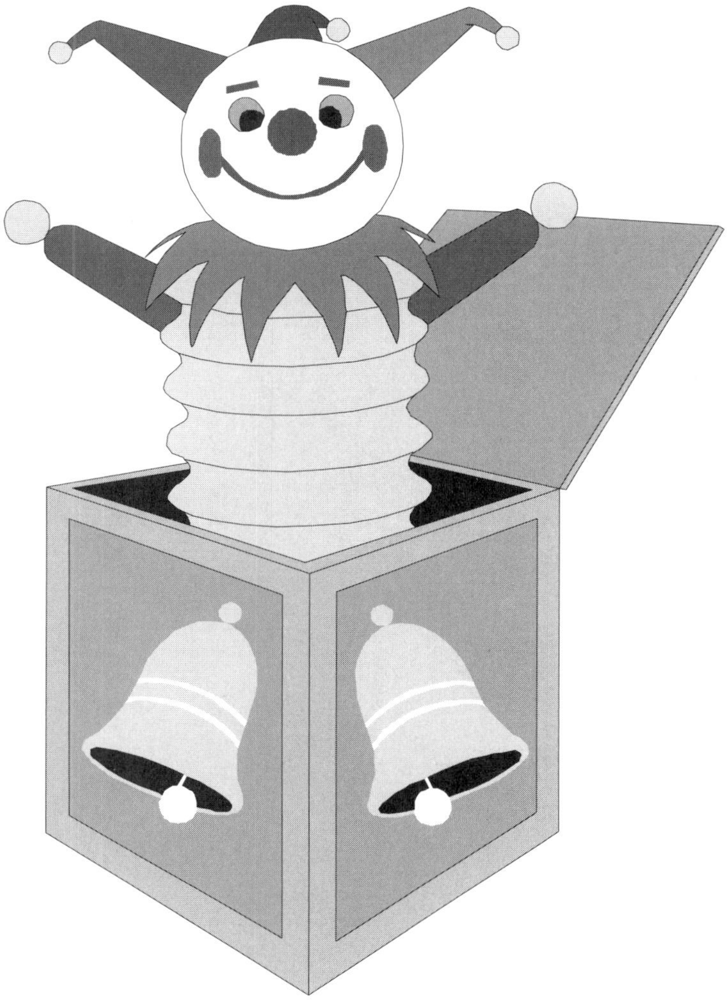

Puff!

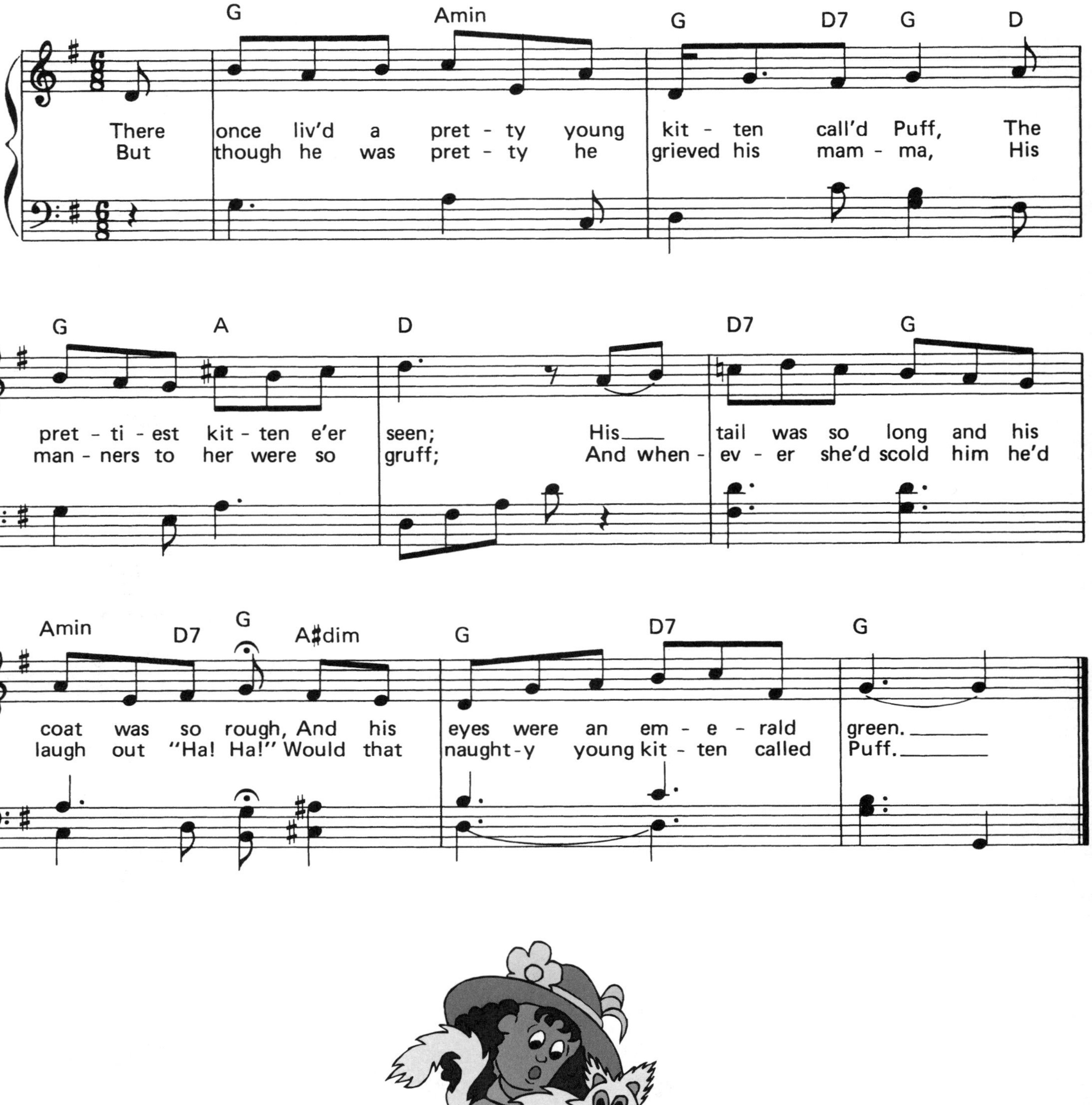

There once liv'd a pret-ty young kit-ten call'd Puff, The
But though he was pret-ty he grieved his mam-ma, His

pret-ti-est kit-ten e'er seen; His tail was so long and his
man-ners to her were so gruff; And when-ev-er she'd scold him he'd

coat was so rough, And his eyes were an em-e-rald green.
laugh out "Ha! Ha!" Would that naught-y young kit-ten called Puff.

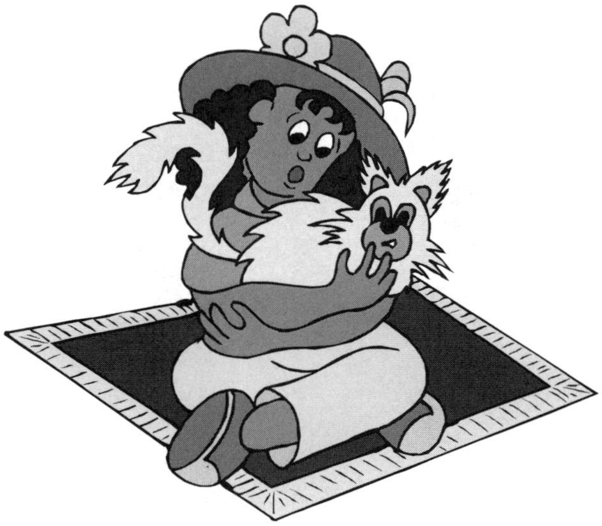

Pussy Cat, Pussy Cat

Pus - sy cat, pus - sy cat, where have you been? I've

been ___ to Lon - don to vis - it the Queen. Pus - sy cat, pus - sy cat,

what did you there? I frightened a lit - tle mouse un - der her chair.

Raccoon and Possum

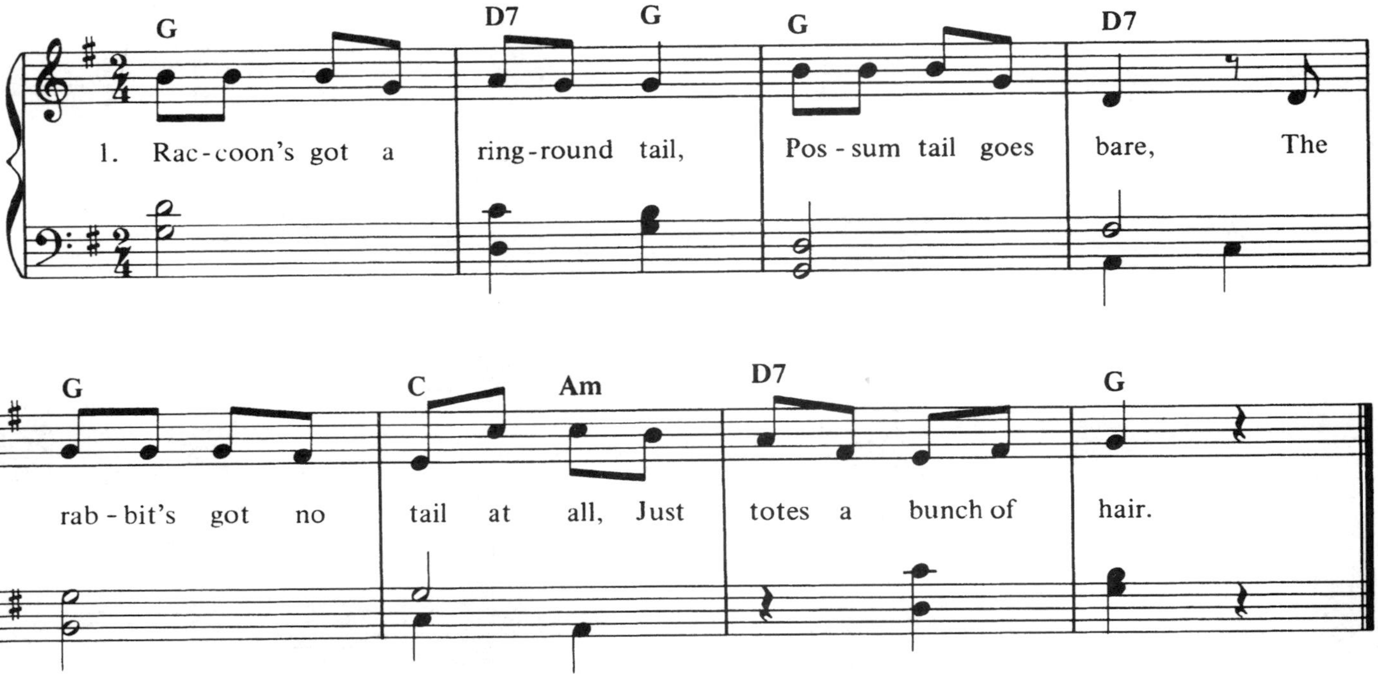

1. Rac-coon's got a ring-round tail, Pos-sum tail goes bare, The rab-bit's got no tail at all, Just totes a bunch of hair.

2. The raccoon is a mighty man,
He rambles through the dark,
You ought to see him find his den
When he hears old Ranger bark.

3. Possum up the 'simmon tree,
Raccoon on the ground,
Raccoon says to the possum,
"Won't you shake them 'simmons down?"

4. I met the possum in the road,
"Possum, where you goin'?"
"Look out, man, don't bother me,
I feel a cold wind blowin'."

5. Rabbit up the tree stump
Raccoon in the hollow,
Possum in the 'tater patch
As fat as he can wallow.

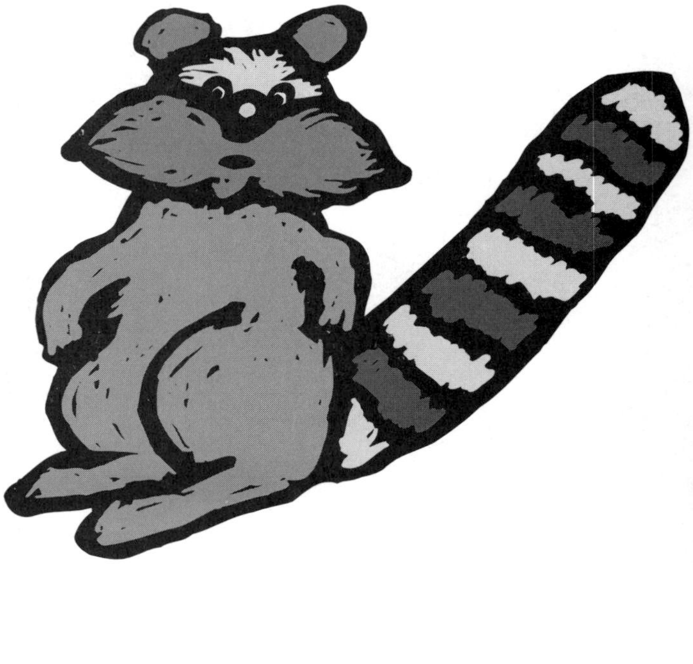

Six Little Ducks

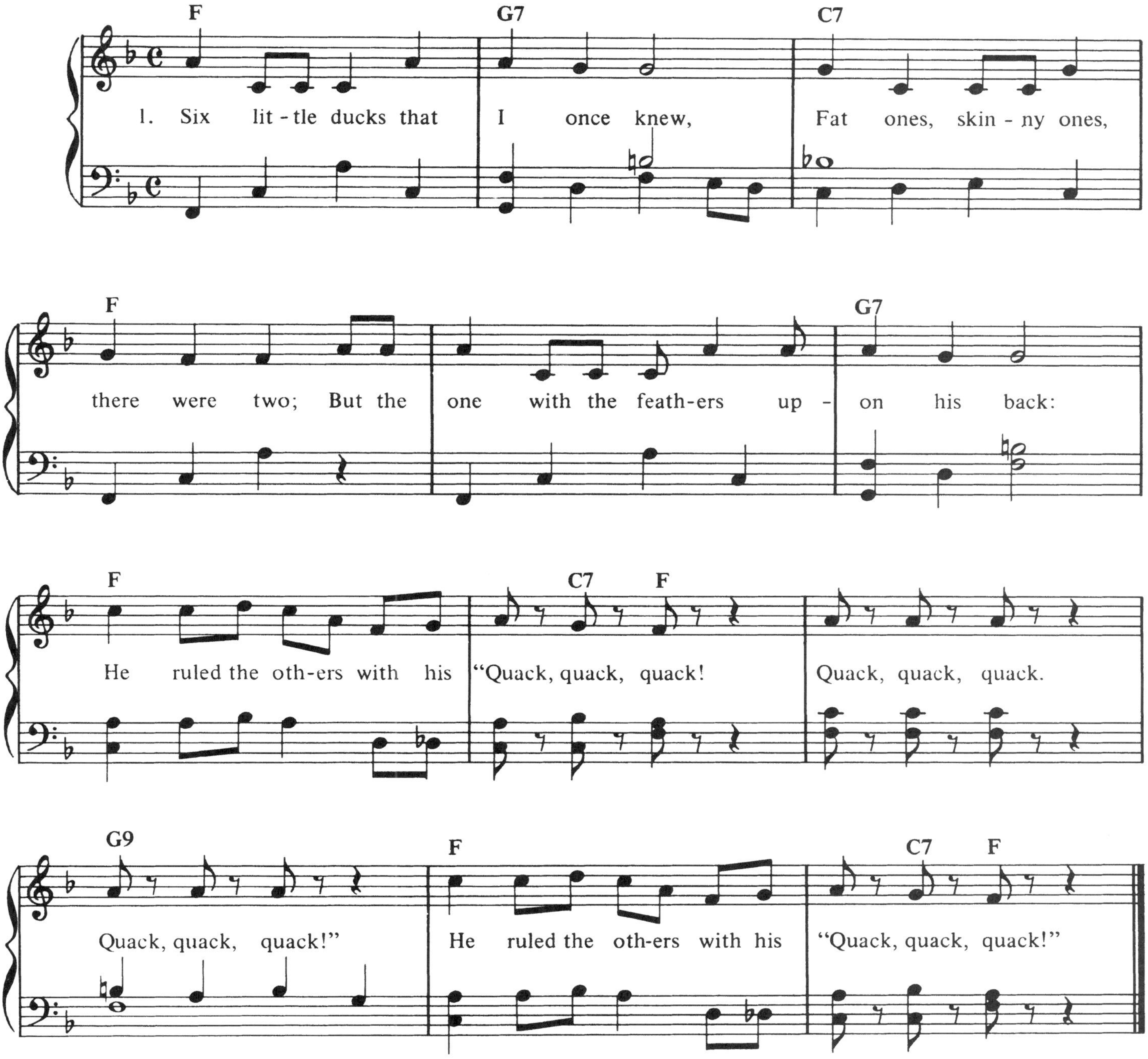

2. Down to the water they would go,
   Wibble-wobble, wibble-wobble, to and fro,
   But the one with the feathers upon his back:
   He ruled the others with his "Quack, quack quack!
   Quack quack quack. Quack quack, quack!"
   He ruled the others with his "Quack, quack quack!"

3. Home from the water they would come,
   Wibble-wobble, wibble-wobble, ho ho hum,
   But the one with the feathers upon his back:
   He ruled the others with his "Quack, quack quack!
   Quack quack quack. Quack quack, quack!"
   He ruled the others with his "Quack, quack quack!"

The Song of the Birds

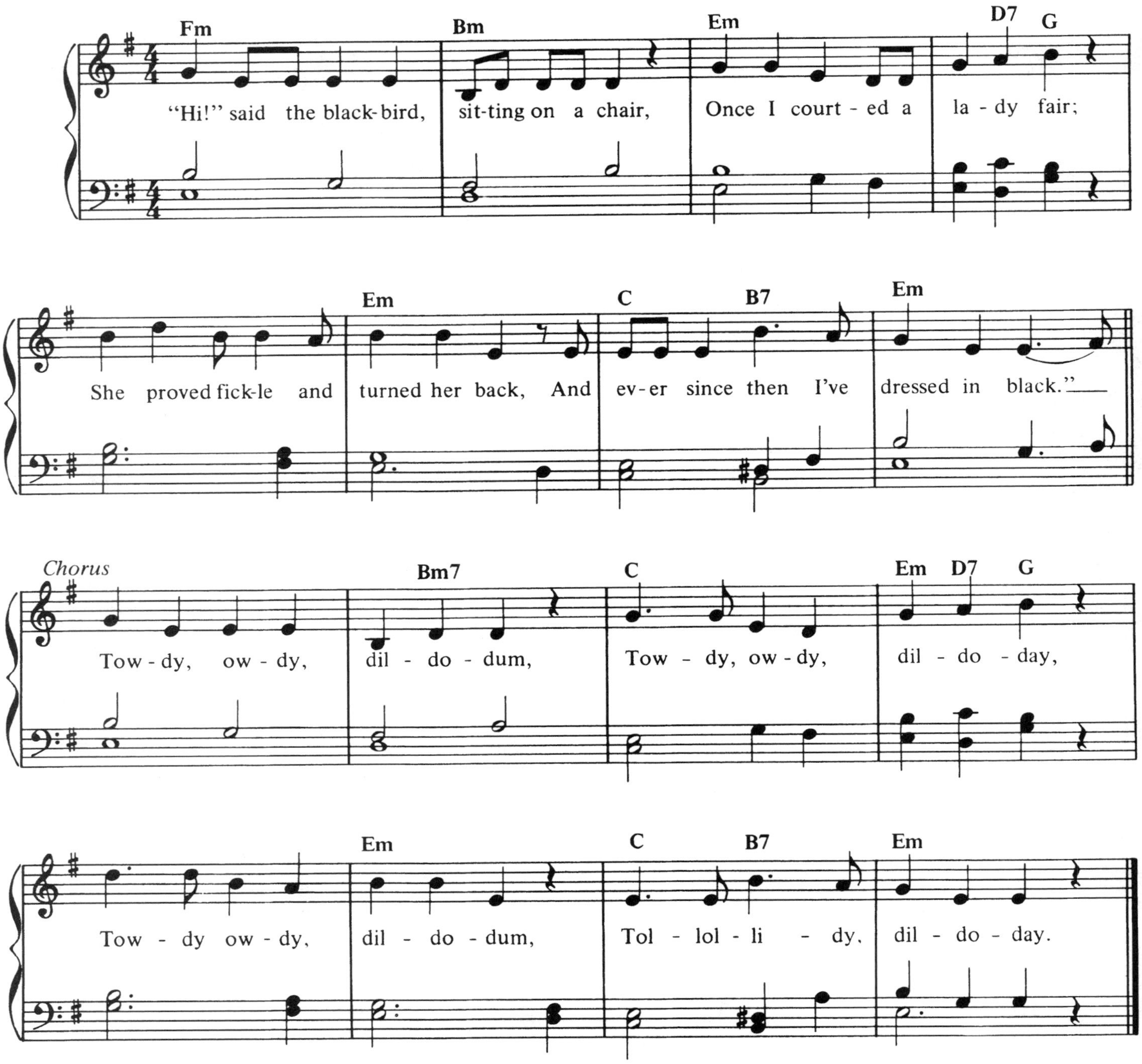

2. "Hi!" said the little leather-winged bat,
   "I will tell you the reason that,
   The reason that I fly in the night
   Is because I've lost my heart's delight."
   Chorus

3. "Hi!" said the little mourning dove,
   "I'll tell you how to regain her love,
   Sing to her both night and day,
   She will find you where you play."
   Chorus

The Sow Got the Measles

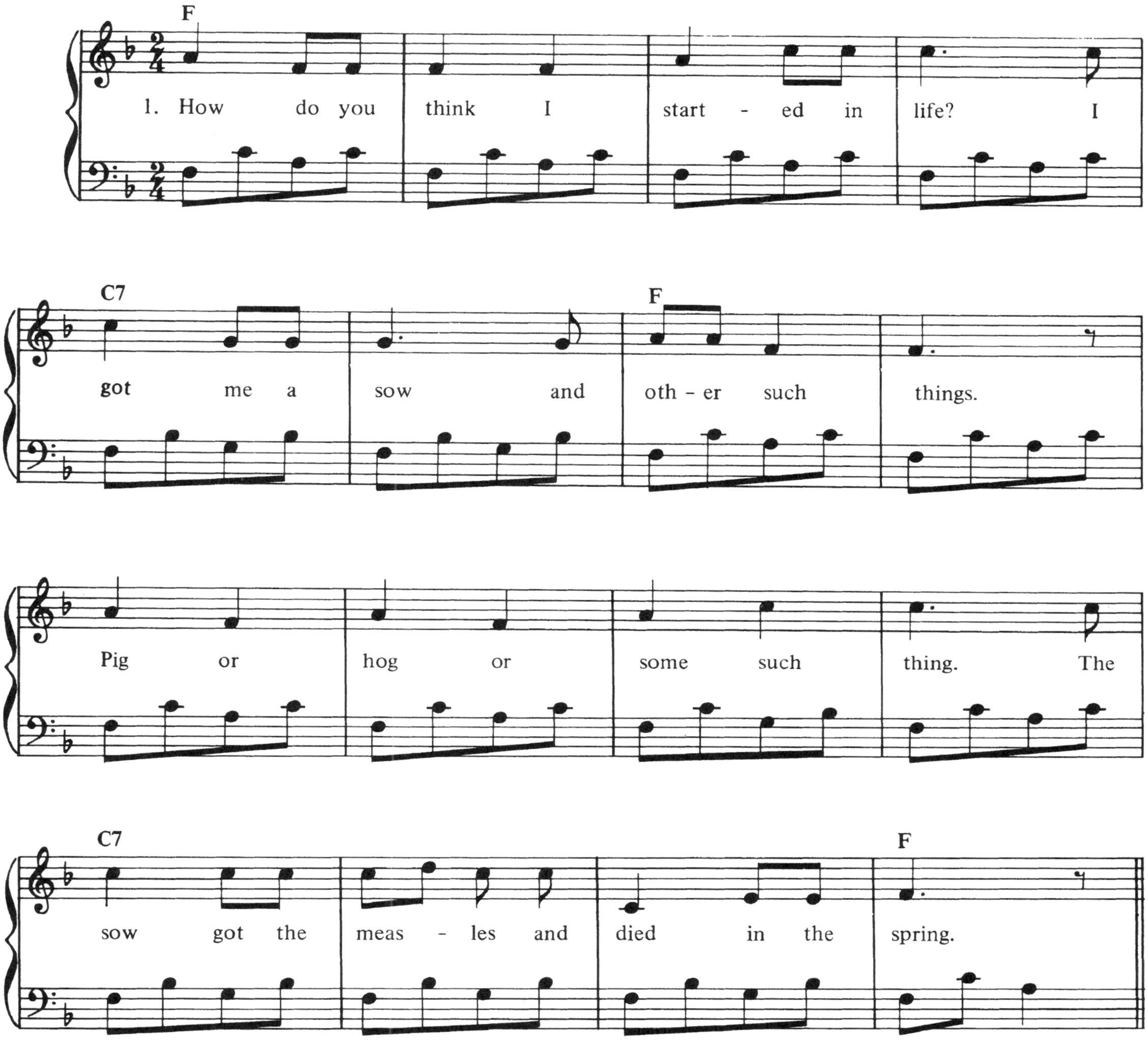

2. What do you think I did with her hide?
Made the best saddle you ever did ride;
Saddle or bridle or some such thing,
The sow got the measles and she died in
the spring.

3. What do you think I did with her hair?
Made the best satin you ever did wear;
Satin or silk or some such thing.
The sow got the measles and she died in
the spring.

Sweetly Sings the Donkey

F Bb C7 F
Sweet-ly sings the don - key At the break of day.
Aminor Bb C7 F
If you do not feed him, This is what he'll say: "Hee -
F#dim7 Gminor F C7 F
haw, hee - haw, hee - haw, hee-haw, hee - haw."

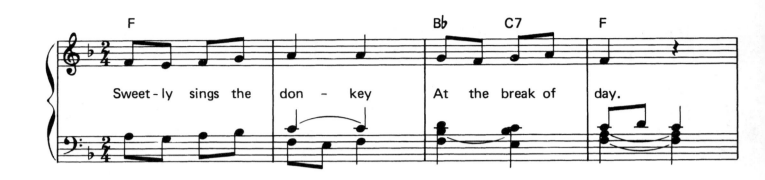

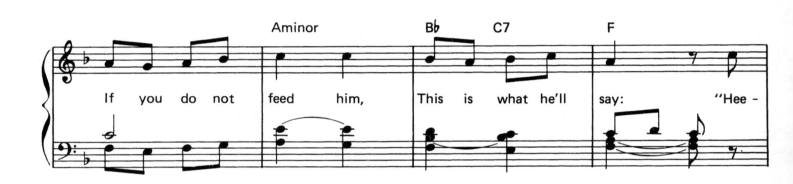

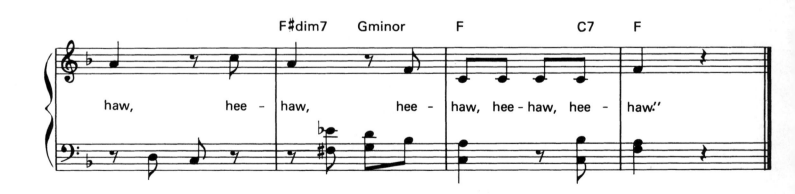

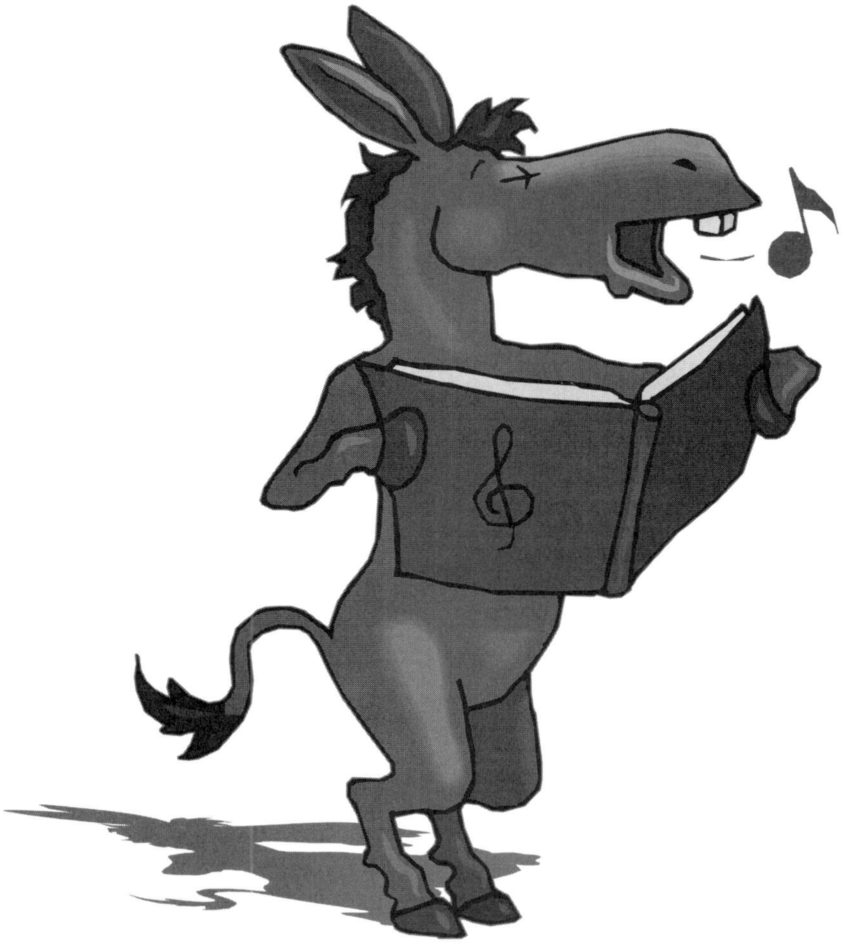

The Teddy Bears' Picnic

Words and music by John W. Bratton
and James B. Kennedy

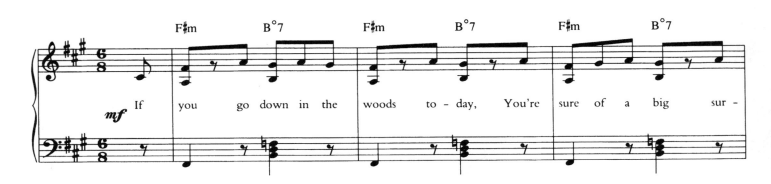

If you go down in the woods to-day, You're sure of a big sur-

prise. _____ If you go down in the woods to-day, You'd bet-ter go in dis-

guise; _____ For ev-'ry bear that ev-er there was Will gath-er there for

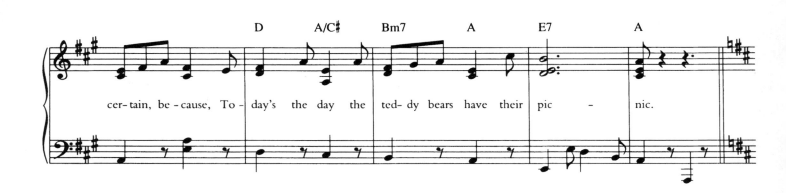

cer-tain, be-cause, To-day's the day the ted-dy bears have their pic - nic.

Chorus
D C♯ D D6
Pic - nic time for ted - dy bears; The lit - tle
A7
ted - dy bears are hav-ing a love - ly time to-day.
A°7 A7
Watch them, catch them un - a-wares, And see them
D A°/E♭ A/E A
pic - nic on their hol - i - day.
D C♯ D D6
See them gai - ly gad - a-bout; They love to

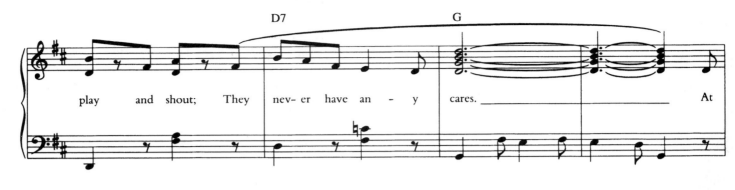

play and shout; They nev- er have an - y cares. _____ At

six o'- clock their mum – mies and dad – dies will take them home to bed, Be – cause they're

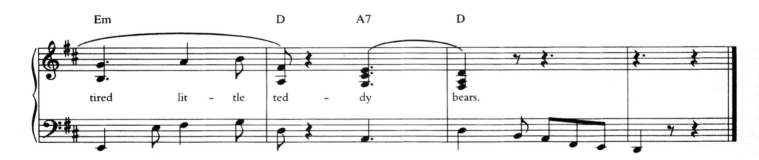

tired lit - tle ted – dy bears.

2. Ev'ry teddy bear who's been good
Is sure of a treat today.
There's lots of marvelous things to eat,
And wonderful games to play.
Beneath the trees where nobody sees,
They'll hide and seek as long as the please,
'Cause that's the way the teddy bears have their picnic.
Chorus

3. If you go down to the woods today,
You'd better not go alone.
It's lovely down in the woods tonight,
But safer to stay at home,
For ev'ry bear that ever there was
Will gather there for certain, because
Today's the day the teddy bears have their picnic.
Chorus

There Was an Old Frog

2. I grabbed him by the leg and pulled him out.
   Ching-a chang-a polly mitch-a cow-me-o,
   He hopped and skipped and bounced all about,
   Ching-a chang-a polly mitch-a cow-me-o.
   Chorus

3. Cheese in the spring house nine days old.
   Ching-a chang-a polly mitch-a cow-me-o,
   Frogs and skippers getting mighty bold.
   Ching-a chang-a polly mitch-a cow-me-o.
   Chorus

This Little Pig Went to Market

C G C
This lit-tle pig went to mar - ket, this lit-tle pig stayed at home.
F G7 C G
This lit - tle pig ___ had roast beef, this lit-tle pig ___ had none, and
C F C G C F G7 C
this lit - tle pig ___ cried we - we, we - we, we, all the way home.

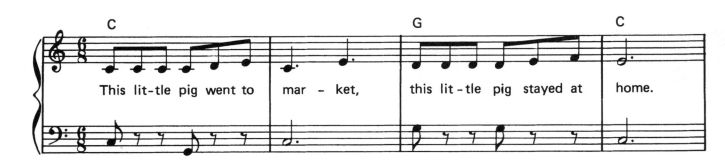

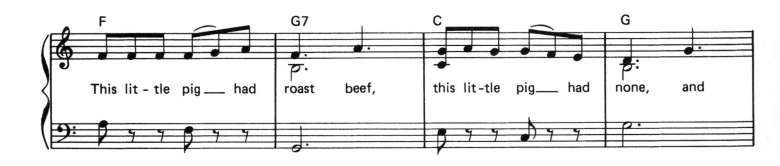

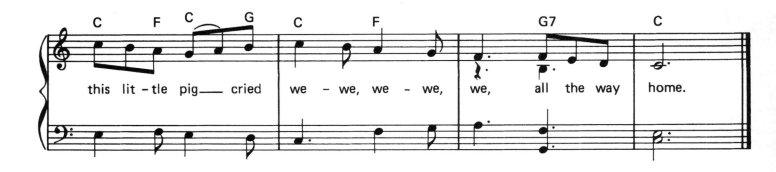

Three Blind Mice

C
Three blind mice, three blind
mice. See how they run, see how they
Am G F C
run. They all ran af - ter the farm - er's wife. She
Dm7 G7 C Dm7 G
cut up a cheese with a carv - ing knife. Did you e - ver see such a
C A7 Dm G C
sight in your life as three blind mice.

130

Three Little Kittens

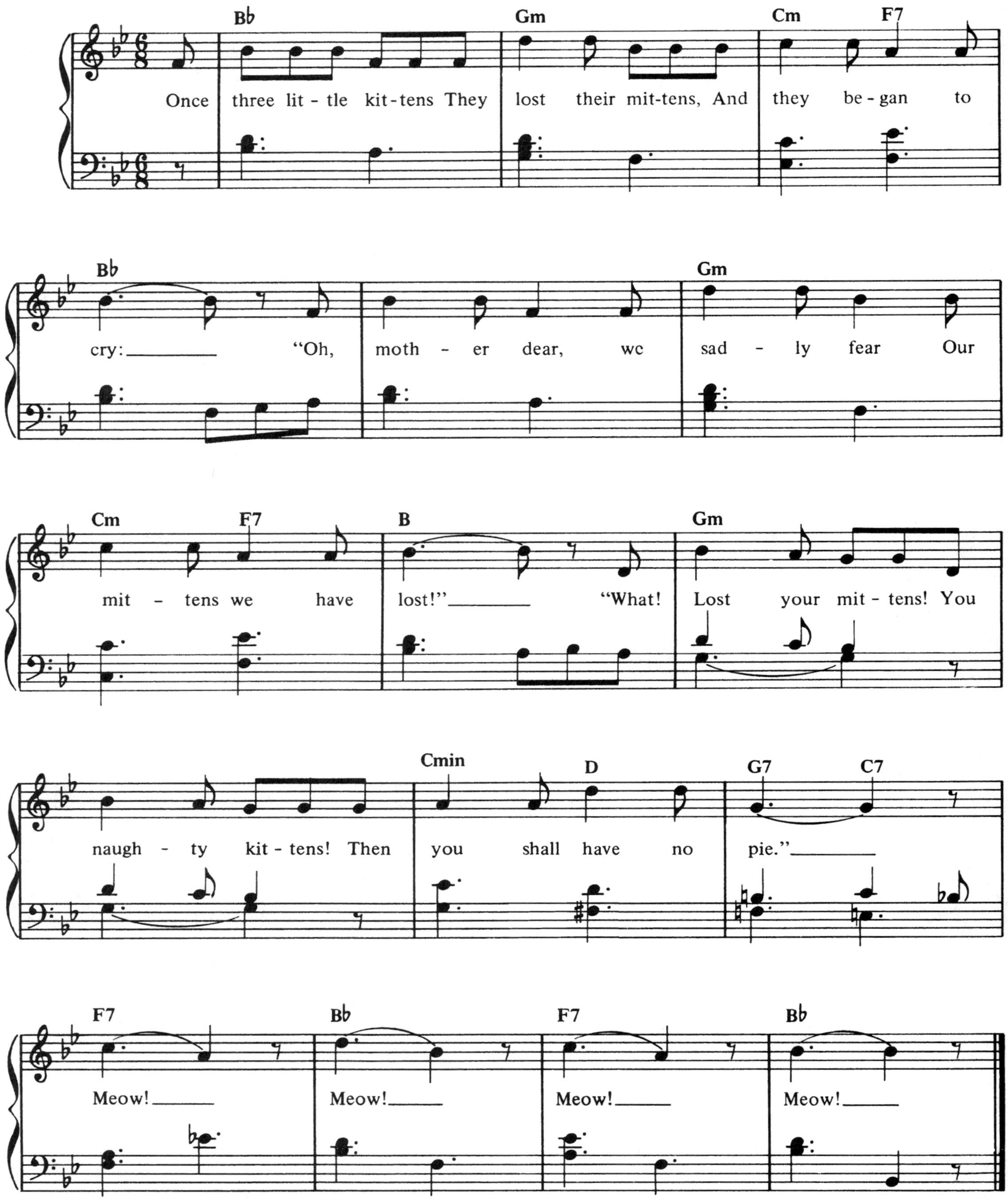

2. The three little kittens, they found their mittens,
    And they began to cry:
    "Oh, mother dear, see here, see here!
    Our mittens we have found!"
    "What! Found your mittens? You darling kittens!
    Then you shall have some pie!"
    Meow! Meow! Meow! Meow!

3. The three little kittens put on their mittens,
    And soon ate up the pie.
    "Oh, mother dear, we greatly fear
    Our mittens we have soiled."
    "What! Soiled your mittens? You naughty kittens!"
    Then they began to sigh,
    Meow! Meow! Meow! Meow!

4. The three little kittens, they washed their mittens,
    And hung them up to dry.
    "Oh, mother dear, look here, look here!
    Our mittens we have washed."
    "What! Washed your mittens? You darling kittens!
    But I smell a rat close by!"
    Hush! Hush! Hush! Hush!

Two Little Dickey Birds

F
Bb
Two lit - tle dick - ey birds, sit - ting on a wall;
C
F
One named Pe - ter, one named Paul.
F
Bb
Fly a - way, Pe - ter! Fly a - way, Paul!
C
F
Come back, Pe - ter! Come back, Paul!

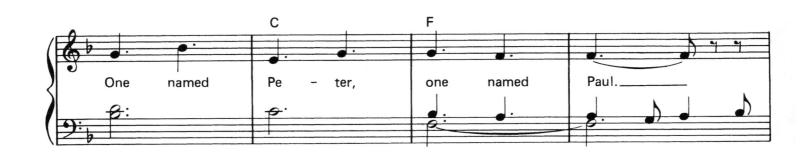

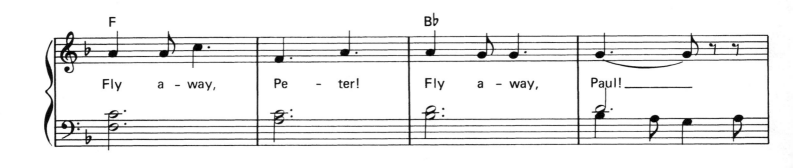

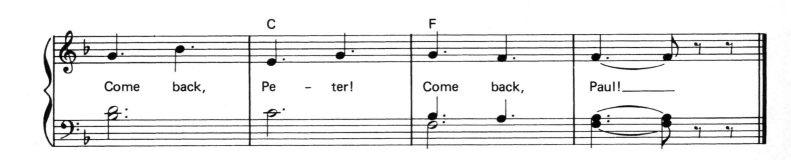

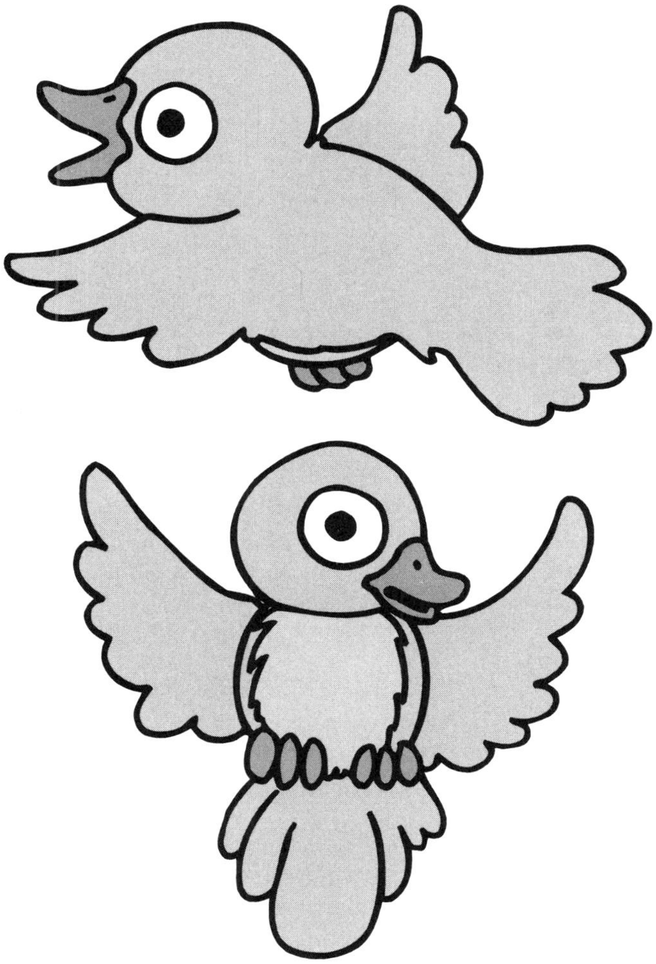

Who Killed Cock Robin?

Dm
Am/
Who killed Cock Ro-bin?
"I," said the Spar-row with my
Chorus
Dm C7 Dm Am Dm C7
bow and ar - row I killed Cock Ro-bin. Then the
F Bb
birds of the air Fell a - sigh - ing and a - sob - bing when they
Gm C7 F
heard of the death of poor Cock Ro - bin When they heard of the
Bb Gm F C7 F
death of poor Cock Ro - bin.

2. Who saw him die?
   "I," said the Fly,
   "With my little eye,
   I saw him die."
   Chorus

3. Who'll dig his grave?
   "I," said the Owl,
   "With my little trowel,
   I'll dig his grave."
   Chorus

4. Who will mourn him?
   "I," said the Rook,
   "Because I can croak,
   I will mourn him."
   Chorus

Whoa, Mule! Can't Get the Saddle On

1. Whoa, mule! Can't get the sad-dle on, Whoa, mule! Can't get the sad-dle on.
2. Catch that mule! Can't get the sad-dle on, Catch that mule! Can't get the sad-dle on.
3. Ride that mule! Can't keep the sad-dle on, Ride that mule! Can't keep the sad-dle on.

4. Run, mule! Can't keep the sad-dle on, Run, mule! Can't keep the sad-dle on.
5. Run, mule! Can't keep the sad-dle on, Run, mule! Can't keep the sad-dle on.

Will You Walk a Little Faster

Words by Louis Carroll

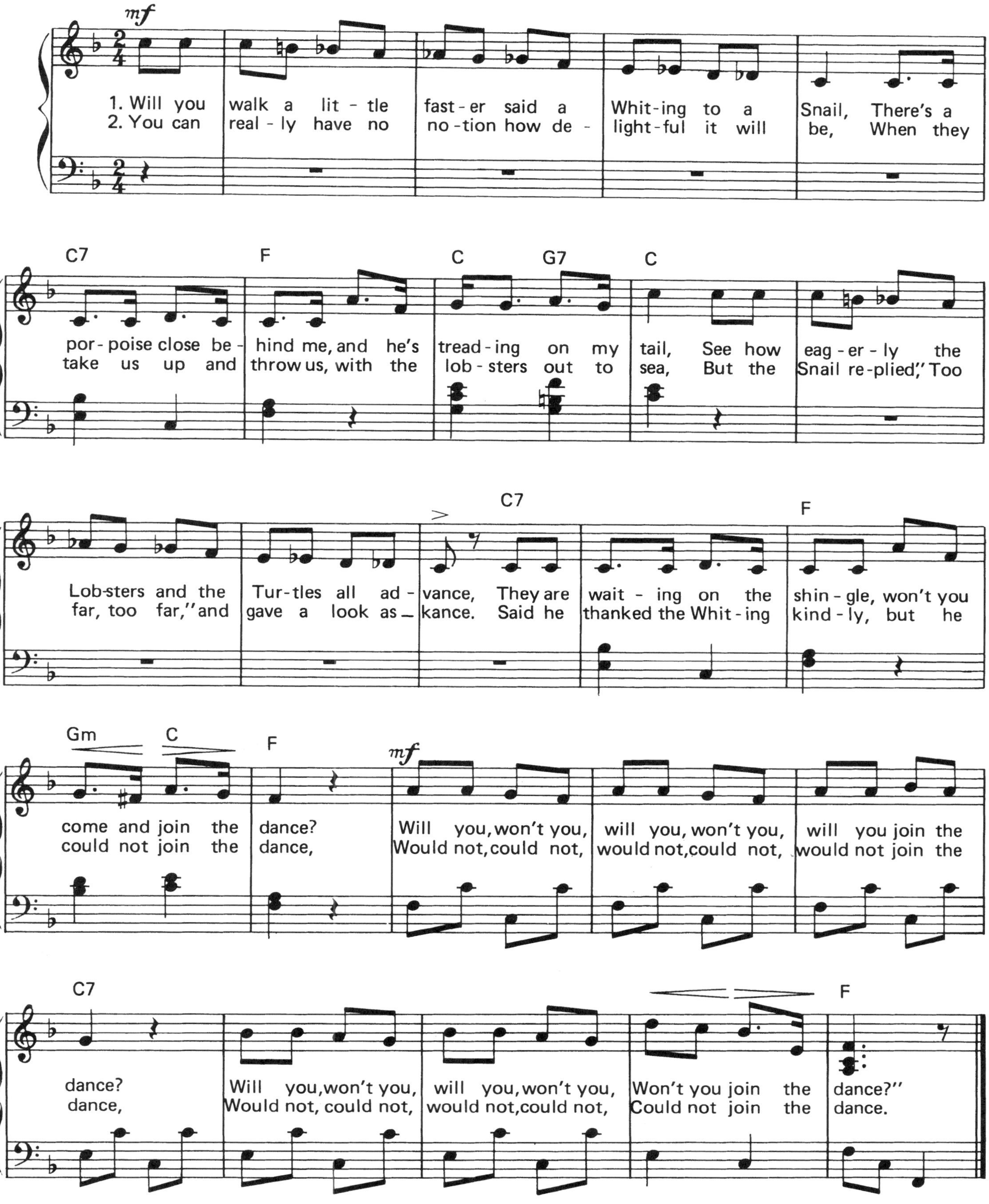

Storybook People

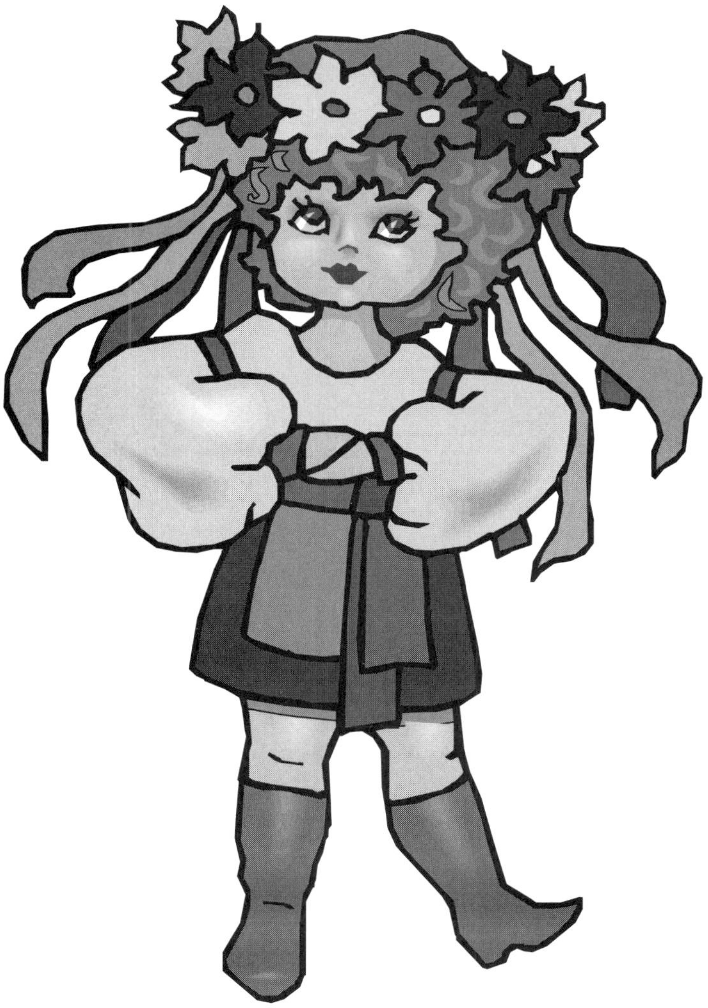

Aiken Drum

There — was a man lived in the moon, lived

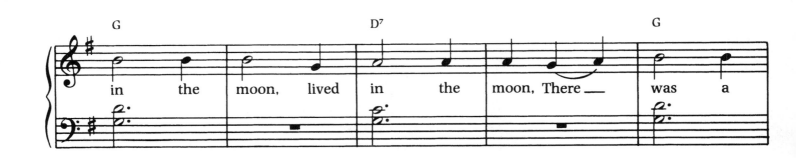

in the moon, lived in the moon, There — was a

man lived in the moon, And his name was Ai - ken

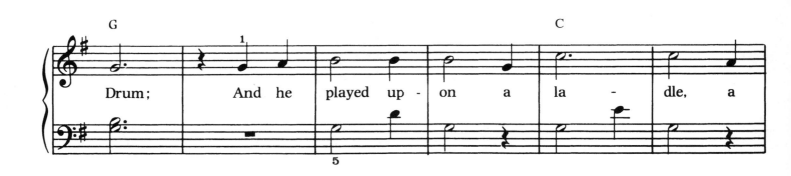

Drum; And he played up - on a la - dle, a

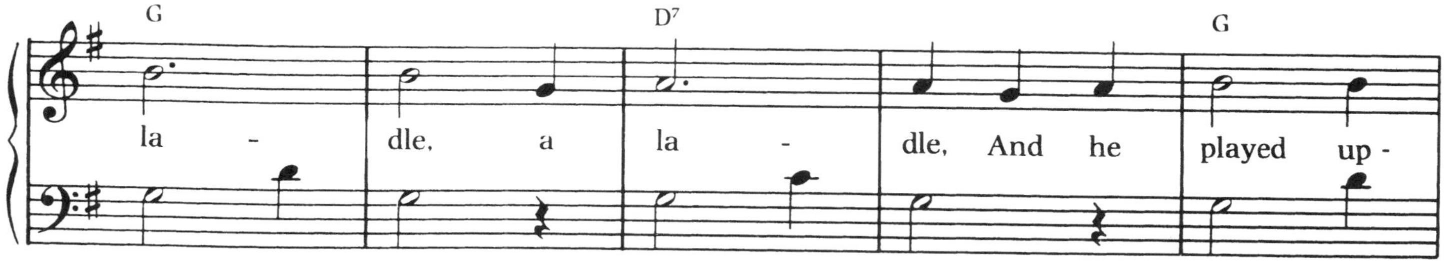

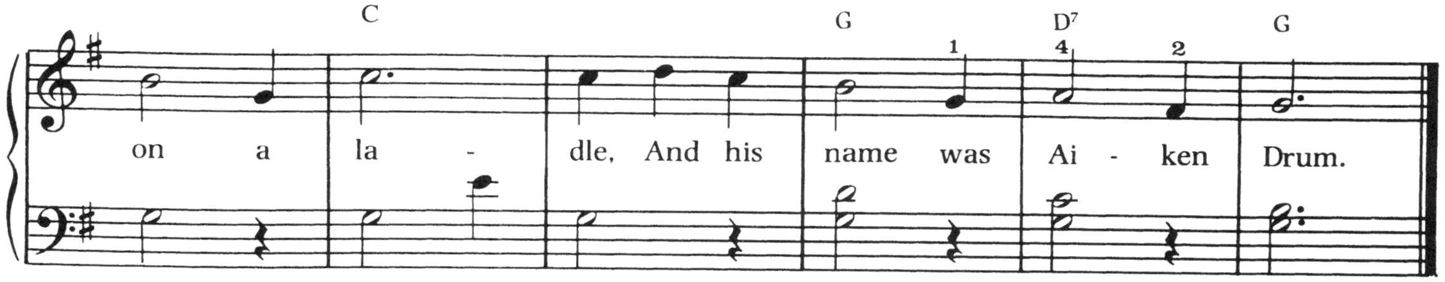

2. And his hat was made of good cream cheese,
Good cream cheese, good cream cheese.
And his hat was made of good cream cheese,
And his name was Aiken Drum.
And he played upon a ladle, a ladle, a ladle,
And he played upon a ladle,
And his name was Aiken Drum.

3. And his coat was made of good roast beef,
Good roast beef, good roast beef.
And his coat was made of good roast beef,
And his name was Aiken Drum.
And he played upon a ladle, a ladle, a ladle,
And he played upon a ladle,
And his name was Aiken Drum.

4. And his buttons were made of penny loaves,
Penny loaves, penny loaves,
And his buttons were made of penny loaves,
And his name was Aiken Drum.
And he played upon a ladle, a ladle, a ladle,
And he played upon a ladle,
And his name was Aiken Drum.

5. His waistcoat was made of crust of pies,
Crust of pies, crust of pies,
His waistcoat was made of crust of pies,
And his name was Aiken Drum.
And he played upon a ladle, a ladle, a ladle,
And he played upon a ladle,
And his name was Aiken Drum.

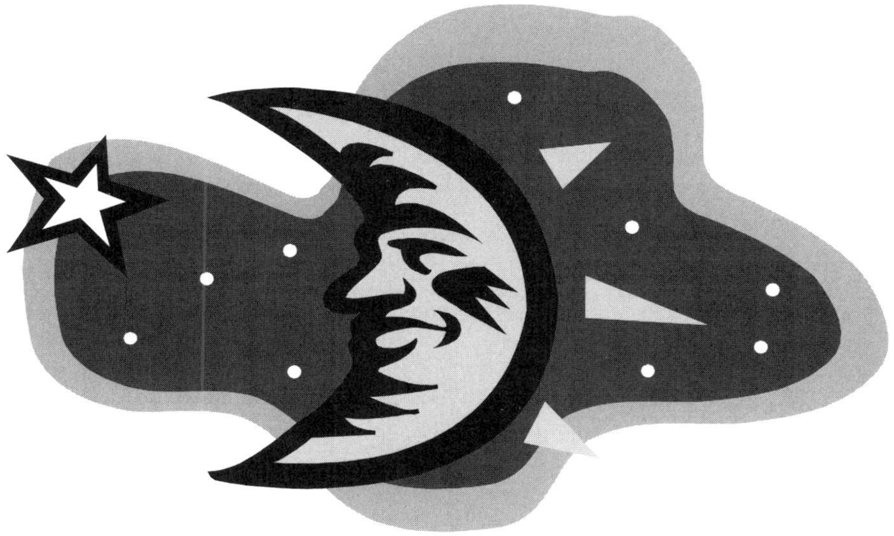

Doctor Foster

Doc - tor Fos - ter went to Glouces-ter in a show-er of rain, he

stepped in a pud - dle, right up to his mid-dle, and nev - er went there a - gain.

Georgie Porgie

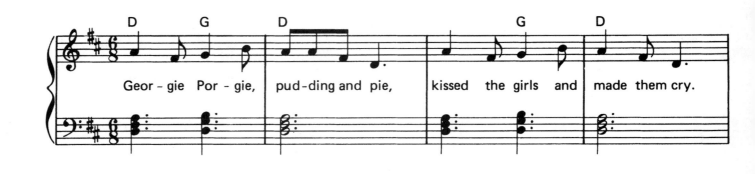

Geor - gie Por - gie, pud-ding and pie, kissed the girls and made them cry.

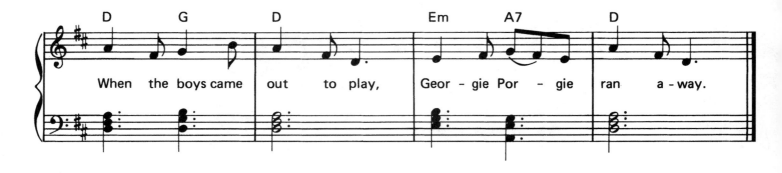

When the boys came out to play, Geor - gie Por - gie ran a - way.

Handy Spandy

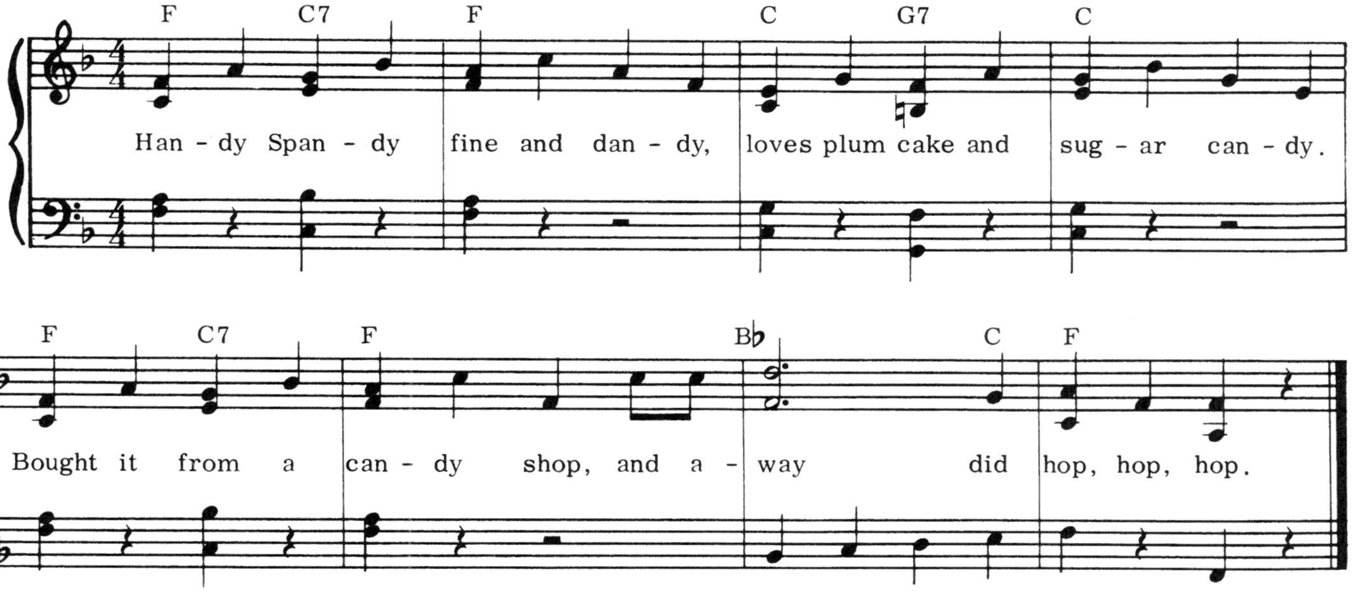
F C7 F C G7 C
Han - dy Span - dy fine and dan - dy, loves plum cake and sug - ar can - dy.
F C7 F B♭ C F
Bought it from a can - dy shop, and a - way did hop, hop, hop.

Humpty Dumpty

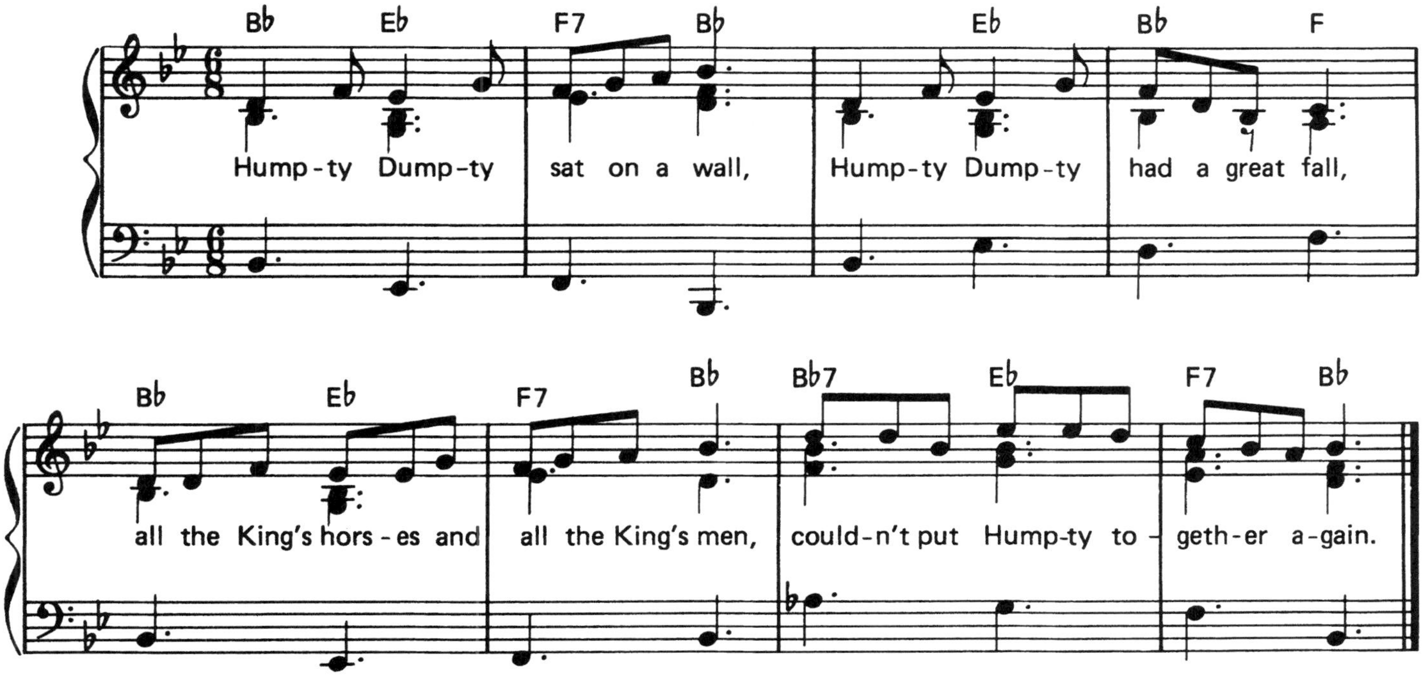
B♭ E♭ F7 B♭ E♭ B♭ F
Hump-ty Dump-ty sat on a wall, Hump-ty Dump-ty had a great fall,
B♭ E♭ F7 B♭ B♭7 E♭ F7 B♭
all the King's hors - es and all the King's men, could-n't put Hump-ty to - geth-er a-gain.

Jack and Jill

C G Am C F6 G C
Jack and Jill went up the hill to fetch a pail of wa - ter.
C F G C
Jack fell down, and broke his crown, and Jill came tumb - ling af - ter.

Jack Spratt

D E A
Jack Spratt could eat no fat, His wife could eat no lean; and
D7 G F♯7 Bmin D A7 D
so be-twixt them both, you see, They made the plat - ter clean.

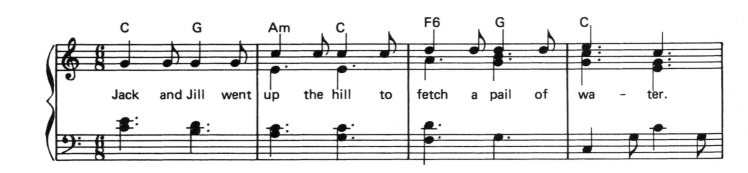

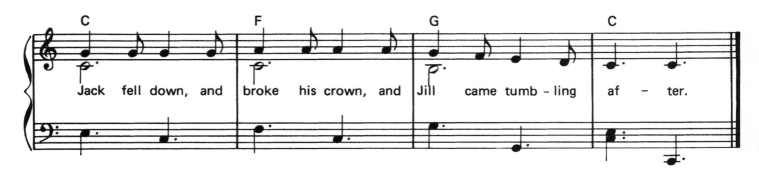

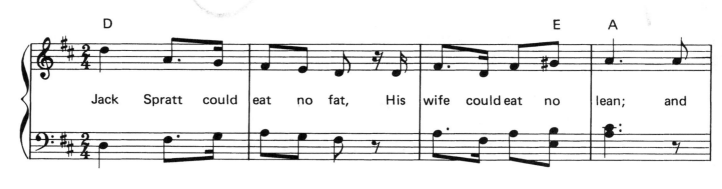

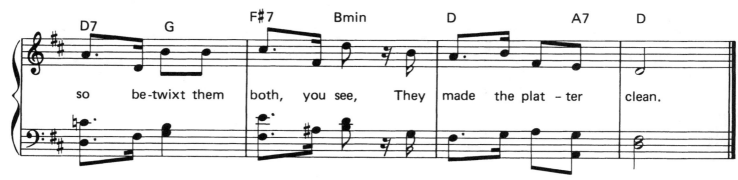

Lazy Katy

La - zy Ka - ty, will you get up, You get up, you get up?

La - zy Ka - ty, will you get up This cold and fros - ty morn - ing?

Little Bo-Peep

G Em C6 D
Lit - tle Bo - Peep has lost her sheep and
G D7 G Am7 G A7 D7
can't tell where to find them.
G Dm6 E Am7 Cm6 D7
Leave them a - lone and they'll come home and
G C G D7 Am7 D7 G Am7 G
bring their tails be - hind them.

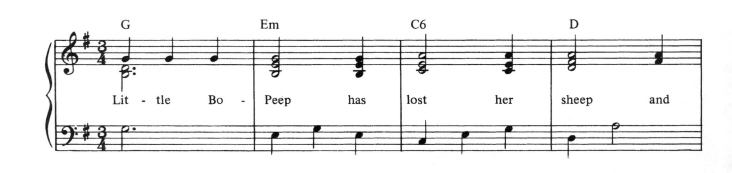

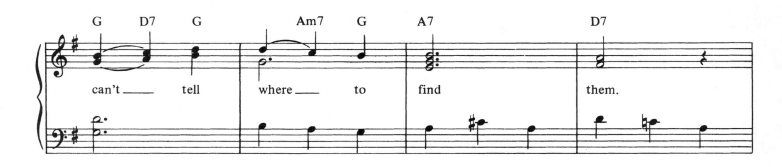

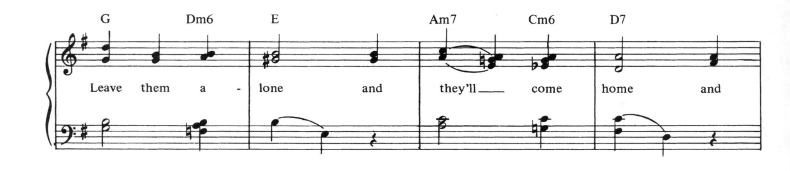

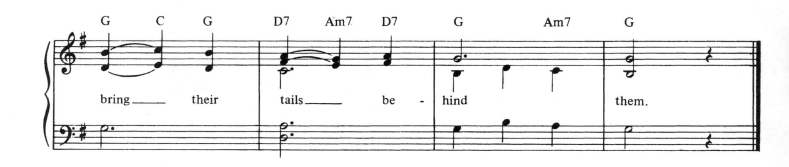

Little Miss Muffet

F
C7
F
Lit - tle Miss Muf - fet sat on a tuf - fet,
F7
Gm7
C7
eat - ing her curds and whey. There
F
C7
F
came a great spi - der and sat down be - side her, which
G7
C7
B♭6
F
fright - en'd Miss Muf - fet a - way.

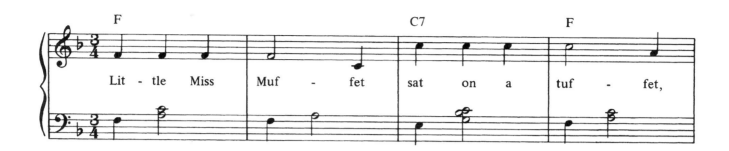

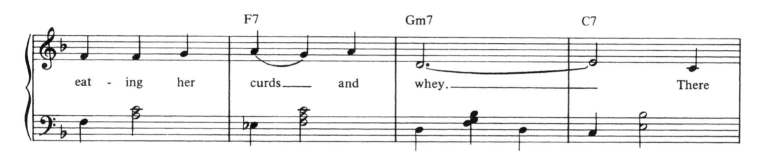

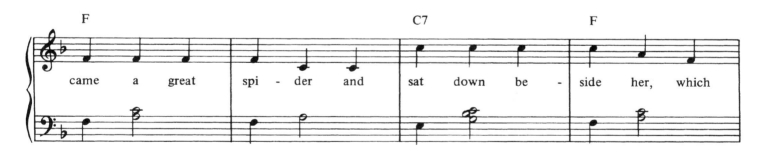

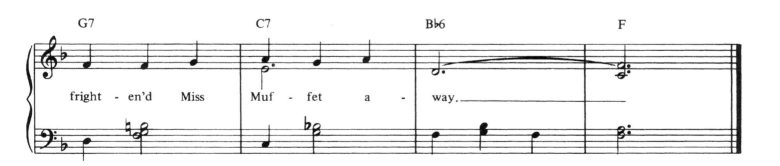

Little Boy Blue

Lit-tle Boy blue, come blow your horn, the sheep's in the mead-ow, the cow's in the corn.

Where's the boy who looks af-ter the sheep? He's un-der the hay-stack fast a-sleep.

Will you wak-en him? No, not I, for if I do,— he's sure to cry.

Little Tommy Tucker

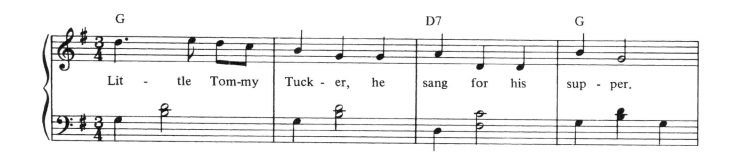

Lit - tle Tom-my Tuck - er, he sang for his sup - per.

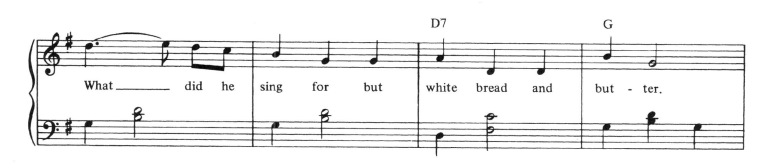

What ___ did he sing for but white bread and but - ter.

How can he cut it with - out an - y knife? ___

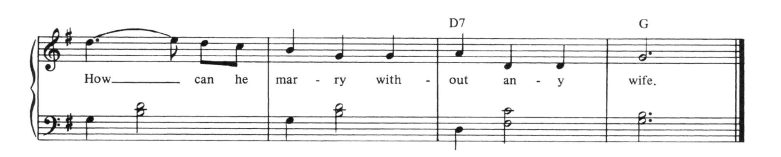

How ___ can he mar - ry with - out an - y wife.

Lucy Locket

Lu — cy Lock — et lost her pock — et, Kit — ty Fish — er found it. Not a pen — ny was there in it But a rib — bon round it. Dree, dree, drop it, drop it....

Michael Finnegan

I know a man named Mi-chael Fin-ne-gan. He had whis-kers

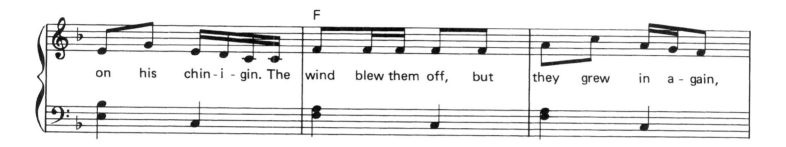

on his chin-i-gin. The wind blew them off, but they grew in a-gain,

Poor old Mi-chael Fin-ne-gan (be - gin a-gain)

2. I know a man named Michael Finnegan,
   He went fishing with a pin-igin,
   Caught a fish and dropped it in-igin
   Poor old Michael Finnegan (begin again).

3. I know a man named Michael Finnegan.
   Climbed a tree and barked his shin-agin,
   Slid back down and scraped his skin-igin,
   Poor old Michael Finnegan (begin again).

4. I know a man named Michael Finnegan,
   He kicked up an awful din-igin,
   Because they said he could not sing-igin,
   Poor old Michael Finnegan (begin again).

5. I know a man named Michael Finnegan.
   He got fat and then got thin again,
   Then he slept and had to begin again,
   Poor old Michael Finnegan (begin again).

Mary Had a Little Lamb

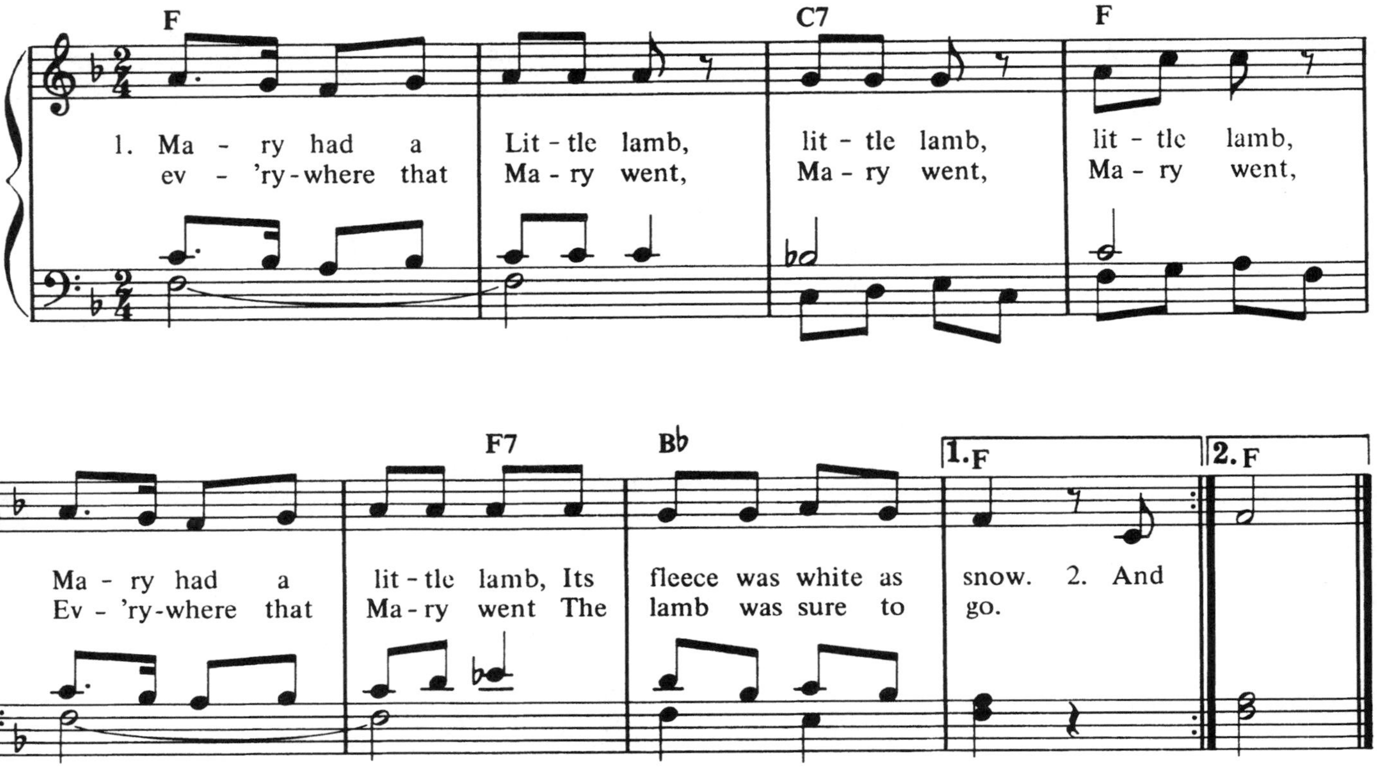
F
C7
F
1. Ma - ry had a Lit - tle lamb, lit - tle lamb, lit - tle lamb,
ev - 'ry-where that Ma - ry went, Ma - ry went, Ma - ry went,
F7
Bb
1.F
2.F
Ma - ry had a lit - tle lamb, Its fleece was white as snow. 2. And
Ev - 'ry-where that Ma - ry went The lamb was sure to go.

Mary, Mary, Quite Contrary

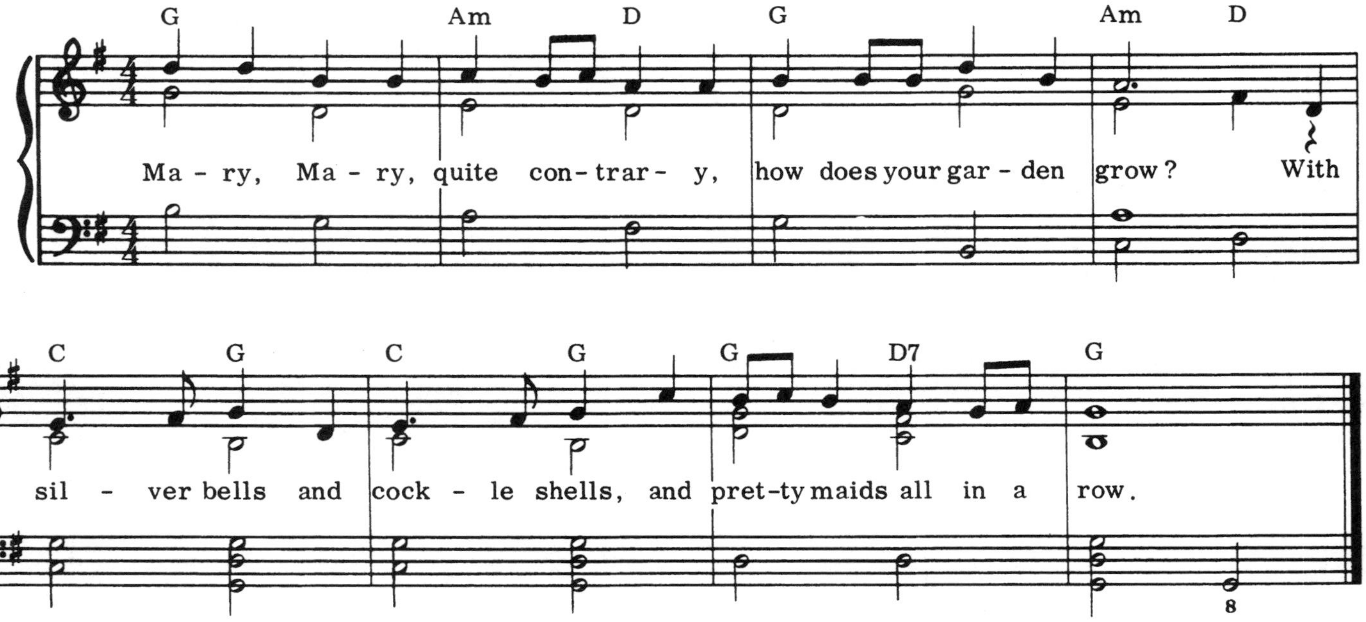
G
Am
D
G
Am
D
Ma - ry, Ma - ry, quite con - trar - y, how does your gar - den grow? With
C
G
C
G
G
D7
G
sil - ver bells and cock - le shells, and pret - ty maids all in a row.
8

The Muffin Man

Do you know the Muf-fin Man, the Muf-fin Man, the Muf-fin Man? Oh,

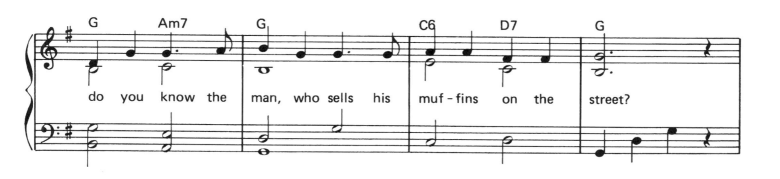

do you know the man, who sells his muf-fins on the street?

Do you know the Muf-fin Man, the Muf-fin Man, the Muf-fin Man? Oh,

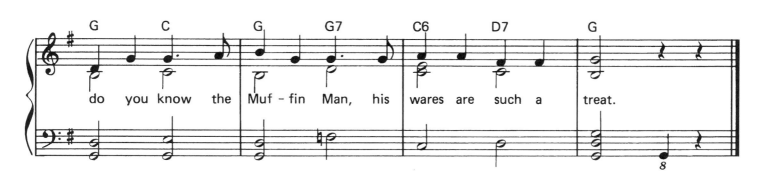

do you know the Muf-fin Man, his wares are such a treat.

The Noble Duke of York

Oh, the no-ble Duke of York, He had ten thous-and men. He marched them up to the top of the hill and he marched them down a-gain. And when they were up, they were up, And when they were down, they were down, And when they were on-ly half-way up, They were neith-er up nor down.

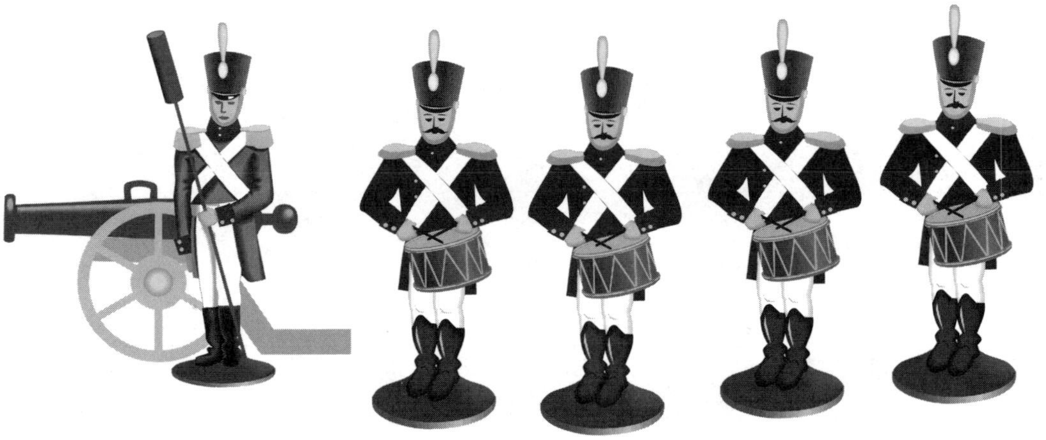

Old King Cole

Gm Gm6 D Gm D Gm Cm
Old King Cole was a mer-ry old__ soul, and a mer-ry old soul was
D B F Gm D D7
he; He__ called for his pipe, and he called for his bowl, and he
Gm Cm7 D7 Gm Gm
called for his fid - dlers__ three. Ev - 'ry__ fid-dler had a
Cm D Gm E♭ F B♭ D7
fid-dle so__ fine, and a ve - ry fine__ fid - dle had he; Oh there's
B♭ F Gm D D7 Gm Cm7 D7 Gm
none so__ rare as__ can com - pare with King Cole and his fid - dlers__ three.

Old Mother Hubbard

Verses 2–10

3. She went to the market
   To buy him some fish
   But when she came back
   He was licking the dish.

4. She went to the farmstand
   To buy him some fruit;
   But when she came back
   He was playing the flute.

5. She went to the tailor's
   To buy him a coat;
   But when she came back
   He was riding a goat.

6. She went to the hatter's
   To buy him a hat;
   But when she came back
   He was feeding the cat.

7. She went to the barber's
   To buy him a wig;
   But when she came back
   He was dancing a jig.

8. She went to the cobbler's
   To buy him some shoes
   But when she came back
   He was reading the news.

9. She went to the seamstress
   To buy him some linen;
   But when she came back
   The dog was a-spinnin'.

10. The dame made a curtsy,
    The dog made a bow;
    The dame said, "Your servant."
    The dog said, "Bow-wow."

Simple Simon

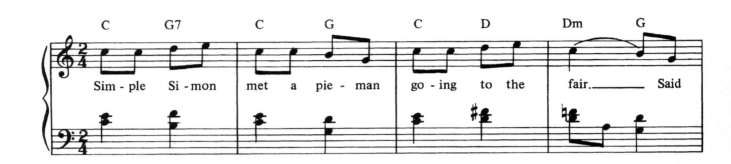

Sim - ple Si - mon met a pie - man go - ing to the fair.____ Said

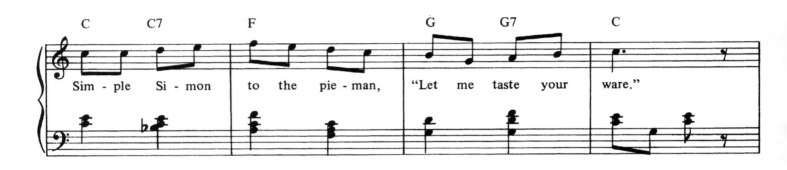

Sim - ple Si - mon to the pie - man, "Let me taste your ware."

Says the man to Sim - ple Si - mon "Do you mean to pay?" Says

Si - mon, "Yes of course I do," and then he ran a - way.____

There Was an Old Man Who Lived in a Wood

Turn Again, Whittington

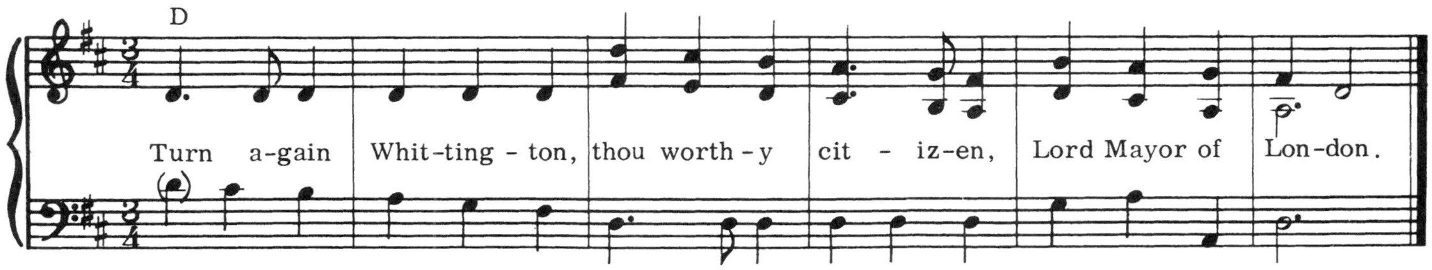

160

There Was an Old Woman Tossed Up in a Basket

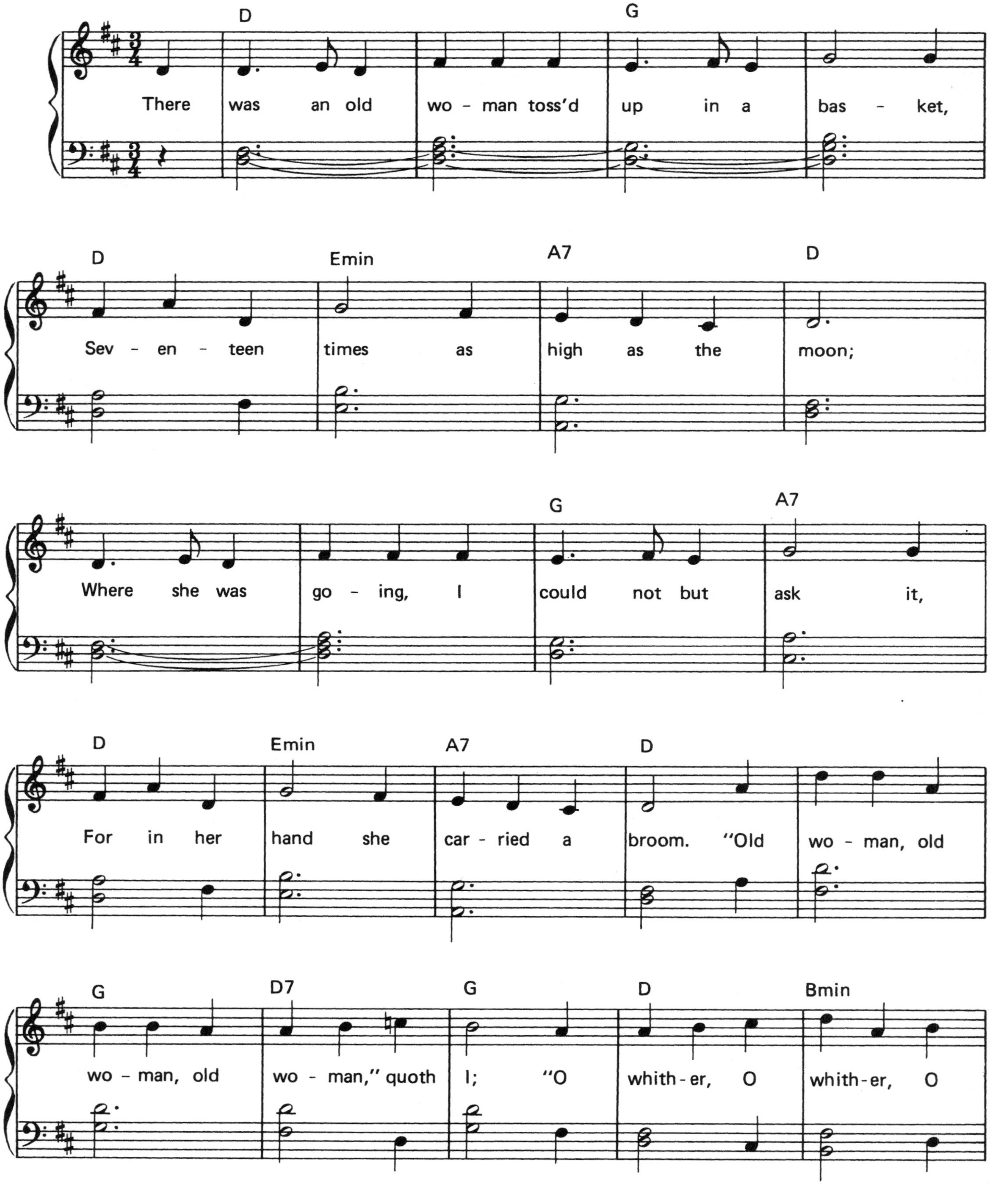

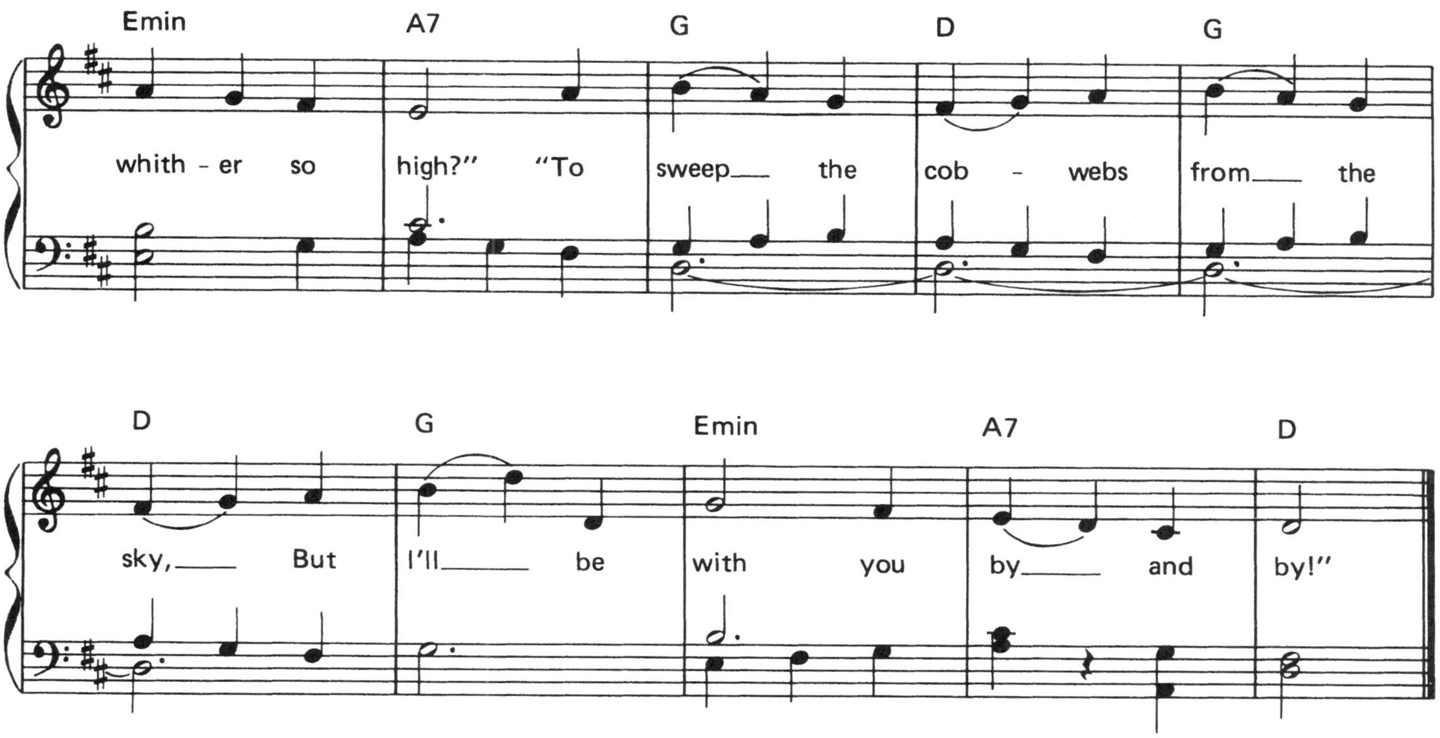

Emin A7 G D G
whith - er so high?" "To sweep the cob - webs from the
D G Emin A7 D
sky, But I'll be with you by and by!"

There Was an Old Woman Who Lived in a Shoe

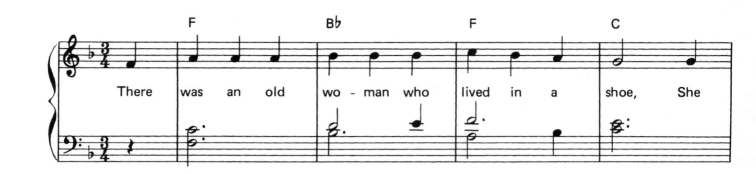

There was an old wo - man who lived in a shoe, She

had so ma - ny child - ren she didn't know what to do. She

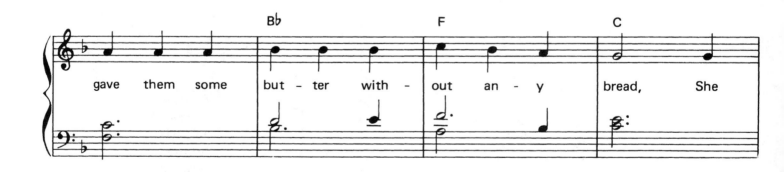

gave them some but - ter with - out an - y bread, She

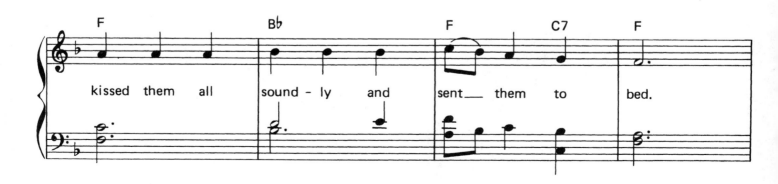

kissed them all sound - ly and sent___ them to bed.

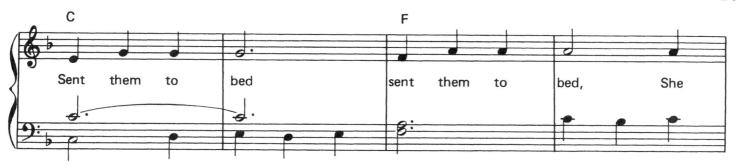

Sent them to bed sent them to bed, She

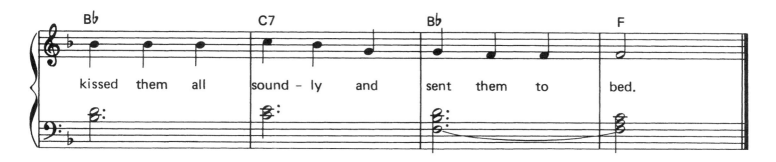

kissed them all sound-ly and sent them to bed.

Wee Willie Winkie

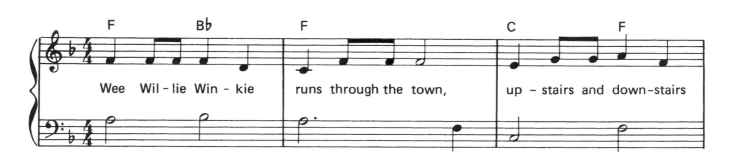

Wee Wil-lie Win-kie runs through the town, up – stairs and down-stairs

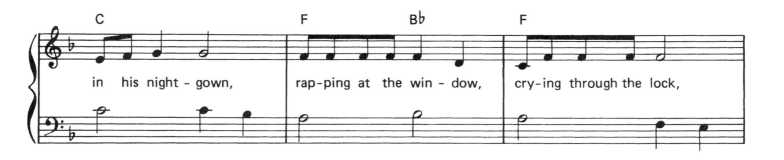

in his night-gown, rap-ping at the win-dow, cry-ing through the lock,

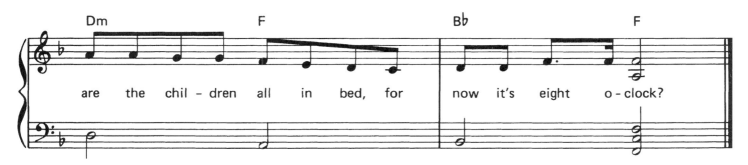

are the chil-dren all in bed, for now it's eight o-clock?

Holiday Songs

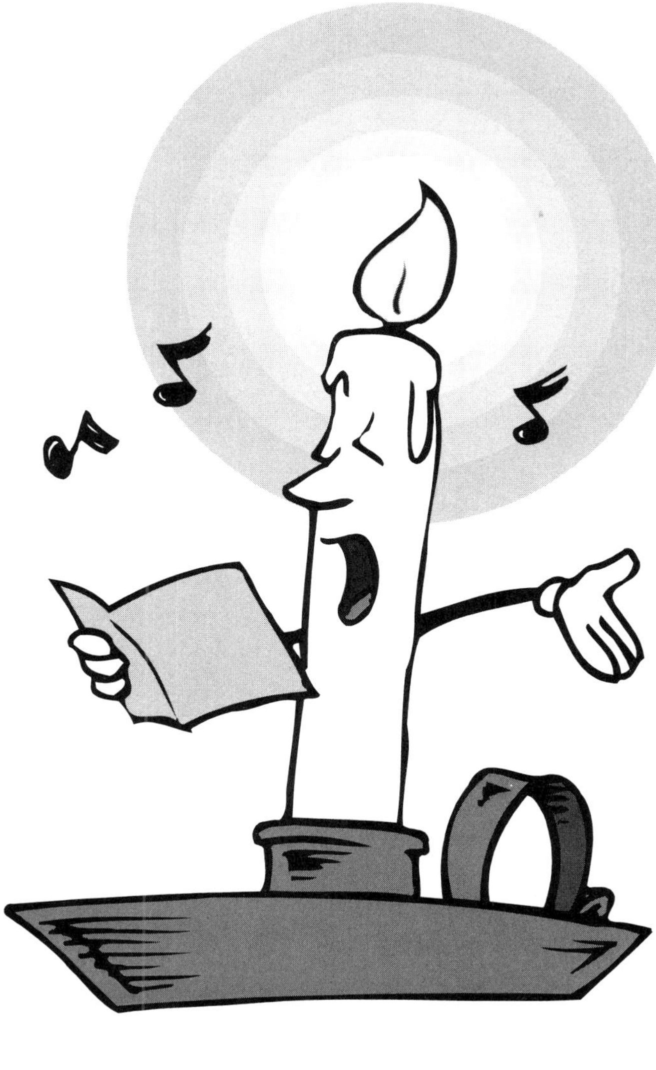

Deck the Hall

Welsh carol

1. Deck the hall with boughs of hol - ly, Fa-la-la-la la, la la - la - la.

'Tis the sea - son to be jol - ly, Fa-la-la-la la, la la - la - la.

Don we now our gay ap-par - el, Fa-la-la, la-la-la, la - la - la.

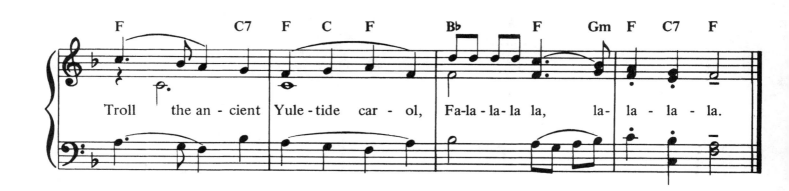

Troll the an - cient Yule - tide car - ol, Fa-la-la-la la, la - la - la - la.

2. See the blazing Yule before us,
   Fa-la-la-la la, la la-la-la.
   Strike the harp and join the chorus,
   Fa-la-la-la la, la la-la-la.
   Follow me in merry measure,
   Fa-la-la, la-la-la, la-la-la.
   Troll the ancient Yuletide treasure.
   Fa-la-la-la la, la la-la-la.

3. Fast away the old year passes,
   Fa-la-la-la la, la la-la-la.
   Hail the new, ye lads and lasses,
   Fa-la-la-la la, la la-la-la.
   Sing we joyous all together,
   Fa-la-la, la-la-la, la-la-la.
   Heedless of the wind and weather,
   Fa-la-la-la la, la la-la-la.

Ding Dong! Merrily on High

French carol

Bb C7 F Bb Cm7 F Bb
1. Ding dong, mer - ri - ly on high, The Christ - mas bells are ring - ing;
2. Ding dong, car - ol all the bells, Ring out the Christ - mas sto - ry;
C7 F Bb Cm7 F Bb
Ding dong, joy - ous - ly re - ply, The an - gels all a - sing - ing.
Ding dong, sound the good now - ells, God's Son has come in glo - ry.
Refrain
Gm7 Cm7 F7 Bbmaj7 Ebmaj7 Am7 Dm7
Glo - - - - - - - - - - - -
Gm7 C7 F C F Bb Cm7 F Bb
- - - - - ri - a, Ho - san - na in ex - cel - sis.

3. Ring to people far and near,
   And join our happy singing.
   Ding dong, everywhere we hear
   The Christmas bells a-ringing.

4. Hear them ring this happy morn!
   A precious gift is given;
   Ding dong, melody is borne
   Across the land to heaven.

Hanukkah Song

Israeli folk song

Dm
G
mf
Oh, Ha - nuk - kah, oh, Ha - nuk - kah, come light the me - no - rah,
Dm
B♭
Dm
Let's have a par - ty, we'll all dance the *ho - ra.* Gath-er 'round the ta - ble, we'll
Gm
Dm6
B♭
Dm
Gm
Dm
give you a treat, *S'vi - vo - nim* to play with, *le - vi - vot* to eat. And
while we are play-ing, The can - dles are burn - ing ___ low;

171

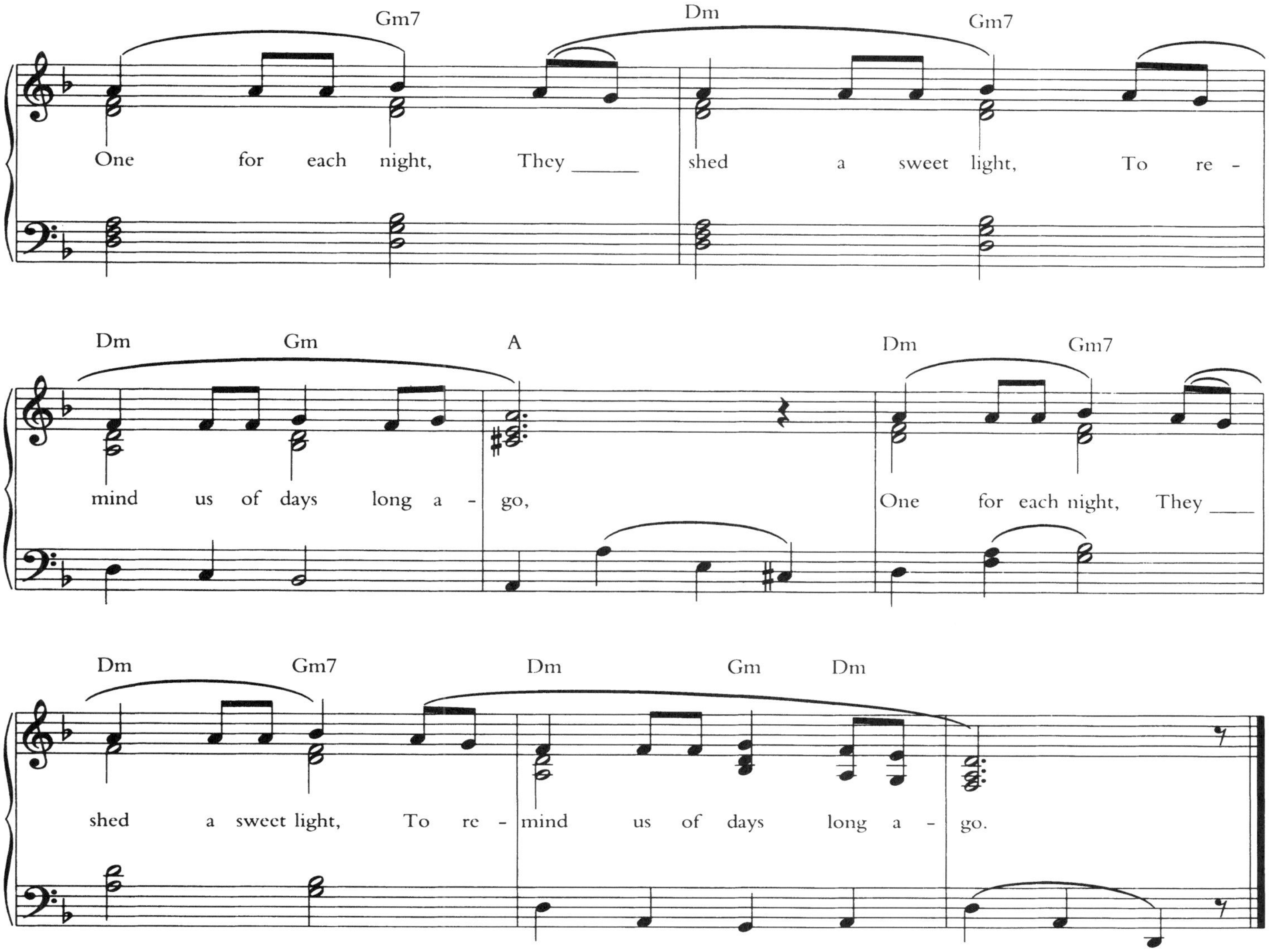

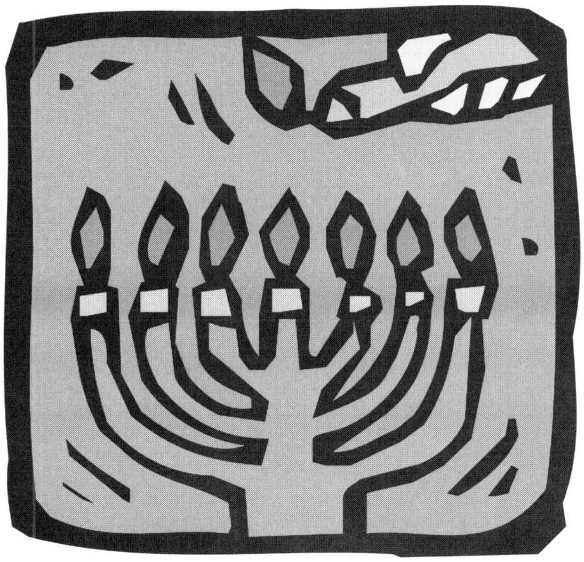

Havah Nagilah

Israeli hora

Ha - vah _____ na - gi - lah, Ha - vah _____ na - gi - lah,

Ha - vah _____ na - gi - lah, Sing! Let us re- joice!

Ha - vah _____ na - gi - lah, Ha - vah _____ na - gi - lah,

Fine
Ha - vah na - gi - lah, Sing! Let us re - joice!
Ha - vah n' - ra - ne - nah, Ha - vah n' - ra - ne - nah,
Ha - vah n' - ra - ne - nah, Sing! Let us re - joice!
Ha - vah n' - ra - ne - nah, Ha - vah n' - ra - ne - nah,
Wake with a hap - py heart, Sing! Let us re - joice!

U - ru, U - ru a - chim,
gradually faster
U-ru a - chim, b' lev sa - me - ach, u-ru a - chim, b'
lev sa - me - ach, U-ru a - chim, b' lev sa - me - ach,
u-ru a - chim, b' lev sa - me - ach, U-ru a - chim!
8-
dim.
D.S. al Fine
b'-lev sa-me - ach.

Hatikvoh

Israeli anthem

Em Am Am Em B7 Em
Kol - od ba - le - vou p' ni - moh ne fesh ye hu - di ho - mi yoh, ul
Em Am Em Am Em B7
fa - a semis - roch ko - di - moh a - in le - zi - von zo - fi - yoh
Em D7 Em D7 G
Od lo ou - doh tik voh se - nu ha - tik - voh ha no sho - noh
Dm Em D7 G Am Em D7 Em
lo shuv le - e - rez a vo - se nu lo ir bo do vid cho noh.

Here We Come A-Wassailing

English carol

C Dm
1. Here we come a - was - sail - ing, a - mong the leaves so
2. Our was - sail cup is made of the rose - mar - y
Em C F C Dm7 G/B G7
green, Here we come a - wan - dering, So fair to be seen:
tree, And so is your beer of the best bar - ley:
Chorus
C G7 C F C D7 G C
Love and joy come to you, And to you your was - sail too, And God bless you, and
Dm G C F Em A Dm G7 C
send you a hap - py new year, And God send you a hap - py new year.

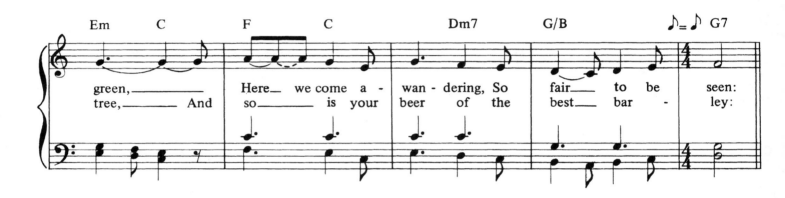

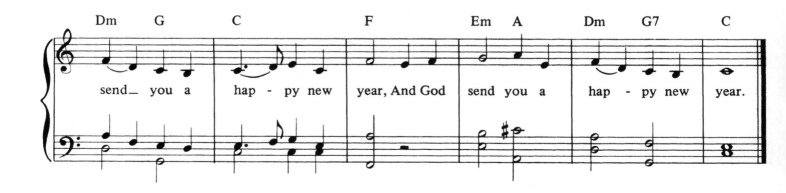

I Saw Three Ships

French carol

I saw three ships come sail-ing by, on Christ-mas Day, on Christ-mas Day. I

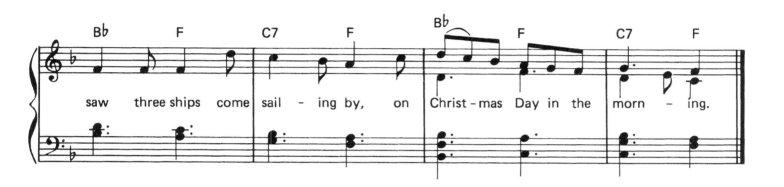

saw three ships come sail - ing by, on Christ-mas Day in the morn - ing.

Jingle Bells

Words and music by J.S. Pierpont

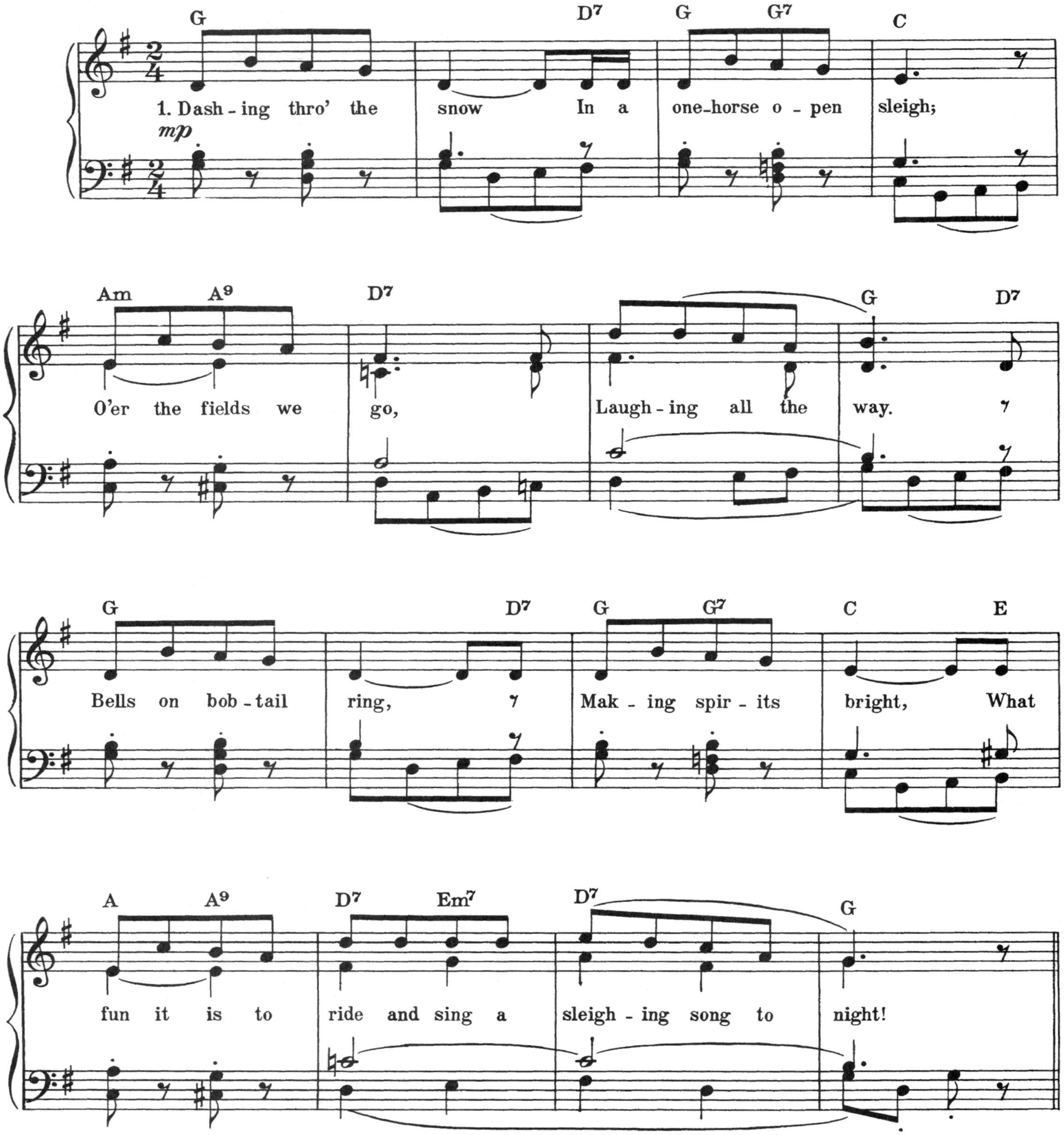
G D7 G G7 C
1. Dash - ing thro' the snow In a one-horse o - pen sleigh;
mp
Am A9 D7 G D7
O'er the fields we go, Laugh - ing all the way.
G D7 G G7 C E
Bells on bob - tail ring, Mak - ing spir - its bright, What
A A9 D7 Em7 D7 G
fun it is to ride and sing a sleigh - ing song to night!

Chorus

Jin - gle bells! Jin - gle bells! Jin - gle all the

way! Oh, what fun it is to ride In a

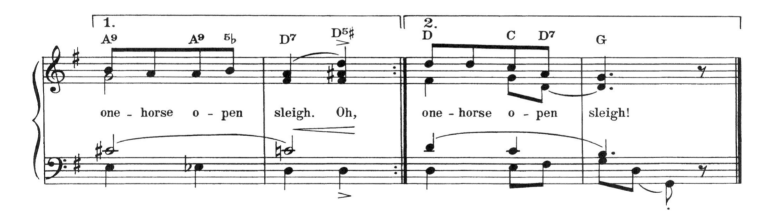

one - horse o - pen sleigh. Oh, one - horse o - pen sleigh!

2. A day or two ago
   I thought I'd take a ride,
   Soon Miss Fanny Bright
   Was seated at my side.
   The horse was lean and lank,
   Misfortune seemed his lot,
   He got into a drifted bank,
   And we, we got upsot.
   Chorus

3. Now the ground is white,
   Go it while you're young!
   Take the kids tonight,
   And sing this sleighing song.
   Just get a bob-tailed bay,
   Two-forty for his speed,
   Then hitch him to an open sleigh
   And crack! You'll take the lead.
   Chorus

Jolly Old Saint Nicholas

American Christmas song

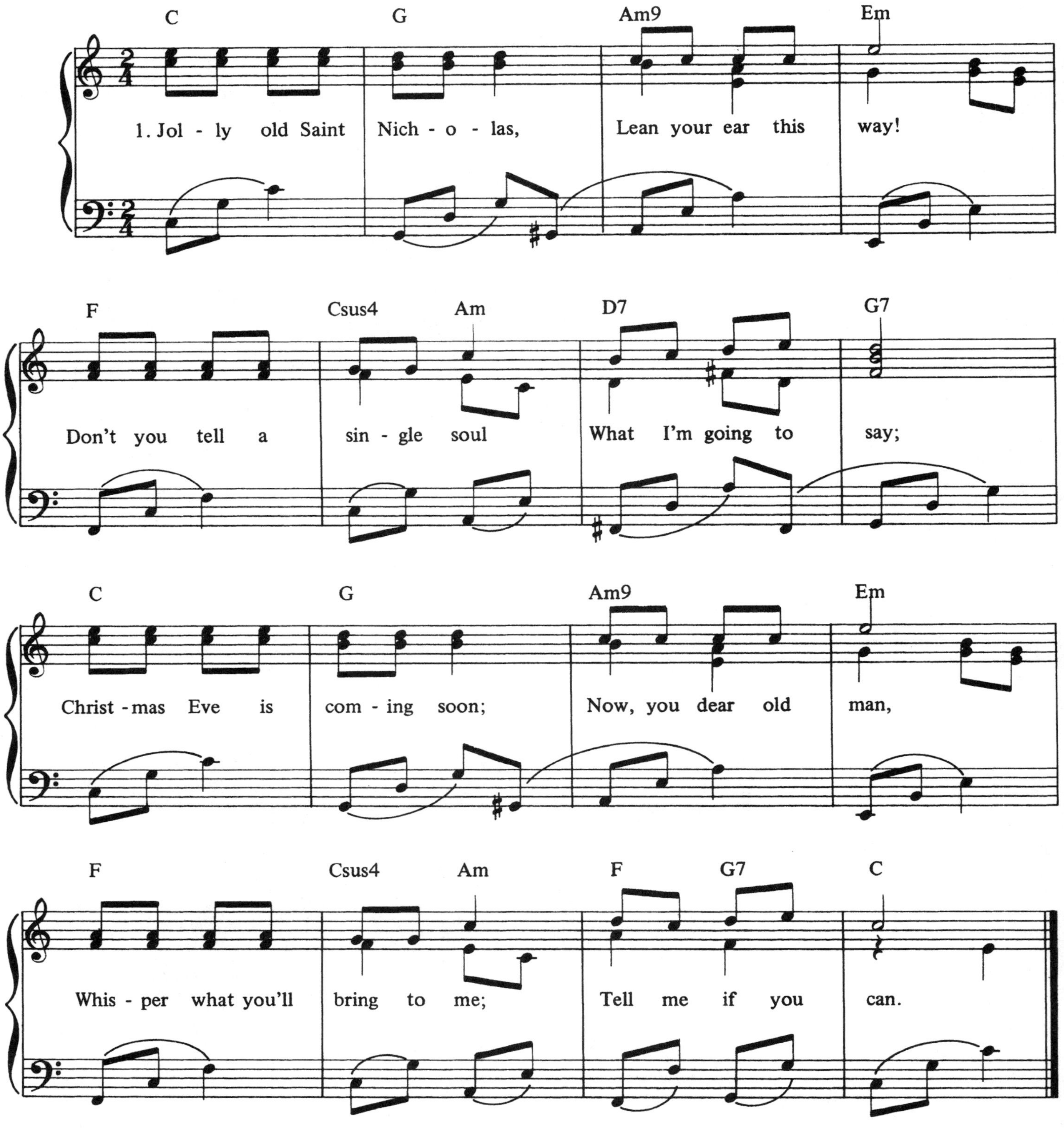

2. When the clock is striking twelve,
   When I'm fast asleep,
   Down the chimney broad and black,
   With your pack you'll creep;
   All the stockings you will find
   Hanging in a row;
   Mine will be the shortest one,
   You'll be sure to know

3. Johnny wants a pair of skates;
   Susy wants a doll;
   Nellie wants a storybook,
   She thinks dolls are folly;
   As for me, my thinking cap
   Isn't very bright;
   Choose for me, old Santa Claus,
   What you think is right.

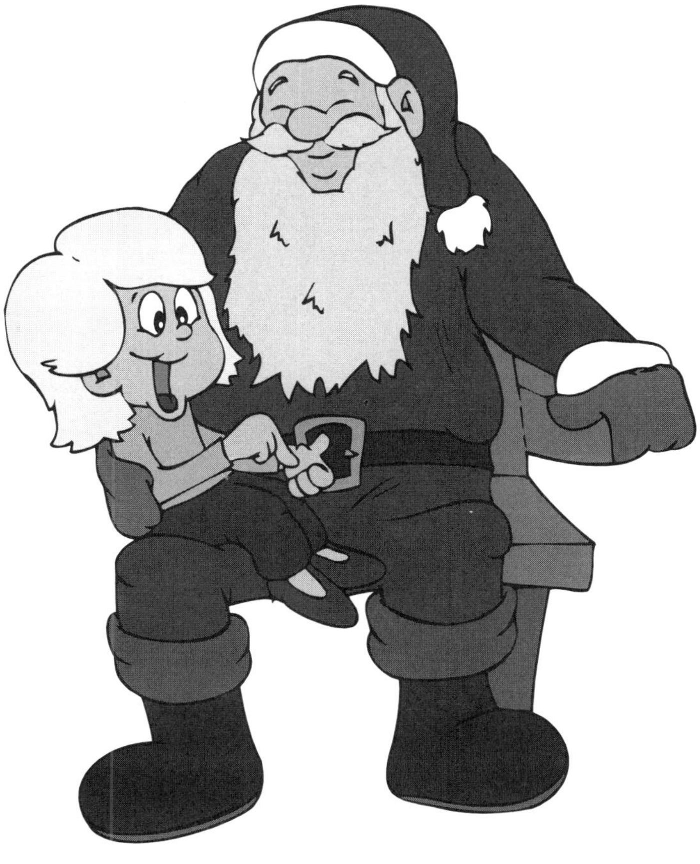

Over the River and Through the Wood

American Thanksgiving song

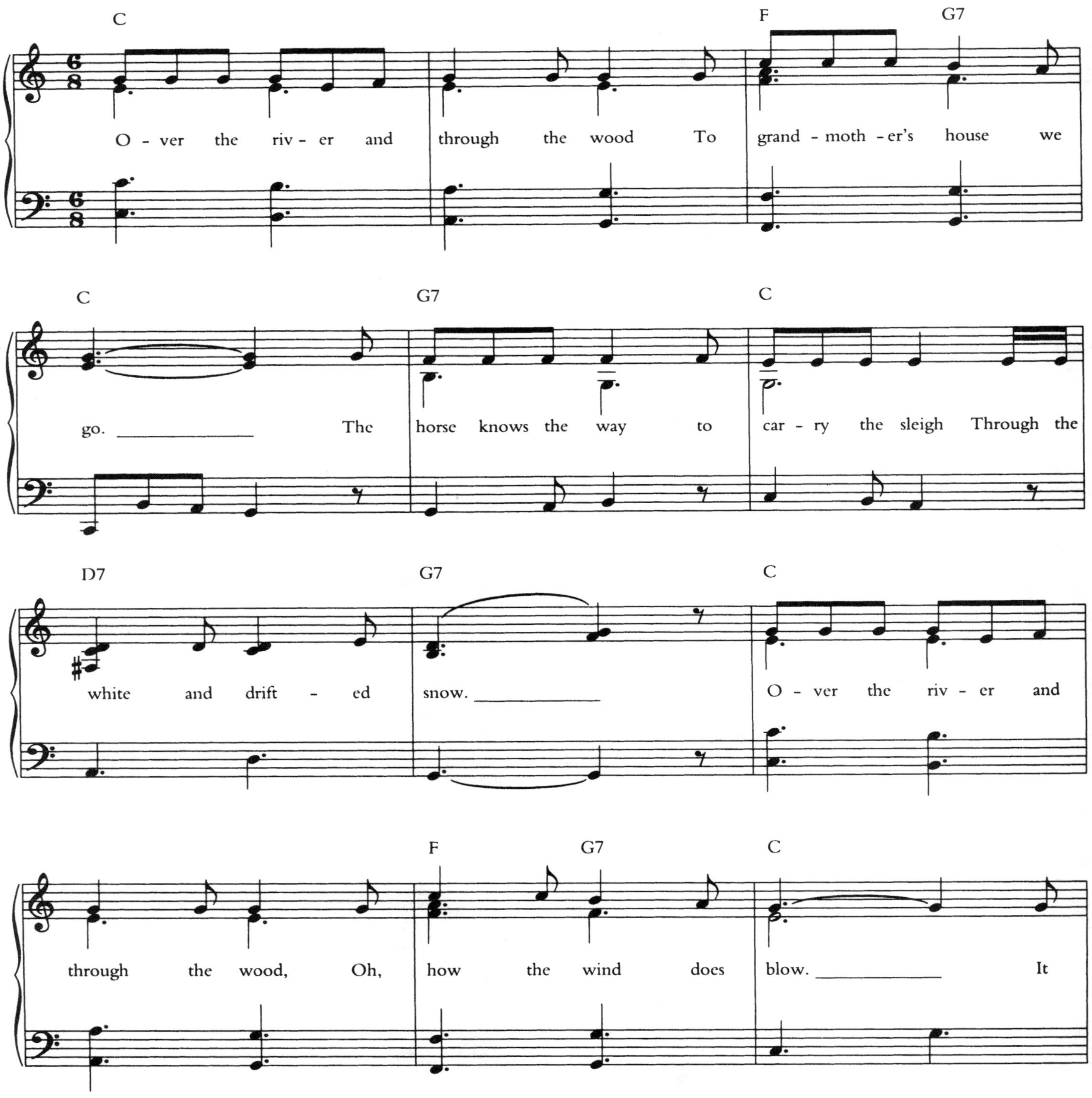

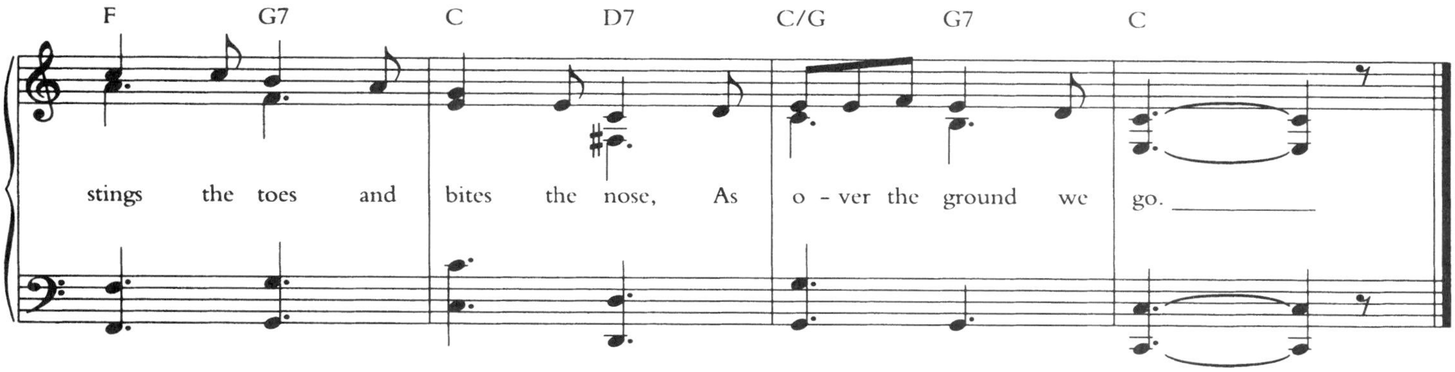

stings the toes and bites the nose, As o-ver the ground we go. _____

2. Over the river and through the wood,
   To have a full day of play.
   Oh hear the bells ringing "ting-a-ling ling."
   For it's Thanksgiving Day.
   Over the river and through the wood,
   Trot fast, my dapple gray.
   Spring o'er the ground just like a hound.
   Hurrah for Thanksgiving Day!

3. Over the river and through the wood,
   And straight through the barnyard gate.
   It seems that we go so dreadfully slow,
   It is so hard to wait.
   Over the river and through the wood,
   Now grandma's cap I spy.
   Hurrah for fun, the pudding's done,
   Hurrah for the pumpkin pie!

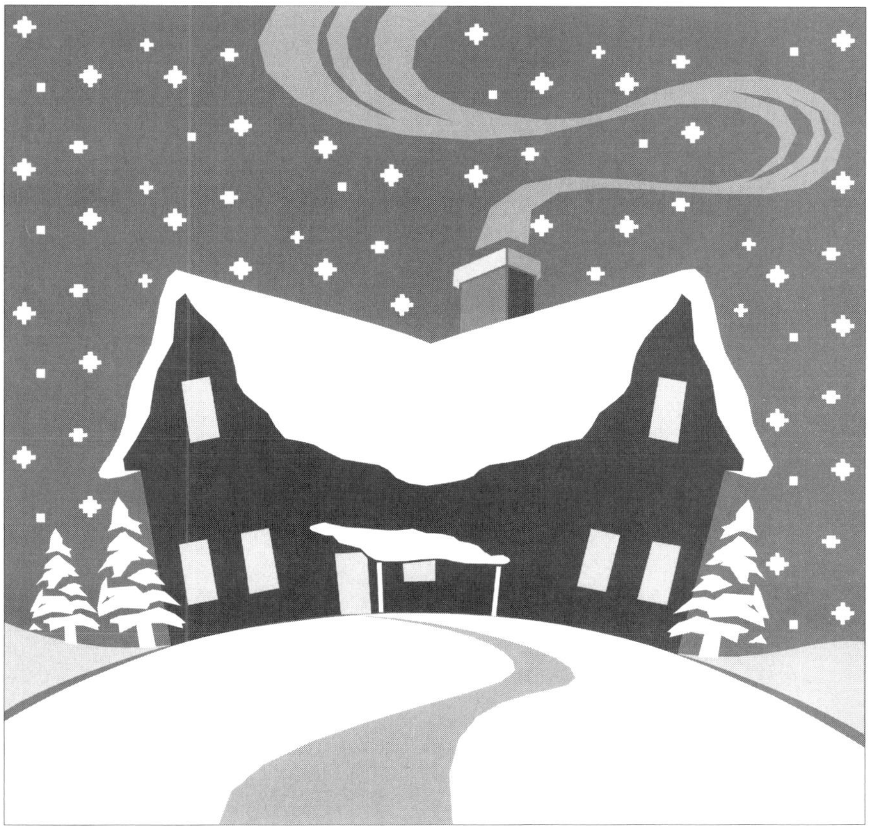

O Christmas Tree

German carol

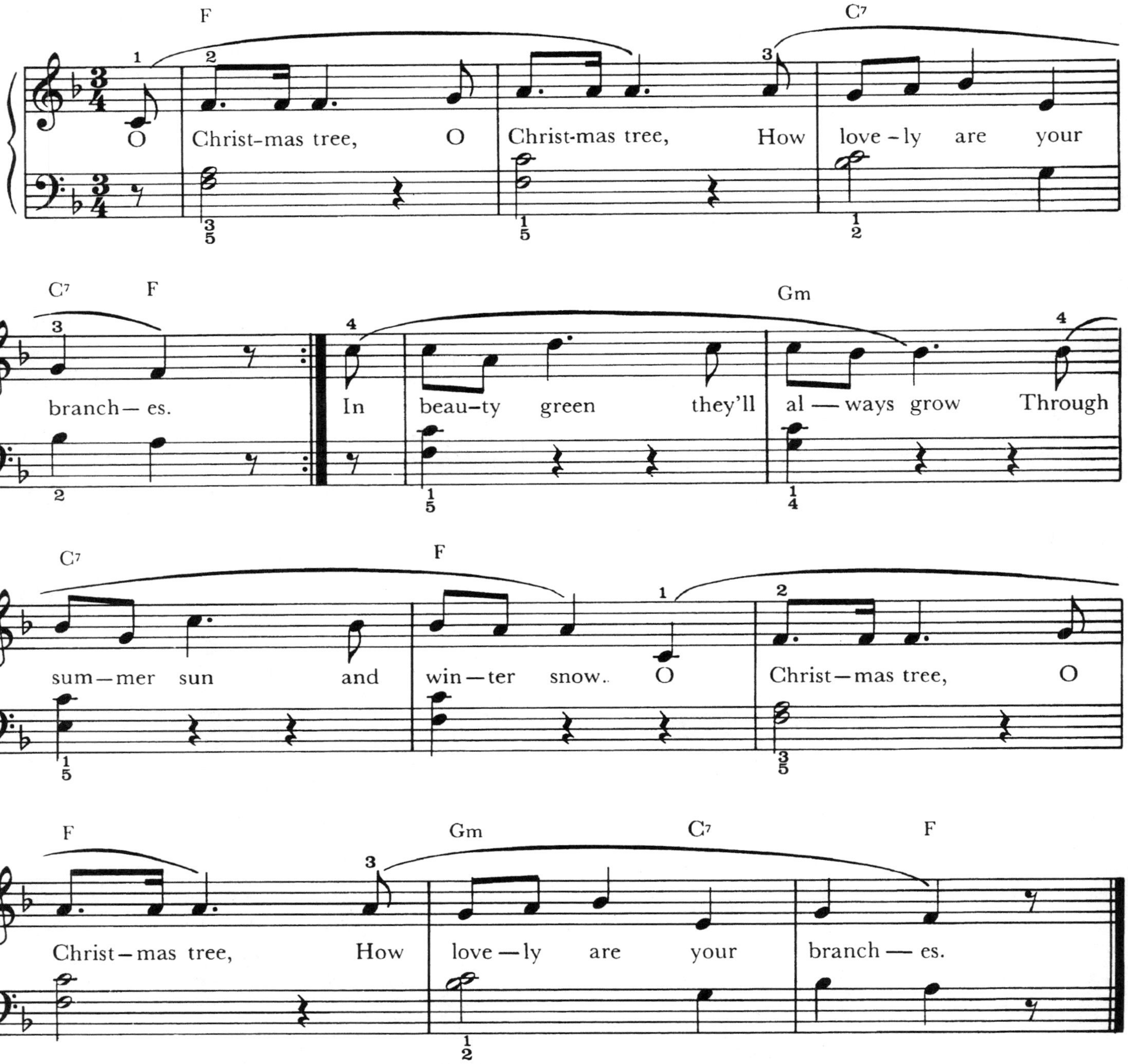

2. O Christmas tree, O Christmas tree,
   Of all the trees most lovely;
   Each year you bring to me delight
   Shining bright on Christmas night.
   O Christmas tree, O Christmas tree,
   Of all the trees most lovely.

3. O Christmas tree, O Christmas tree,
   Your beauty green will teach me
   That hope and joy will ever be
   The way to joy and peace for me.
   O Christmas tree, O Christmas tree,
   Your beauty green will teach me.

Pat-a-Pan

French carol

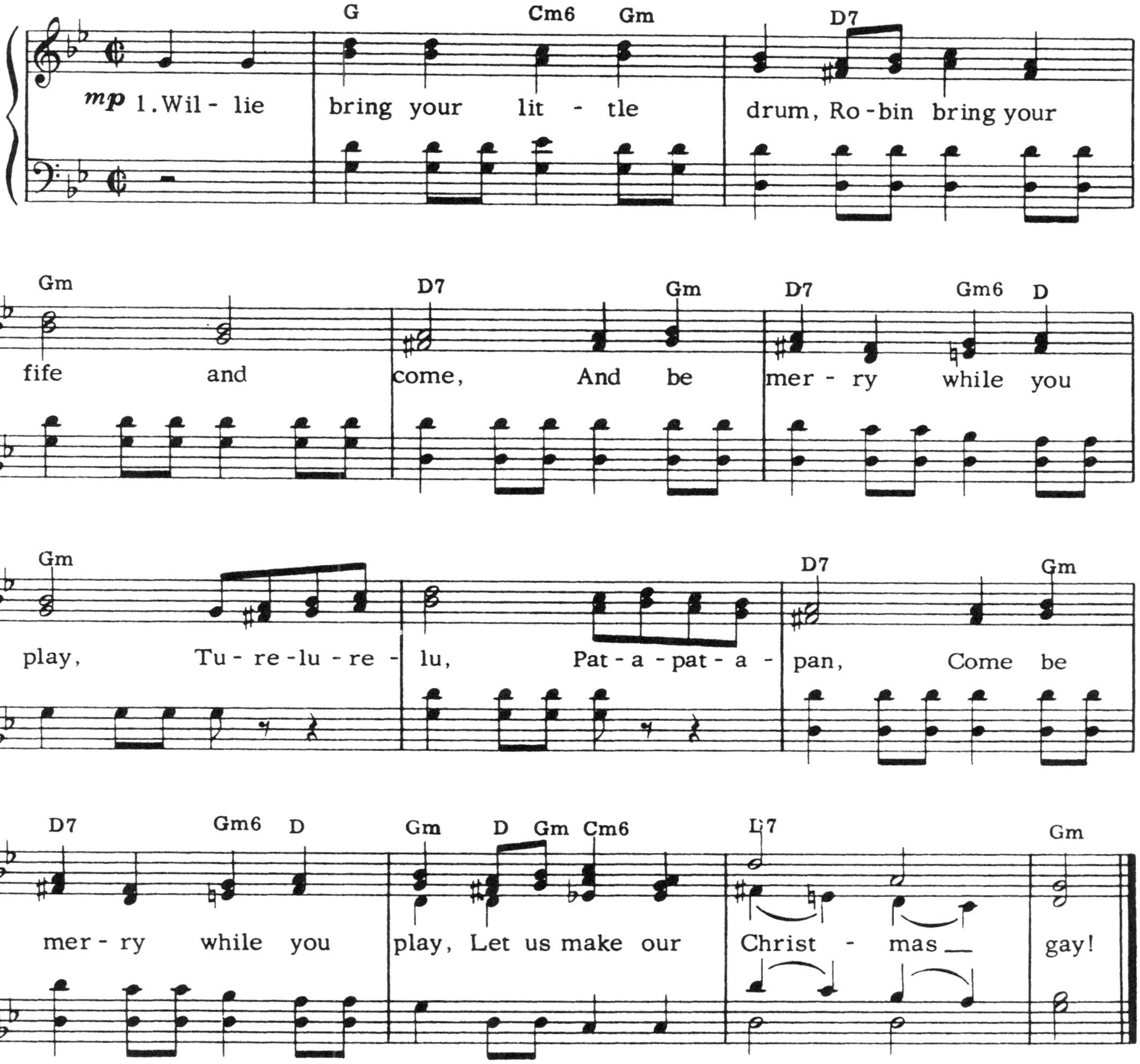

2. When the men of olden days
   On Christmas Day gave praise,
   On the fife and drum did play,
   Tu-re-lu-re-lu,
   Pat-a-pat-a-pan,
   On the fife and drum did play,
   So their hearts were glad and gay!

3. All the world today become
   More in tune than fife and drum,
   So be merry while you play,
   Tu-re-lu-re-lu,
   Pat-a-pat-a-pan,
   So be merry while you play
   On this joyous Christmas Day.

'Twas the Night Before Christmas

Words by Clement Moore

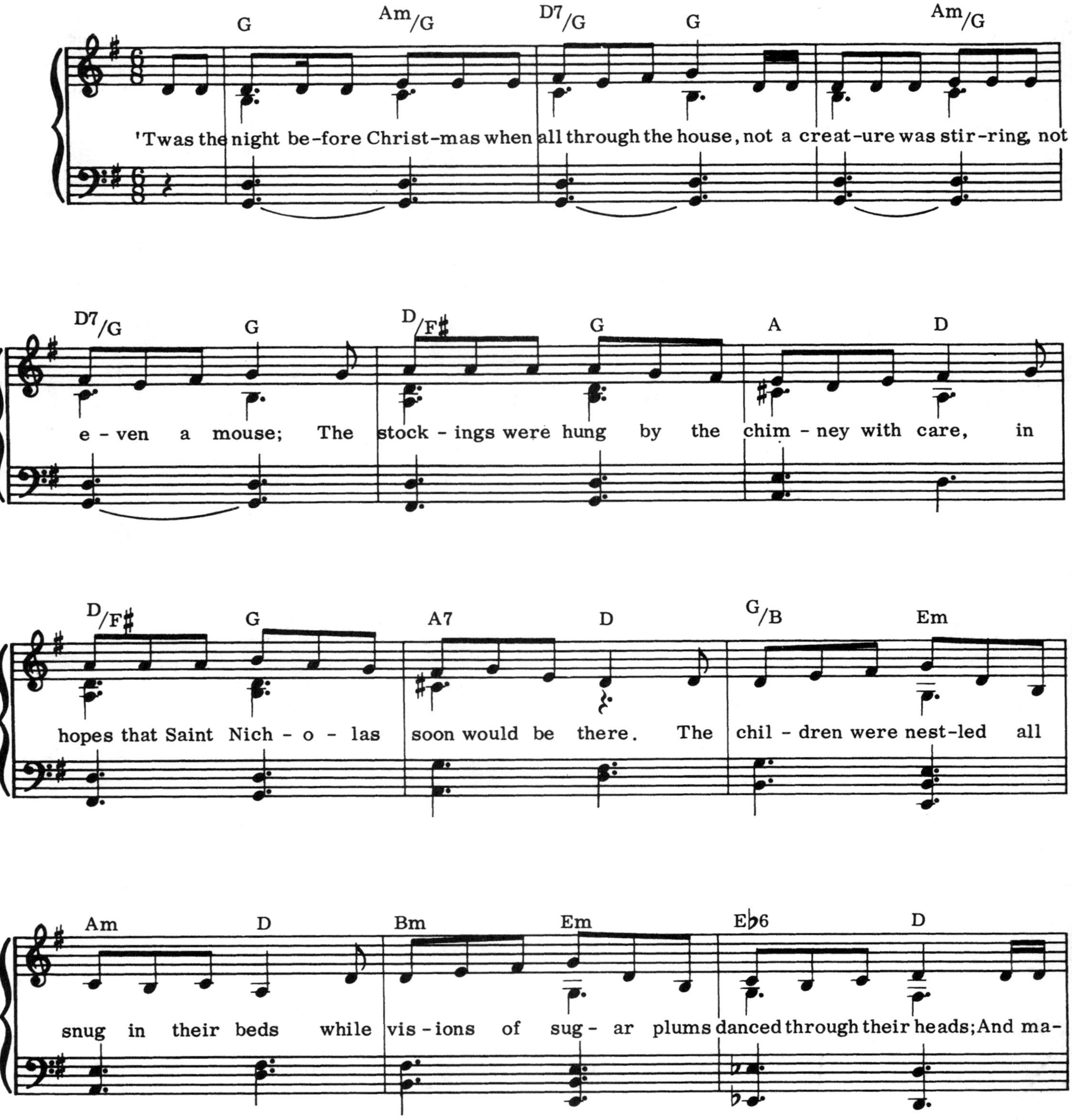

ma in her 'ker - chief, and I in my cap, had just set - tled our brains for a

long win - ter's nap.

2. When out on the lawn there arose such a clatter,
I sprang from my bed to see what was the matter.
Away to the window I flew like a flash,
Tore open the shutters and threw up the sash.
The moon on the breast of the new-fallen snow,
Gave a lustre of midday to objects below,
When, what to my wondering eyes should appear,
But a miniature sleigh, and eight tiny reindeer.

3. With a little old driver, so lively and quick,
I knew in a moment it must be St. Nick.
More rapid than eagles his coursers they came,
And he whistled and shouted and called them by name;
"Now Dasher! now Dancer! now Prancer and Vixen!
On Comet! on Cupid! on Donner and Blitzen!
To the top of the porch, to the top of the wall!
Now, dash away, dash away, dash away all!"

4. As dry leaves that before the wild hurricane fly,
When they meet with an obstacle, mount to the sky
So up to the housetop the coursers they flew,
With the sleigh full of toys, and St. Nicholas, too.
And then in a twinkling, I heard on the roof
The prancing and pawing of each little hoof.
As I drew in my head, and was turning around,
Down the chimney St. Nicholas came with a bound.

5. He was dressed all in fur from his head to his foot,
And his clothes were all tarnished with ashes and soot,
A bundle of toys he had flung on his back,
And he looked like a peddler just opening his pack.
His eyes how they twinkled! His dimples, how merry!
His cheeks were like roses, his nose like a cherry,
His droll little mouth was drawn up like a bow,
And the beard of his chin was as white as the snow.

6. The stump of a pipe he held tight in his teeth,
And the smoke, it encircled his head like a wreath,
He had a broad face and a round little belly
That shook when he laughed like a bowl full of jelly.
He was chubby and plump, a right jolly old elf,
And I laughed when I saw him, in spite of myself.
A wink of his eye, and a twist of his head,
Soon gave me to know I had nothing to dread.

7. He spoke not a word, but went straight to his work,
And filled all the stockings; then turned with a jerk,
And laying his finger aside of his nose,
And giving a nod, up the chimney he rose.
He sprang to his sleigh, to his team gave a whistle,
And away they all flew like the down of a thistle;
But I heard him exclaim, ere he drove out of sight,
"Happy Christmas to all, and to all a good night!"

The Twelve Days of Christmas

English carol

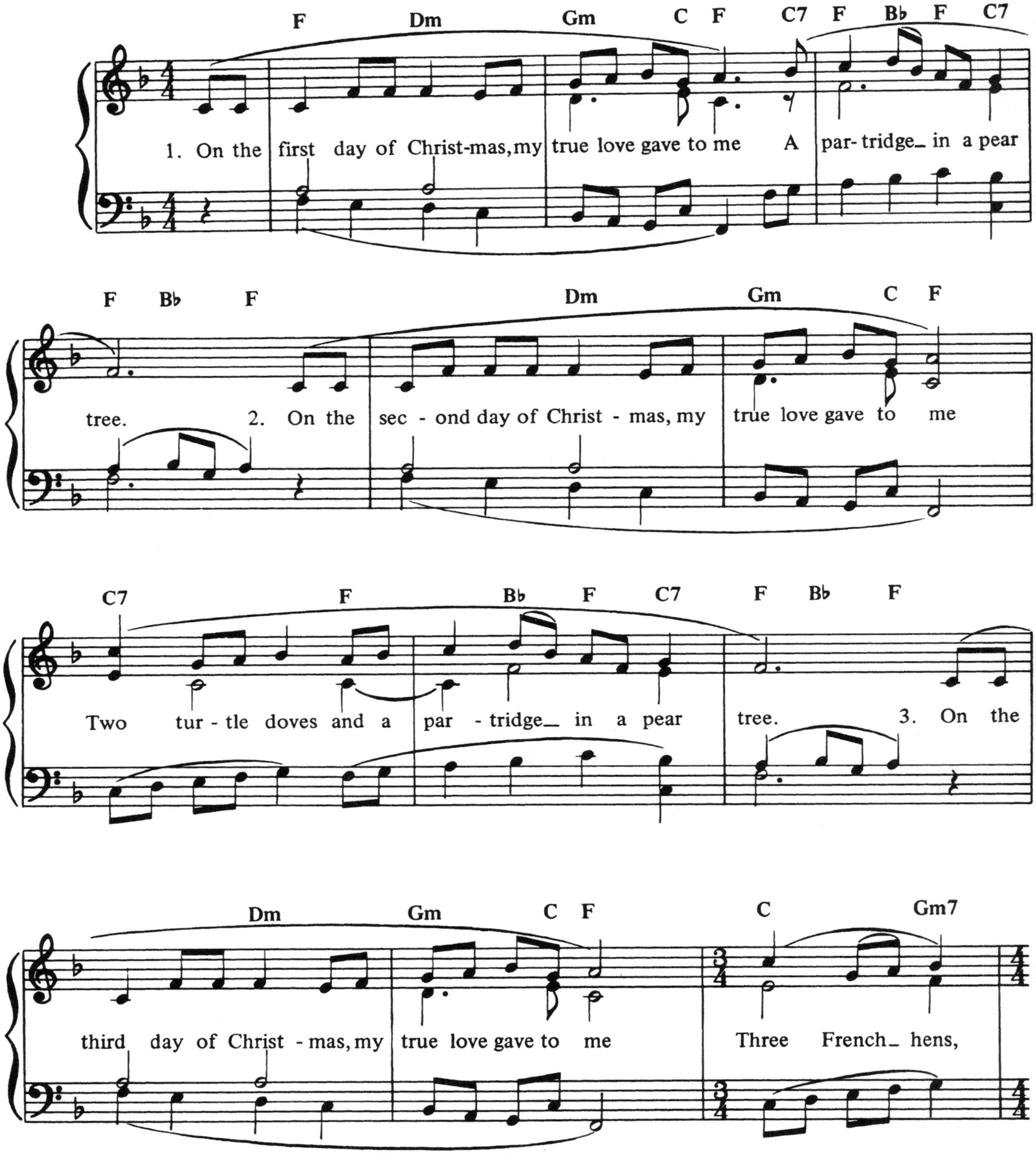

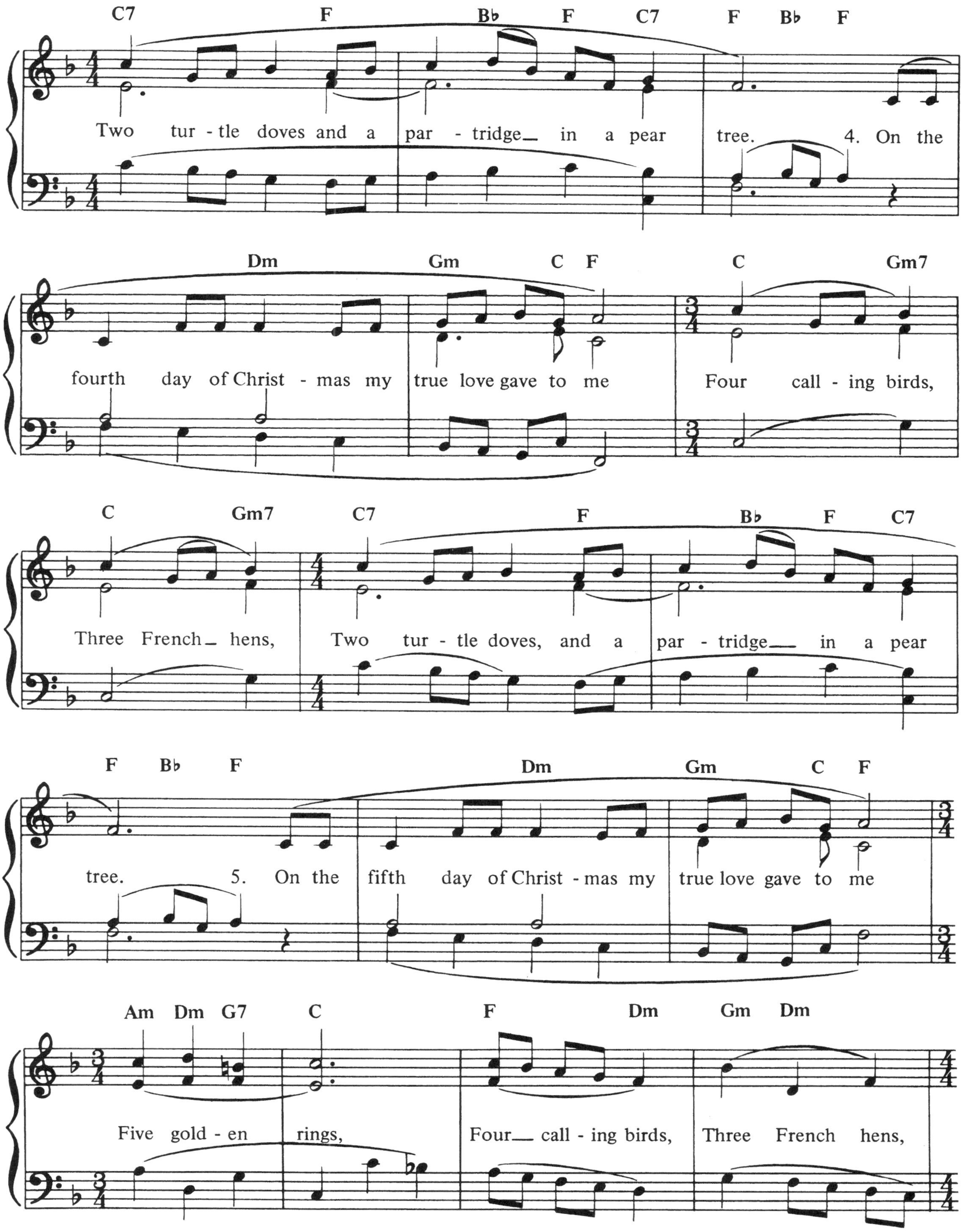
C7 F B♭ F C7 F B♭ F
Two tur - tle doves and a par - tridge in a pear tree. 4. On the
Dm Gm C F C Gm7
fourth day of Christ - mas my true love gave to me Four call - ing birds,
C Gm7 C7 F B♭ F C7
Three French hens, Two tur - tle doves, and a par - tridge in a pear
F B♭ F Dm Gm C F
tree. 5. On the fifth day of Christ - mas my true love gave to me
Am Dm G7 C F Dm Gm Dm
Five gold - en rings, Four call - ing birds, Three French hens,

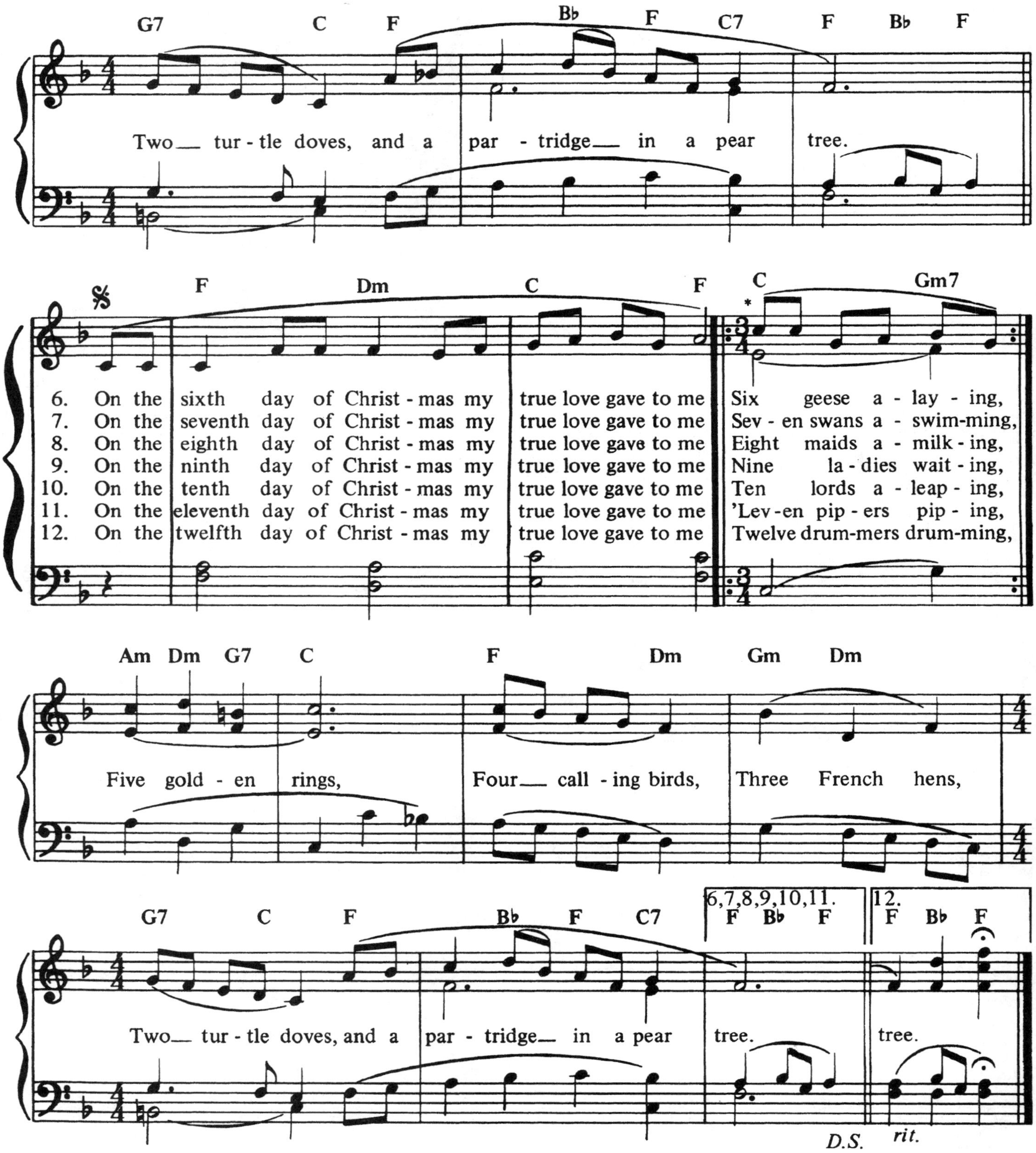

* Repeat this measure as often as necessary, so that these lines may be sung in reverse order,
  each time ending with "Six geese a-laying."

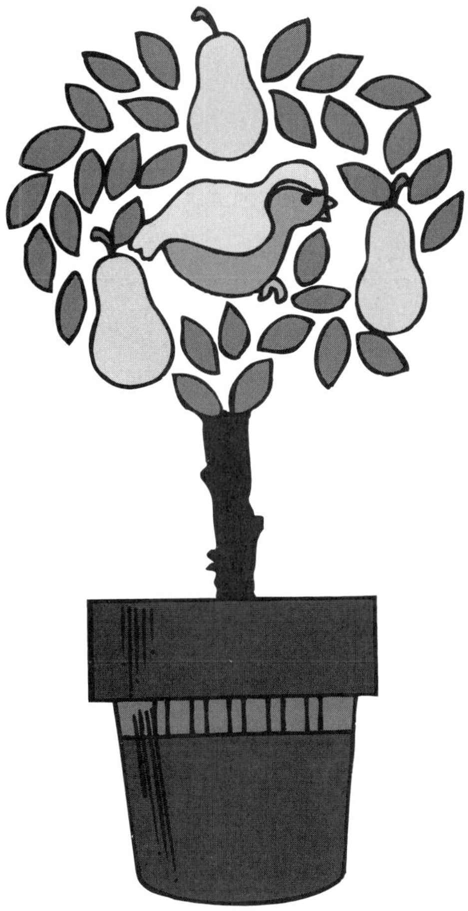

Up on the Housetop

Words and music by B.R. Hanby

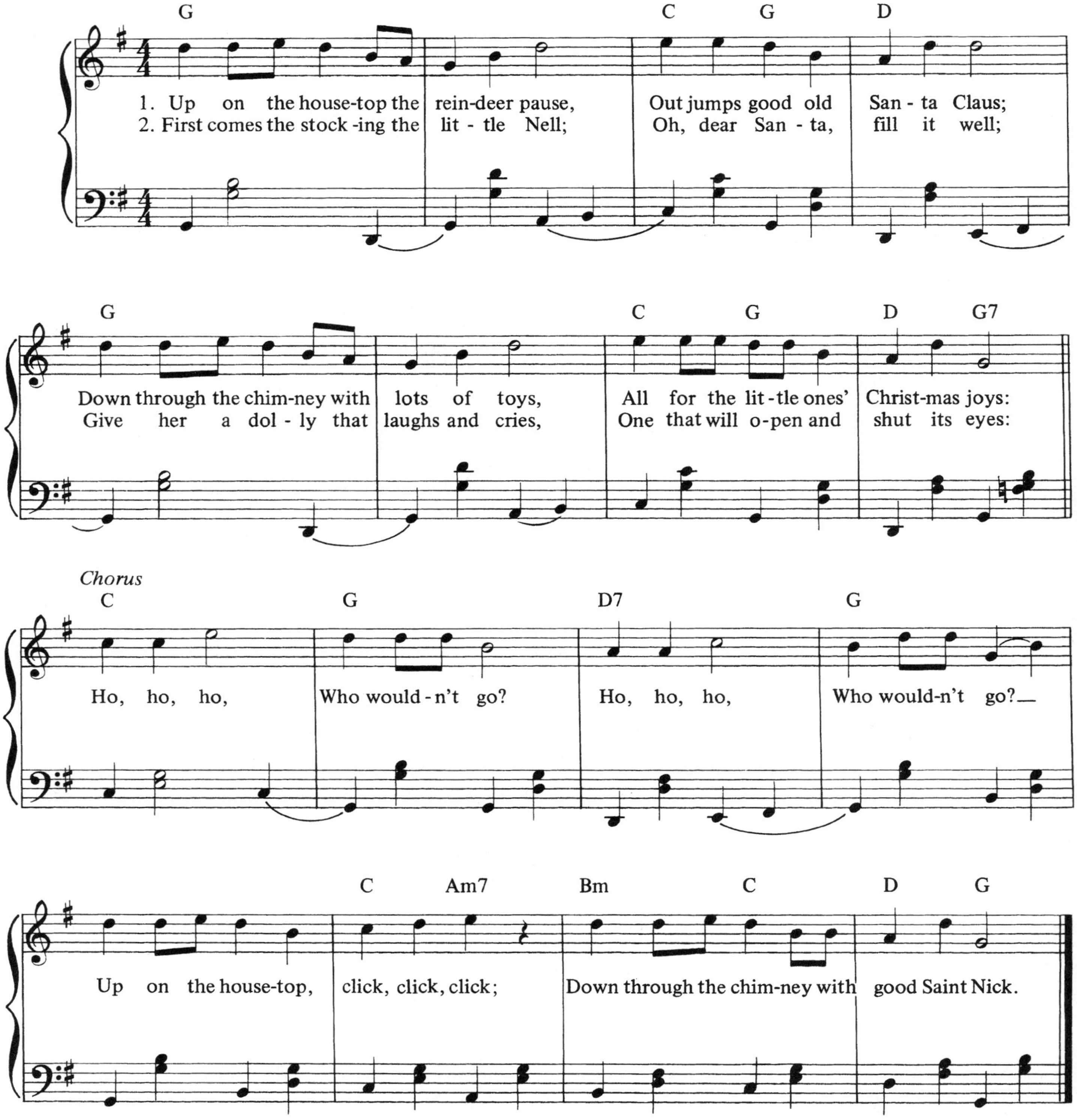
G C G D
1. Up on the house-top the rein-deer pause, Out jumps good old San - ta Claus;
2. First comes the stock -ing the lit - tle Nell; Oh, dear San - ta, fill it well;
G C G D G7
Down through the chim-ney with lots of toys, All for the lit-tle ones' Christ-mas joys:
Give her a dol - ly that laughs and cries, One that will o-pen and shut its eyes:
Chorus
C G D7 G
Ho, ho, ho, Who would - n't go? Ho, ho, ho, Who would-n't go?
C Am7 Bm C D G
Up on the house-top, click, click, click; Down through the chim-ney with good Saint Nick.

3. Next comes the stocking of little Will;
   Oh, just see what a glorious fill:
   Here is a hammer and lots of tacks,
   Also a bell and a whip that cracks.

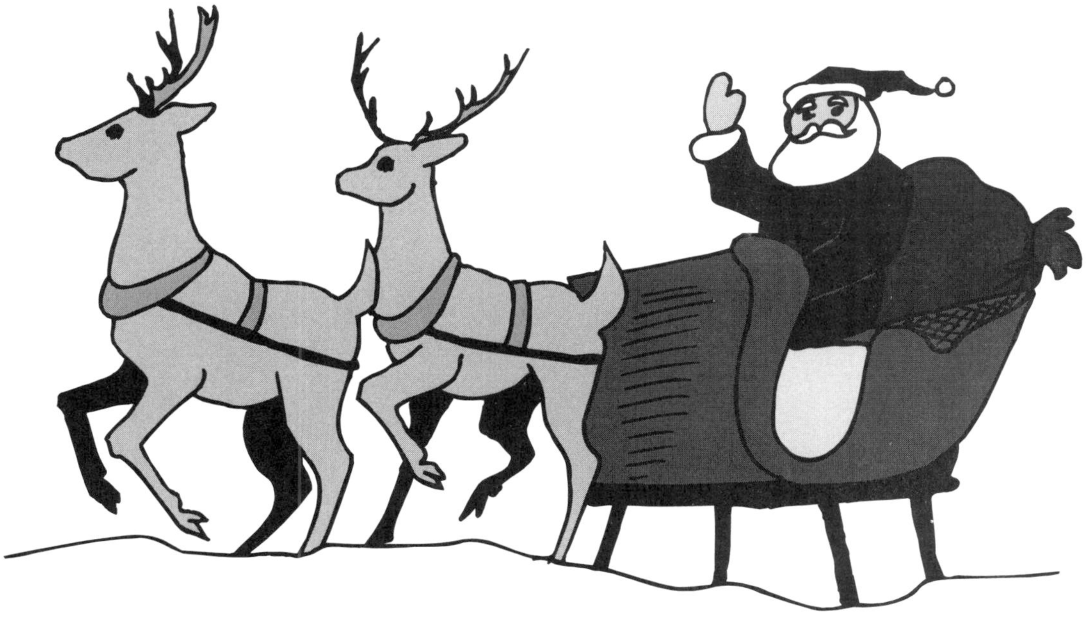

We Wish You a Merry Christmas

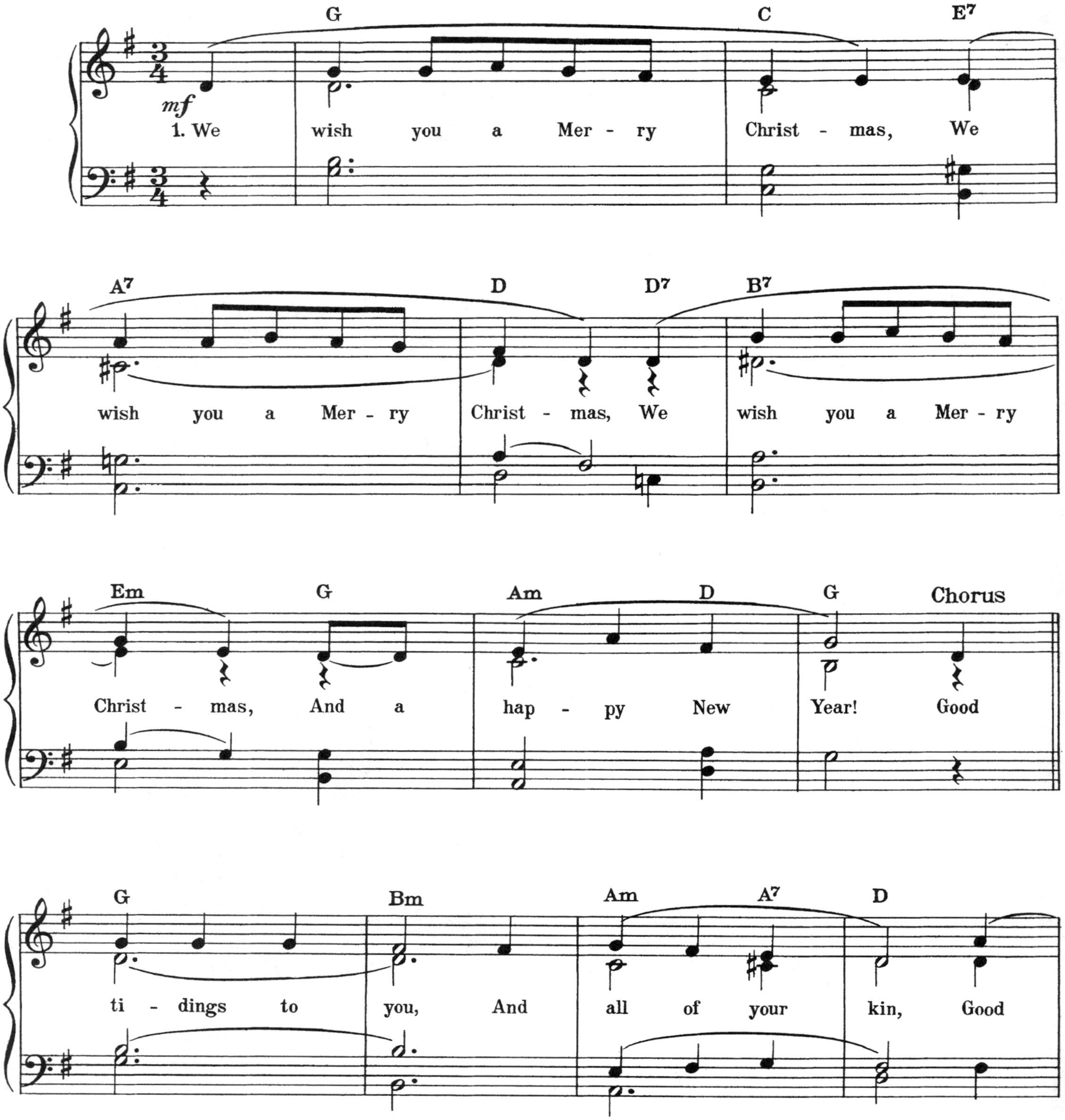
G C E7
mf
1. We wish you a Mer - ry Christ - mas, We
A7 D D7 B7
wish you a Mer - ry Christ - mas, We wish you a Mer - ry
Em G Am D G Chorus
Christ - mas, And a hap - py New Year! Good
G Bm Am A7 D
ti - dings to you, And all of your kin, Good

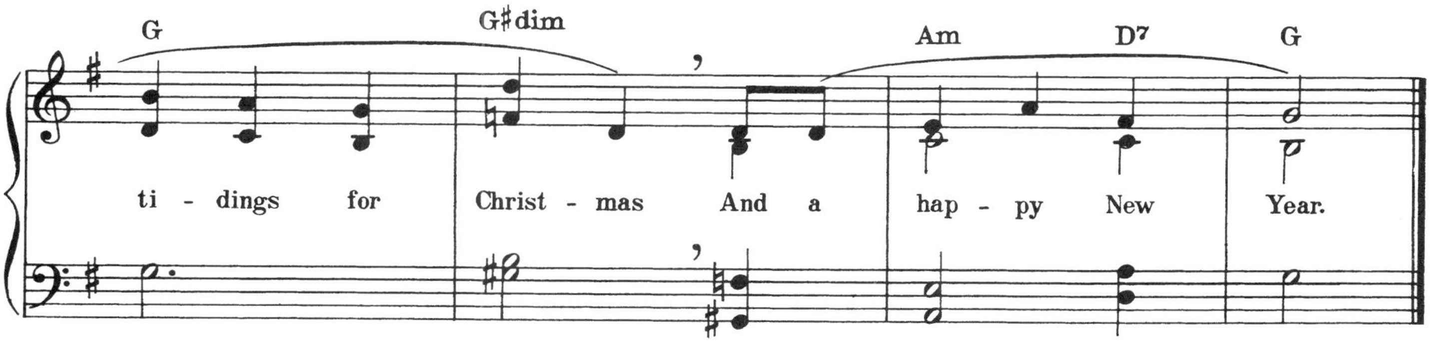

ti - dings   for   Christ - mas   And a   hap - py   New   Year.

2. Oh, bring us some figgy pudding,
   Oh, bring us some figgy pudding,
   Oh, bring us some figgy pudding,
   Yes, bring it right here.

3. We won't go until we get some,
   We won't go until we get some,
   We won't go until we get some,
   So bring it right here.

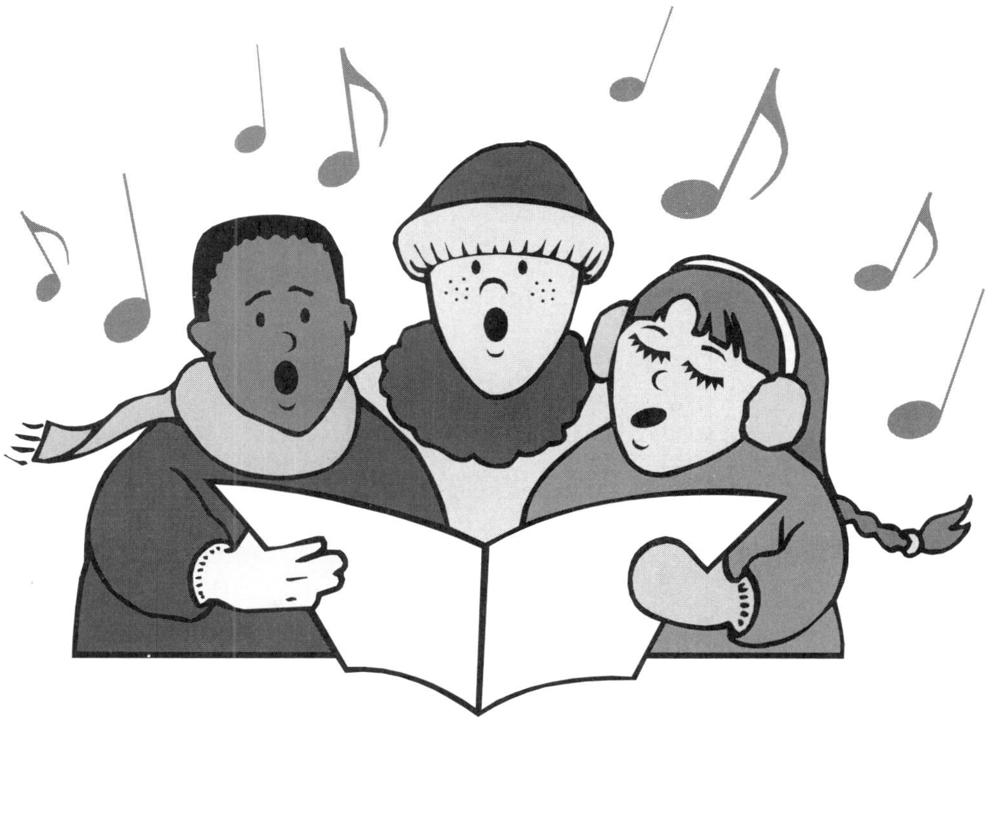

Golden Showstoppers

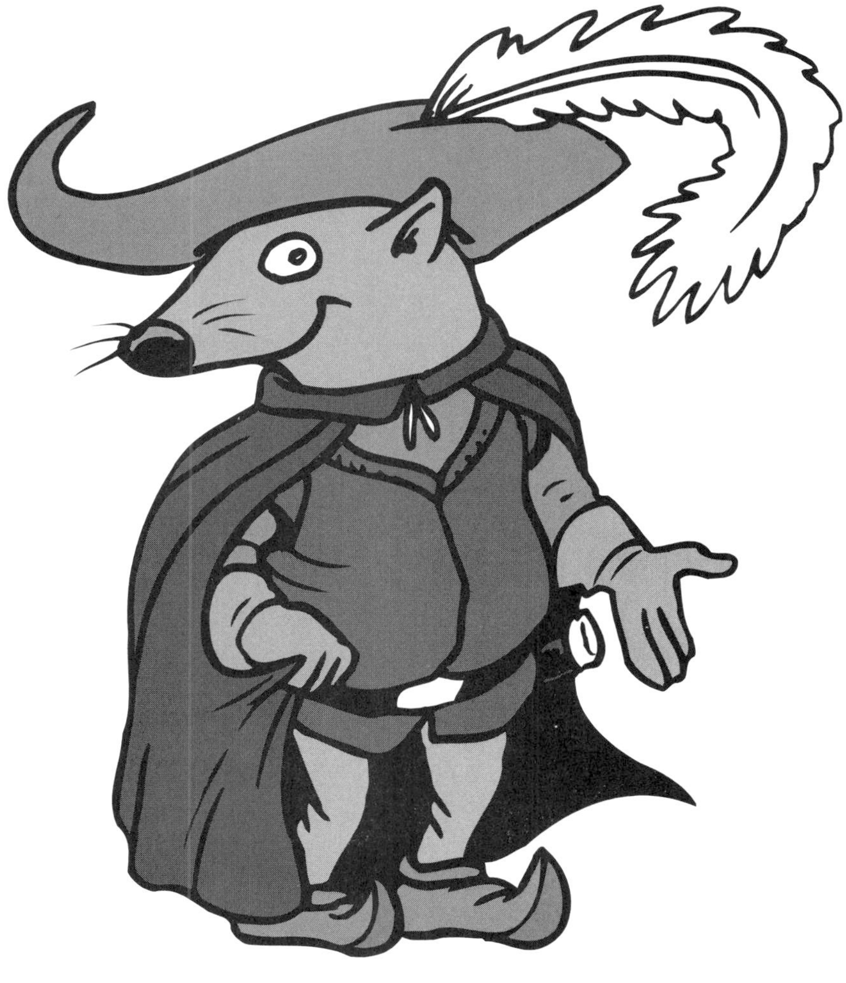

The Flowers That Bloom in the Spring

(from *The Mikado*)

Words by W.S. Gilbert

Music by Arthur Sullivan

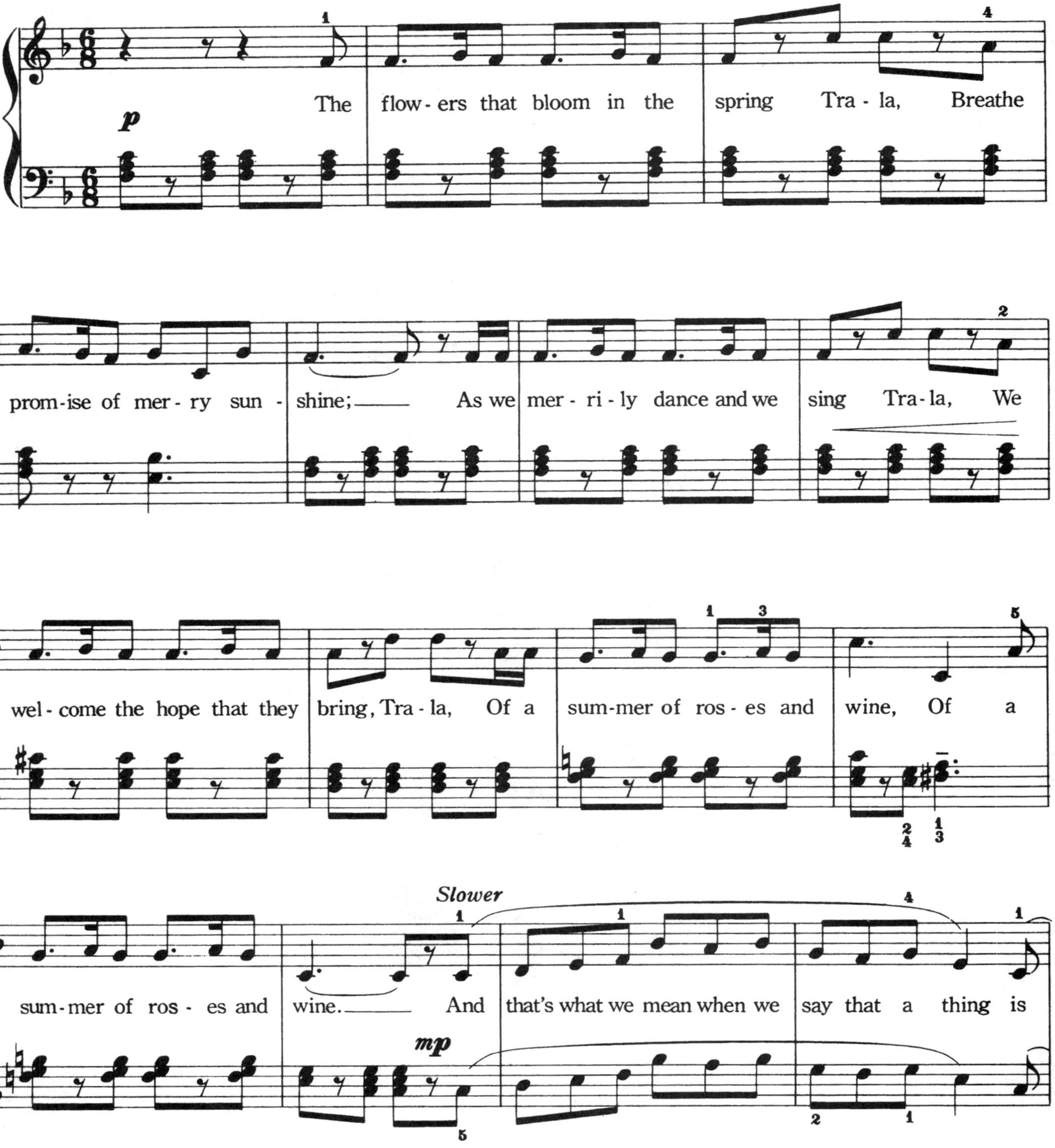

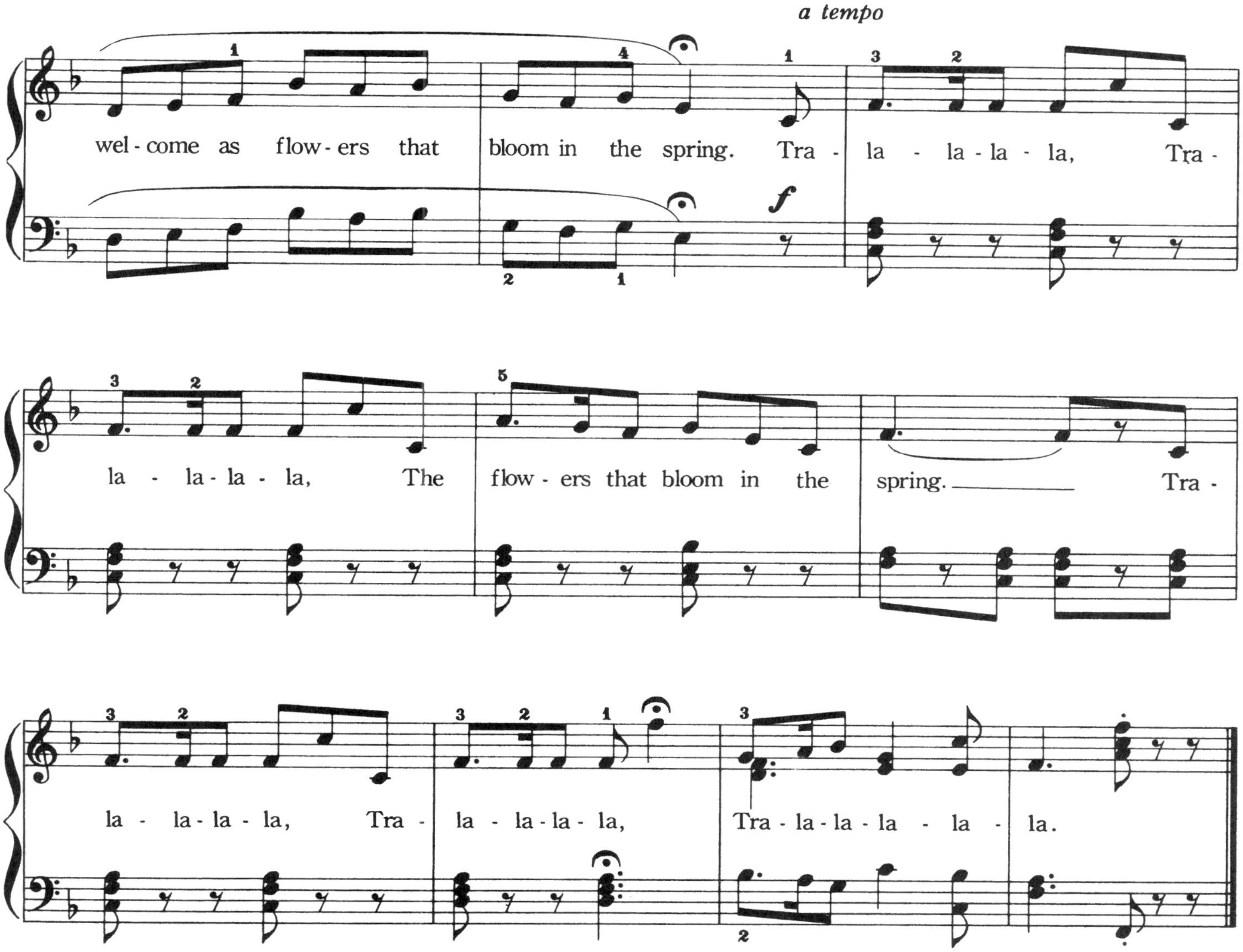

welcome as flowers that bloom in the spring. Tra-la-la-la-la, Tra-la-la-la-la, The flowers that bloom in the spring. Tra-la-la-la-la, Tra-la-la-la-la, Tra-la-la-la-la.

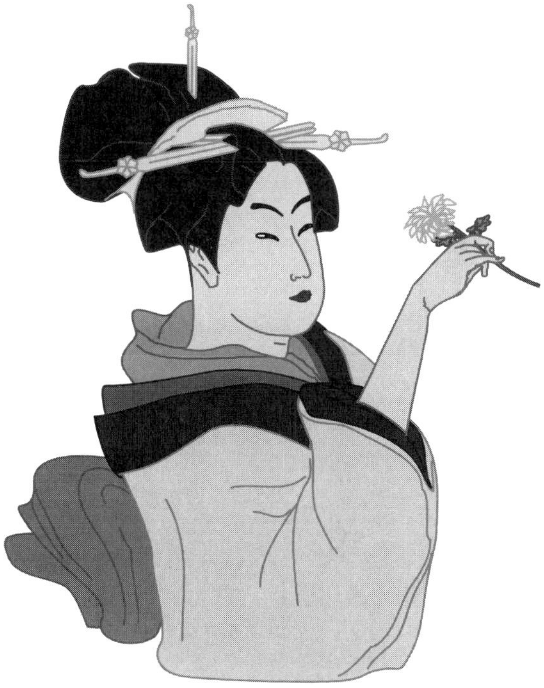

Give My Regards to Broadway

(from *Little Johnny Jones*)

Words and music by George M. Cohan

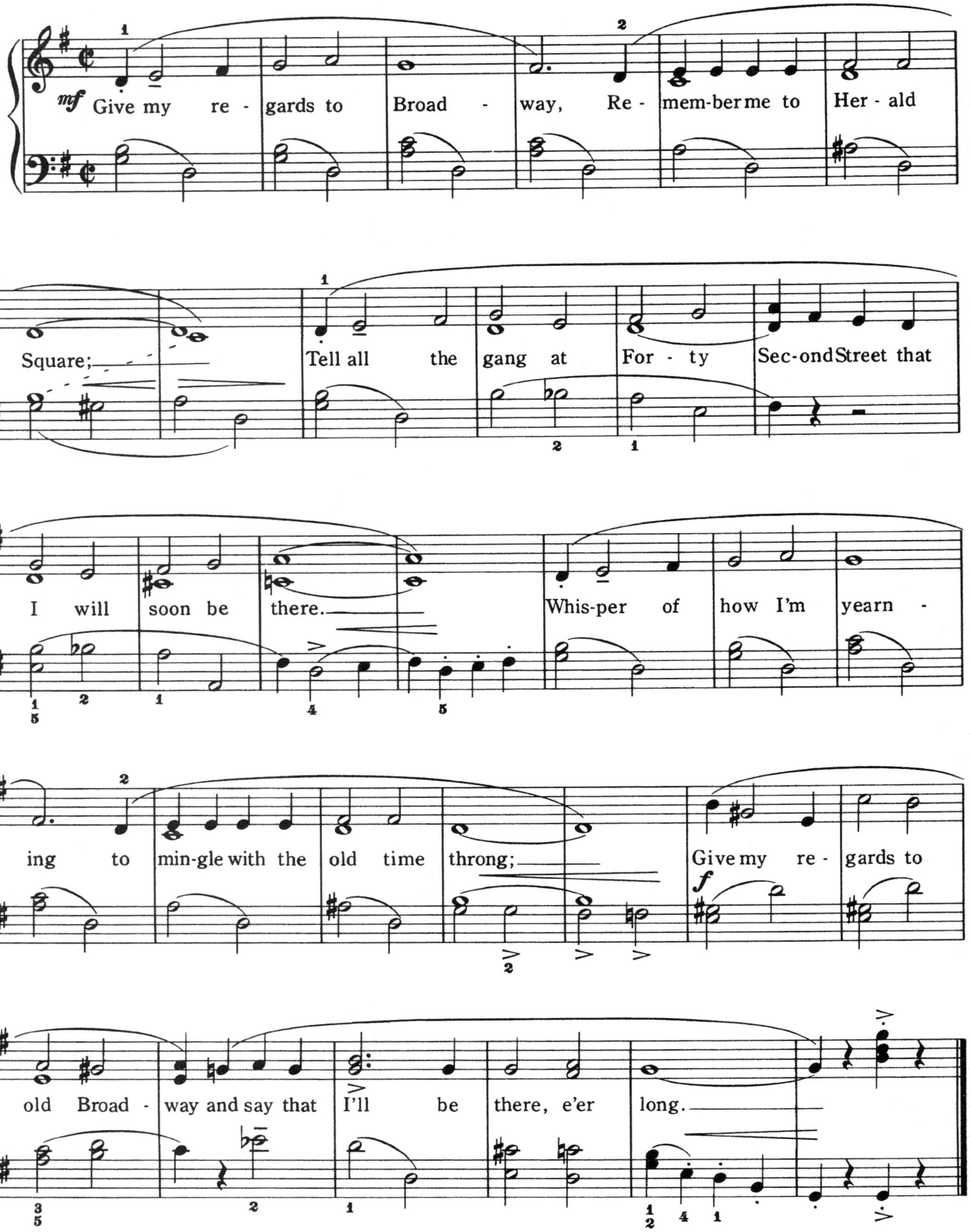

Hail! Hail! The Gang's All Here

(adapted from *The Pirates of Penzance*)

Words by D.A. Esrom Morse

Music by Arthur Sullivan

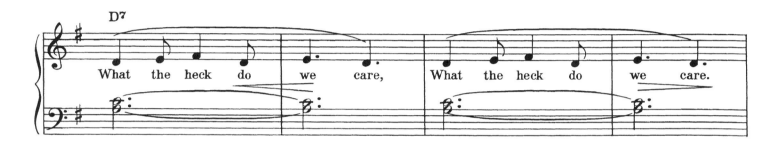

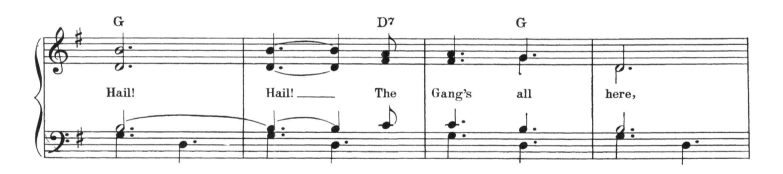

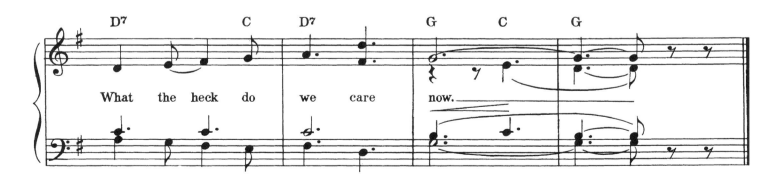

I Am the Very Model of a Modern Major General

(from *H.M.S Pinafore*)

Words by W.S. Gilbert

Music by Arthur Sullivan

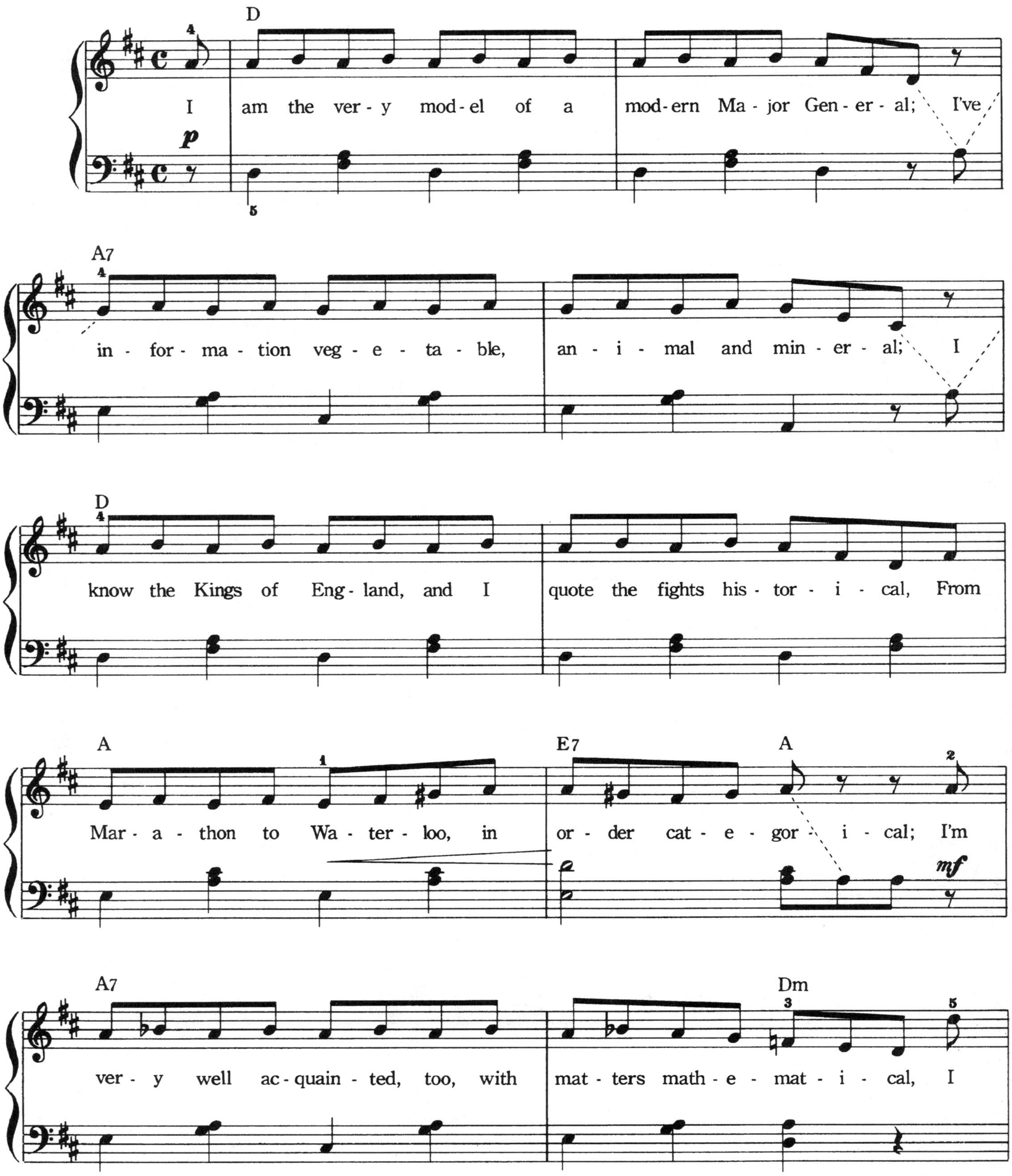

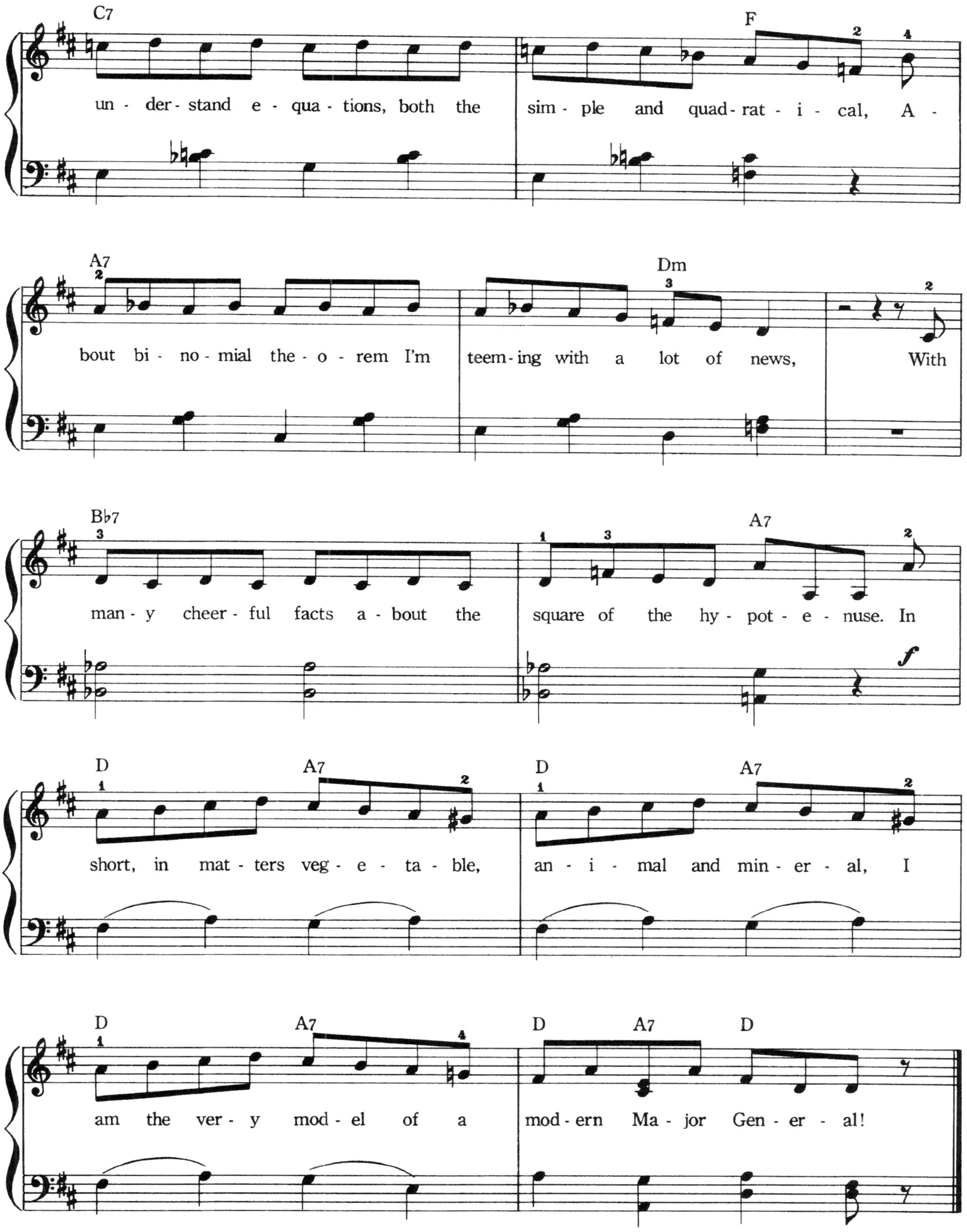
C7
un - der - stand e - qua - tions, both the
F
sim - ple and quad - rat - i - cal, A -
A7
bout bi - no - mial the - o - rem I'm
teem - ing with a lot of news,
Dm
With
B♭7
man - y cheer - ful facts a - bout the
A7
square of the hy - pot - e - nuse. In
D A7
short, in mat - ters veg - e - ta - ble,
D A7
an - i - mal and min - er - al, I
D A7
am the ver - y mod - el of a
D A7 D
mod - ern Ma - jor Gen - er - al!

I Have a Song to Sing-O

(from *The Yeomen of the Guard*)

Words by W. S. Gilbert

Music by Arthur Sullivan

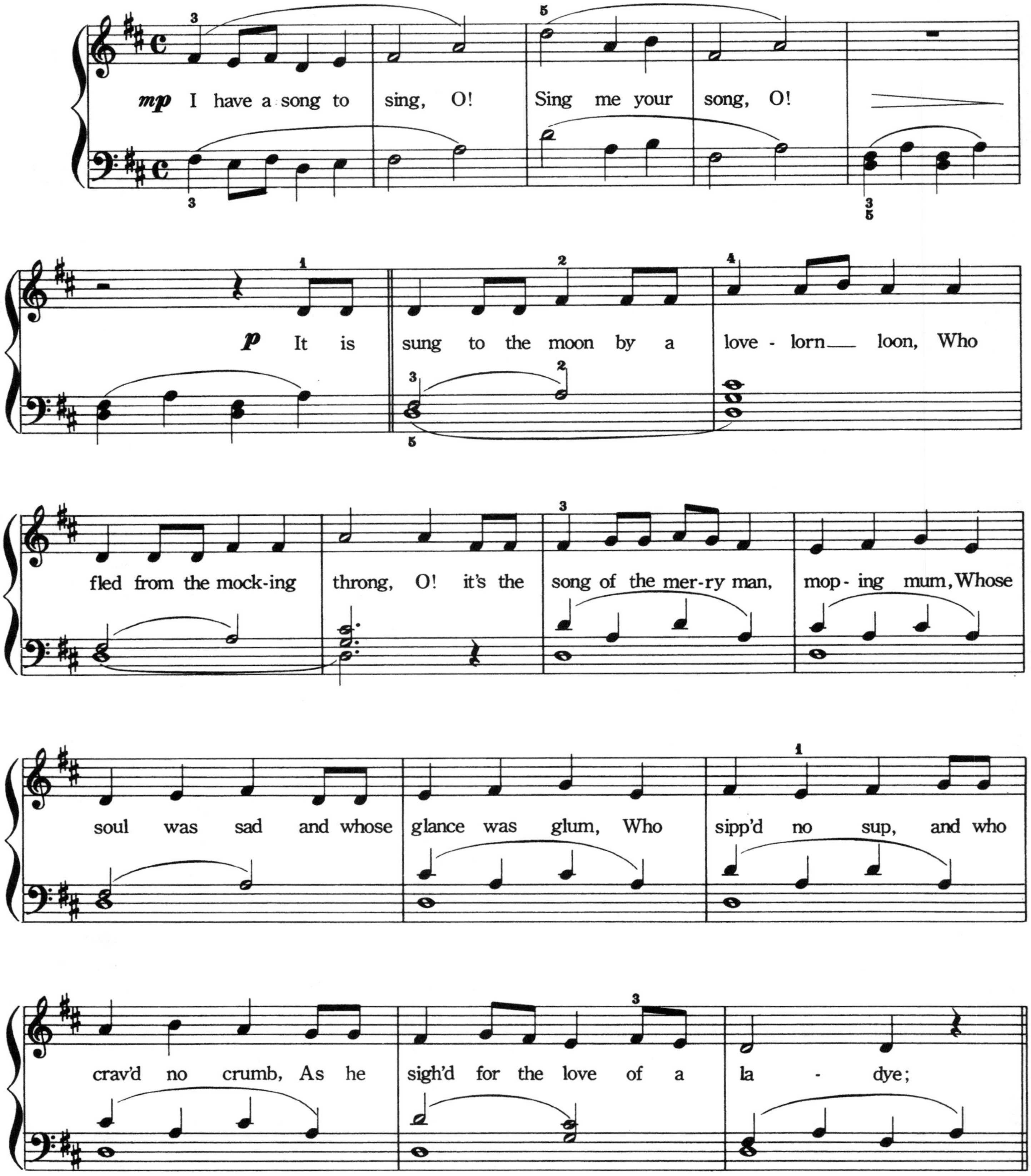

Heigh - dy! Heigh - dy! Mis-er - y me, Lack-a - day - dee! He

sipp'd no sup, and he crav'd no crumb, As he sigh'd for the love of a la - dye!

March of the Toys

(from *Babes in Toyland*)

Words by Glen MacDonough

Music by Victor Herbert

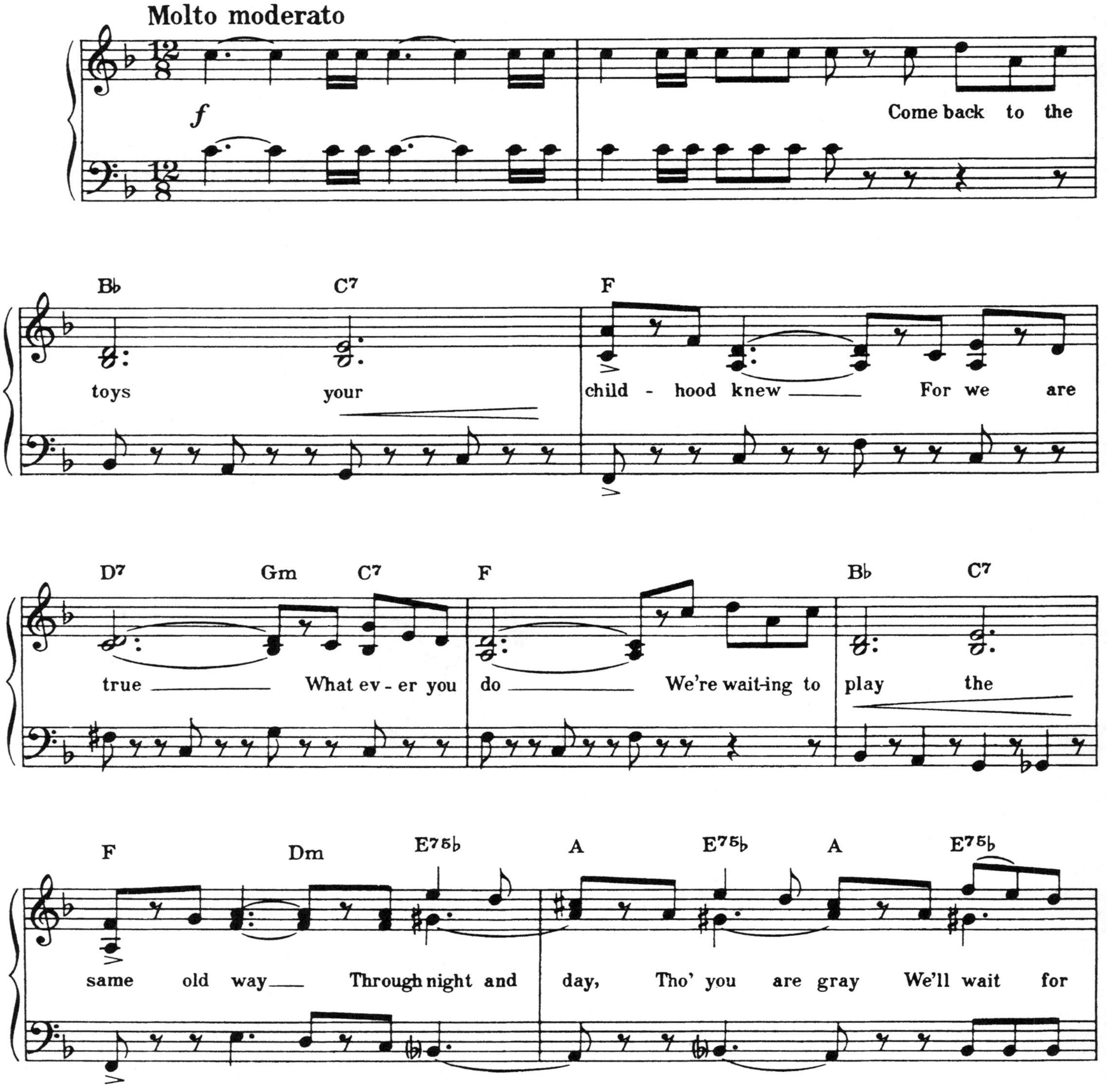

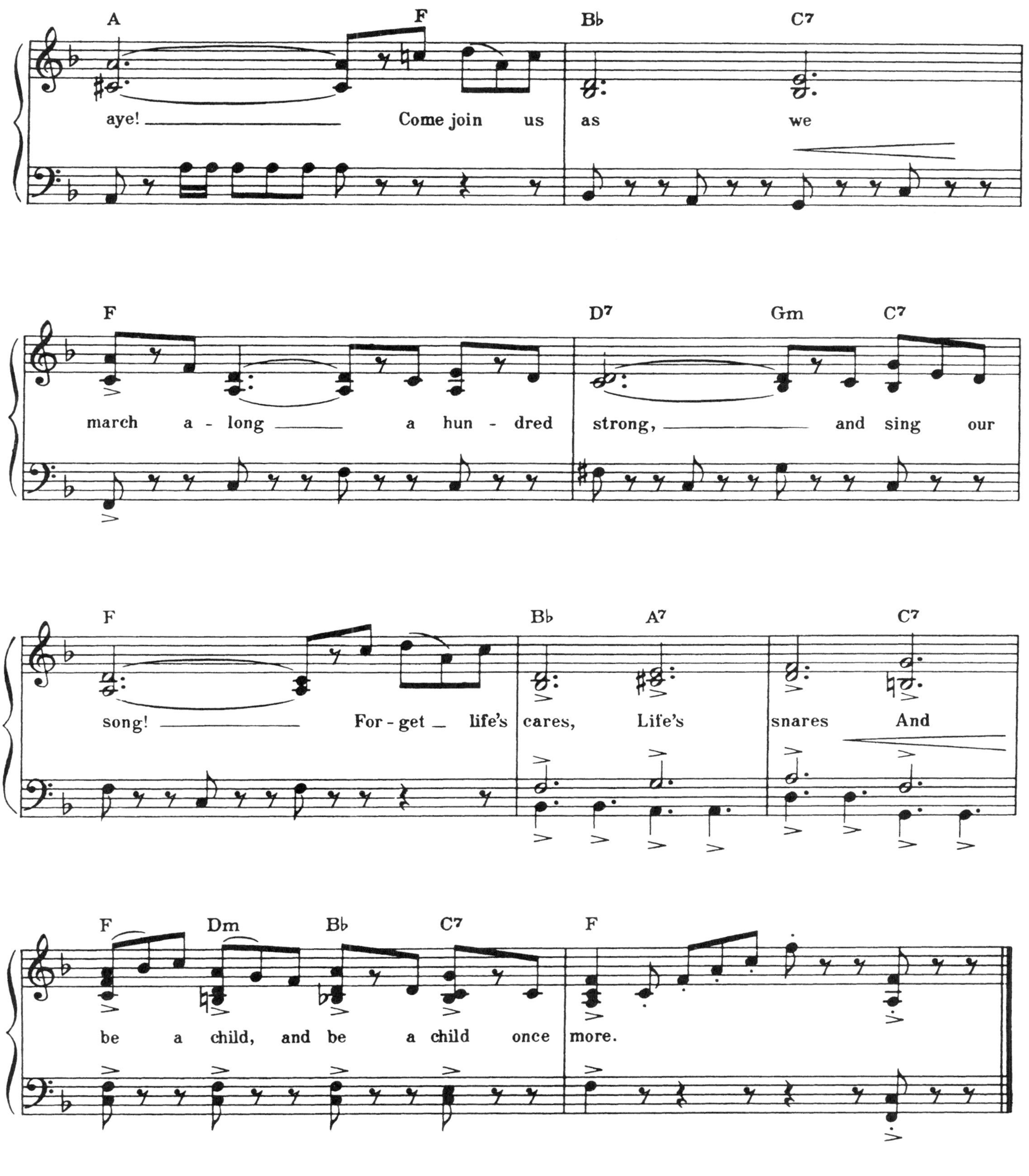
A F Bb C7
aye! Come join us as we
F D7 Gm C7
march a - long a hun - dred strong, and sing our
F Bb A7 C7
song! For - get life's cares, Life's snares And
F Dm Bb C7 F
be a child, and be a child once more.

Mary's a Grand Old Name

Words and music by George M. Cohan

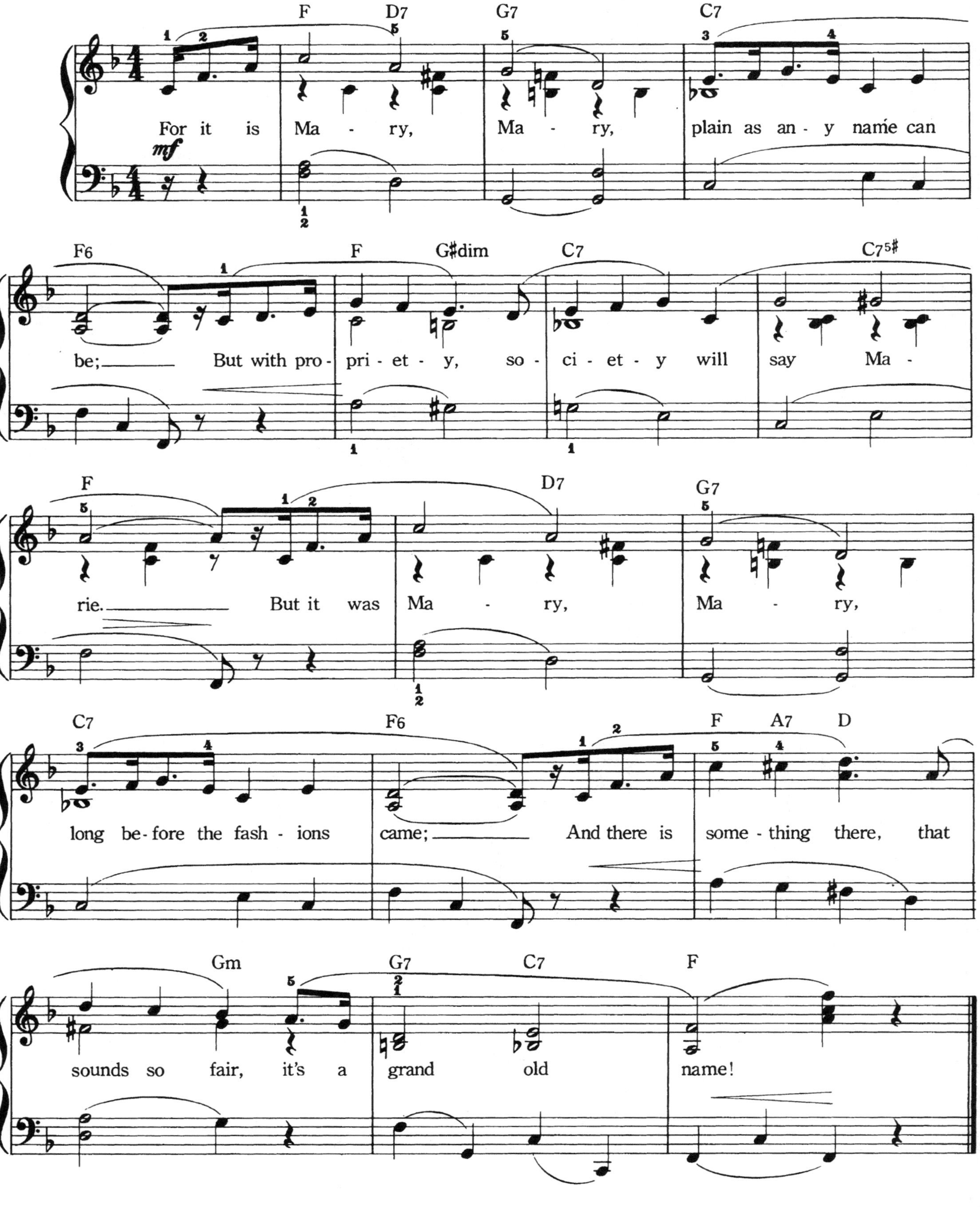

For it is Ma - ry, Ma - ry, plain as an - y name can be; _____ But with pro - pri - et - y, so - ci - et - y will say Ma - rie. _____ But it was Ma - ry, Ma - ry, long be - fore the fash - ions came; _____ And there is some - thing there, that sounds so fair, it's a grand old name!

Ta-Ra-Ra Boom-De-Ay

Words and music by Henry J. Sayers

Toyland

(from *Babes in Toyland*)

Words by Glen MacDonough

Music by Victor Herbert

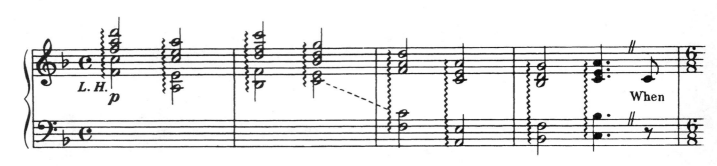

you're grown up, my dears —— And are as old as I —— You'll oft - en pon - der

on the years That roll so swift - ly by, my dears, that roll so swift - ly by —— And

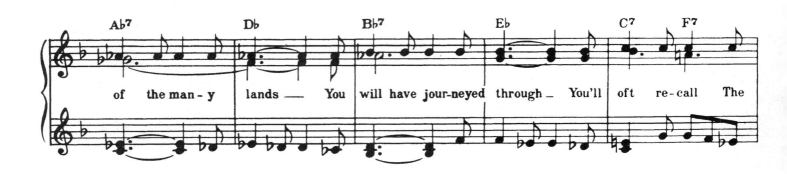

of the man - y lands —— You will have jour - neyed through —— You'll oft re - call The

D7 Gm G7 Em5b C7
best of all, The land your child-hood knew! Your child - hood knew.
rit.
Chorus
Tempo I
F6 Am Gm C7 F Bb Bbm
Toy - land! Toy - land! Lit - tle girl and boy - land, while you dwell with-
Am G7 C7 F6 Am Gm C7
in it You are ev - er hap-py then. Child - hood's Joy - land, Mys-tic mer-ry
F Dm Bbm F D7 Gm C7 F
Toy - land! Once you pass - its bor-ders you can ne'er re-turn a - gain.
rit.

When I Was a Lad

(from *H.M.S. Pinafore*)

Words by W.S. Gilbert

Music by Arthur Sullivan

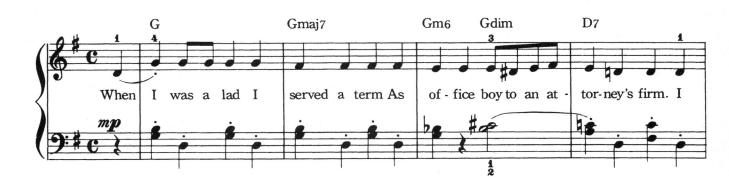

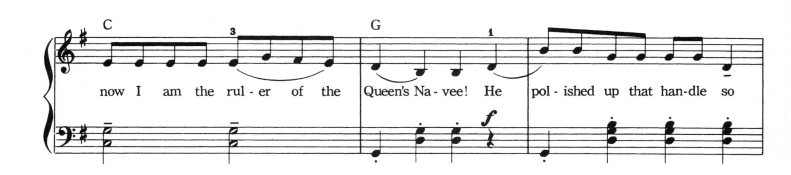

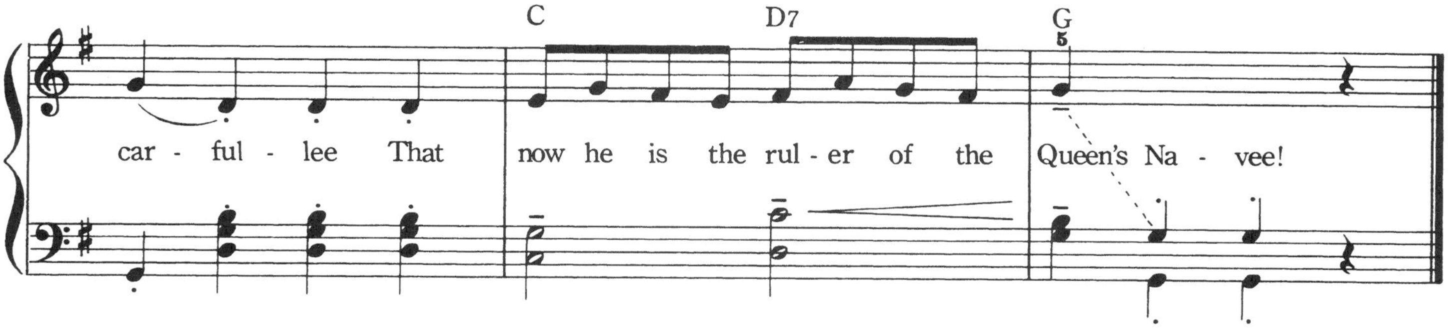

car - ful - lee That now he is the rul - er of the Queen's Na - vee!

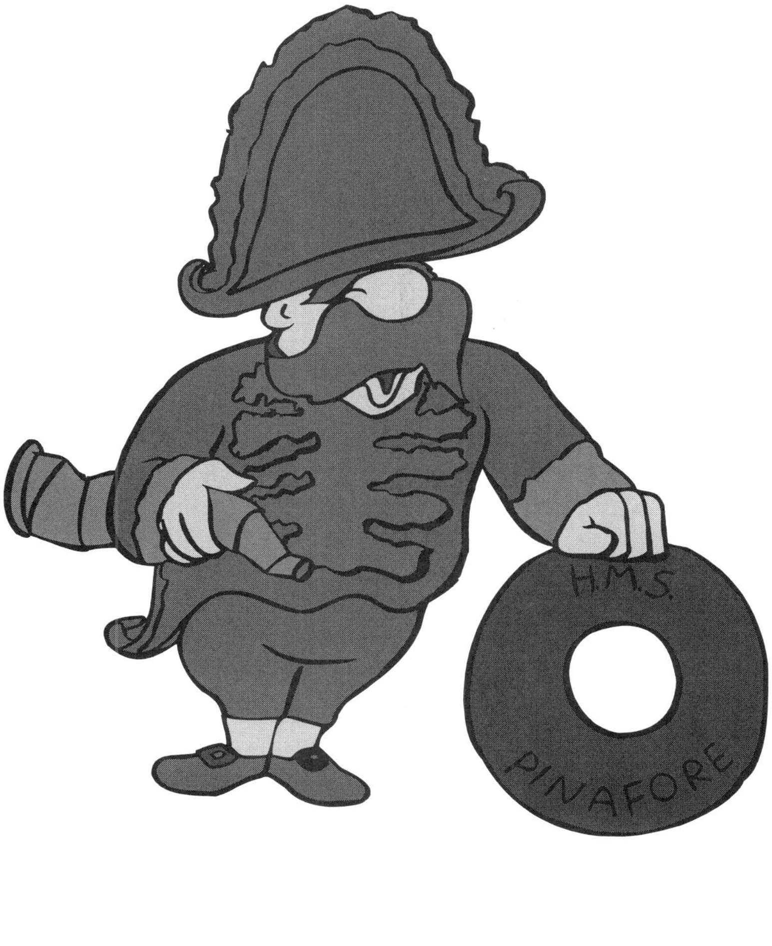

Yankee Doodle Boy

(from *Little Johnny Jones*)

Words and music by George M. Cohan

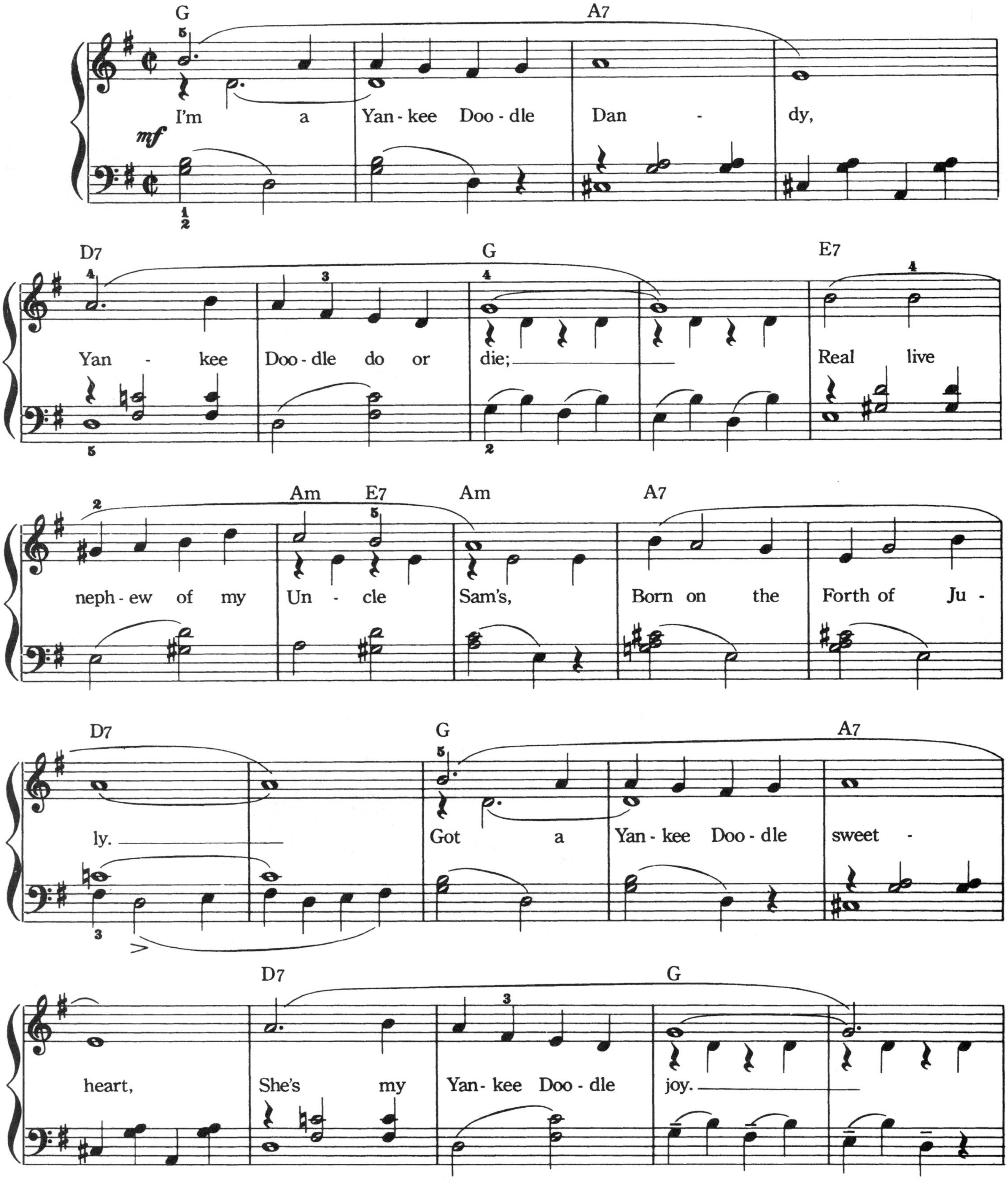

Yan - kee Doo - dle | came to Lon - don | just to ride the | po - nies,

A7   D7   G

I am a | Yan - kee Doo - dle | boy.

You're a Grand Old Flag

Words and music by George M. Cohan

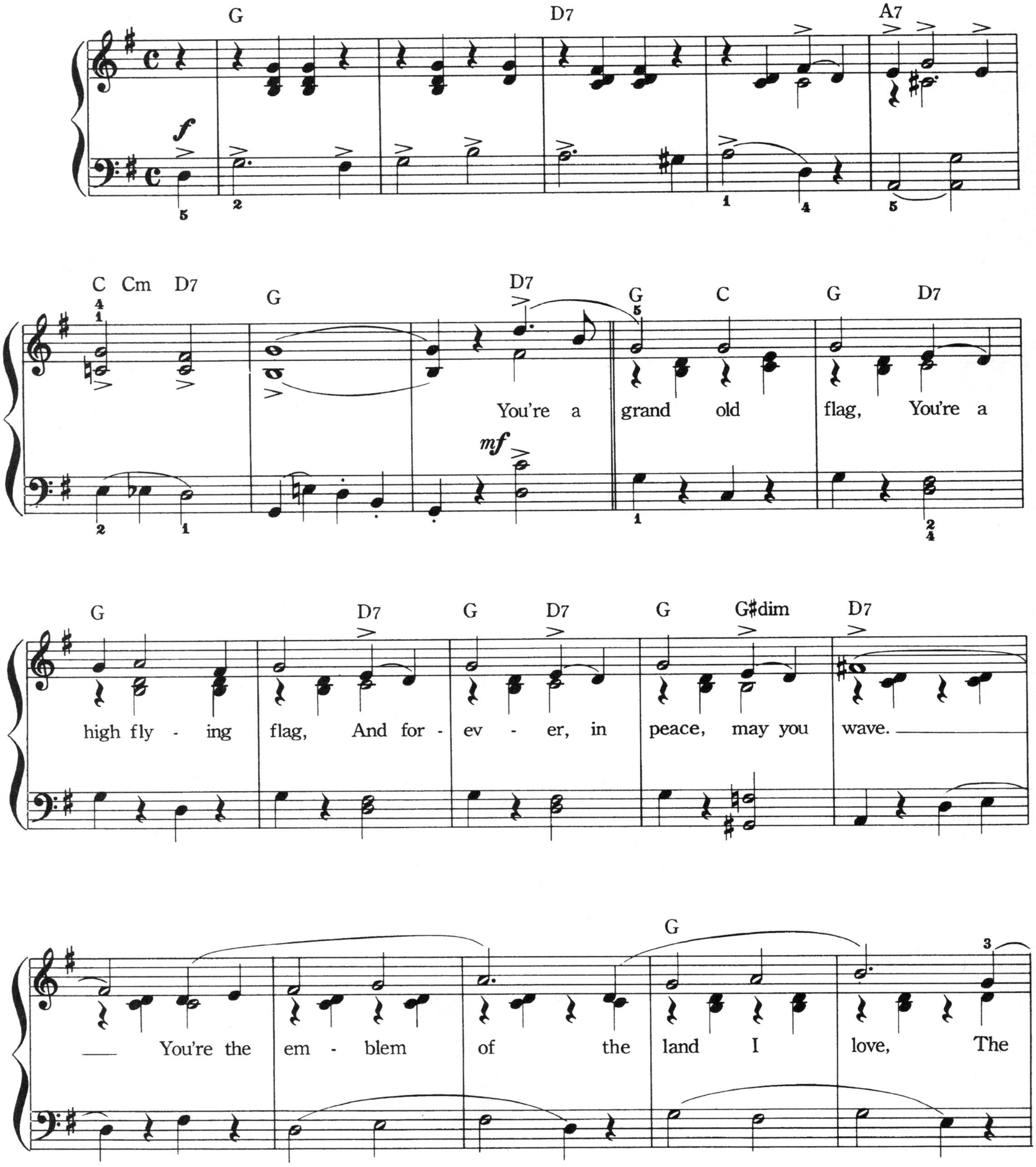

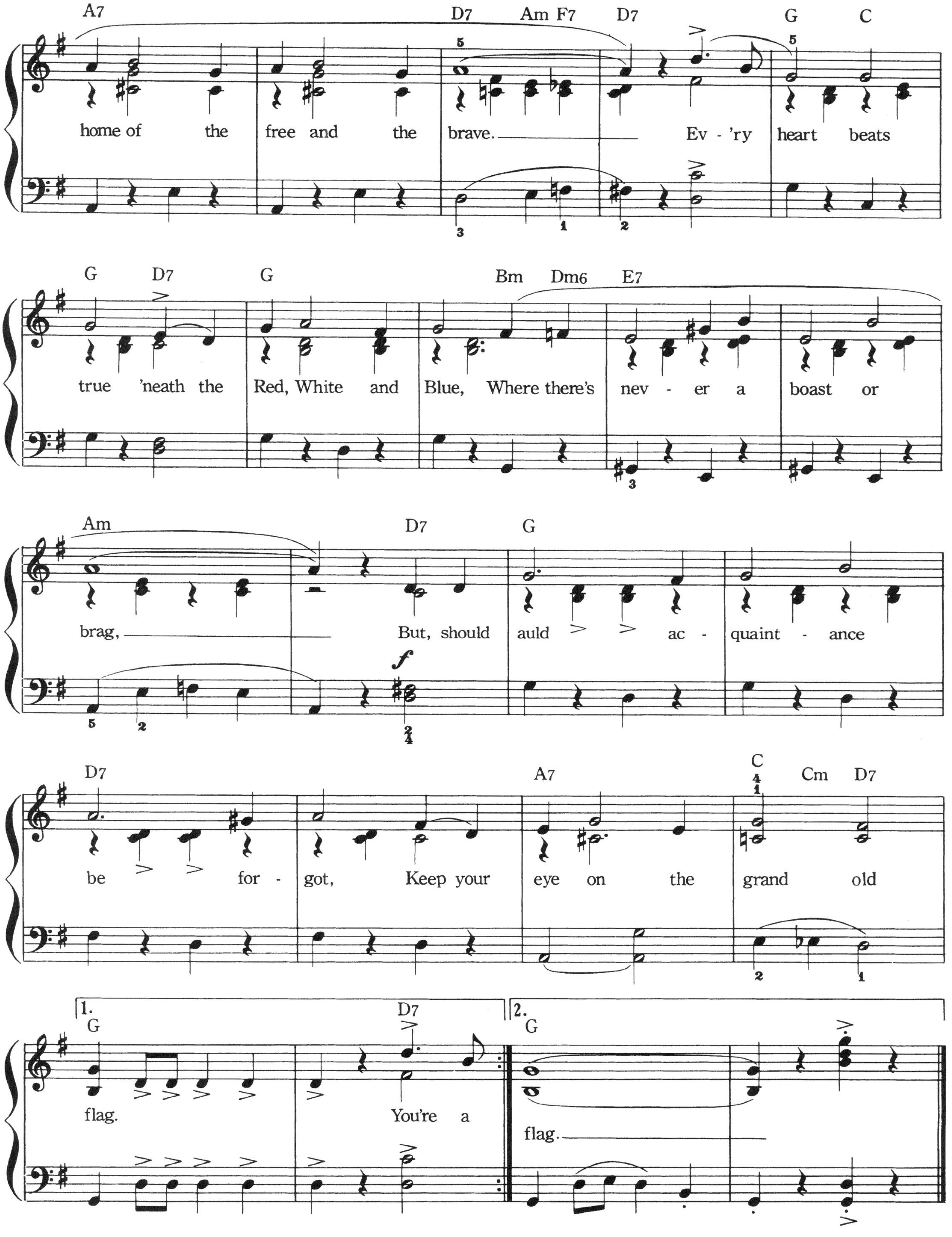
A7 D7 Am F7 D7 G C
home of the free and the brave. Ev - 'ry heart beats
G D7 G Bm Dm6 E7
true 'neath the Red, White and Blue, Where there's nev - er a boast or
Am D7 G
brag, But, should auld ac - quaint - ance
D7 A7 C Cm D7
be for - got, Keep your eye on the grand old
1. G D7 2. G
flag. You're a flag.

Songs of America

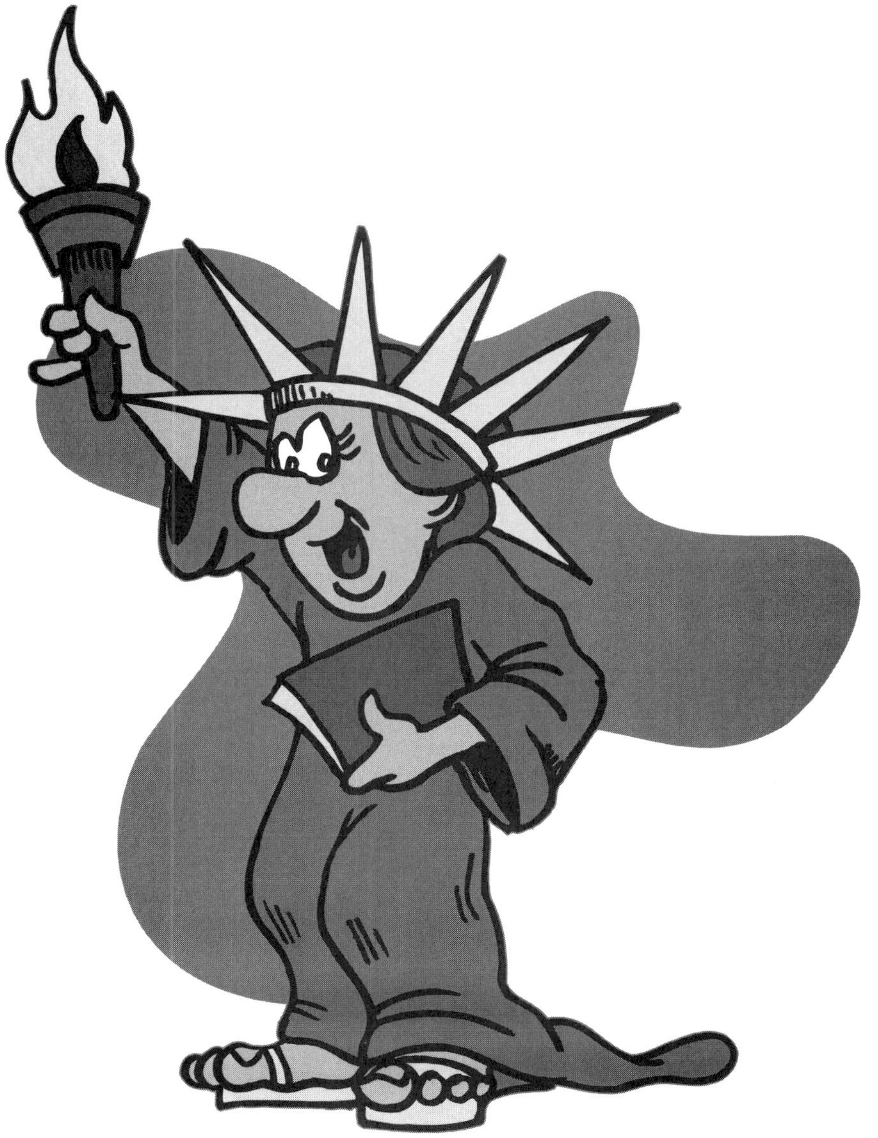

America, the Beautiful

Words by Katherine Lee Bates

Music by Samuel A. Ward

O beau - ti - ful for spa - cious skies, For am - ber waves of grain, For

pur - ple mount - ain maj - es - ties A - bove the fruit - ed plain. A -

mer - i - ca! A - mer - i - ca! God shed His grace on thee, And

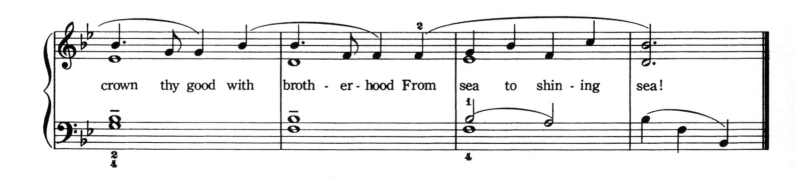

crown thy good with broth - er - hood From sea to shin - ing sea!

2. Oh, beautiful for pilgrim feet,
   Whose stern impassioned stress,
   A thoroughfare for freedom beat,
   Across the wilderness.
   America, America,
   God mend thine ev'ry flaw,
   Confirm thy soul in self-control,
   Thy liberty in law.

3. Oh, beautiful for heroes proved,
   In liberating strife,
   Who more than self their country loved,
   And mercy more than life.
   America, America,
   May God thy gold refine,
   Till all success be nobleness,
   And ev'ry gain divine.

4. Oh, beautiful for patriot dream,
   That sees beyond the years,
   Thine alabaster cities gleam,
   Undimmed by human tears.
   America, America,
   God shed His grace on thee,
   And crown thy good with brotherhood,
   From sea to shining sea.

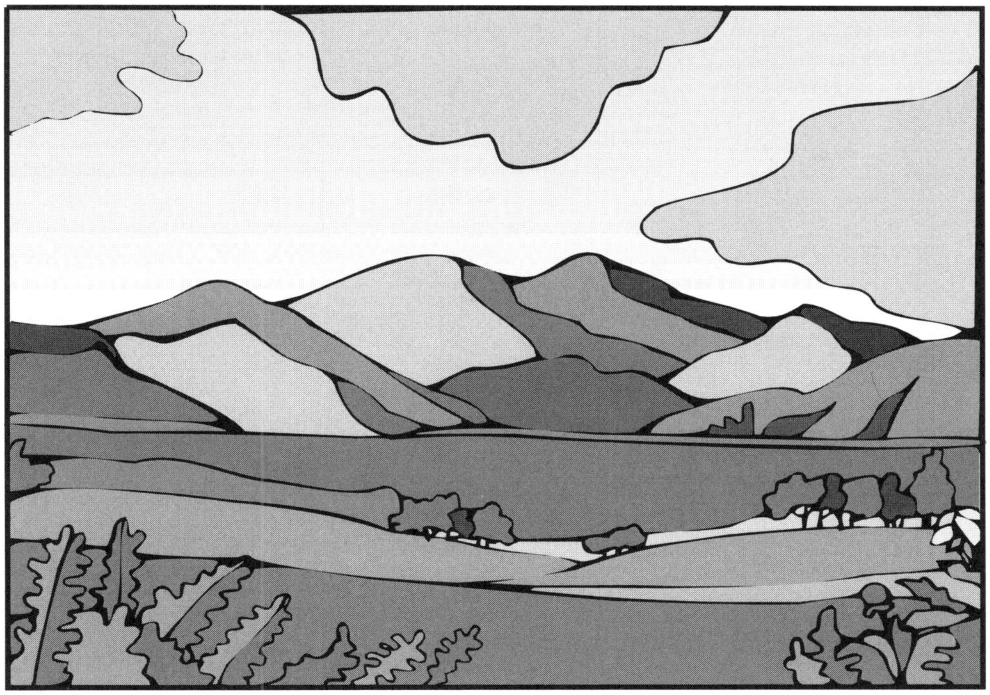

Down in the Valley

American Folk Song

2. If you don't answer, answer my pleas;
   Throw your arms round me, give my heart ease.
   Throw your arms round me, feel my heart ache.
   Throw your arms round me, so it won't break.

3. Build me a castle forty feet high,
   So I can you as you ride by.
   Roses love sunshine, violets love dew,
   Angels in heaven, know I love you.

The Big Rock Candy Mountain

American folk song

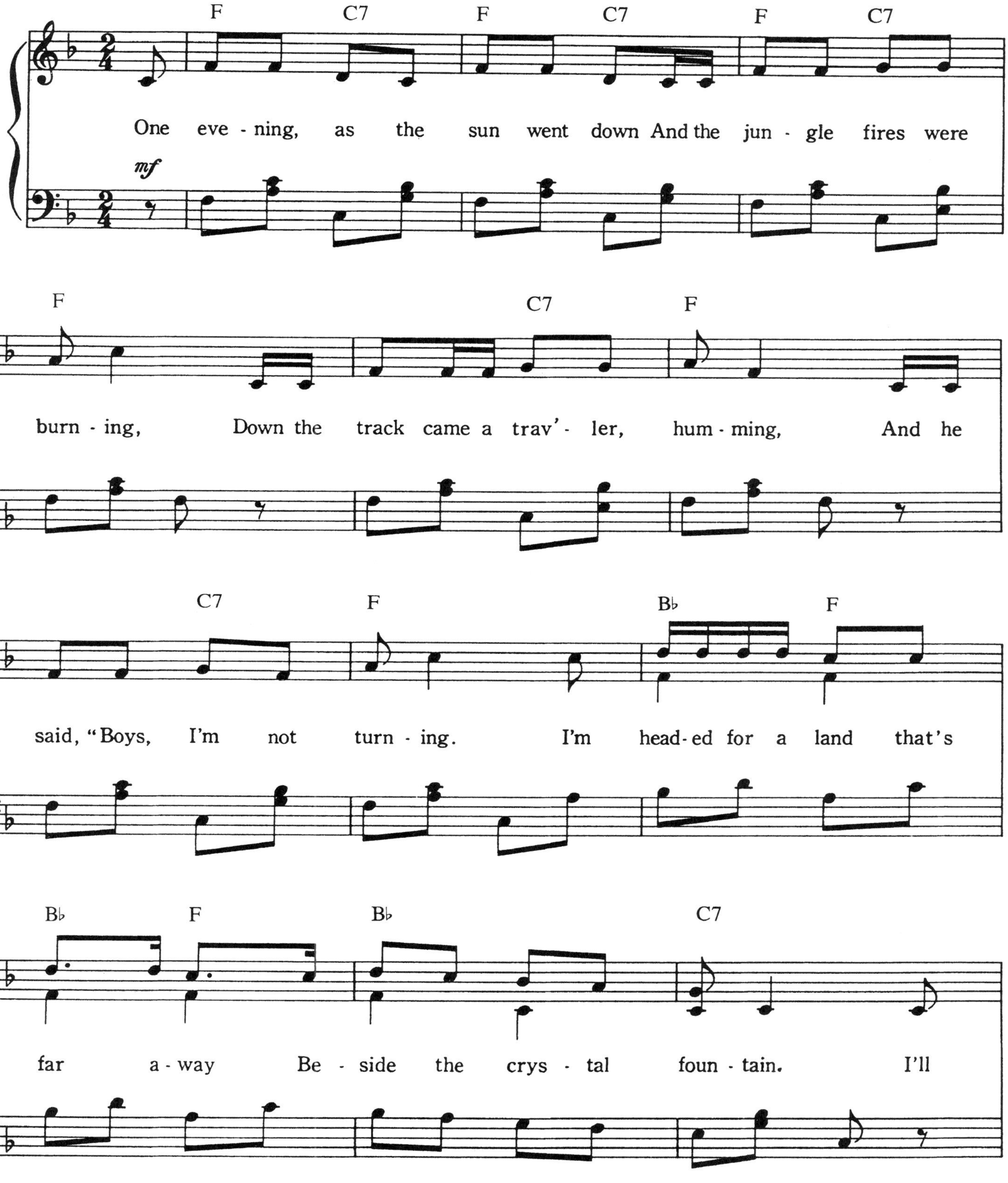
F C7 F C7 F C7
One eve - ning, as the sun went down And the jun - gle fires were
mf
F C7 F
burn - ing, Down the track came a trav' - ler, hum - ming, And he
C7 F B♭ F
said, "Boys, I'm not turn - ing. I'm head - ed for a land that's
B♭ F B♭ C7
far a - way Be - side the crys - tal foun - tain. I'll

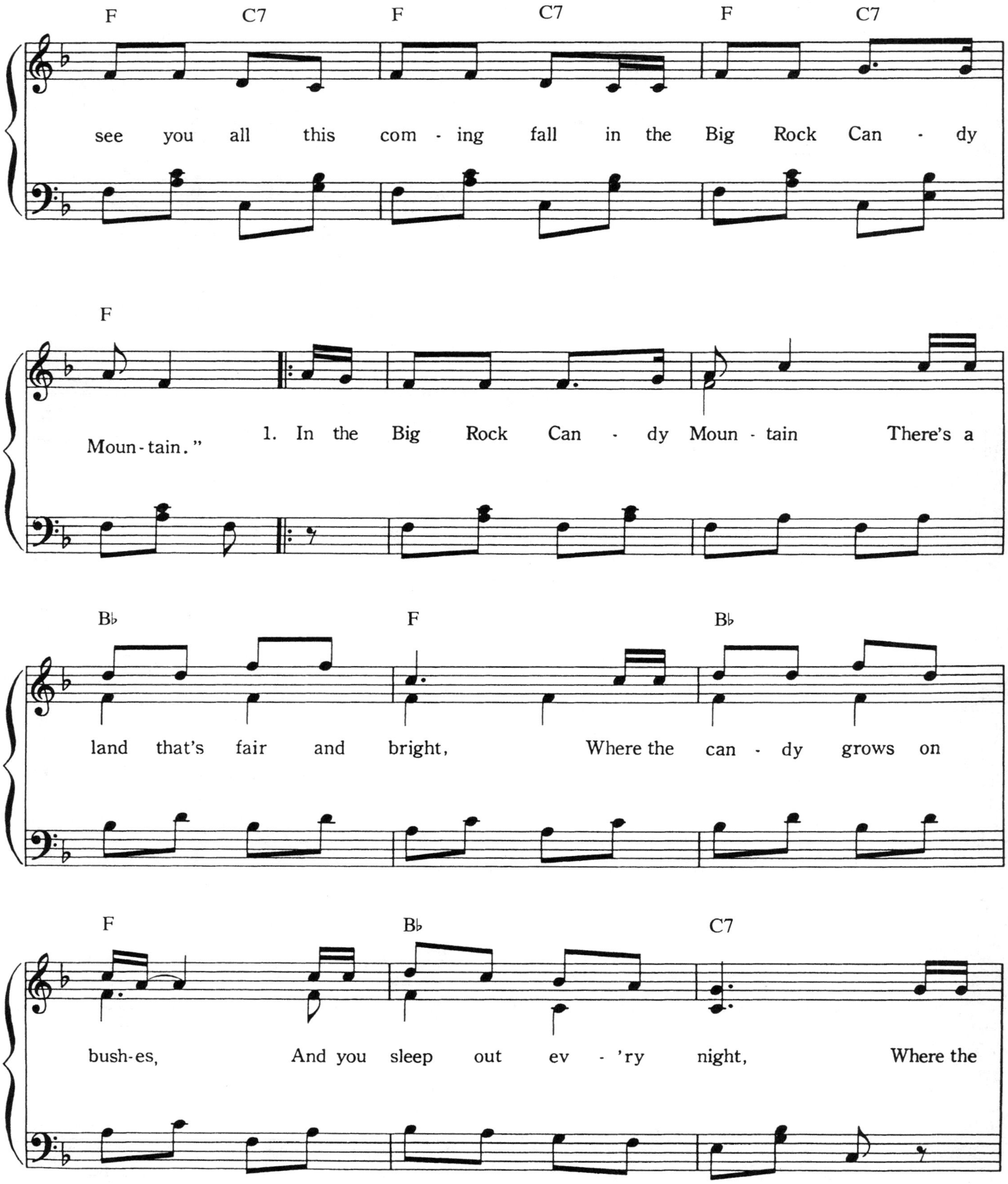
F C7 F C7 F C7
see you all this com - ing fall in the Big Rock Can - dy
F
Moun - tain."
1. In the Big Rock Can - dy Moun - tain There's a
B♭ F B♭
land that's fair and bright, Where the can - dy grows on
F B♭ C7
bush - es, And you sleep out ev - 'ry night, Where the

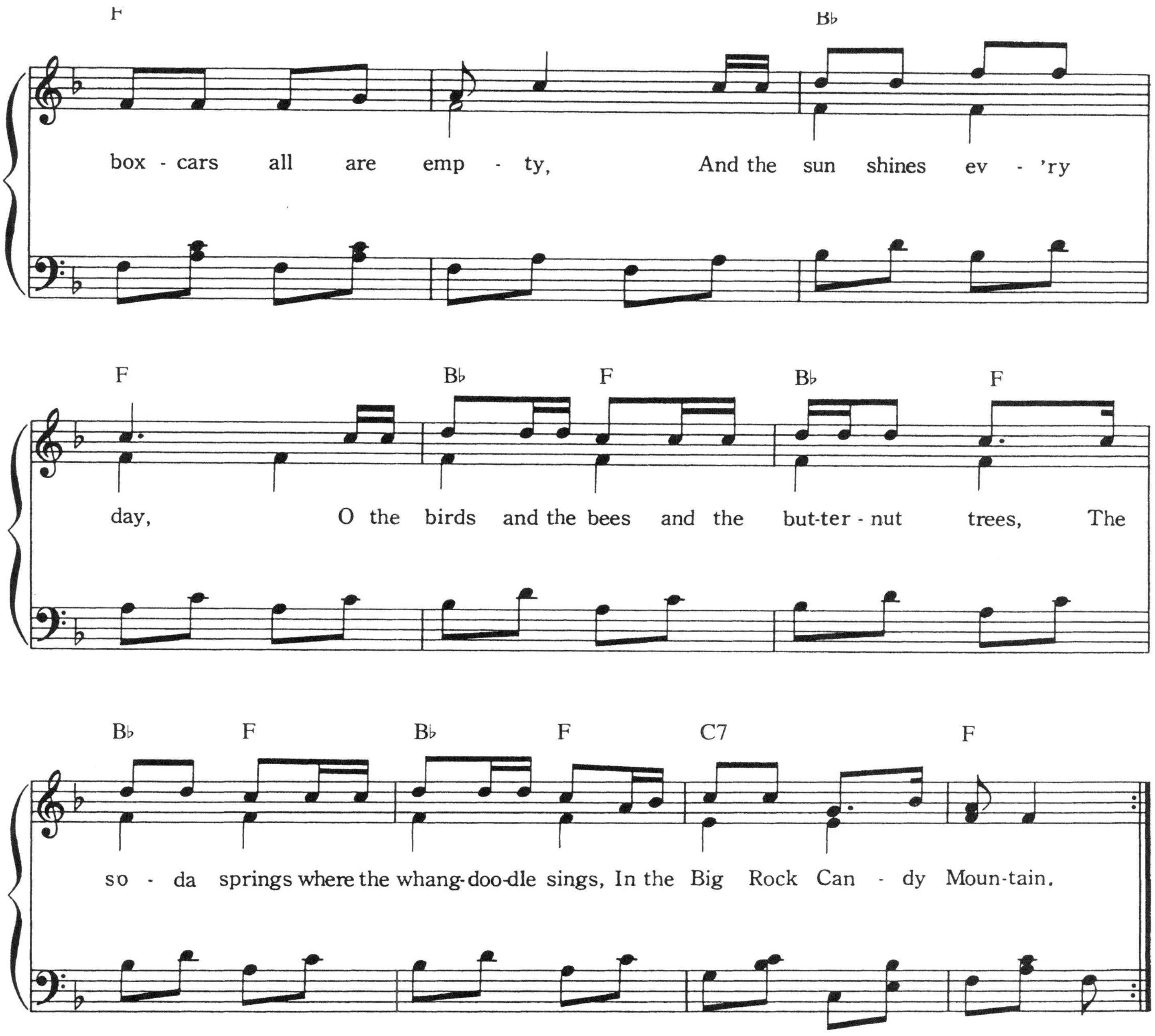

2. In the Big Rock Candy Mountain
   You never change your socks,
   And the little streams of lemonade
   Come trickling down the rocks.
   The farmers' trees are full of fruit,
   And the barns are full of hay;
   Yes, I want to go where there ain't no snow,
   Where the sleet don't fall and the wind don't blow,
   In the Big Rock Candy Mountain.

Dixie

Words and music by Daniel Decatur Emmett

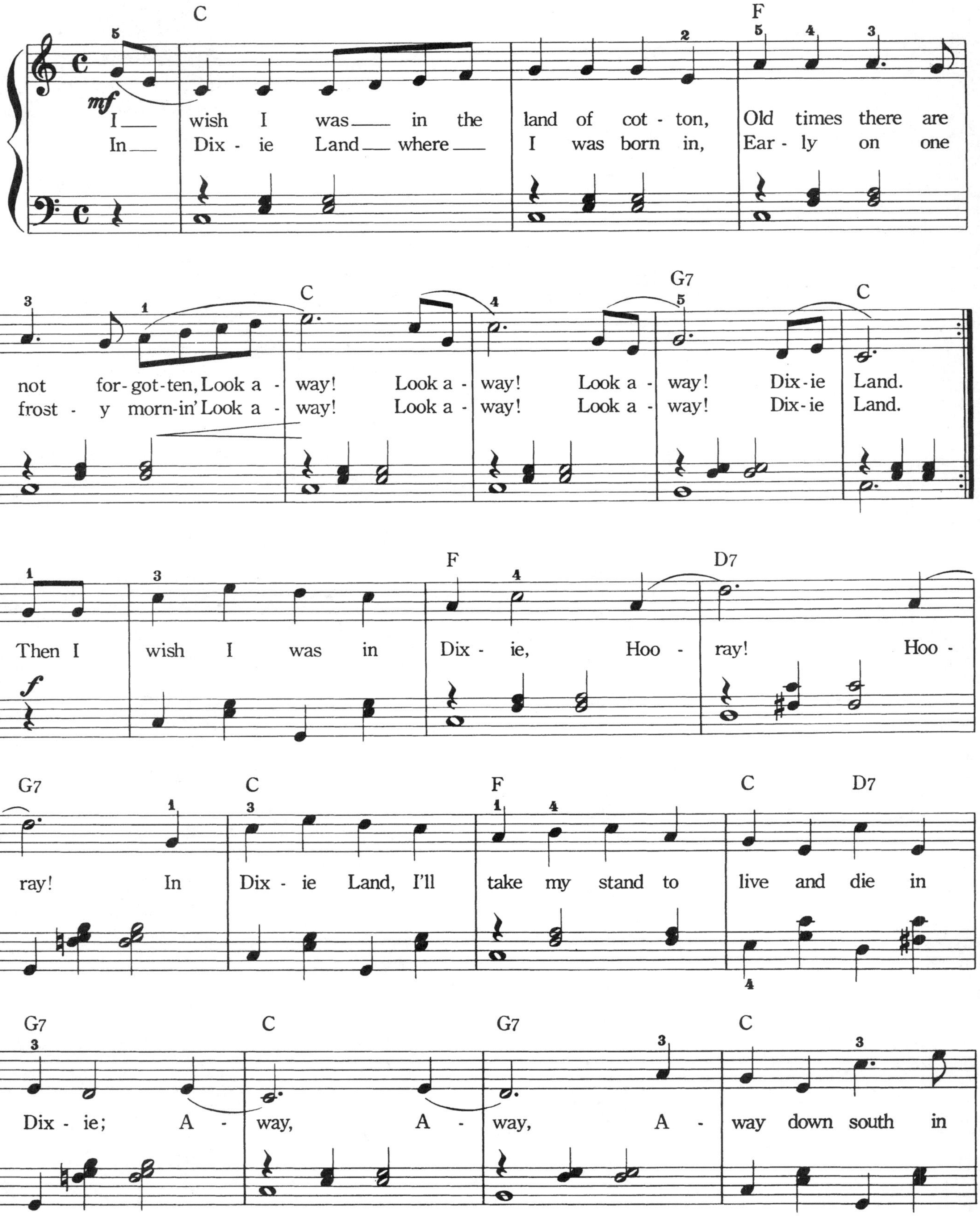
C F
mf
I wish I was in the land of cot - ton, Old times there are
In Dix - ie Land where I was born in, Ear - ly on one
C G7 C
not for - got - ten, Look a - way! Look a - way! Look a - way! Dix - ie Land.
frost - y morn - in' Look a - way! Look a - way! Look a - way! Dix - ie Land.
F D7
f
Then I wish I was in Dix - ie, Hoo - ray! Hoo -
G7 C F C D7
ray! In Dix - ie Land, I'll take my stand to live and die in
G7 C G7 C
Dix - ie; A - way, A - way, A - way down south in

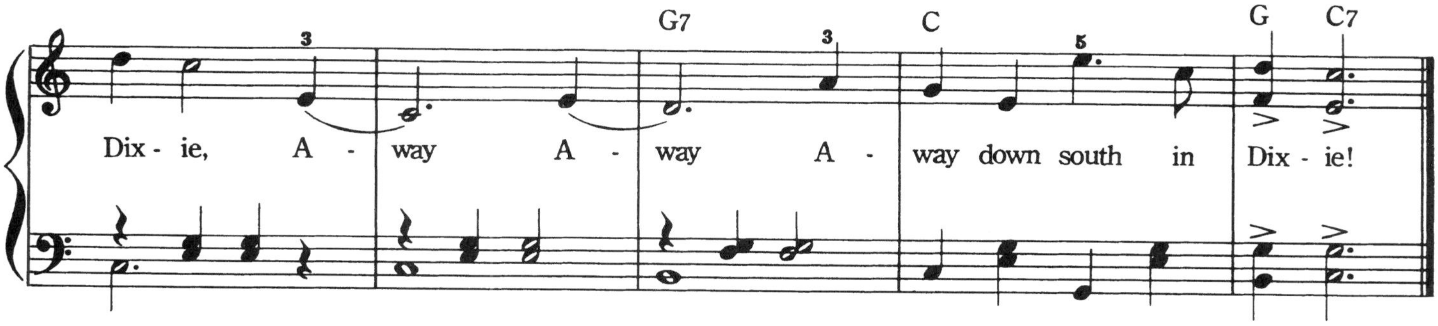
G7
C
G
C7
Dix - ie, A - way A - way A - way down south in Dix - ie!

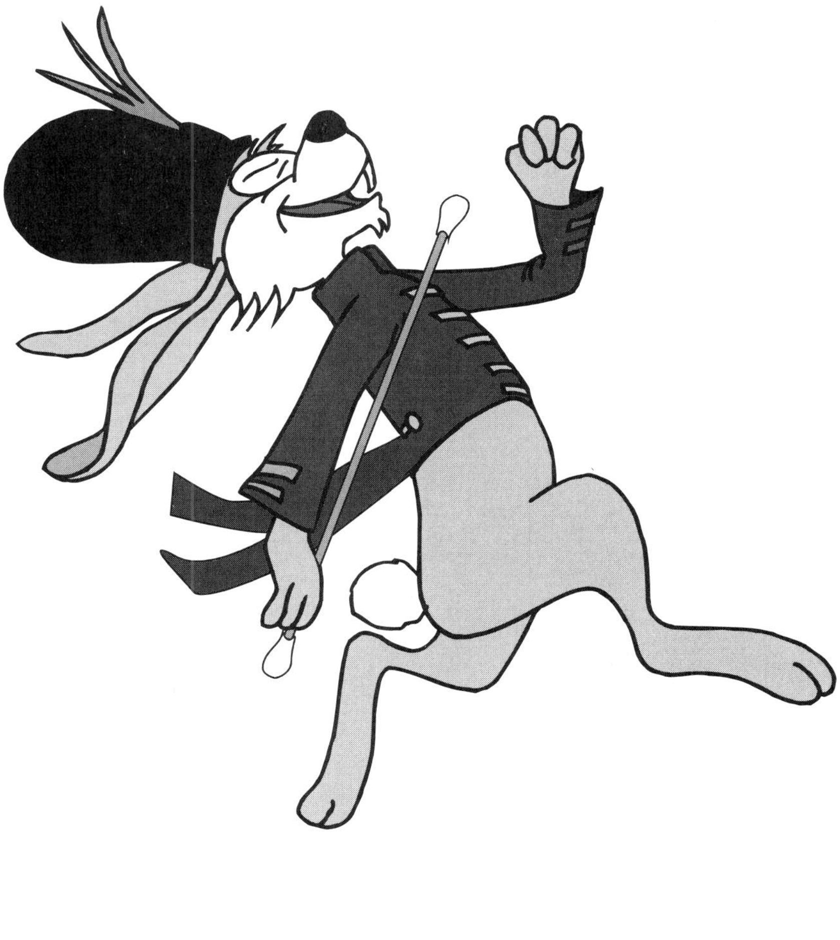

Git on Board, Little Children

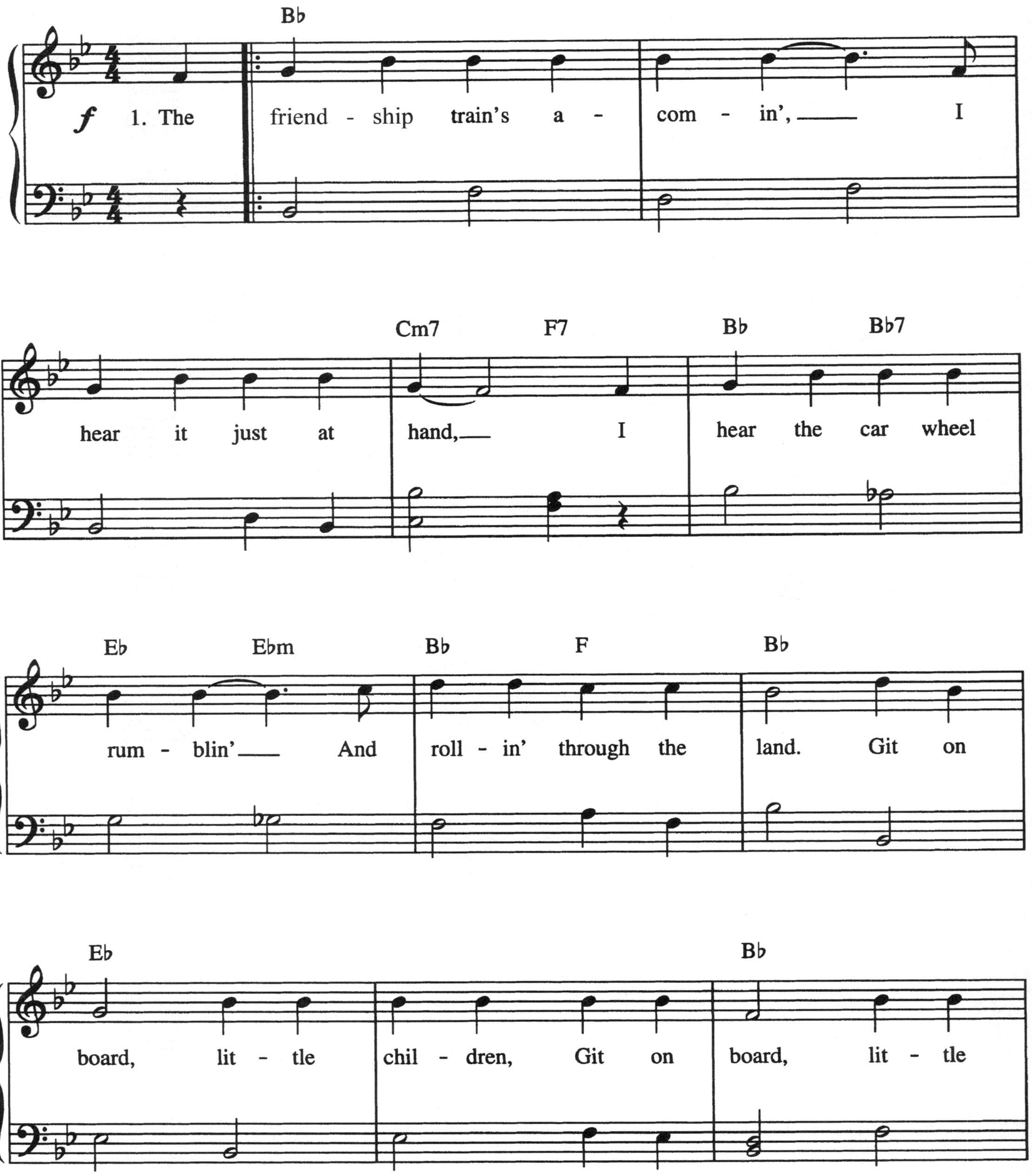
Bb
f 1. The friend - ship train's a - com - in', I
Cm7 F7 Bb Bb7
hear it just at hand, I hear the car wheel
Eb Ebm Bb F Bb
rum - blin' And roll - in' through the land. Git on
Eb Bb
board, lit - tle chil - dren, Git on board, lit - tle

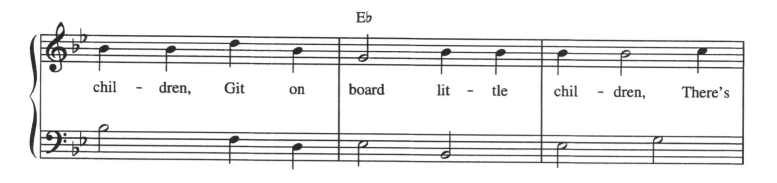

chil - dren,   Git   on   board   lit - tle   chil - dren,   There's

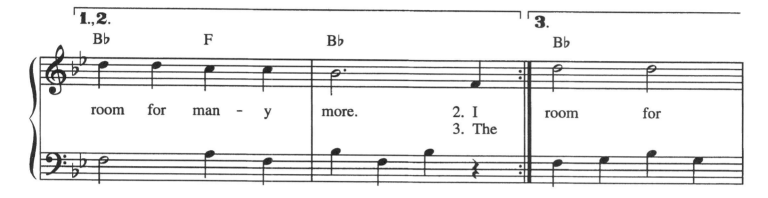

1., 2.   **3.**

room   for   man - y   more.   2. I   room   for
                                3. The

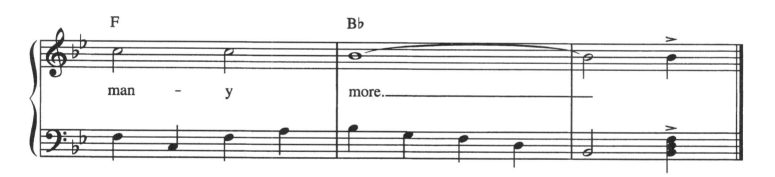

man - y   more._____

2. I heard the train's a-comin',
   She's comin' round the curve,
   She's loosened all her steam and brakes,
   And strainin' every nerve.
   Chorus

3. The fare is cheap and all can go,
   The rich and poor are there,
   No second class aboard this train,
   No difference in the fare.
   Chorus

Home on the Range

American folk song

1. Oh ___ give me a home, where the buf - fa - lo roam ___ where the
2. Where the air is so pure, the ___ zeph - yrs so free, the ___

deer and the an - te - lope play, ___ where sel - dom is
breez - es so balm - y and light, ___ that I'd not ex -

heard a dis - cour - ag - ing word And the skies are not cloud - y all
change my - home on the range For ___ all ___ the cit - ies so

day. ___
bright. ___

Chorus

Home, home on the range, ___

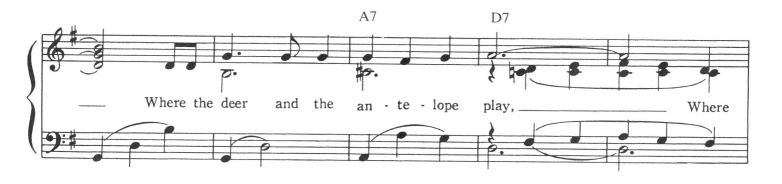

A7   D7

Where the deer and the an-te-lope play, _____ Where

G   C   Cm

sel - dom is heard a dis - cour - ag - ing word, And the

G   D7   G

skies are not cloud - y all day. _____

I Ride an Old Paint

American folk song

G
mf
I ride an old Paint, I lead an old
D7
Dan, I'm goin' to Mon - tan' For to
G D7
throw the hoo - li - han. They feed in the
C D7 G
cou - lees, They wa - ter in the drow, Their

tails are all mat - ted, Their backs are all

raw. **Refrain** Ride a - round, lit - tle do - gies, Ride a

round _____ them _ slow, For the fi - ery and

snuf - fy are a - rar - in' to go.

I've Been Workin' on the Railroad

American folk song

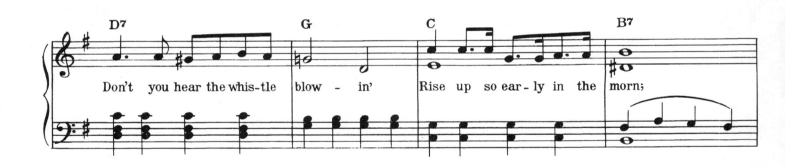

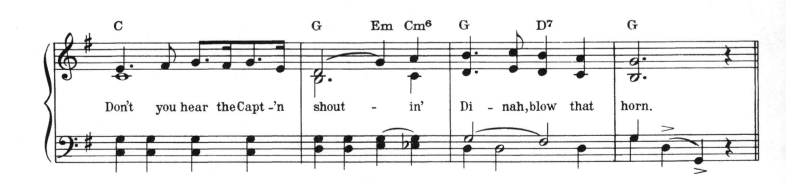

G Am D7 G D7 G
Di-nah, won't you blow, Di-nah, won't you blow, Di-nah, won't you blow that horn, — Di-nah, won't you blow,
mp
Am D7 G G
Di-nah, won't you blow, Di-nah, won't you blow that horn. Some-one's in the kitch-en with
mf
D7 G C C♯dim
Di - nah, Some-one's in the kitch-en I know-o - o - o. Some-one's in the kitchen with Di - nah!
clap hands
G D7 G G
Strum-min' on the old ban - jo, Fee Fi fidd-lee-i - o Fee-fi-fidd-le-i -
f
D7 G C C♯dim G D7 G
o - o - o - o. Fee Fi fidd-lee - i - o Strum-min' on the old ban - jo.

Jimmy Crack Corn

African-American folk song

1. Big owl with your eyes so bright, On man-y a dark and storm-y night, I've

of - ten heard my true love say, Sing all night and sleep all day.

Chorus:

Jim-my crack corn, I don't care, Jim-my crack corn, I don't care,

Jim-my crack corn, I don't care, the Mas-ter's gone a - way.

2. When I was young I used to wait
On my master and give him his plate,
And pass the bottle when he got dry,
And brush away the blue tail fly.
Chorus

3. And when he'd ride in the afternoon,
I'd follow with a hickory broom;
The pony being rather shy,
When bitten by a blue tail fly.
Chorus

4. One day he rode around the farm,
The flies so numerous they did swarm;
One chanced to bite him on thigh,
That miserable blue tail fly.
Chorus

5. The pony run, he jump, he pitch,
He threw my master in the ditch;
He died and the jury wondered why;
The verdict was the blue tail fly.
Chorus

Li'l Liza Jane

African-American folk song

1. I know a gal that you don't know, Li'l Li - za Jane.
2. Li - za Jane looks good to me, Li'l Li - za Jane.

'Way down south in Bal - ti - mo,' Li'l Li - za Jane.
Sweet - es' one I ev - er see, Li'l Li - za Jane.

Chorus

Oh! E - li - za, Li'l Li - za Jane

Oh! E - li - za, Li'l Li - za Jane. *D.C.*

3. Where she lives, the posies grow,
   L'il Liza Jane.
   Chickens round the kitchen door,
   L'il Liza Jane,
   Chorus

4. What do I care how far we roam,
   L'il Liza Jane?
   Where she's at is home sweet home,
   L'il Liza Jane,
   Chorus

Look Down That Lonesome Road

African-American folk song

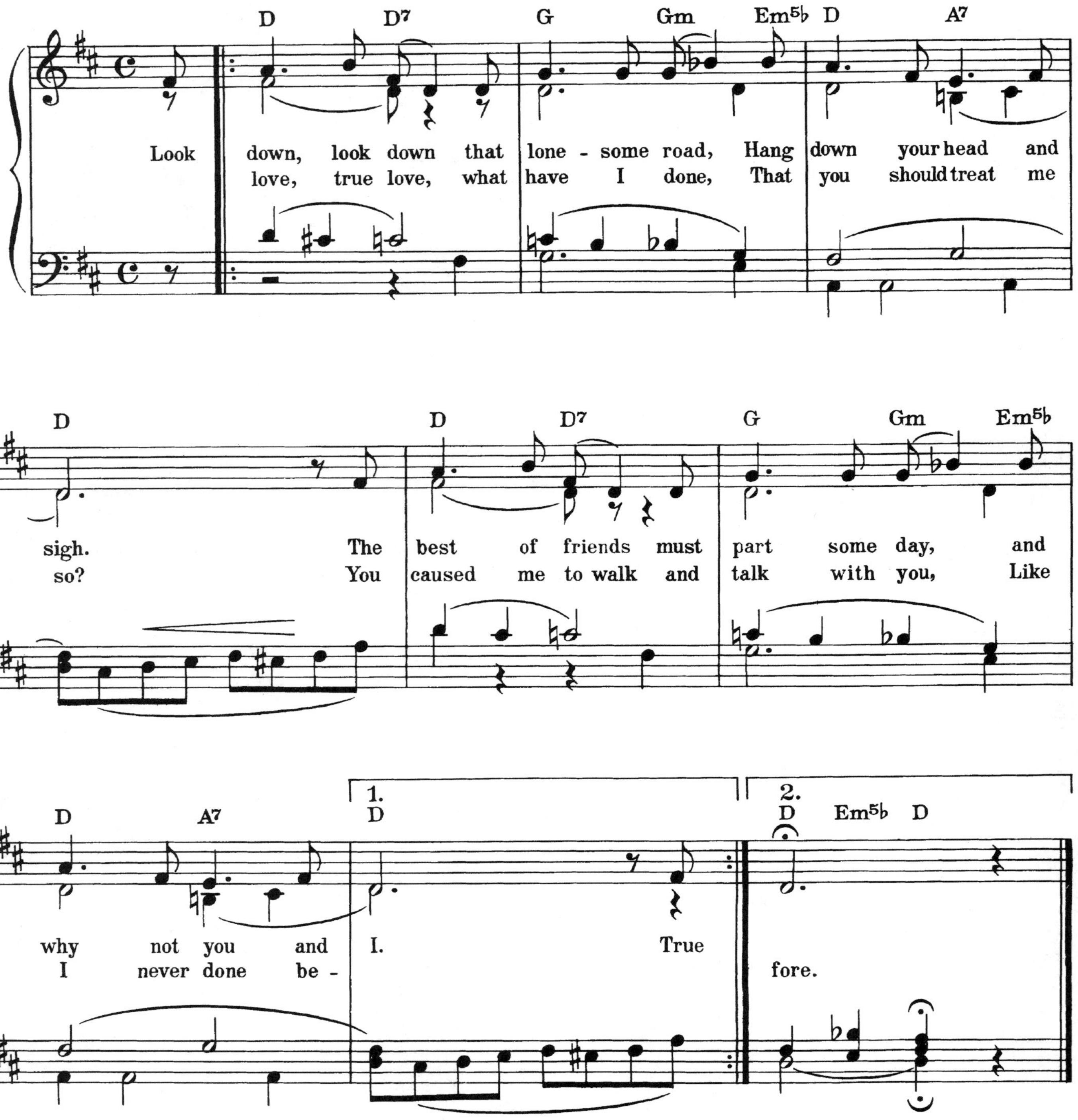

The Old Chisholm Trail

American folk song

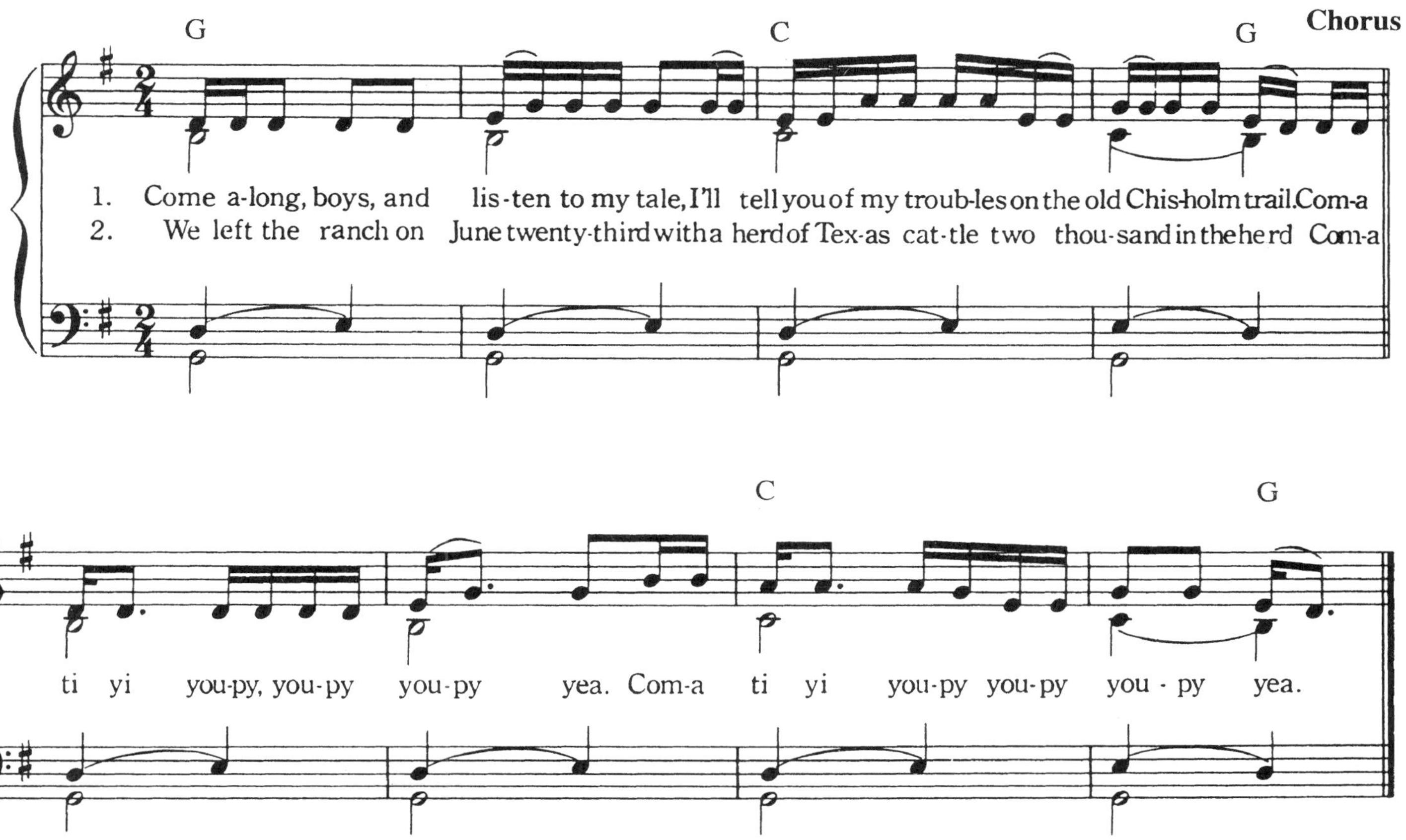

3. It's bacon and beans most every day,
   I'd as soon be eatin' prairie hay.
   Chorus

4. Saddle up boys and saddle up right,
   For I think these cattle have scattered out of sight.
   Chorus

5. With lightnin' in his eye and thunder in his heels,
   He went spinnin' round like a hoop in a reel.
   Chorus

6. Make a circle, boys, don't lose no time,
   I'm sure that they'll be easy to find.
   Chorus

7. We hit the junction and we hit her on the fly,
   And bedded down the cattle on the hill nearby.
   Chorus

Oh Dear! What Can the Matter Be?

American folk song

Eb Fm Bb7
Oh Dear! What can the mat-ter be? Dear dear! What can the mat-ter be?
Eb Ab6 Bb7
Oh Dear! What can the mat - ter be? John-ny's so long at the
Eb Eb
fair. He prom - ised to buy me a bunch of blue rib-bons, he
Fm B° Bb7 Eb
prom - ised to buy me a bunch of blue rib - bons, he prom - ised to buy me a
Ab6 Bb7 Eb
bunch of blue rib - bons, to tie up my bon - nie brown hair.

On the Banks of the Wabash

Words and music by Paul Dresser

Oh, the moon-light's fair to-night a-long the Wa-bash, From the fields there comes the breath of new mown hay; Thro' the syc-a-mores the can-dle-lights are gleam-ing On the banks of the Wa-bash, far a-way.

Polly-Wolly-Doodle

African-American folk song

1 Oh, I went down South for to see my Sal, Sing Pol-ly-wol-ly-doo-dle all the day. My
2 Oh, my Sal, she am a __ maid-en fair, Sing Pol-ly-wol-ly-doo-dle all the day. With

Sal - ly am a __ spun-ky gal, Sing Pol-ly-wol-ly-doo-dle all the day.
cur - ly eyes and laugh-ing hair, Sing Pol-ly-wol-ly-doo-dle all the day. Fare thee

Chorus

well, fare thee well, Fare thee well my fair-y fay, For I'm

going to Louisi-a - na, For to see my Su-sy-an-na, Singing Pol-ly-wol-ly-doo-dle all the day.

3. Oh, a grasshopper sittin' on a railroad track,
   Sing Polly-wolly-doodle all the day,
   A-pickin' his teeth with a carpet tack,
   Sing Polly-wolly-doodle all the day.
   Chorus

4. Oh, I went to bed, but it wasn't no use,
   Sing Polly-wolly-doodle all the day,
   My feet stuck out for a chicken roost,
   Sing Polly-wolly-doodle all the day.
   Chorus

5. Behind the barn, down on my knees,
   Sing Polly-wolly-doodle all the day,
   I thought I heard that chicken sneeze,
   Sing Polly-wolly-doodle all the day.
   Chorus

6. He sneezed so hard with whooping cough,
   Sing Polly-wolly-doodle all the day,
   He sneezed his head and tail right off,
   Sing Polly-wolly-doodle all the day.
   Chorus

Red River Valley

American folk song

mf
1. From this val - ley they say you are go - ing, I will miss your bright eyes and your smile, For they say you are tak - ing the sun - shine That bright - ened our path - way a - while. 2. Come and
sit by my side if you love me, Do not has - ten to bid me ad - ieu, But re - mem - ber the Red Riv - er Val - ley And the cow - boy who loved you so true.
1.
2.

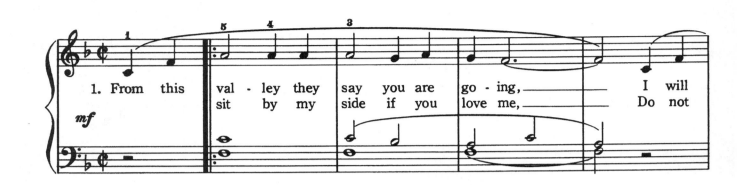

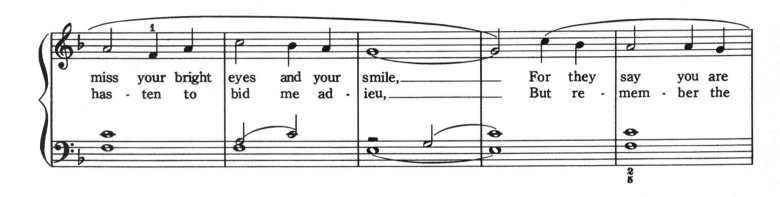

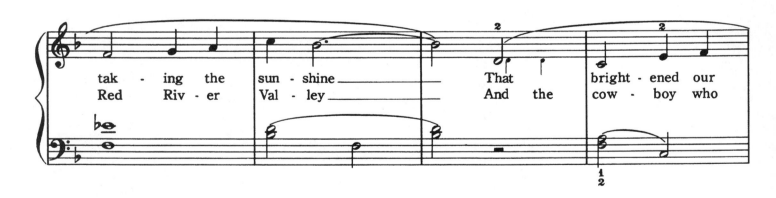

The Riddle Song

American folk song

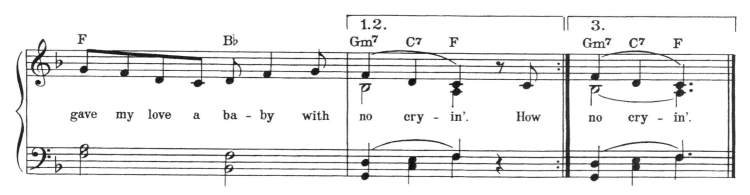

2. How can there be a cherry that has no stone?
   How can there be a chicken that has no bone?
   How can there be a ring that has no end?
   How can there be a baby with no cryin'?

3. A cherry when it's bloomin', it has no stone.
   A chicken when it's pippin', it has no bone.
   A ring when it's rollin', it has no end.
   A baby when it's sleepin' has no cryin'.

She'll Be Comin' Round the Mountain

American folk song

She'll be com-in' round the moun-tain when she comes,

She'll be com-in' round the moun-tain when she comes,

She'll be steam-in' and a - puff-in', Oh Lawd, she won't stop for

noth-in', She'll be com-in' round the moun-tain when she comes.

2. She'll be drivin' six white horses when she comes,
   She'll be drivin' six white horses when she comes,
   She'll be drivin' six white horses,
   She'll be drivin' six white horses,
   She'll be drivin' six white horses when she comes.

3. Oh, we'll all go out to meet her when she comes, *etc.*

4. We will all have chicken and dumplings when she comes, *etc.*

Shenandoah

American folk song

F
Bb
Oh Shen-an-doah, I long to hear you, Way hay, my roll-ing
p
F
Bb
F C7
riv-er! Oh, Shen-an-doah, I can't be near you, Way
Dm
Am
Bb Bdim C7
F
hay, I'm bound a way, 'Cross the wide Mis-sou-ri.

The Streets of Laredo

American folk song

1. As I ___ walked out in the streets of La - re - do, As I walked out in La - re - do one day, I spied a poor cow - boy all wrapped in white lin - en, ___ wrapped in white lin - en as cold as the clay.

2. "I see by your out - fit that you are a cow boy" These words he did say as I bold - ly walked by, "Come sit down be - side me and hear my sad sto - ry, I'm shot in the breast and I know I must die."

3. "'Twas once in the saddle I used to go dashing,
With no one as quick on the trigger as I.
I sat in a card game in back of the barroom,
Got shot in the back and today I must die."

4. "Get six of my buddies to carry my coffin,
With six pretty maidens to sing a sad song.
Take me to the valley and lay the sod o'er me,
For I'm a young cowboy who knows he's
done wrong."

5. "Oh, beat the drum slowly and play the fife lowly,
And play the dead march as they carry my pall.
Put bunches of roses all over my coffin,
The roses will deaden the clods as they fall."

6. We beat the drum slowly and played the fife lowly,
And bitterly wept as we carried him along,
For we all loved our comrade, so brave, young,
and handsome,
We all loved our comrade, although he done
wrong.

When Johnny Comes Marching Home

American folk song

When John-ny comes march-ing home a-gain, Hur - rah,_____ hur - rah!_____ We'll

give him a heart - y wel - come then, Hur-rah,_____ hur - rah!_____ The

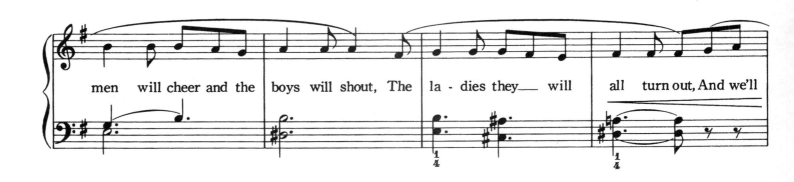

men will cheer and the boys will shout, The la-dies they_ will all turn out, And we'll

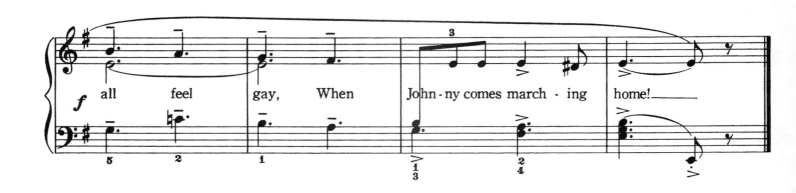

all feel gay, When John-ny comes march - ing home!_____

2. The old church bell will peal with joy,
   Hurrah! hurrah!
   To welcome home our darling boy,
   Hurrah! Hurrah!
   The village lads and lassies say,
   With roses they will strew the way,
   And we'll all feel gay
   When Johnny comes marching home.

3. Get ready for the jubilee,
   Hurrah! hurrah!
   We'll give the hero three times three,
   Hurrah! hurrah!
   The laurel wreath is ready now,
   To place upon his loyal brow,
   And we'll all feel gay
   When Johnny comes marching home.

When the Saints Come Marchin' In

African-American folk song

Chorus

2. Come and join me in my journey,
   Cause it's time that we begin
   And we'll be there for that fine day,
   When the saints go marching in.

   Chorus:
   I want to join the heav'nly band,
   I want to join the heav'nly band,
   Want to hear the trumpets a-blowing,
   When the saints go marching in.

3. So I hope each day for spirit,
   And the strength to help me win;
   Want to be in that procession,
   When the saints go marching in.

   Chorus:
   I want to wear a happy smile,
   I want to wear a happy smile,
   Want to sing and shout all over,
   When the saints go marching in.

Yankee Doodle

English-American folk song

Yan - kee Doo - dle came to town up - on a lit - tle po - ny, he

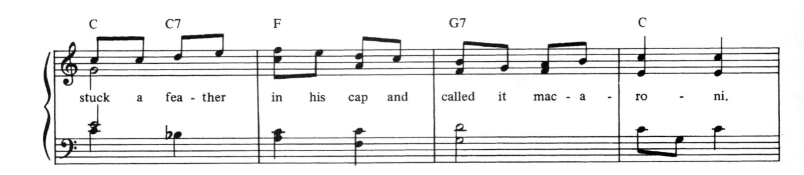

stuck a fea - ther in his cap and called it mac - a - ro - ni.

Yan - kee Doo - dle, doo - dle do, Yan - kee Doo - dle dan - dy,

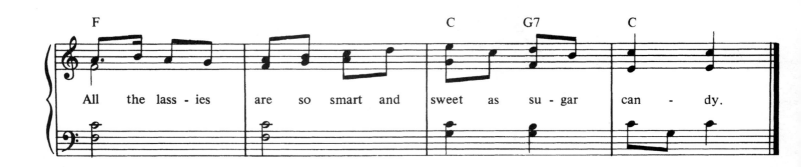

All the lass - ies are so smart and sweet as su - gar can - dy.

Songs of Many Lands

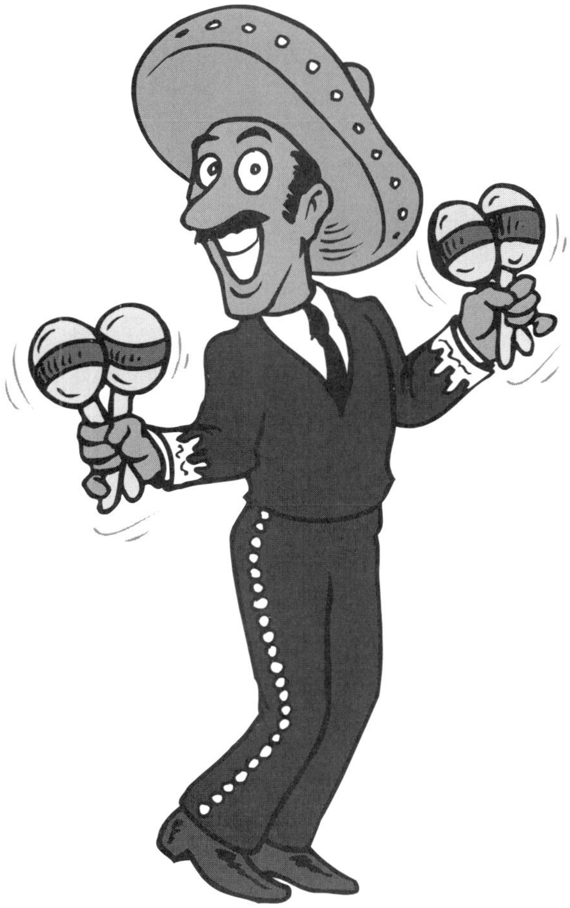

Alouette

French-Canadian folk song

A - lou-et - te, gen - tille A - lou-et - te, A - lou-et - te,

Je te plu - me-rai. Je te plu-me-rai la tête, Je te plu-me-rai la tête,

Et la tête, Et la tête, Oh! A - lou-et - te,

Et la tête, Et la tête,

gen - tille A - lou-et - te, A - lou-et - te, Je te plu - me-rai.

Au Clair de la Lune

French folk song

D A D A D A D
p f p
Good Pier - rot, I beg you, In the moon - light bright,
A D A D A D
p f
Your quill pen to lend me, for I long to write.
A E A
Burned out is my can - dle, And my fire's out too,
D A D A D A D
f p
Come, Thy door please o - pen Let me in, pray do!

Bendeemer's Stream

Irsh folk song

1. There's a bow-er of ros-es by Ben-de-meer's stream, And the
2. Time of my child-hood 'twas like a sweet dream, To

night-in-gale sings 'round it all the day long, In the
sit in the ros-es and hear the bird's song, That

bow'r and its mus-ic I'll nev-er for-get, But

oft when a-lone in the bloom of the year, I

think, "Is the night-in-gale sing - ing there yet? Are the

ros - es still bright by the calm Ben-de - meer?"

Beautiful Skies
(Ay, Ay, Ay, Ay)

Mexican song by C. Fernandez

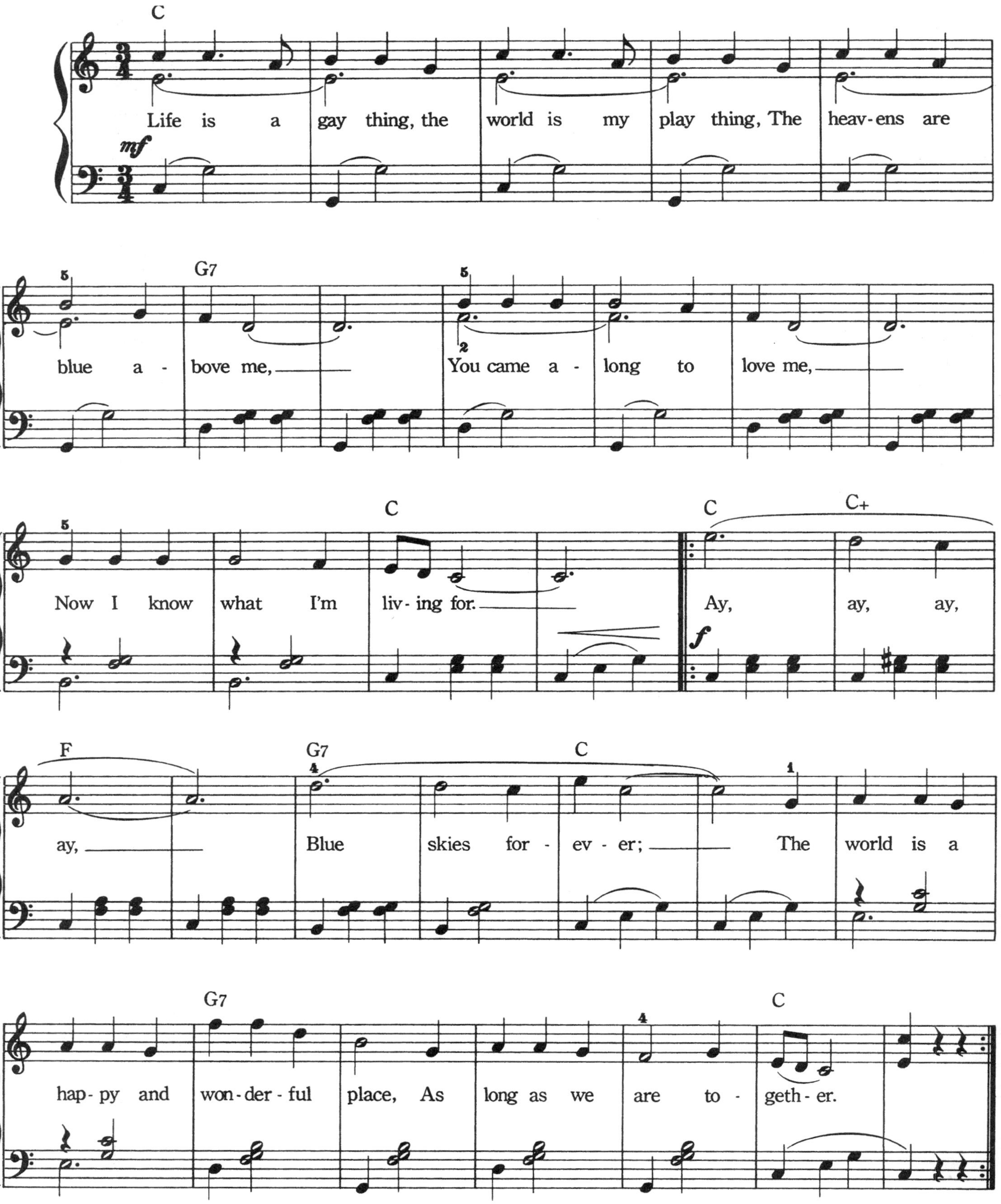

Chiapanecas

Mexican folk dance

F
Down in Mex - i - co There's a dance they know 'Round a som-bre - ro
So come join the throng, While we dance a - long, And we sing the song
mf
C7
Chia-pan - e - cas, They will form a ring While they dance and sing
Chia-pan - e - cas, We will form a ring, While we dance and sing
F
— Does - n't mean a thing, Chia - pan - e - cas.
— Let your voi - ces ring, Chia - pan - e - cas.
Chorus
C7
(Clap hands)
Sing Chia - pan - e - cas, Ay, Ay, Ay, Ay, Sing Chia - pan -
F
(Clap hands)
e - cas, Ay, Ay, Ay, Ay, Sing Chia - pan - e - cas. Ay,
C7
(Clap hands)
F
(Clap hands)
Ay, Ay, Ay, Sing Chia - pan - e - cas, Ay, Ay, Ay, Ay!

The Cuckoo

English folk song

Bb C Dm Gm
mp
3
Dm C
1. O the cuc - koo she's a pret - ty bird, she
F Gm Dm Bb Am
sing - eth as she flies. She bring - eth good
C F Gm Dm
tid - ings, she tell - eth no lies. She

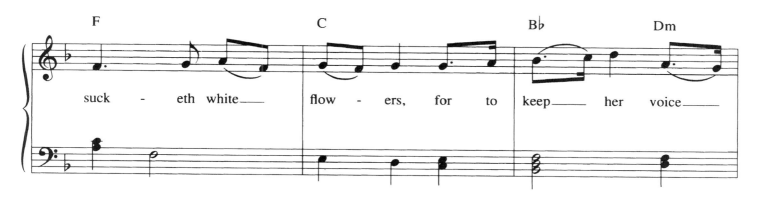

suck - eth white____ flow - ers, for to keep____ her voice____

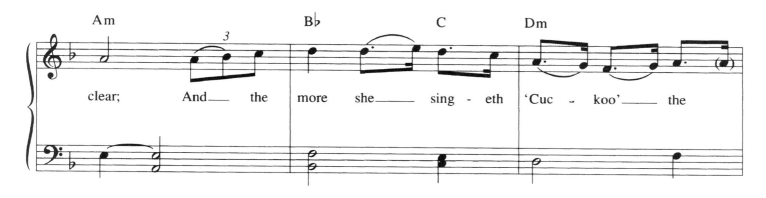

clear; And____ the more she____ sing - eth 'Cuc - koo'____ the

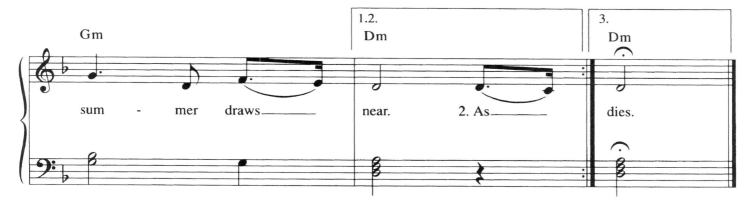

sum - mer draws____ near. 2. As____ dies.

2. As I was a-walking and a-talking one day,
   I heard a poor cuckoo a-singing away,
   She sucketh white flowers for to keep her voice clear;
   And the more she sings 'Cuckoo' the summer draws near.

3. I wish I were a scholar and could handle the pen,
   I would write to all women and all roving men.
   I would bring them glad tidings and tell them no lies,
   I would wish them have pity on the flower when it dies.

Danny Boy

Irish folk song

C7 F Am Dm G7 C7
mf
1. Oh, Dan - ny
mp
F C7 F B♭ C7 F C9 F Dm
Boy, the pipes, the pipes are call - ing, From glen to glen and down the moun-tain
Gm7 C F F7 B♭ Gm
side, The sum-mer's gone and all the ros - es fall - ing, It's you it's
F B♭ C7
you must go and I must bide. But come ye back when sum-mer's in the
mf

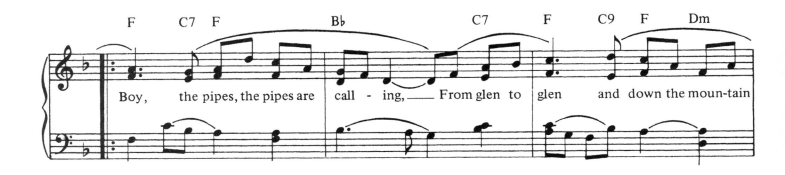

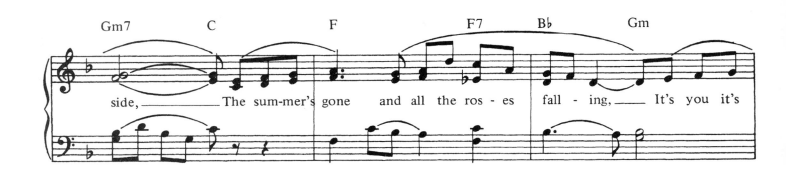

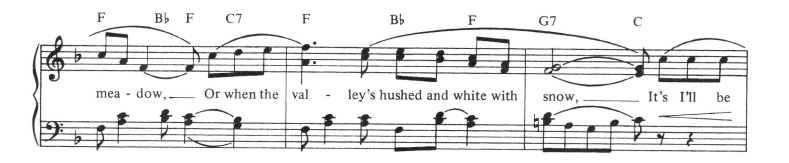

2. But when you come when all the flowers are dying,
And I am gone, as gone I well may be,
You'll come and find the place where I am lying,
And kneel and say a prayer there for me.
And I shall hear, though soft you tread above me,
And all my dreams will warm and sweeter be.
If you will only tell me that you love me,
Then I will sleep in peace until you come to me.

The Derby Ram

English folk song

C G Am C F Gsus4 G C
f
1. As
C Dm C F Em
I was going to Der - by, Sir, 'twas on a sum - mer's
Dm G C G Am C F C
day. I met the fin - est ram, Sir, that ev - er was fed on
G Chorus C F C
hay; And in - deed, Sir, 'tis true, Sir, I

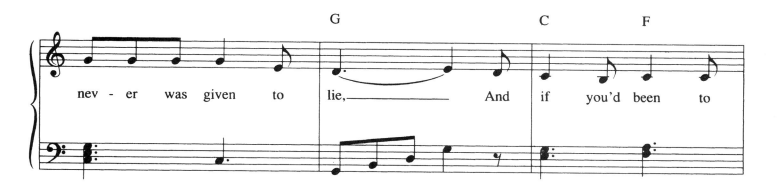

2. It had four feet to walk on, Sir,
It had four feet to stand,
And every foot it had, Sir,
Did cover an acre of land.

3. The ram was fat behind, Sir,
The ram was fat before.
He measured ten yards round, Sir,
I think it was no more.

4. The horns upon his head, Sir,
Were high as a man could reach.
And there they built a pulpit, Sir,
The sages for to teach.

5. The wool upon his belly, Sir,
It reached down to the ground.
It was sold in Derby, Sir,
For forty thousand pounds.

6. The tail was fifty yards, Sir,
As near as I could tell,
And it was sent to Rome, Sir,
To ring Saint Peter's bell.

7. The mutton that the ram made, Sir,
Gave the whole army meat,
And what was left, I'm told, Sir,
Was served out to the fleet.

The Kerry Dance

Irish folk dance

O the days of the Ker-ry danc-ing, O the ring of the

pi-per's tune! O for one of those hours of glad-ness, Gone a-las like our youth, too soon.

Fine

When the boys be-gan to gath-er in the glen, of a sum-mer night,

And the Ker-ry pi-per's tun-ing made us long— with wild de-light;

O to think of it, O to dream of it, Fills my heart with tears!

D.S. al Fine

Loch Lomond

Scottish folk song

By yon bonnie banks and by yon bonnie braes, Where the sun shines bright on Loch
Lomond, Where me and my true love were ever wont to be, On the
bonnie, bonnie banks of Loch Lomond. Oh, you'll take the high road And
I'll take the low road, And I'll be in Scotland before you; But
me and my true love will never meet again, On the bonnie, bonnie banks of Loch Lomond.
p
mf

O Mein Lieber, Augustine

German folk song

O mein lie-ber Au-gus-tin, Au-gus-tin, Au-gus-tin, O mein lie-ber Au-gus-tin al-les ist weg:

Bock ist weg stock ist weg Auch ich bin in dem dreck O mein lie-ber Au-gus-tin, al-lest is weg.

Santa Lucia

Italian folk song

Calm o'er the o-cean blue Moon - light is shin - ing
While from the blue ex-panse Fair stars are gleam - ing

And with it's sil - ver light Stray cloud is lin - ing;
O - ver the night be-neath, In sweet - ness beam - ing.

Come pret - ty mai - den, Look from thy lat - tice, love,
As o'er the stream we glide, Borne by the rol - ling tide,

List to the boat - men chant - ing and row - ing.
San - ta Lu - ci - a, San - ta Lu - ci - a.

Skye Boat Song

Scottish folk song

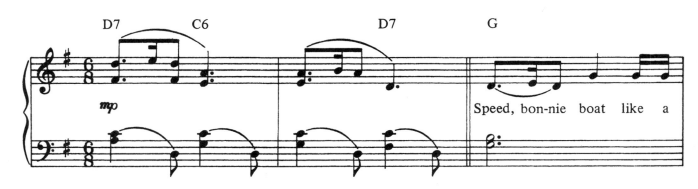

Speed, bon-nie boat like a

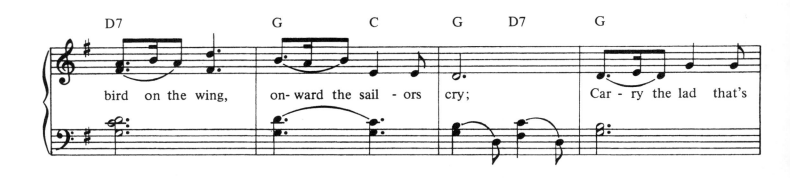

bird on the wing, on-ward the sail -ors cry; Car - ry the lad that's

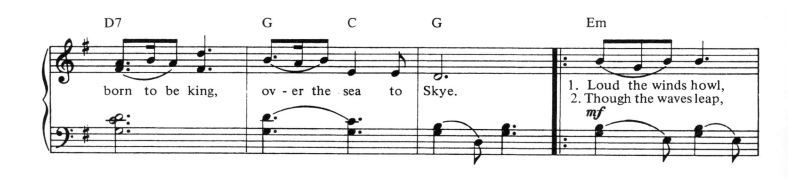

born to be king, ov - er the sea to Skye.
1. Loud the winds howl,
2. Though the waves leap,

loud the waves roar, Thun - der - claps rend the air.
soft shall ye sleep, O - cean's a roy - al bed.

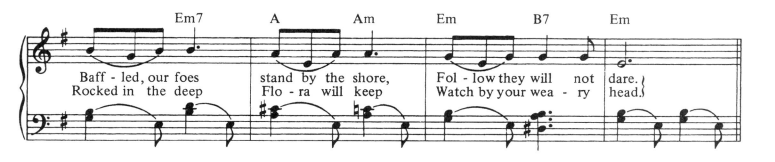

Baff - led, our foes stand by the shore, Fol - low they will not dare.
Rocked in the deep Flo - ra will keep Watch by your wea - ry head.

Chorus

Speed, bon - nie boat like a bird on the wing, On - ward the sail - ors

cry; Car - ry the lad that's born to be king,

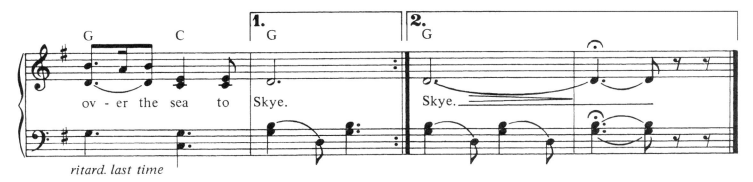

ov - er the sea to Skye. | **1.** Skye. | **2.** Skye.

ritard. last time

Song of the Volga Boatman

Russian folk song

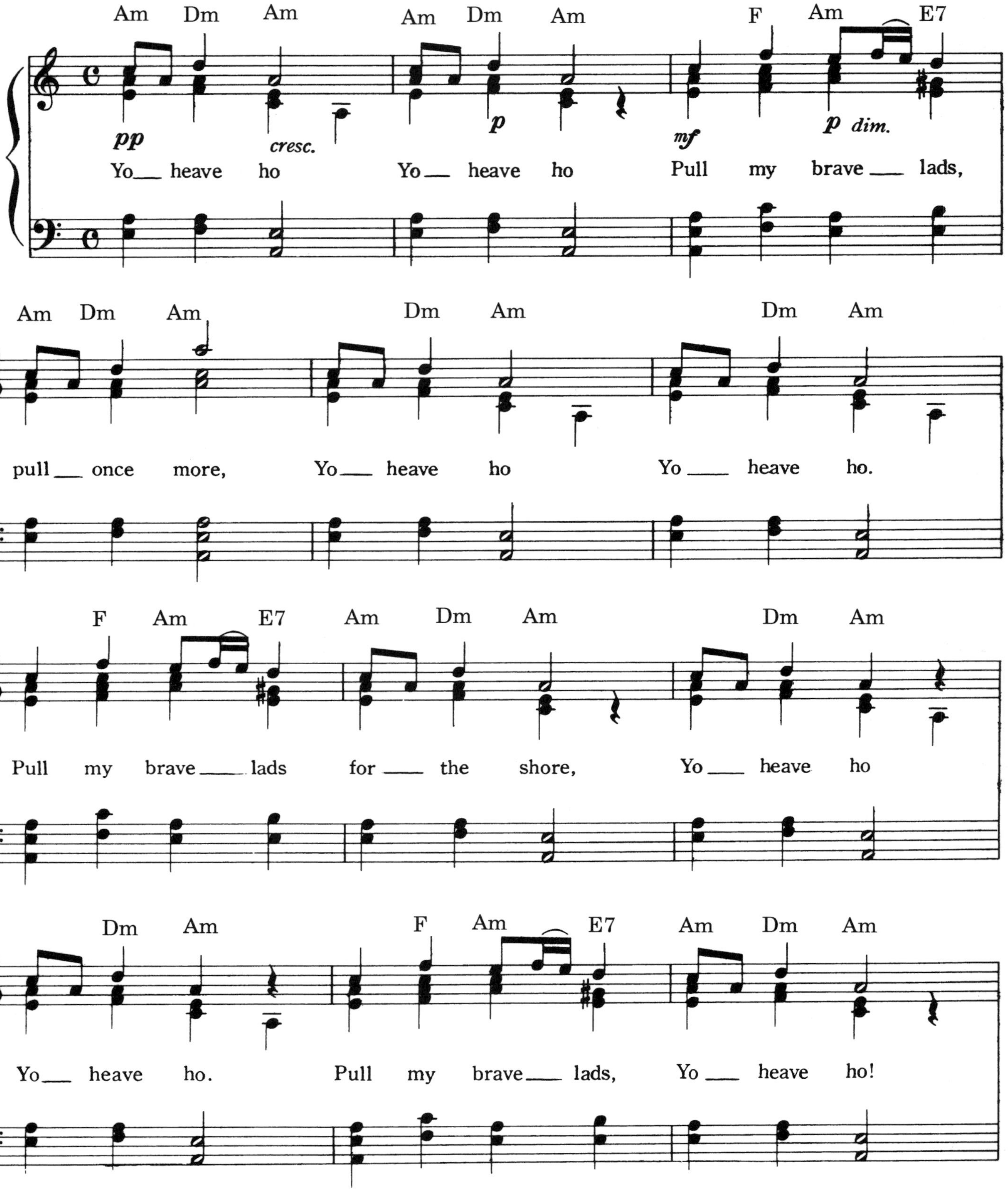
Am Dm Am Am Dm Am F Am E7
pp cresc. p mf p dim.
Yo heave ho Yo heave ho Pull my brave lads,
Am Dm Am Dm Am Dm Am
pull once more, Yo heave ho Yo heave ho.
F Am E7 Am Dm Am Dm Am
Pull my brave lads for the shore, Yo heave ho
Dm Am F Am E7 Am Dm Am
Yo heave ho. Pull my brave lads, Yo heave ho!

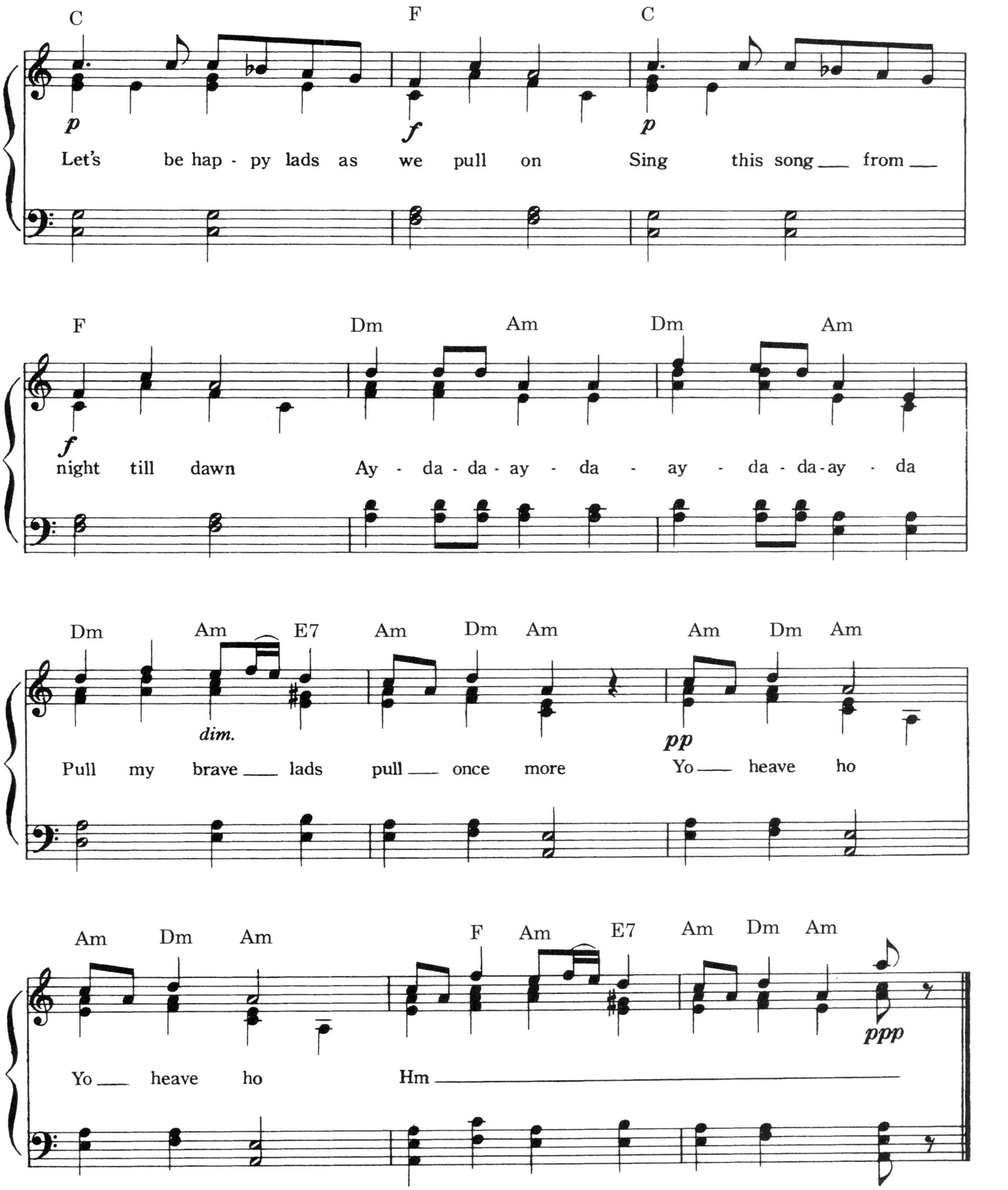
C F C
p f p
Let's be hap - py lads as we pull on Sing this song from
F Dm Am Dm Am
f
night till dawn Ay - da - da - ay - da - ay - da - da - ay - da
Dm Am E7 Am Dm Am Am Dm Am
dim. pp
Pull my brave lads pull once more Yo heave ho
Am Dm Am F Am E7 Am Dm Am
ppp
Yo heave ho Hm

Tum-Balalayka

Yiddish folk song

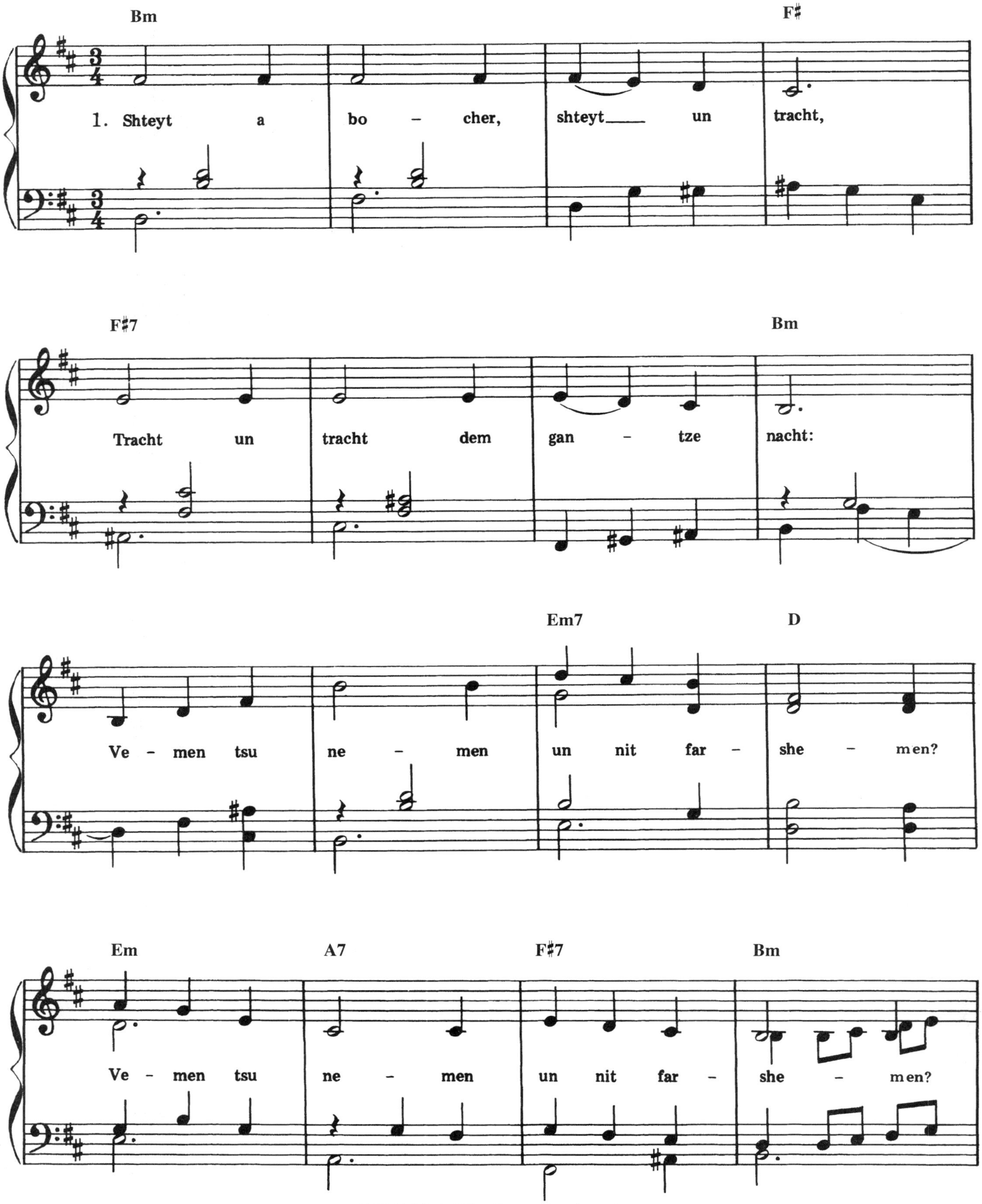
Bm
F♯
1. Shteyt a bo - cher, shteyt un tracht,
F♯7
Bm
Tracht un tracht dem gan - tze nacht:
Em7
D
Ve - men tsu ne - men un nit far - she - men?
Em
A7
F♯7
Bm
Ve - men tsu ne - men un nit far - she - men?

Chorus

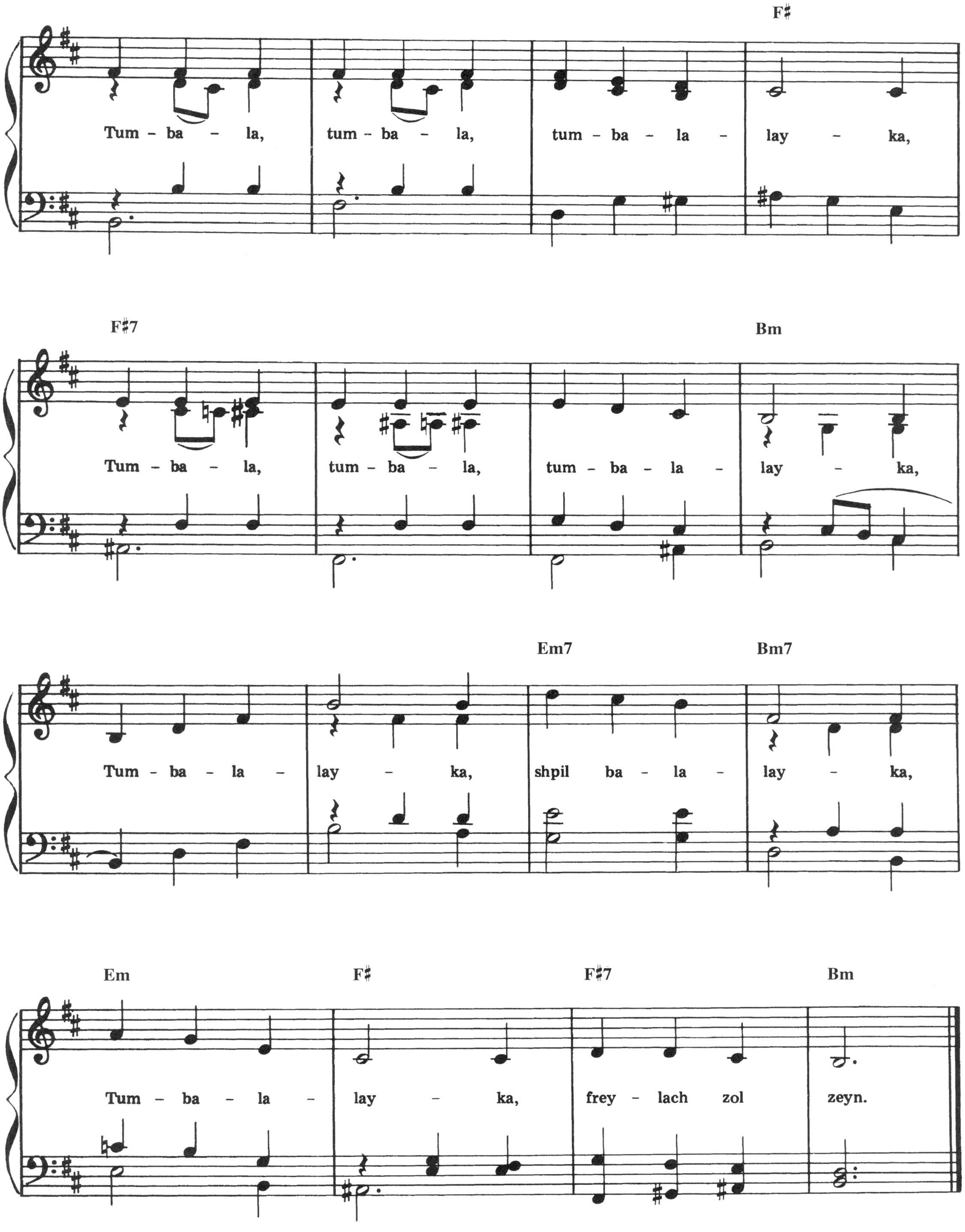
F♯
Tum – ba – la, tum – ba – la, tum – ba – la – lay – ka,
F♯7
Bm
Tum – ba – la, tum – ba – la, tum – ba – la – lay – ka,
Em7
Bm7
Tum – ba – la – lay – ka, shpil ba – la – lay – ka,
Em
F♯
F♯7
Bm
Tum – ba – la – lay – ka, frey – lach zol zeyn.

Extra Verses

2. Meydl, meydl, ch'vel bay dir fregn:
   Vos kon vaksn, vaksn on regn?
   Vos kon brenen un nit oyfhern?
   Vos kon benken, veynen on trern?

3. Narisher bocher, vos darfstu fregn?
   A shteyn kon vaksn, vaksn on regn.
   Libe kon brenen, un nit oyfhern.
   A harts kon benken, veynen on trern.

English Lyrics

1. A lad stood thinking all the night through,
   Thinking, thinking, what to do?
   Whose heart to take? Whose heart not to break?
   Whose heart to take? Whose heart not to break?

   Tum-bala, tum-bala, tum-balalayka
   Tum-bala, tum-bala, tum-balalayka
   Tum-balalayka, strum balalayka.
   Tum-balalayka, may we find joy.

2. Maiden, maiden, tell me true,
   What can grow, grow without dew?
   What can burn for years and years?
   What can cry and shed no tears?

3. Listen lad, here's the answer true:
   A stone can grow, grow without dew.
   Love can burn for years and years.
   A heart can cry and shed no tears.

Rounds

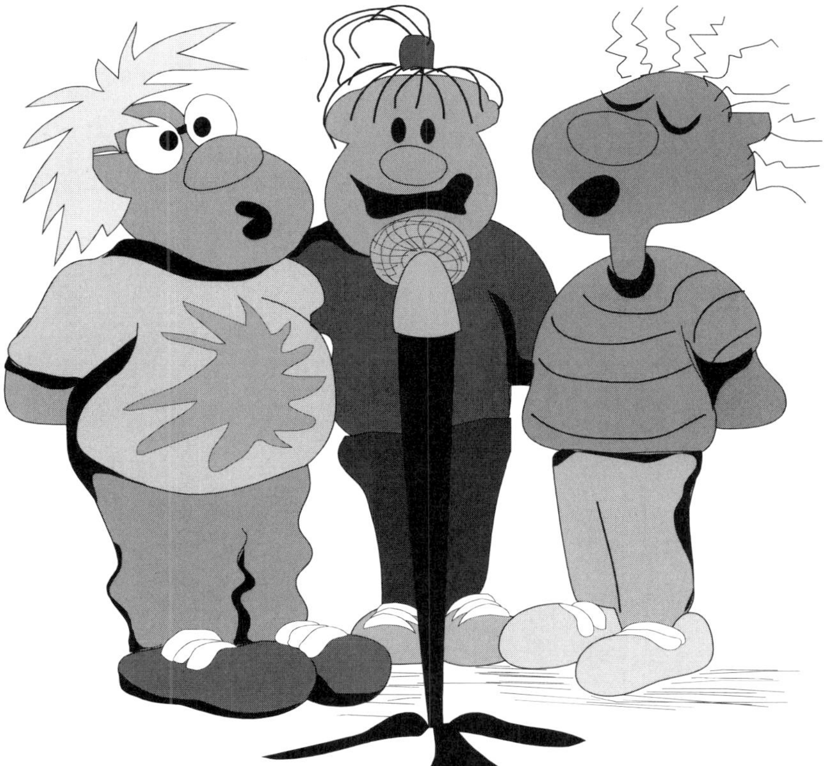

Three-Part Rounds

All in a Fairy Ring

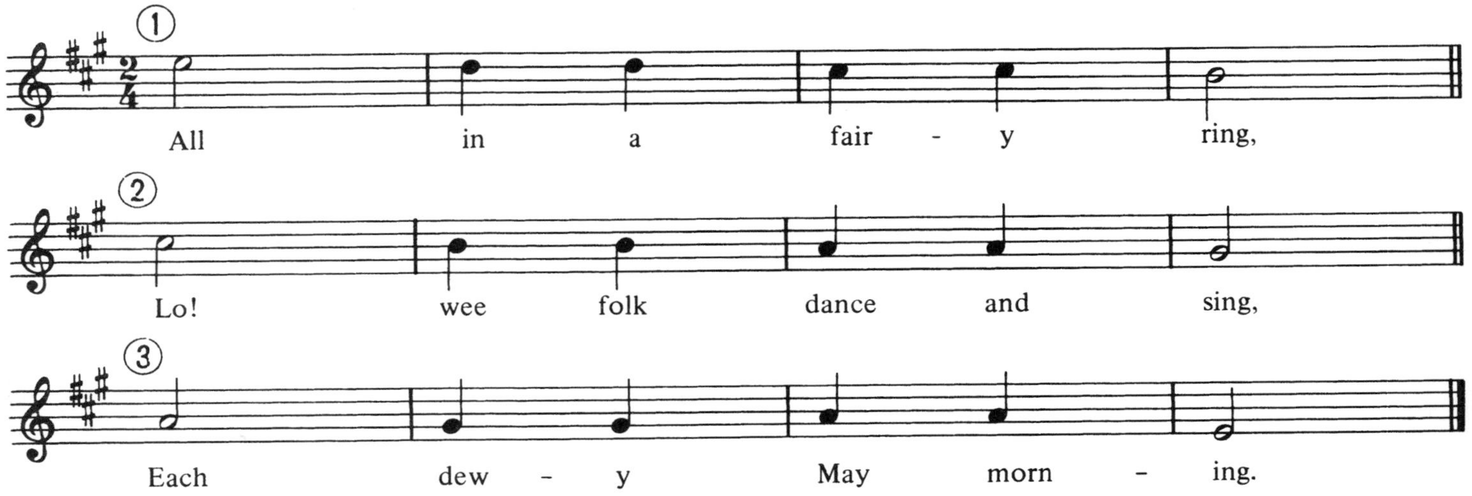

All Work and No Play

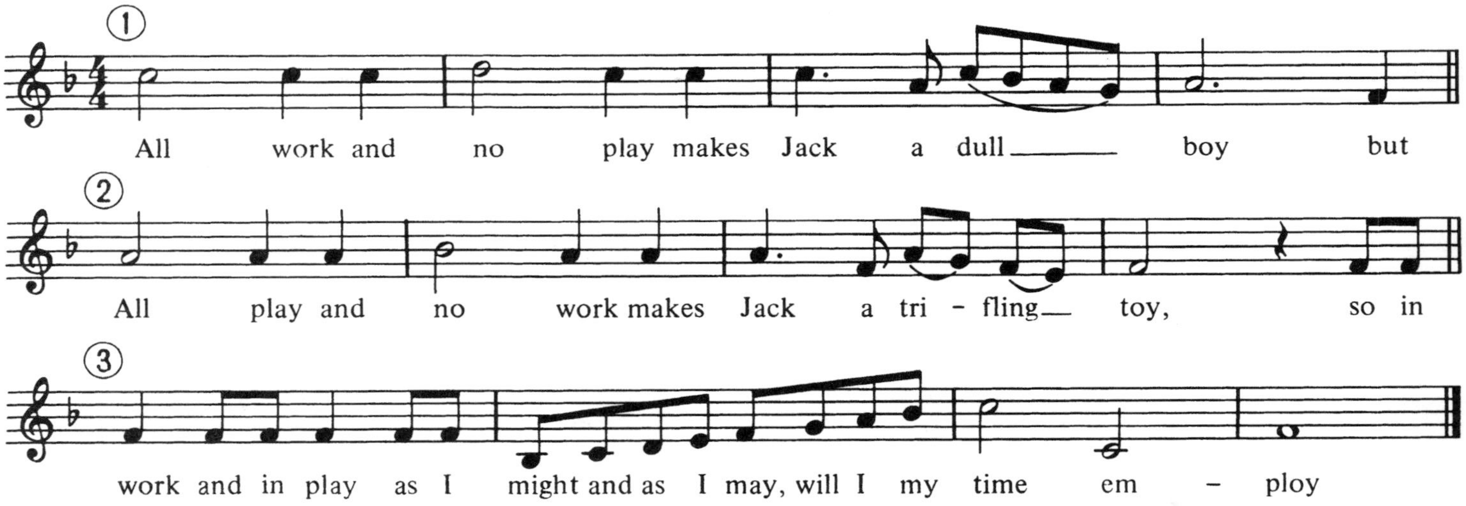

At Summer Morn

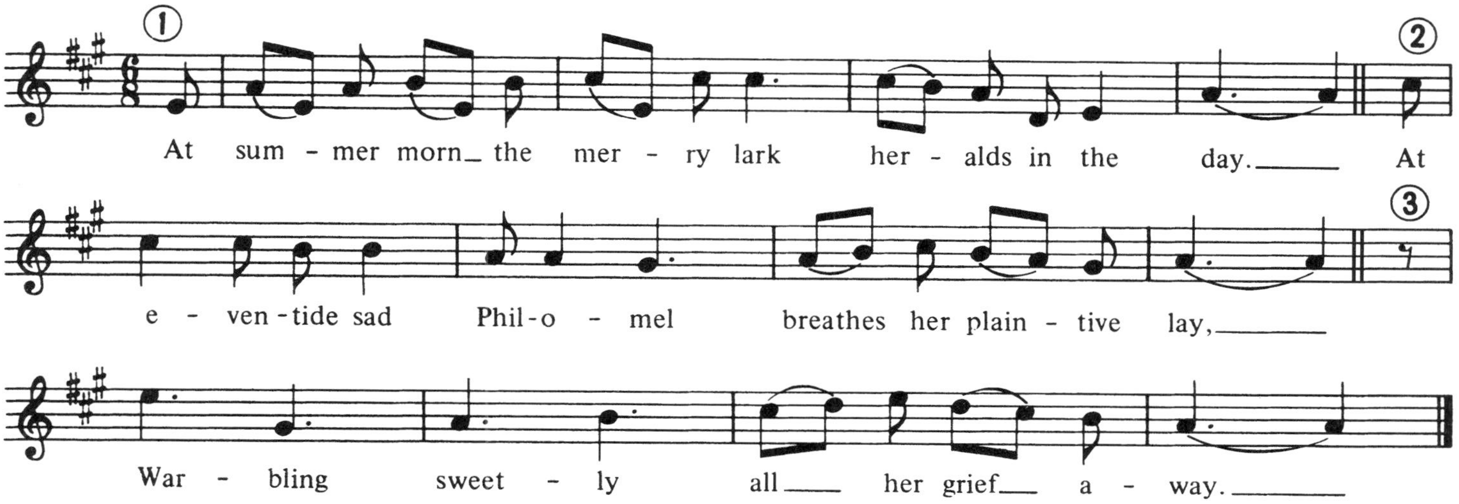

①
At sum - mer morn_ the mer - ry lark her - alds in the day._____
②
At e - ven - tide sad Phil - o - mel breathes her plain - tive lay,_____
③
War - bling sweet - ly all___ her grief___ a - way._____

Beauty's but an Idle Boast

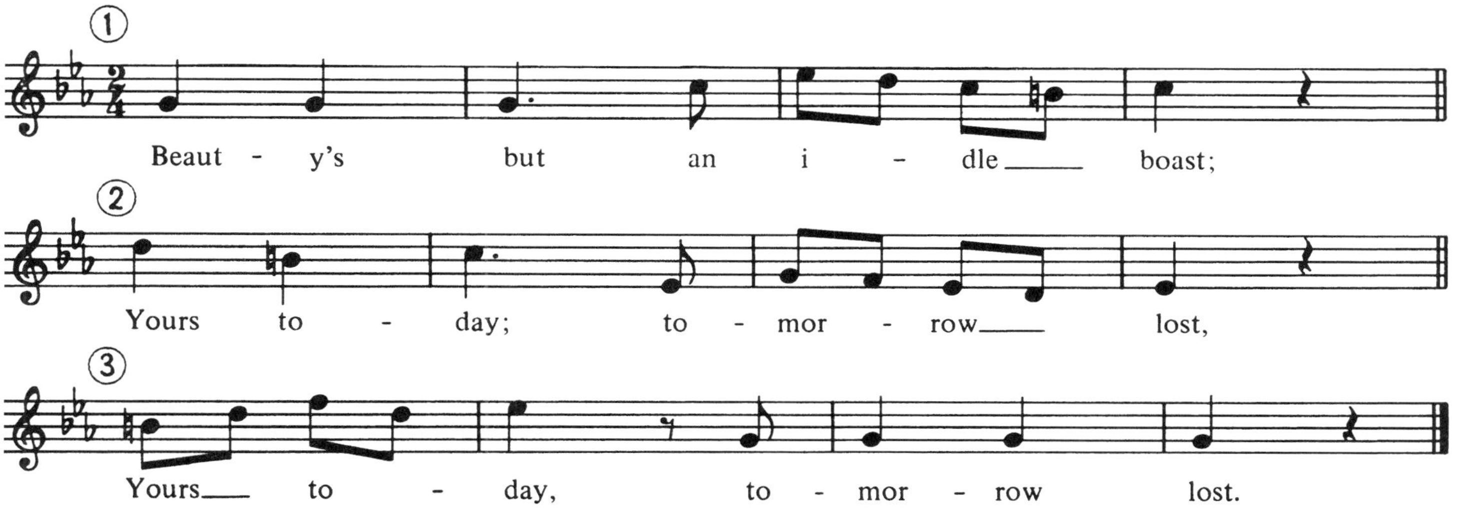

①
Beaut - y's but an i - dle_____ boast;
②
Yours to - day; to - mor - row_____ lost,
③
Yours___ to - day, to - mor - row lost.

The Bell Doth Toll

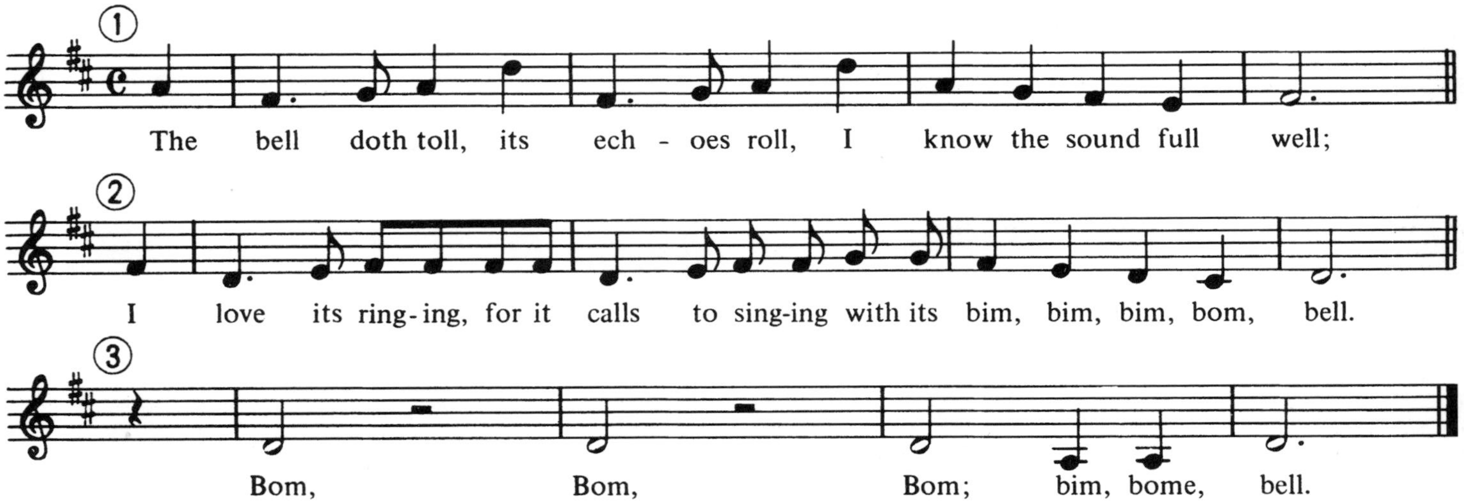
1
The bell doth toll, its ech - oes roll, I know the sound full well;
2
I love its ring-ing, for it calls to sing-ing with its bim, bim, bim, bom, bell.
3
Bom, Bom, Bom; bim, bome, bell.

A Boat, A Boat

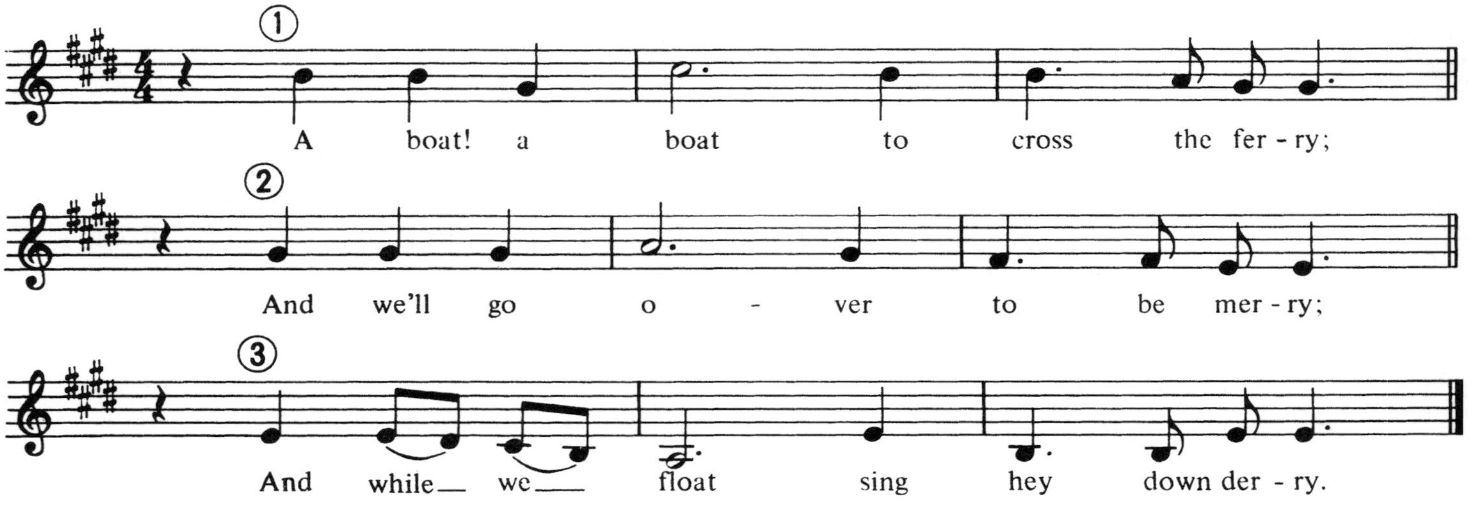
1
A boat! a boat to cross the fer - ry;
2
And we'll go o - ver to be mer - ry;
3
And while— we— float sing hey down der - ry.

Bow Wow Wow

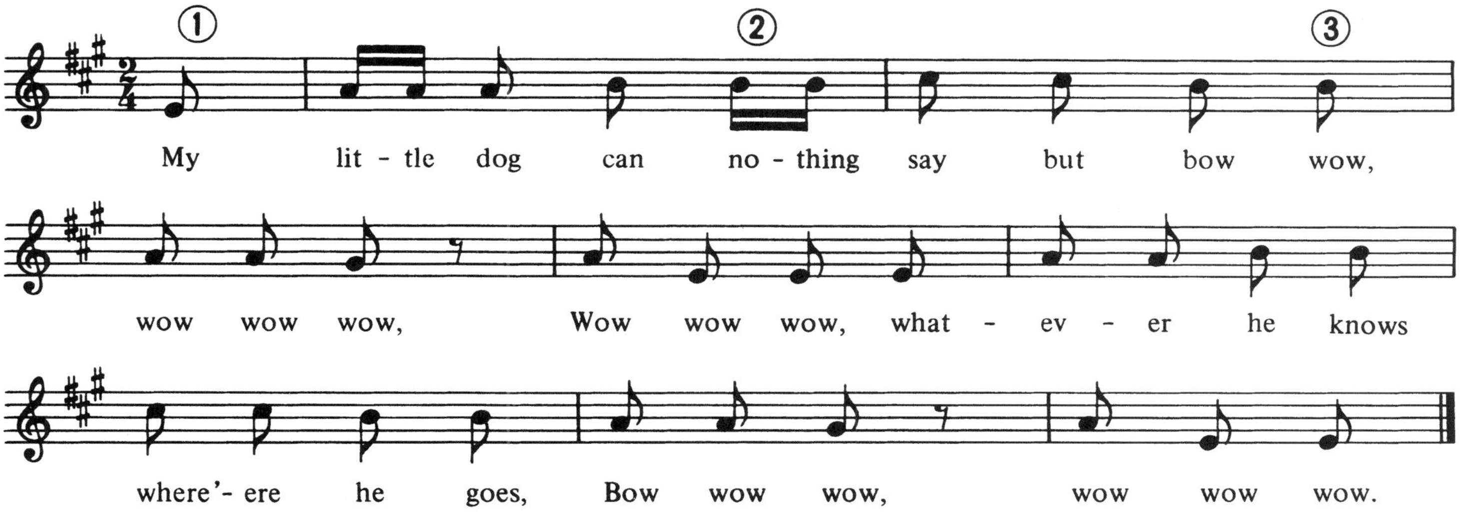
My lit - tle dog can no - thing say but bow wow,
wow wow wow, Wow wow wow, what - ev - er he knows
where'- ere he goes, Bow wow wow, wow wow wow.

Bring in the Tea Tray

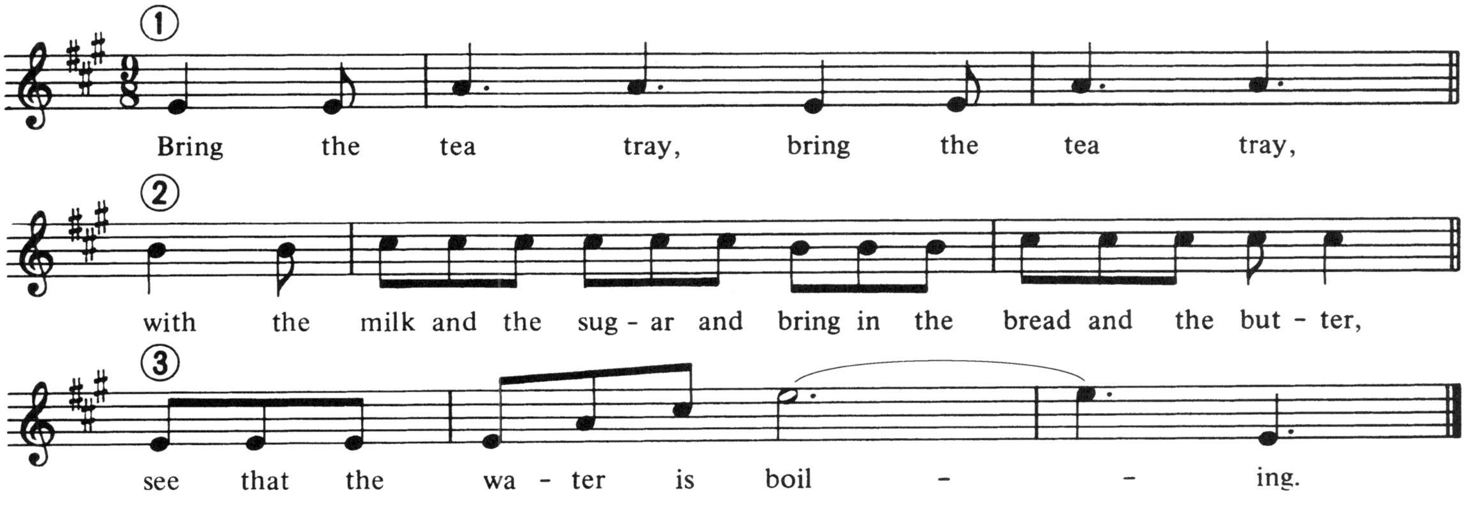
Bring the tea tray, bring the tea tray,
with the milk and the sug - ar and bring in the bread and the but - ter,
see that the wa - ter is boil - - ing.

Birds Are Singing

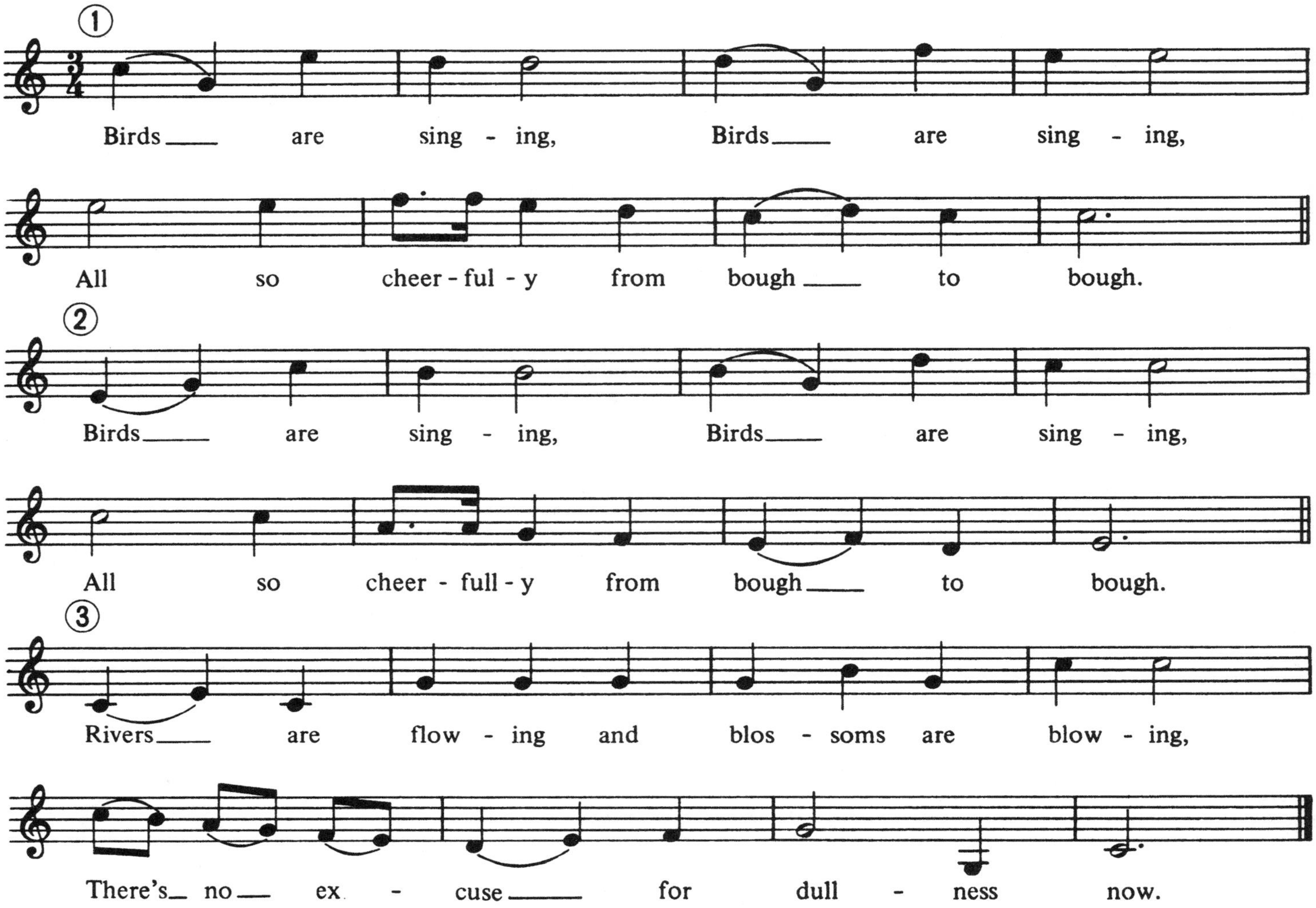

Birds ____ are sing - ing, Birds ____ are sing - ing,

All so cheer - ful - y from bough ____ to bough.

Birds ____ are sing - ing, Birds ____ are sing - ing,

All so cheer - full - y from bough ____ to bough.

Rivers ____ are flow - ing and blos - soms are blow - ing,

There's ____ no ____ ex - cuse ____ for dull - ness now.

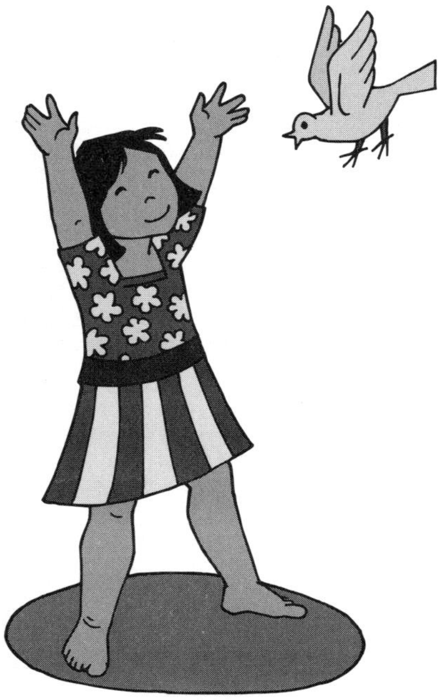

Call John

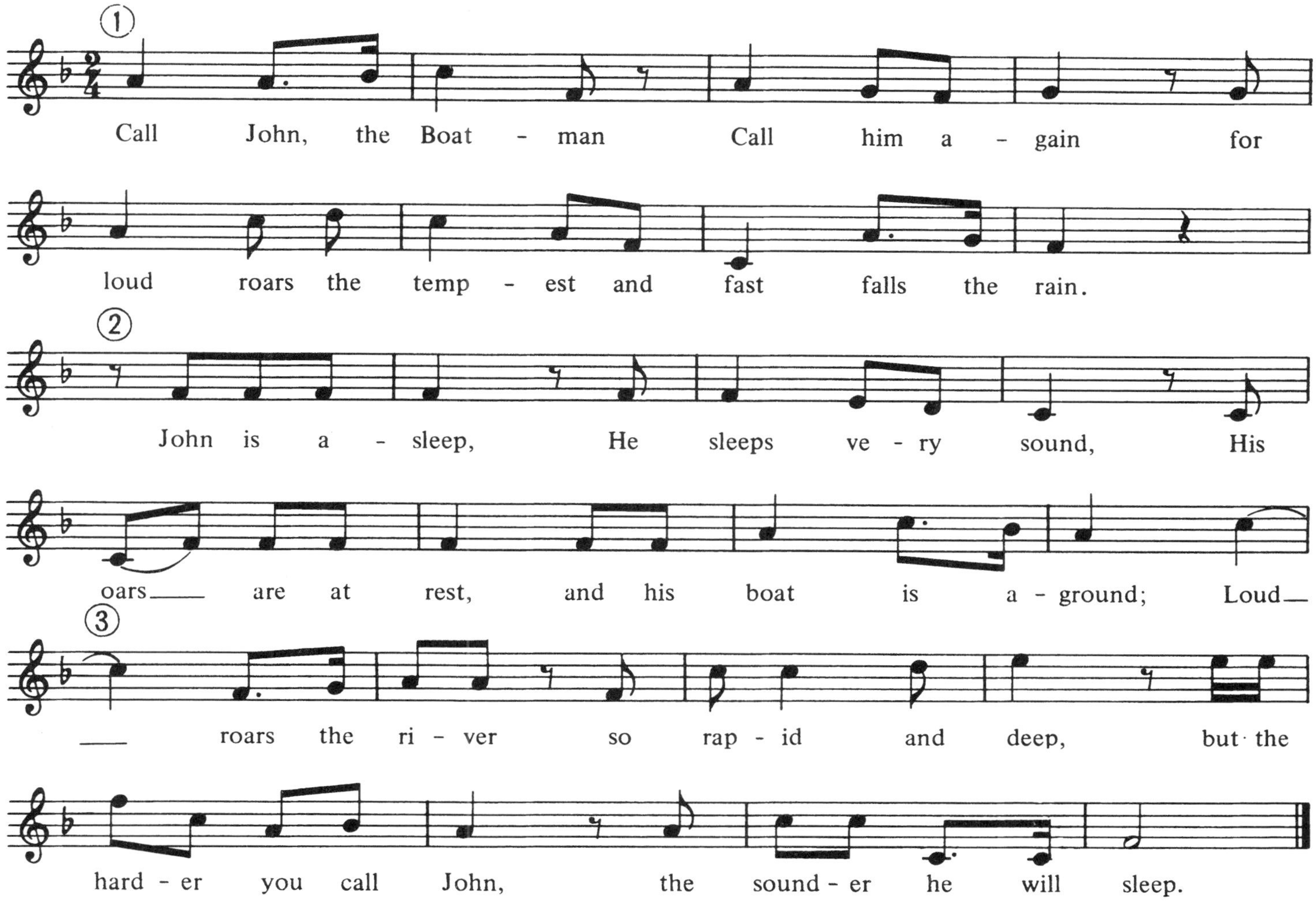

Call John, the Boat - man Call him a - gain for
loud roars the temp - est and fast falls the rain.
John is a - sleep, He sleeps ve - ry sound, His
oars___ are at rest, and his boat is a - ground; Loud__
__ roars the ri - ver so rap - id and deep, but the
hard - er you call John, the sound - er he will sleep.

Come Away

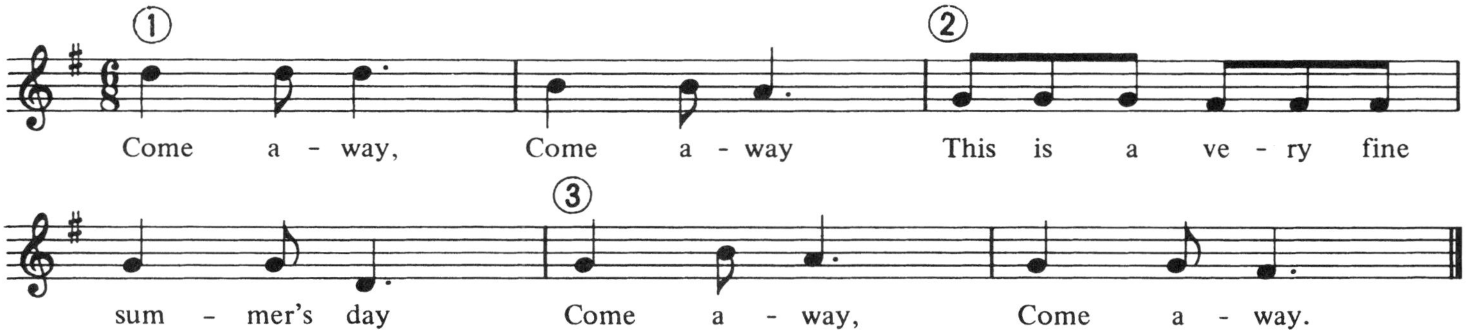

Come a - way, Come a - way This is a ve - ry fine
sum - mer's day Come a - way, Come a - way.

Buy My Dainty Fine Beans

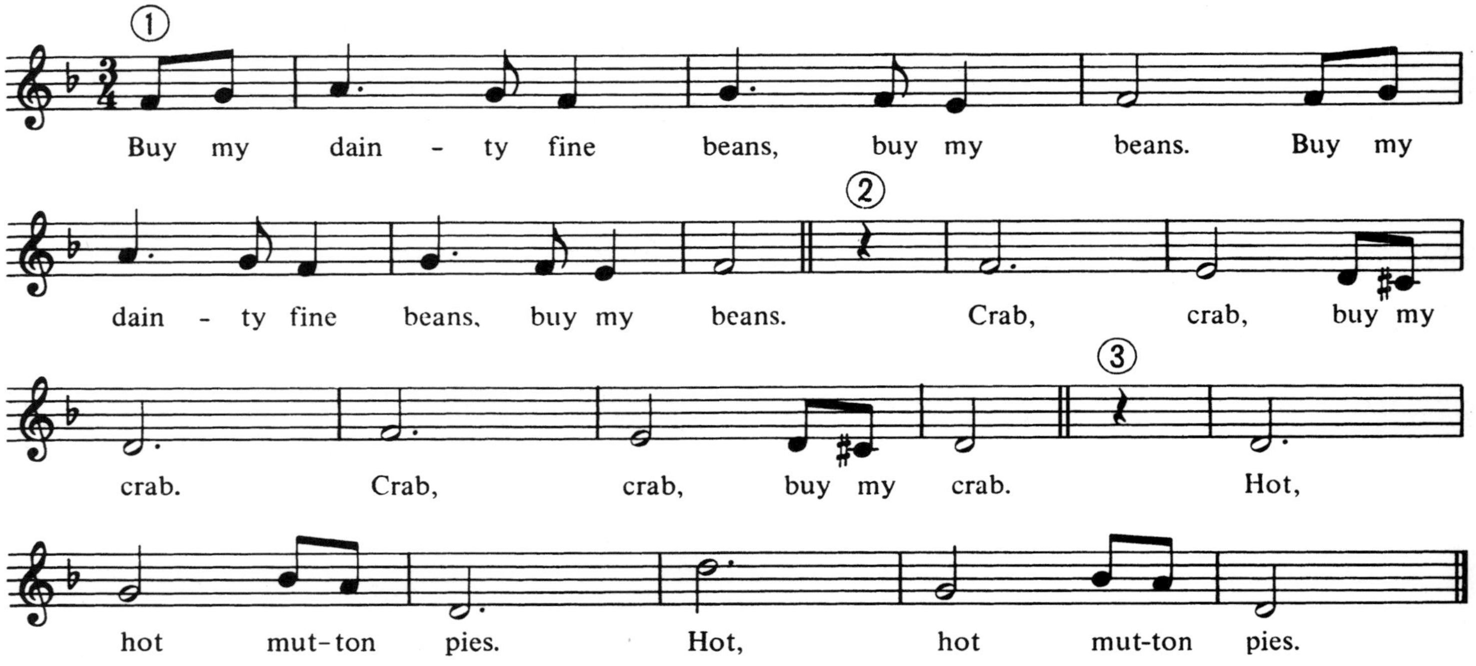

Buy my dain - ty fine beans, buy my beans. Buy my

dain - ty fine beans, buy my beans. Crab, crab, buy my

crab. Crab, crab, buy my crab. Hot,

hot mut-ton pies. Hot, hot mut-ton pies.

Come, Count the Time for Me

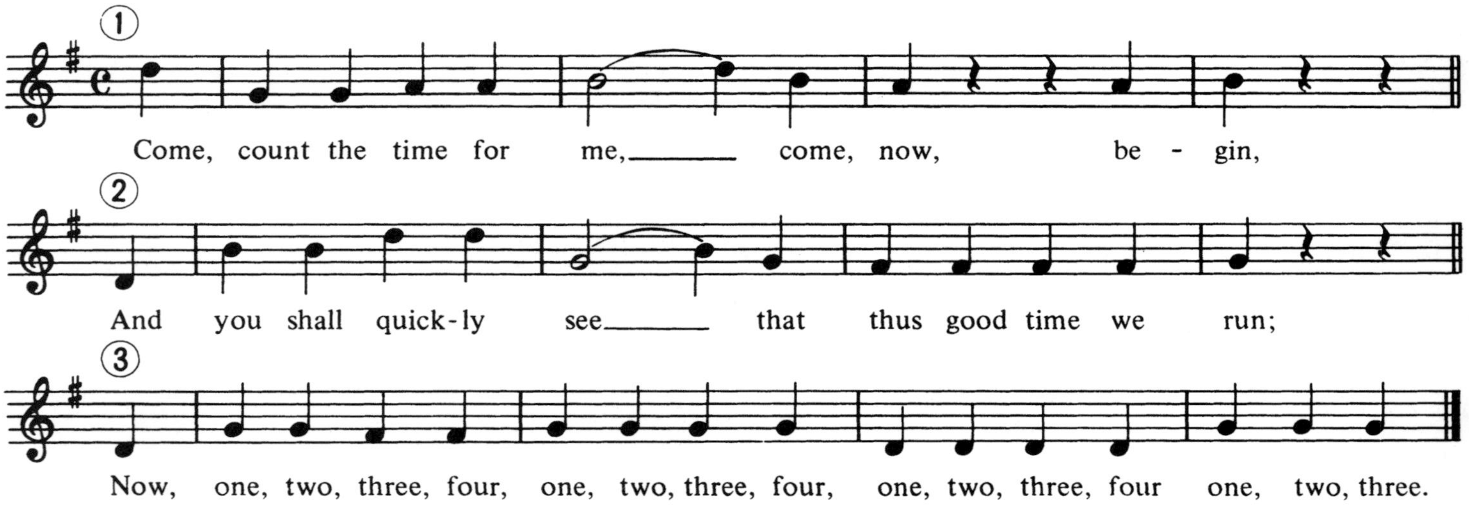

Come, count the time for me,_____ come, now, be - gin,

And you shall quick-ly see_____ that thus good time we run;

Now, one, two, three, four, one, two, three, four, one, two, three, four one, two, three.

Come Follow

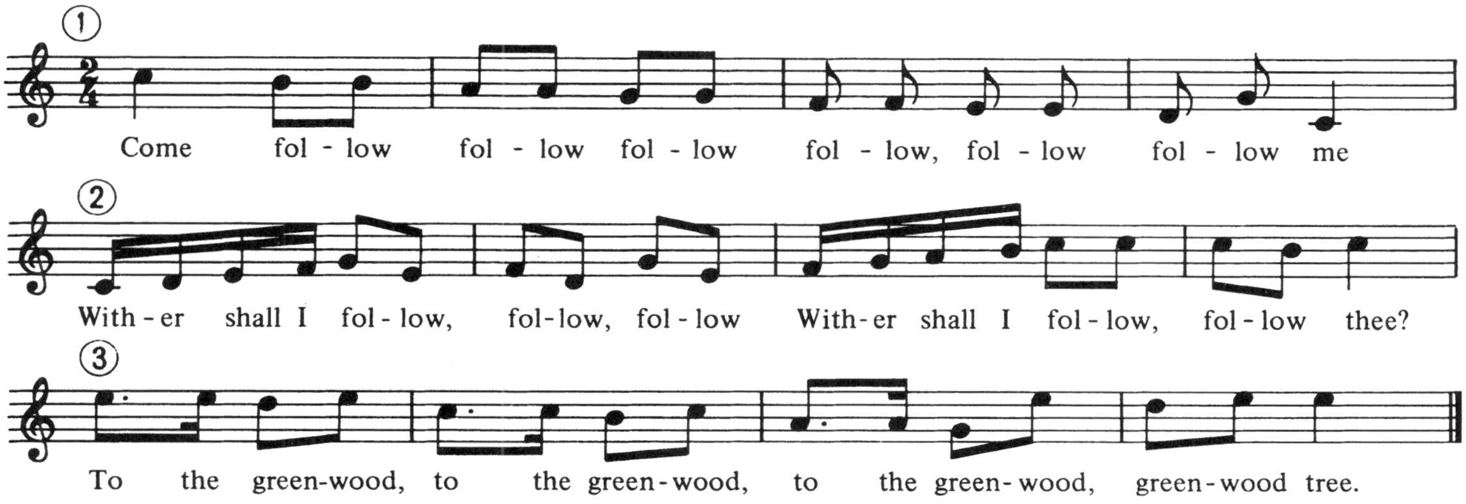
1
Come fol - low fol - low fol - low fol - low, fol - low fol - low me
2
With - er shall I fol - low, fol - low, fol - low With - er shall I fol - low, fol - low thee?
3
To the green-wood, to the green - wood, to the green - wood, green - wood tree.

Come and Sing a Merry Song

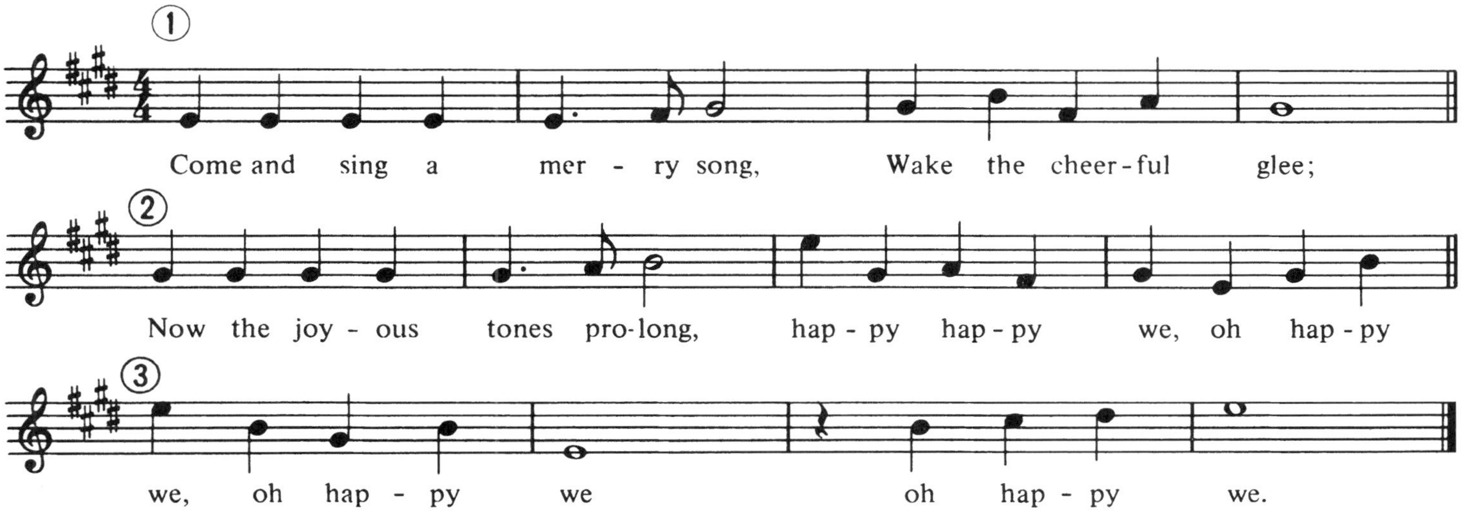
1
Come and sing a mer - ry song, Wake the cheer - ful glee;
2
Now the joy - ous tones pro - long, hap - py hap - py we, oh hap - py
3
we, oh hap - py we oh hap - py we.

Dona Nobis Pacem

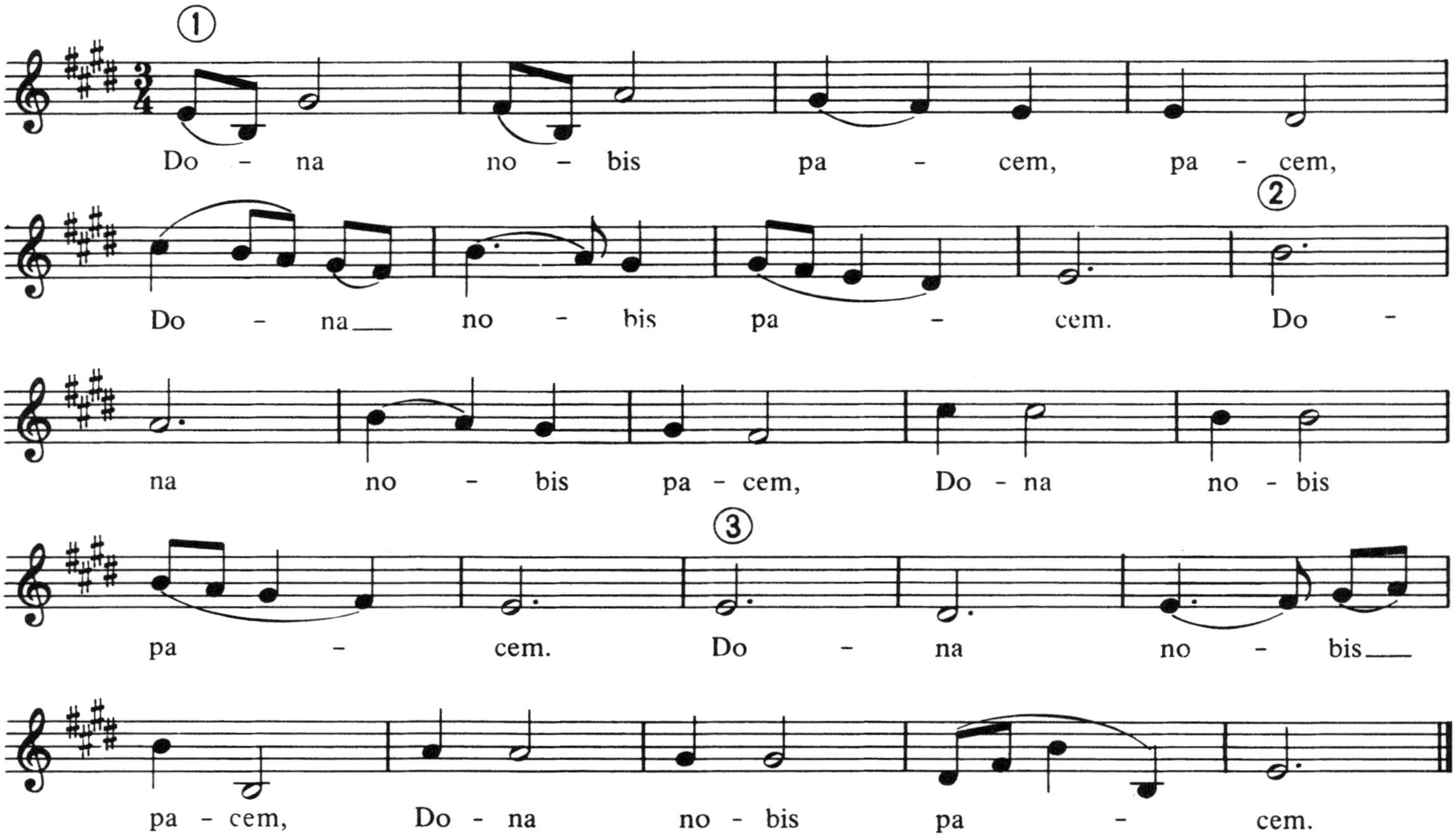
①
Do - na no - bis pa - cem, pa - cem,
Do - na no - bis pa - cem.
②
Do - na no - bis pa - cem, Do - na no - bis
pa - cem.
③
Do - na no - bis
pa - cem, Do - na no - bis pa - cem.

Great Tom Is Cast

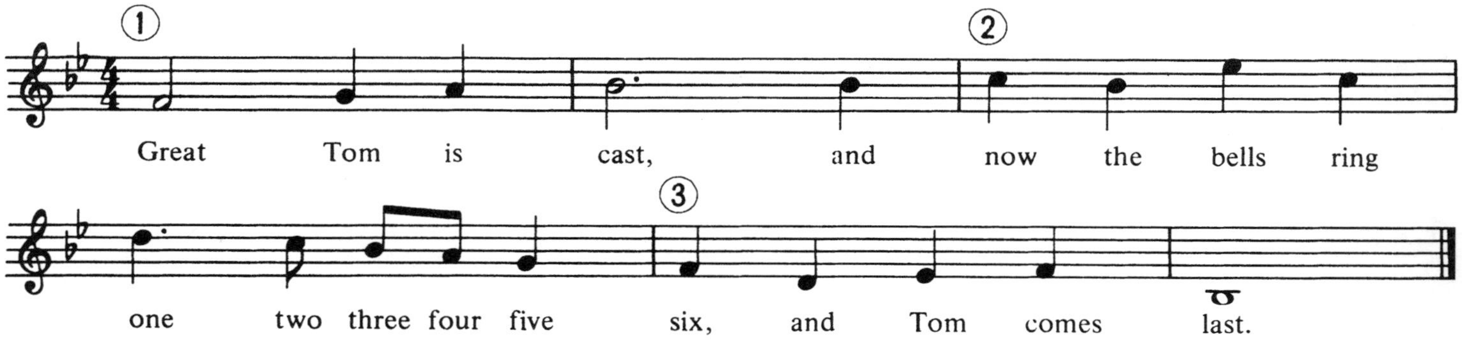
①
Great Tom is cast, and
②
now the bells ring
one two three four five
③
six, and Tom comes last.

Glide Along

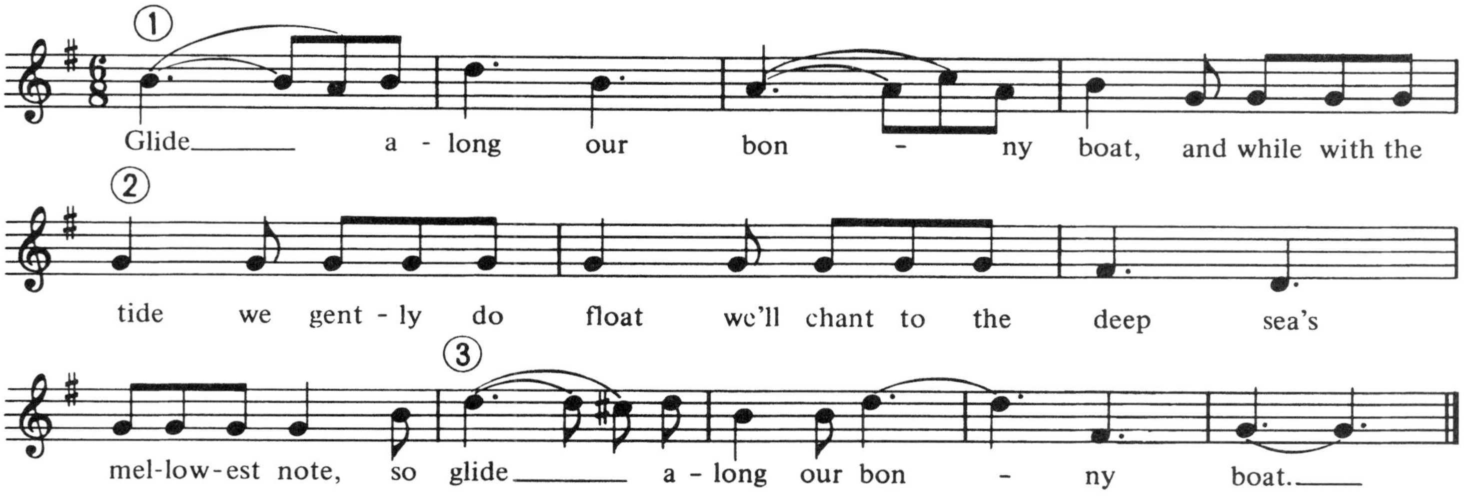

Glide____ a - long our bon - ny boat, and while with the
tide we gent - ly do float we'll chant to the deep sea's
mel-low-est note, so glide____ a - long our bon - ny boat.____

Grasshoppers Three

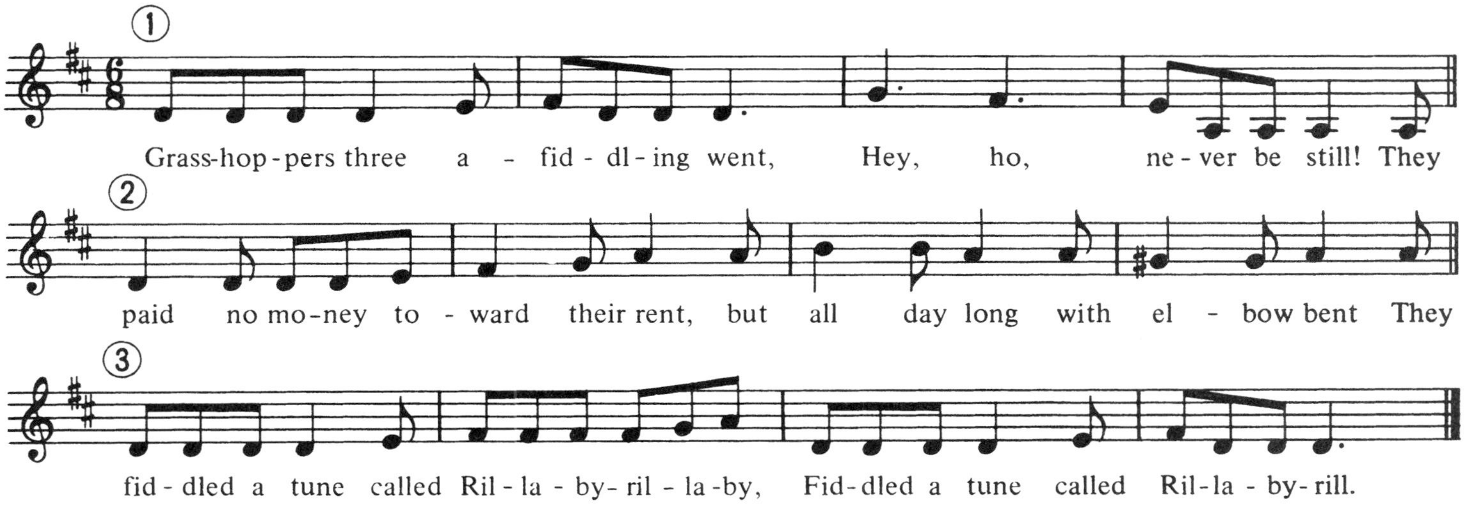

Grass-hop-pers three a - fid-dl-ing went, Hey, ho, ne - ver be still! They
paid no mo-ney to - ward their rent, but all day long with el - bow bent They
fid-dled a tune called Ril-la-by-ril-la-by, Fid-dled a tune called Ril-la-by-rill.

Happy to Meet

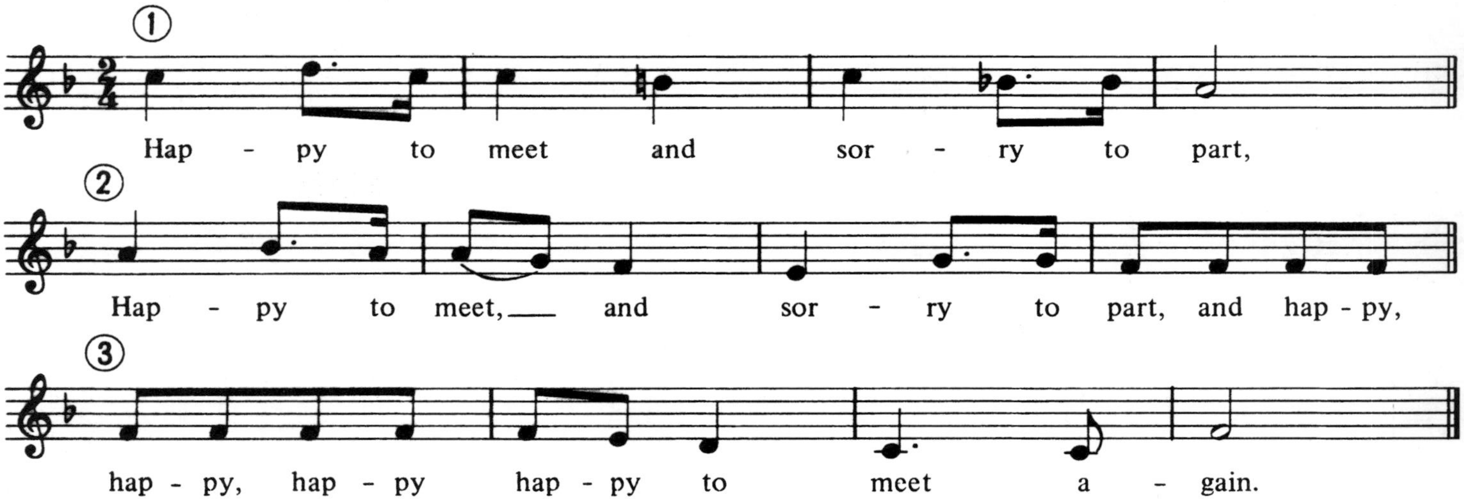

① Hap - py to meet and sor - ry to part,

② Hap - py to meet, ___ and sor - ry to part, and hap - py,

③ hap - py, hap - py hap - py to meet a - gain.

Here I Go

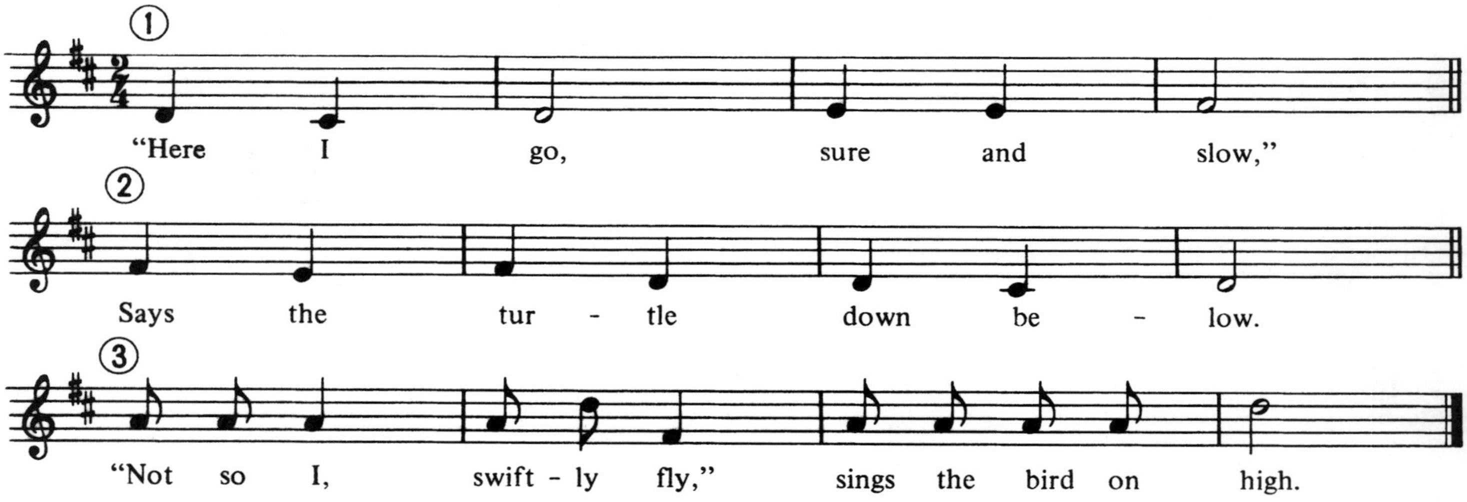

① "Here I go, sure and slow,"

② Says the tur - tle down be - low.

③ "Not so I, swift - ly fly," sings the bird on high.

Hey Ho, Nobody's Home

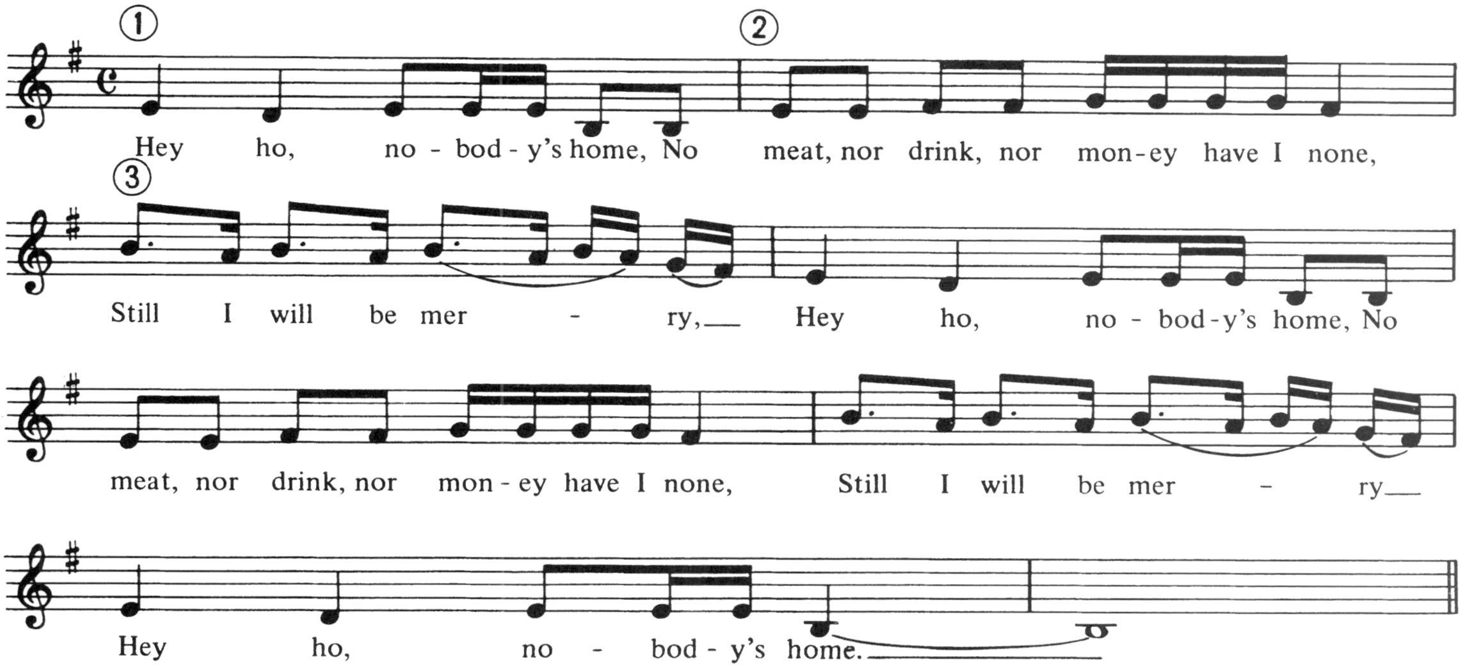
①
②
Hey ho, no - bod - y's home, No meat, nor drink, nor mon-ey have I none,
③
Still I will be mer - ry, Hey ho, no - bod-y's home, No
meat, nor drink, nor mon - ey have I none, Still I will be mer - ry
Hey ho, no - bod - y's home.

Hi! Cheerily Ho

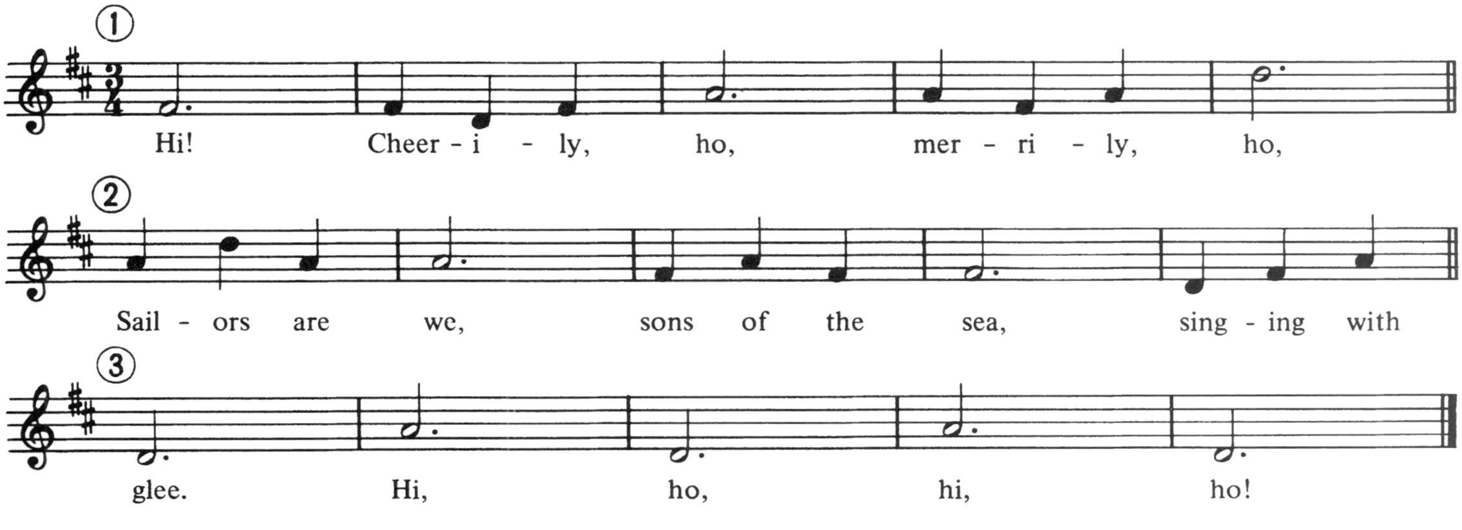
①
Hi! Cheer - i - ly, ho, mer - ri - ly, ho,
②
Sail - ors are we, sons of the sea, sing - ing with
③
glee. Hi, ho, hi, ho!

Horse to Trot

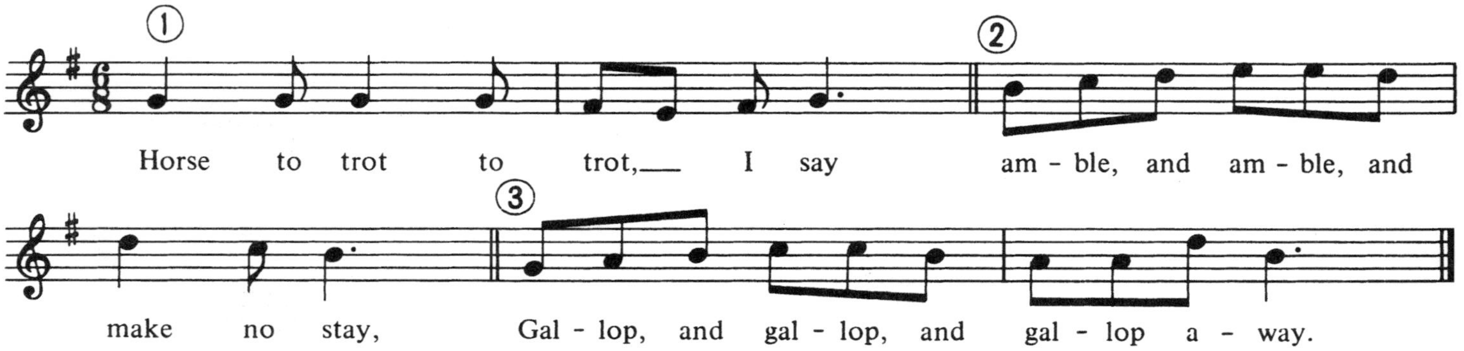

Horse to trot to trot,___ I say am - ble, and am - ble, and make no stay, Gal - lop, and gal - lop, and gal - lop a - way.

If I Know What You Know

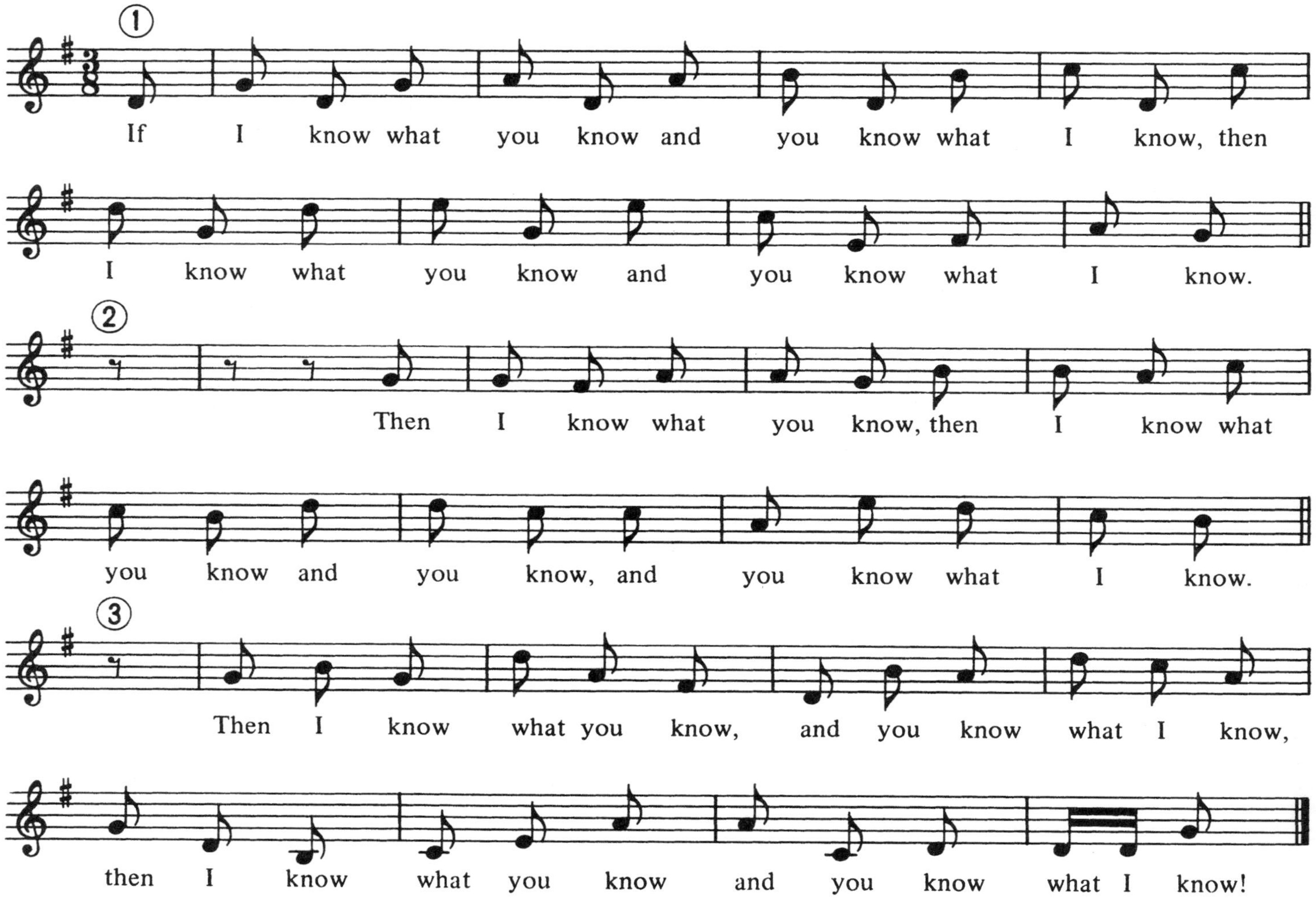

If I know what you know and you know what I know, then I know what you know and you know what I know.

Then I know what you know, then I know what you know and you know, and you know what I know.

Then I know what you know, and you know what I know, then I know what you know and you know what I know!

Laughter Makes the World Go Round

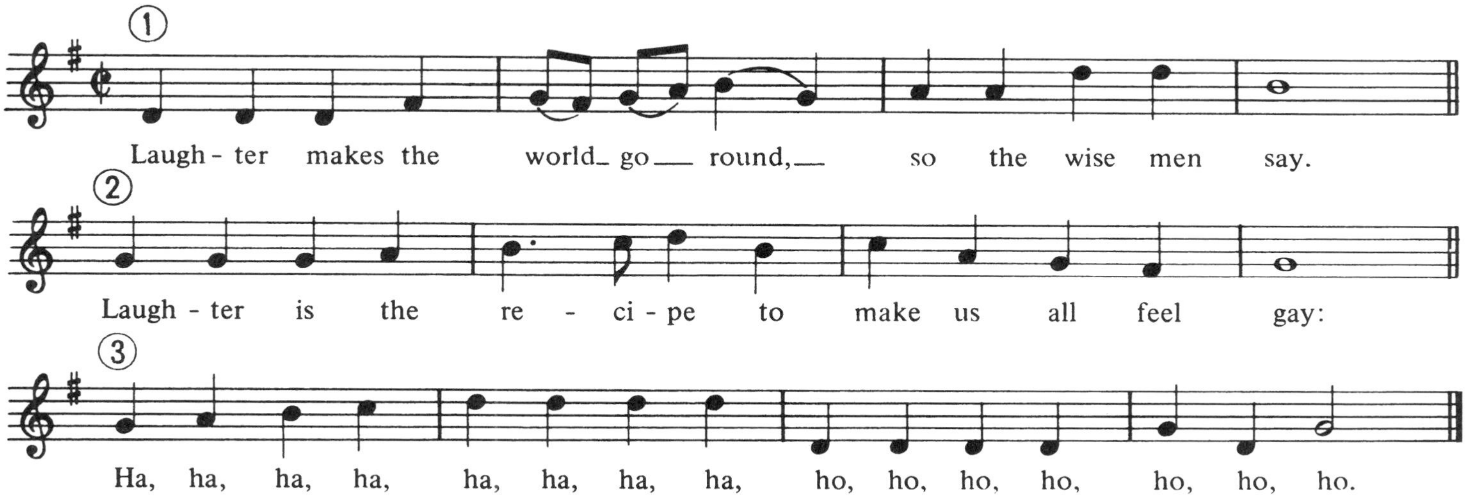

① Laugh-ter makes the world go round, so the wise men say.

② Laugh-ter is the re - ci - pe to make us all feel gay:

③ Ha, ha, ha, ha, ha, ha, ha, ha, ho, ho, ho, ho, ho, ho, ho.

The Millwheel

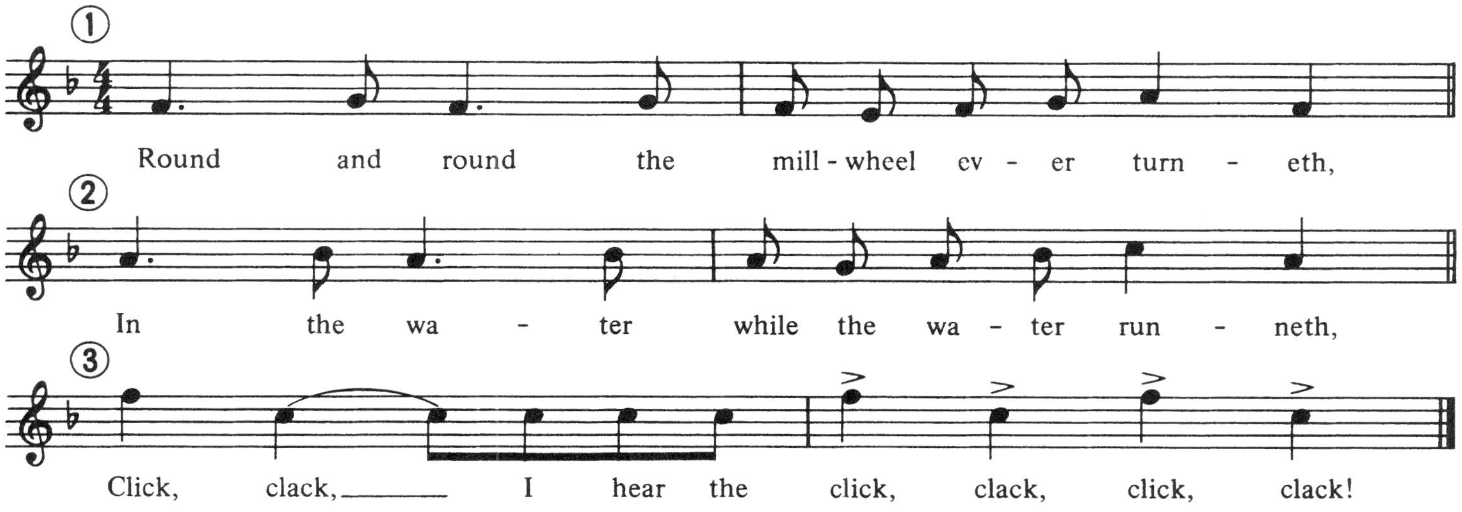

① Round and round the mill - wheel ev - er turn - eth,

② In the wa - ter while the wa - ter run - neth,

③ Click, clack, I hear the click, clack, click, clack!

The Merry Bells of Hamburg Town

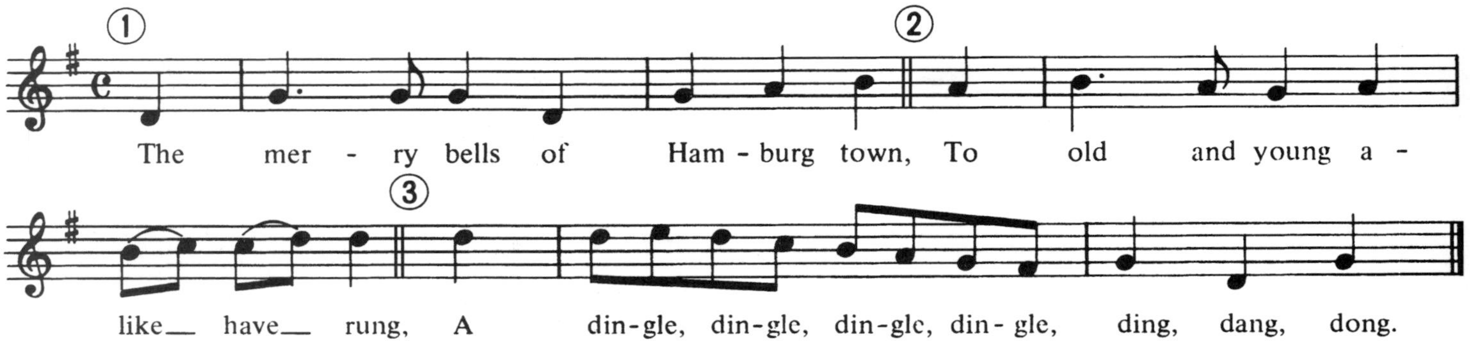

The mer - ry bells of Ham - burg town, To old and young a -
like__ have__ rung, A din - gle, din - gle, din - gle, din - gle, ding, dang, dong.

Morning Papers

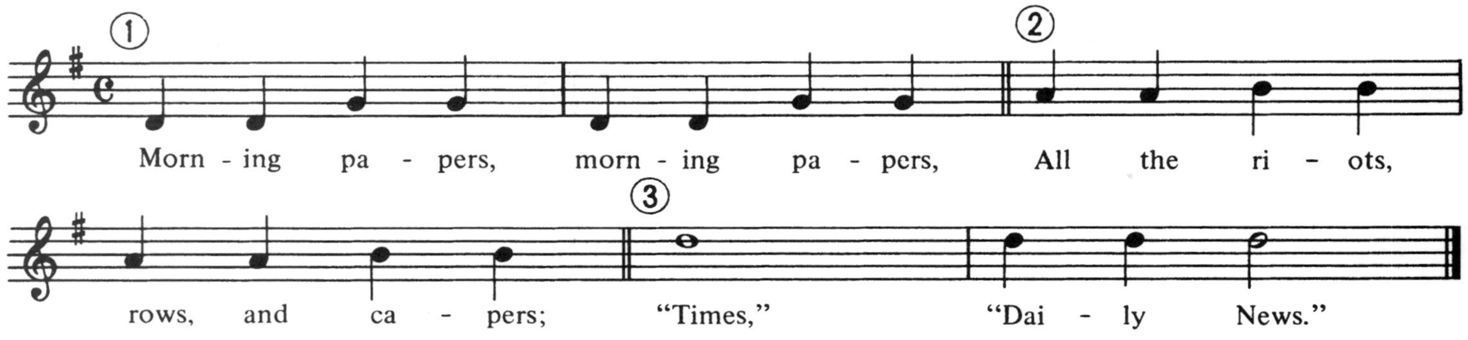

Morn - ing pa - pers, morn - ing pa - pers, All the ri - ots,
rows, and ca - pers; "Times," "Dai - ly News."

Not Too Great

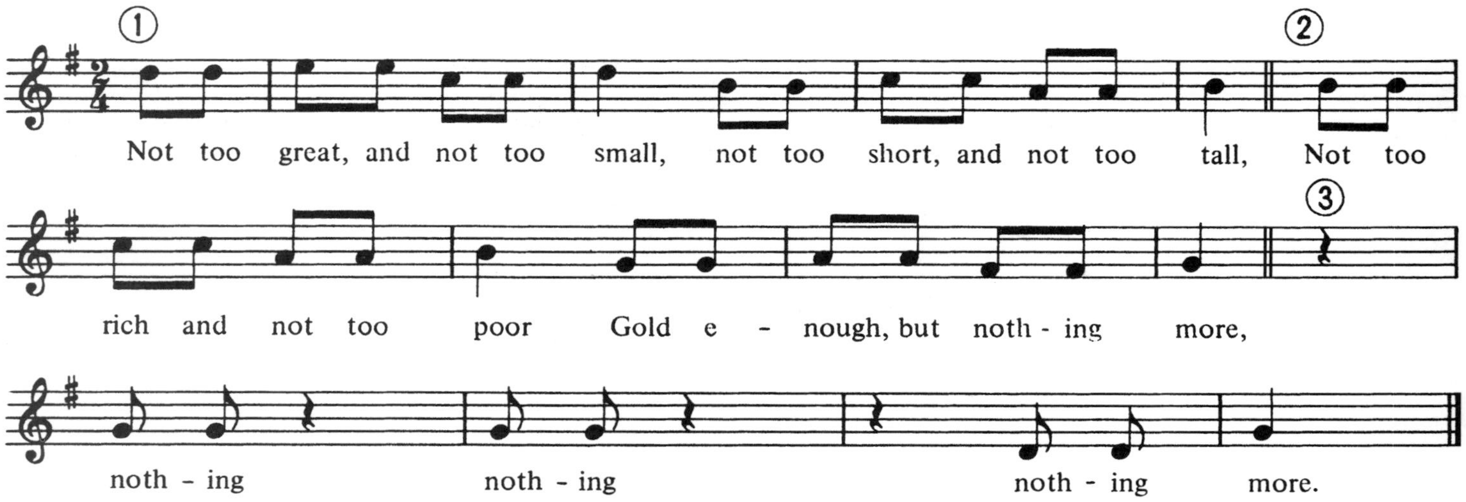

Not too great, and not too small, not too short, and not too tall, Not too
rich and not too poor Gold e - nough, but noth - ing more,
noth - ing noth - ing noth - ing more.

Now the Sun Sinks

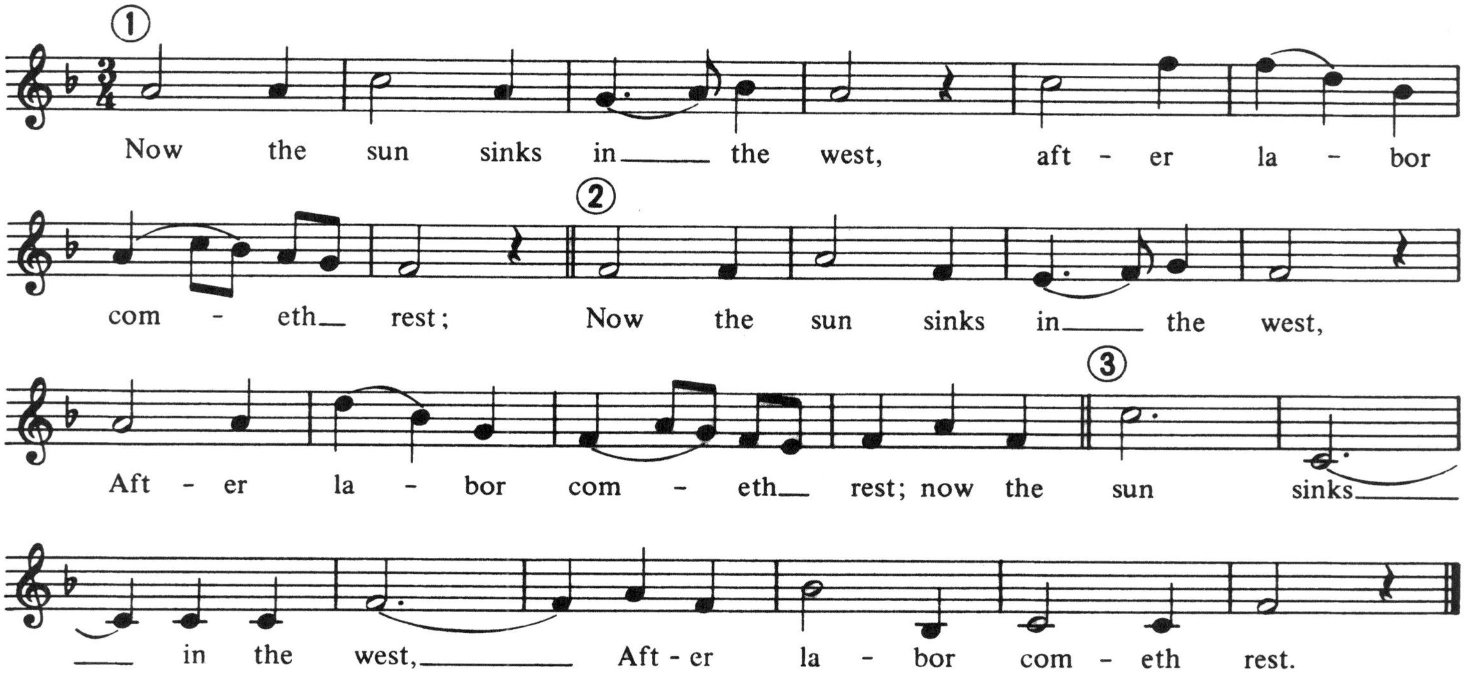

Now the sun sinks in the west, aft - er la - bor com - eth rest; Now the sun sinks in the west, Aft - er la - bor com - eth rest; now the sun sinks in the west, Aft - er la - bor com - eth rest.

O How Lovely Is the Evening

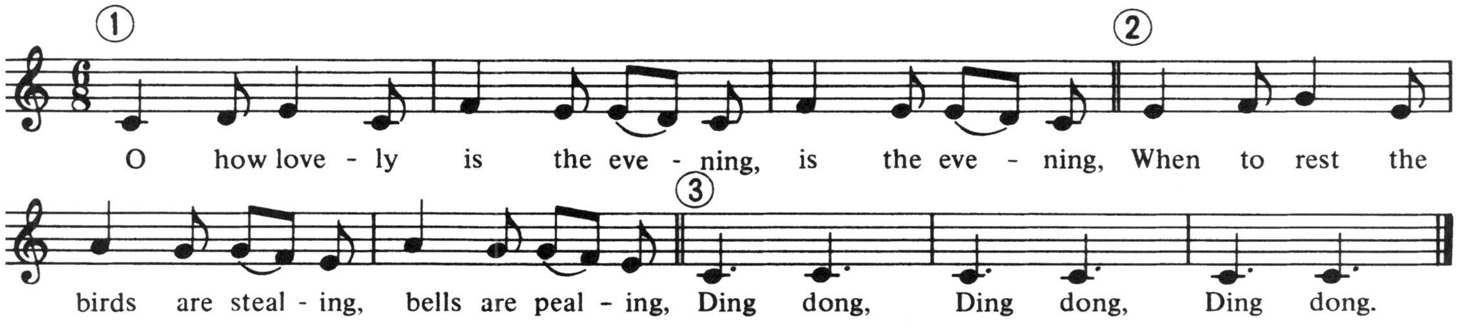

O how love - ly is the eve - ning, is the eve - ning, When to rest the birds are steal - ing, bells are peal - ing, Ding dong, Ding dong, Ding dong.

Packing Up

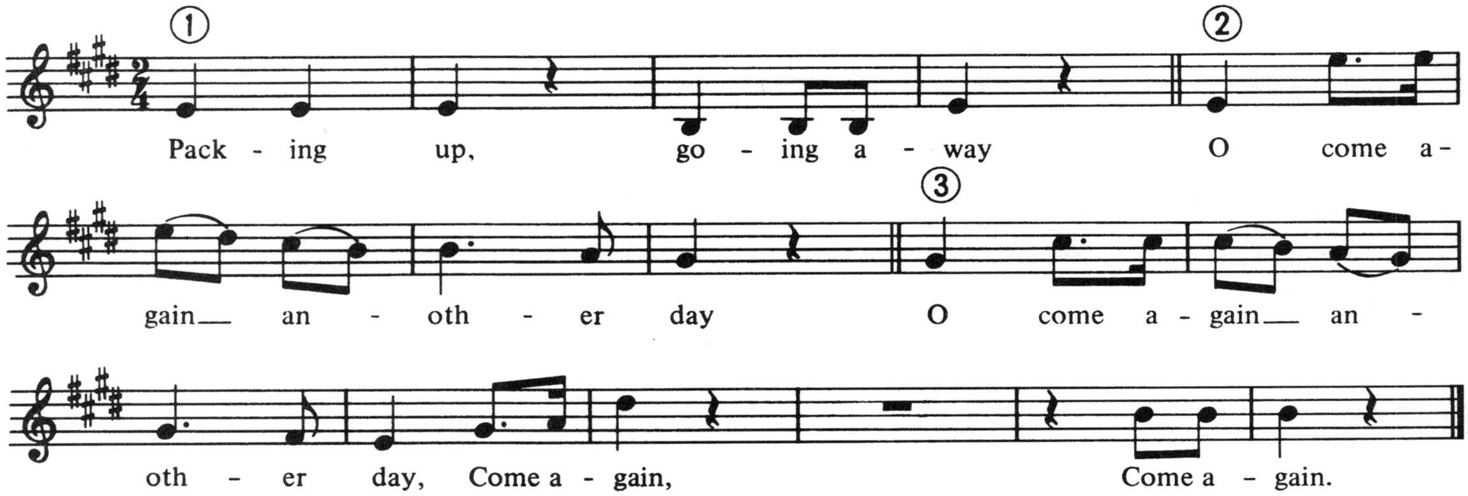

Pack - ing up, go - ing a - way O come a-
gain __ an - oth - er day O come a - gain __ an -
oth - er day, Come a - gain, Come a - gain.

Sandy McNab

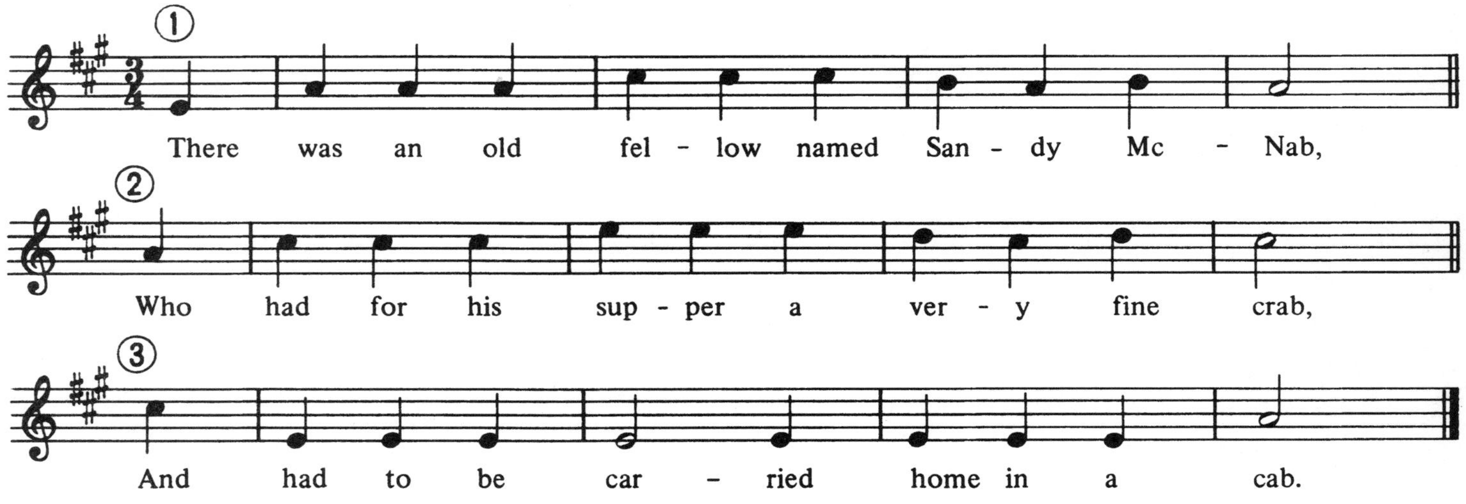

There was an old fel - low named San - dy Mc - Nab,
Who had for his sup - per a ver - y fine crab,
And had to be car - ried home in a cab.

Shut the Door

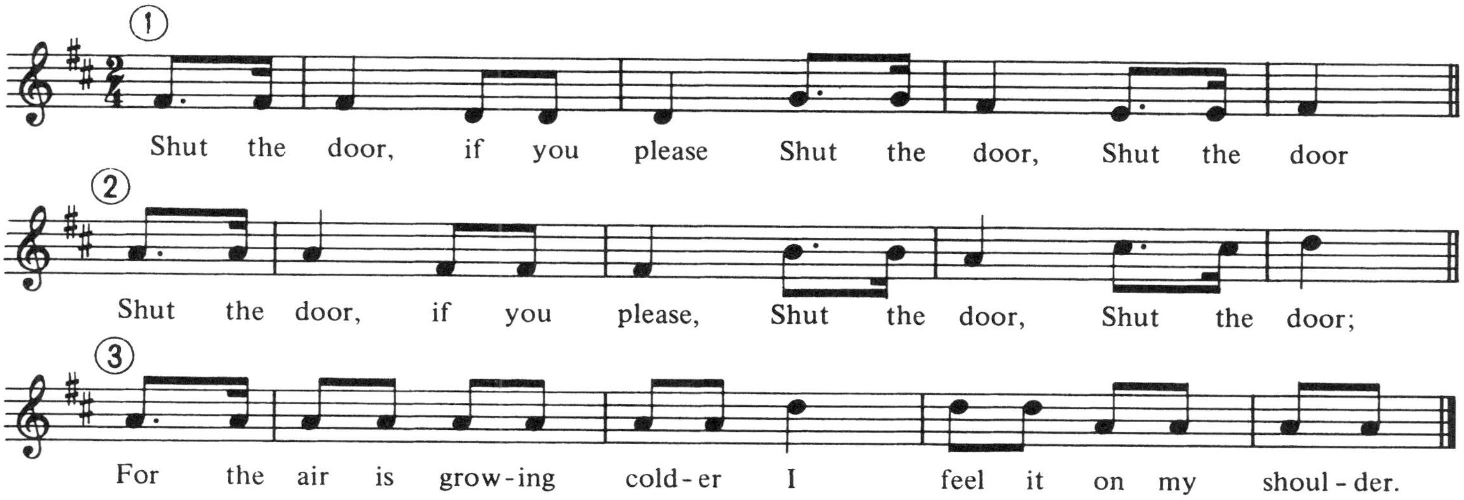

Shut the door, if you please Shut the door, Shut the door

Shut the door, if you please, Shut the door, Shut the door;

For the air is grow-ing cold-er I feel it on my shoul-der.

Sing We Now Our Morning Song

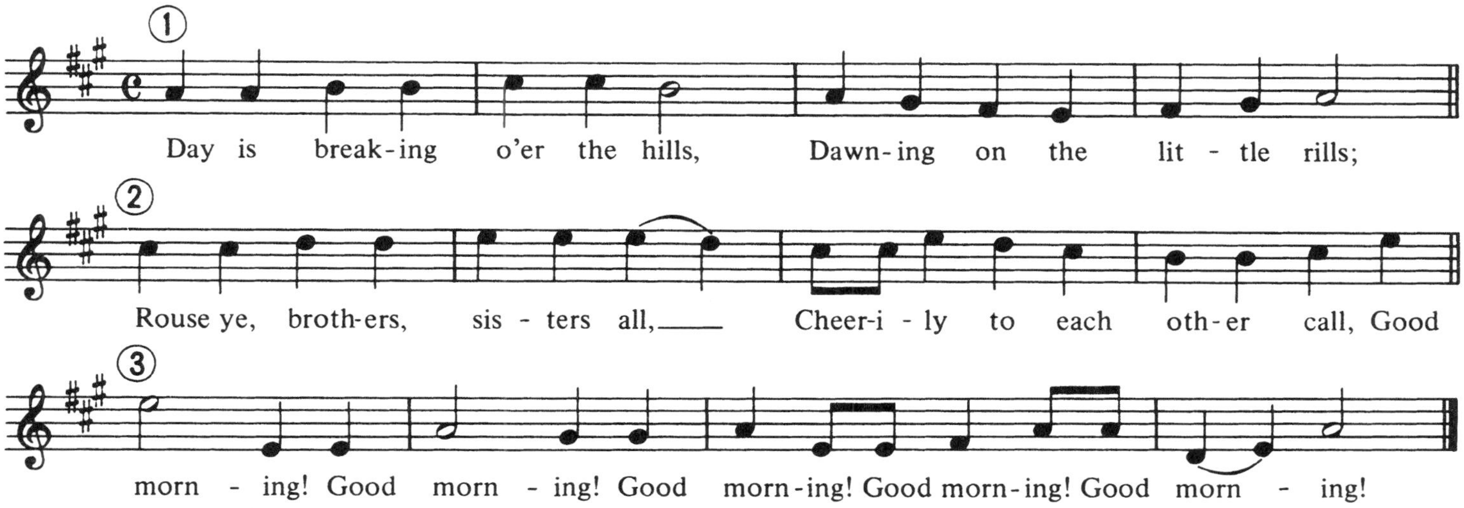

Day is break-ing o'er the hills, Dawn-ing on the lit-tle rills;

Rouse ye, broth-ers, sis-ters all,___ Cheer-i-ly to each oth-er call, Good

morn - ing! Good morn - ing! Good morn-ing! Good morn-ing! Good morn - ing!

298

Spring Is Coming

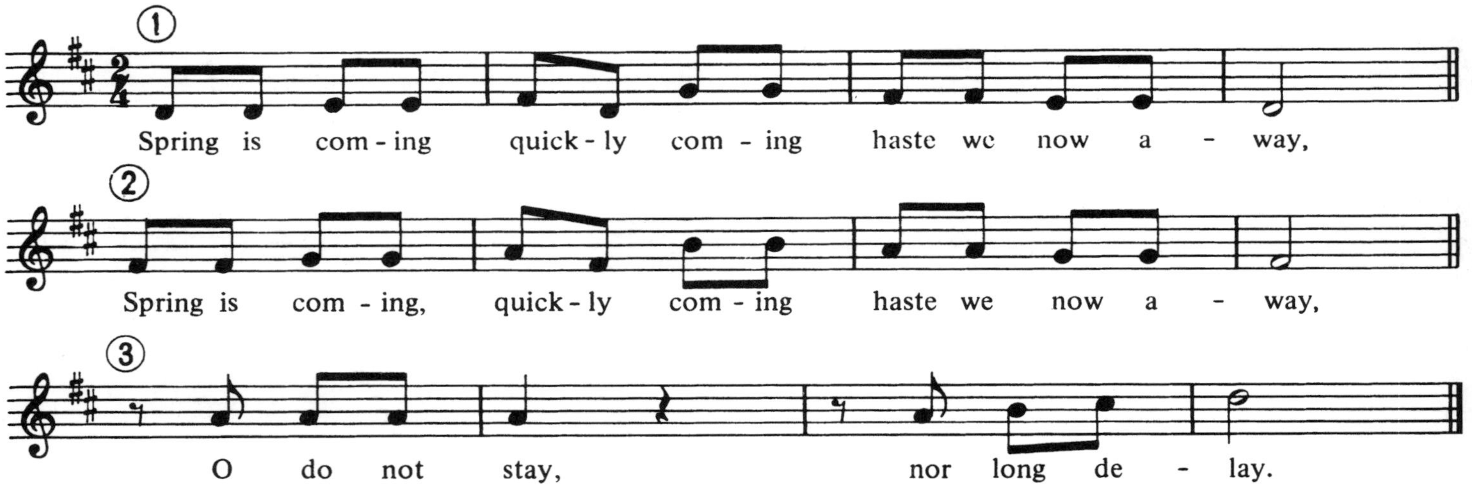

Spring is com-ing quick-ly com-ing haste we now a - way,

Spring is com-ing, quick-ly com-ing haste we now a - way,

O do not stay, nor long de - lay.

Three Bulls and a Bear

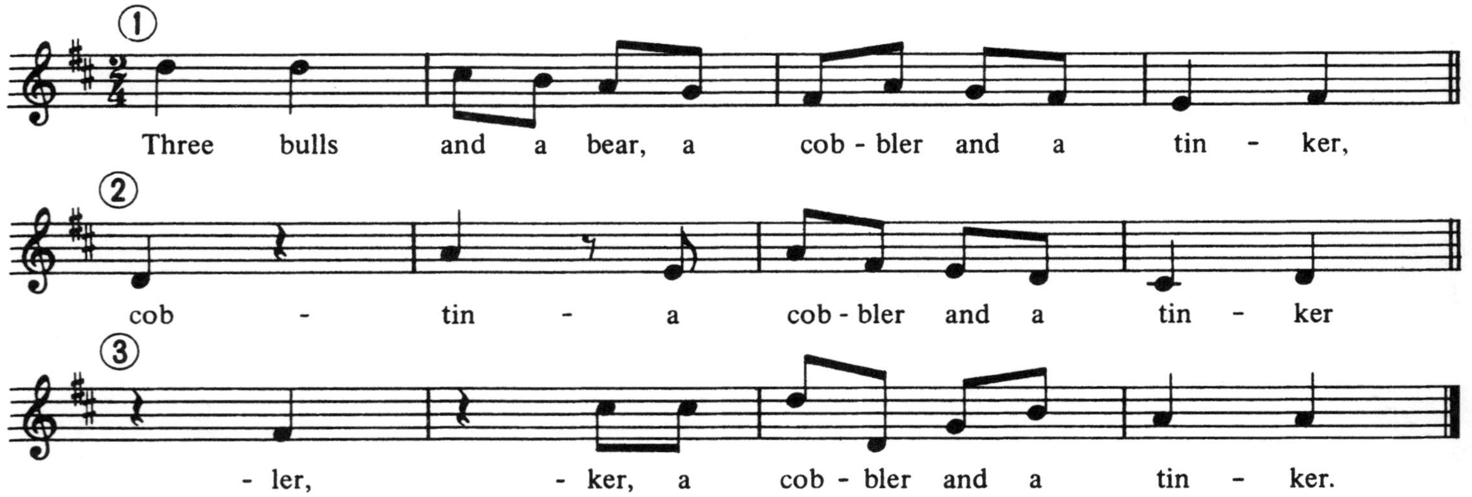

Three bulls and a bear, a cob - bler and a tin - ker,

cob - tin - a cob - bler and a tin - ker

- ler, - ker, a cob - bler and a tin - ker.

© 2001 Music Sales Corporation (ASCAP)
International Copyright Secured. All Rights Reserved.

They March, They March

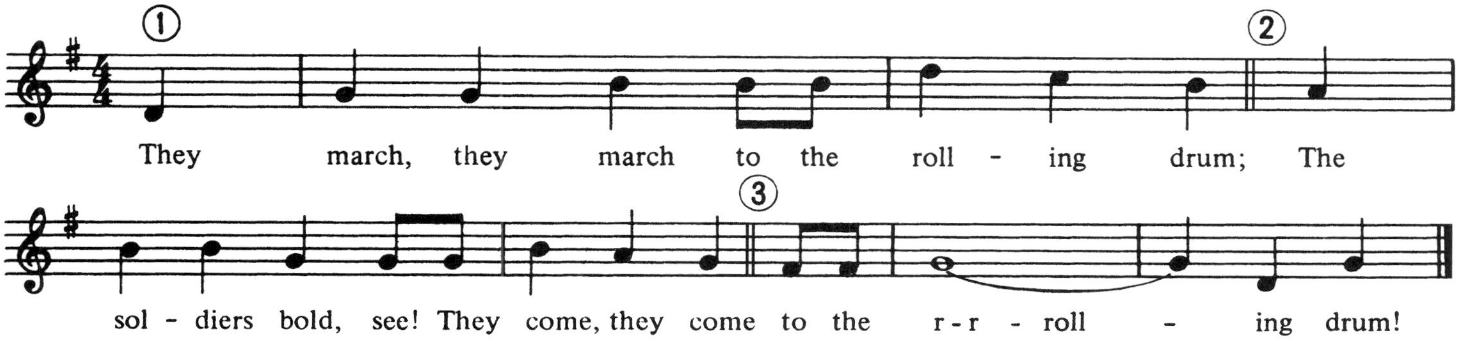

They march, they march to the roll - ing drum; The

sol - diers bold, see! They come, they come to the r-r - roll - ing drum!

When Spring Returns Again

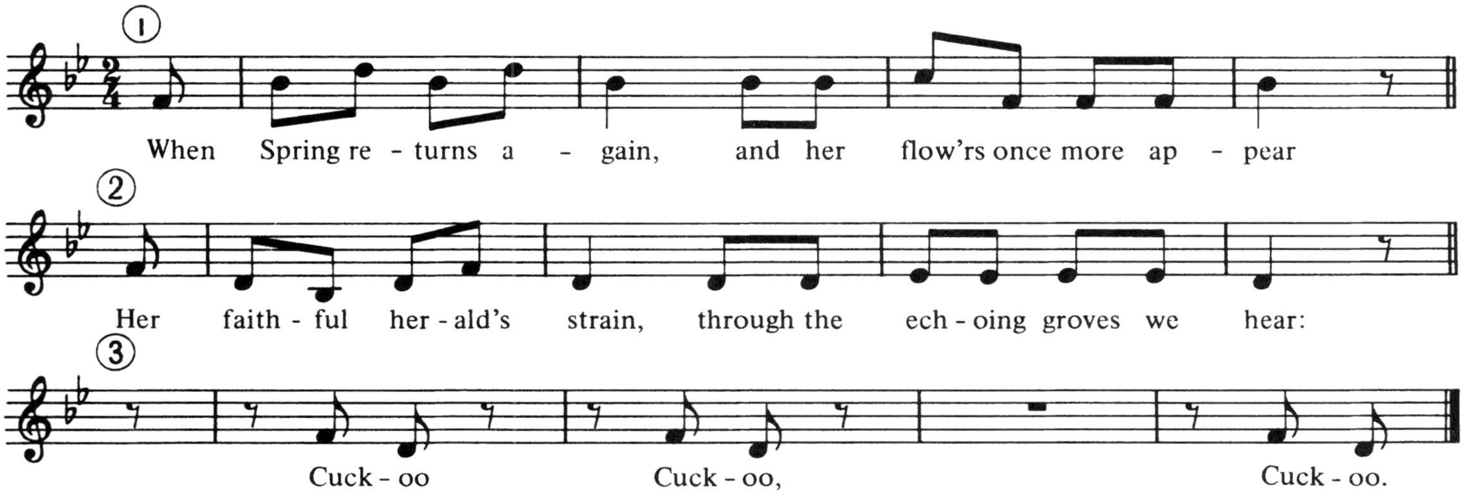

When Spring re - turns a - gain, and her flow'rs once more ap - pear

Her faith - ful her - ald's strain, through the ech - oing groves we hear:

Cuck - oo　　Cuck - oo,　　Cuck - oo.

When a Weary Task

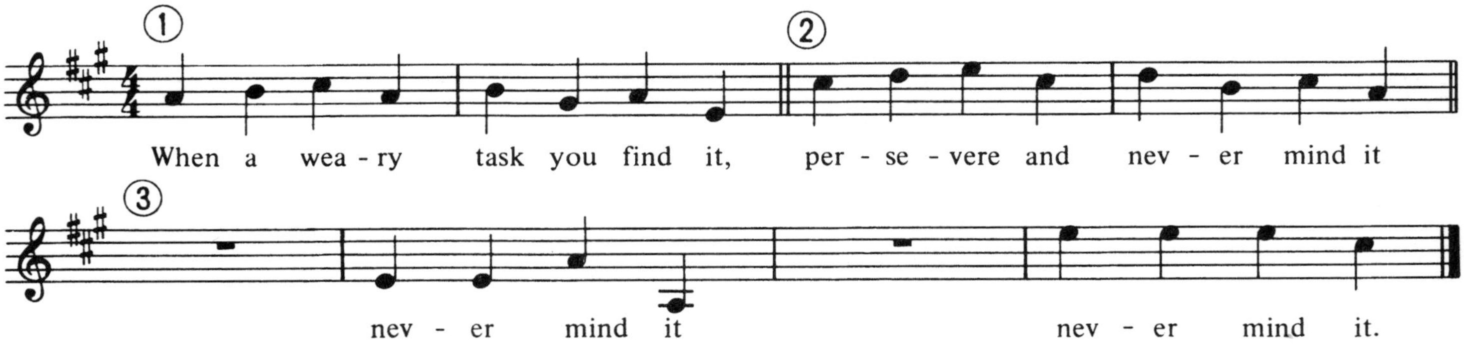

When a wea-ry task you find it, per-se-vere and nev-er mind it nev-er mind it nev-er mind it.

Where Is John

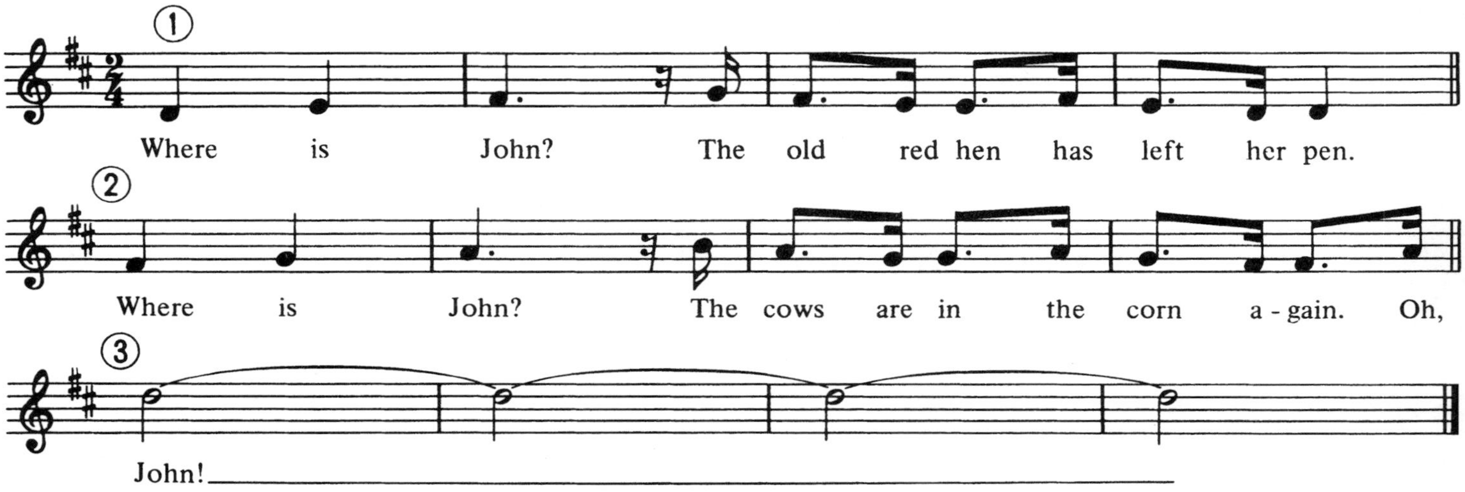

Where is John? The old red hen has left her pen.
Where is John? The cows are in the corn a-gain. Oh,
John!

White Sand and Gray Sand

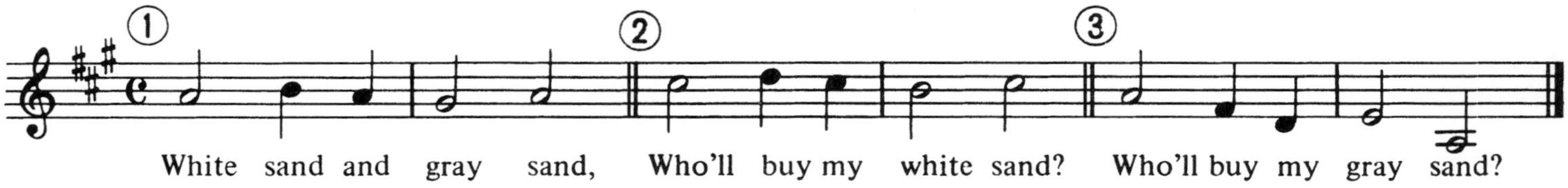

White sand and gray sand, Who'll buy my white sand? Who'll buy my gray sand?

Who Comes Laughing?

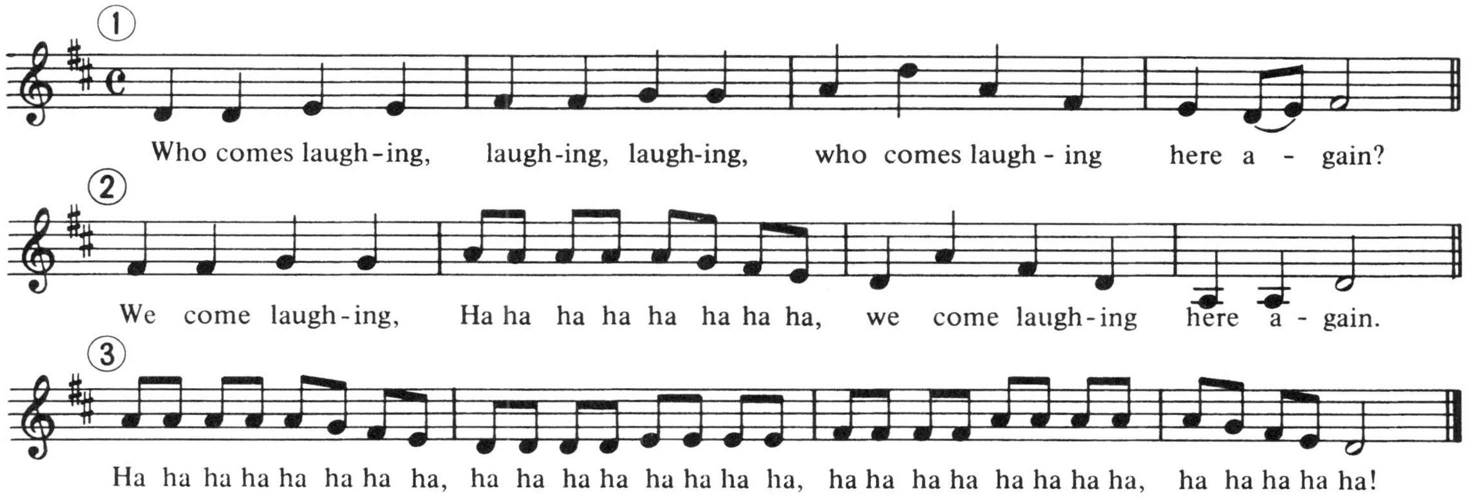

① Who comes laugh-ing, laugh-ing, laugh-ing, who comes laugh - ing here a - gain?

② We come laugh-ing, Ha ha ha ha ha ha ha ha, we come laugh-ing here a - gain.

③ Ha ha ha ha ha ha ha ha, ha ha ha ha ha ha ha ha, ha ha ha ha ha ha ha ha, ha ha ha ha ha!

Yes! 'Tis Raining

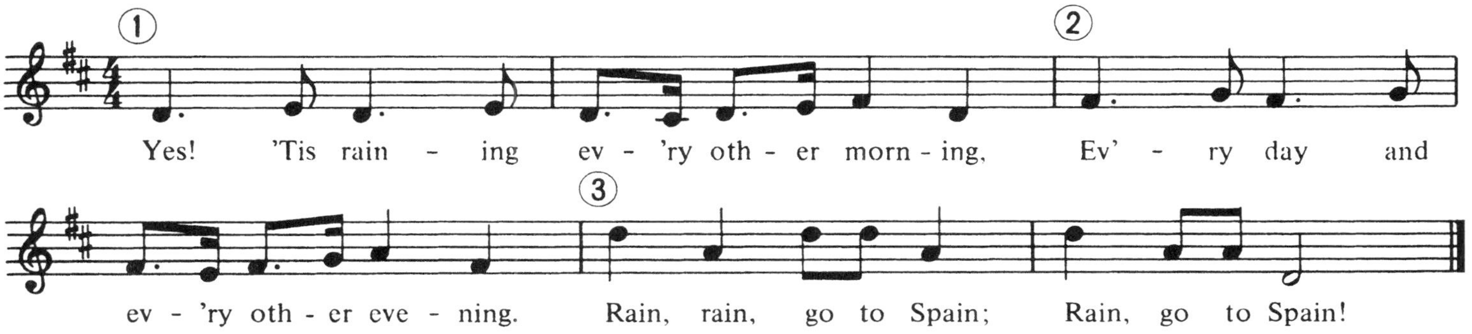

① Yes! 'Tis rain - ing ev - 'ry oth - er morn - ing, ② Ev' - ry day and

③ ev - 'ry oth - er eve - ning. Rain, rain, go to Spain; Rain, go to Spain!

Ye Sportive Birds

1
Ye sport - ive birds, in cir - cles high, Your
fight for - ev - er wing - ing.
2
And ye who make the woods more high, All
vo - cal with your sing - ing.
3
May joy be yours, in flight and
song, To - day, and long.

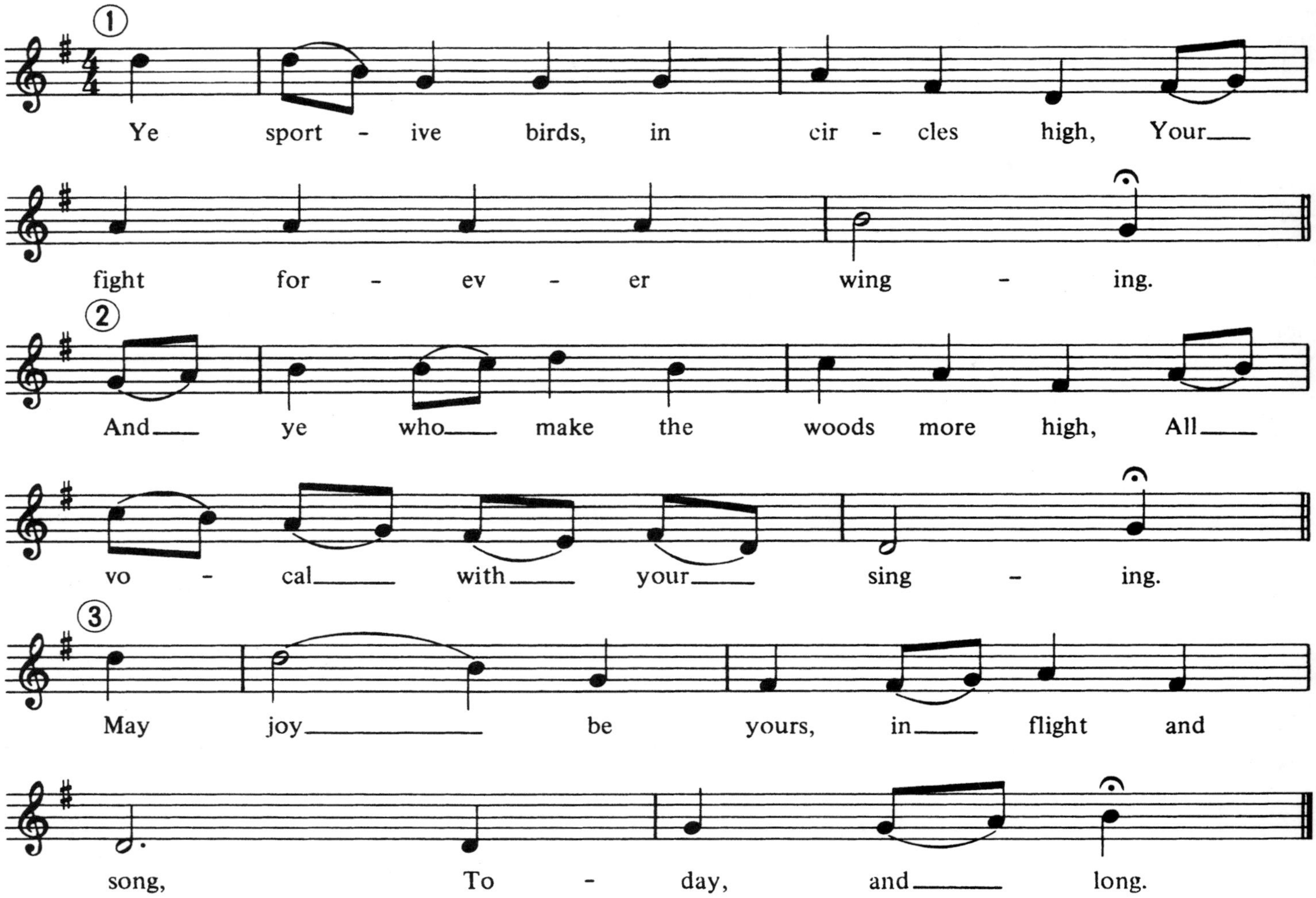

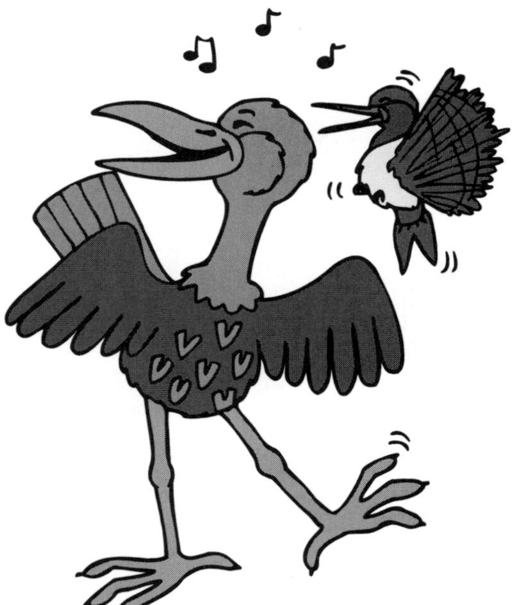

Two-Part Rounds

A Cuckoo and an Owl

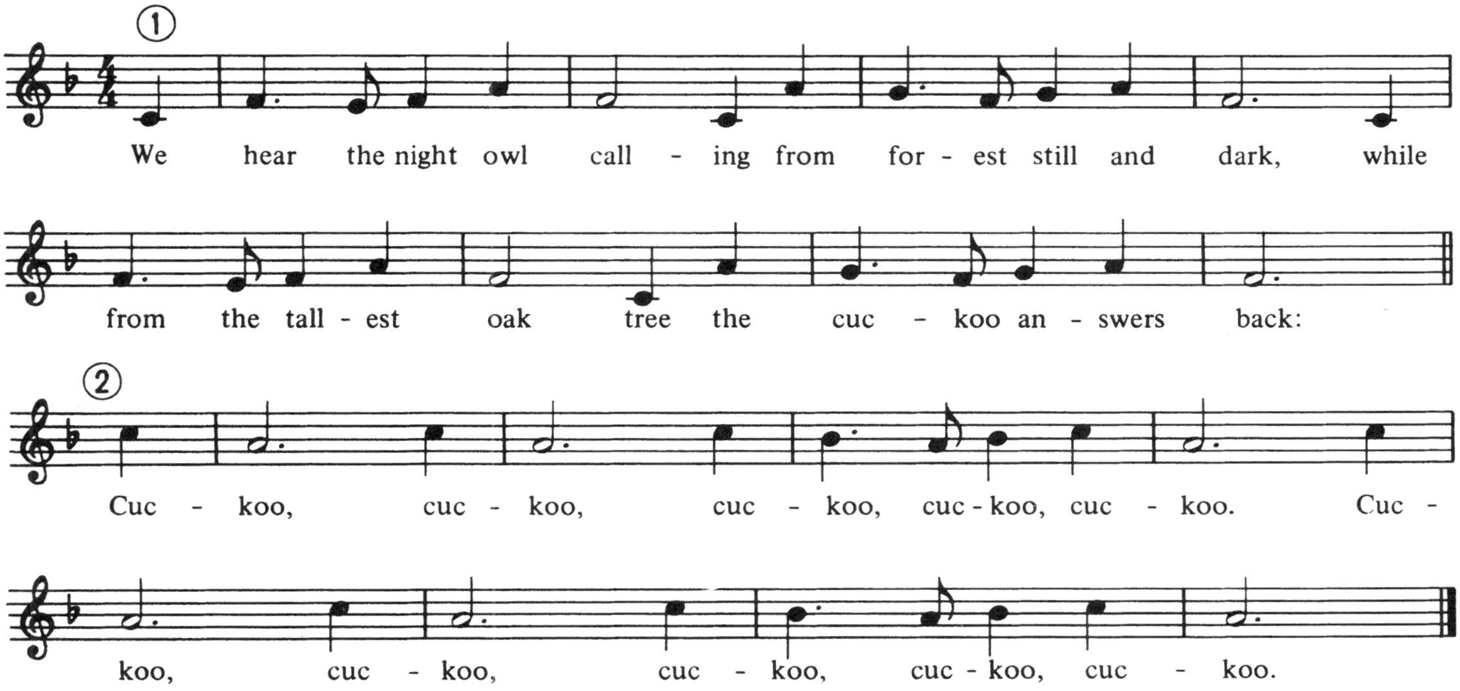
①
We hear the night owl call - ing from for - est still and dark, while
from the tall - est oak tree the cuc - koo an - swers back:
②
Cuc - koo, cuc - koo, cuc - koo, cuc - koo, cuc - koo. Cuc -
koo, cuc - koo, cuc - koo, cuc - koo, cuc - koo.

Echo Sweet

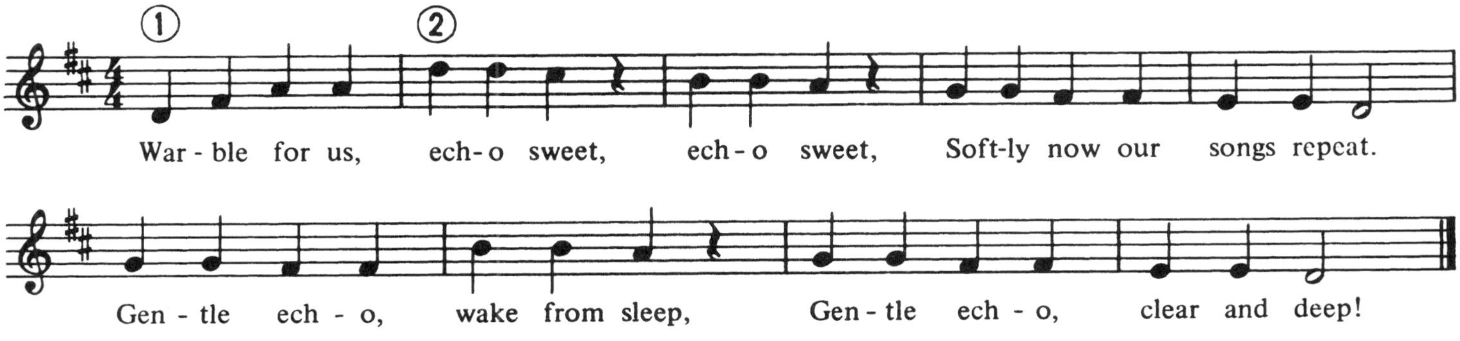
①
②
War - ble for us, ech - o sweet, ech - o sweet, Soft-ly now our songs repeat.
Gen - tle ech - o, wake from sleep, Gen - tle ech - o, clear and deep!

Fruitful Fields Are Waving

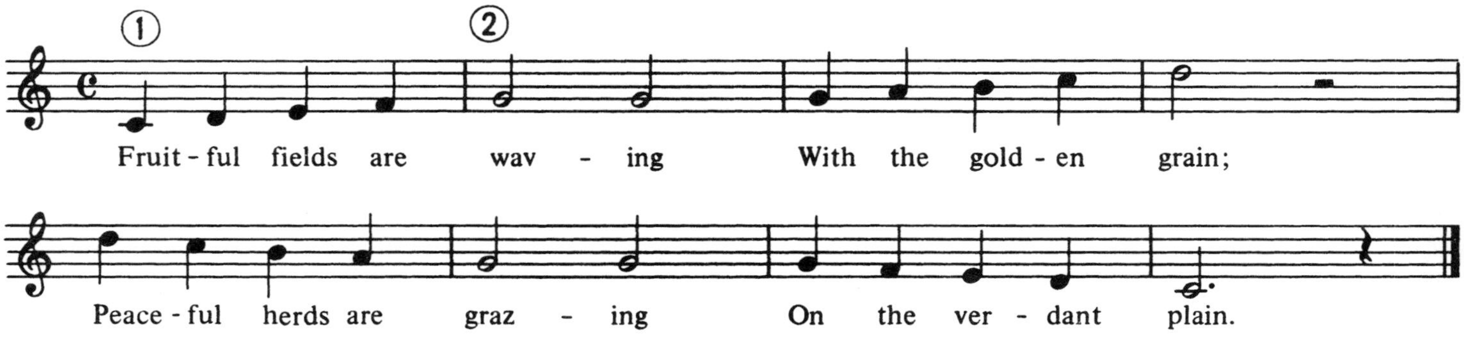

Fruit-ful fields are wav — ing With the gold-en grain;

Peace-ful herds are graz — ing On the ver-dant plain.

Goodbye

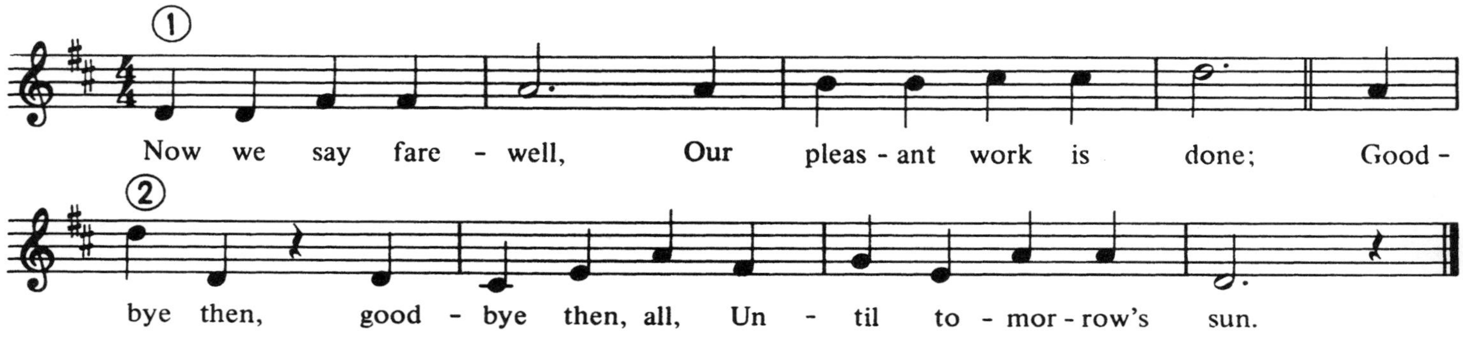

Now we say fare-well, Our pleas-ant work is done; Good-

bye then, good-bye then, all, Un-til to-mor-row's sun.

Here Where Rippling Waters

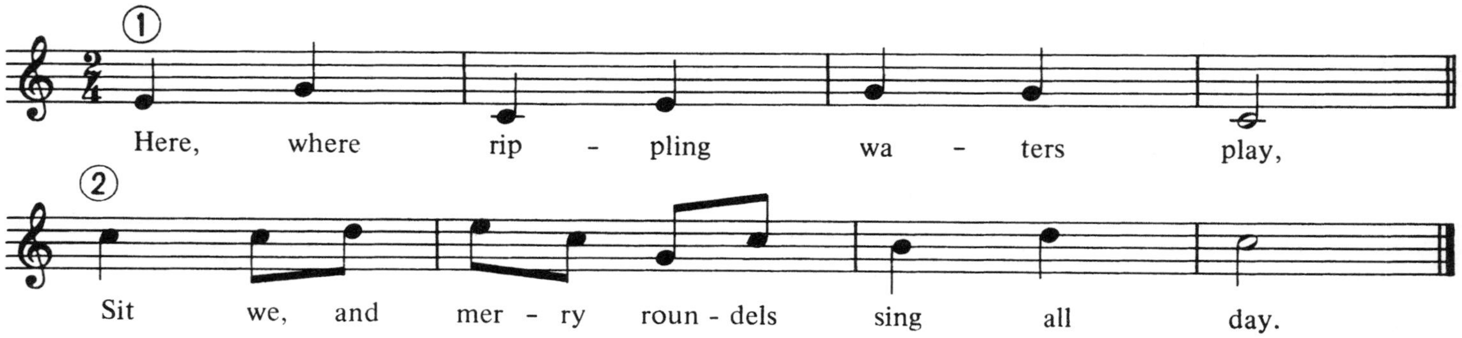

Here, where rip — pling wa — ters play,

Sit we, and mer-ry roun-dels sing all day.

Onward, Upward

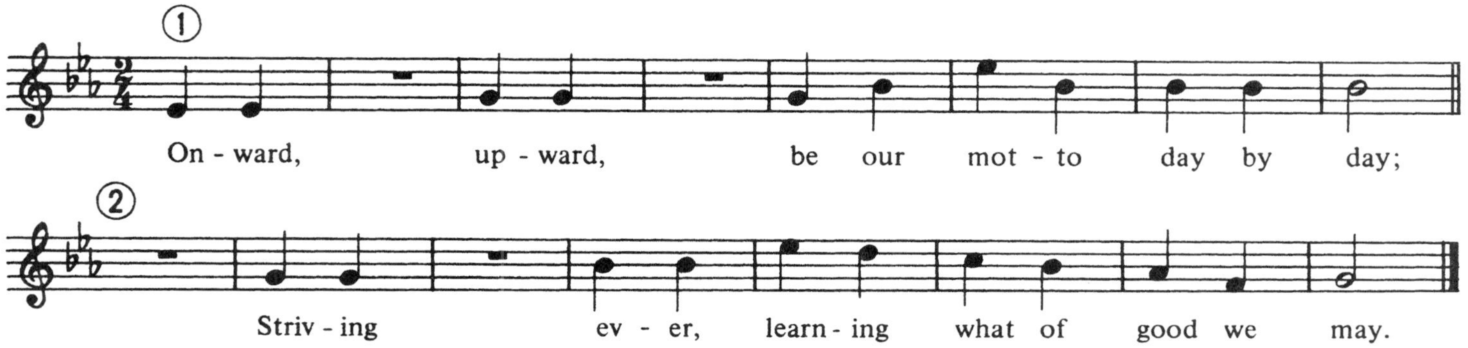

On - ward,   up - ward,   be   our   mot - to   day   by   day;

Striv - ing   ev - er,   learn - ing   what   of   good   we   may.

Over the Mountain

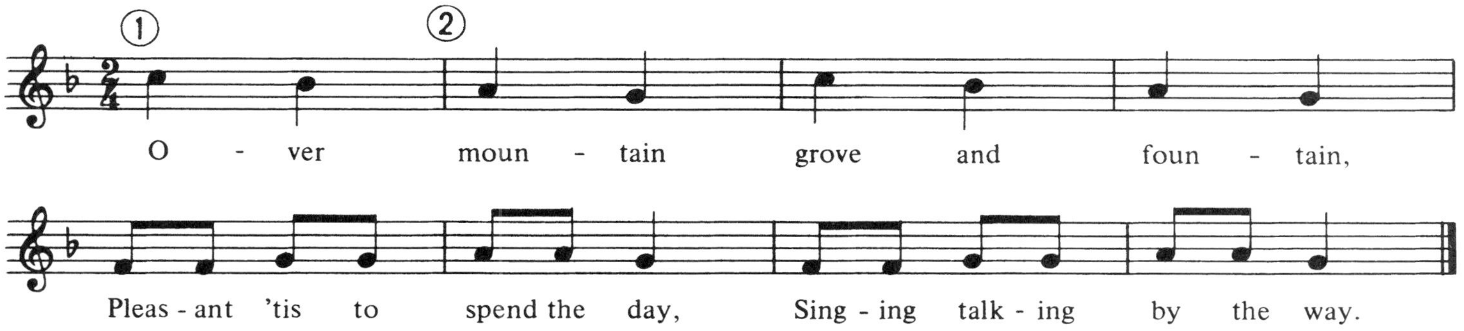

O - ver   moun - tain   grove   and   foun - tain,

Pleas - ant 'tis   to   spend   the   day,   Sing - ing   talk - ing   by   the   way.

Past Ten O'Clock

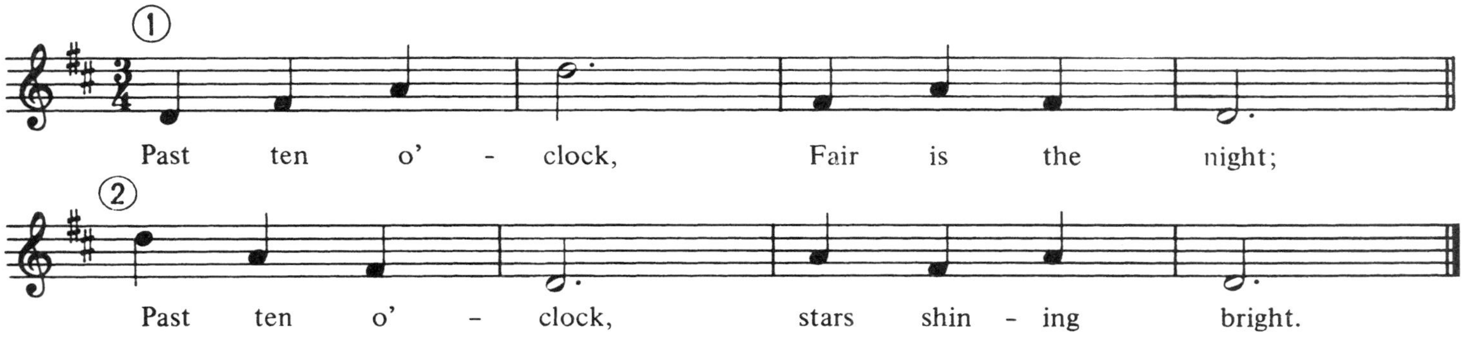

Past   ten   o' - clock,   Fair   is   the   night;

Past   ten   o' - clock,   stars   shin - ing   bright.

Whether You Whisper Low

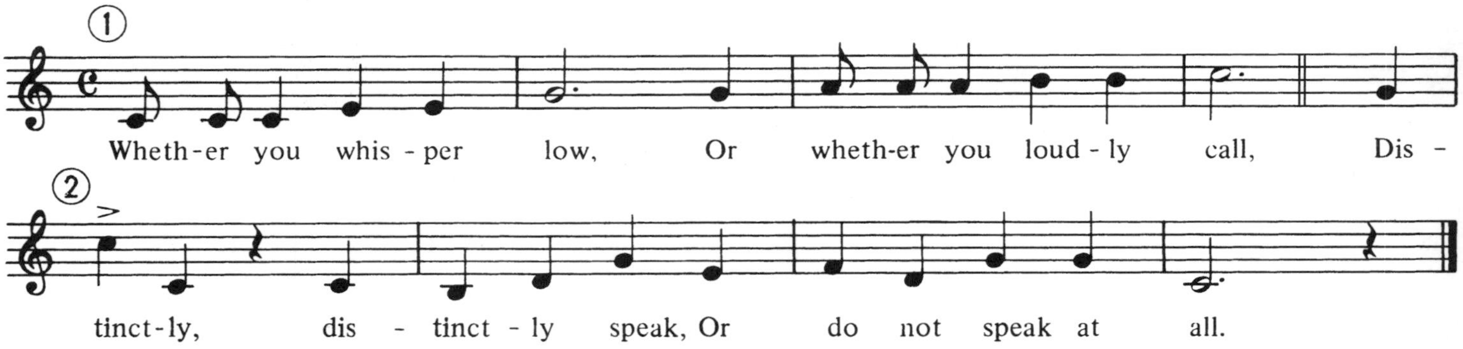

Wheth-er you whis-per low, Or wheth-er you loud-ly call, Dis-

tinct-ly, dis-tinct-ly speak, Or do not speak at all.

Water Falling

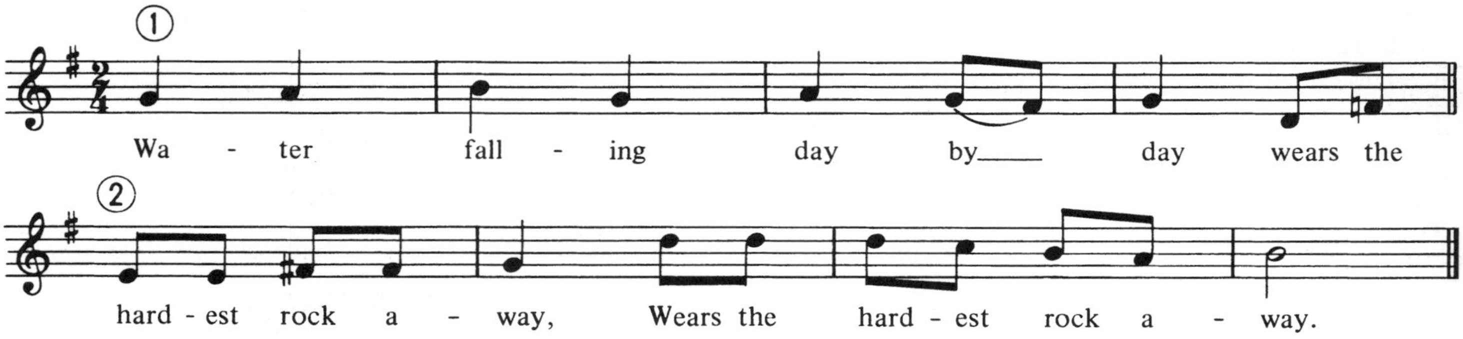

Wa-ter fall-ing day by day wears the

hard-est rock a-way, Wears the hard-est rock a-way.

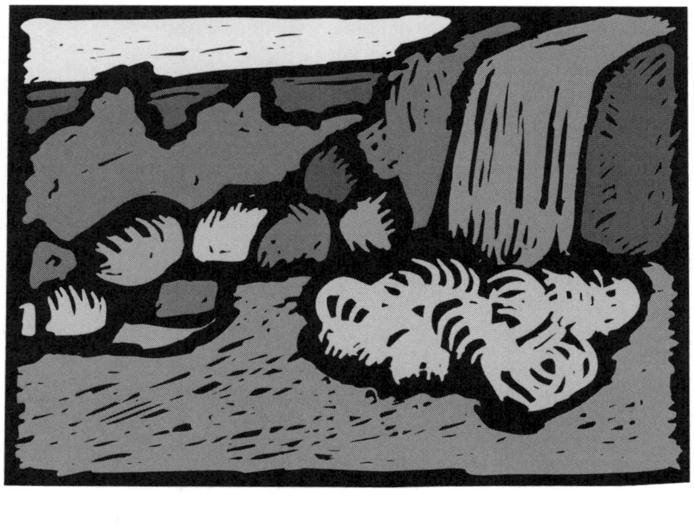

Four- and Five-Part Rounds

Cat in the Plum Tree

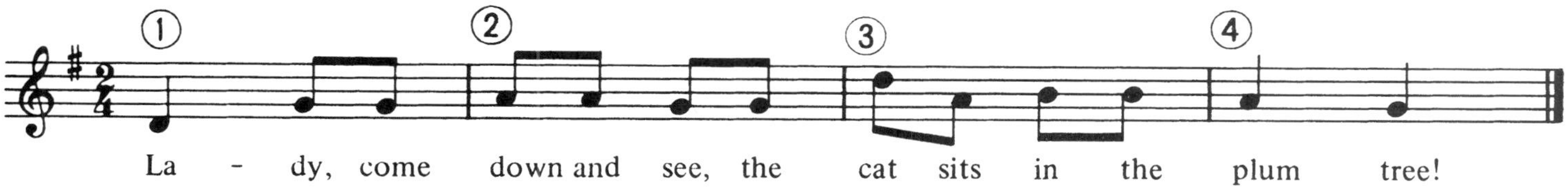

La - dy, come down and see, the cat sits in the plum tree!

Come, Let's Sing a Merry Round

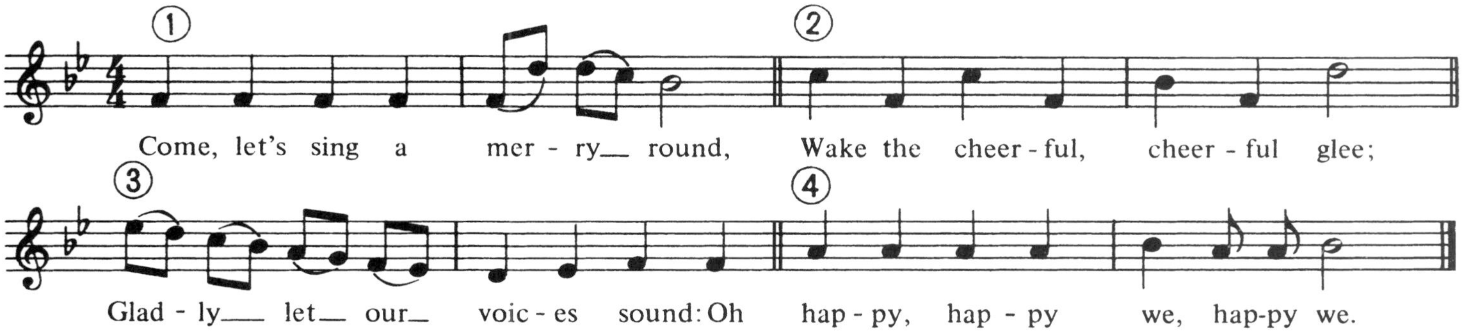

Come, let's sing a mer - ry round, Wake the cheer - ful, cheer - ful glee;

Glad - ly let our voic - es sound: Oh hap - py, hap - py we, hap-py we.

Do, Re, Mi, Fa

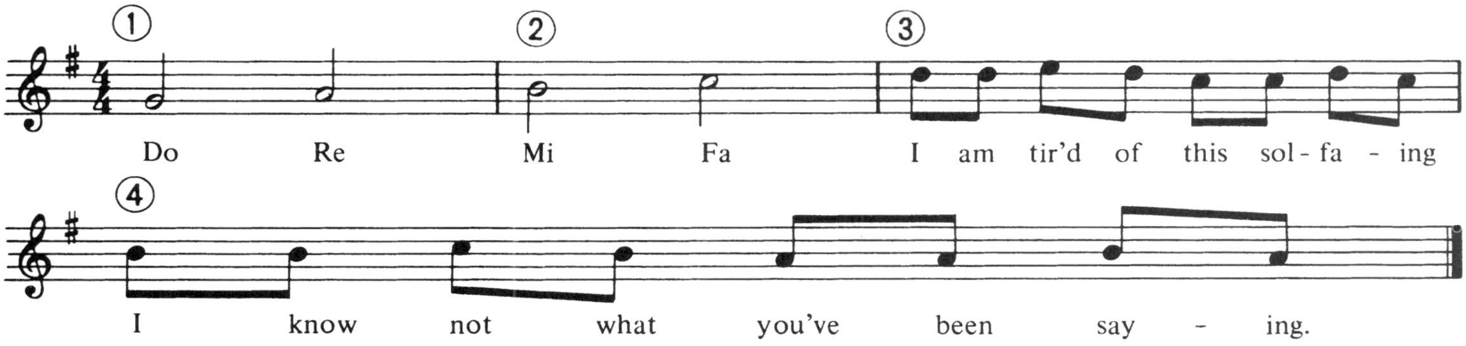

Do Re Mi Fa I am tir'd of this sol-fa - ing

I know not what you've been say - ing.

Donkeys Love Carrots

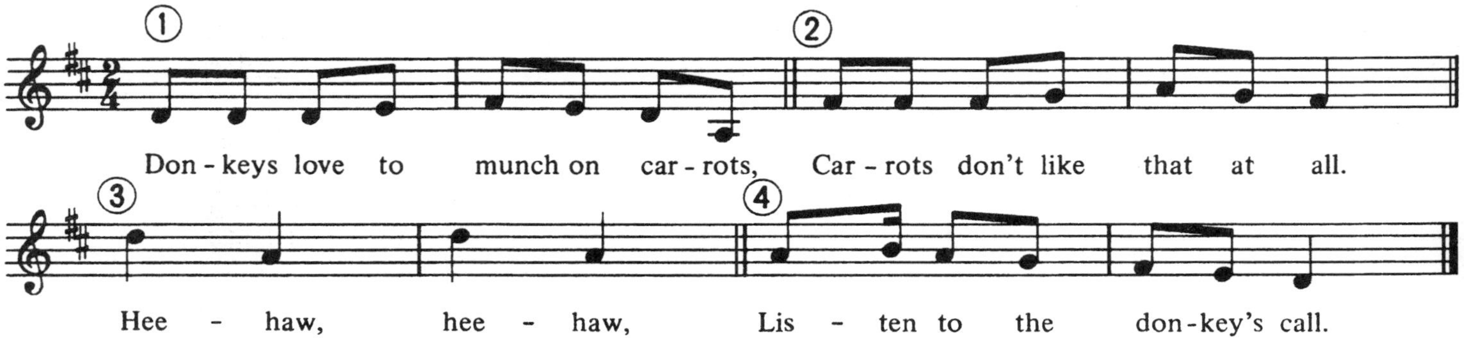

Frère Jacques
(Brother John)

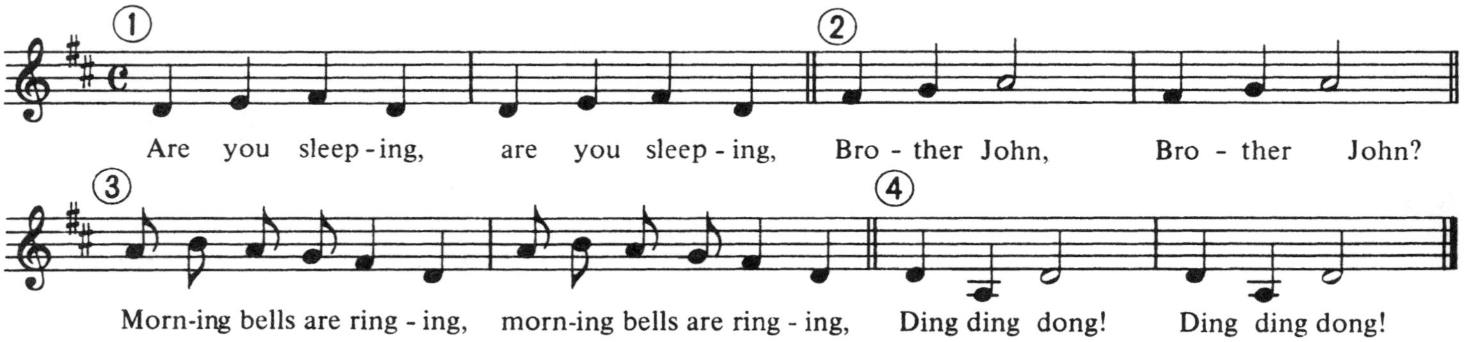

Good Morning

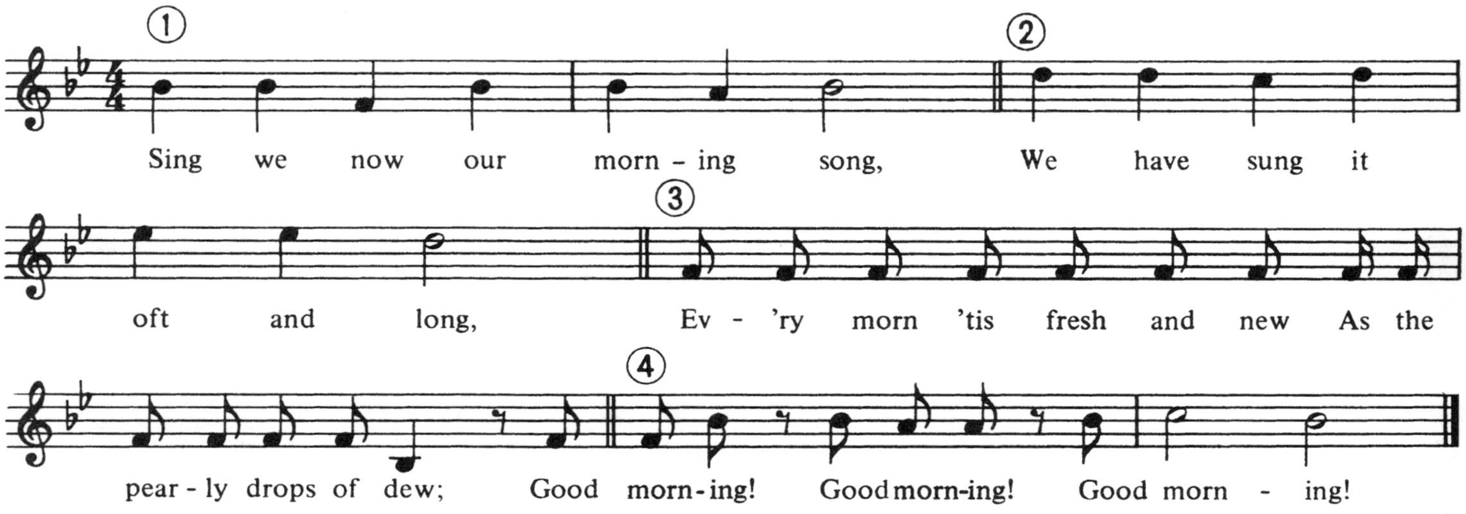

Good Night, Good Night

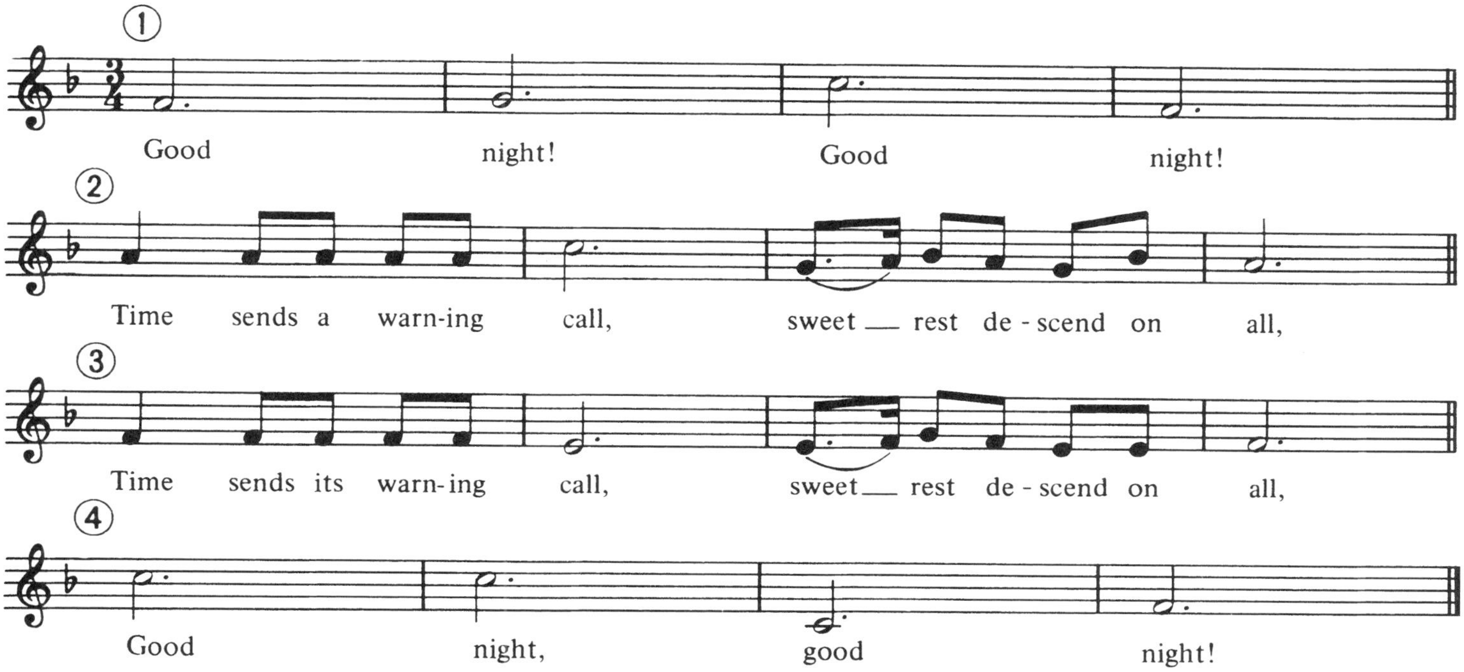

Good night! Good night!

Time sends a warn-ing call, sweet rest de-scend on all,

Time sends its warn-ing call, sweet rest de-scend on all,

Good night, good night!

Haste Makes Waste

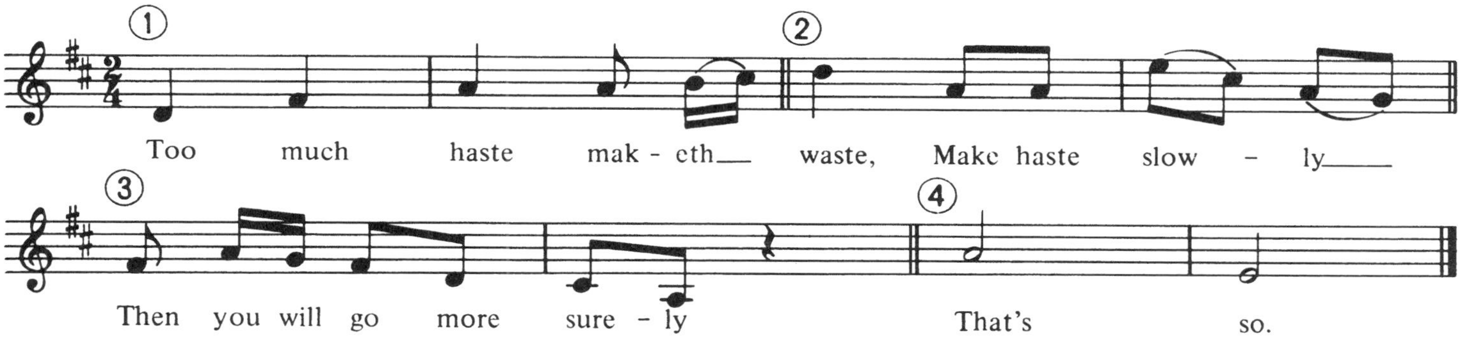

Too much haste mak-eth waste, Make haste slow - ly

Then you will go more sure - ly That's so.

Hear the Lively Song of the Frogs

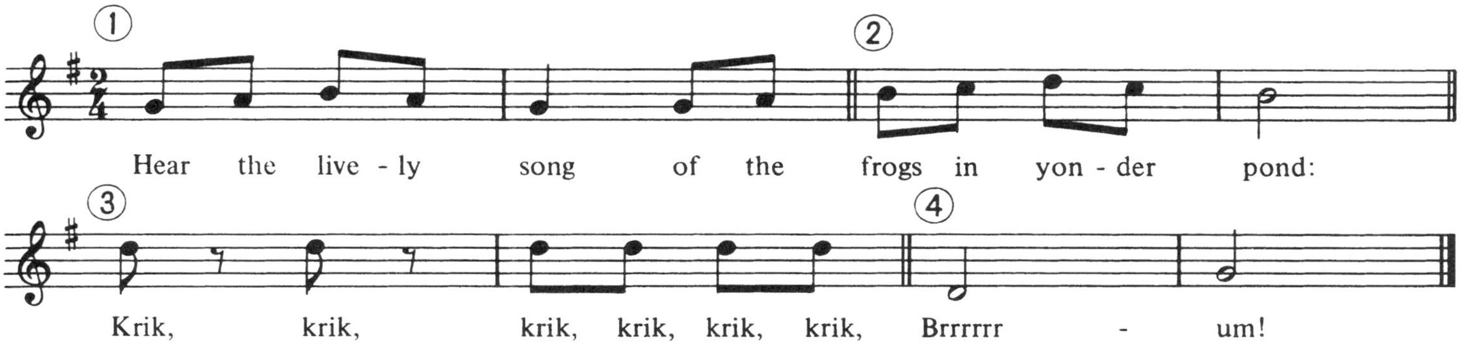

Hear the live - ly song of the frogs in yon - der pond:

Krik, krik, krik, krik, krik, krik, Brrrrr - um!

310

If Thou Tell

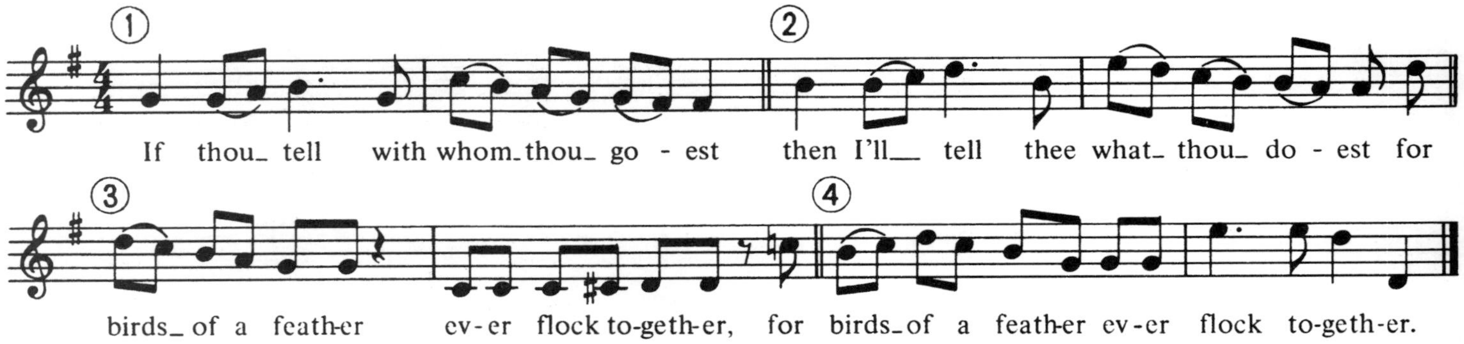

If thou_ tell with whom_thou_ go - est then I'll_ tell thee what_ thou_ do - est for birds_ of a feath-er ev-er flock to-geth-er, for birds_of a feath-er ev-er flock to-geth-er.

I'll Begin

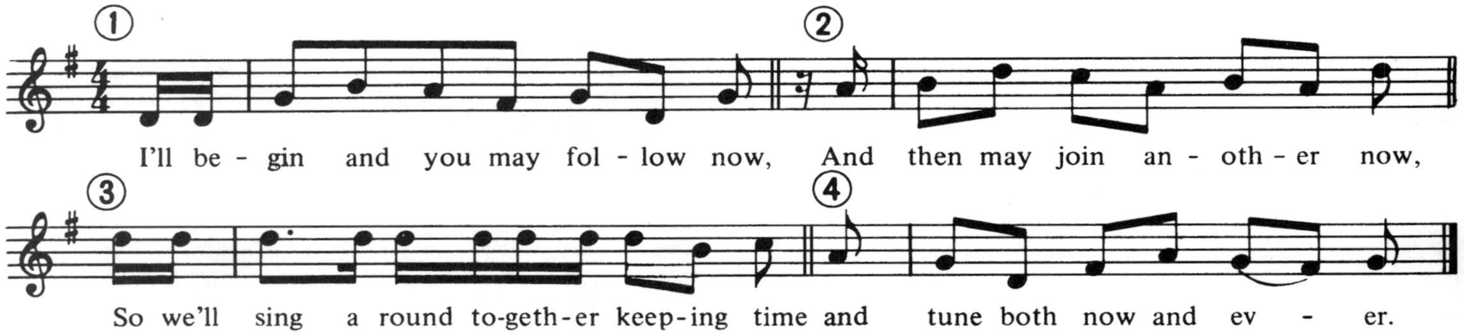

I'll be - gin and you may fol - low now, And then may join an - oth - er now, So we'll sing a round to-geth-er keep-ing time and tune both now and ev - er.

Jolly Round

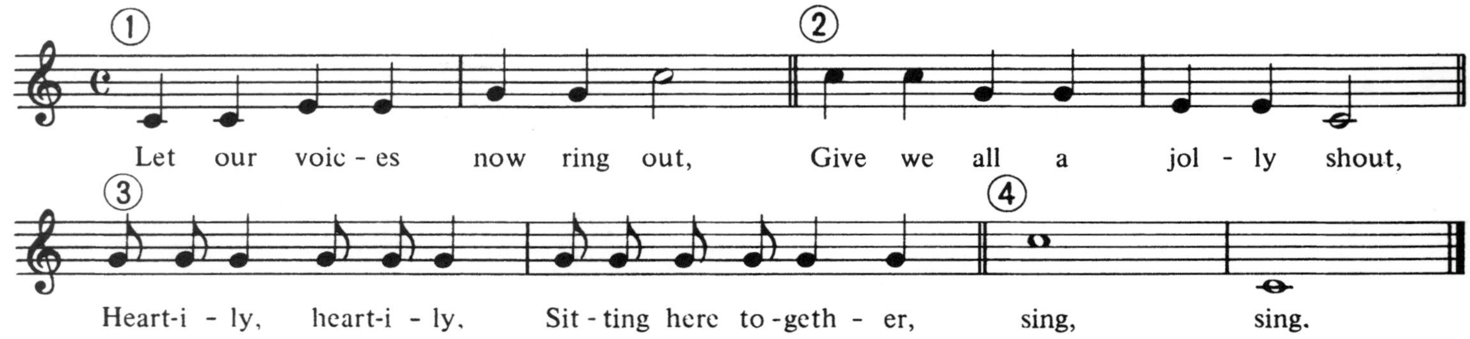

Let our voic - es now ring out, Give we all a jol - ly shout, Heart-i - ly, heart-i - ly, Sit-ting here to-geth - er, sing, sing.

Jinkin the Jester

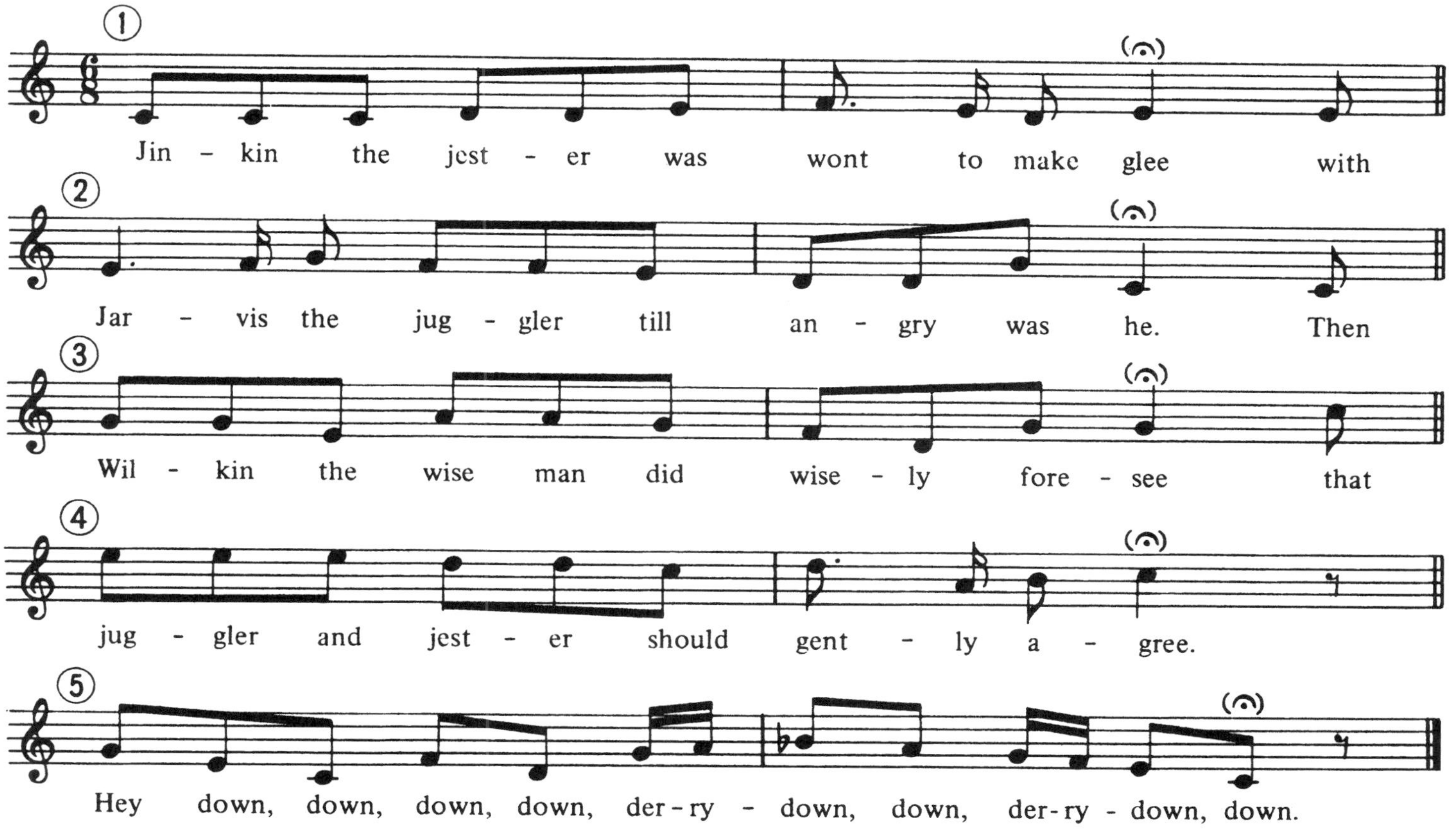
① Jin - kin the jest - er was wont to make glee with
② Jar - vis the jug - gler till an - gry was he. Then
③ Wil - kin the wise man did wise - ly fore - see that
④ jug - gler and jest - er should gent - ly a - gree.
⑤ Hey down, down, down, down, der - ry - down, down, der - ry - down, down.

A Lame, Tame Crane

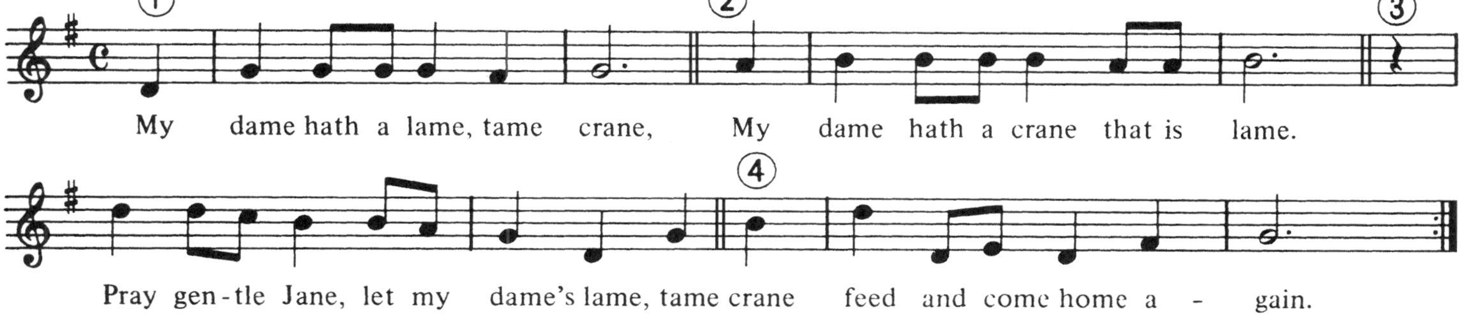
① My dame hath a lame, tame crane, ② My dame hath a crane that is lame. ③
Pray gen - tle Jane, let my dame's lame, tame crane ④ feed and come home a - gain.

The Lark, Linnet, and Nightingale

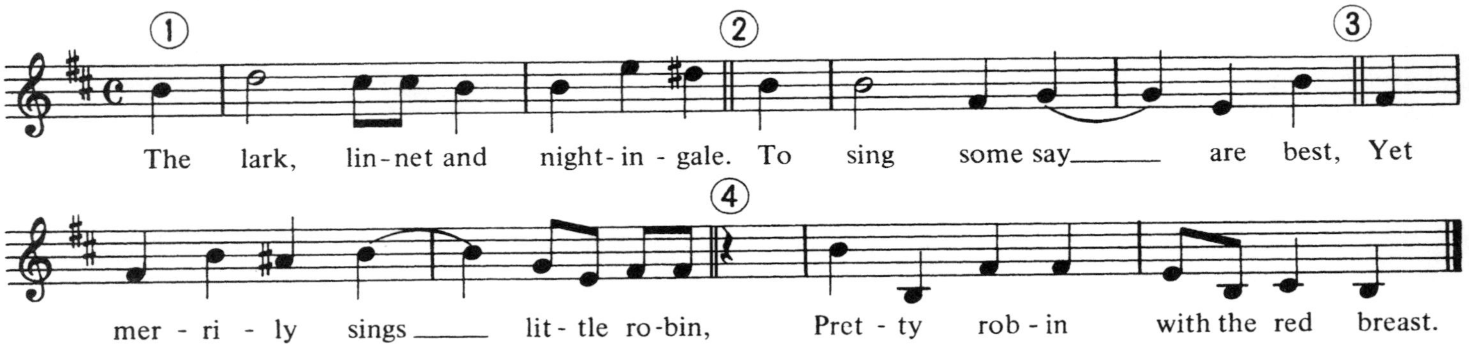

The lark, lin-net and night-in-gale. To sing some say____ are best, Yet mer-ri-ly sings____ lit-tle ro-bin, Pret-ty rob-in with the red breast.

Laughing May Is Here

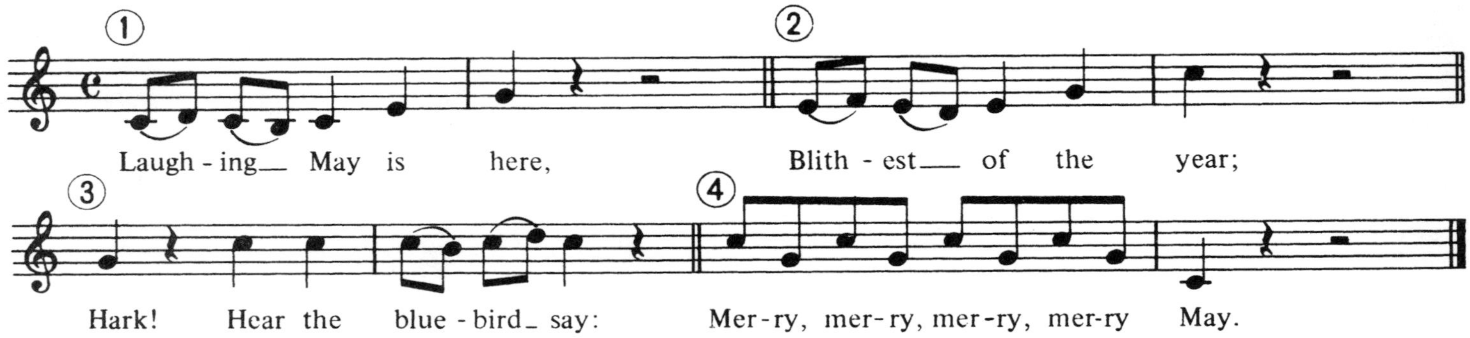

Laugh-ing__ May is here, Blith-est__ of the year; Hark! Hear the blue-bird_ say: Mer-ry, mer-ry, mer-ry, mer-ry May.

Let the Wind Blow

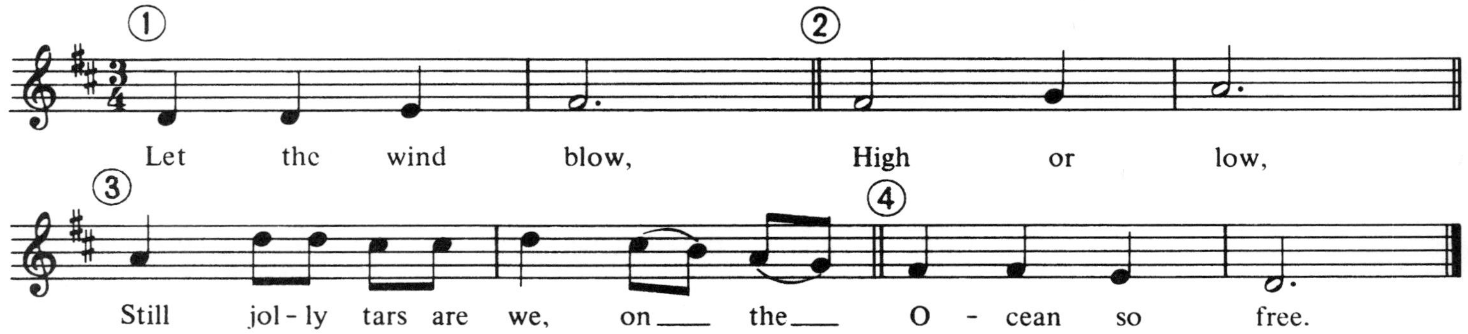

Let the wind blow, High or low, Still jol-ly tars are we, on__ the__ O-cean so free.

Love Your Neighbor

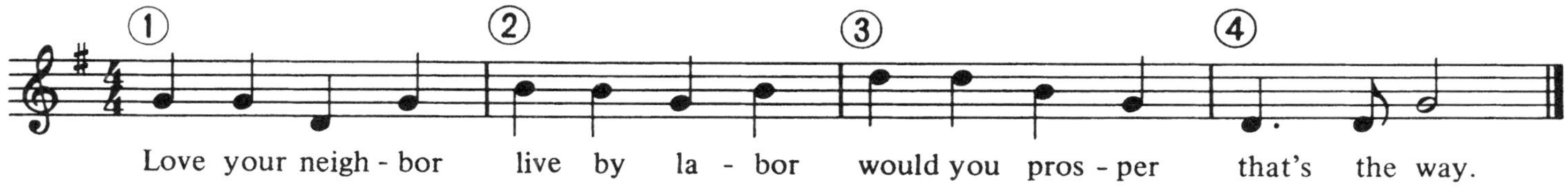

Love your neigh-bor live by la-bor would you pros-per that's the way.

May-Day

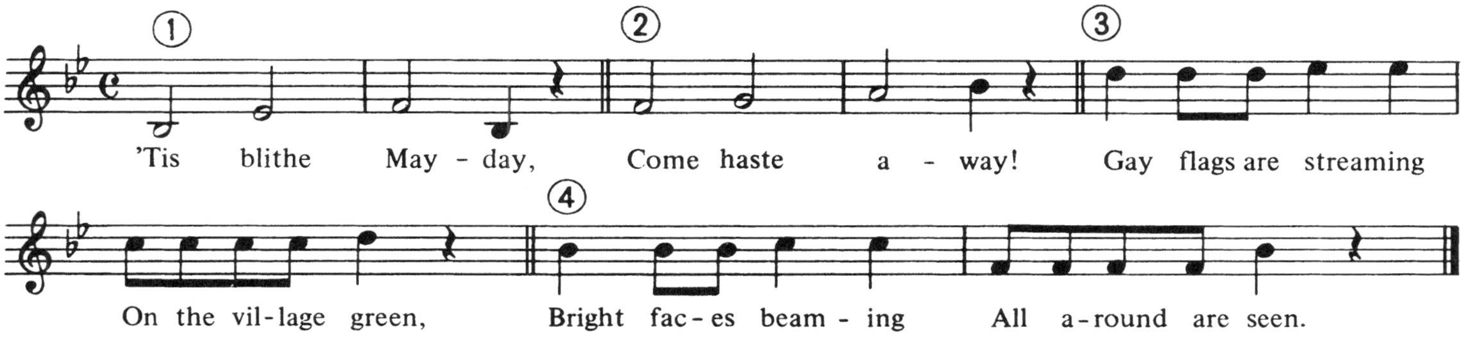

'Tis blithe May-day, Come haste a-way! Gay flags are streaming On the vil-lage green, Bright fac-es beam-ing All a-round are seen.

Merrily, Merrily Greet the Morn

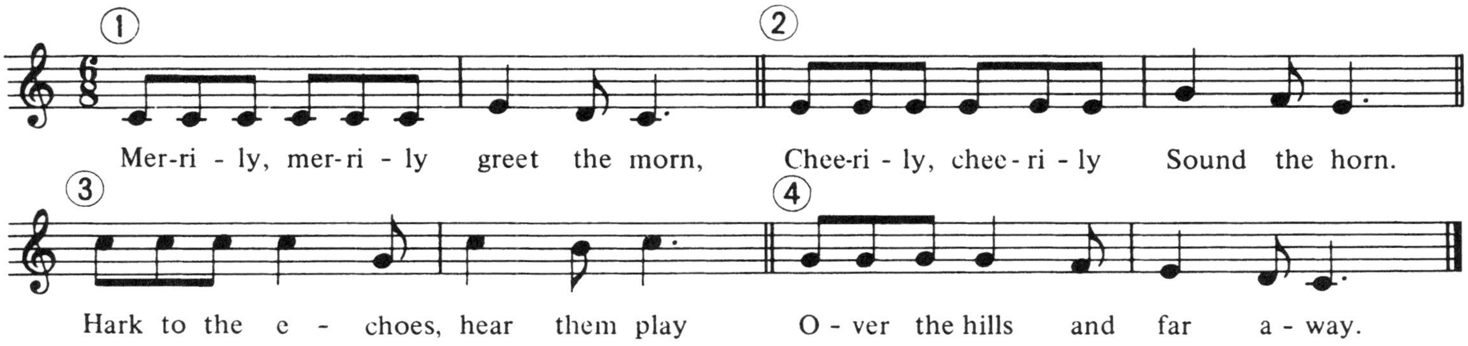

Mer-ri-ly, mer-ri-ly greet the morn, Chee-ri-ly, chee-ri-ly Sound the horn. Hark to the e-choes, hear them play O-ver the hills and far a-way.

Morning Is Come

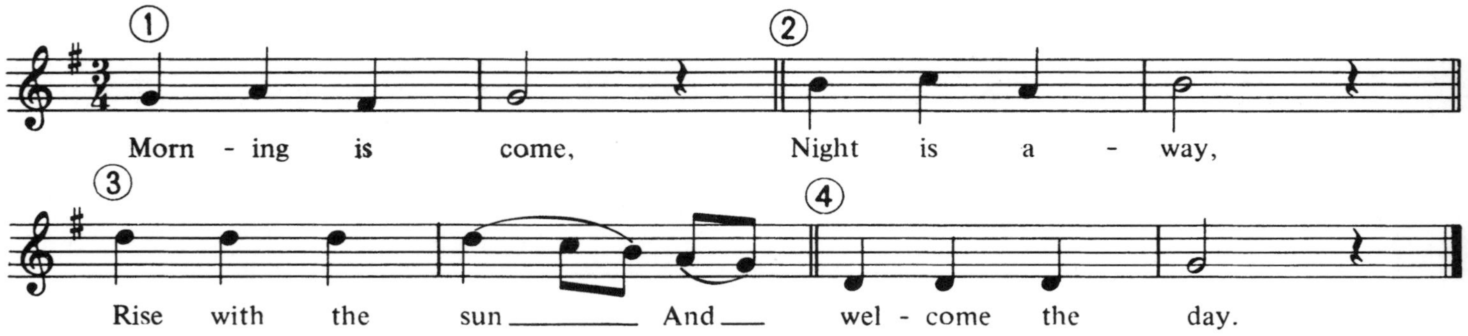

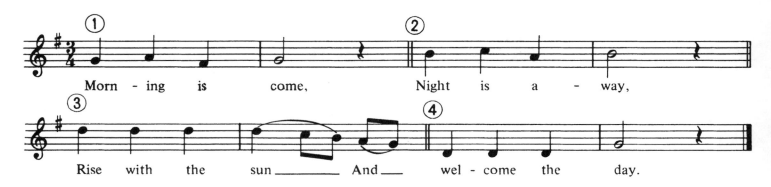

Morn - ing is come, Night is a - way,

Rise with the sun ___ And ___ wel - come the day.

My Goose and Thy Goose

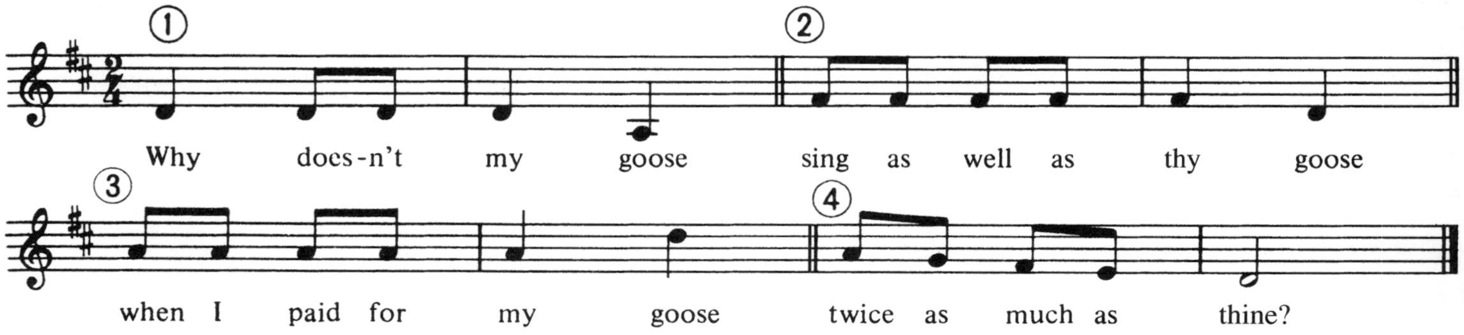

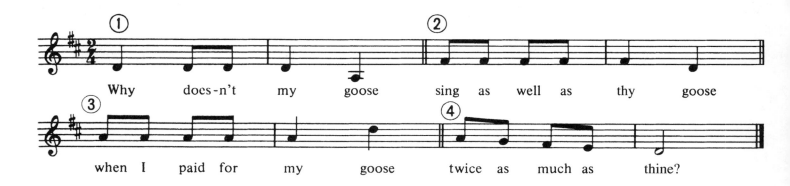

Why does-n't my goose sing as well as thy goose

when I paid for my goose twice as much as thine?

My Paddle's Keen and Bright

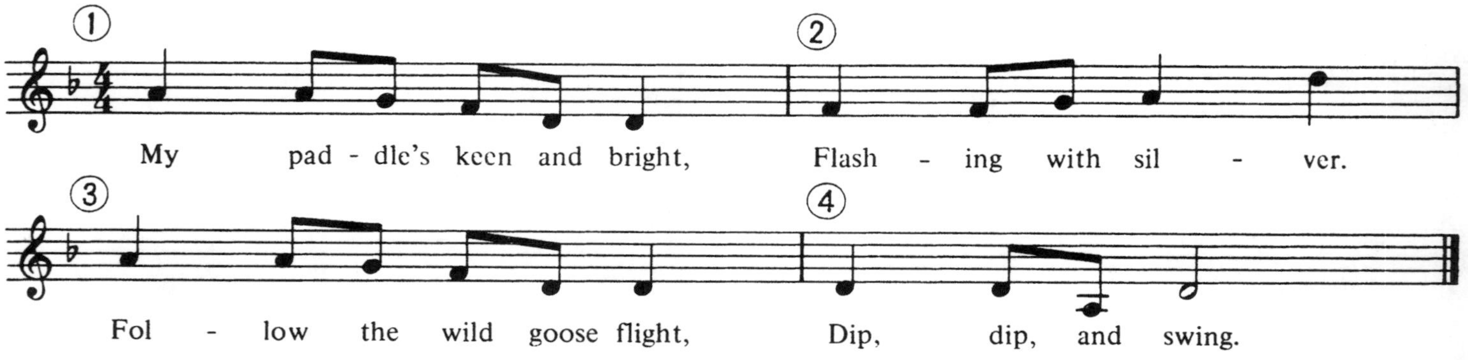

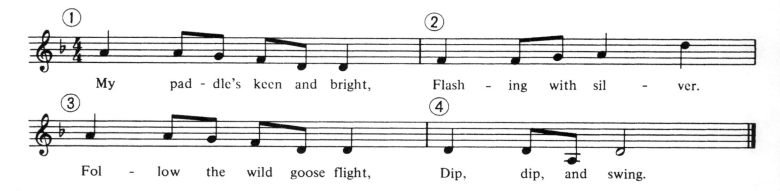

My pad - dle's keen and bright, Flash - ing with sil - ver.

Fol - low the wild goose flight, Dip, dip, and swing.

Now the Day Is Nearly Done

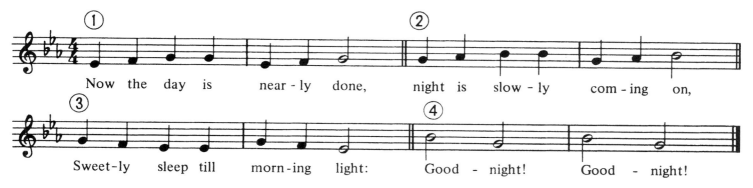

Now the day is near-ly done, night is slow-ly com-ing on,

Sweet-ly sleep till morn-ing light: Good - night! Good - night!

Now We'll Make the Rafters Ring

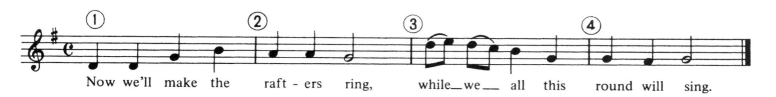

Now we'll make the raft-ers ring, while we all this round will sing.

On Mules We Find

On mules we find two legs be-hind, and two we find be - fore.

We stand be - hind be - fore we find what the two be - hind be for.

When we're be-hind the two be - hind, we find what these be for.

So stand be - fore the two be - hind, and be-hind the two be - fore.

Scotland's Burning

Scot-land's burn-ing, Scot-land's burn-ing! Look out! look out!
Fire! fire! fire! fire! Pour on wa-ter, pour on wa-ter!

Sing It Over

Sing it o - ver With your might;
Ne - ver leave it, ne - ver leave it Till 'tis right.

Sing One, Two, Three

Sing one, two, three, Come fol - low me, And so shall we Good fel - lows_ be.

Sweet Is the Hour

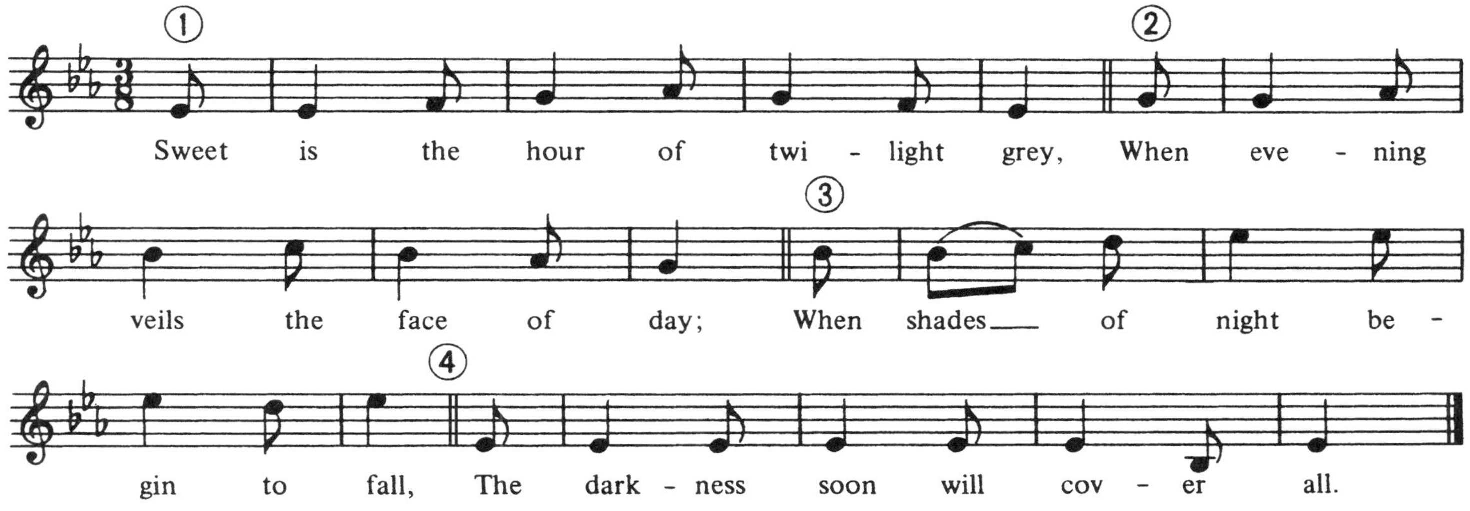

Sweet is the hour of twi-light grey, When eve-ning veils the face of day; When shades___ of night be-gin to fall, The dark-ness soon will cov-er all.

Thirty Days Hath September

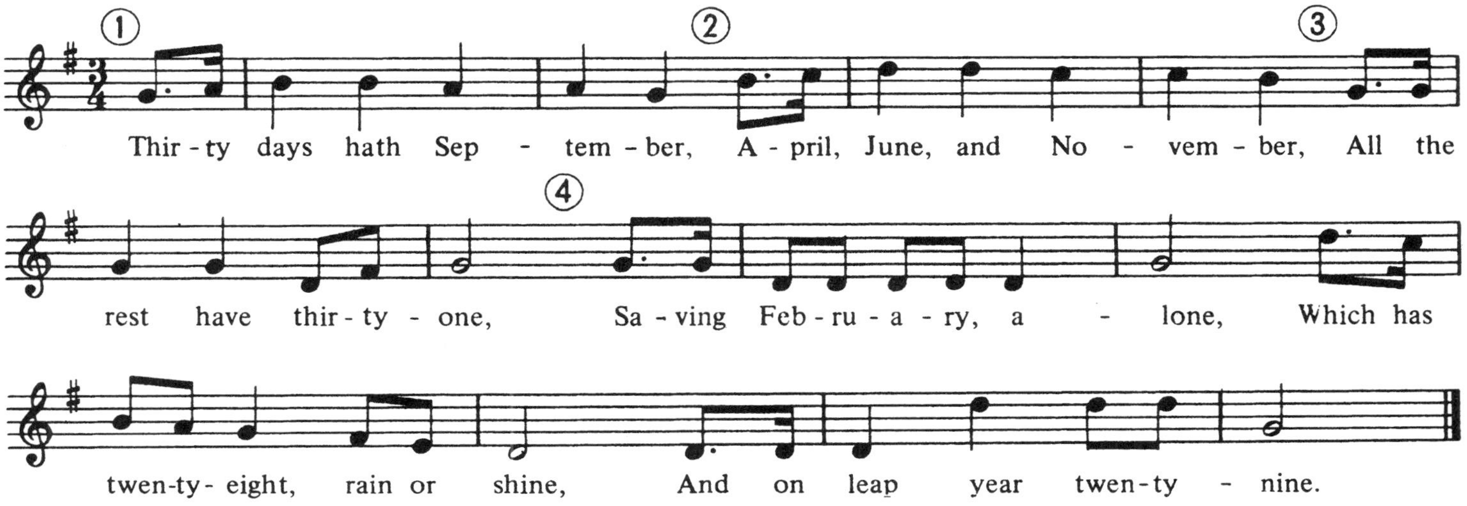

Thir-ty days hath Sep-tem-ber, A-pril, June, and No-vem-ber, All the rest have thir-ty-one, Sa-ving Feb-ru-a-ry, a-lone, Which has twen-ty-eight, rain or shine, And on leap year twen-ty-nine.

Those Evening Bells

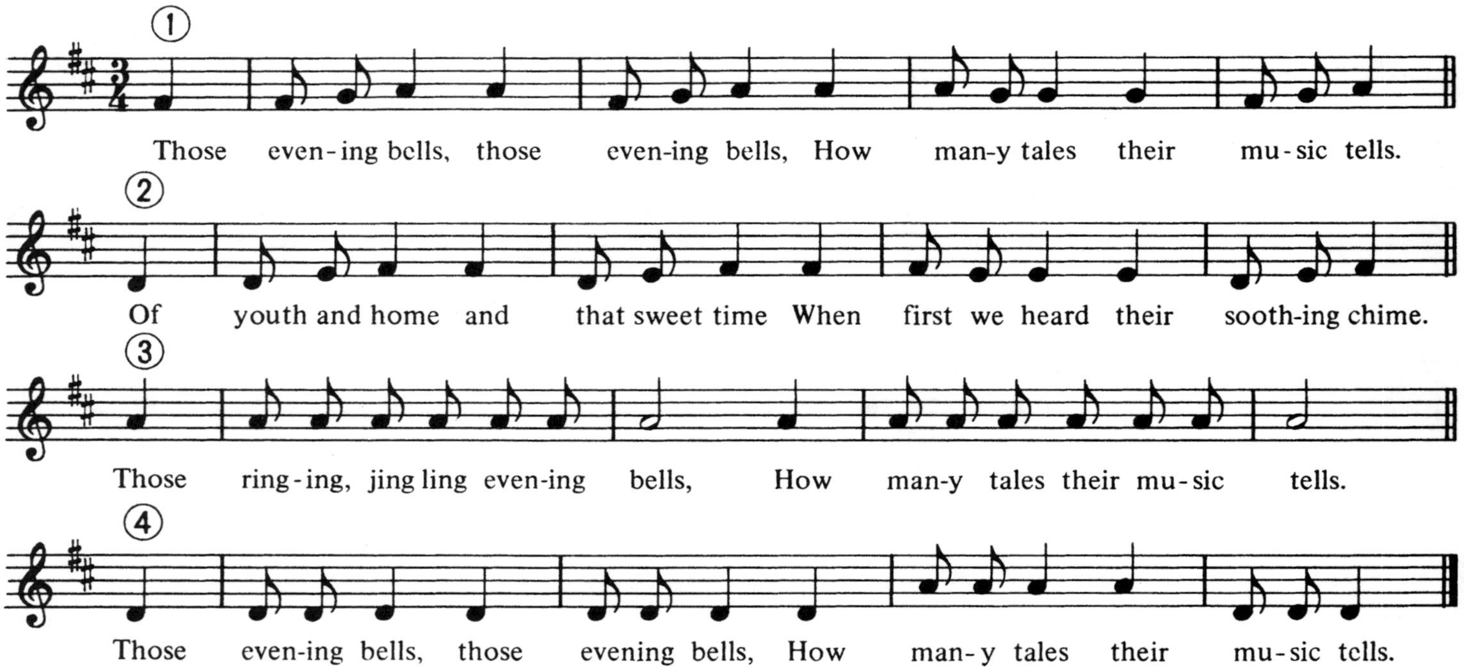
Those even-ing bells, those even-ing bells, How man-y tales their mu-sic tells.
Of youth and home and that sweet time When first we heard their sooth-ing chime.
Those ring-ing, jing ling even-ing bells, How man-y tales their mu-sic tells.
Those even-ing bells, those evening bells, How man-y tales their mu-sic tells.

Thou Poor Bird

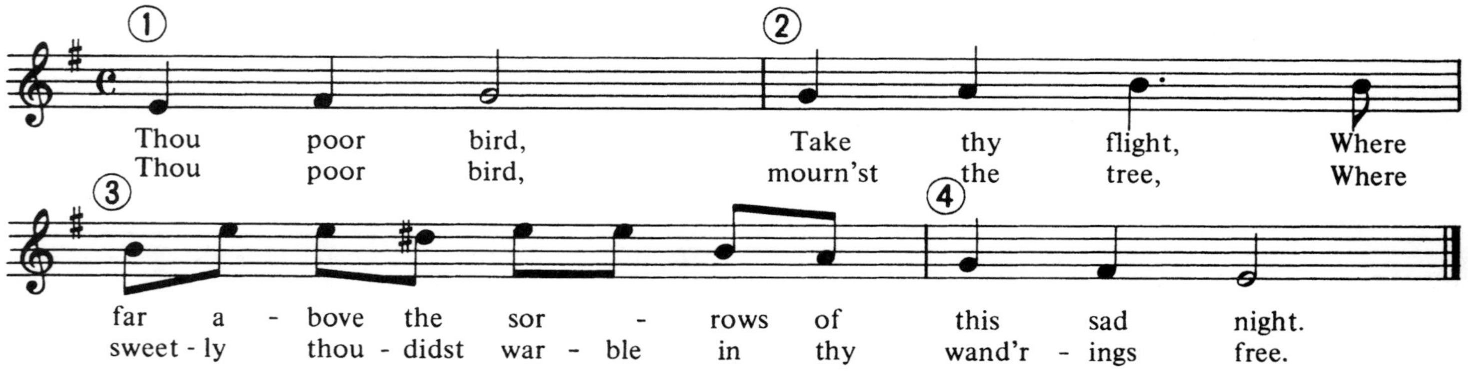
Thou poor bird, Take thy flight, Where
Thou poor bird, mourn'st the tree, Where
far a - bove the sor - rows of this sad night.
sweet - ly thou - didst war - ble in thy wand'r - ings free.

Wake and Sing

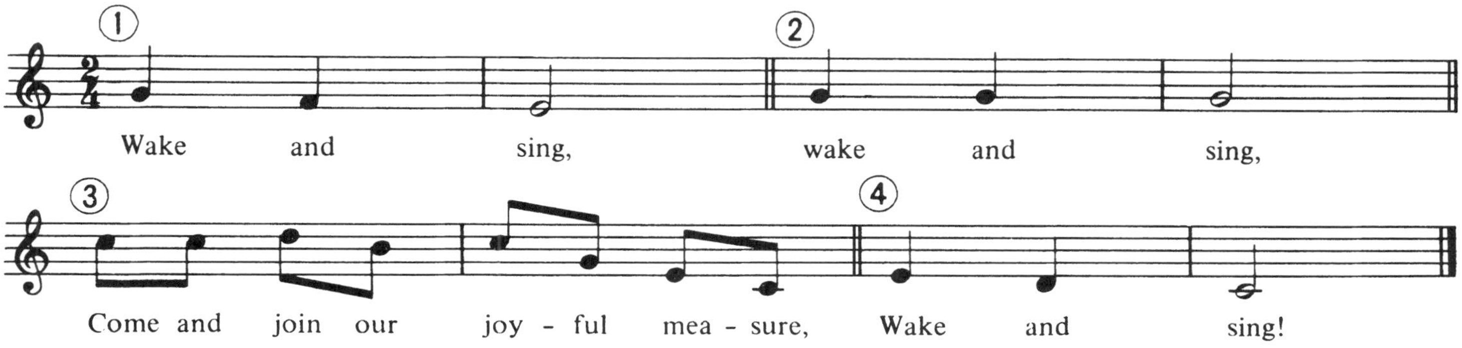

Wake and sing, wake and sing,
Come and join our joy-ful mea-sure, Wake and sing!

Well Rung, Tom

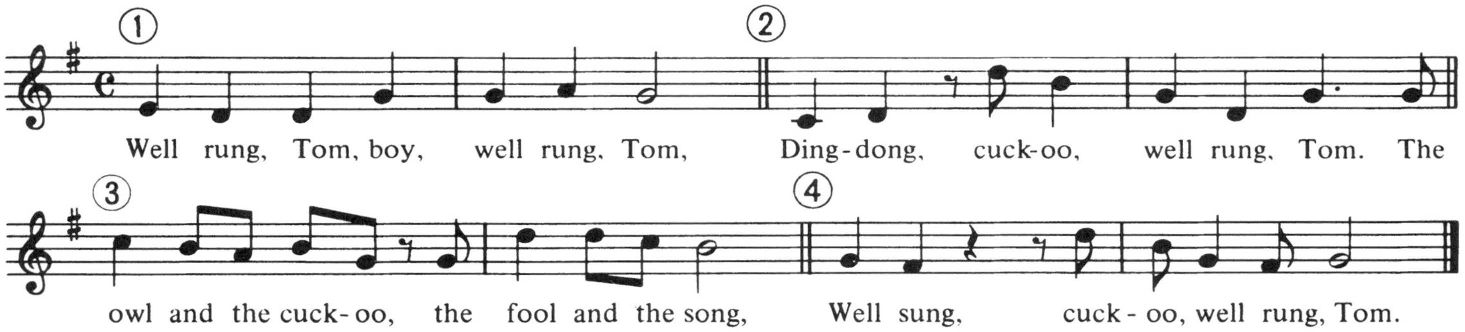

Well rung, Tom, boy, well rung, Tom, Ding-dong, cuck-oo, well rung, Tom. The
owl and the cuck-oo, the fool and the song, Well sung, cuck-oo, well rung, Tom.

The White Hen

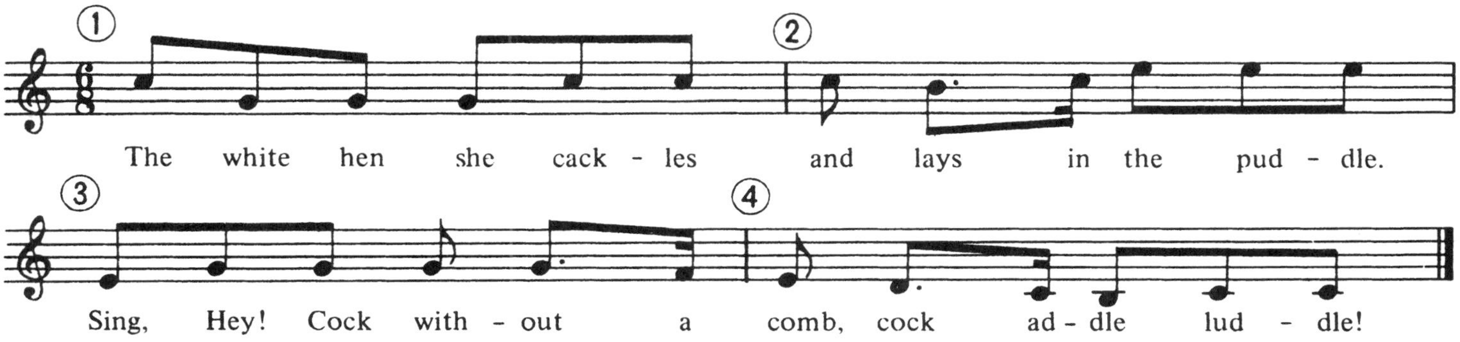

The white hen she cack-les and lays in the pud-dle.
Sing, Hey! Cock with-out a comb, cock ad-dle lud-dle!

White Coral Bells

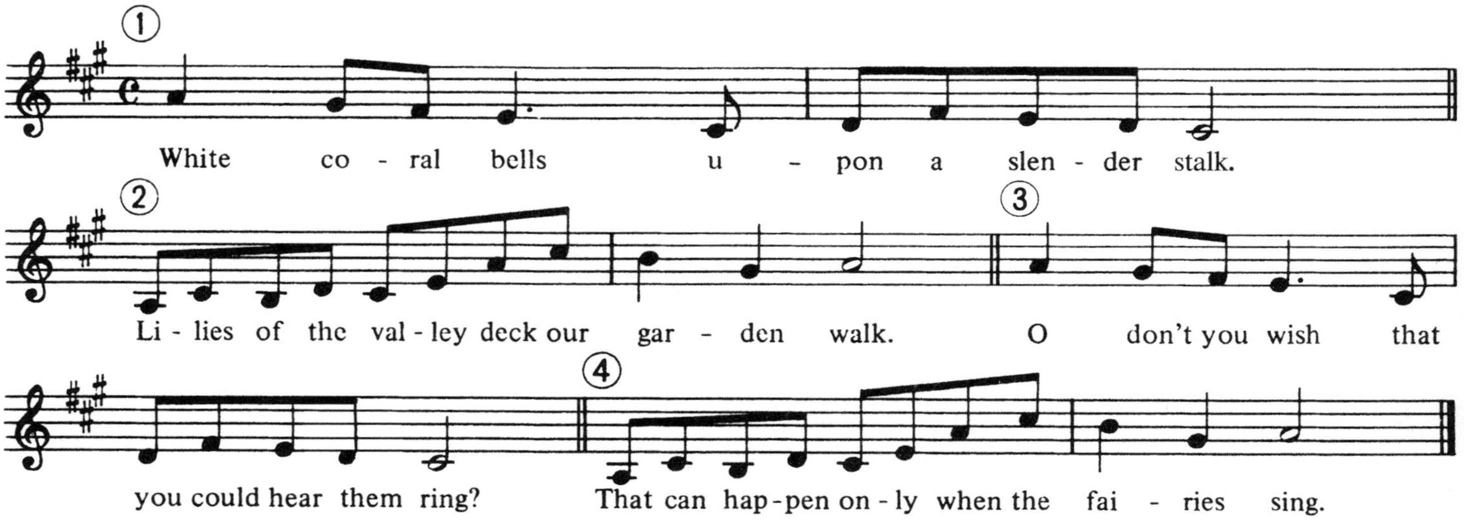

White co-ral bells u-pon a slen-der stalk. Li-lies of the val-ley deck our gar-den walk. O don't you wish that you could hear them ring? That can hap-pen on-ly when the fai-ries sing.

Who'll Buy My Posies

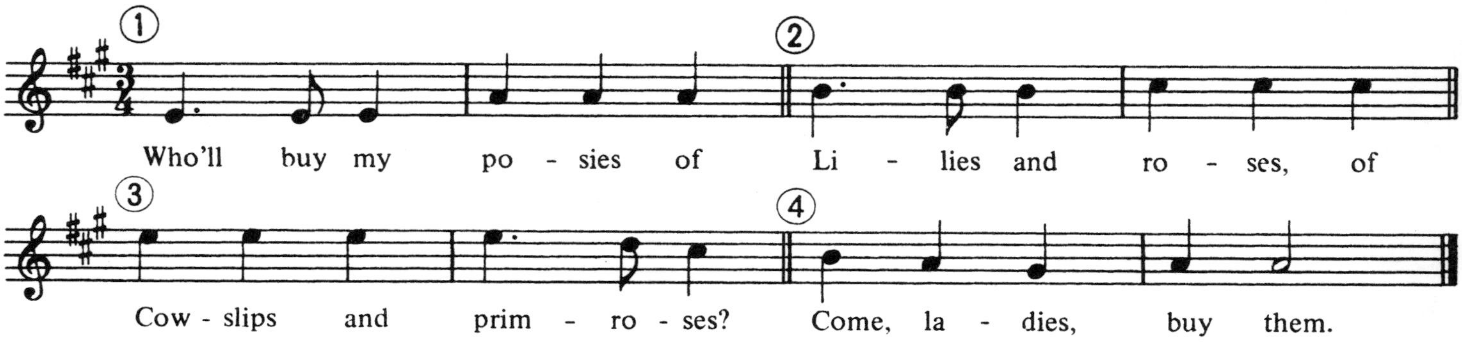

Who'll buy my po-sies of Li-lies and ro-ses, of Cow-slips and prim-ro-ses? Come, la-dies, buy them.

Singing with Grandma

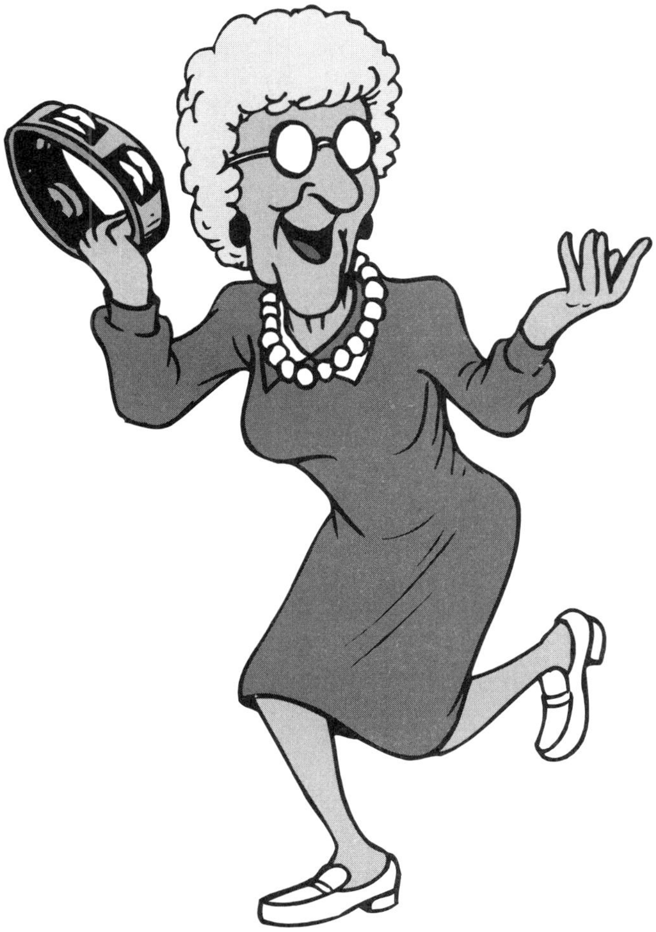

Aura Lee

Words by W.W. Fosdick

Music by George R. Poulton

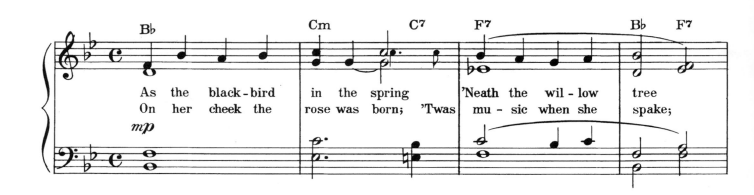

As the black-bird in the spring 'Neath the wil-low tree
On her cheek the rose was born; 'Twas mu - sic when she spake;

Sat and piped, I heard him sing, Sing - ing Au - ra Lee.
In her eyes the rays of morn, With sud - den splen - dor break.

Chorus

Au - ra Lee, Au - ra Lee Maid with gold - en hair

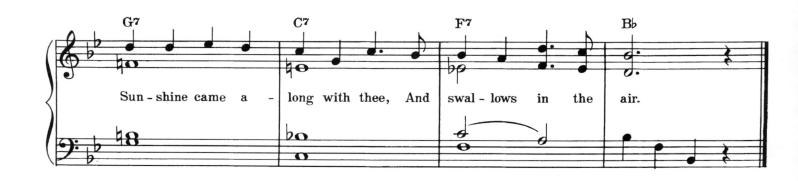

Sun-shine came a - long with thee, And swal - lows in the air.

3. From my the heart the answer came,
   Sure and sweet and clear,
   On my lips, there breathes a name,
   Aura Lee, my dear.
   Chorus

4. Aura Lee, the bird may flee
   The willow's golden hair,
   Then the wintry winds may be
   Blowing ev'rywhere.
   Chorus

5. Yet if thy blue eyes I see,
   Gloom will soon depart,
   For to me, sweet Aura Lee
   Is sunshine to the heart.
   Chorus

The Band Played On

Words by John F. Palmer

Music by Charles B. Ward

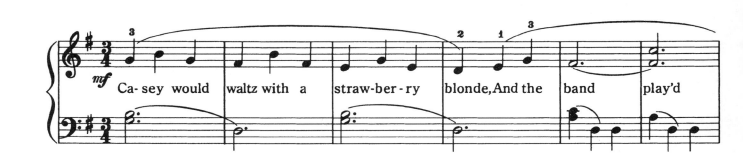

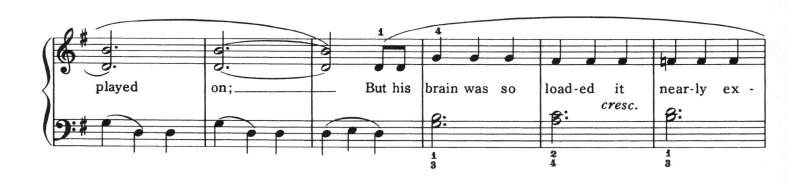

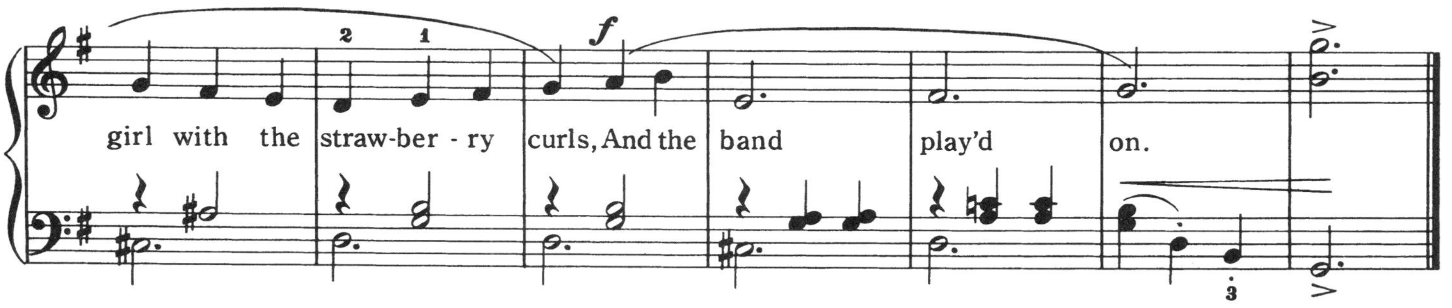

girl with the straw-ber - ry curls, And the band play'd on.

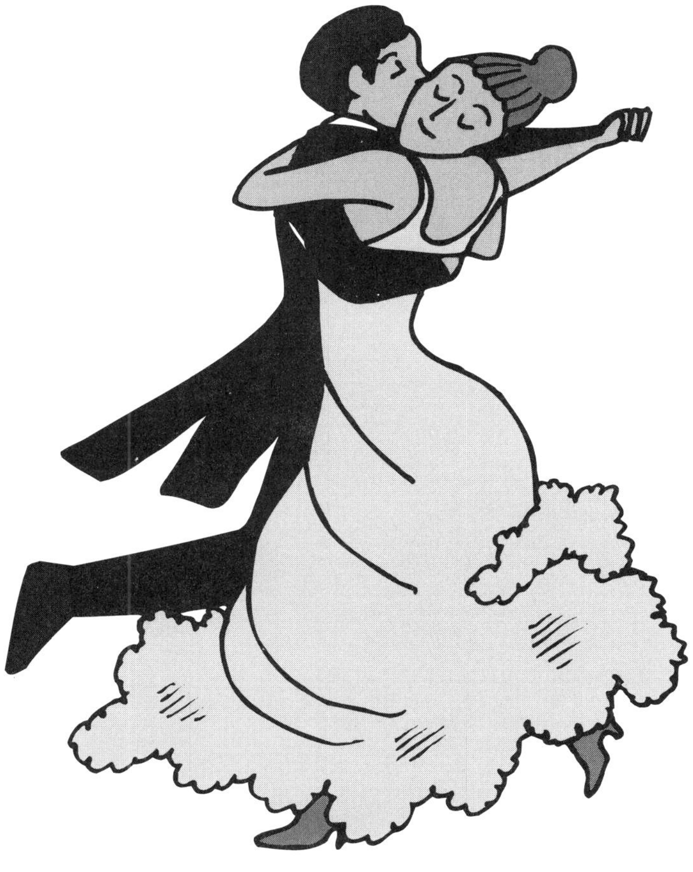

Beautiful Dreamer

Words and music by Stephen Foster

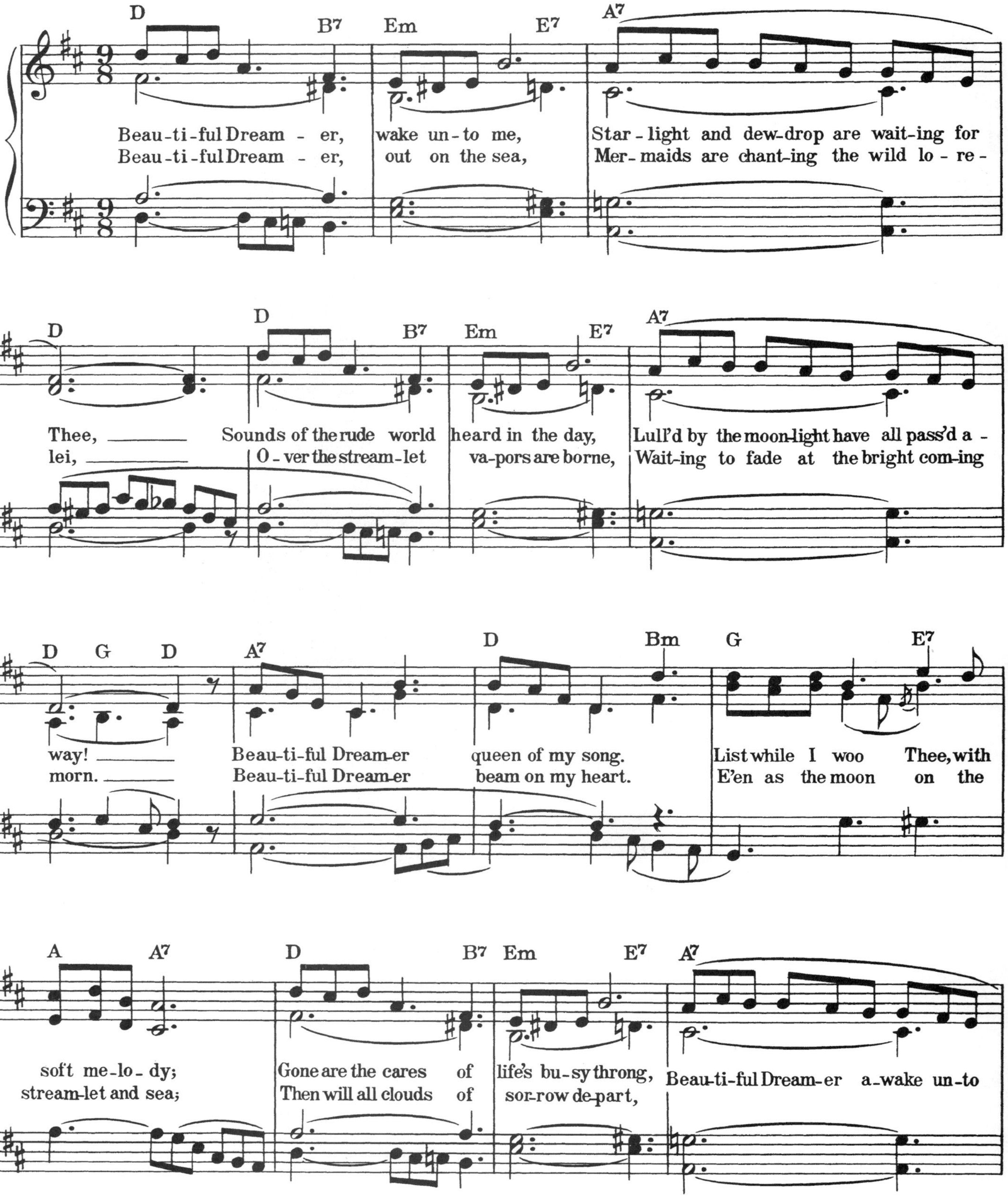

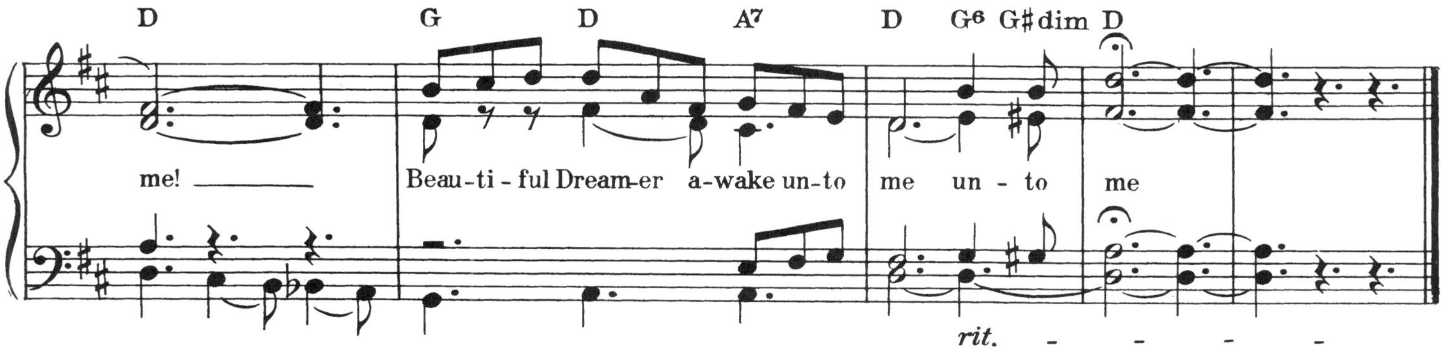
D G D A7 D G6 G#dim D
me! Beau-ti-ful Dream-er a-wake un-to me un-to me
rit.

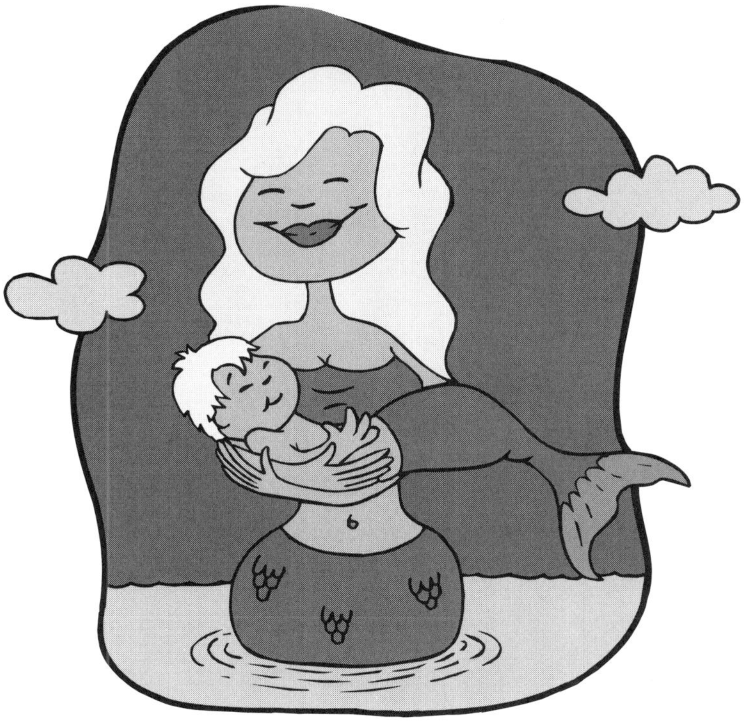

Dear Old Daddy Whiskers

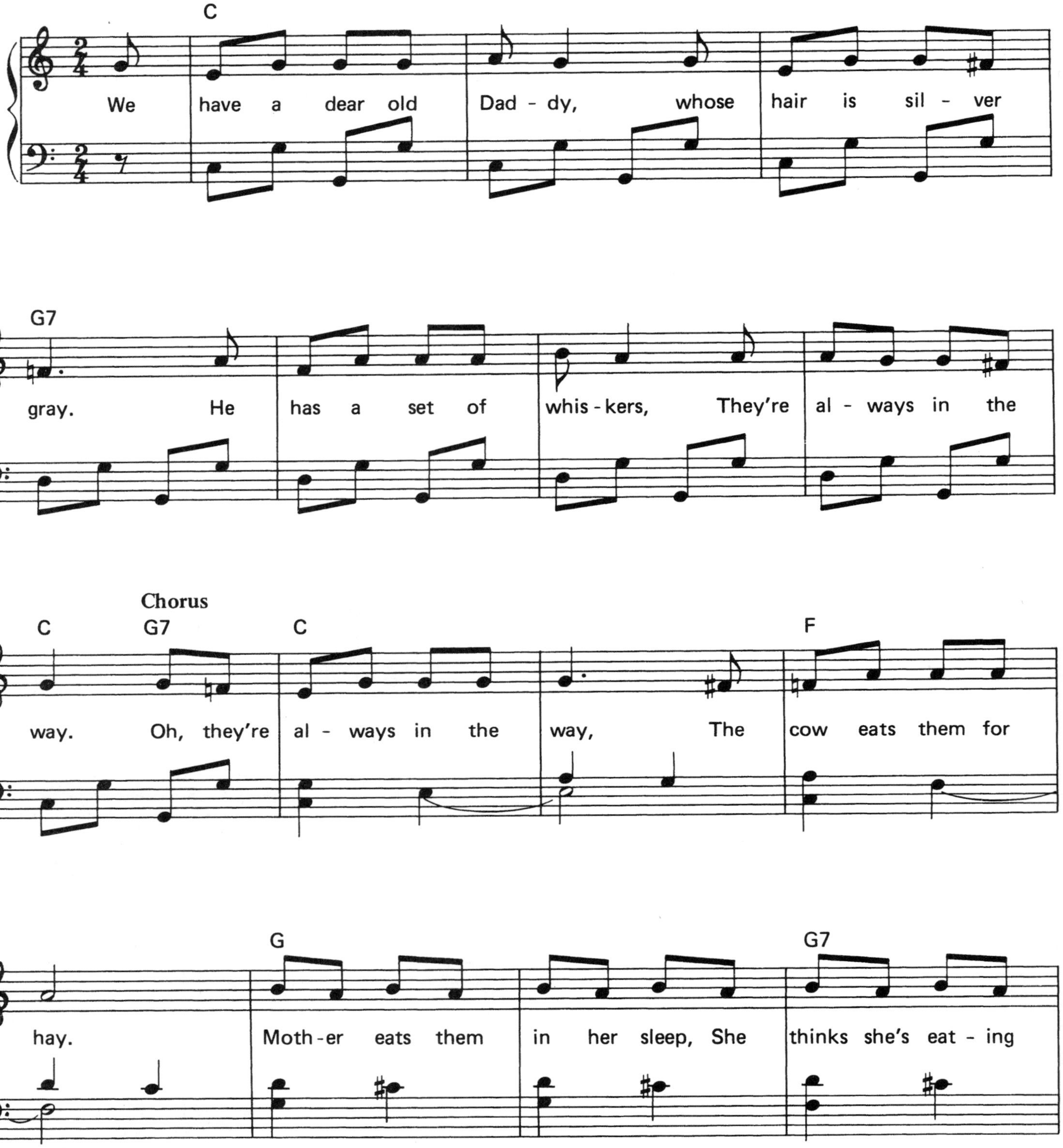
C
We have a dear old Dad - dy, whose hair is sil - ver
G7
gray. He has a set of whis - kers, They're al - ways in the
Chorus
C G7 C F
way. Oh, they're al - ways in the way, The cow eats them for
G G7
hay. Moth - er eats them in her sleep, She thinks she's eat - ing

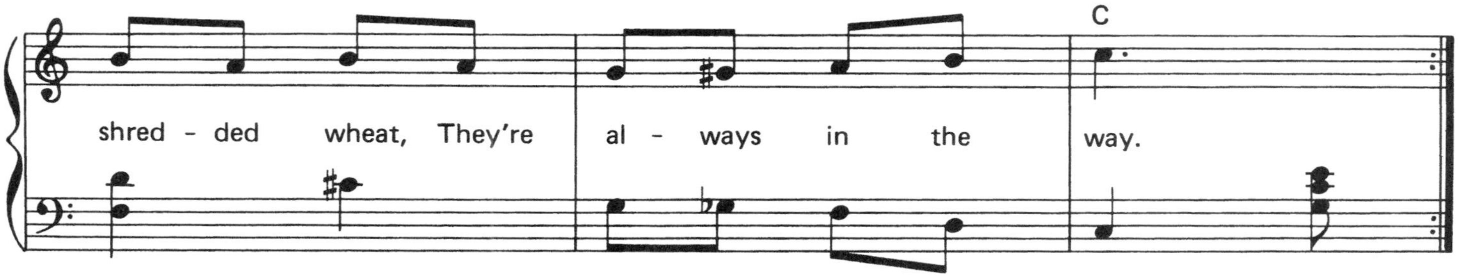

shred - ded   wheat,   They're   al - ways   in   the   way.

2. We have a dear old Mommy,
   She likes his whiskers, too.
   She uses them for cleaning
   And stirring up a stew.
   Chorus

3. We have a dear old brother,
   Who has a Ford machine.
   He uses Daddy's whiskers
   To strain the gasoline.
   Chorus

4. We have a dear old sister
   Her name is Ida Mae.
   She climbs up Daddy's whiskers
   And braids them every day.
   Chorus

5. Around the supper table,
   We make a merry group,
   Until dear Daddy's whiskers
   Get tangled in the soup.
   Chorus

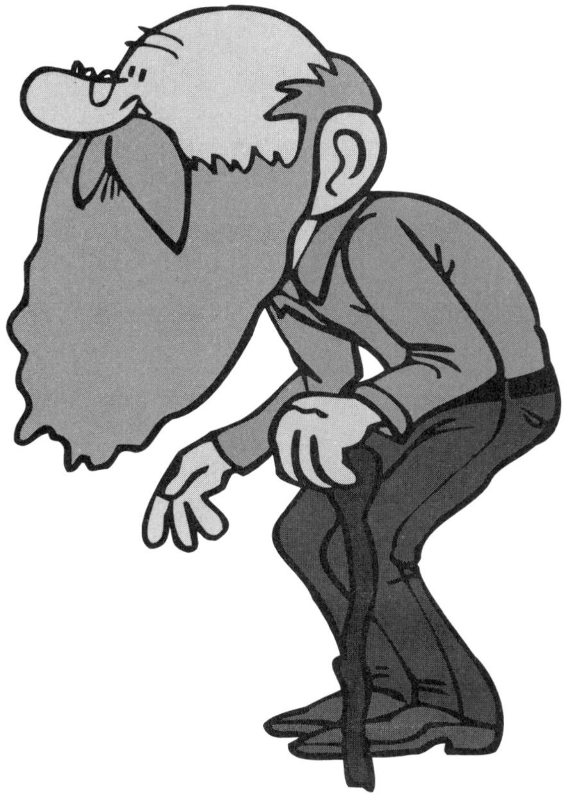

Grandfather's Clock

Words and music by Henry C. Work

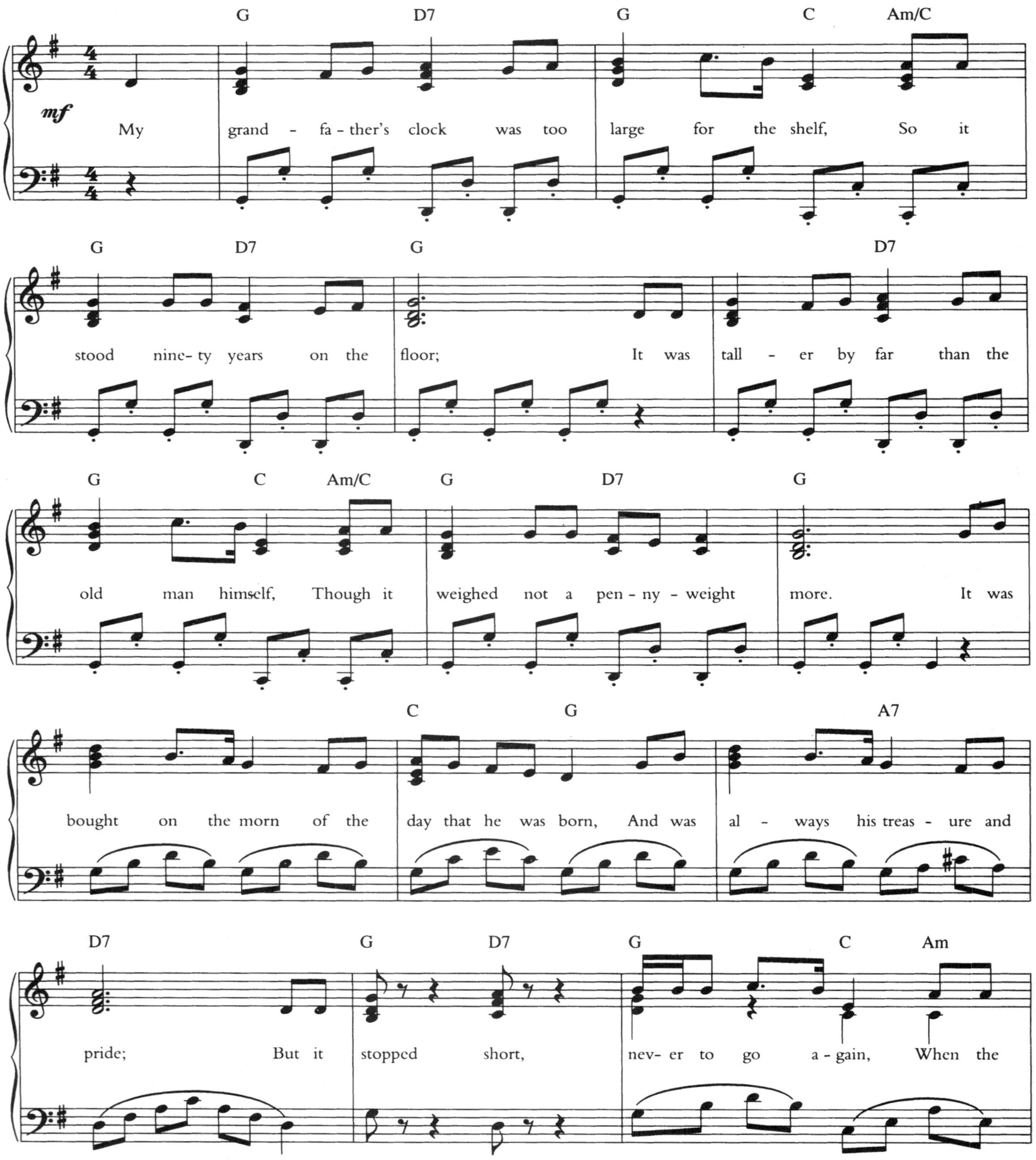

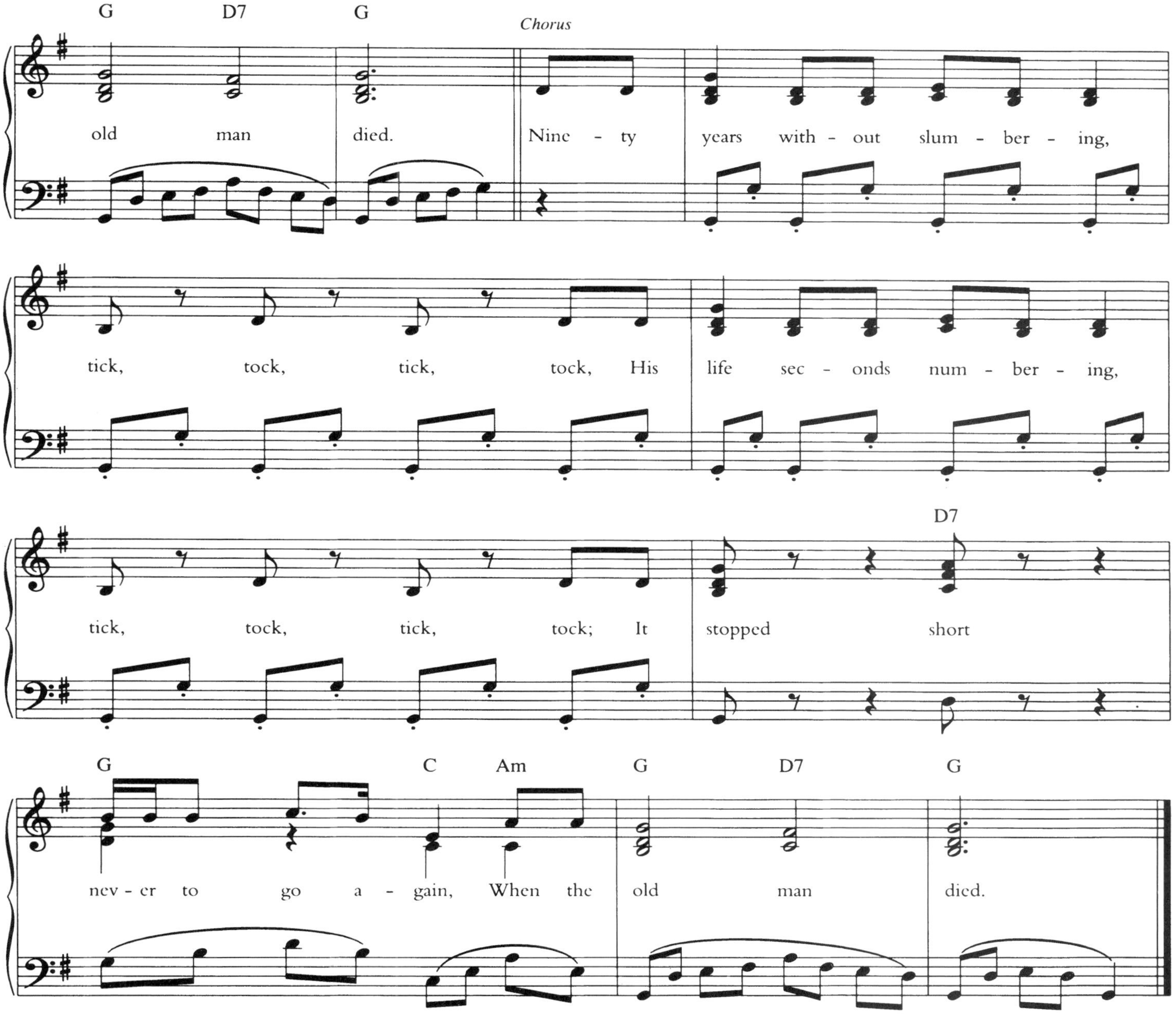

G   D7   G   *Chorus*

old   man   died.   Nine - ty   years   with - out   slum - ber - ing,

tick,   tock,   tick,   tock,   His   life   sec - onds   num - ber - ing,

tick,   tock,   tick,   tock;   It   stopped   short

G   C Am   G   D7   G

nev - er   to   go   a - gain,   When   the   old   man   died.

2. In watching its pendulum swing to and fro,
Many hours had he spent while a boy;
And in childhood and manhood, the clock seemed to know,
And to share both his grief and his joy;
For it struck twenty-four when he entered at the door,
With a blooming and beautiful bride;
But it stopped short, never to go again,
When the old man died.
Chorus

3. My grandfather said that of those he could hire,
Not a servant so fauthful he found;
For it wasted no time, and had but one desire,
At the close of each week, to be wound;
And it kept in its place, not a frown upon its face,
And its hands never hung by its side;
But it stopped short, never to go again,
When the old man died.
Chorus

4. It rang an alarm in the dead of the night,
An alarm that, for years, had been dumb;
And we knew that his spirit was pluming its flight,
That his hour of departure had come.
Still the clock kept the time, with a soft and muffled chime,
As we silently stood by his side;
But it stopped short, never to go again,
When the old man died.
Chorus

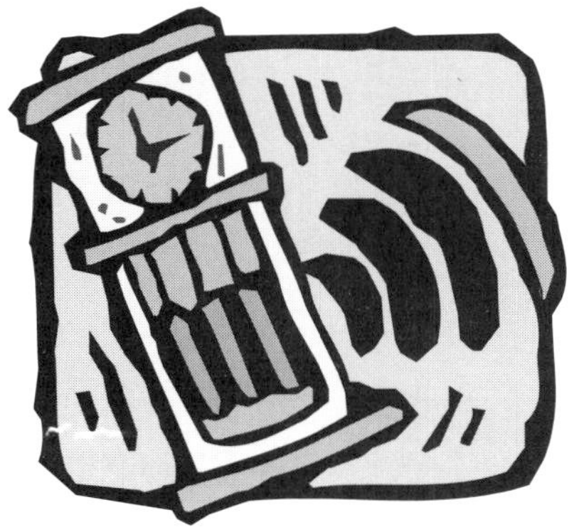

Home, Sweet Home

Words by John Howard Payne

Music by Henry R. Bishop

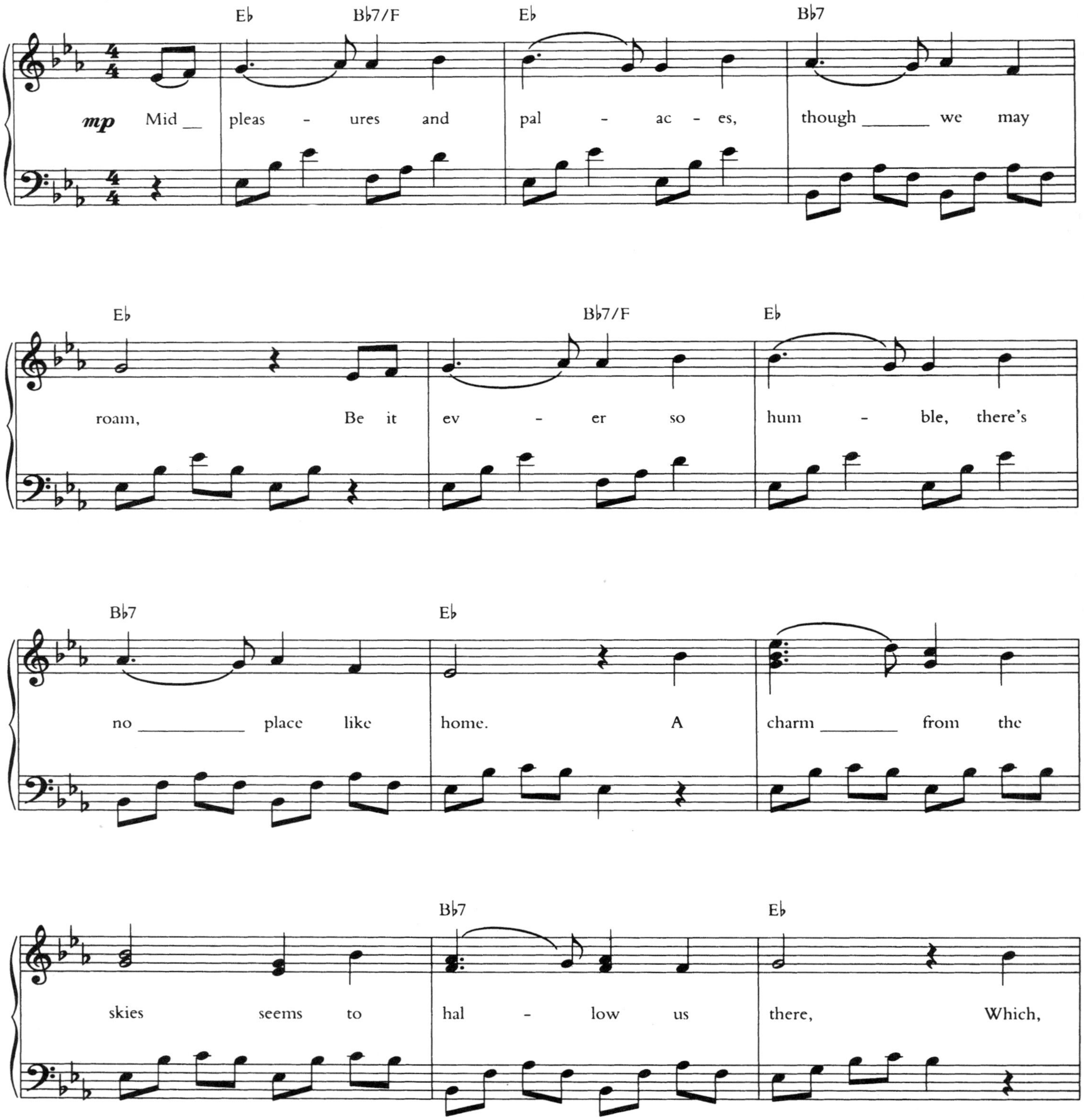

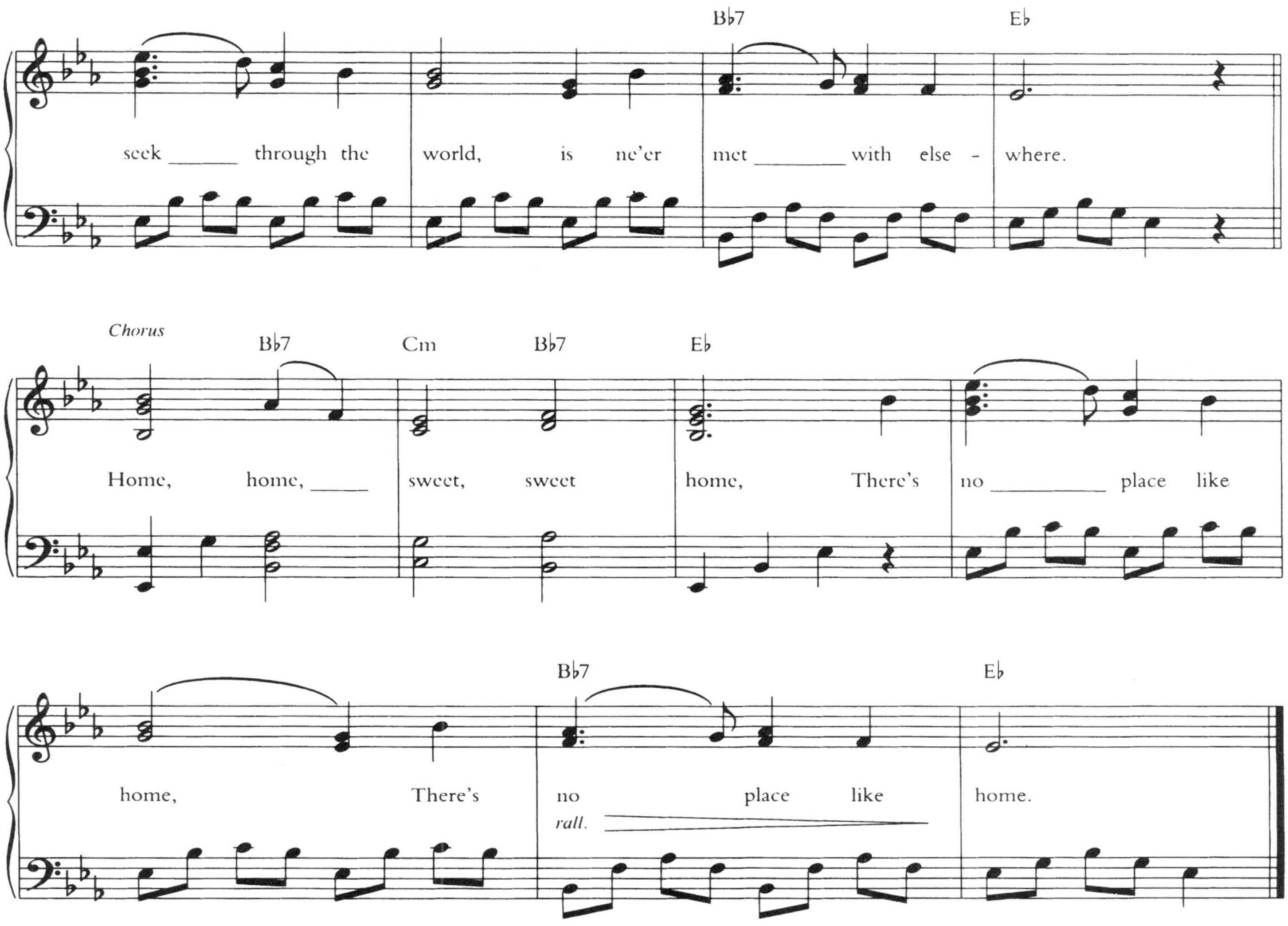

seek _____ through the world, is ne'er met _____ with else - where.

Chorus

Home, home, _____ sweet, sweet home, There's no _____ place like

home, There's no _____ place like home.

rall.

2. I gaze on the moon as I tread the drear wild,
   And feel that my mother now thinks of her child,
   As she looks on that moon from our own cottage door,
   Through the woodbine whose fragrance shall cheer me
       no more.
   Chorus

3. An exile from home, splendor dazzles in vain;
   Oh, give me a lowly thatched cottage again;
   The birds singing gaily, that came at my call,
   Give me them, and that peace of mind, dearer than all.
   Chorus

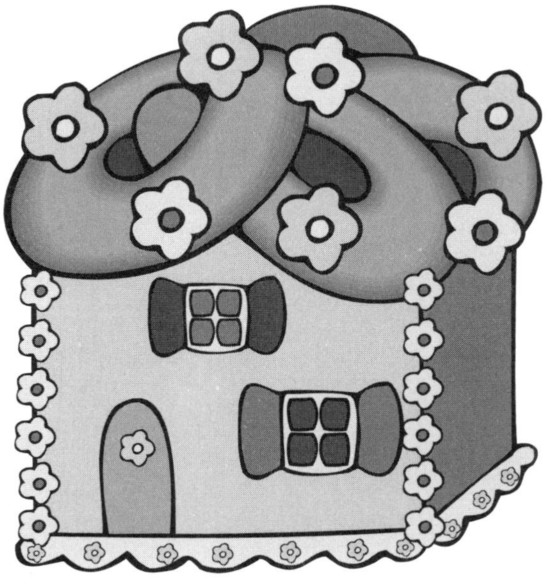

I Dream of Jeanie with the Light Brown Hair

Words and music by Stephen Foster

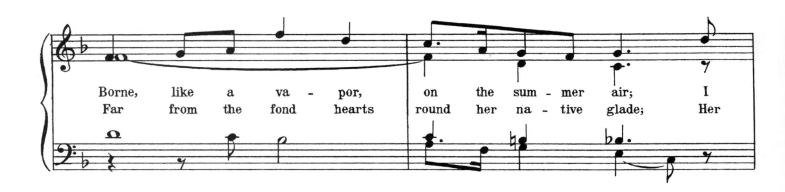

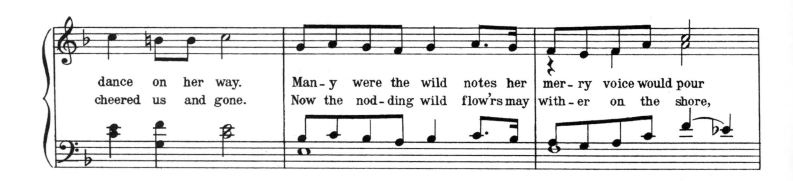

Man - y were the blithe birds that war - bled them o'er: I dream of Jean-ie With The
While her gen - tle fin - gers will cull them no more; I sigh for Jean-ie With The

Light Brown Hair, Float-ing like a va - por on the soft, sum-mer air.
Light Brown Hair, Float-ing like a va - por on the soft, sum-mer air.

I Love a Piano

Words by Glen MacDonough

Music by Irving Berlin

i - vor - ies. And with the ped - al I love to med - dle. When Pa - de -
rew - ski comes this way, I'm so de - light - ed, If I'm in -
vit - ed To hear that long - haired ge - nius play. So you can keep your fid - dle
and your bow, Give me a P - I - A - N - O, oh, oh, I love to
stop right be - side an up - right, Or a high - toned ba - by grand.
sfz

I Love You Truly

Words and music by Carrie Jacobs-Bond

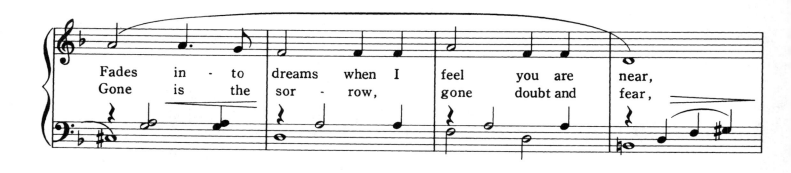

In the Evening by the Moonlight

Words and music by James A. Bland

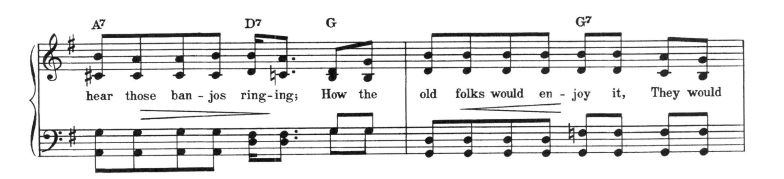

In the Good Old Summer Time

Words by Ren Shields

Music by George Evans

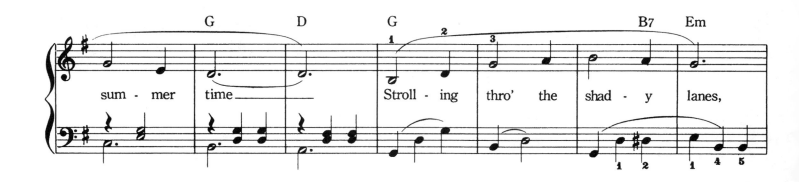

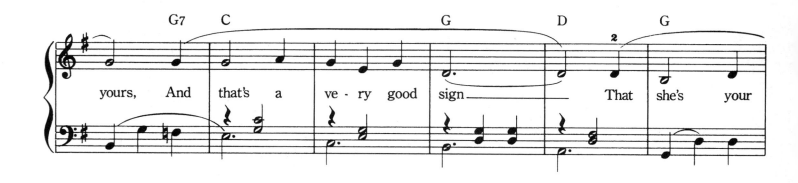

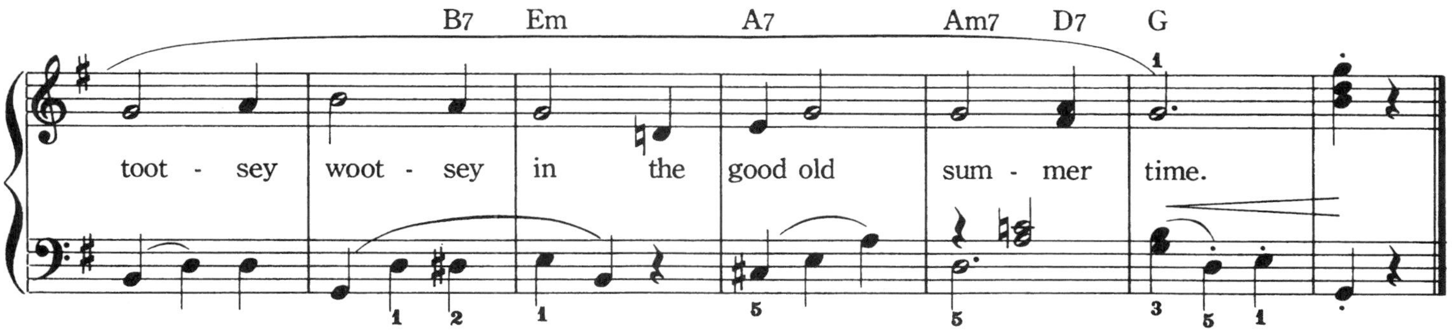

toot - sey   woot - sey   in   the   good old   sum - mer   time.

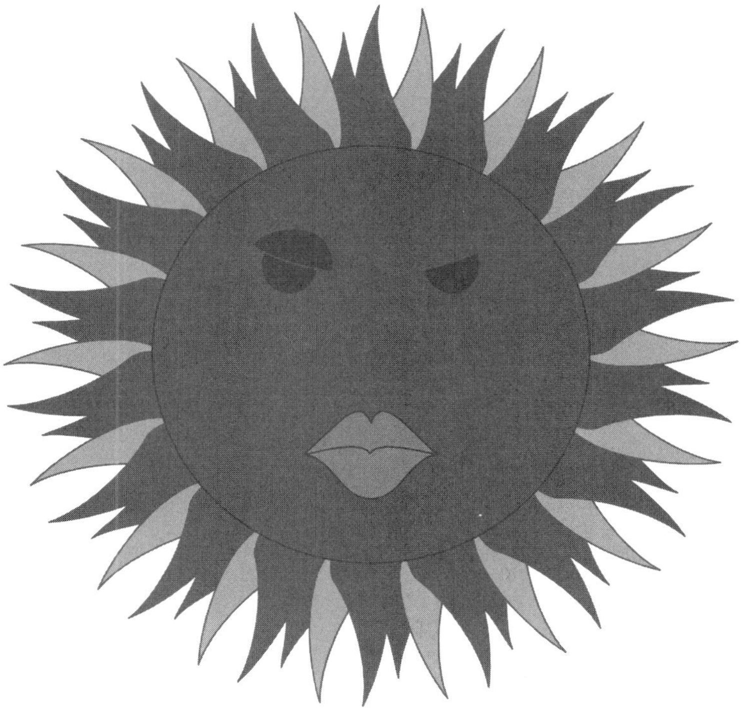

My Wild Irish Rose

Words and music by Chauncey Olcott

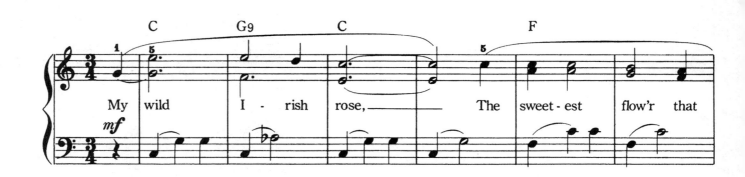

My wild I - rish rose,_____ The sweet - est flow'r that

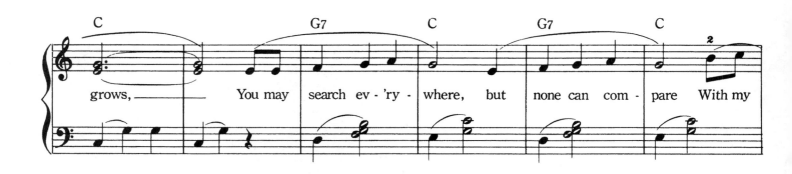

grows,_____ You may search ev - 'ry - where, but none can com - pare With my

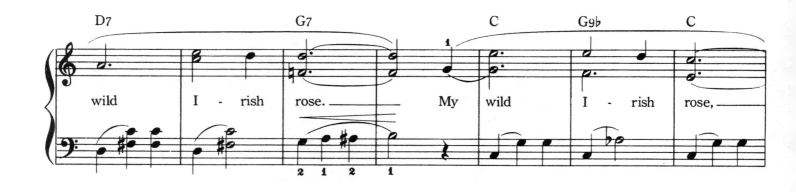

wild I - rish rose._____ My wild I - rish rose,_____

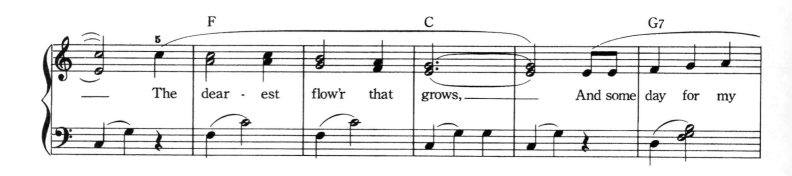

_____ The dear - est flow'r that grows,_____ And some day for my

sake, she | may let me | take The | bloom from my | wild I - rish | rose.

Old Folks at Home

Words and music by Stephen Foster

2. All 'round the little farm I wandered,
When I was young,
Then many happy days I squandered,
Many the songs I sung.
When I was playing with my brother,
Happy was I.
Oh! take me to my kind old mother,
There let me live 'neath the sky.
Chorus

3. One little hut among the bushes,
One that I love,
Still sadly to my mem'ry rushes,
No matter where I rove.
When will I see the bees a-humming,
All 'round the comb?
When will I hear the banjo strumming,
Down in my good old home?
Chorus

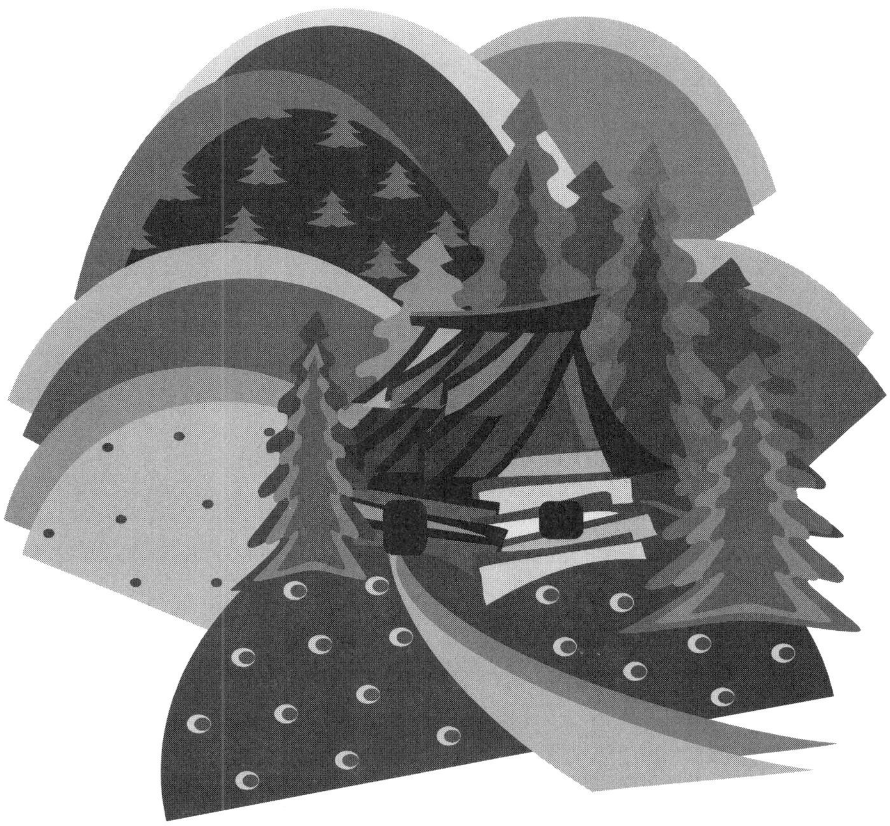

The Sidewalks of New York

Words and music by
James W. Blake & Charles B. Lawlor

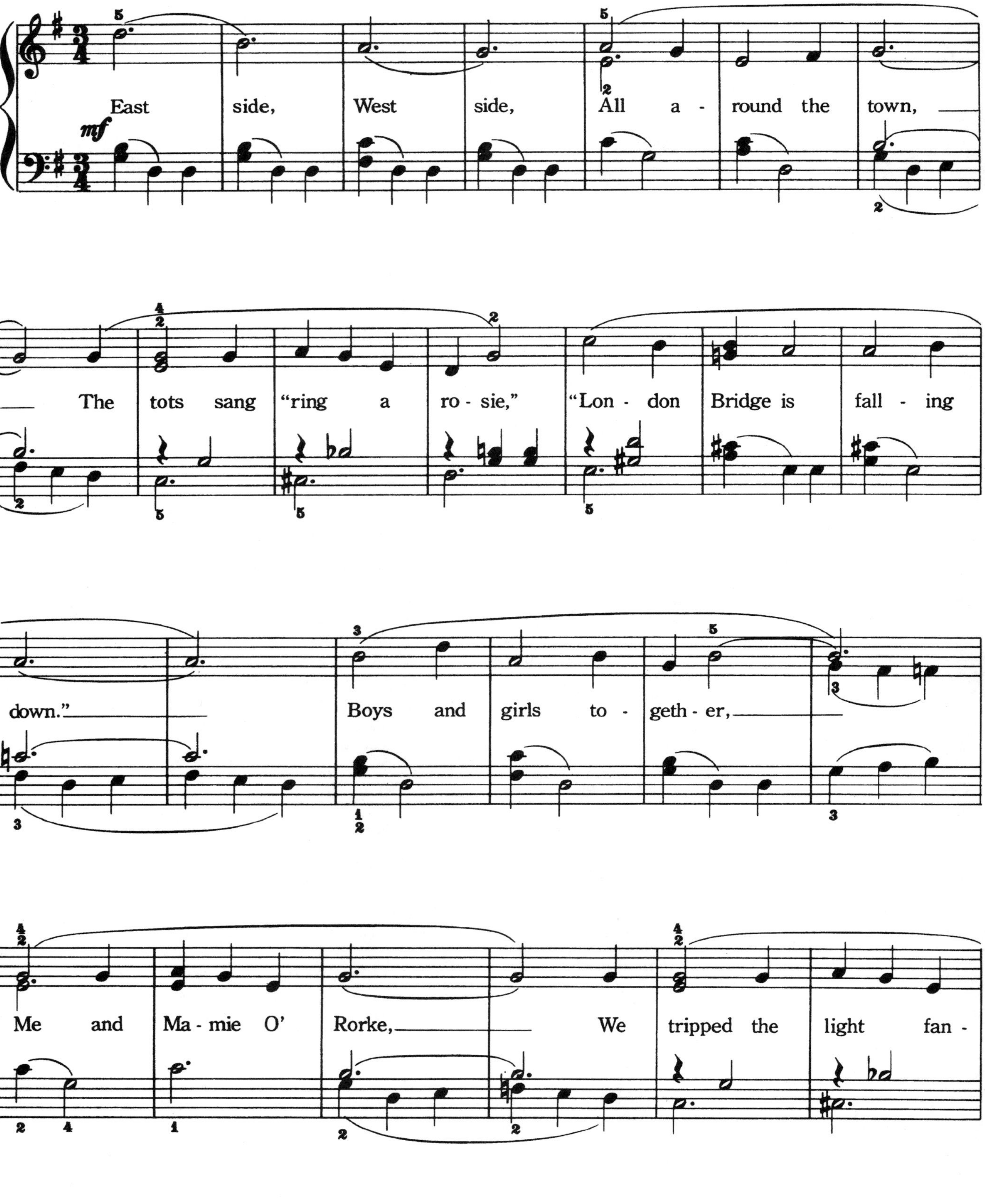

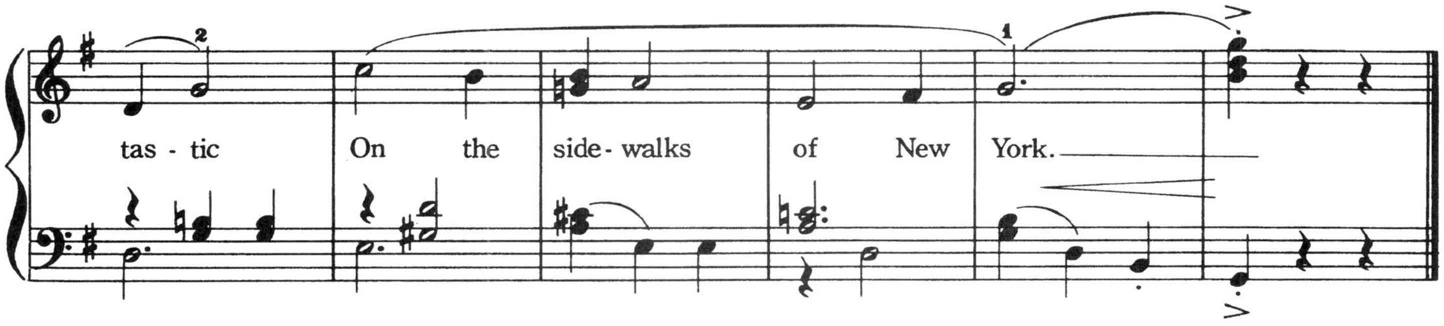

tas - tic On the side - walks of New York.

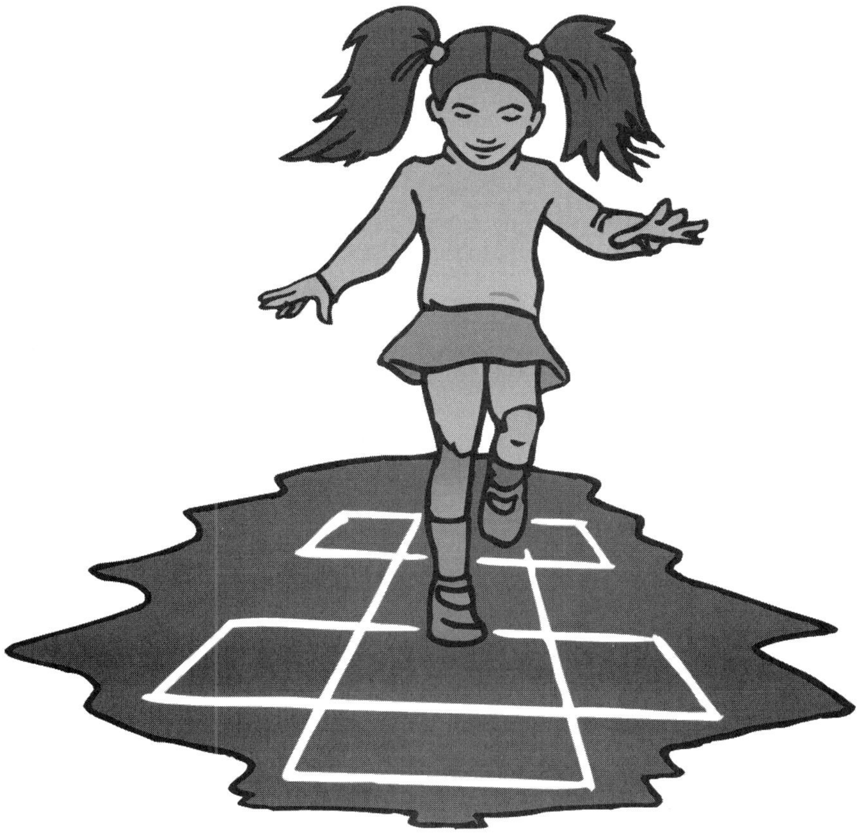

Quiet Songs
and Lullabies

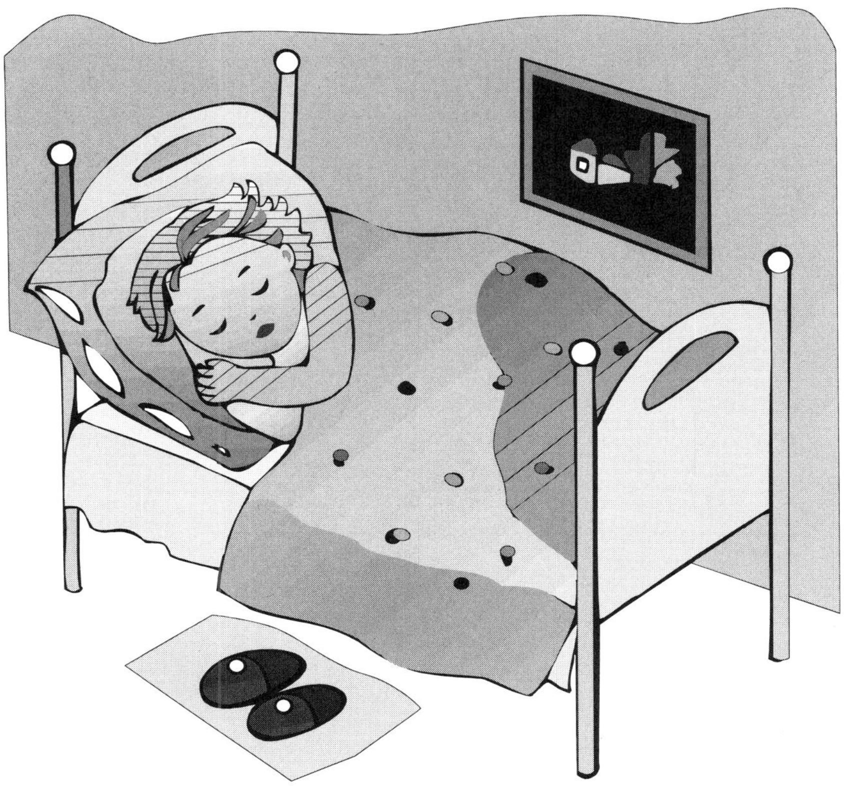

All Through the Night

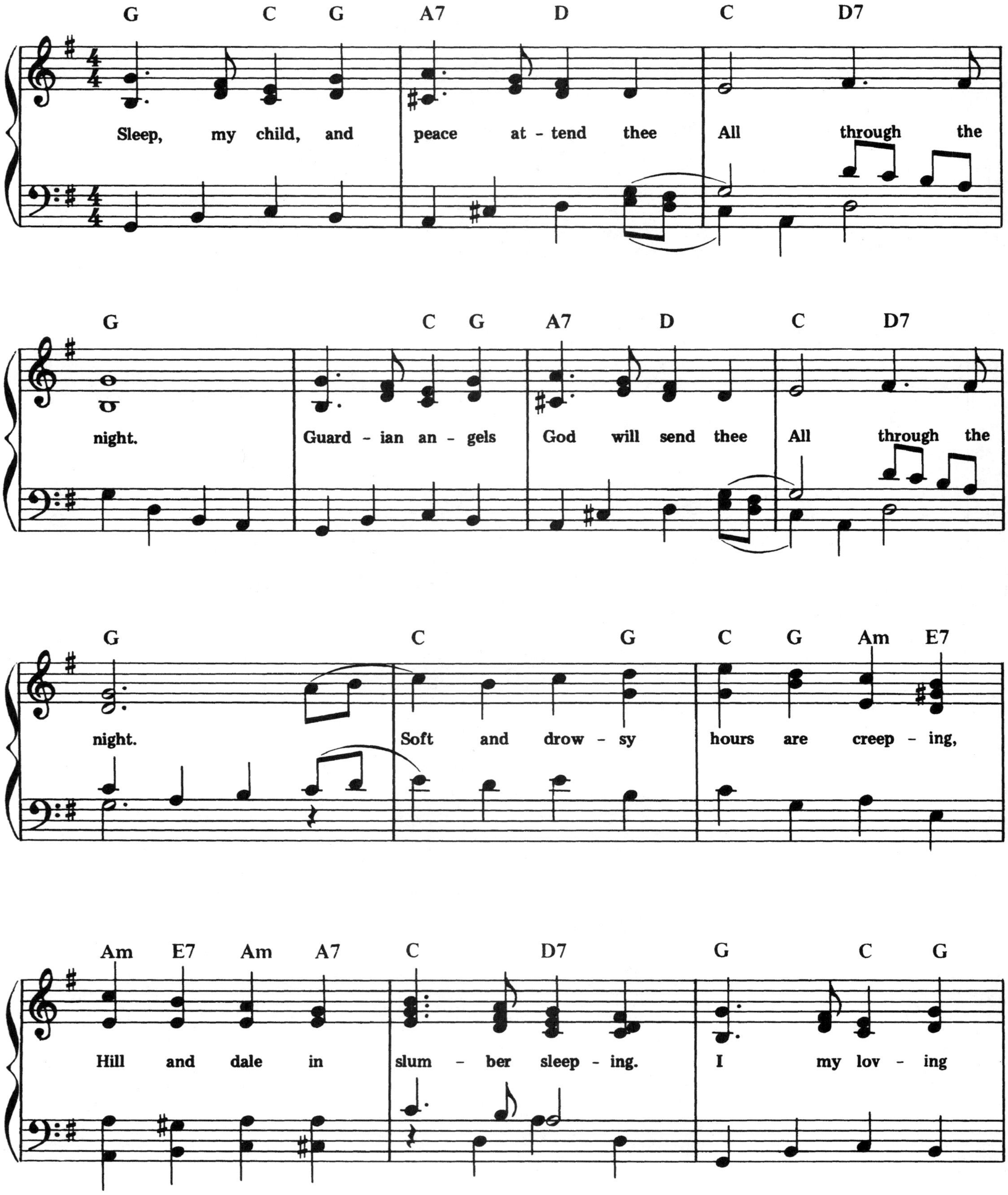
G C G A7 D C D7
Sleep, my child, and peace at - tend thee All through the
G C G A7 D C D7
night. Guard - ian an - gels God will send thee All through the
G C G C G Am E7
night. Soft and drow - sy hours are creep - ing,
Am E7 Am A7 C D7 G C G
Hill and dale in slum - ber sleep - ing. I my lov - ing

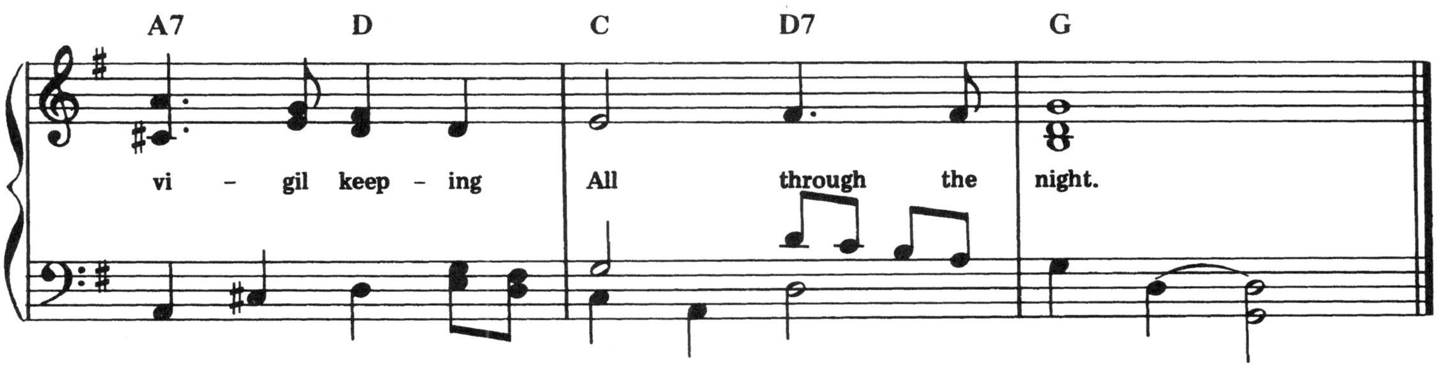

vi - gil keep - ing All through the night.

2. Angels watching ever round thee,
   All through the night;
   In thy slumbers close surround thee,
   All through the night.
   They should of all fears disarm thee,
   No forebodings should alarm thee,
   They will let no peril harm thee,
   All through the night.

3. While the moon her watch is keeping,
   All through the night;
   While the weary world is sleeping,
   All through the night.
   O'er thy spirit gently stealing,
   Visions of delight revealing,
   Breathes a pure and peaceful feeling,
   All through the night.

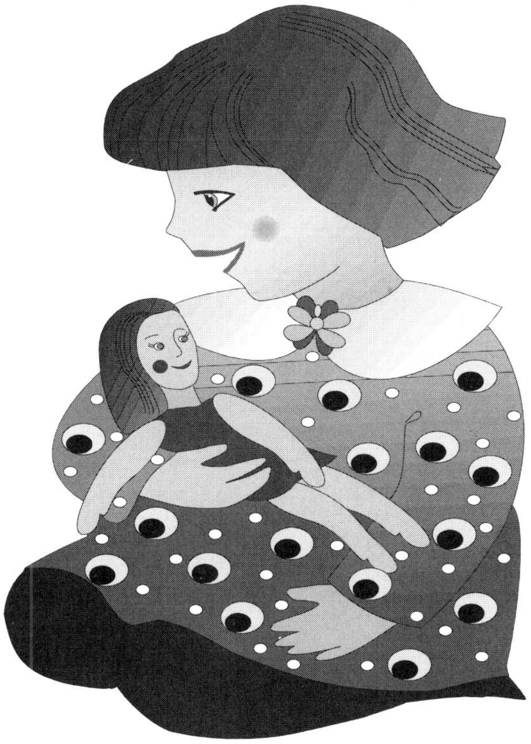

All the World Is Sleeping

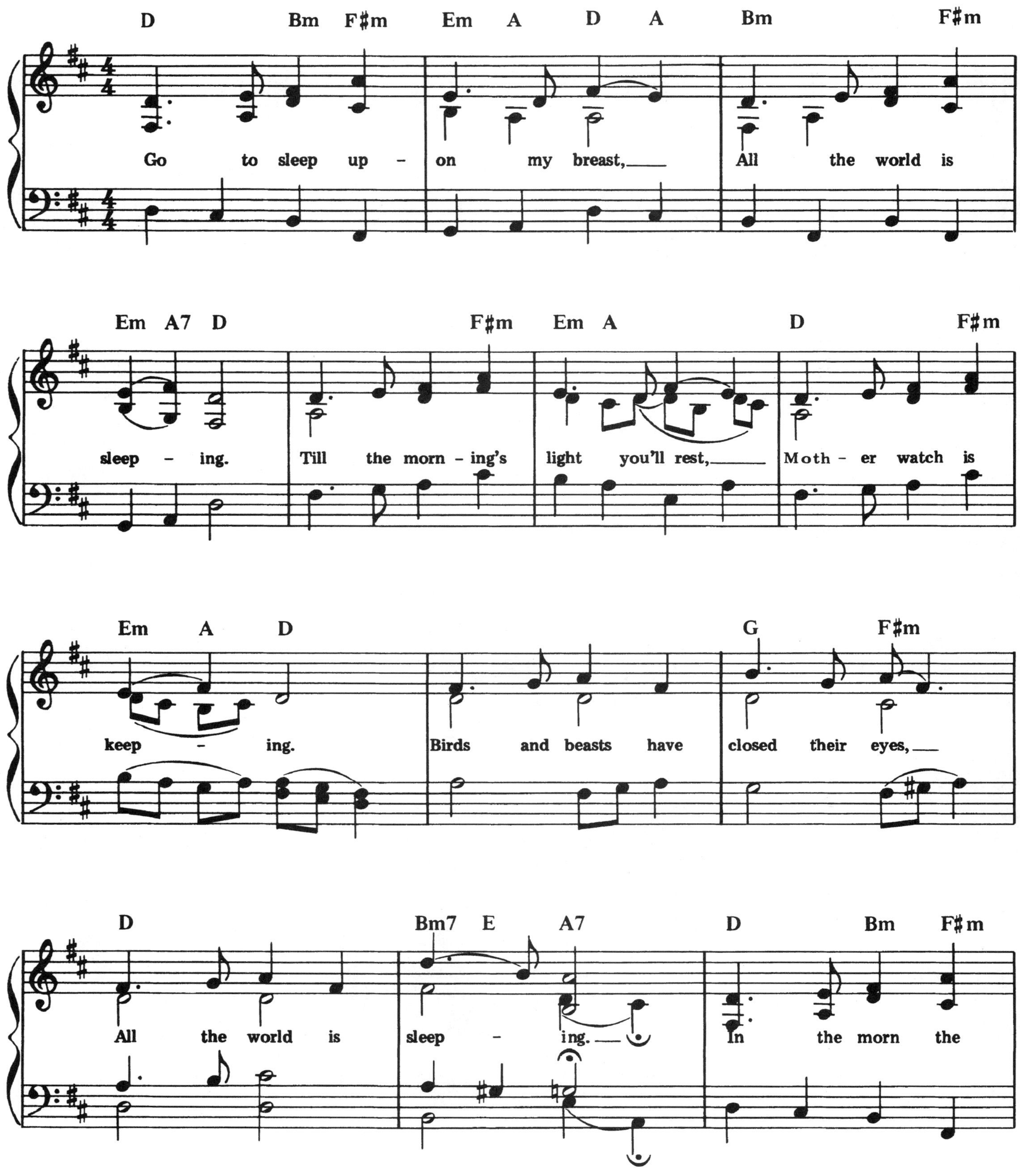
D Bm F♯m Em A D A Bm F♯m
Go to sleep up - on my breast, All the world is
Em A7 D F♯m Em A D F♯m
sleep - ing. Till the morn - ing's light you'll rest, Moth - er watch is
Em A D G F♯m
keep - ing. Birds and beasts have closed their eyes,
D Bm7 E A7 D Bm F♯m
All the world is sleep - ing. In the morn the

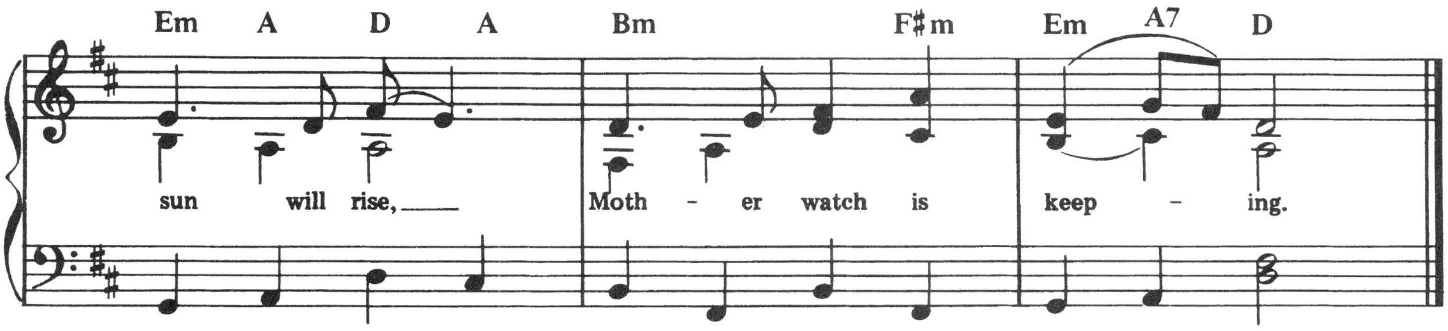

sun will rise, ____ Moth - er watch is keep - ing.

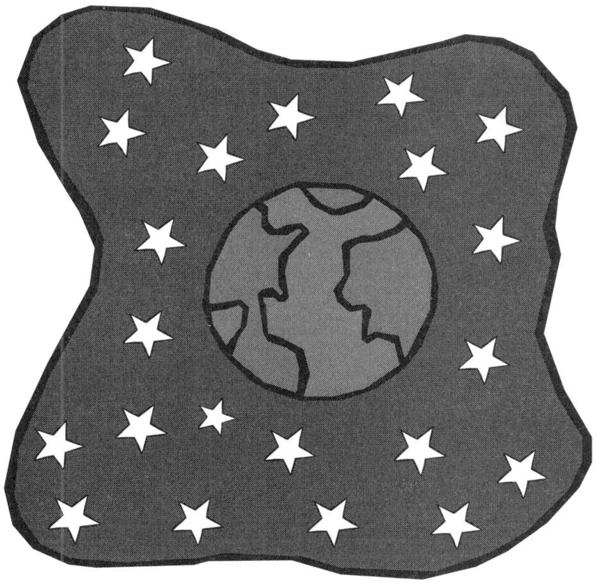

All the Pretty Little Horses

Dm
Hush - a - by
When you wake,
Gm7
don't you cry,
you shall have,
go to sleep - y lit - tle
All the pret - ty lit - tle
Dm
bay - by.
hors - ses.
Refrain
Gm
Black and bays,
C
dap - ples and grays,
Am7
all the pret - ty lit - tle
Dm
hors - es.

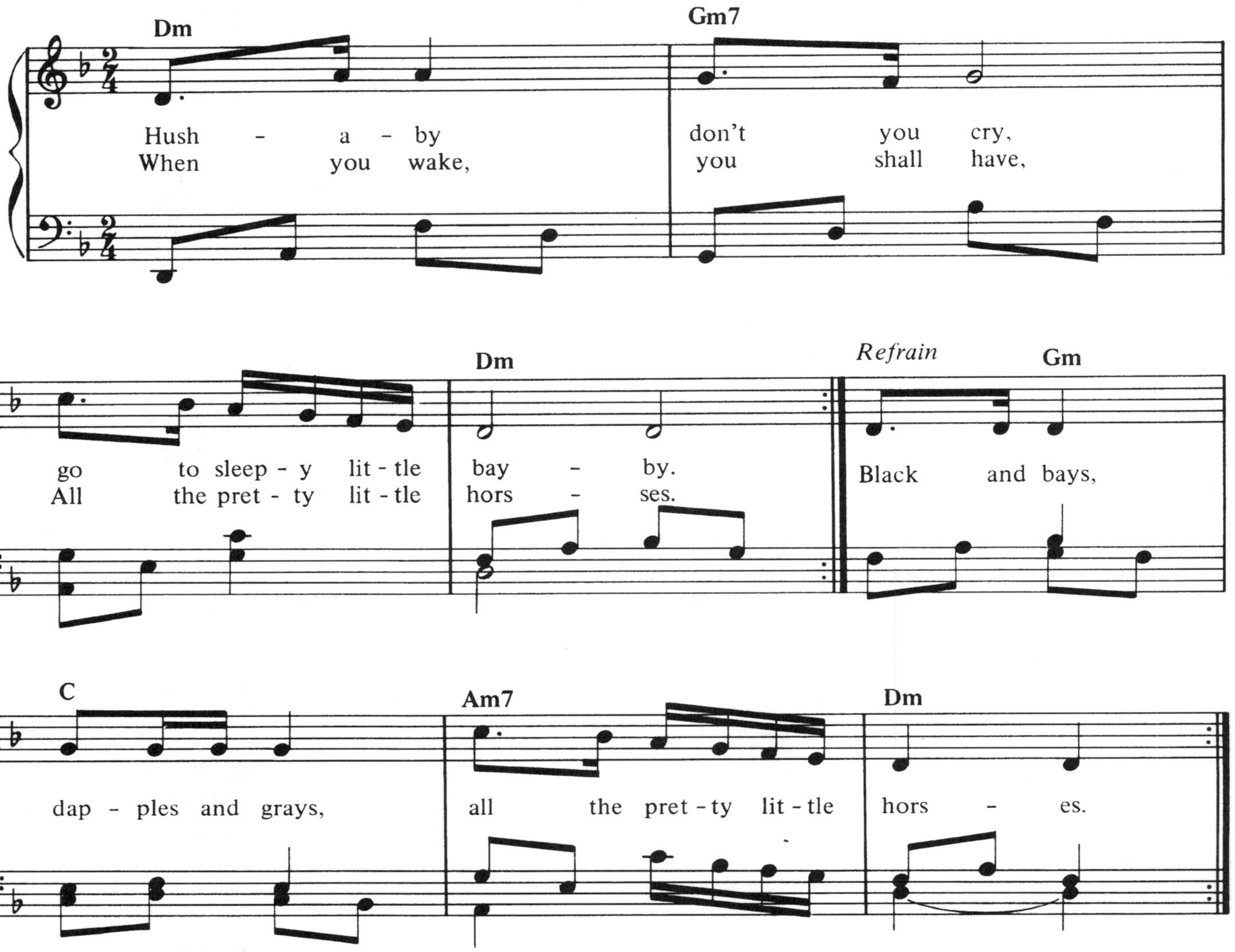

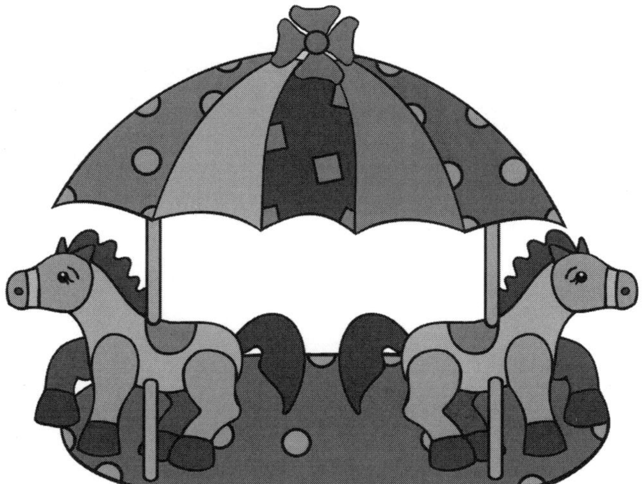

Baby Bye, Here's a Fly

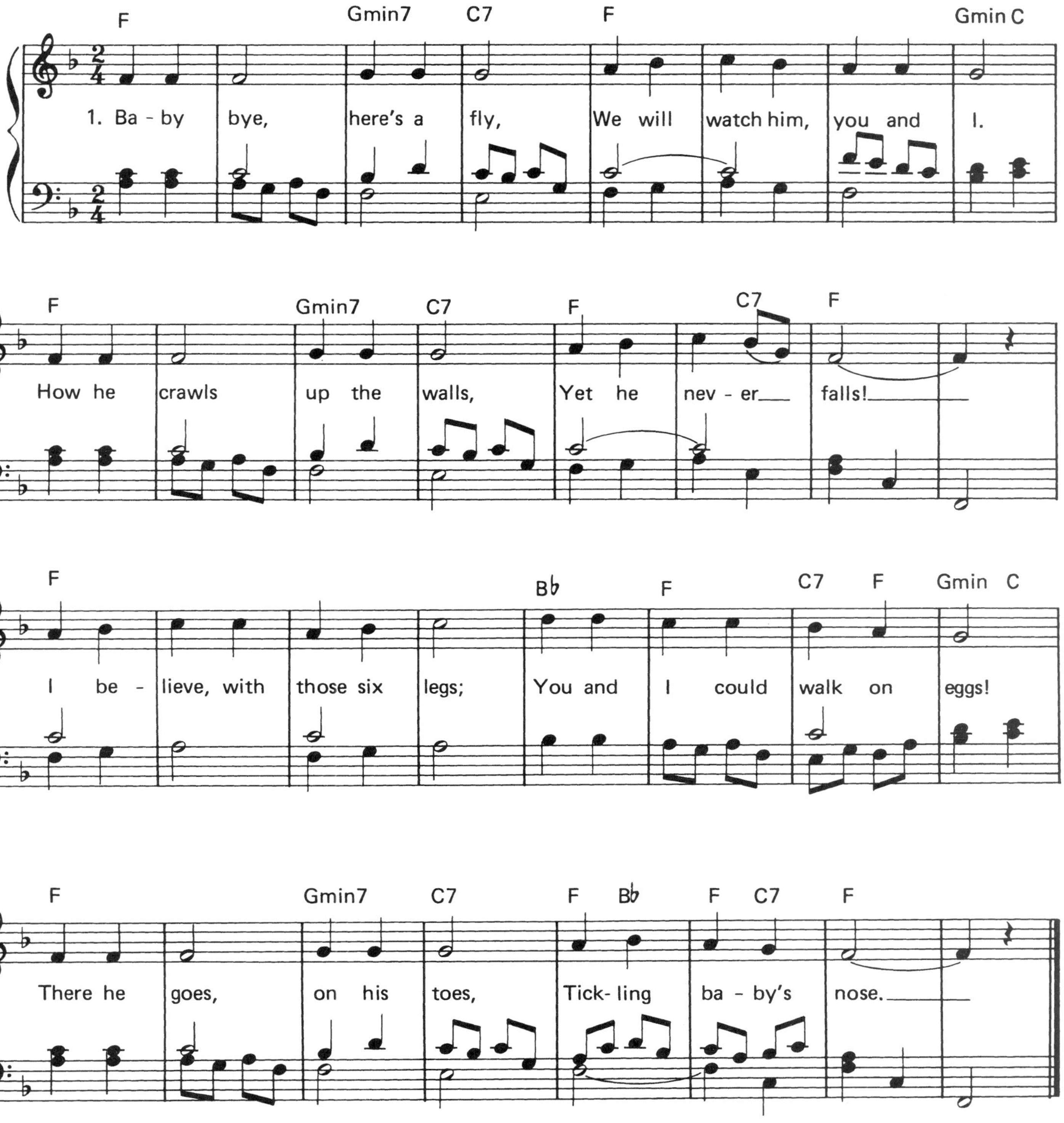
F Gmin7 C7 F Gmin C
1. Ba - by bye, here's a fly, We will watch him, you and I.
F Gmin7 C7 F C7 F
How he crawls up the walls, Yet he nev - er falls!
F B♭ F C7 F Gmin C
I be - lieve, with those six legs; You and I could walk on eggs!
F Gmin7 C7 F B♭ F C7 F
There he goes, on his toes, Tick- ling ba - by's nose.

Bedtime

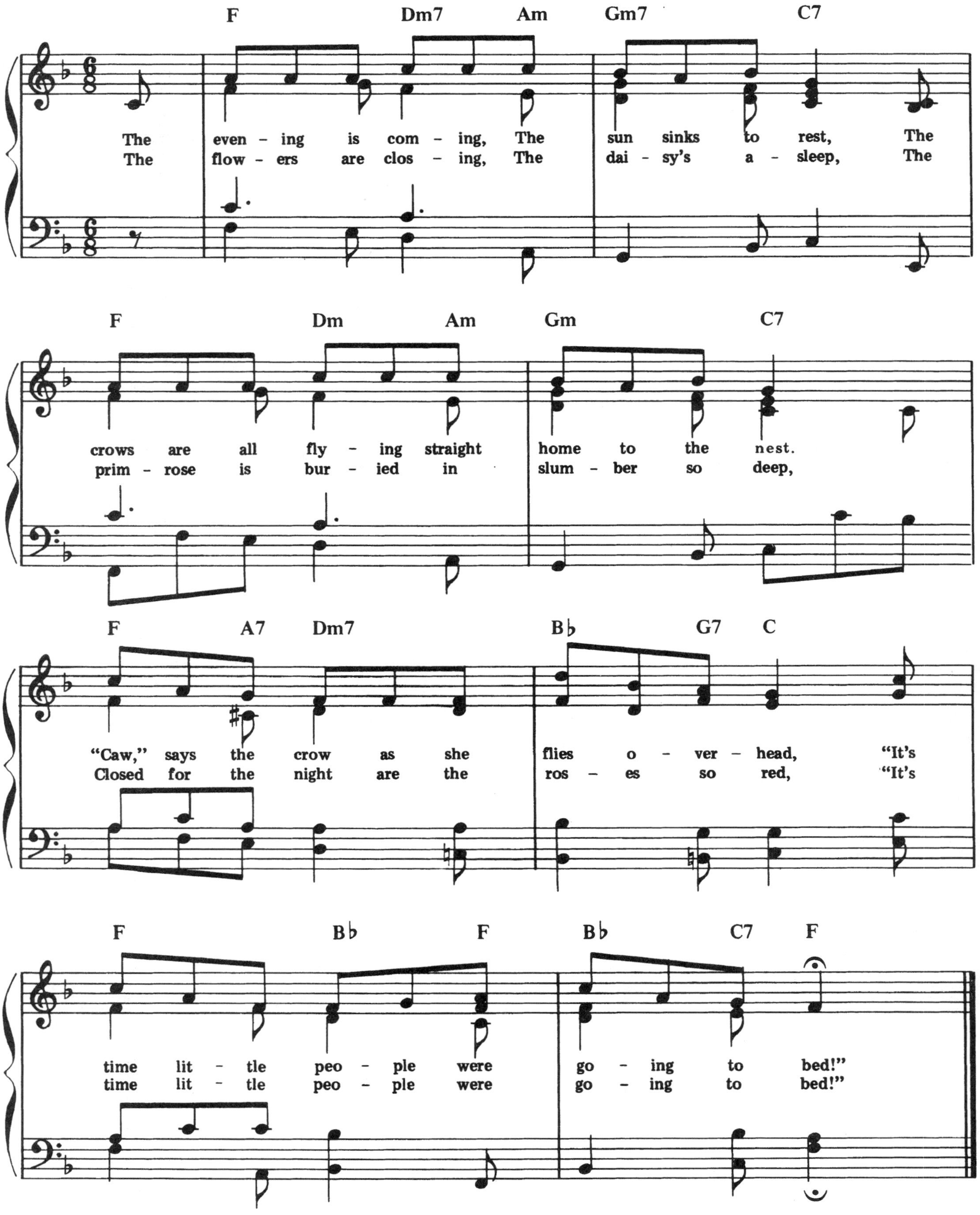
F Dm7 Am Gm7 C7
The even – ing is com – ing, The sun sinks to rest, The
The flow – ers are clos – ing, The dai – sy's a – sleep, The
F Dm Am Gm C7
crows are all fly – ing straight home to the nest.
prim – rose is bur – ied in slum – ber so deep,
F A7 Dm7 B♭ G7 C
"Caw," says the crow as she flies o – ver – head, "It's
Closed for the night are the ros – es so red, "It's
F B♭ F B♭ C7 F
time lit – tle peo – ple were go – ing to bed!"
time lit – tle peo – ple were go – ing to bed!"

Brahms's Lullaby

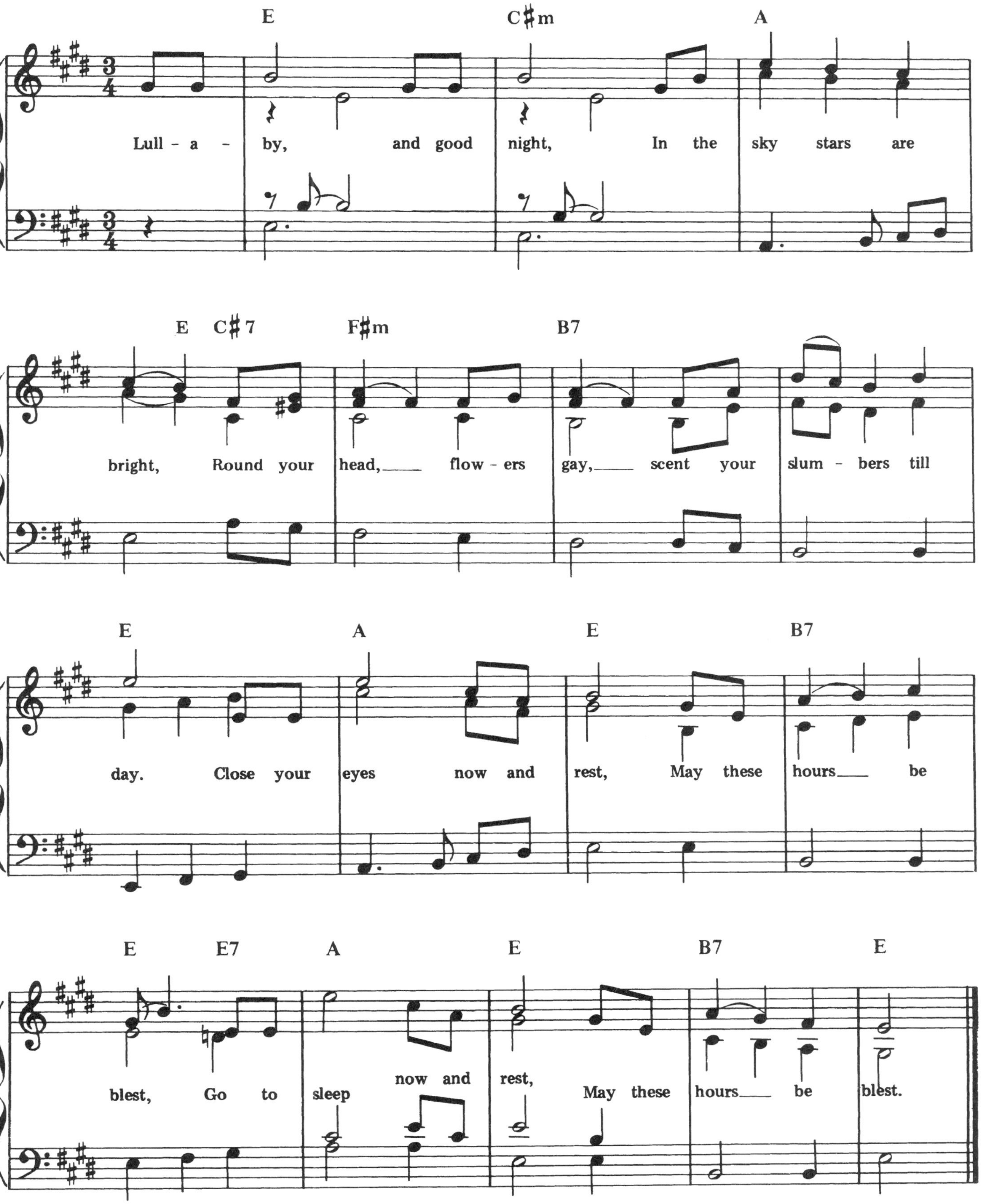
E C♯m A
Lull - a - by, and good night, In the sky stars are
E C♯7 F♯m B7
bright, Round your head, flow - ers gay, scent your slum - bers till
E A E B7
day. Close your eyes now and rest, May these hours be
E E7 A E B7 E
blest, Go to sleep now and rest, May these hours be blest.

Coventry Lullaby

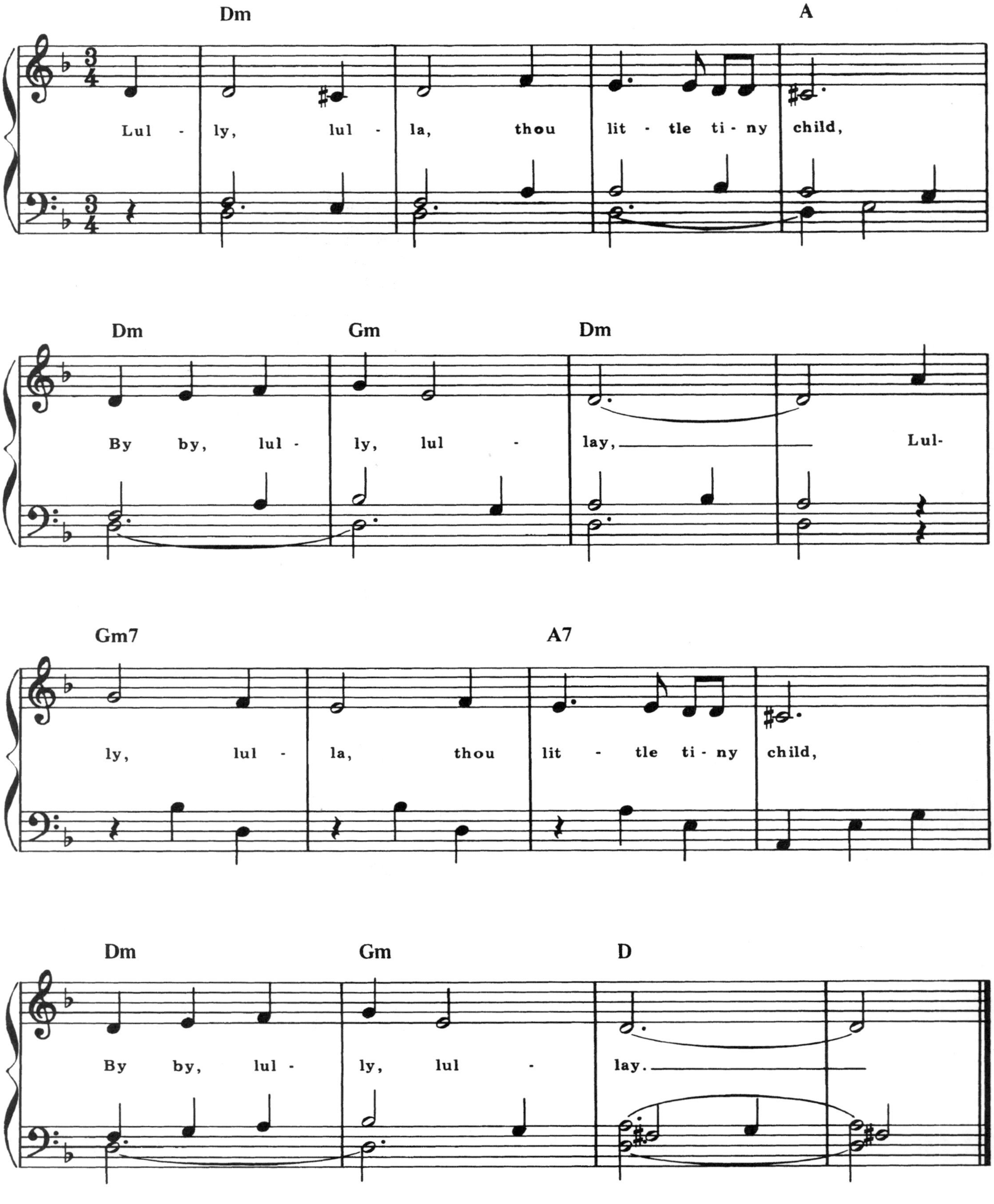
Dm
A
Lul - ly, lul - la, thou lit - tle ti - ny child,
Dm
Gm
Dm
By by, lul - ly, lul - lay, Lul-
Gm7
A7
ly, lul - la, thou lit - tle ti - ny child,
Dm
Gm
D
By by, lul - ly, lul - lay.

Dance, My Baby Diddy

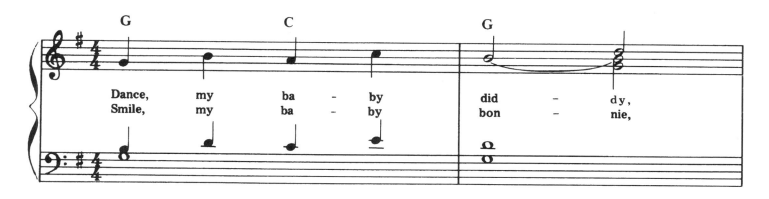

Dance, my ba - by did - dy,
Smile, my ba - by bon - nie,

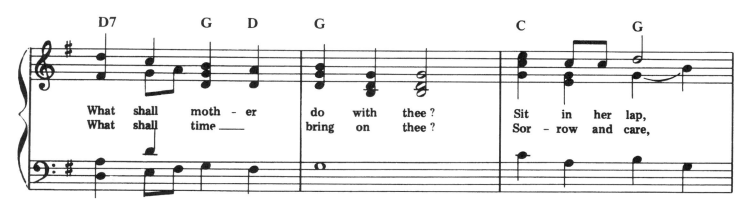

What shall moth - er do with thee? Sit in her lap,
What shall time bring on thee? Sor - row and care,

give thee some pap, Dance, my ba - by did - dy.
frowns and grey hair, Smile, my ba - by bon - nie.

3. Laugh, my baby beauty,
What will time do to thee?
Furrow our cheek, wrinkle your neck,
Laugh my baby beauty.

4. Dance my baby deary,
Mother will not be weary,
Frolic and play, while you may,
Dance my baby deary.

Dance to Your Daddy

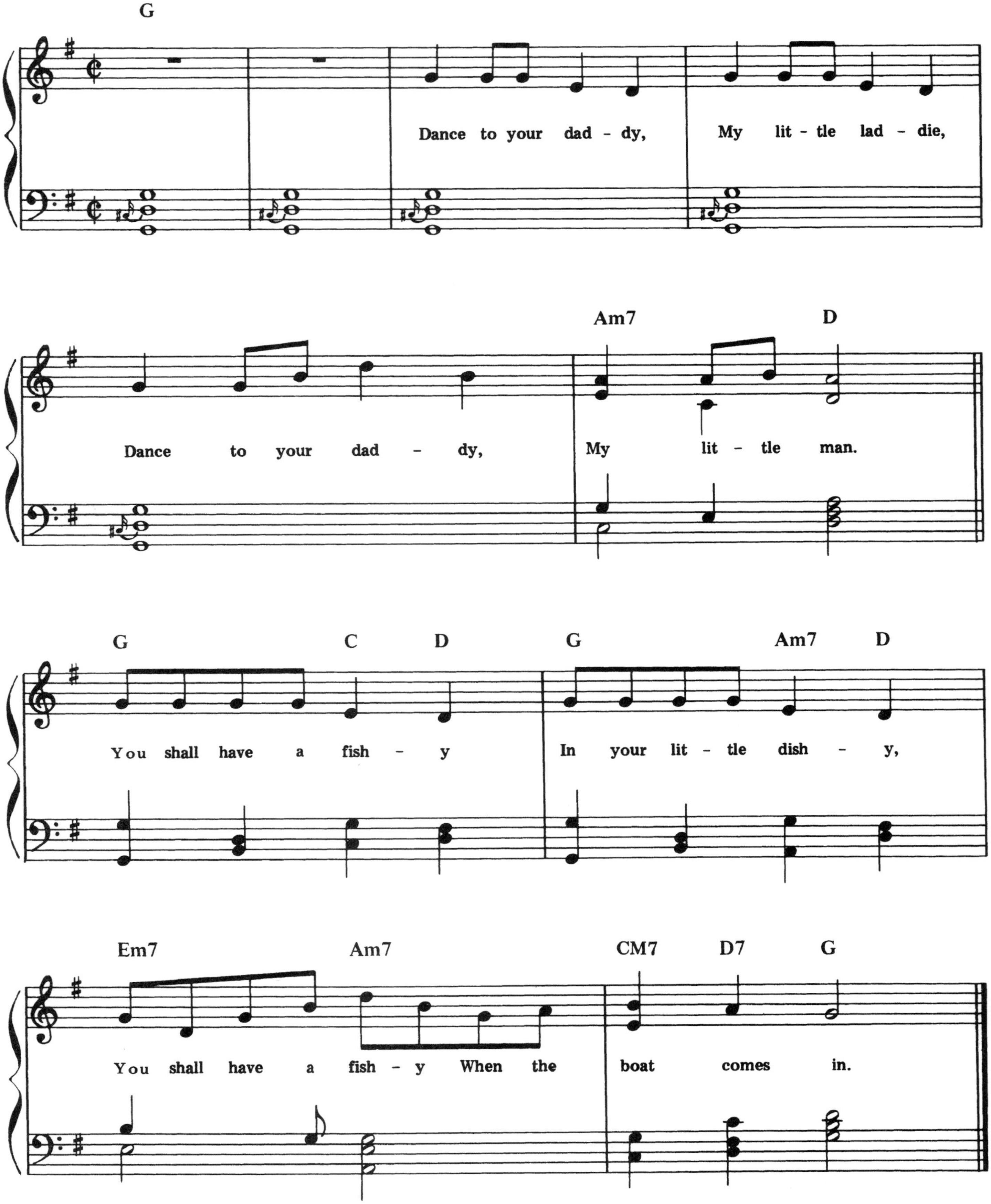
G
Dance to your dad - dy, My lit - tle lad - die,
Am7 D
Dance to your dad - dy, My lit - tle man.
G C D G Am7 D
You shall have a fish - y In your lit - tle dish - y,
Em7 Am7 CM7 D7 G
You shall have a fish - y When the boat comes in.

Day and Night

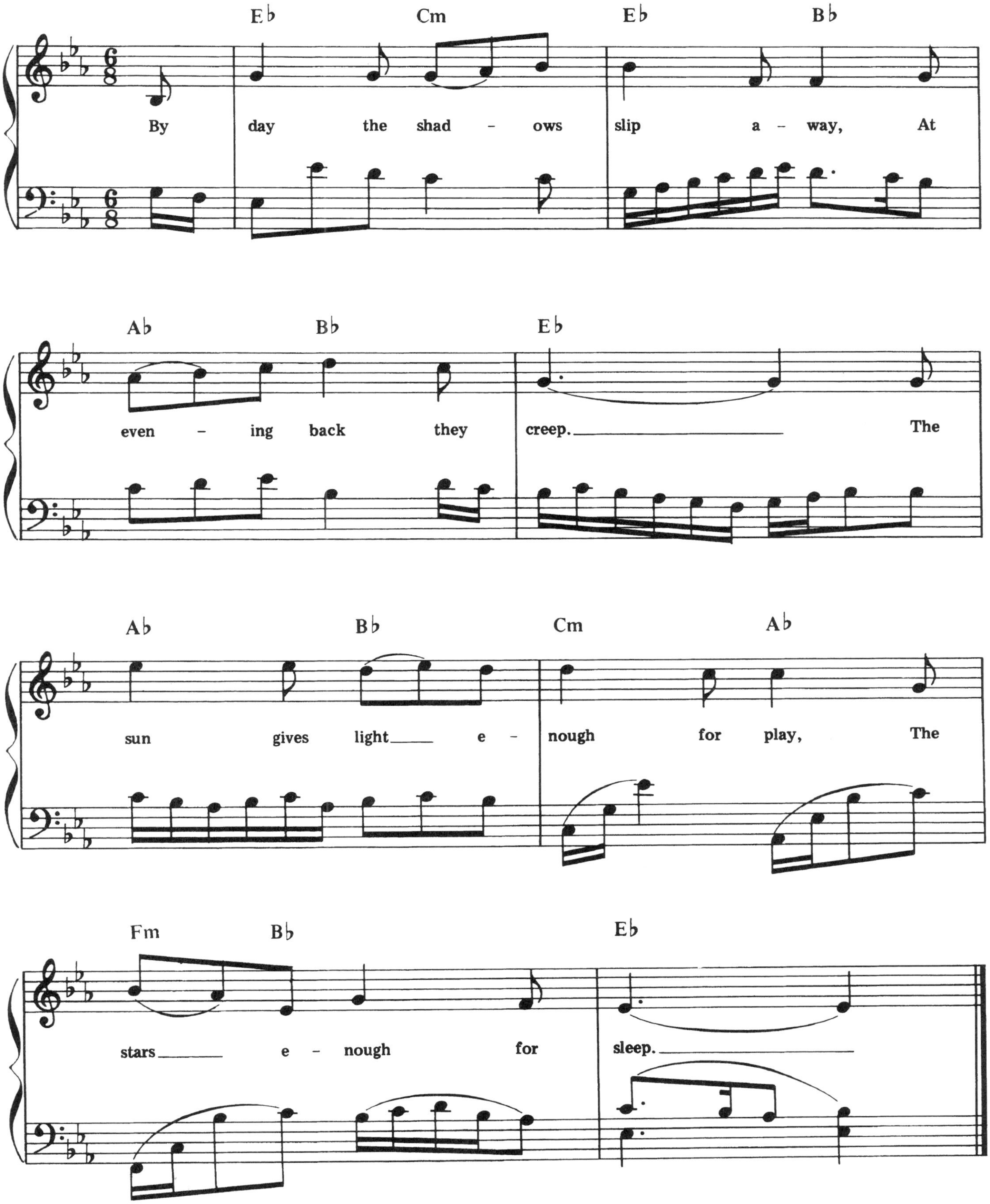
E♭ Cm E♭ B♭
By day the shad - ows slip a - way, At
A♭ B♭ E♭
even - ing back they creep. The
A♭ B♭ Cm A♭
sun gives light e - nough for play, The
Fm B♭ E♭
stars e - nough for sleep.

Diddle, Diddle Dumpling, My Son John

Did - dle, did - dle dump - ling, my son John,

Went to bed with his trou - sers____ on.

One shoe off, the oth - er shoe on.

Did - dle, did - dle dump - ling, my son John.

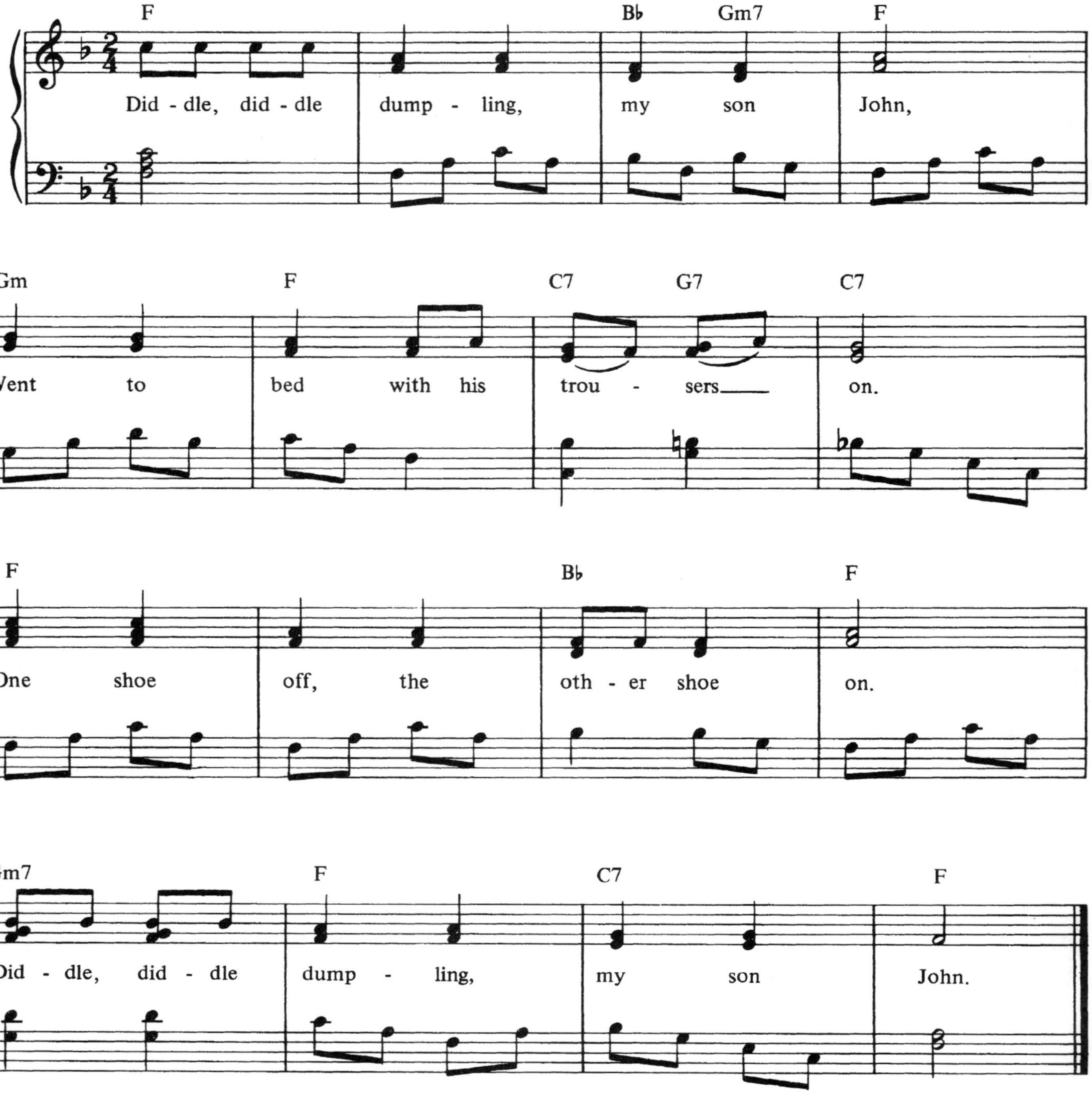

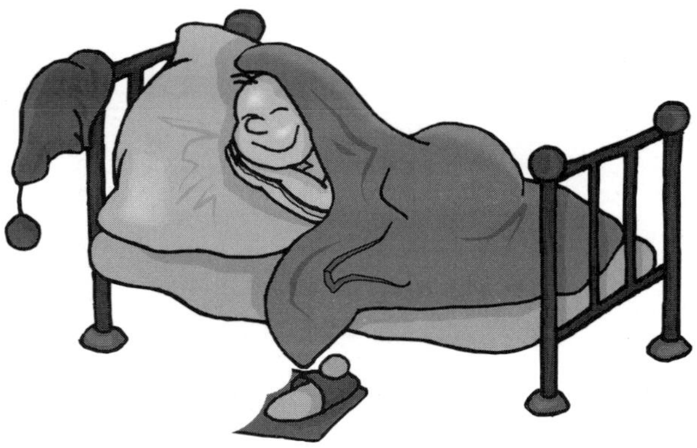

Dodo, Baby, Do

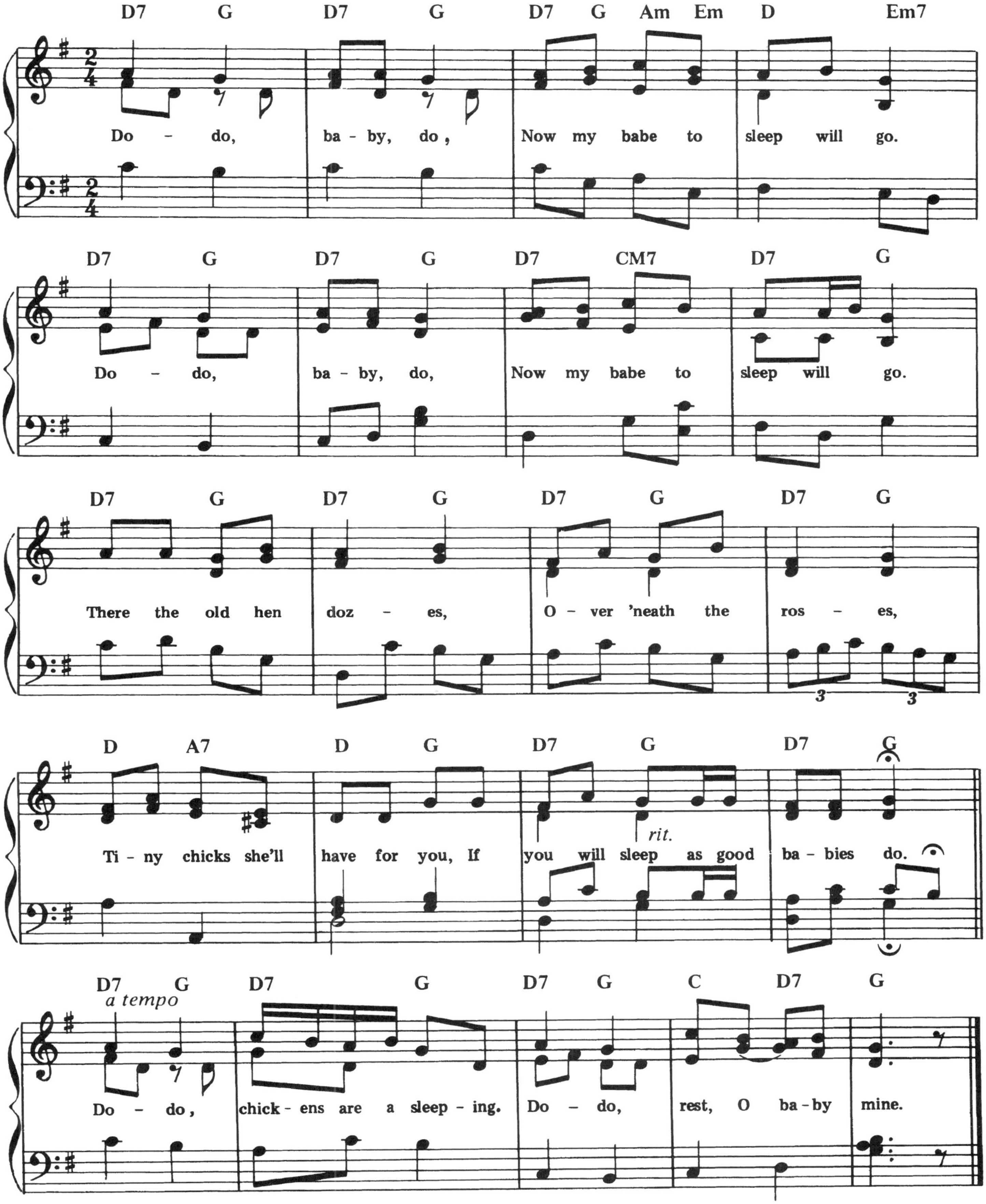
D7 G D7 G D7 G Am Em D Em7
Do - do, ba - by, do, Now my babe to sleep will go.
D7 G D7 G D7 CM7 D7 G
Do - do, ba - by, do, Now my babe to sleep will go.
D7 G D7 G D7 G D7 G
There the old hen doz - es, O - ver 'neath the ros - es,
D A7 D G D7 G D7 G
Ti - ny chicks she'll have for you, If you will sleep as good ba - bies do.
rit.
a tempo
D7 G D7 G D7 G C D7 G
Do - do, chick - ens are a sleep - ing. Do - do, rest, O ba - by mine.

Far in the Wood

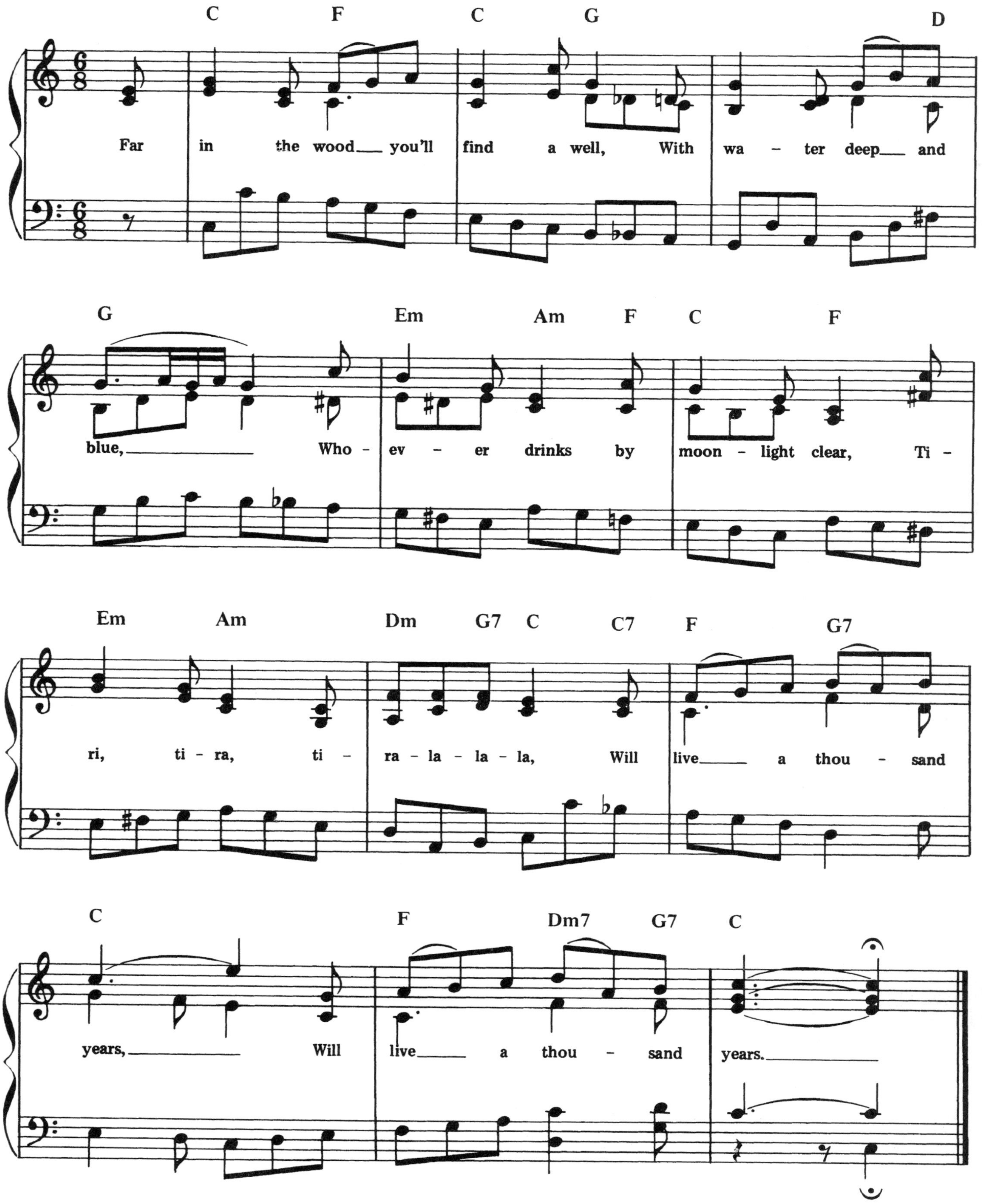
C F C G D
Far in the wood___ you'll find a well, With wa - ter deep___ and
G Em Am F C F
blue,___ Who - ev - er drinks by moon - light clear, Ti -
Em Am Dm G7 C C7 F G7
ri, ti - ra, ti - ra - la - la - la, Will live___ a thou - sand
C F Dm7 G7 C
years,___ Will live___ a thou - sand years.___

Gaelic Cradle Song

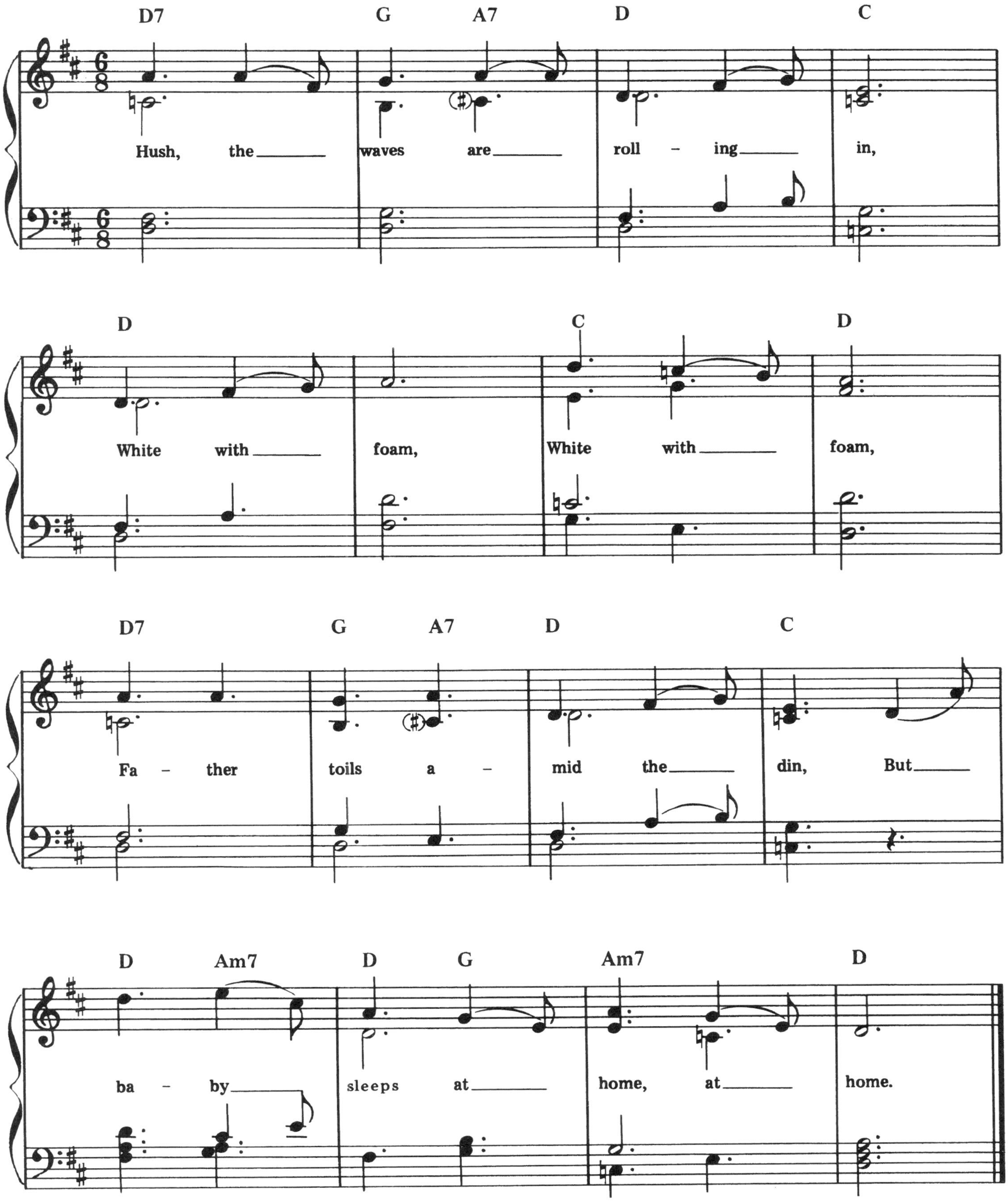
D7 G A7 D C
Hush, the waves are rolling in,
D C D
White with foam, White with foam,
D7 G A7 D C
Fa - ther toils a - mid the din, But
D Am7 D G Am7 D
ba - by sleeps at home, at home.

The Gartan Mother's Lullaby

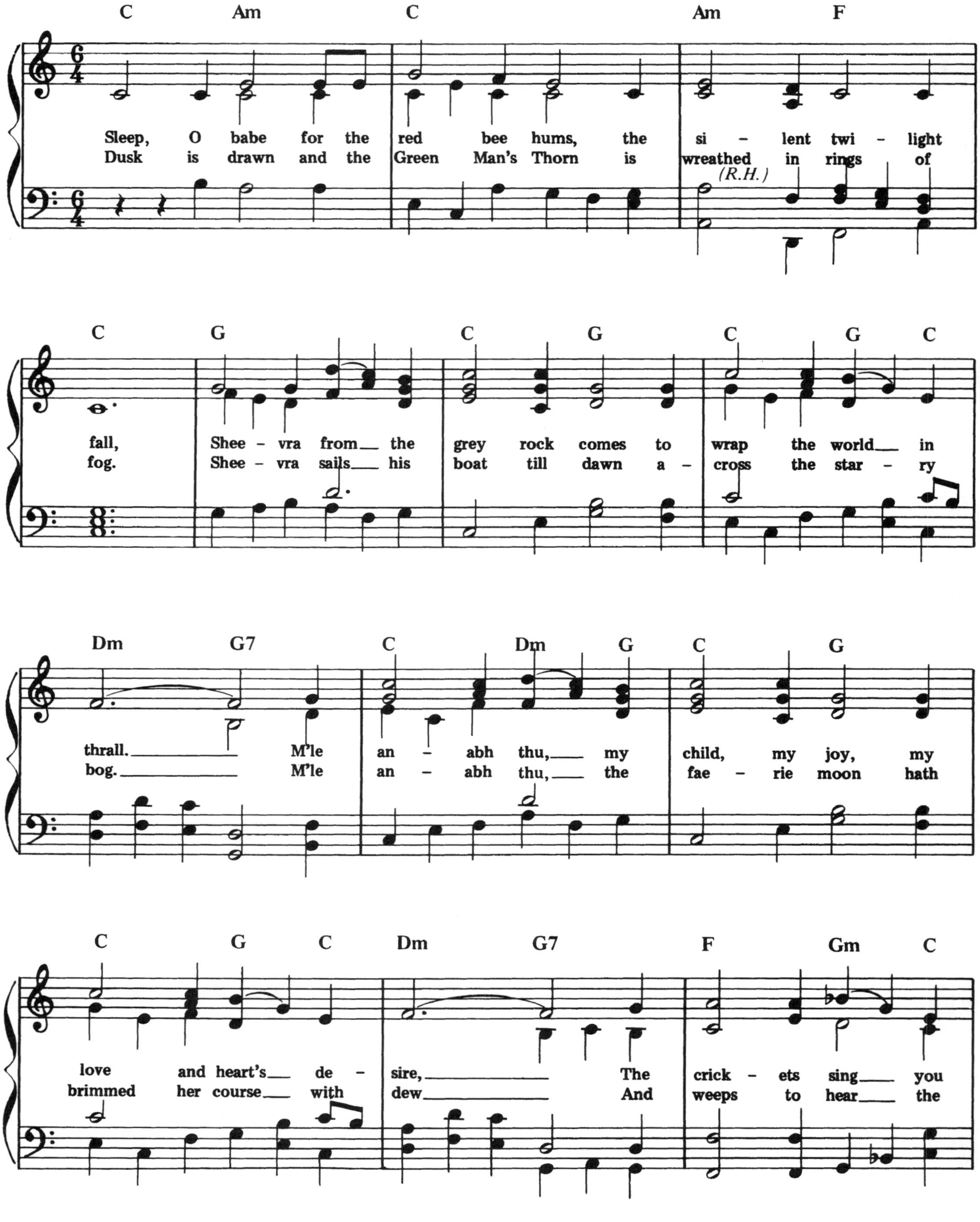
C Am C Am F
Sleep, O babe for the red bee hums, the si - lent twi - light
Dusk is drawn and the Green Man's Thorn is wreathed in rings of
(R.H.)
C G C G C G C
fall, Shee - vra from the grey rock comes to wrap the world in
fog. Shee - vra sails his boat till dawn a - cross the star - ry
Dm G7 C Dm G C G
thrall. M'le an - abh thu, my child, my joy, my
bog. M'le an - abh thu, the fae - rie moon hath
C G C Dm G7 F Gm C
love and heart's de - sire, The crick - ets sing you
brimmed her course with dew And weeps to hear the

lull - a - by be - side the dy - ing fire.
sad, sweet song I sing, O love, to you.

Bye, Baby Bunting

Bye, ba - by bunt – ing, Dad – dy's gone a – hunt – ing.

Gone to get a rab - bit skin To wrap his ba – by bunt – ing in.

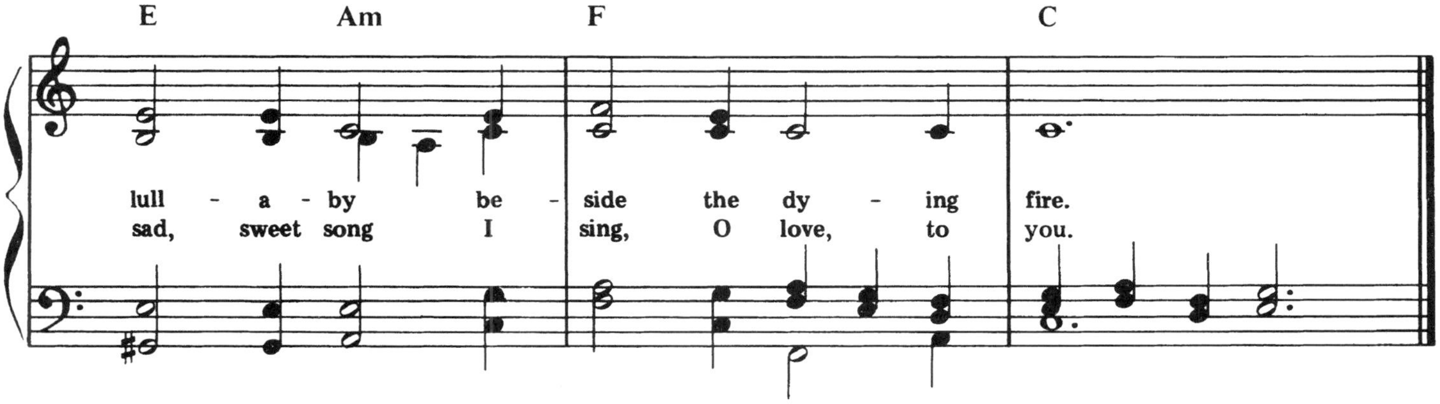

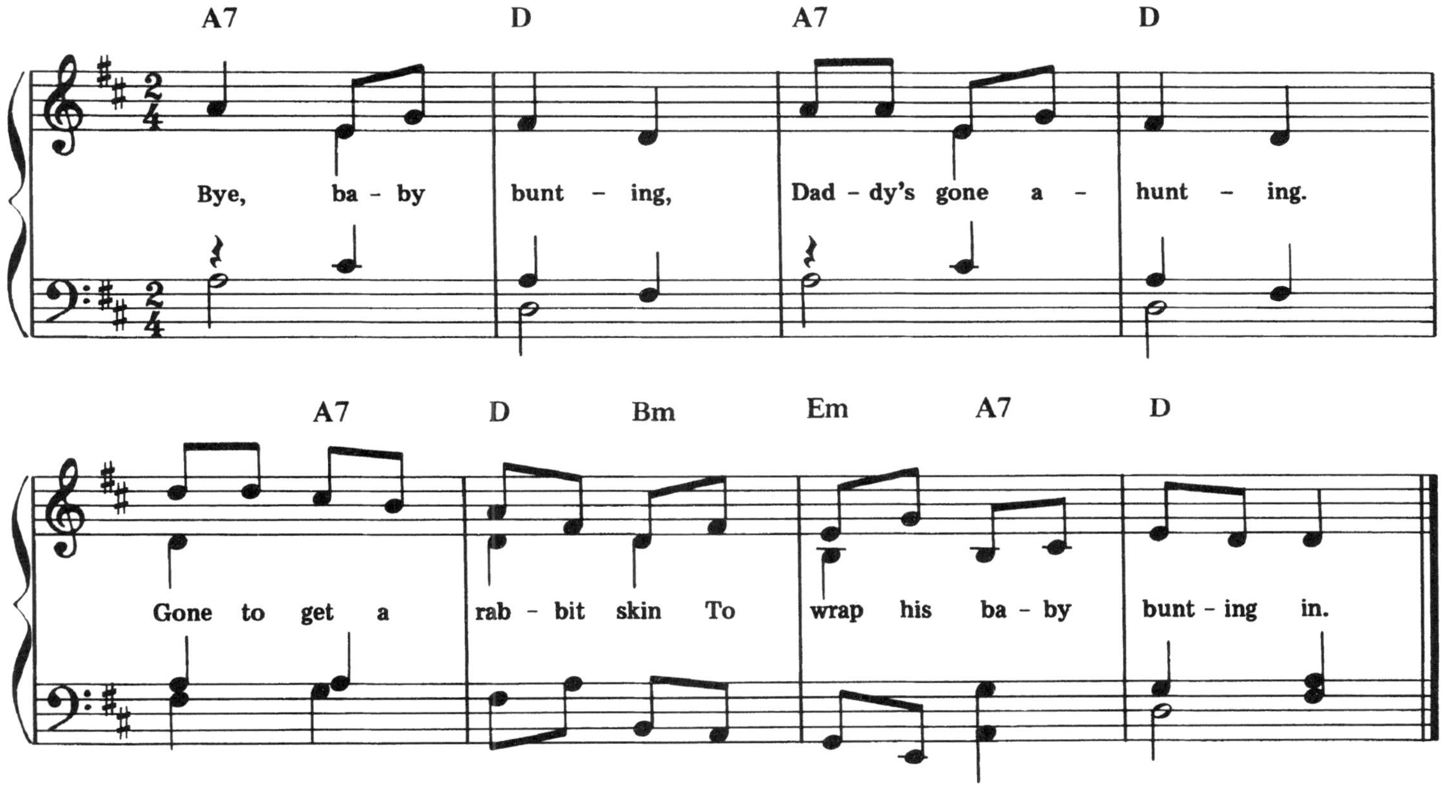

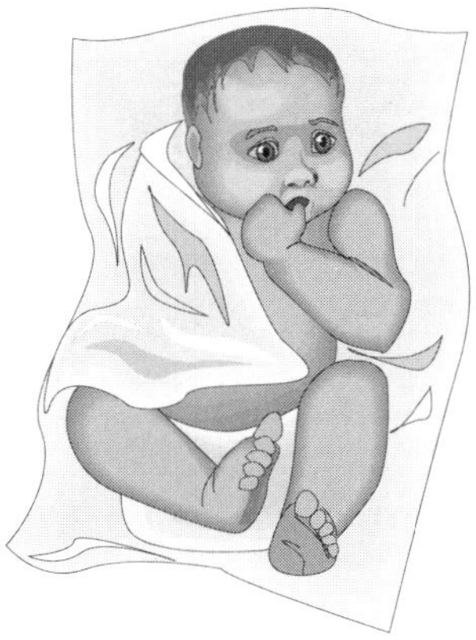

Go Away, Little Fairies

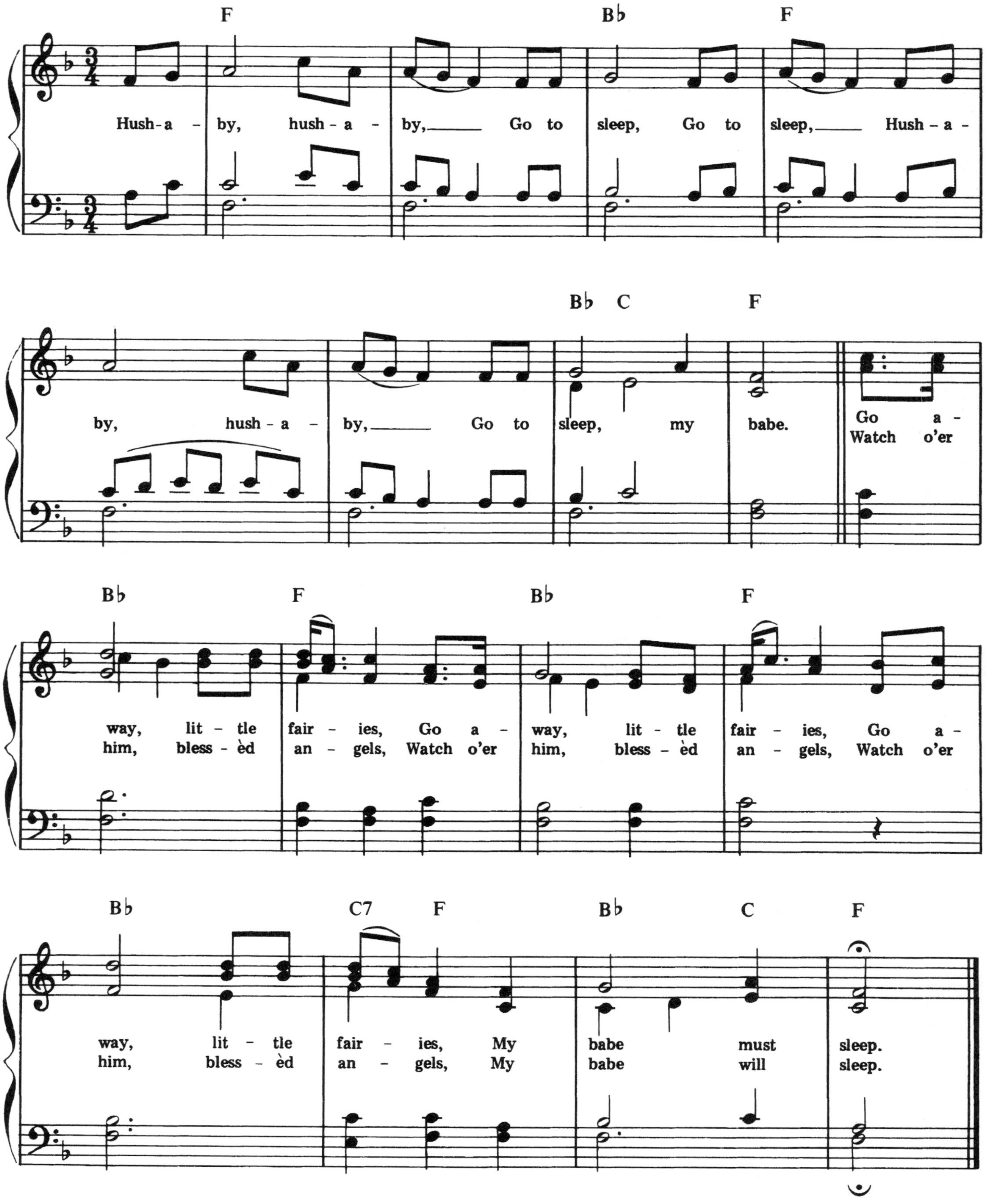
F Bb F
Hush-a - by, hush - a - by, Go to sleep, Go to sleep, Hush - a -
Bb C F
by, hush - a - by, Go to sleep, my babe. Go a - / Watch o'er
Bb F Bb F
way, lit - tle fair - ies, Go a - way, lit - tle fair - ies, Go a -
him, bless - èd an - gels, Watch o'er him, bless - èd an - gels, Watch o'er
Bb C7 F Bb C F
way, lit - tle fair - ies, My babe must sleep.
him, bless - èd an - gels, My babe will sleep.

Golden Cradle

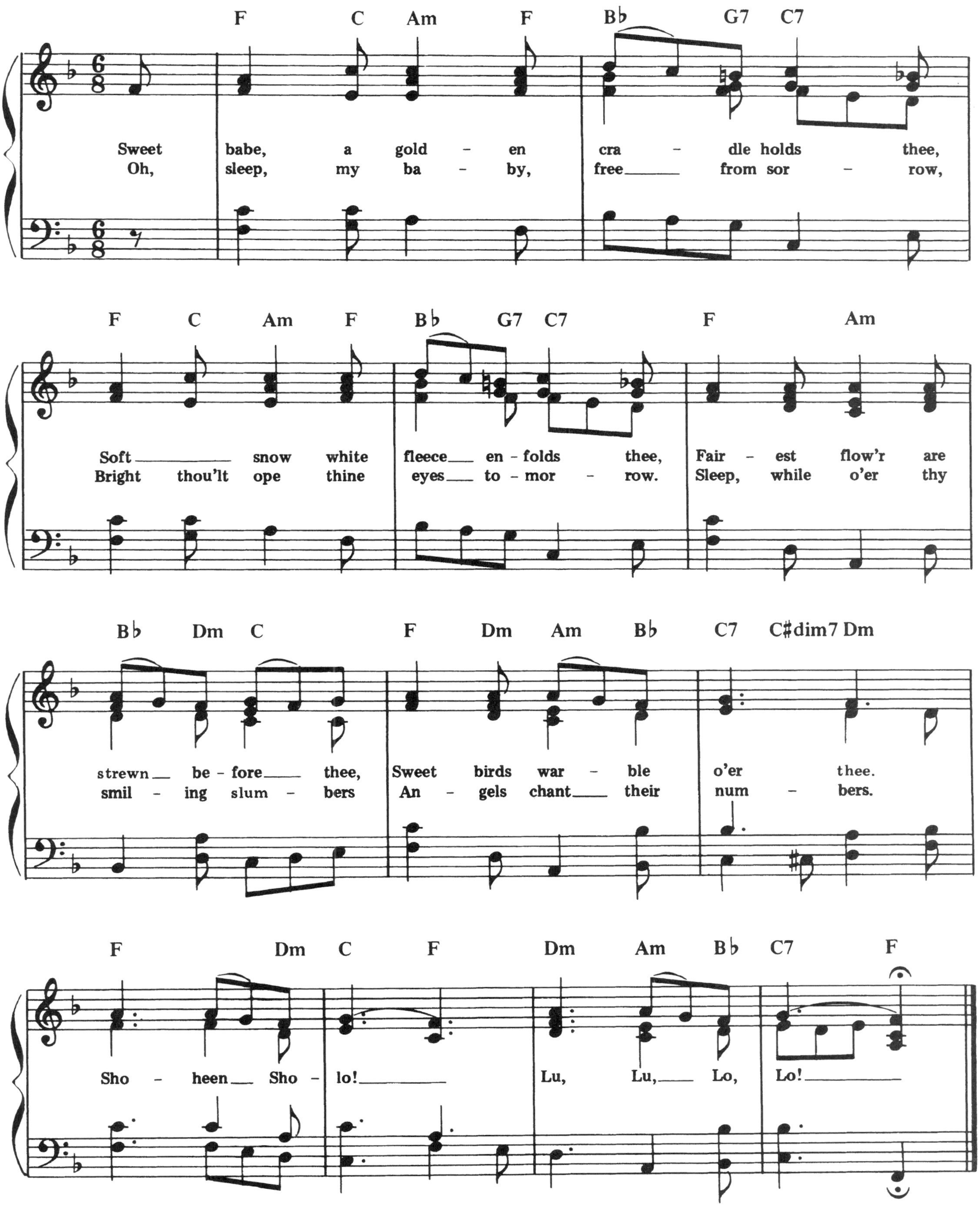
F C Am F B♭ G7 C7
Sweet babe, a gold - en cra - dle holds thee,
Oh, sleep, my ba - by, free from sor - row,
F C Am F B♭ G7 C7 F Am
Soft snow white fleece en - folds thee, Fair - est flow'r are
Bright thou'lt ope thine eyes to - mor - row. Sleep, while o'er thy
B♭ Dm C F Dm Am B♭ C7 C♯dim7 Dm
strewn be - fore thee, Sweet birds war - ble o'er thee.
smil - ing slum - bers An - gels chant their num - bers.
F Dm C F Dm Am B♭ C7 F
Sho - heen Sho - lo! Lu, Lu, Lo, Lo!

Golden Slumbers

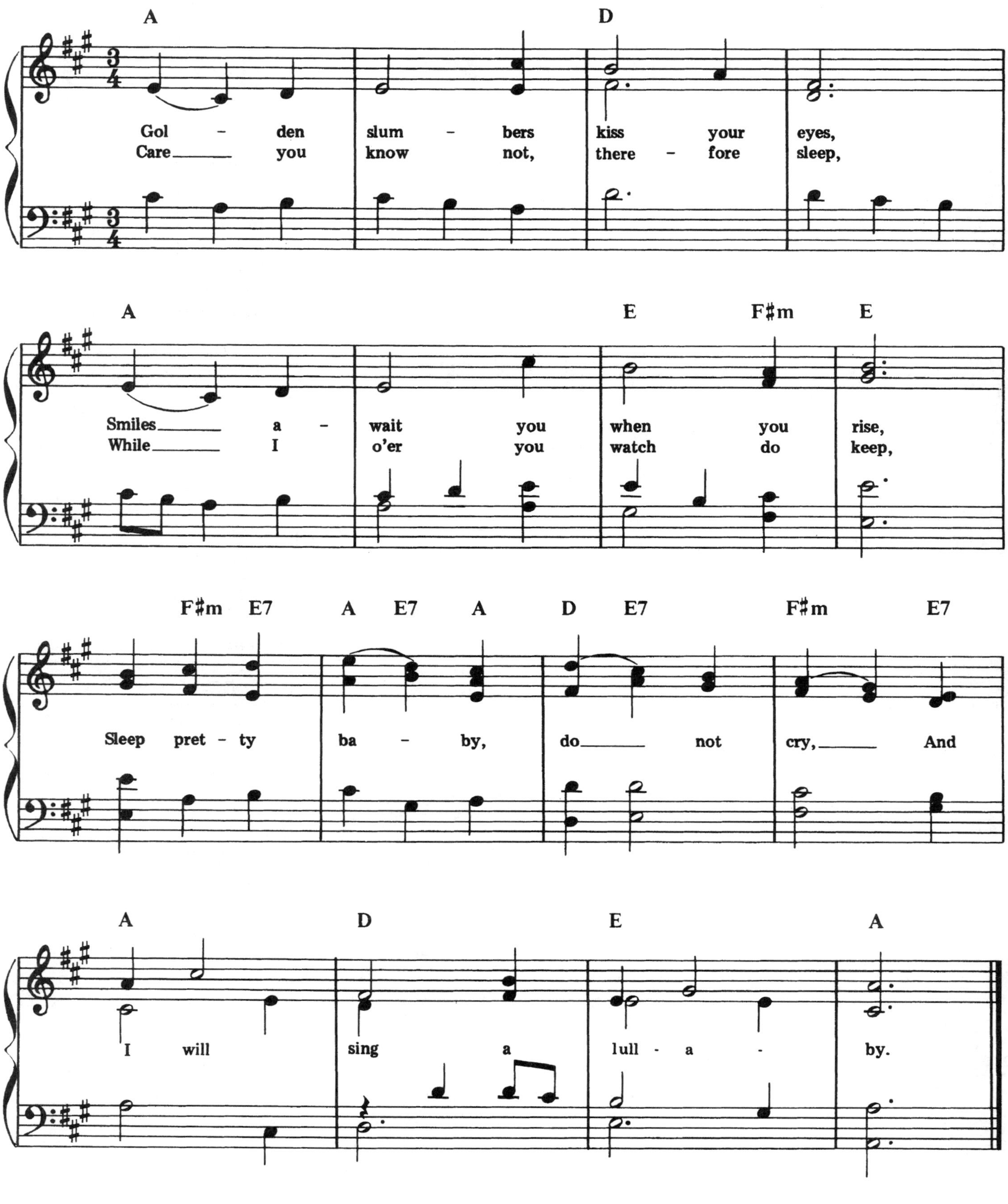
A D
Gol - den slum - bers kiss your eyes,
Care you know not, there - fore sleep,
A E F♯m E
Smiles a - wait you when you rise,
While I o'er you watch do keep,
F♯m E7 A E7 A D E7 F♯m E7
Sleep pret - ty ba - by, do not cry, And
A D E A
I will sing a lull - a - by.

Hush, Little Baby

1. Hush, lit-tle ba-by don't say a word, Ma-ma's gon-na buy you a

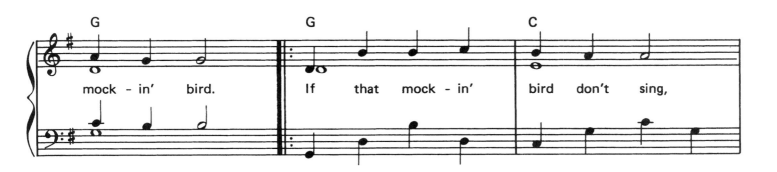

mock-in' bird. If that mock-in' bird don't sing,

Pa-pa's gon-na buy you a dia-mond ring. ba-by in town!

2. If that diamond ring turns to brass,
Papa's gonna buy you a looking glass.

3. If that looking glass gets broke,
Papa's gonna buy you a billy goat.

4. If that billy goat don't pull,
Papa's gonna buy you a cart and bull.

5. If that cart and bull turn over,
Papa's gonna buy you a dog named Rover.

6. If that dog named Rover won't bark,
Papa's gonna buy you a horse and cart.

7. If that horse and cart fall down,
You'll still be the sweetest little baby in town.

Kentucky Babe

Words by Richard H. Buck

Music by Adam Geibel

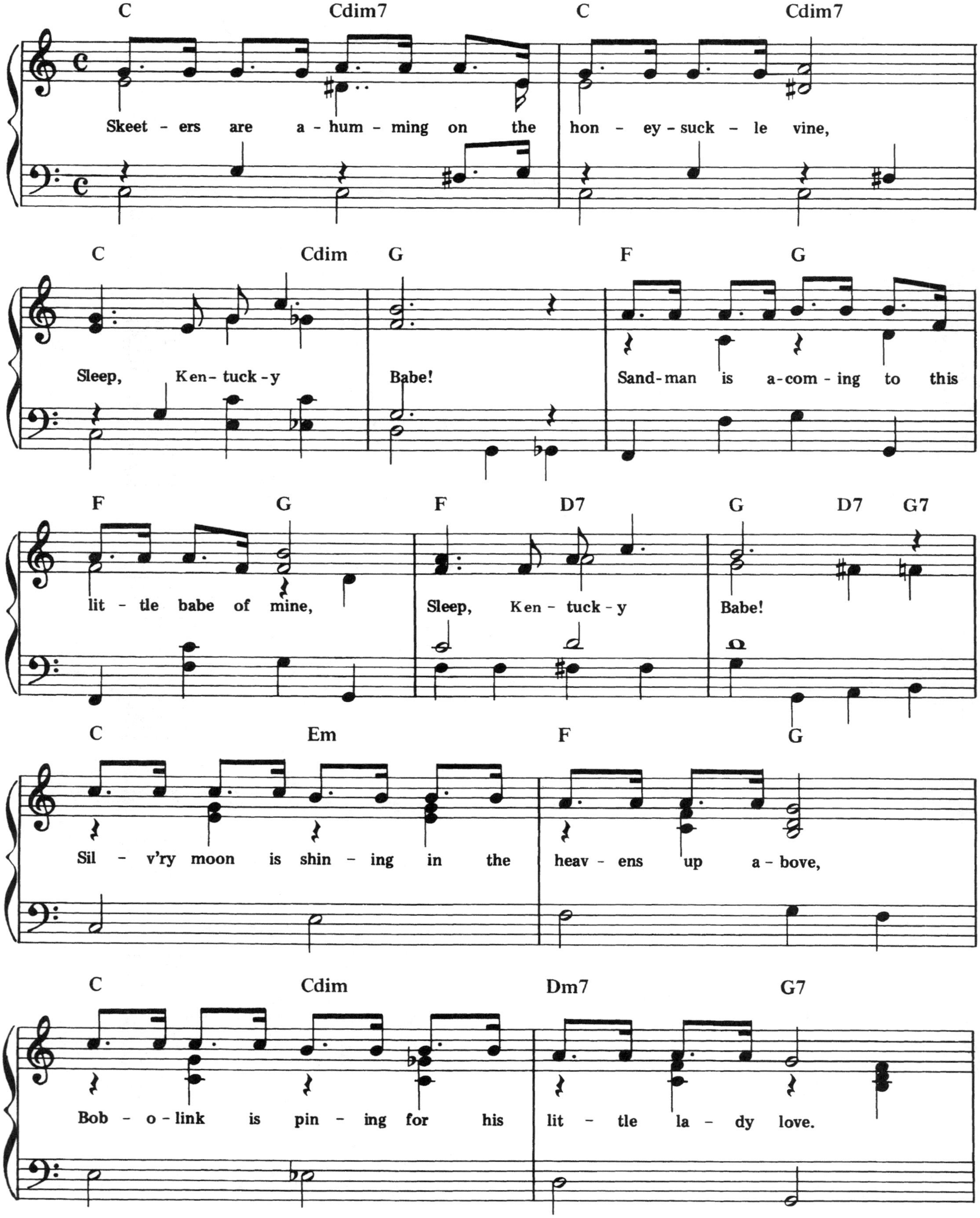

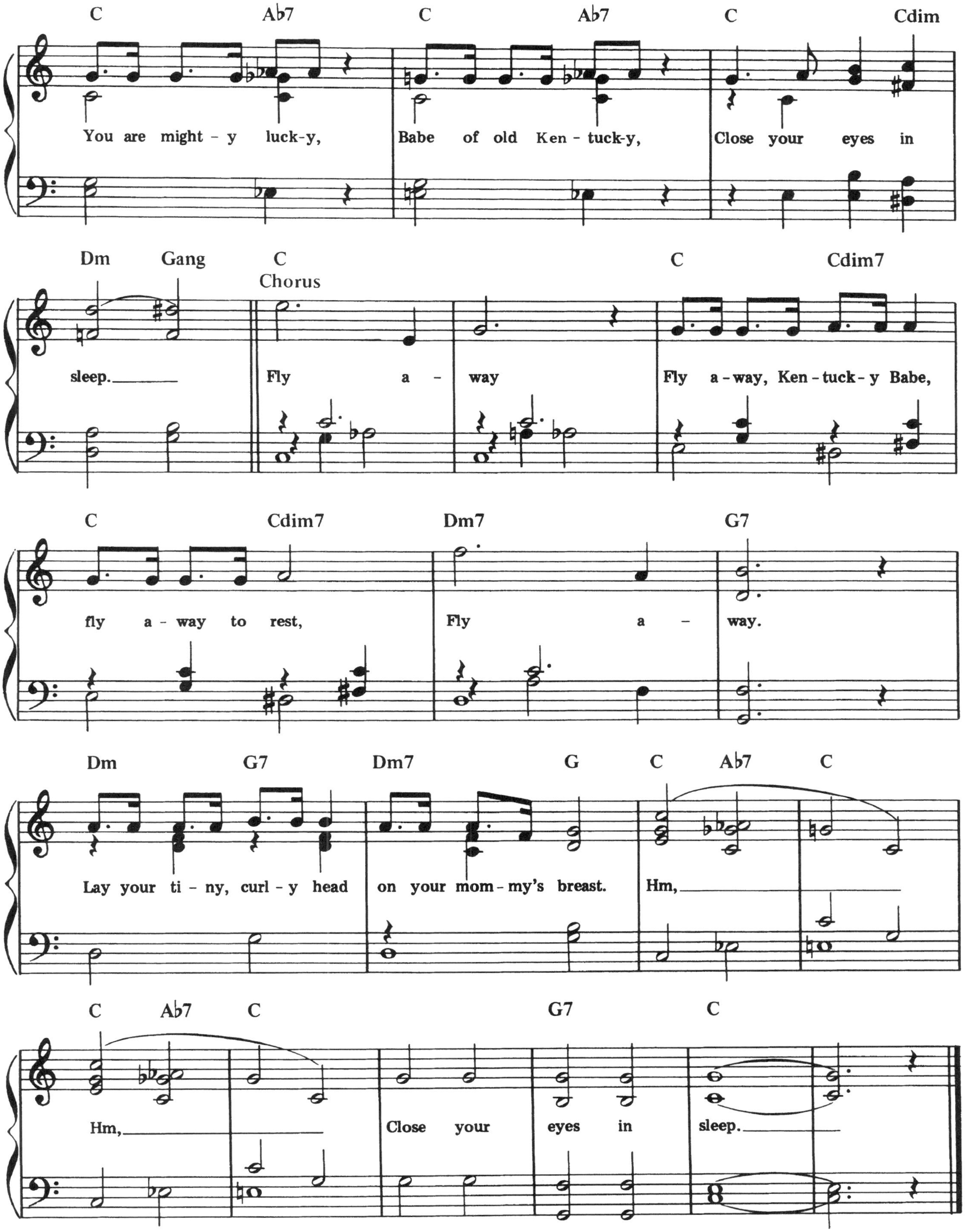
C Ab7 C Ab7 C Cdim
You are might - y luck-y, Babe of old Ken - tuck-y, Close your eyes in
Dm Gang C C Cdim7
Chorus
sleep. Fly a - way Fly a - way, Ken - tuck - y Babe,
C Cdim7 Dm7 G7
fly a - way to rest, Fly a - way.
Dm G7 Dm7 G C Ab7 C
Lay your ti - ny, curl - y head on your mom - my's breast. Hm,
C Ab7 C G7 C
Hm, Close your eyes in sleep.

Kerry Lullaby

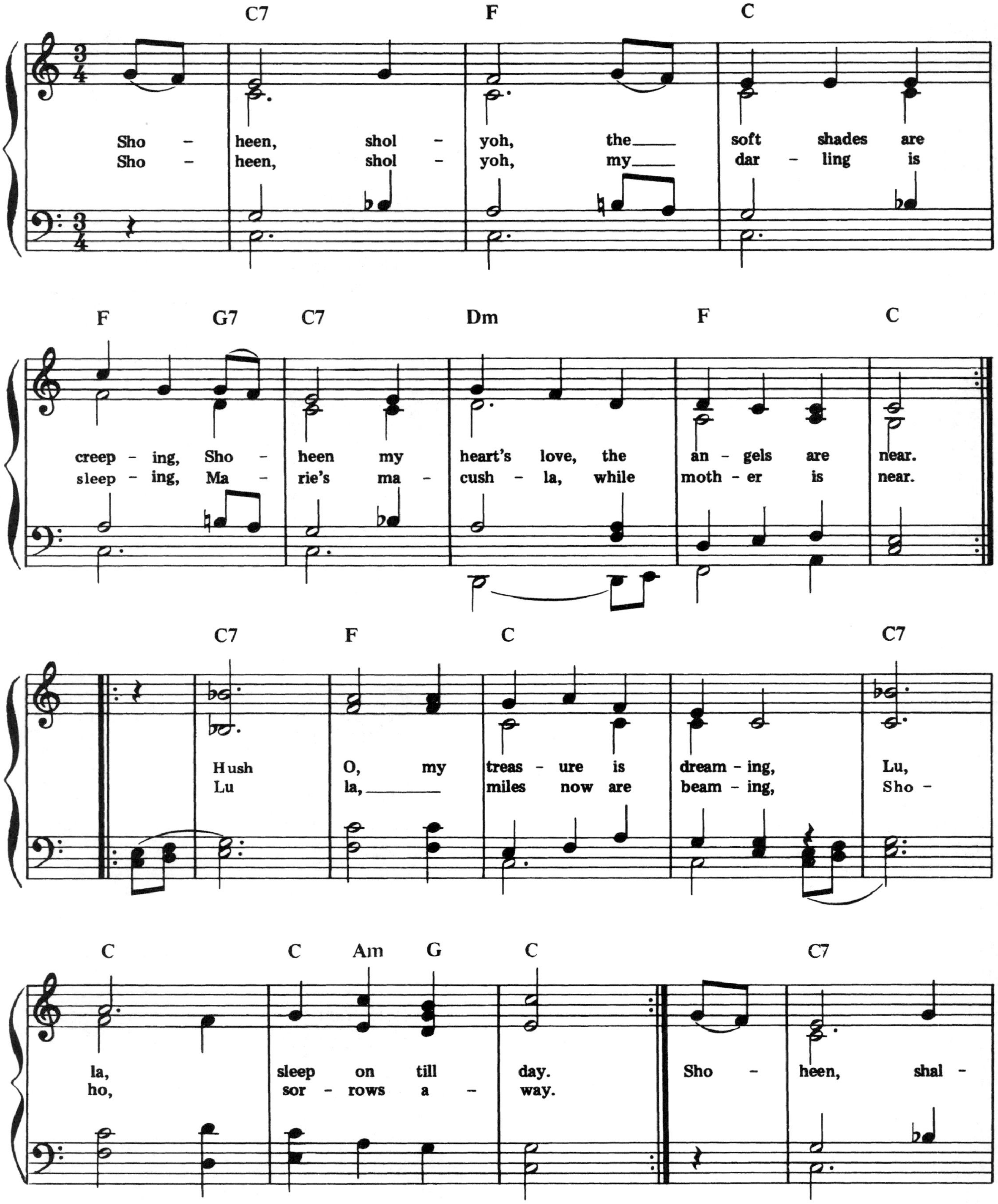
C7 F C
Sho – heen, shol – yoh, the___ soft shades are
Sho – heen, shol – yoh, my___ dar – ling is
F G7 C7 Dm F C
creep – ing, Sho – heen my heart's love, the an – gels are near.
sleep – ing, Ma – rie's ma – cush – la, while moth – er is near.
C7 F C C7
Hush O, my treas – ure is dream – ing, Lu,
Lu la,___ miles now are beam – ing, Sho –
C C Am G C C7
la, sleep on till day. Sho – heen, shal –
ho, sor – rows a – way.

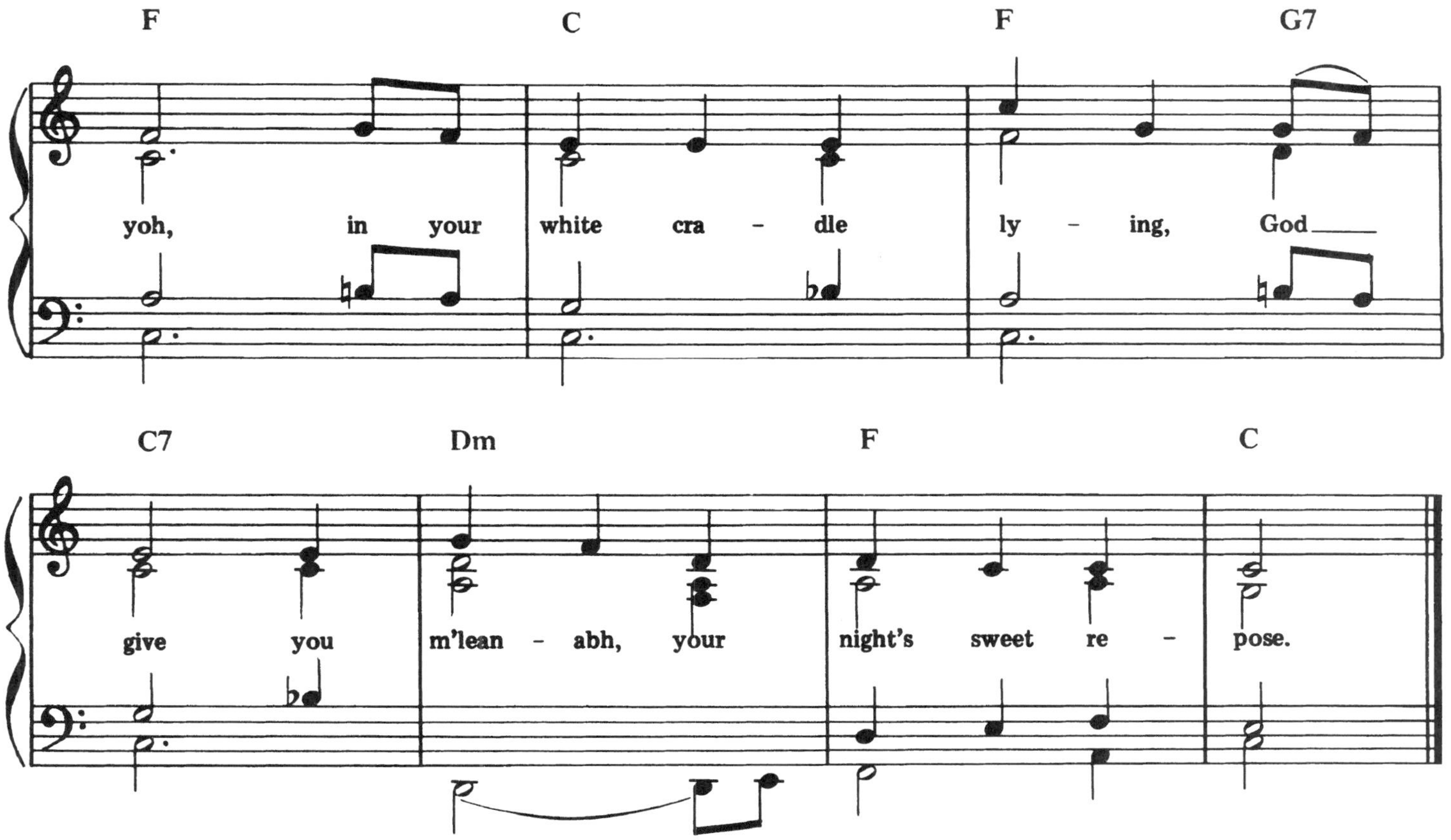
F C F G7
yoh, in your white cra - dle ly - ing, God
C7 Dm F C
give you m'lean - abh, your night's sweet re - pose.

The Man in the Moon

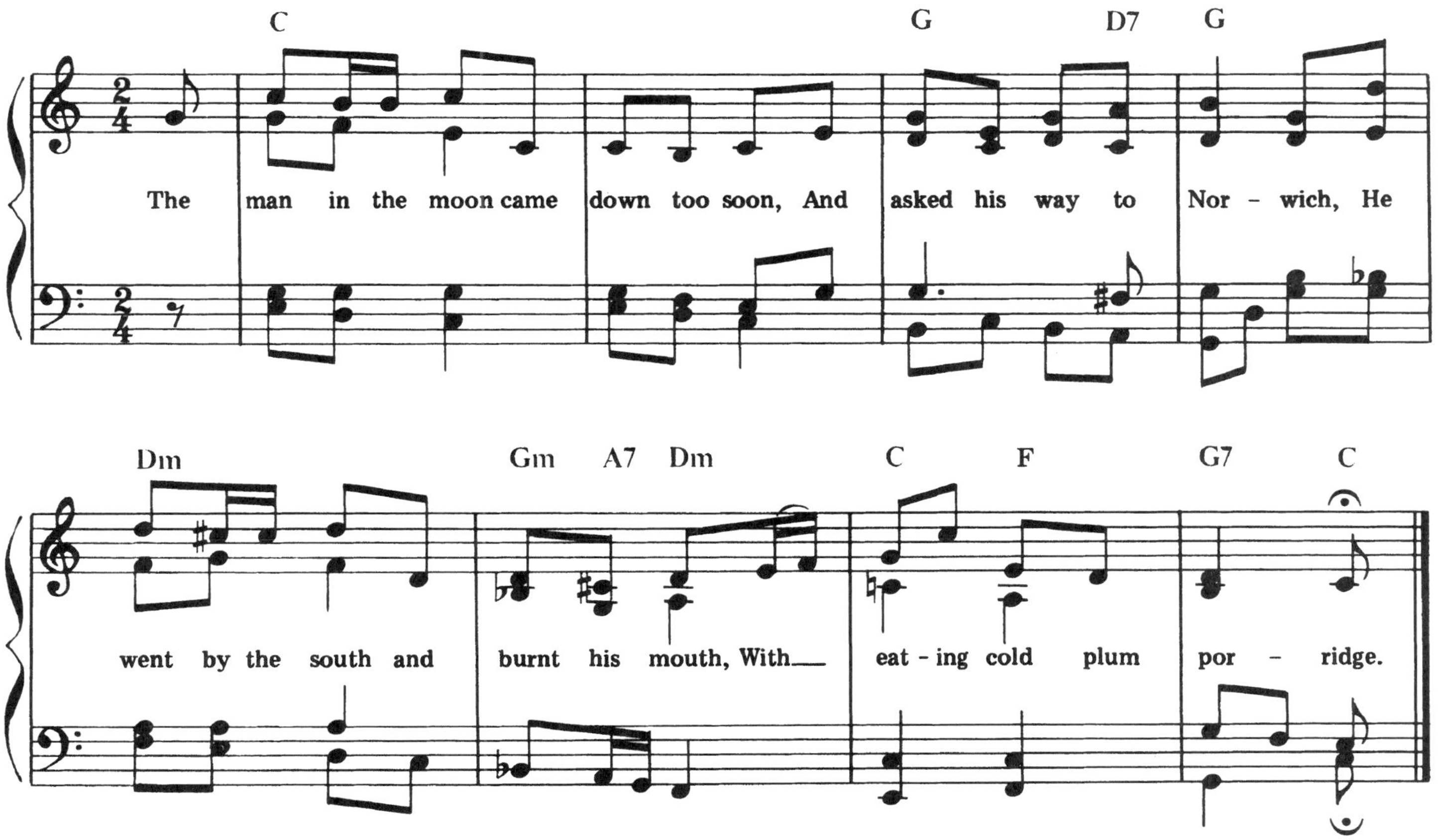
C G D7 G
The man in the moon came down too soon, And asked his way to Nor - wich, He
Dm Gm A7 Dm C F G7 C
went by the south and burnt his mouth, With eat - ing cold plum por - ridge.

Lambs Are Sleeping

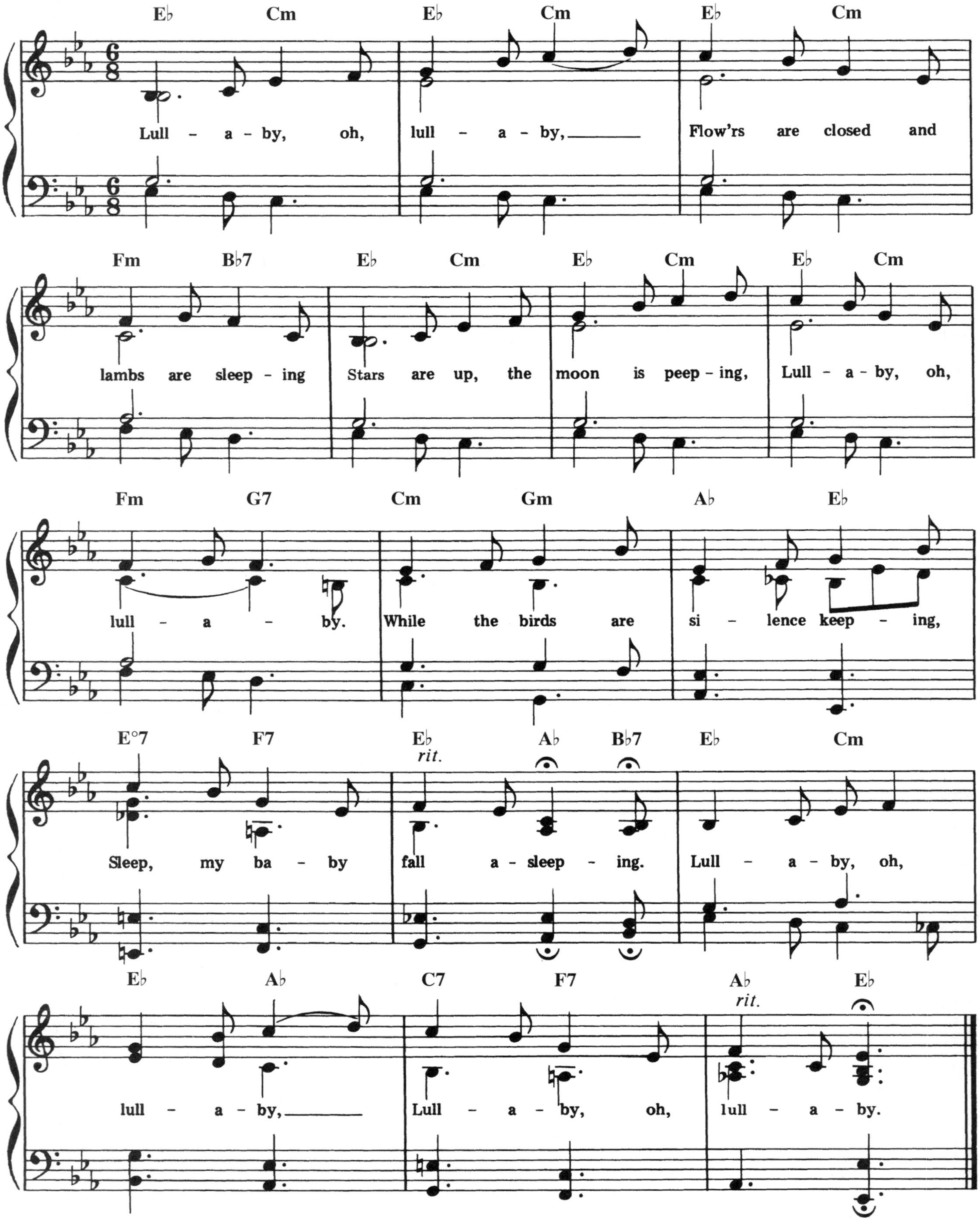

E♭ Cm E♭ Cm E♭ Cm
Lull - a - by, oh, lull - a - by, Flow'rs are closed and
Fm B♭7 E♭ Cm E♭ Cm E♭ Cm
lambs are sleep - ing Stars are up, the moon is peep - ing, Lull - a - by, oh,
Fm G7 Cm Gm A♭ E♭
lull - a - by. While the birds are si - lence keep - ing,
E°7 F7 E♭ A♭ B♭7 E♭ Cm
rit.
Sleep, my ba - by fall a - sleep - ing. Lull - a - by, oh,
E♭ A♭ C7 F7 A♭ E♭
rit.
lull - a - by, Lull - a - by, oh, lull - a - by.

Manx Lullaby

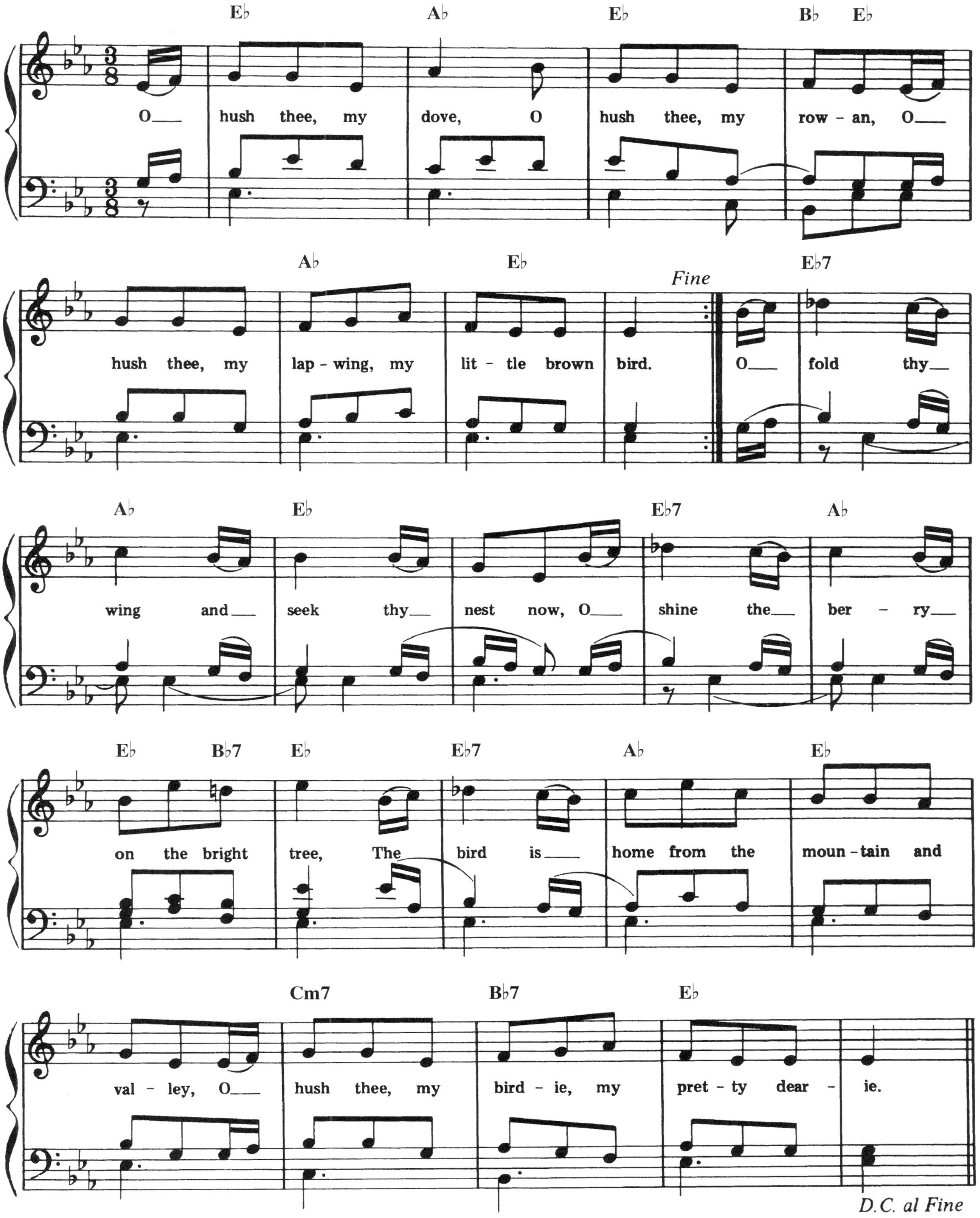
E♭ A♭ E♭ B♭ E♭
O hush thee, my dove, O hush thee, my row - an, O
A♭ E♭ Fine E♭7
hush thee, my lap - wing, my lit - tle brown bird. O fold thy
A♭ E♭ E♭7 A♭
wing and seek thy nest now, O shine the ber - ry
E♭ B♭7 E♭ E♭7 A♭ E♭
on the bright tree, The bird is home from the moun - tain and
Cm7 B♭7 E♭
val - ley, O hush thee, my bird - ie, my pret - ty dear - ie.
D.C. al Fine

Little Children

Music by Wolfgang Amadeus Mozart

Little chil - dren, ti - ny chil - dren, So
In their bed with down - y pil - lows, The

tired and so sleep - y. Wea - ry chil - dren, drow - sy
chil - dren's so heads rest on. Sleep - y chil - dren, wea - ry

chil - dren, To dream - land will go.
chil - dren, To dream - land will have gone.

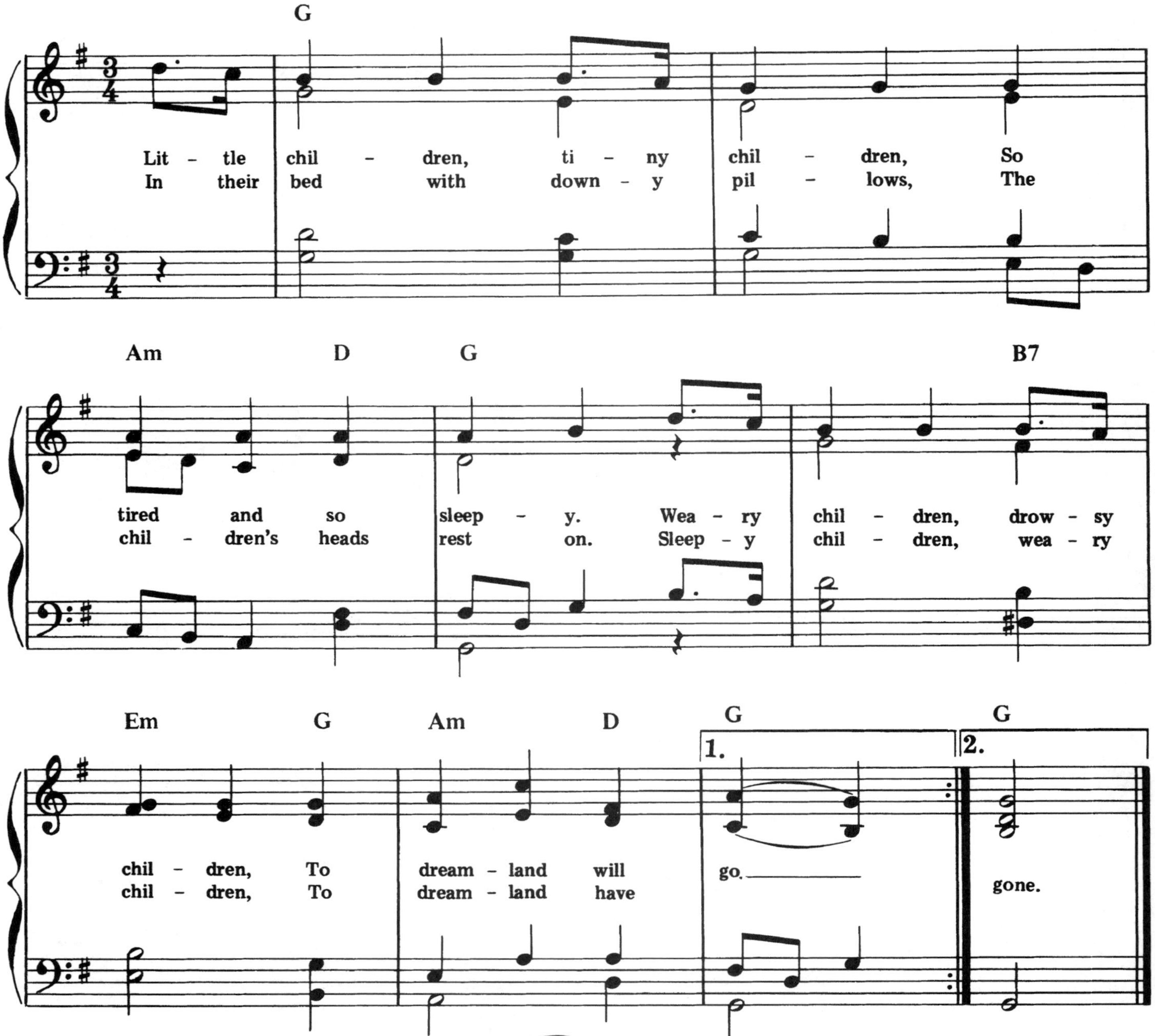

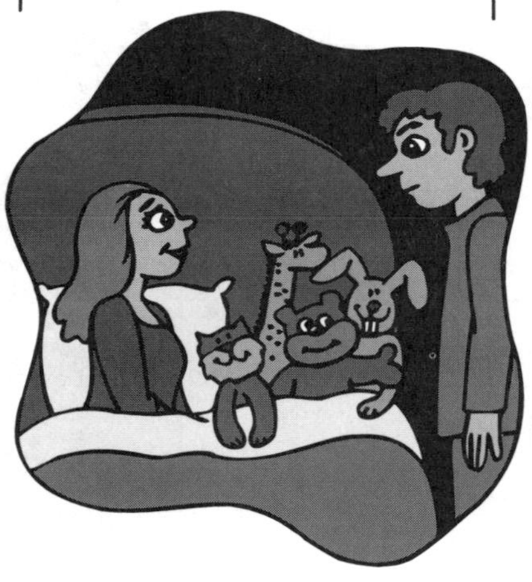

Moon and Sun

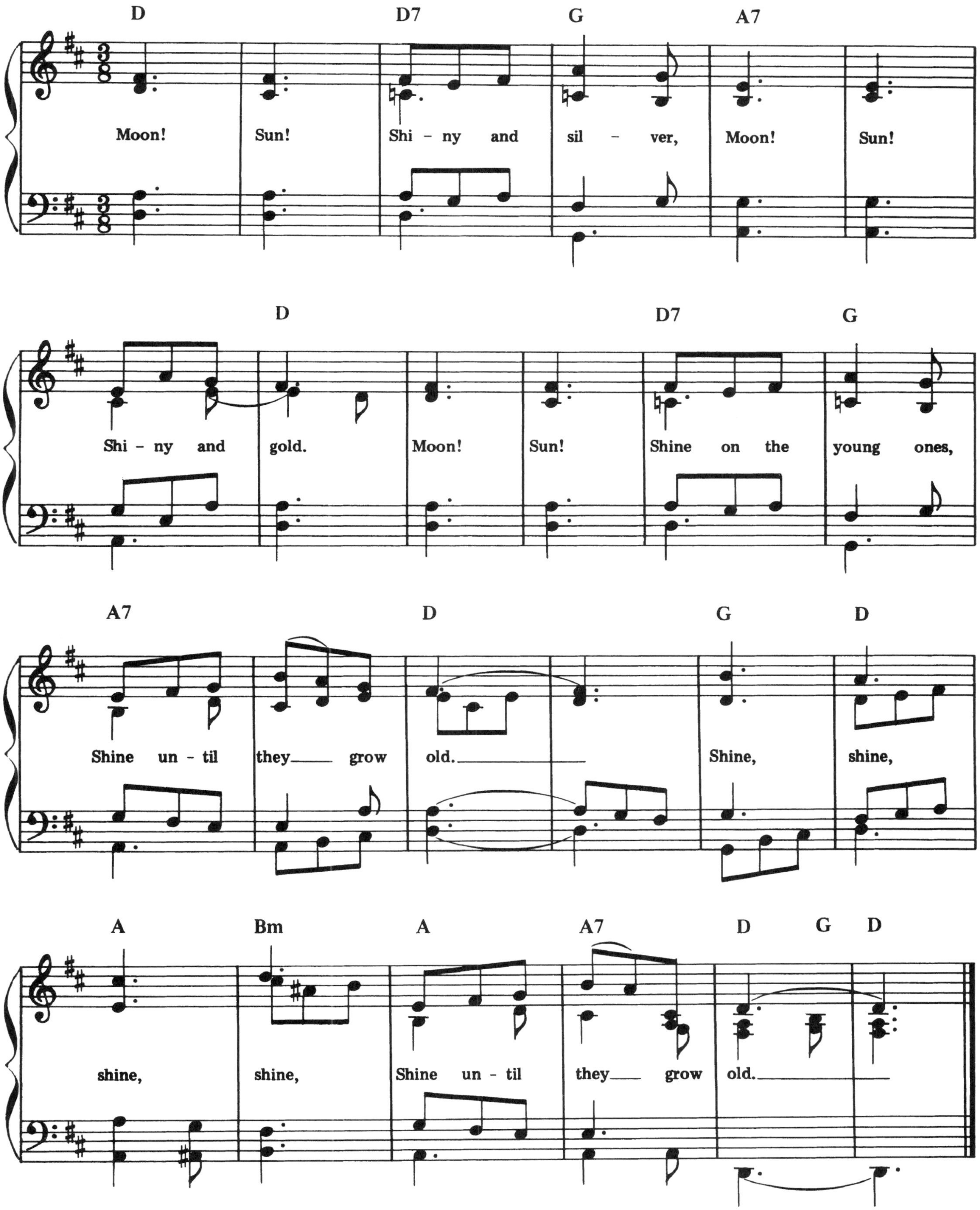
D D7 G A7
Moon! Sun! Shi - ny and sil - ver, Moon! Sun!
D D7 G
Shi - ny and gold. Moon! Sun! Shine on the young ones,
A7 D G D
Shine un - til they grow old. Shine, shine,
A Bm A A7 D G D
shine, shine, Shine un - til they grow old.

Nature's Goodnight

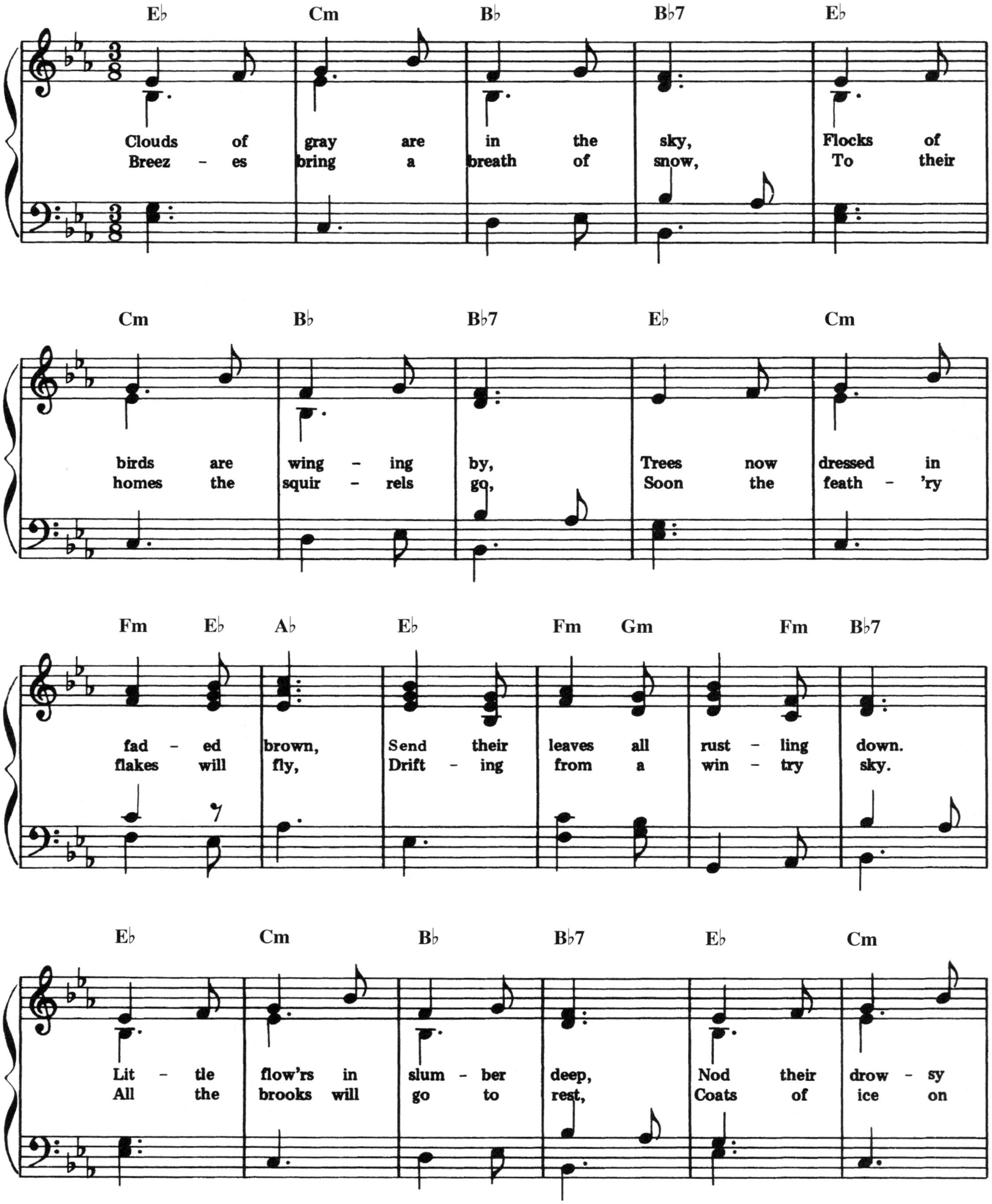
E♭ Cm B♭ B♭7 E♭
Clouds of gray are in the sky, Flocks of
Breez - es bring a breath of snow, To their
Cm B♭ B♭7 E♭ Cm
birds are wing - ing by, Trees now dressed in
homes the squir - rels go, Soon the feath - 'ry
Fm E♭ A♭ E♭ Fm Gm Fm B♭7
fad - ed brown, Send their leaves all rust - ling down.
flakes will fly, Drift - ing from a win - try sky.
E♭ Cm B♭ B♭7 E♭ Cm
Lit - tle flow'rs in slum - ber deep, Nod their drow - sy
All the brooks will go to rest, Coats of ice on

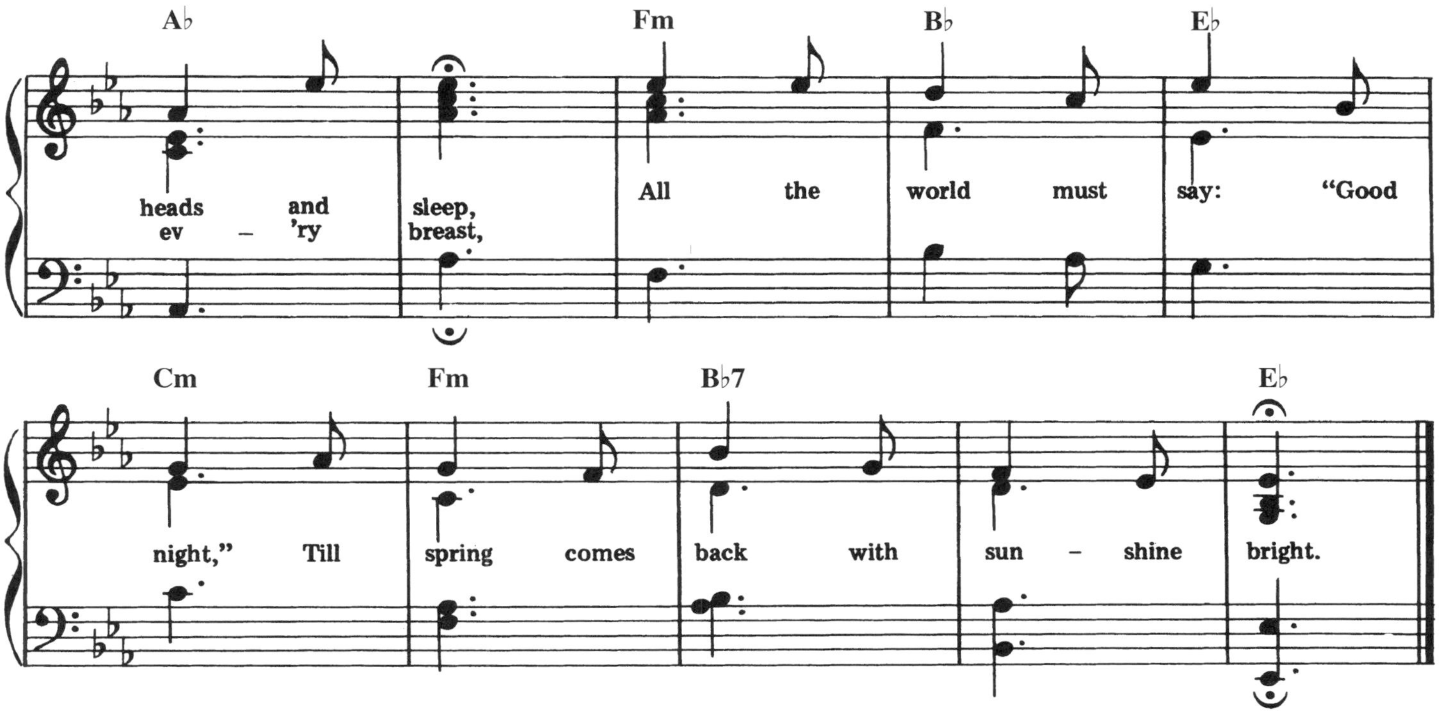

Now the Day Is Over

Words by Sabine Baring-Gould

Music by Joseph Barnby

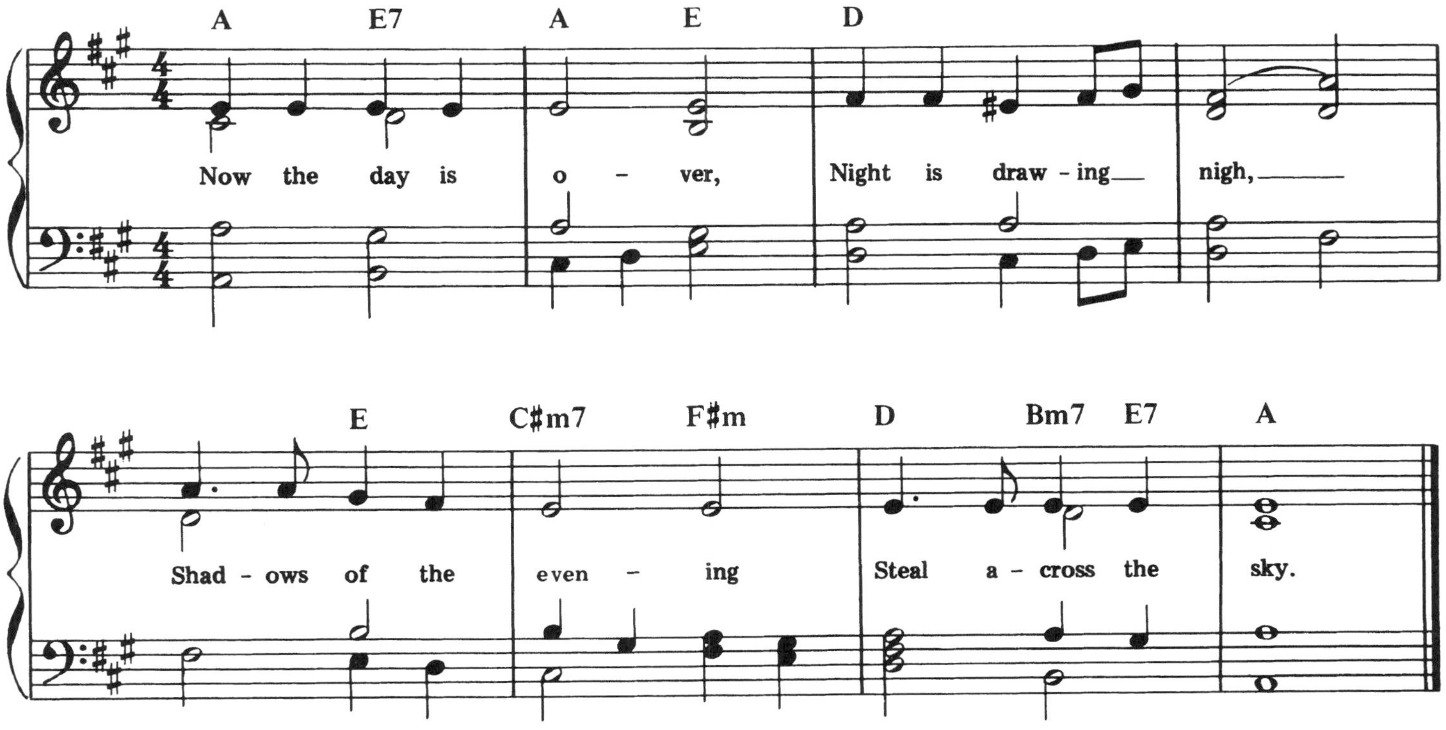

Oh Hush Thee, My Baby

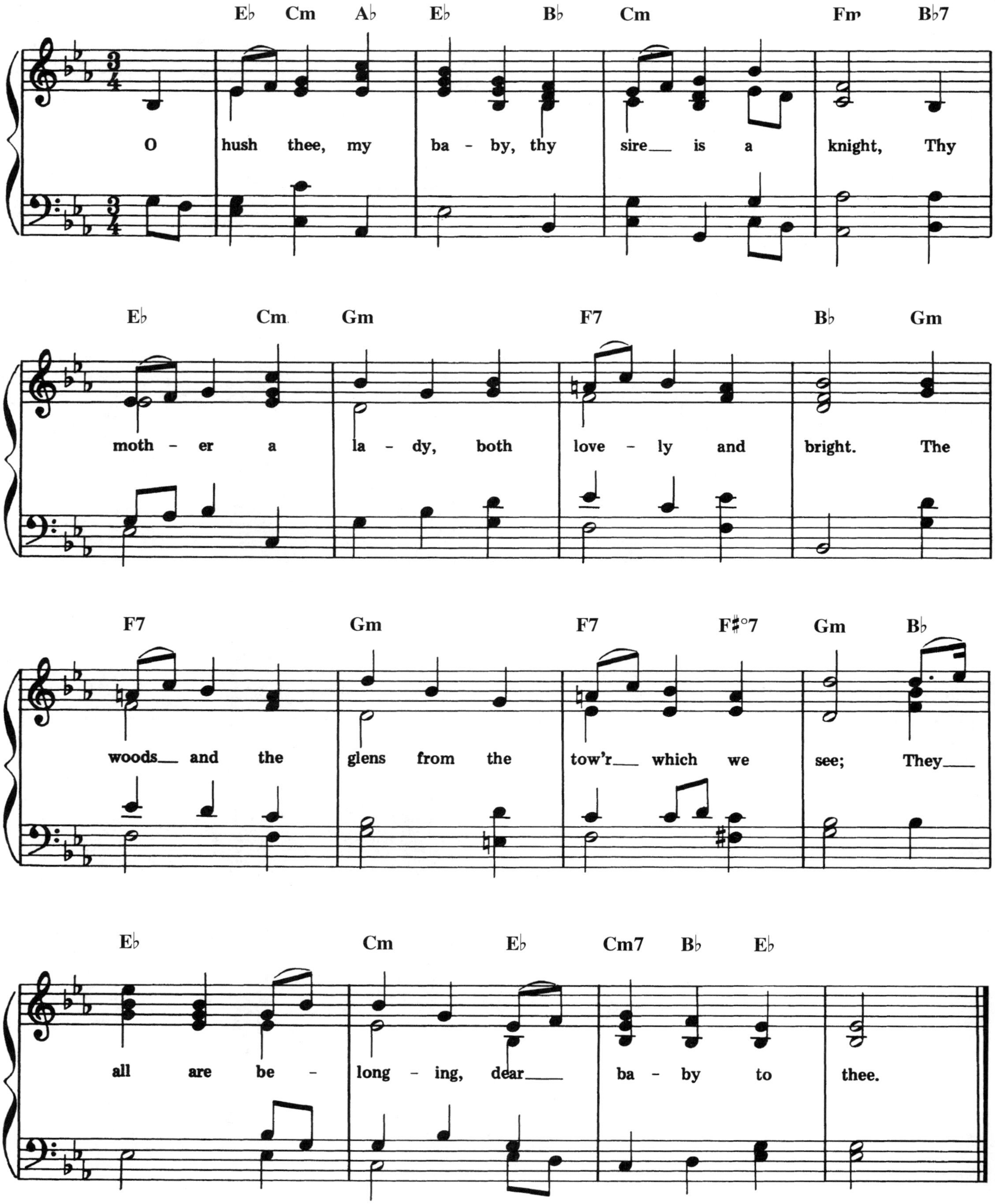
E♭ Cm A♭ E♭ B♭ Cm Fm B♭7
O hush thee, my ba - by, thy sire is a knight, Thy
E♭ Cm Gm F7 B♭ Gm
moth - er a la - dy, both love - ly and bright. The
F7 Gm F7 F♯°7 Gm B♭
woods and the glens from the tow'r which we see; They
E♭ Cm E♭ Cm7 B♭ E♭
all are be - long - ing, dear ba - by to thee.

2. O fear not the bugle, though loudly it blows,
   It calls but the wardens that guard thy repose;
   Their bows would be bended, their blades would be red,
   Ere the step of a foeman draws near thy bed.

3. O hush thee, oh baby, the time soon will come,
   When thy sleep be broken by trumpet and drum,
   Then hush thee, my darling, take rest while you may,
   For cares come with manhood, and waking with day.

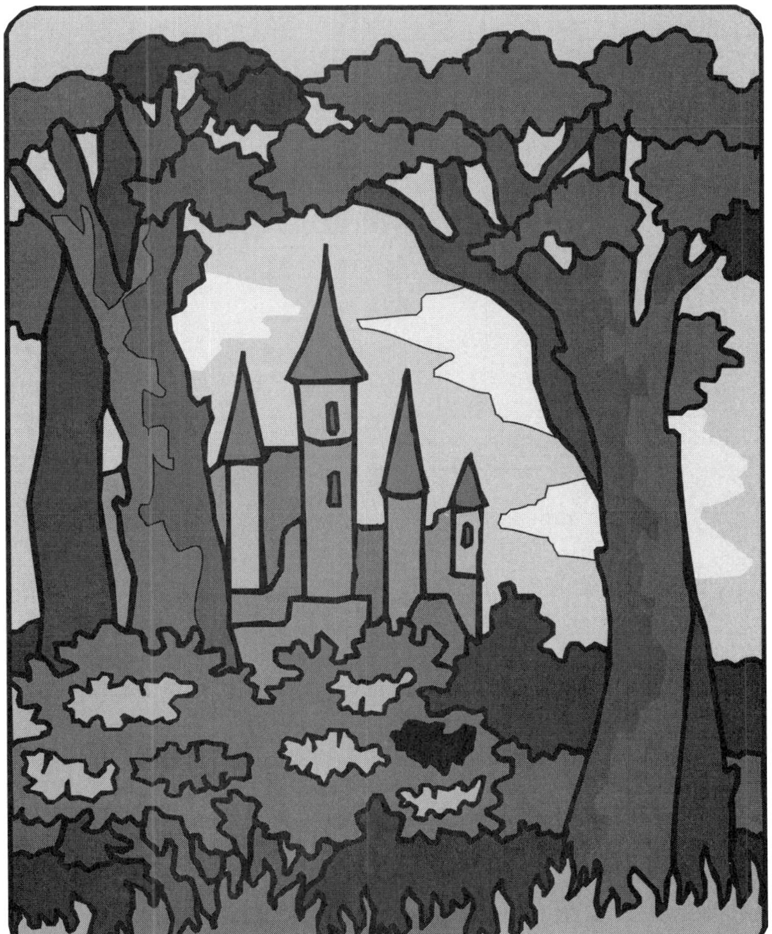

Rock-a-bye Baby

Words and music by Effie I. Crockett

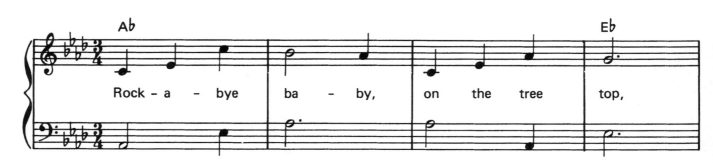

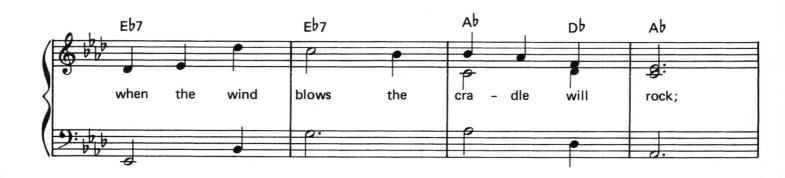

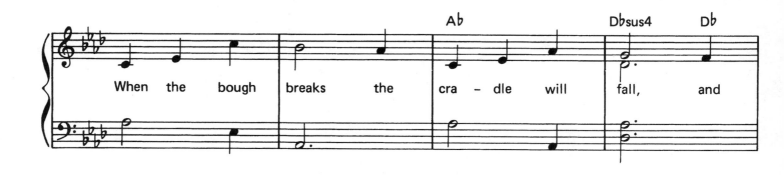

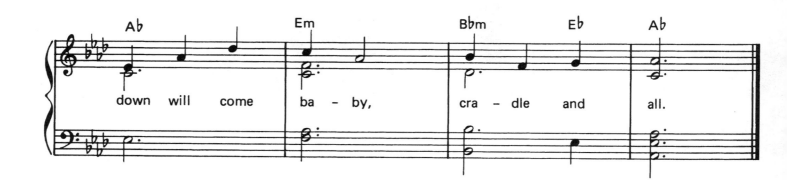

Rock the Cradle

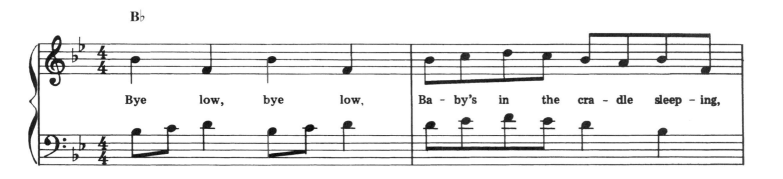

Bye low, bye low, Ba - by's in the cra - dle sleep - ing,

Tip toe, tip toe, still as pus - sy sly - ly creep - ing, Bye low, bye low,

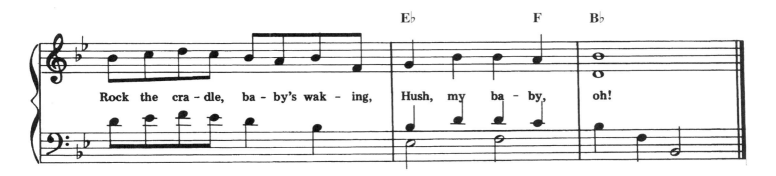

Rock the cra - dle, ba - by's wak - ing, Hush, my ba - by, oh!

Sleep, Little Child

Music by Wolfgang A. Mozart

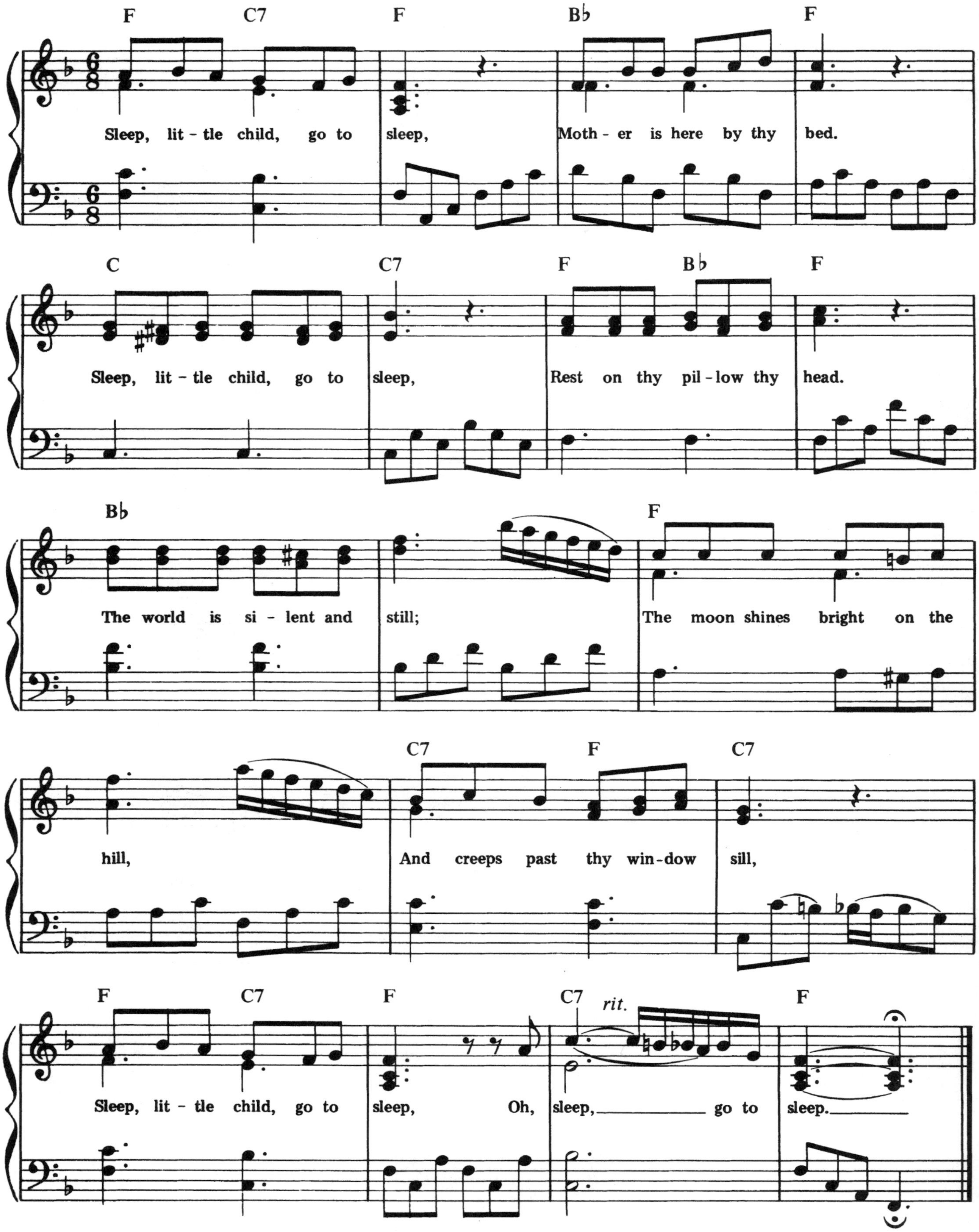

Sleep, lit – tle child, go to sleep, Moth – er is here by thy bed.

Sleep, lit – tle child, go to sleep, Rest on thy pil – low thy head.

The world is si – lent and still; The moon shines bright on the

hill, And creeps past thy win – dow sill,

Sleep, lit – tle child, go to sleep, Oh, sleep,_____ go to sleep._____

Sleep On, Little One

Music by Johannes Brahms

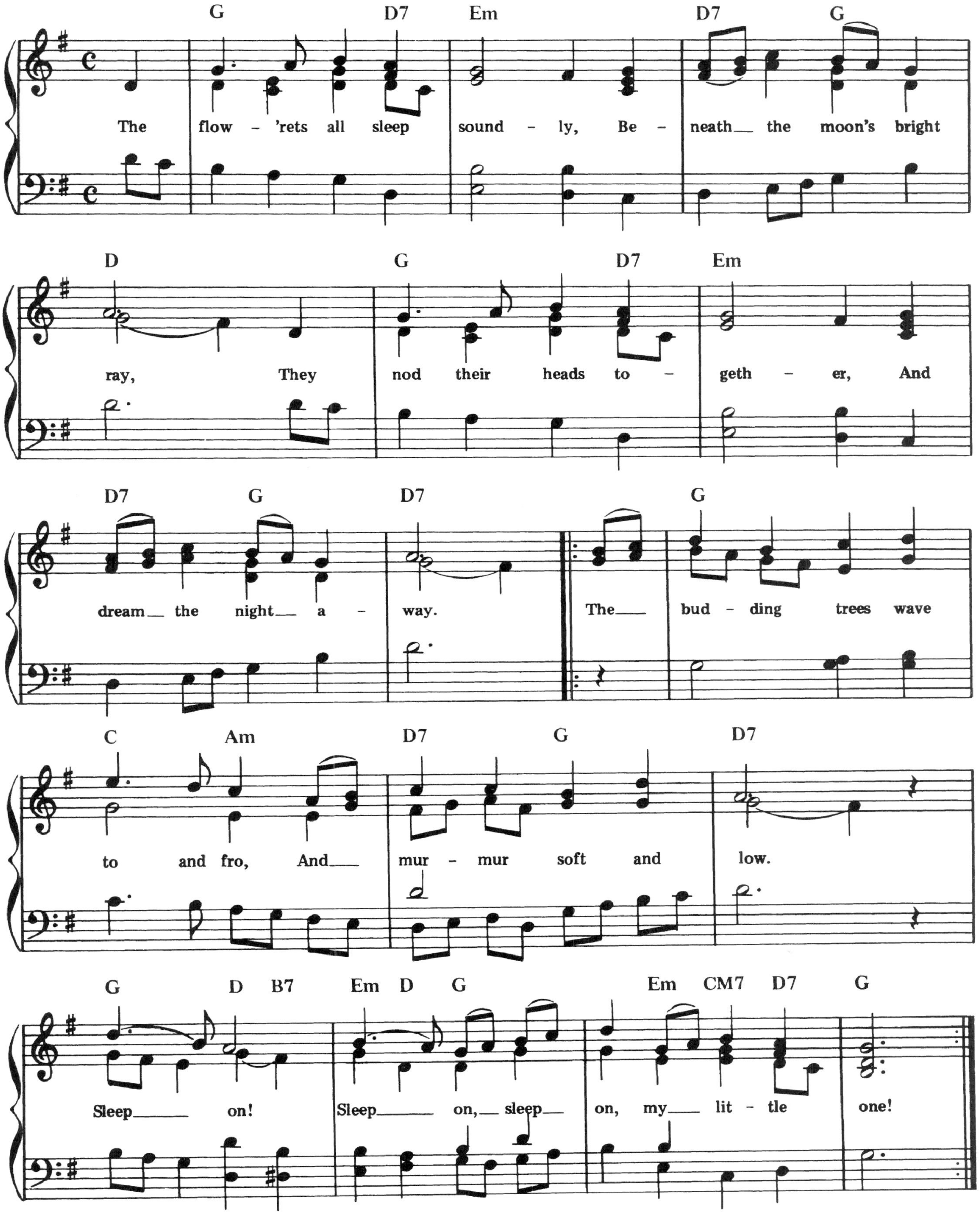
G D7 Em D7 G
The flow – 'rets all sleep sound – ly, Be – neath the moon's bright
D G D7 Em
ray, They nod their heads to – geth – er, And
D7 G D7 G
dream the night a – way. The bud – ding trees wave
C Am D7 G D7
to and fro, And mur – mur soft and low.
G D B7 Em D G Em CM7 D7 G
Sleep on! Sleep on, sleep on, my lit – tle one!

Sleep, Sweet Babe

Words by Samuel Taylor Coleridge

Chilean folk tune

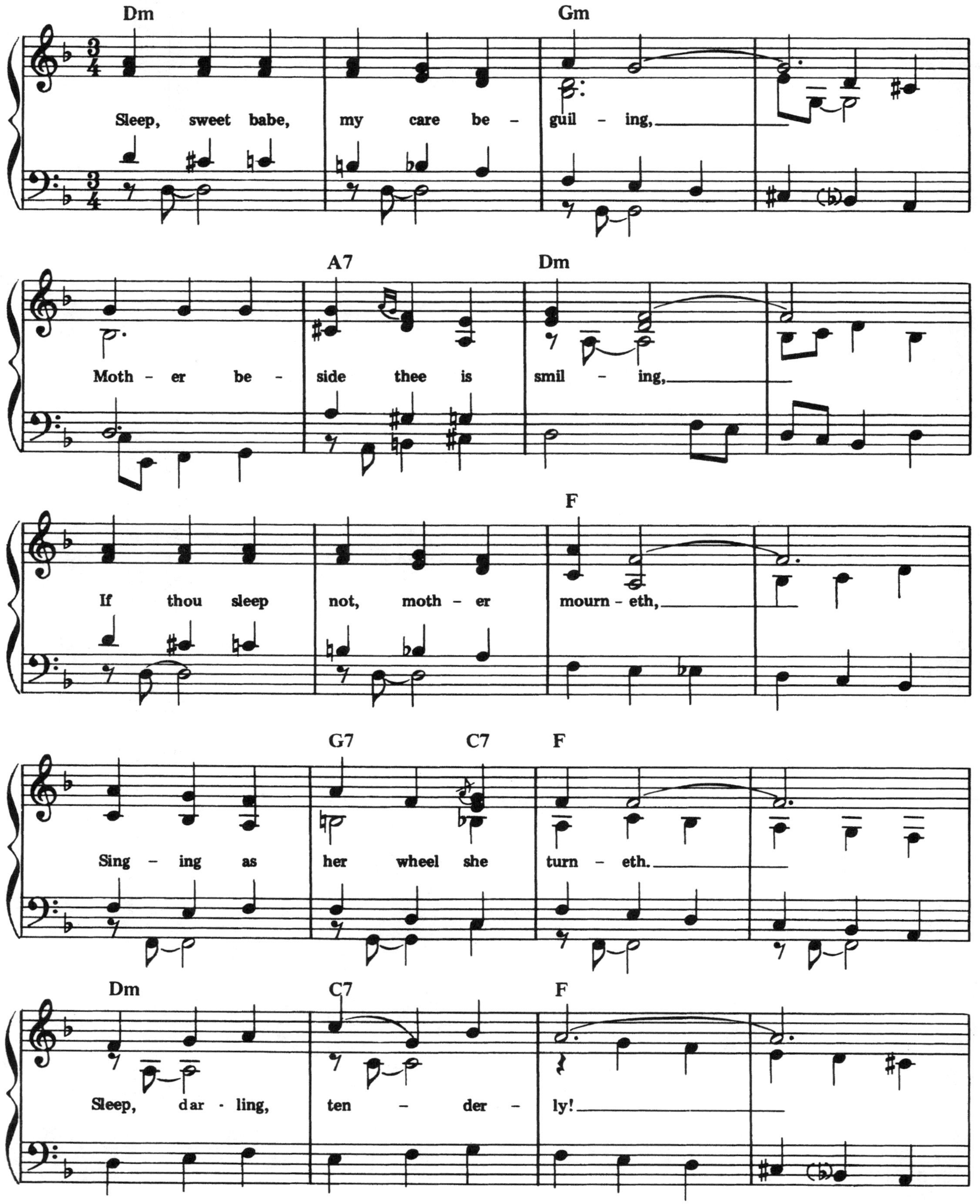

Sleep, sweet babe, my care be-guil-ing,

Moth-er be-side thee is smil-ing,

If thou sleep not, moth-er mourn-eth,

Sing-ing as her wheel she turn-eth.

Sleep, dar-ling, ten-der-ly!

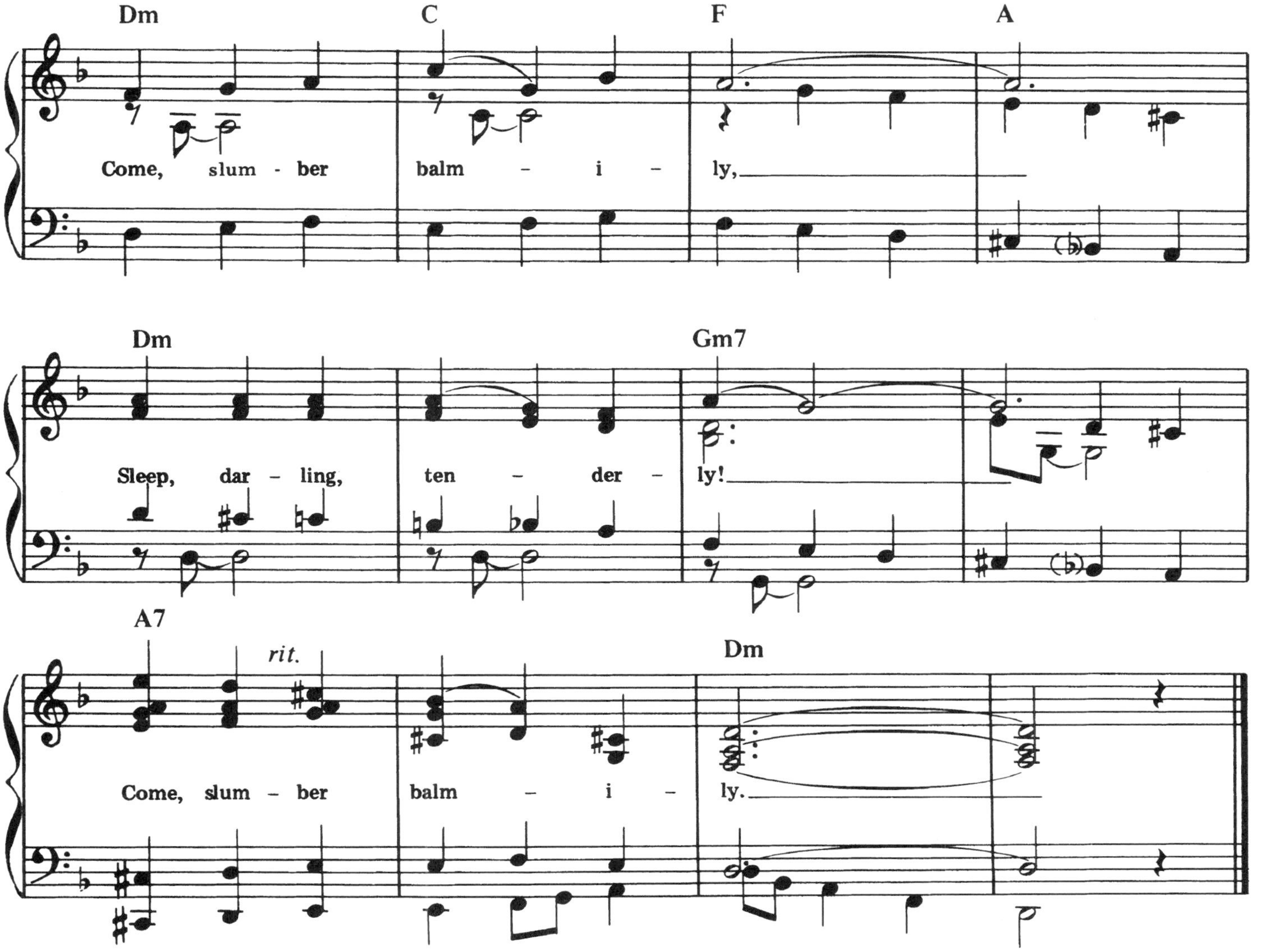
Dm
C
F
A
Come, slum - ber balm - i - ly,
Dm
Gm7
Sleep, dar - ling, ten - der - ly!
A7
rit.
Dm
Come, slum - ber balm - i - ly.

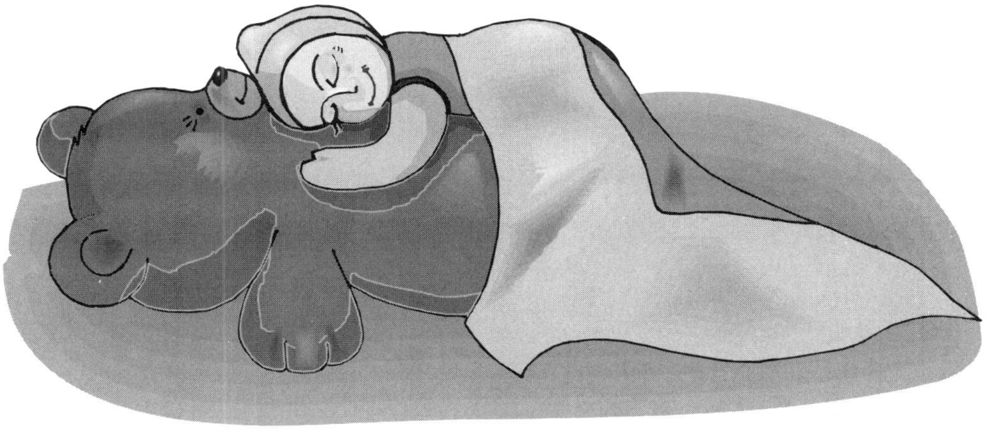

Sleepytime

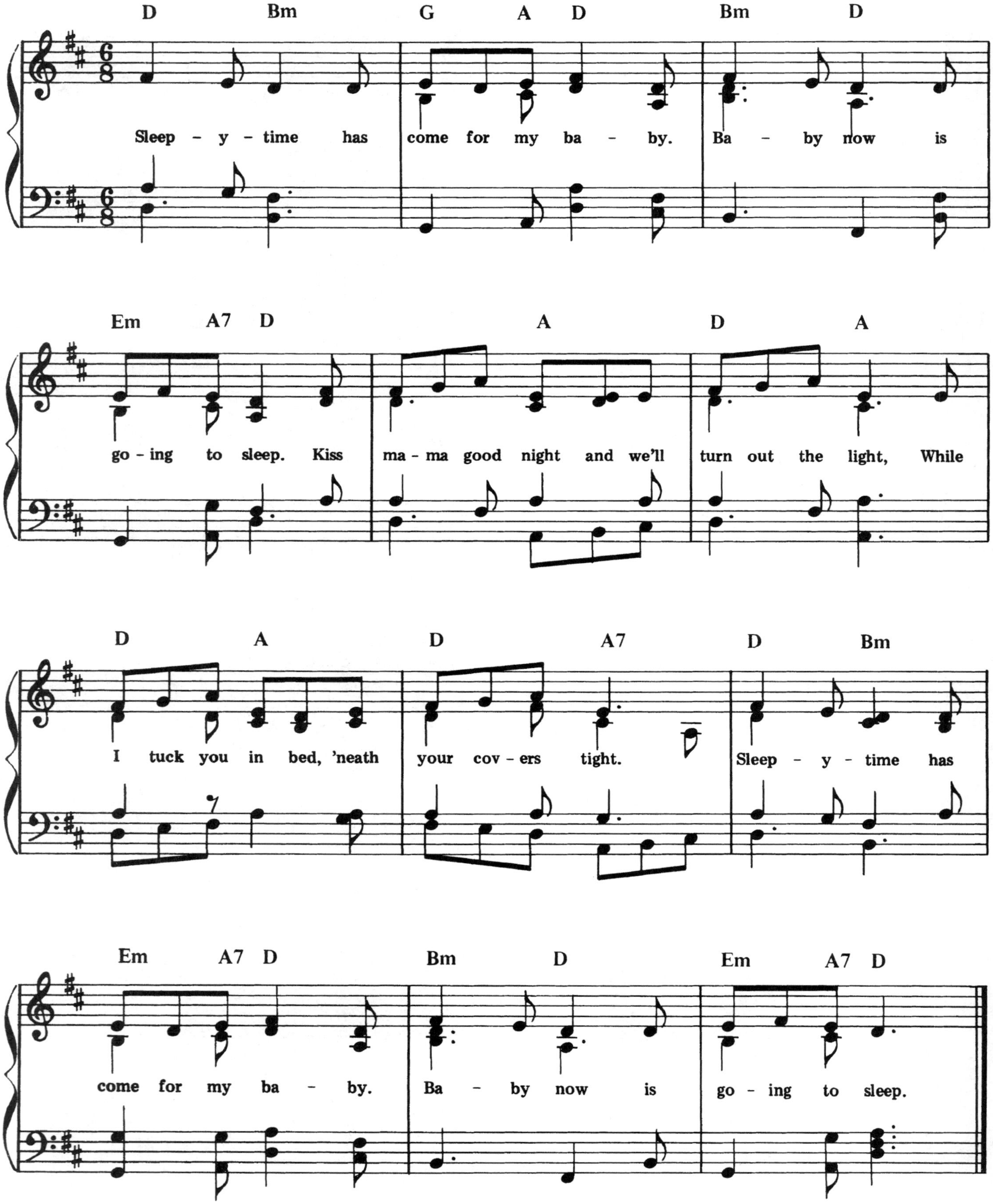
D Bm G A D Bm D
Sleep - y - time has come for my ba - by. Ba - by now is
Em A7 D A D A
go - ing to sleep. Kiss ma - ma good night and we'll turn out the light, While
D A D A7 D Bm
I tuck you in bed, 'neath your cov - ers tight. Sleep - y - time has
Em A7 D Bm D Em A7 D
come for my ba - by. Ba - by now is go - ing to sleep.

The Sun Is Down

D A D G A D A
Sun is down, stars in the skies; Close your drow - sy
D G A G D
lit - tle eyes. Time for one more song to sing, How
Em B Em A D
fast the happy even - ing flies.

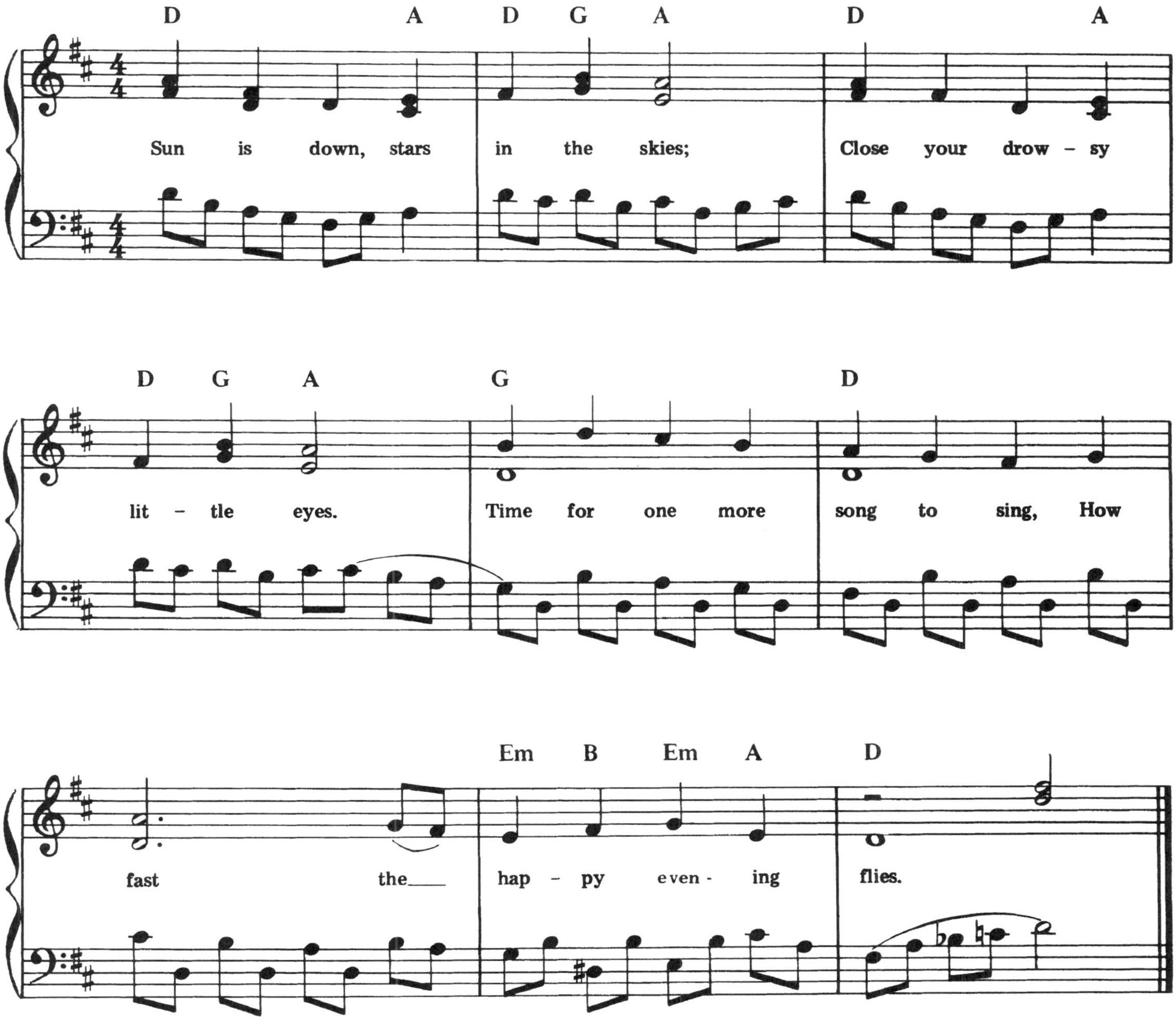

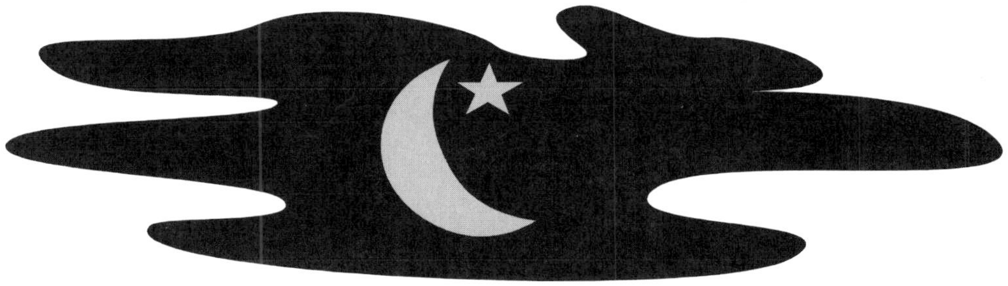

Sweet and Low

Words by Alfred, Lord Tennyson

Music by Joseph Barnby

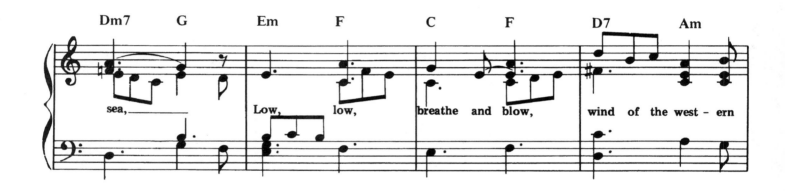

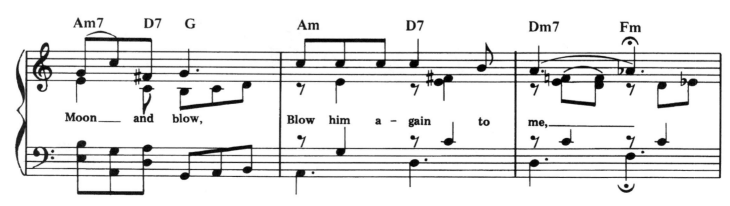

While   my lit – tle one,   while my   pret-ty one,   sleeps.

2. Sleep and rest, sleep and rest,
   Father will come to thee soon,
   Rest, rest on mother's breast,
   Father will come to thee soon.
   Father will come to his babe in the nest,
   Silver sails all out of the west,
   Under the silver moon,
   Sleep, my little one, sleep my pretty one, sleep.

Sweet Be Your Sleep

F C7 F C7
Good night to you all and sweet be your
F B♭ Gm Am Dm7
sleep, May an - gels a - round you their
Gm C7 F B♭ C
si - lent watch keep. Good night, good
F C F
night, good night, good night.

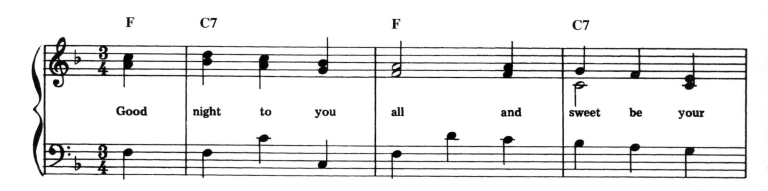

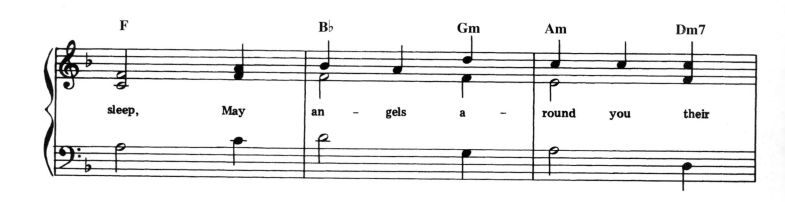

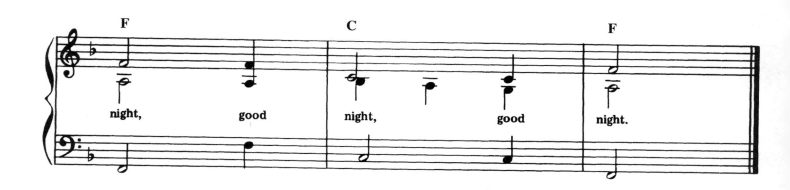

Winkum, Winkum

C Dm7 G C G
Wink - um, wink - um, shut___ your eye, Sweet, my ba - by,
Chick - ens long have gone___ to rest, Birds lie snug with -
D7 G C G
lull - a - by, For the dews are fall - ing soft,
in___ their nest, And my bir - die soon will be
C G C
Light are flick - 'ring up a - loft. And the moon - light's
Sleep - ing like a chick - a - dee. For with on - ly
Dm7 G C Dm G C
peep - ing o - ver, yon - der hill - top___ capped with clo - ver.
half___ a try,______ Wink - um, wink - um___ shuts her eye.______

Underneath the Spreading Chestnut Tree

C G7 C
Un - der - neath the spread-ing chest - nut tree
F G7 C
I'm as hap - py as can be
F C F C
with my ban - jo on my knee
G7 C
Un - der - neath the spread - ing chest - nut tree.

Index